Contents

COURSE 4   TRUST ACCOUNTS AND RECORD KEEPING

COURSE 5   CLOSINGS AND SETTLEMENT

Colorado
REAL ESTATE
Principles
VOLUME 2, SECOND EDITION UPDATE

Sherry Steele, Contributing Editor

This publication is designed to provide accurate and authoritative information in regard to the subject matter covered. It is sold with the understanding that the publisher is not engaged in rendering legal, accounting, or other professional advice. If legal advice or other expert assistance is required, the services of a competent professional should be sought.

President: Dr. Andrew Temte
Chief Learning Officer: Dr. Tim Smaby
Vice President, Real Estate Education: Asha Alsobrooks
Development Editor: Kari Domeyer

COLORADO REAL ESTATE PRINCIPLES VOLUME 2, SECOND EDITION UPDATE
© 2013 Kaplan, Inc.
Published by DF Institute, Inc., d/b/a Kaplan Real Estate Education
332 Front St. S., Suite 501
La Crosse, WI 54601
www.kapRE.com

All rights reserved. The text of this publication, or any part thereof, may not be reproduced in any manner whatsoever without written permission from the publisher.

Printed in the United States of America
11   12   13   10   9   8   7   6   5   4   3   2   1
ISBN: 978-1-4277-1455-8 / 1-4277-1455-X
PPN: 2139-1003

PRACTICAL APPLICATIONS

Before Class:

■ Review the following units to become familiar with the topics that will be covered in the lecture. You do not need to memorize this material. Use the PowerPoint presentation lecture slides reproduced for you in Unit 12 at the end of the Practical Application material when you come to class or view the lecture online.

After Class:

■ Home Study students take the Practical Applications Final Exam online.

U N I T

Finding a Brokerage Firm and Achieving Professionalism

■ **LEARNING OBJECTIVES**   *Upon completion of this unit, you should be able to*

■ **interview** with a brokerage firm and know the five most important points to consider when looking for a firm,

■ **explain** why a real estate broker associate needs additional knowledge and experience to become a professional,

■ **list** three types of communication skills that the professional real estate broker associate must master,

■ **list** the three types of knowledge a real estate broker associate needs and distinguish the differences between each type,

■ **list** the five requirements for effective goal setting, and

■ **list** at least ten services that an unlicensed personal assistant can perform.

■ OVERVIEW

Finding a brokerage firm and starting a successful business are by far the most important first steps for new broker associates. Upon completion of this unit, new licensees will know how to look for a firm and the questions to ask to determine the best fit between them and their new employing broker.

Real estate brokers are, for the most part, self-employed and in charge of their own small business. Developing the habits and skills to start and keep a successful business are among the challenges facing a new licensee. In this unit, the new broker associate will find information on acquiring these habits and planning to begin a successful career.

■ FINDING A BROKERAGE FIRM AND AN EMPLOYING BROKER

New Colorado licensees (broker associates) are required to work under an employing broker for the first two years after licensing. For a new broker associate the decision of which firm to join can seem nearly as difficult as passing the state licensing exam. But do not worry. If you interview a number of firms and take the time to get to know the employing broker, sales manager, and other brokers of the firm prior to joining, you will undoubtedly find the right fit. Moreover, while Colorado law requires that the broker associate work under an employing broker for two years, it does not have to be for the same employing broker or for the same firm. If a broker associate changes firms, the broker associate and the employing brokers, both the old and new, simply notify the Colorado Real Estate Commission about the change of address for the broker associate.

The five major areas broker associates should be concerned with as they start the interview process are the following:

■ Training
■ The relationship with the employing broker or manager
■ Location of the firm
■ Costs to start
■ Commission splits and desk fees

Training

Upon completing the required pre-licensing education, most broker associates have a basic understanding of real estate law, Colorado contracts, trust accounting, and closings. Each of these topics involves concepts that are required once a buyer or seller is found. The training most new broker associates need involves how to find business in the first place (i.e., buyers and sellers) and how to work with buyers and sellers once you find them. As in any type of sales there are a variety of ways to develop a client base. Training programs present broker associates with multiple approaches and help them develop a personal business plan that identifies specific, measurable goals and the approaches that licensees will use to achieve those goals. Many effective training programs combine lecture/book learning with hands-on application to help get new licensees off to a fast start. Additionally, many companies offer mentors or training coaches to help new licensees get started.

Most new broker associates are surprised to learn that they are solely responsible for determining their success—including what they do every day. With no formal boss to report to, the broker associate alone decides what time to begin work each morning, what to do each day, which evenings to work late, which weekends to work, and so on. Keep in mind, though, that most real estate brokers are self-employed independent contractors and get paid on a commission-only basis. If they don't sell, they don't get paid. It is incumbent upon broker associates to develop a work schedule and learn to meet the goals they've set each day. A good training program can provide the tools needed to earn a living selling real estate, but, of course, it's up to broker associates to implement what they learn.

The Relationship with the Employing Broker, Sales Manager, Mentor, and Other Brokers

Training is imperative to getting a good start in business. Still, the first time a new broker associate has to give a listing or buyer presentation or fill out a purchase contract can be daunting. Having a seasoned professional to help is invaluable. In many offices, the new broker associate is expected to turn to the employing broker or sales manager for assistance. The broker associate should make sure there is a complete understanding of the expectations of both of these parties. Is it acceptable to call the sales manager on a Sunday afternoon for help with writing an offer? Will the sales manager go to the first listing appointment, closing, or other appointment with the new broker associate?

Many firms have mentor programs that give new broker associates access to a top-producing broker to help them as they grow their business. Each firm handles these relationships differently. Often, broker associates will share part of their commission from a sale with their mentor. New broker associates should have the same understanding of what assistance the mentor will give them as they would with a sales manger or employing broker. Putting the understanding between the mentor and broker associate in writing should make misunderstandings less likely.

It is also important that the broker associate feels comfortable with the office style. There are a variety of office policies and styles that address issues such as required office hours (if any), frequency of office meetings, and acceptable office attire. Before joining the firm, the broker associate should try to attend a sales meeting or walk around the office and meet the other broker associates to determine whether the office fits a personal style.

Location of the Firm

Electronic access allows most real estate brokers to do much of their business from home. Nevertheless, new broker associates may wish to select an office relatively close to their home since they may be expected to attend office trainings or take floor duty (if applicable), and may want to use the office equipment. Many broker associates also use the office conference rooms to meet clients. New broker associates may find that having an office close to home makes getting in early and getting started every day easier.

Costs to Start

Compared to costs of starting most businesses, the start-up costs for broker associates are relatively low; however, there are important costs to be aware of. It takes many new broker associates several months to earn their first commission; therefore, new broker associates must be certain to have enough personal savings to live on until they begin generating income from their real estate sales activities. Some of the costs involved in doing business as a broker associate include errors and omissions insurance, license fees, board of REALTOR® dues, multiple listing service (MLS) fees, self-employment taxes, computer and related equipment, contract and database software, digital camera, cell phone, Web site fees, and automobile-related expenses. Other costs may include marketing, lawn signs, lockboxes, business cards, letterhead, envelopes, and postage. Some firms may charge the broker associate for portions of the office training as well. The broker associate should discuss with each potential employing broker estimated start-up costs with the company and if the company helps new brokers with any of the expenses. Many companies have computer systems and software available at the office, which will save the broker associate the cost of acquiring these items on their own.

Commission Splits and Desk Fees

When a sale is made, the broker associate is required to relinquish a portion of the commission earned to the employing brokerage firm. This is called the commission split. Nearly every employing brokerage company has different ways of splitting fees with their broker associates. Typically, as a new, unproven real estate salesperson, the broker associate will not be able to negotiate a different split than the standard split that the firm offers all new broker associates. However, after time, experience, and success meeting sales quotas and proving that they have the skills and ability to sell real estate, broker associates will likely be in a position to negotiate a more advantageous commission split with their employing broker.

Many real estate firms offer a straight 50 percent commission split plan where new broker associates agree to pay the employing brokerage firm 50 percent of the commissions they generate. Other firms may offer a higher split (i.e., 70 percent) but require broker associates to pay monthly fees or cover more of their own business expenses. If the brokerage firm says they offer a 70 percent split, broker associates keep 70 percent of their commissions and agree to pay the employing brokerage firm 30 percent. Many firms have an annual cap that allows broker associates to keep more of their commissions after reaching certain specified earnings levels. These arrangements vary with each brokerage firm.

Some companies offer plans that allow broker associates to keep a higher percentage of their commissions, but require that they pay a monthly desk fee or other monthly fee. These fees are usually based on what it costs the employing broker to provide the office space, equipment, and marketing that benefits everyone in the firm. Still other firms offer a combination desk fee and commission split. While it is important to understand the commission split plan of the firm the broker associate chooses, it is equally important that the firm the broker associate selects fits her professional style, provides adequate support and training, and provides an opportunity for growth. After all, even the most attractive commission split plan will mean little if the broker associate has not positioned herself for success.

See Figure 1.1 for a list of issues and questions to ask employing brokers during the process of interviewing firms.

■ ACHIEVING PROFESSIONALISM

Customers of real estate licensees expect them to be knowledgeable, organized, and effective; however, professionalism is not easily achieved. Professional knowledge and behavior result from additional study and hard work and go beyond minimum legal requirements.

The broker associate who provides honesty, service, diligence, and knowledge tends to be more successful than the stereotypical hard sell broker associate who uses manipulative techniques to try to close deals. The following are the basic qualities needed to better serve clients and customers:

- Professional ethics
- Communication skills
- Professional education
- Goal-setting skills and time management skills

F I G U R E   1.1

**Questions to Ask
Employing Brokers**

As a new broker associate, to activate your license you must have an employing broker that agrees to hire you. There are a number of issues that need to be considered before signing with a brokerage firm:

1. Are you planning on working full- or part-time?
2. Do you plan to work mostly from home or do you need to have an office at the brokerage?
   - How far are you willing to travel to get to your office?
3. What do you need and expect the brokerage to offer you?
   - Do you want training?
   - Do you want to work with a mentor?
   - Do you want to be part of a team or work on your own?

Sample Questions to Ask Brokers

Here are some questions you might want to ask as you interview with firms. Add any others that are a concern for you.

1. How long has the firm and/or office been in business?
2. How long has the broker/manager been in the real estate business?
3. How long has the secretarial/office staff been with the company?
4. Does the office belong to the Board of REALTORS®? Which one?
5. What was last year's gross sales volume?
6. What are office hours?
7. Is the office open weekends or holidays?
8. How many agents are currently affiliated with the firm?
9. What is the average educational level of the agents?
10. How long have the current associates been with the firm?
11. What advanced REALTOR® designations are there in the office?
12. Is there a formal training program?
    - How long is it?
    - What does it cover?
    - Is there a charge?
    - What is the success rate?
    - Is there a company-sponsored follow-up program or ongoing training?
13. How many new brokers make a sale in the first three months?
14. What is the new agent retention and success rate for the last year?
15. Does the firm encourage or pay for advanced training?
16. What is the desk/office arrangement?
17. Is floor time offered to or required of new agents?
18. Are there regularly scheduled office meetings?
19. Does the office tour new listings?
20. What is the commission structure?
    - Is it graduated based on production?
    - Are there franchise fees?
    - Transaction fees?
    - Processing fees?
    - Any other fees?
    - Is there a desk or office rental fee?
21. What does the firm pay for?
    - Business cards?
    - Yard signs?
    - Stationery?
    - Copies?
    - Postage?
    - Telephones?
    - Long distance?
    - Direct lines?
    - Voice mail?

FIGURE   1.1

**Questions to Ask
Employing Brokers
(continued)**

22. What equipment does the firm have available for associates to use?
    - Computers?
    - Laser printer?
    - Color laser printer?
    - Scanner?
    - Digital camera?
    - Copier?
    - What software does the firm have available to agents?
23. Is the office wired for a network or does it offer Wi-fi?
    - Does the office have an Internet presence?
    - Does the office have a Web site?
    - Is there high-speed Internet access?
    - What other office equipment is available for agent use?
24. Does the firm specialize in a particular area?
25. Does the firm specialize in a specific type of property?
    - Will I be restricted from prospecting any particular area?
26. What is the firm's marketing program?
27. Is there an in-office transaction coordinator?
28. Does the firm have a relocation department?
    - What percentage of the firm's business is relocation?
29. Is there an in-office loan officer?
30. Does the firm offer health insurance?
31. Does the firm offer a retirement plan?
32. Does the firm have a mentor program?
33. How much are the estimated cost to get started?
34. How do I get started finding leads?
35. How does the firm help their broker associates keep up with industry changes while continuing to maintain a profitable business?

Professional Ethics

A distinct difference exists between what is *ethical* and what is *legal*. License laws set a minimum standard of professional behavior, while codes of ethics set the higher standard of what is honest and fair to all parties involved in a real estate transaction.

Even the appearance of impropriety may cause customers to avoid doing business with a broker associate and the brokerage firm. The expression "perception is reality" is true; such shortcomings are very damaging to a real estate career.

The National Association of REALTORS® (NAR) has standardized a code of **professional ethics** so that all members are aware of and follow their professional responsibilities. NAR's Code of Ethics is extremely influential, not only for REALTORS® but for other licensees, because ethical codes often later become license laws. The code may be the best available guideline for ethical behavior, whether or not a licensee is a member of NAR.

Communication Skills

Communication is the core of the real estate brokerage business. A licensee may be knowledgeable, competent, and ethical, yet because of a lack of communication skills, be unable to help customers successfully. The three types of communication skills necessary are:

- Verbal communication skills
- Written communication skills
- Nonverbal communication skills

Verbal communication skills   Talking to buyers, sellers, appraisers, surveyors, and other licensees enables the professional to share information, ask questions, and better understand the needs of others. The professional must be able to express information completely, honestly, and clearly. The individual who fails to master **verbal communication skills** may be misunderstood, appearing incompetent or even dishonest.

Community colleges and universities offer communication and public speaking classes to the public. One inexpensive way to learn to speak effectively is by joining a Toastmasters Club, a nonprofit service organization devoted to enhancing verbal communication skills. Many real estate licensees point to their years in Toastmasters as a key factor in their success.

■ RELATED WEB SITE

Toastmasters International: *www.toastmasters.com*

When licensees prepare for oral presentations they should organize the presentation logically and know exactly what they are going to say. Word choice is important. For instance, the statement "We can finish the deal by the end of the month" would sound better as "We should be able to close the transaction by the end of the month."

Jargon is a word or expression related to a specialized vocation that a layperson might not understand. Licensees should avoid using jargon. For example, the term *floor duty* describes the period during which a broker associate is entitled to take all customer calls. While it's a well-known expression in real estate circles, it is not as familiar to consumers. A customer who calls the office for information on a listed property and is told "Just a minute, I'll let you talk to the associate on the floor" may wonder whether there has been an accident or just a lack of chairs. By avoiding jargon, a real estate professional helps clients and customers better understand the information the professional is trying to relate.

Written communication skills   Letters, e-mail, flyers, and other forms of written communication are often the first impression the public has of a licensee. Bad grammar and misspellings may reflect poorly on the licensee and the brokerage firm. Written communication skills are even more important for writing a contract provision. An ambiguous clause may result in a lost sale, a lawsuit, or disciplinary action by the Colorado Real Estate Commission.

■ **EXAMPLE 1.1**   Les shows a town home to a married couple who are interested in purchasing it despite the fact that the property has been poorly maintained. The seller has told Les that he would be willing to make reasonable repairs if the buyers include them in the sales contract. So Les writes the following special clause in the contract:

"Seller agrees to remodel the townhome and put everything into first-class condition."

Based on this clause, what will the buyer expect?

What will the seller want to do?

Is there a possibility for miscommunication here?

How should this clause have been written?

Written communication skills may be enhanced by taking courses at a community college, reading books to improve writing skills, or purchasing a book of ready-made real estate letters, such as *Power Real Estate Letters*, by William H. Pivar and Corinne Pivar (Dearborn Real Estate Education). A dictionary and spelling and grammar check on a software program are minimum requirements for achieving better written communication.

Nonverbal communication skills   **Nonverbal communication,** often called **body language,** is also very important in sales. The real estate broker associate who understands body language will be better able to read the attitudes of customers and develop body language that can make a customer comfortable and establish rapport. Often, nonverbal communication can be far more revealing than what a person says. Some obvious body language styles include those described in Figure 1.2.

A real estate broker associate who wants to be more effective might consider using the following body language:

- A firm, but not hard handshake
- Usually, direct eye contact when you are talking or listening. Staring without blinking or looking away or down all the time may be disconcerting to the listener. Persons from certain cultures may perceive constant direct eye contact as disrespectful.
- Don't cross arms or legs. Keep arms open and relaxed.
- Lean forward into the conversation to display your interest. Leaning backward, especially if hands are joined behind the head, may be perceived as a sign of superiority or aloofness.

■ RELATED WEB SITE

The Web site for the Center for Nonverbal Studies is rich in observations of nonverbal communication: *http://members.aol.com/nonverbal2/index.htm.*

■ **EXAMPLE 1.2**   Larry is making a listing presentation to Jack, a for-sale-by-owner. He notices Jack has faced to the side, folded his arms over his chest, and looked in another direction.

What feedback is Jack giving Larry about his presentation?

Professional Education

Licensees enhance their professionalism through continuing education. The law requires continuing education before renewal of a license, but many professionals take more courses than are required by the law. National organizations award professional designations to graduates of their educational programs. These designations make consumers aware of those persons who have exceeded the legally required continuing education.

FIGURE 1.2

Body Language Indicators

Body Language	Probably Means...	Comments
Pyramiding fingertips—the classic "banker" look	I'm superior to you, and I'm making some judgments about you	Don't do this when talking to a customer
Pyramiding, leaning back in the chair with hands joined behind the head—the "boss"	I'm superior to you; you have less status here	Don't do this when talking to a customer
Arms folded across the chest	Closed, defensive	Bad sign; you'll get nowhere in this presentation until you get the listener loosened up
Legs crossed at the knee away from the listener with body facing to the side	Closed, defensive	Bad sign; you'll get nowhere in this presentation until you get the listener loosened up
Customer looking away (no eye contact) during a sales presentation	Closed, often unfriendly	Bad sign; unlikely to buy until you can establish rapport
Palms toward the person just before speaking	Stop talking; I have more important things to say	Don't do this when talking to a customer
Stroking the chin (mostly males); fingertips to the neck (mostly females)	Sign of seriously considering the proposal	Get ready to write the offer
Scratching the head	Thinking; may be about to make a decision	Ask to help with any questions the customer may have
Staring at the ceiling	Thinking; trying to remember a fact	Ask to help with any questions the customer may have
Leaning forward into sales presentation	Interested, attentive	Good sign; you're doing something right
Customer frowning during sales presentation	May indicate the customer disagrees or does not understand some point	Trouble; try to ask a question to find out what's happening here
Hands hiding mouth while person is talking	Sometimes a habit of persons who are not speaking honestly	Probably OK, but some information may be incorrect
Hands on hips, head bowed, staring at you	Aggressive stance; challenge	This could mean trouble

Other types of education, when combined with formal instruction, also enhance a licensee's competence. In *Real Estate Brokerage: A Success Guide*, by Cyr, Sobeck, and McAdams, the authors describe three types of knowledge broker associates need:

- Technical knowledge
- Marketing knowledge
- Product knowledge

Technical knowledge   Technical knowledge provides the tools of the business, such as completing contracts properly, knowing sellers' and buyers' costs, and understanding the comparative market analysis process. This text provides technical knowledge in the following areas:

- State and federal laws
- Preparing a comparative market analysis
- Preparing a listing contract
- Qualifying a buyer
- Understanding financing plans
- Preparing a sales contract
- Reviewing closing statements
- Analyzing real estate investments

Broker associates should not work in the field without the appropriate technical knowledge. For example, broker associates will feel quite incompetent if they cannot fill out the cost disclosure statement or contract form. Technical knowledge also includes knowledge about state and federal laws, such as fair housing and antitrust laws.

■ **EXAMPLE 1.3**   Traci has been in the real estate business for about a month and is working with her first buyer customers, referred to her by a close friend. She shows them a home listed by another broker associate in her office. The buyers immediately start to talk about where to place their furniture. "We think this is the one," they tell Traci.

It is Saturday afternoon and Traci is unable to contact the broker to answer some questions about how to complete the required forms. Nervously, she tells the buyers, "You know, I hate to see you rush into anything. There are some other houses out there you might like better. I can show them to you tomorrow, if you like. That'll give you time to think about it all, too!"

What is Traci's main objective at this moment?

How could Traci have been better prepared for this situation?

Marketing knowledge   Learning how to sell real estate comes from **marketing knowledge**. It encompasses the knowledge of psychology and the ability to assess a consumer's specific housing needs. This text provides marketing knowledge in the following areas:

- Business planning (self-marketing)
- Prospecting for listings
- Making an effective listing presentation
- Prospecting for buyers
- Showing and selling the property

Many sales training books and tapes are available commercially. Kaplan Professional Schools, institutes and societies of the National Association of REALTORS®, as well as local Boards of REALTORS® offer sales training classes. Many brokerage firms and franchise companies hold regular sales training courses for sales personnel. Marketing knowledge is an important tool and a major part of the service consumers expect when buying and selling real estate.

Product knowledge   Customers expect their real estate broker associates to know the market. They want the benefits of that **product knowledge** in marketing a property or finding the right property for purchase. A new practitioner should work hard to obtain that knowledge as quickly as possible to best serve the consumer. This text cannot help you acquire product knowledge because it is so area-specific.

How does one gain product knowledge? Outstanding trainers say the most important step a new licensee can take is to become familiar with the marketplace, which means looking at properties. Some firms recommend their new broker associates take at least two weeks to see as many listings as possible. They suggest maintaining that product knowledge by regularly scheduling time to look at properties.

Setting Goals, Business Planning, and Time Management

Setting realistic goals is extremely important in real estate sales. Because real estate broker associates are usually independent contractors, they receive little supervision. Without a clear set of goals and a strong business plan, the licensee may lose focus and direction. Goals should be written, measurable, attainable, and flexible and should contain deadlines. Once goals have been set, the business plan shows how to achieve the goals. Time management is an important part of that plan.

A distinction can be made between goals, plans, and time management. For example, an automobile trip from Orlando to St. Louis requires all three.

- The goal is St. Louis.
- The plan is the road map on which is drawn the route and mileage.
- **Time management** consists of the daily objectives: When do we leave, when do we stop for food, and how far should we go today?

Goal setting should begin with a long-term view: What accomplishments does a person want to achieve in his lifetime? Once this long-term view is established, the next step is to work back to the present, using smaller increments of time. By working from the long term to the short term, it becomes clear what a licensee, must do this year, this week, and today to achieve the long-term goal.

Sample Long-Range Plan

Year 5	CRS designation	Own brokerage firm	$150,000 net worth
Year 3	Finish two courses	Open office	$90,000 net worth
Year 1	Finish first course	Pass course and state exam	Must save at least $30,000 this year
Month 1	Check class schedule	Check class schedule	Must save at least $2,500 this month

When setting these goals, the professional should always include personal and family objectives. An example of professional goal setting follows. (See Figure 1.3.)

A licensee's five-year goals are

■ earning the GRI and CRS professional education designations,
■ obtaining a broker's license,
■ owning a brokerage firm with 15 associates, and
■ acquiring $150,000 in additional net worth.

Once the licensee establishes the one-year goal, it is converted into monthly and weekly goals—short-term tasks.

A new broker associate must remember that setting income goals as an independent contractor in real estate sales is different from what it would be in a salaried position. Because of the independent contractor relationship, the broker does not pay the normal employee's share of Social Security and Medicare taxes, and does not pay for health insurance or other benefits. Also, the broker associate will have expenses such as Board of REALTORS® dues, license fees, education, office supplies, and advertising. To be safe, the broker associate should estimate those costs at 35 percent of gross earnings. So, if the broker associate plans to earn a net income of $31,200 in the first year, the gross income goal should be $48,000 ($31,200 ÷ 0.65).

Use the worksheet shown in Figure 1.4 to see what must be done today to achieve a $48,000 gross income. If the assumptions shown are appropriate for your market area, it is simple to project how you can accomplish the goal. This example focuses on income goals, but the same exercise could be completed for other goals.

A blank worksheet for *your* personal goals is included on the following page.

When the licensee is aware of what must be done today to achieve a long-term goal, the goals should be written out in contract form. It can be a private contract or a public document, with copies delivered to the broker and a mentor. Giving a copy to another person usually strengthens the commitment to succeed in the goals. A sample goals contract might look like the one in Figure 1.5.

The licensee then posts the goals where they are visible. The adage "out of sight, out of mind" is true where goals are concerned.

F I G U R E   1.4

Goals Worksheet

1. During the next 12 months, I want to earn: $ _____

2. That works out to be monthly earnings of: $ _____
   (Line 1 ÷ 12)

3. Approximately 60% of my earnings should come from listings sold $ _____
   (Line 2 × 0.60)

4. Approximately 40% of my earnings should come from sales made $ _____
   (Line 2 × 0.40)

Achieving my listing income:

5. In my market area, the average listing commission amount is: $ _____
   (Get this amount from your broker.)

6. So I must have the following number of listings sold: _____
   (Line 3 ÷ Line 5)

7. If only 75% of my listings sell, I have to get this many listings: _____
   (Line 6 ÷ 0.75)

8. It may take this many listing appointments to get a listing: _____
   (Get this number from your broker.)

9. So I need to go on this many listing appointments: _____
   (Line 7 × Line 8)

10. It may take this many calls to get an appointment: _____
    (Get this number from your broker.)

11. So I have to make this many calls per month: _____
    (Line 9 × Line 10)

12. Which means this many calls per week: _____
    (Line 11 ÷ 4.3 weeks per month)

Achieving my sales income:

13. In my market area, the average sales commission is: $ _____
    (Get this amount from your broker.)

14. So I've got to make this many sales per month: _____
    (Line 4 ÷ Line 13)

15. It takes about this many showings to make a sale: _____
    (Get this number from your broker.)

16. So I must show this many properties per month: _____
    (Line 14 × Line 15)

FIGURE 1.4

Goals Worksheet (continued)

1. During the next 12 months, I want to earn $48,000
2. That works out to be monthly earnings of (Line 1 ÷ 12) $4,000
3. Probably 60% of my earnings should come from listings sold (Line 2 × 0.60) $2,400
4. Probably 40% of my earnings should come from sales made (Line 2 × 0.40) $1,600

Achieving my listing income:

5. In my market area, the average listing commission amount is (Figure used here
   should be changed to fit your market.) $1,800
6. So I must have the following number of listings sold (Line 3 ÷ Line 5)   1.5
7. If only 75% of my listings sell, I have to get this many listings (Line 6 ÷ 0.75)   2
8. It may take this many listing appointments to get a listing (Get this number from your broker.)   5
9. So I need to go on this many listing appointments (Line 7 × Line 8)   10
10. It may take this many calls to get an appointment (Get this number from your broker.)   15
11. So I have to make this many calls per month (Line 9 × Line 10)   150
12. Which means I must make this many calls per week (Line 11 ÷ 4.3 weeks per month)   35

Achieving my sales income:

13. In my market area, the average sales commission is $1,800
    (Figure used here should be changed to fit your market.)
14. So I've got to make this many sales per month (Line 4 ÷ Line 13)   0.9
15. It takes about this many showings to make a sale (Get this number from your broker.)   20
16. So I must show this many properties per month (Line 14 × Line 15)   18

Source: *30-Day Track to Success* by Edward J. O'Donnell, O'Donnell Publishing, Tallahassee, 2003

Daily goals and time management Time management goes hand in hand with goal setting. Goals don't work without a schedule. Besides being measurable and attainable, a deadline must be set for achieving the goals. For example, the goal of "making as many calls as possible to prospective sellers" is attainable, but immeasurable because no time deadline has been established. The statement "I will make five calls to prospective sellers by 6 PM today" is clear, measurable, and more likely to accomplish the goal.

The licensee should make a **to-do list** before each workday starts, keep the list nearby throughout the day, and check off each item as it is completed. This provides a sense of accomplishment and motivation to continue. Some helpful points to remember about the list include the following:

- Transfer unfinished tasks from the previous day
- Include those daily tasks from the goals worksheet that are necessary to achieve long-term goals
- **Prioritize** items on the list
- Start with the least pleasant items. ("Eat the frog first.") Completing the tough tasks first results in the ability to get on with achieving important goals.
- Establish times for completing each task. Even if they need to be adjusted later, you have established a basic guideline to follow.
- Make notes for items to include on tomorrow's list.

FIGURE 1.5

Goals Contract

I, _____, have determined my career and financial goals voluntarily, independently, and without coercion. I now formally commit to the following:

During the next 12 months, I will earn (from Line 1)	$48,000
I will obtain at least this number of listings per month (from Line 7)	2
I will go on this number of listing appointments weekly (Line 9 ÷ 4.3)	2.3
I will make this many listing calls weekly (from Line 12)	35
I will make this many sales each month (from Line 14)	0.9
I will show this many properties each week (Line 16 ÷ 4.3)	4

If I begin to fall behind, I request that my broker remind me of this commitment and prod me to stay on schedule so that I can achieve my goals.

Date _____   My signature _____

Date _____   My broker's signature _____

Date _____   My mentor's signature _____

Source: *30-Day Track to Success* by Edward J. O'Donnell, O'Donnell Publishing, Tallahassee, 2003

Time management hints   A licensee can do many things to help manage time more effectively:

- Schedule time off for family, recreation, exercise, and relaxation. Failing to plan for these items can result in guilt feelings, discontent, poor health, or burnout.
- Make a time log of all activities in 15-minute segments for about two weeks. This will show where time is wasted and may give clues for being a more effective time manager. Your time can be rated as A, B, or C with respect to productivity. A time is most productive because it represents time actually spent with customers. B time is necessary work that can sometimes be handled by a personal assistant. C time is wasted time. Doubling your income may require only moving more of your workday to A time, not working twice as many total hours. See Figure 1.6 for a sample daily activity log.
- Qualify sellers and buyers based on their financial ability to complete a transaction, as well as on their motivation. Working with unqualified buyers and sellers is both a disservice to the consumers and a nonproductive use of time.

Sample Daily Activity Log

A Direct $	Hours [Goal]	Hours [Actual]	Comments
Prospecting for sellers	1	1	Pretty good. Got a lead for a listing.
Prospecting for buyers	1	0	Just couldn't get to this.
Making appointments with buyers or sellers			
Showing homes			
Presenting offers			
Making listing presentation			
Other activities that will directly produce $:			
Calling friends for referrals			
	1	1	Jane said she has a good friend who needs to sell a house. Maybe I'll call her tomorrow.
TOTAL	3	2	I need to do better at this.

B Office and Administrative			
Prepare CMAs			
Write ads	0.5	0	
Attend office meetings	1	1	
Look at properties	2	1	Just didn't have time to see more.
Attend education meeting			
Other administrative activities:			
Prepare announcement and mail out			
	1	0	I'll try to do this tomorrow.
TOTAL	4.5	2	

C Wasted Time			
Stopped to shop at Dillard's	0	1	Had a sale; shouldn't have, but...
Friend stopped by office	0	1	She had a day off and wanted to talk. Should have arranged to see her at lunch.
TOTAL		2	Makes me mad at myself

? Personal			
Scheduled time off			
Other (Describe):			
Renew driver's license	0.5	1.5	Went to tax collector's office, traffic snarled. Should have just mailed it.
TOTAL	0.5	1.5	

| **GRAND TOTAL HOURS** | **8.0** | **7.5** | |

- Be on time for appointments. Being late is the quickest way to lose the confidence of customers. Plan for contingencies such as rush hour traffic, last-minute phone calls, and weather-related inconveniences.
- Understand how much each hour of your day is worth. For example, if you earn $48,000 per year and work 290 days per year, nine hours per day, you work 2,610 hours and the hourly rate is approximately $18.40.
- Make cost-effective decisions. If you make $18.40 per hour, hiring a personal assistant for $10 per hour is more cost-effective than doing your own mail-outs and clerical work. Going home to wash the car Monday afternoon may cost you $18.40 versus $9.95 at a car wash.
- Utilize technology to increase productivity.

Power prospecting   Setting high income goals requires a commitment to prospect. The three keys to prospecting success are the following:

- Numbers
- Consistency
- Organization

Numbers   The difference between making a living and becoming a superstar is numbers. Figure 1.7 shows the real estate sales process. Notice the first activity is prospecting. Following these tips will help you become a successful prospector:

- Follow all laws when prospecting, paying particular attention to the National Do-Not-Call Registry list.
- A cross-reference directory can give you information on area residents and businesses. Cross-reference directories are arranged by street addresses and numerically by phone number. Listings arranged by street addresses allow you to find all the residents and businesses on a particular street in sequence. Listings arranged by phone number allow you to find all the numbers and names for a particular area code and exchange. The product is available in print or on CD. An annual subscription (costing from $150 to $400, depending on location) will give current information, and can filter out phone numbers that appear on the do-not-call list.

■ RELATED WEB SITE

Hill-Donnelly Corp. sells cross-reference directories for many market areas: *www.hill-donnelly.com*

- Use a prospecting tool such as The Daily 100 Power Prospecting Points Chart. (See Figure 1.8.) Note that this chart awards more weight to activities that are more likely to result in a listing or a sale. For example, sending a mailing to for-sale-by-owners is worth one point, but visiting in person gives five points because it is a more productive activity.
- Stay out of the office as much as possible. The only people you'll see there are other broker associates.

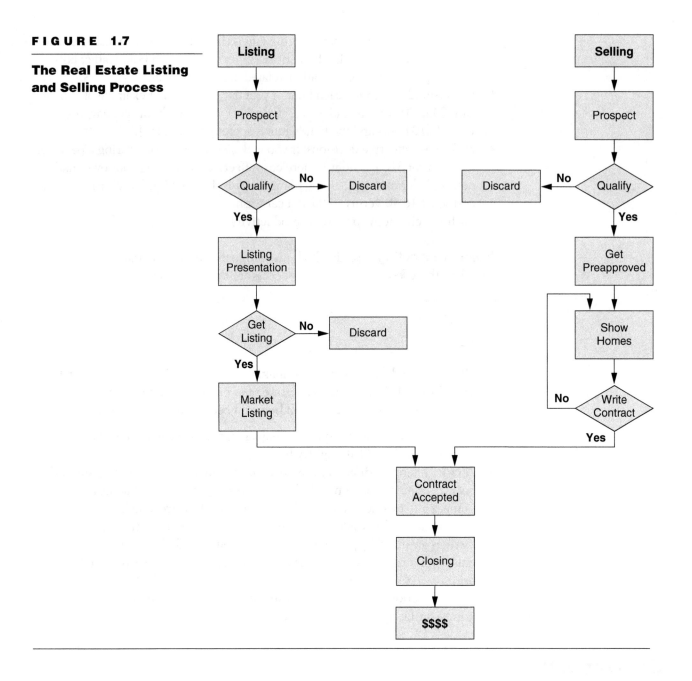

FIGURE 1.7

The Real Estate Listing and Selling Process

- Avoid time-wasting activities such as idle conversation, poor organization and planning, and uncontrolled interruptions. If you're worth $18.40 per hour, four hours per week of idle conversation with associates in the office costs you nearly $75!

It's all about prospecting. If a broker associate can reduce wasted hours and hours spent on administrative support functions and shift them to A-level activities, income should show a dramatic increase.

FIGURE 1.8

The Daily 100 Power Prospecting Points Chart—How to Survive and Make Money Selling Real Estate

Directions: Complete any combination of the activities listed below. If you consistently "earn" at least 100 Daily Power Prospecting points, your personal income will increase dramatically!

Name: _____ Week Beginning: _____ Goal for Week: $_____

Suggested Activity	Points	Mon.	Tue.	Wed.	Thu.	Fri.	Sat.	Sun.	Total
Listings:									
FSBO (For Sale by Owner)—Mail	1								
FSBO—Phone	2								
FSBO—Visit	5								
Expired Listing—Mail	1								
Expired Listing—Phone	2								
Expired Listing—Visit	5								
Notice of Listing—Mail	1								
Notice of Listing—Phone	2								
Notice of Sale—Mail	1								
Notice of Sale—Phone	2								
FRBO (For Rent by Owner)—Mail	1								
FRBO—Phone	2								
Cold Call Completed	2								
Follow Up on Listing Prospect	2								
Listing Presentation Made	10								
Listing Taken	20								
Servicing Listing by Mail	2								
Servicing Listing by Phone	3								
Servicing Listing by Visit	5								
Listing Price Change	5								
Listing Term Extended	5								
Contract on Listing Presented	10								
Listing Sold	20								
Sales:									
Office Caravan (per home seen)	3								
Previewing Listings	3								
Prospecting Calls to Renters	2								
Open House	10								
Name and Phone from Ad Call	5								
Follow Up on Buying Prospect	2								
Property Shown to Buyer	5								
Contract Written	10								
Contract Accepted	20								
Sales Servicing Call	3								
Referral Requested from Buyer	2								
Referral Sent to Another City	5								
Closing Attended	10								
Other:									
Attend Office Meeting	10								
Attend MLS Marketing Session	10								
Attend Education Meeting (hr)	10								
Past Customer Contacted	3								
Phone Friend about Real Estate	3								
Lunch with a Prospect	5								
Attend Civic Club Meeting	5								
Thank-You Card Mailed	3								
Personal Referral Received	5								
Newsletter Mailed	2								
Other Productive Activities	?								
Total Points									

FIGURE   1.9

John's Power Prospecting Program

	Month 1	Month 2	Month 3	Month 4	Month 5	Month 6	Month 7
Points on Daily 100	700	1,000	1,200	1,400	2,000	2,200	2,500
Following month business results							
Listings taken	1	1	1	2	2	2	3
Sales made	0	0	1	1	2	2	3
Listings sold	0	1	1	2	2	3	4
Total transactions	1	2	3	5	6	7	10
Commissions: ($150,000 price with a 1.5% commission to sales assoc.)	$0	$2,250	$4,500	$6,750	$9,000	$11,250	$15,750

If a broker associate decides to make a commitment to do power prospecting and is able to increase contacts, the associate's income should show a geometric increase. Figures 1.9 and 1.10 show what can happen to the income stream in seven months if a person goes from little or no prospecting to power prospecting. The figures shown won't magically work for every broker associate but depend on the following assumptions:

■   The broker associate is articulate, likes people, and is disciplined.
■   The broker associate has finished training and knows how to
  — prepare a CMA,
  — make an effective listing presentation,
  — show properties,
  — ask closing questions, and
  — ask for the order.

For example, John is a broker associate who has been "drifting" through his start up training program. After he completes the program, he decides to work smarter and increase his prospecting time. The first month he works 20 days and gets 700 points (35 per day). He continues to work the program, becomes more focused, and is finally able to achieve a 2,500-point month. His business increases dramatically. He finally understands that "prospecting is the name of the game." While some licensees may be skeptical of the income levels shown in Figures 1.9 and 1.10, power prospectors know the numbers work.

Time management and the use of a personal assistant   Many broker associates use licensed and unlicensed personal assistants to help complete many of the administrative duties that must be completed around a real estate transaction.

Licensed personal assistants   Licensed personal assistants are invaluable and can provide all real estate services for the customers of the employing licensee, including showing and listing properties, calling prospects, and providing access to a listed property. A licensed personal assistant must be registered under the employing broker and may be paid for brokerage activities only by the employing broker.

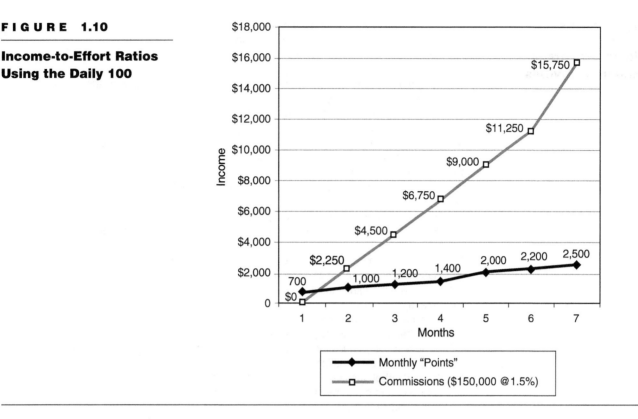

FIGURE 1.10

Income-to-Effort Ratios Using the Daily 100

Unlicensed personal assistants   Some licensees now employ unlicensed assistants to help complete routine office activities, such as mass mailings, writing ads, and preparing comparative market analyses. Broker associates who employ unlicensed assistants must ensure that the assistant does not perform any activities that violate the law.

An unlicensed individual may *not* negotiate or agree to any commission split or referral fee on behalf of a licensee. The unlicensed assistant may be paid as an employee or as an independent contractor. However, licensees should not share commissions with unlicensed assistants. The licensee hiring an unlicensed assistant must be very careful to avoid putting them in a position where they would be asked to offer an opinion or negotiate with a member of the public. A list of activities that may be performed by unlicensed personal assistants is shown in Figure 1.11.

If the assistant is to be paid as an employee the employer must withhold and pay FICA and income taxes and file withholding tax reports on a timely basis. Penalties for noncompliance can be substantial. A licensed assistant who is paid a salary or assigned specific working hours or told how to do the work is an employee rather than an independent contractor. For further clarification review Commission Position Statement 20 in the Colorado Real Estate Manual (CREM).

A licensee also should be aware of the liability of having employees. An accident on the job could make the licensee's employer liable, as could an employee who injures another person while running errands for the licensee.

FIGURE 1.11

Unlicensed Personal Assistant Activities

1. Answer and forward telephone calls.
2. Fill out and submit listings and changes to any multiple listing service.
3. Follow up on loan commitments.
4. Assemble documents for closing.
5. Secure public information documents from courthouse, utility district, etc.
6. Make keys for company listings.
7. Write ads for approval of licensee and supervising broker, place advertising in newspapers, and so forth.
8. Receive, record, and deposit earnest money, security deposits, and advance rents.
9. Type contract forms for approval by licensee and supervising broker.
10. Monitor licenses and personnel files.
11. Compute commission checks.
12. Place signs on property.
13. Order items of repair as directed by the licensee.
14. Prepare flyers and promotional information for approval by licensee and supervising broker.
15. Act as a courier service to deliver documents, pick up keys.
16. Place routine telephone calls on late rent payments.
17. Schedule appointments for licensees to show listed property.
18. Be at an open house
    - for security purposes,
    - to hand out materials (brochures), and
    - to respond to questions that may be answered with objective information from preprinted information.
19. Answer verbal questions concerning a listing if the answer to the question may be obtained from preprinted information, and is objective in nature, and if no subjective comments are made.
20. Gather information for a comparative market analysis (CMA).
21. Gather information for an appraisal.
22. Hand out objective, written information on a listing or rental.
23. Drive a customer or client to a listing or rental.
24. Give a key to a prospect at the licensee's office and nowhere else.

■ **EXAMPLE 1.4**   Do a role-playing session, assigning parts to Sharon, John, and the broker.

Sharon *(Excited)*   I did it! I got that FSBO over on Killearney Way! Now I have another showing appointment. I love this business. Gotta go! See you later!

John *(Dejected, shaking head)*   How does she keep doing it? She seems to get one appointment after another. I'm still slogging along trying to finish up my daily plan. I've got eight more things to do!

Broker *(Sympathetically)* Tell me what you have done today, John.

John   Well, I had to make copies of the plat book pages for my farm area, make up a list of all the people on Scenic Drive, take my clothes to the cleaners, shop for a financial calculator, go to the title insurance company to get a rate card, and get my car washed. I did all that.

Broker   What is still on the to-do list?

John   I still need to find listings for the guy who called while I was on floor duty yesterday and tell him about some property. I've got to get back in touch with the buyer I showed property to last week to set up another appointment. Oh! And I need to get a market report back to my wife's friends who said they're interested in selling their house. I also got a response to the notice of sale cards I mailed last week. I need to call those people back. They said they might consider selling. And the tenants on Jackson Bluff Road think they may be ready to buy. I need to call them and set up a time. There's just not enough time in the day!

Can you help John evaluate his time management skills so he can be as productive as Sharon?

■ SUMMARY

Licensees who meet only the minimum education requirements of the license law cannot be called professionals in the true sense of the word. To be perceived as a professional, a real estate broker associate will do the following:

■ Acquire verbal, written, and nonverbal communication skills to share information clearly in order to reduce the chance of misunderstandings or misrepresentation

■ Acquire technical knowledge, marketing knowledge, and product knowledge

■ Set goals that are written, measurable, attainable, flexible, and that establish deadlines (Setting goals allows new licensees to achieve those business and personal objectives that provide the ability to grow professionally and provide better customer service.)

■ Practice effective time management (Time management allows broker associates to meet commitments and maximize their efforts to provide good service.)

■ KEY TERMS

body language	professional ethics	written communication skills
jargon	technical knowledge	
marketing knowledge	time management	
nonverbal communication	to-do list	
prioritize	verbal communication skills	
product knowledge		

■ APPLY WHAT YOU'VE LEARNED

The following actions reinforce the material in Course 3, Unit 1. Use this list as you start your new business:

■ Write a concise description of each brokerage relationship disclosure form that you could use to explain forms to customers.

■ List the customer contacts you have had in the previous two weeks. If you acted as a transaction broker, did you tend to favor one party over another?

■ Write a short list of each of the fiduciary responsibilities required of a single agent. Analyze each carefully, then select the responsibility you believe is most likely to be violated in the real world. Explain why.

■ Write a script that you could use with a seller for introducing and explaining the property condition disclosure statement.

■ Using the Daily 100 chart, begin recording your success in making contacts with as many potential customers as possible. Involve your broker in the program and ask for help to stay on track.

■ List your personal characteristics that you believe will be of most value to you in your real estate career, then refine the list by showing which activities will best use those strengths.

■ List your personal characteristics that you believe need improvement to enhance your career. Make one action plan focusing on ways to achieve those improvements and another focusing on ways to reduce the impact of those personal characteristics that are hard to change.

■ At the next meeting of your Board of REALTORS®, don't hesitate to give an opinion on the subject under discussion or to market your listing during the marketing time.

■ Prepare a to-do list for tomorrow, arranged by priority.

■ Set a goal of getting one new listing within the next seven days, and write out an action plan to achieve the goal.

■ Prepare a short-term goal that includes the number of customer contacts you intend to make each day for the next ten days.

2
UNIT

Prospecting for Listings

Upon completion of this unit, you should be able to

- ■ **list** the five principal sources of listings,

- ■ **describe** at least three types of properties a licensee should not attempt to list,

- ■ **explain** why a listing commission seems much higher than the stated percentage to the seller,

- ■ **list** at least three circumstances under which an FSBO might be ready to list right away,

- ■ **describe** the three transactions that can be generated from a call to a for-rent-by-owner,

- ■ **state** the principal reason that listings expire, and

- ■ **list** the five categories in a leads database.

■ OVERVIEW

Learning how to be an effective and productive listing broker can make the difference between average and above average income in real estate. This unit shows you how to be above average by showing how a strong prospecting program can help build an income-producing listing inventory. The top-producing broker associate is the one who has a strong ongoing prospecting system that allows for effectively finding ready and willing sellers and buyers. This unit shows how to start the process.

■ YOU DON'T WANT THEM ALL

When prospecting for listings, qualify the properties and prioritize your efforts. Be picky. Your time is limited, and there are only so many listings you can work to get. The amount of effort required for prospecting and making a listing presentation is the same for a good listing as for a poor one. Don't spend time working to get a listing

■ if the seller is not motivated,

■ if the seller suggests you break the law by nondisclosure or discriminatory practices,

■ in a market area you don't service, such as in an adjoining community,

■ outside of your preferred price range,

■ if the property condition is so bad you would be embarrassed to show it, or

■ if the owners are so rude or demanding you don't want to work with them.

The secret is to prioritize your efforts and focus only on those listings that will sell within a reasonable time with reasonable effort on your part.

■ PROSPECTING OBJECTIVES

The main objective when prospecting for listings is to get an appointment to make a listing presentation. Because listings are the lifeblood of the real estate business, broker associates must know how to find sellers who need their professional services. In this unit, the new broker associate will learn the most productive sources of listings and how to effectively approach the sellers and obtain an appointment to make a listing presentation.

The most important sources of listings for a new broker associate are

■ for-sale-by-owner (FSBO),

■ for-rent-by-owner (FRBO),

■ expired listing,

■ farming, and

■ canvassing.

Canvassing includes cold calls, knocking on doors, and direct mail. Other sources for listings are your spheres of influence, personal contacts, notices of listings, and sales to neighbors and out-of-town owners. Notice that the discussion began with sources of listings for *new* broker associates. In two, three, or four years, the new broker associate who uses these sources will have the most powerful listing source of all: previous customers.

No matter which method a broker associate uses to locate prospective listings, the broker must prepare for listing appointments carefully. The comparative market analysis (CMA) is necessary to help price the listing. The broker associate also must understand which costs the seller can be expected to pay, how to complete and explain the listing agreement, and how to market and service the listing.

■ WHY FSBOS ARE FSBOS

If you were an owner of a property, try to think why you might consider selling the property yourself rather than listing it. Assume your home is worth $200,000. A broker's commission of 6 percent would result in your paying $12,000, a pretty substantial amount. But if you further assume you bought the home two years ago for $185,000, with a 10 percent down payment, your equity is approximately $35,000.

Calculation: $200,000 minus the original mortgage of $166,500 ($0.90 \times \$185,000$) less the principal paid back.

Now, the $12,000 is much greater than 6 percent. It's actually closer to 34 percent of the equity, perhaps explaining why sellers might want to try it alone. It also explains why you will need a good presentation to show them why they need you.

For-Sale-by-Owner

The only potential prospect we know for sure who wants to sell is the **for-sale-by-owner**. It is surprising that so few new broker associates use this outstanding source of listings in their daily plan. The myths many broker associates quote to avoid prospecting the FSBO market include the following.

- It takes more organizational skills to make the prospecting pay off.
- Sometimes FSBOs are not courteous to licensees who phone or visit (but remember, you can phone only if the owner is not on the National Do Not Call Registry).
- They won't agree to add the commission to their price.
- It takes significant selling skills to get a listing from a FSBO.
- FSBO houses are overpriced already.
- The FSBO does not need a broker because they have the Internet.

Broker associates who master the FSBO market by adapting to its unique characteristics are able to significantly increase their listing inventories.

FSBO characteristics   First, anyone in sales can be much more effective with a healthy supply of *empathy*. **Empathy** is sensitivity to the thoughts and feelings of others. To be able to persuade an owner to list, the licensee must first understand the mindset of that owner.

Those of us who have sold a car directly, rather than trading it in, usually did it to make more money from the sale. Whether that savings occurs is not the point; the fact is we did it for that purpose.

It's fair to assume that of all the FSBOs out there, at least 90 percent are trying to sell without a broker in order to save the commission. It's also likely that only a certain set of circumstances will change that mind-set. The FSBO may be ready to list if the owner

- is moving out of town right away,
- is concerned about personal security,
- is baffled by the home-selling process,

- is not available during normal hours to show the home,
- does not like negotiating with people, or
- is convinced that a buyer will reduce the price offered by at least the amount of the commission.

The broker associate who has made a positive contact with the sellers when those circumstances exist is most likely to get the listing. While the first item on the list is based on external conditions, the licensee may be able to change the sellers' mind on the others during the listing presentation (see Course 3, Unit 4).

Finding and tracking FSBOs An important part of the FSBO prospecting process is finding and tracking FSBOs. Most sellers use a yard sign, classified ad, or a note on a community bulletin board.

Most broker associates locate FSBOs in the classified ads. The licensee may assume that all ads that don't have the name of a brokerage firm are FSBOs. A broker's ad without the firm name is a *blind ad*, a violation of Rule C-19 (g).

Because not all FSBOs advertise in the newspaper, the licensee can find those properties by driving through neighborhoods and asking friends and family to call when they see a sign or notice on a bulletin board.

Even though this is the age of technology, many broker associates keep index cards with the phone number prominently placed in the upper right corner of the card. You then sort the cards by the number. When going through the paper, look for the number, then compare it with the cards. If it's not there, this is a new property. See Figure 2.1 for an example of the file card system. To find the owners' information, use a cross-reference directory.

It's easier to sort the ads if the records are on your computer. A spreadsheet or a database program like Access makes it easier. Even your word processor makes it simple to sort using the table function. (See Table 2.1.) Contact programs like *Top Producer* or *Act!* are specifically designed for this purpose, have many more functions, and are user-friendly.

FSBO prospecting techniques Licensees who work the FSBO market must be persistent, organized, and disciplined (POD). The first approach to a FSBO can be done by

- direct mail,
- telephone, or
- visit.

Direct mail is a low-risk technique that is likely to have a fairly low reward ratio. Direct mail is **passive prospecting** and should always be followed by a phone call or a visit. When used in conjunction with one of the other methods, it can be an effective way to prospect. The objective of sending direct mail is to introduce you to the seller.

FIGURE 2.1

FSBO Index Card

W. H. Lister   (303) 555-4369
0123 Street Way
Denver, 80218

Contacts:
4/15   Phoned, said he did not want to list now.
4/20   Stopped by and gave him sample contracts. "Thanks!"
4/25   He got my "thanks" card. Called to ask me if I could give him an opinion of value.
4/26   Went over my CMA with him at the house.
4/27   He called me to come over and list his house at $220,000.

TABLE 2.1

Sample Table for FSBO Information Sorted by Phone Number

Phone	Name/Address	Price	Contacts
(303) 555-2527	J. B. House 1111 Another St. Denver, 80219	$175,000	4/12 Phoned. Made listing appointment. 4/13 Got listing at $175,000.
(303) 555-2421 <DO NOT CALL LIST!>	Mary Mover 2222 Avenue Denver, 80205	$215,000	4/16 Stopped by. Told me she wasn't interested, but took sample contract.
(303) 555-4369	W. H. Lister 0123 Street Way Denver, 80206	$220,000	4/15 Phoned, said he did not want to list now. 4/20 Stopped by and gave him sample contracts. "Thanks!" 4/25 He got my "thanks" card. Called to ask me if I could give him an opinion of value. 4/26 Went over my CMA with him at the house. 4/27 He called me to come over and list his house at $220,000.

Before telephoning a FSBO, be certain that you understand and are complying with the National Do-Not-Call Registry. The liability for a violation of the law is quite substantial. If a FSBO's phone number is on the list, make a note in all data such as <DO NOT CALL LIST> so that the number is not accidentally called.

The objective for the call is to get an appointment to give a listing presentation. (See Figure 2.2.)

The most effective way to get a listing is by visiting the house. Many licensees don't like to do this because of the risk of rejection. When you see a FSBO sign, just stop the car and walk to the door. You can also set up the visits by geographic area, using your FSBO data cards. Asking questions is the best approach. The objective for the visit is to get an appointment to give the seller a listing presentation. (See Figure 2.3.)

FIGURE   2.2

FSBO Telephone Calling Guide

1. Check the National Do Not Call Registry before calling.
2. Introduce yourself and your company and say why you're calling.
3. Ask to visit the home at a specific time.
4. If the seller declines, you could ask if the seller would agree to pay a commission if you bring a buyer.
5. If the seller agrees to pay a commission, get an appointment to see the home.
6. If the seller doesn't agree, ask if he'd sell if the buyer agreed to pay the commission.
7. If the seller says no, ask if you can call again in the future.

FIGURE   2.3

So, You've Got a FSBO Appointment?

If an owner accepts your request to visit, set the appointment for a time when both parties will be home and available to talk. Ask that the sellers have several items ready for you, if possible:

- A copy of the paperwork when they purchased, especially the deed and title insurance documents
- Their homeowners' insurance policy
- A copy of the property survey, if available
- An extra set of front door keys

Why do you need these items now?

- Because they will be helpful when you list the home
- Because when you get there and find all these items neatly stacked on the table, it's your signal that they are ready to list their home

At the FSBO's front door   Questions that may help you build rapport with the sellers include the following:

- How much are you asking for the home?
- How long has it been for sale?
- Are you moving out of town?
- Have you had any offers?
- If I brought a buyer to you, would you pay a commission?
- Do you have a sales contract?
- Would you like to see a market report on your neighborhood?

Don't forget, sellers are also buyers. You have to find out what they intend to buy, and where, when this house is sold. If the seller tells you they are moving to another city, you have an opportunity to send a referral to a broker in that area. Referral commissions can be a significant part of your annual income if you always get the information about where people are moving.

For-Rent-by-Owner

The most common way to find many **for-rent-by-owners** (FRBOs) is by reading the classifieds in the newspaper or other classified publication. Owners trying to rent a house are good prospects for a listing, a sale, or property management.

FRBO as listing prospect   Those who own rental homes experience difficulties such as vacancies, uncollectible rent, evictions, and damage to the property. When the home is currently for rent, the broker associate must understand that some or all of those problems may have occurred very recently.

FRBO as buying prospect   Sometimes investors have factored such problems into their business plan, understanding the characteristics of rental property. Those investors frequently plan to continue investing in rental property.

FRBO as property management prospect   Persons who have their property for rent may be weary of the time and effort involved in managing the property. They may have had difficulty showing the property because of other commitments, and sometimes rental prospects are no-shows. Your call may come at the right moment and may turn into an opportunity for management. If your company does not have a property management department, you can establish a relationship with a local company that will pay a referral fee for the business.

FRBO prospecting techniques   The first approach to a FRBO can be made by

- direct mail,
- telephone, or
- visit.

Because the phone number in the ad is that of the owner's home, not the rental, it's difficult to learn where the rental property is located. The first contact can be direct mail followed by a phone call. Before telephoning a FRBO, be certain to check the National Do Not Call Registry. (See Figure 2.4.)

The objective of this call is to get an appointment to give a listing presentation. Remember, the advertised phone number matches the owner's address, not the rental property. See Figure 2.5 for an illustration of the possible business that can be generated from a call to an FRBO.

Another mailing, a phone call, or a visit should always follow direct mail. When used in connection with one of the other methods, it can be an effective way to prospect. The objective of sending direct mail is to get a call from the seller. Because the owner does not live at the rental property, visiting is probably the least effective method.

Expired Listings

Why listings expire   Some listings don't sell during the listing period for a variety of reasons, including

- market conditions (oversupply of homes available for sale),
- property condition,
- listing period too short,
- uncooperative owner or tenant,
- overpriced, or
- poor marketing effort.

FIGURE 2.4

FRBO Telephone Calling Guide

1. Check the National Do Not Call Registry before calling.
2. Introduce yourself and your company and say why you're calling.
3. Ask if the owner has considered selling rather than renting.
   a. If the answer is yes, suggest you do a market report, and get an appointment.
   b. If the answer is no, go to the next step.
4. Ask if the owner might consider buying other income property.
   a. If the answer is yes, get an appointment to discuss other properties.
   b. If the answer is no, go to the next step.
5. Ask if the owner has considered hiring a professional property manager.
   a. If the answer is yes, get an appointment for your company's property manager.
   b. If the answer is no, thank the owner for his or her time and say goodbye.

FIGURE 2.5

Business Options from FRBO Call

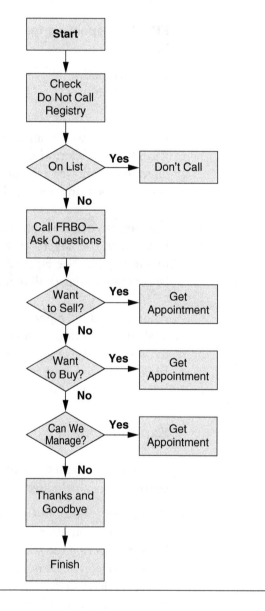

Except for the uncooperative owner or tenant, the major reason listings expire is almost always price. If there is an oversupply of homes, the price should be reduced. If the property condition is poor, the property is likely overpriced. A short listing period also calls for a low price.

Finding expired listings Listings expire from the multiple listing service (MLS) every day. They are shown in the change-of-status section, where you can also find sales and price changes. Without the MLS, it is more difficult to work this market. An excellent way to find expired listings is to get a recommendation from broker associates who have a listing about to expire when the owner won't relist. You can either pay a referral fee or have a cooperative arrangement to send your sellers to them at the end of a listing period.

How to approach owners of expired listings The owner whose property did not sell may be disillusioned with brokers and unreceptive to your approach. To effectively work expired listings, you must have empathy. The seller whose home was on the market for six months and didn't sell might

- wonder why the seller bought a home that no one else likes,
- feel the broker did little or nothing to market the property, or
- believe the home was overpriced during the listing period.

Once you understand how the owner might feel, you will be better able to tailor your approach to the situation.

Licensees can prospect for expired listings using the following methods used with FSBOs or FRBOs:

- Direct mail
- Telephone
- Visit

Direct mail may be ineffective because owners who want to sell often list with another broker immediately after the listing expires. A visit may not be as time-effective as telephoning, but visiting the owner is more likely to result in getting the listing. When the owner answers the door, you might ask the questions in the telephone calling guide in Figure 2.6. Your objective is to be invited inside to view the home, getting an opportunity for a listing presentation.

Farming

Think of farming as the cultivation of listings, much like establishing an orange grove. You can't get rich planting one tree. The more trees you plant, the greater the harvest. The grove takes a lot of work for some time without any apparent return. But when the grove begins to produce, it can shower you with fruit for years to come. And as the trees grow larger, the size of the harvest increases and can make you rich.

A listing **farm** requires lots of hard work to get established and for a time may have no apparent return. Many listing farmers abandon the grove just before it produces. If you decide to farm an area, you must make a commitment to continue for at least three years.

What's the payoff? Farming is a disciplined approach to prospecting. It is intended to expand a broker associate's sphere-of-influence, thus increasing listings and sales. Joyce Caughman's book, *Real Estate Prospecting*, 2nd ed. (Dearborn Real Estate Education, 1994), describes how farming should produce 20 percent

FIGURE 2.6

Expired Listing Telephone Calling Guide

1. Check the National Do Not Call registry before calling.
2. Introduce yourself and your company and say why you're calling.
3. Tell the seller the listing has expired and ask if the seller still wants to sell.
   a. If the answer is yes, get an appointment.
   b. If the answer is no, ask if the seller would like to know why the house didn't sell. Get an appointment, and make a CMA study.
   c. If the answer is no, say thanks and place another call.

of the listings in the farm area in the second year, 50 percent in the third year, and up to 75 percent of the listings after that.

Assume that owners in your farm area move once every six years and your farm has 800 houses. That means 133 homes will be listed this year (800 ÷ 6). If you're in the third year of your farm and get 50 percent of those listings, you'll get 67 listings, or 5½ each month. Assuming further that the average sales price is $200,000, two-thirds of your listings sell, and your share is 1.5 percent, your listing commissions alone would be over $134,000 ($200,000 × 67 × ⅔ × 0.015).

How many homes should be in a farm?   Because the farm may take six months before generating listings, a broker associate must also prospect using other methods. A new licensee should start a farm with no more than 200 homes but should select an area that allows for expansion of the farm. Many successful broker associates ultimately develop farms with 800 to 1,000 homes in several neighborhoods.

How to choose the farm area   You must carefully select your listing farm. It should have the following characteristics:

- Middle to upper price range
- High turnover
- Increasing property values
- Not currently being farmed by any other broker associate

The steps to take are in beginning a farm area are the following:

1. Select at least six potential farm neighborhoods. Check the MLS or the tax appraiser's office for all sales during the previous year.
2. Of those sales, review the listing office and broker associate so you can see if one person is getting a large market share. This would indicate that person is farming the area.
3. Determine the total number of homes in the area by looking at the subdivision plat map.
4. Divide the number of sales by the number of homes in the neighborhood to get the turnover index.
5. Select the neighborhood that is not currently being farmed that has the highest turnover index.

Table 2.2 is an example of the evaluation process. Blackwater Farms and Green Valley are currently being farmed, so it's not worthwhile to try to compete if other good areas are available. Mt. View has a 25 percent turnover ratio, and the home prices are in the $200,000 range. Mt. View is the best choice for farming.

Make contacts now, organize over time   Some broker associates spend too much time preparing to farm and too little time making contacts. While it's nice to have a map wall, a database of information about each homeowner, or prepared mailings for the next six months, that can be done later. It's tempting to "play office" rather than take the risk of talking with prospective sellers.

T A B L E   2.2

Farm Area Evaluation

Neighborhood	Currently Farmed?	Home Prices	Sales Last Year	Homes in Neighborhood	Turnover Index
Rustling Woods	No	$175,000	88	521	17%
Blackwater Farms	Yes	$200,000	86	416	21%
North Gate	No	$150,000	145	740	20%
Cold Springs	No	$250,000	52	345	15%
Mt. View	No	$200,000	172	685	25%
Green Valley	Yes	$250,000	68	534	13%

One task that you should do up-front, however, is to prepare a comparative market analysis (CMA) for the neighborhood, showing listings and sales for at least three years. This will help you discuss prices and also to know what prospective sellers paid when they purchased. Preparation of a CMA is discussed in Course 3, Unit 3.

Making contacts in your farm area   Contacts in your farm area should be a combination of direct mail, telephone, and a visit. Remember, direct mail is passive prospecting that works well as long as personal contact is part of the farming program. A color newsletter with your name and company logo is inexpensive and can result in more business. You can also send a letter of introduction, a postcard, or any other mailing piece that keeps your name in front of owners. Notices of listings and sales in the farm area can be one of the most effective and cost-efficient mailings, but should be followed up with a phone call or a visit. (See Figure 2.7.)

Calling persons in a farm area can be effective, but there should be a good reason for the call. Some reasons include telling owners about a new listing or sale, or that you will be holding an open house in the area.

The best way to cultivate your farm is by visiting owners in the neighborhood. Saturday is a wonderful visit day. A drive through the neighborhood allows you to stop and meet people out walking or doing yard work. A cold drink is a good ice-breaker.

Of course, just knocking on doors is one of the best activities. Give the homeowner a gift such as a calendar or yardstick with your name (and company name) imprinted on it. The owners will remember you when it's time to sell their homes.

You should make at least one contact each month with everyone in your farm area. If you work 25 days each month and farm 500 homes, you must make at least 20 contacts each day. Rotating between mailings, phone, and visits may reduce your workload. After you become fairly well known, you can increase the mail contacts and reduce the personal contacts.

FIGURE 2.7

Notice of Sale Card

We've done it again!

We have just participated in the sale of your neighbor's home located at

724 Oak Street.

Your neighborhood is very attractive and much in demand by buyers. You might be pleasantly surprised when you learn the market value of your home. I'd be glad to furnish information to you about prices and marketability.

Please call me right away if you might be considering selling your home.

Hilda Cummings, Sales Associate
(312) 555-4300 • *Floyd Realty, Inc.*

Canvassing

Canvassing is prospecting by mail, telephone, and in person, not necessarily in your farm. All **power prospecting** programs include canvassing. The Daily 100 prospecting chart in Course 3, Unit 1 is a good reminder list.

Every broker associate who aspires to attaining top-producer status understands the power of canvassing. While this is the last prospecting tool mentioned as a listing source, it is likely the most important.

■ BECOMING A LISTING SUPERSTAR

This section is designed for broker associates who are not satisfied with a median net income, but who want to be in the 90th percentile and above. The average licensee does prospecting in small numbers and the results are modest. The superstar prospects to a huge base of leads and harvests huge rewards. You should go back to your goals worksheet and kick it up a notch! Fill out the worksheet to determine how to make a gross income of $200,000.

Your Leads Database

First, set up a software database. There are many databases available, including MS Outlook and Top Producer. One of the first steps is to organize your potential leads into five database categories:

- Close friends and family
- Friends
- Customers
- Acquaintances
- Targeted strangers

You need the different categories because your prospecting methods depend on your relationship.

There is another category of persons called Others who won't be put in your database. They make up the general population; strangers whom we don't consider prospects.

Close friends and family   This category of leads will be very small, with probably no more than 30 to 50 names. Close friends and members of your family will do business with you and send you referrals, but you may need to ask. The term *close friend* suggests a very strong, usually long-term relationship with mutual trust, care, and respect. Sometimes even close friends are reluctant to do business with friends for fear that the relationship could be affected. Your friends must be convinced of your professionalism and dedication. You must let them know that when you do business you will wear your "professional" hat. The contacts within this group are natural and frequent, and all requests for business should be low key.

Friends and past customers   These are people we know reasonably well but who are not close friends. Perhaps we have had lunch together or worked on a committee together. We should be working hard to move more people to this list from the list of acquaintances and targeted strangers. The size of this category will grow with the number of years you are in real estate. This group is a significant source of new business and referrals. Work it diligently! Each person on the list should hear from you by mail or phone at least twice monthly.

Acquaintances   These are people we've met or spoken to by phone but don't yet know well. We will develop this group into a powerhouse of direct and referral business. One of the major objectives of our prospecting efforts is to move as many targeted strangers to the acquaintance category as possible. We should have a combination of contacts with this group using mail and telephone at least two times per month.

Targeted strangers   Targeted strangers are persons we don't know who are qualified by income, occupation, or residence address. This is by far the largest group in your database. The names might come from mailing list companies based on income levels, from cross-reference directories, or from lists of doctors, attorneys, accountants, and business owners. This list should be very large, starting with at least 5,000 names and addresses. In the beginning you should send a direct mail piece (it could be a postcard or newsletter) at least six times annually. Leads that are generated must be followed up immediately. If you generate one transaction for every 100 names (a modest goal), you will have an additional 50 transactions this year. If your average commission is $2,000 per sale, your income has increased by $100,000.

What Will It Cost?

Postcards can be designed online through companies like VistaPrint.com using one of hundreds of templates. Five thousand glossy finish postcards, printed front and back, cost about $400 plus shipping. You can upload your photo and company logo. Send a different postcard each month. Your software will make label printing easy. Let's check the numbers:

Estimated gross income	$100,000
Less prospecting costs	
Postcards	
$399 (for 5,000) for 12 months (12 × $399)	$4,788
Estimated mailing costs	$612
Postage (60,000 cards × 0.26)	$15,600
Labor 6 hrs. × $8/hr × 12 months	$576
Total costs	<u>$21,576</u>
Net income generated	**$78,424**

Making Contacts

Some important points to remember when prospecting include the following:

1. Success is in the numbers

    Be confident that this process will result in much higher income levels. You will discover that there is a strong correlation between your prospecting and the number of transactions you make. When you discover what your personal ratios are, it's easy to better control your income levels by your daily prospecting. If you get $3,000 extra income, on average, from every 100 contacts you make, you should assume that by making 1,000 additional contacts (20 per week) you can increase your income by $30,000.

2. Be consistent

    Set the same time every day to make your contacts. Stick to the schedule, but if a closing or appointment conflicts, make sure your contact time is rescheduled for later in the day. It's like a diet: you might get off track, but success will come if you get back to the plan.

3. Call at your best time of day

    Some of us are great in the morning. Others are a little grumpy and should set their prospecting time later. Just be sure you have a high energy level when making contacts. Morning may be the best time for a prospecting routine because showing and listing appointments are usually set for afternoons or evening.

4. Make the first call

    The rest will be easier. Think of the athletic slogan "Just do it!" The hardest call is the first call. Just think one call at a time.

5. You'll get better

    As you make your daily calls, your contact skills will get better and your enthusiasm levels will increase.

6. Remember the goal

    Before you make your calls, visualize what you want to happen as a result of the call. Put a sign above the phone that says, "Get an appointment!" Another sign might read "Get a referral!"

Saturate and Remind

When you put a new entry into your acquaintances category, your strategy should be to saturate and remind.

If you watch television, you have undoubtedly seen one or more companies start a major media campaign with saturation broadcasting. A three-hour sports program, for example, might have as many as ten 30-second commercials in the first two hours. For the next hour, the commercial is often abbreviated to 15 seconds, but we know it well enough so that the short ad is as effective as the longer one. This is saturate and remind.

When you meet a new qualified prospect by phone or in person, that person is now put in the saturate mode, with at least a weekly contact for six weeks. Now they know who you are and what you do. If your contacts have been skillful, they also like you, will do business with you, and will send you referrals.

After the saturation period, you can reduce the number of contacts to twice monthly, and you'll have a steady source of business.

■ SUMMARY

The main objective of a licensee when prospecting is to get an appointment. The most important sources of listings for new broker associates are for-sale-by-owners, for-rent-by-owners, expired listings, farms, and canvassing.

Licensees should be selective about which listings to try to obtain and avoid listing property if the seller is not motivated or wants you to break the law. Also avoid listings that are out of your market area or are in poor condition.

Licensees who work the FSBO market must be persistent, organized, and disciplined (POD). Most FSBOs try to sell direct in order to save the commission, and most advertise in the classifieds. The most effective way to get a listing from a FSBO is to pay a visit. Organize the FSBOs by telephone number.

A broker associate who prospects for-rent-by-owners has a chance of three types of transactions: the FRBO might list the house, buy another house, or ask the licensee to manage the property.

Farming is a prospecting activity with long-term results. Persons who farm an area for several years may get up to 75 percent of the listings in a given neighborhood. The farm should be in a large area, but the associate should start with no more than 200 houses. The farm should be in a high-turnover neighborhood that is not currently being farmed.

Canvassing is the process of contacting prospective customers by mail, telephone, or in person. Licensees who want to engage in power prospecting must establish a leads database containing close friends and family, friends and past customers, acquaintances, and targeted strangers. Friends, past customers, and acquaintances should be contacted in some way at least twice monthly. New persons in the acquaintances category should have a contact program called saturate and remind, meaning weekly contacts for at least six weeks, then twice monthly.

■ KEY TERMS

farm	for-sale-by-owner	power prospecting
for-rent-by-owner	passive prospecting	targeted stranger

■ APPLY WHAT YOU'VE LEARNED

The authors suggest the following actions to reinforce the material in Section 1—Laying the Foundation for a Successful Career. Use this list as you start your new business.

■ Write a concise description of each brokerage relationship disclosure form that you could use to explain forms to customers.

■ List the customer contacts you have had in the previous two weeks. If you acted as a transaction broker, did you tend to favor one party over another?

■ Write a short list of each of the fiduciary responsibilities required of a single agent. Analyze each carefully, then select the responsibility you believe is most likely to be violated in the real world. Explain why.

■ Write a script that you could use with a seller for introducing and explaining the property condition disclosure statement.

■ Using the Daily 100 chart, begin recording your success in making contacts with as many potential customers as possible. Involve your broker in the program and ask his or her help in staying on track.

■ List your personal characteristics that you believe will be of most value to you in your real estate career, then refine the list by showing which activities will best use those strengths.

■ List your personal characteristics that you believe need improvement to enhance your career. Make one action plan focusing on ways to achieve those improvements and another focusing on ways to reduce the impact of those personal characteristics that are hard to change.

■ At the next meeting of your Board of REALTORS®, don't hesitate to give an opinion on the subject under discussion or to market your listing during the marketing time.

■ Prepare a to-do list for tomorrow, arranged by priority.

■ Set a goal of getting one new listing within the next seven days, and write out an action plan to achieve the goal.

■ Prepare a short-term goal that includes the number of customer contacts you intend to make each day for the next ten days.

3 UNIT

Pricing the Property to Sell

- **explain** the difference between an appraisal and an opinion of value,
- **list** four conditions that must be met in order to fairly use a comparable sale,
- **list** the three categories of properties shown in a CMA,
- **list** at least three sources of information used in compiling a CMA, and
- **explain** the adjustment process and direction of the adjustment.

OVERVIEW

Two duties owed to the public by real estate brokers are care and diligence. Assisting a seller in setting a realistic listing price or helping a buyer understand the market and assisting in setting a realistic offering price are two of the most important services a broker associate can offer.

Because all real estate activity is related to value, a valid estimate of property value has a significant effect on marketing a listing.

One term—*market value*—is of the most important value in a real estate transaction. The market value of real estate is the most probable price a property should bring in an arm's-length transaction occurring in a competitive and open market.

Real estate licensees use the **appraisal** process of sales comparison to produce opinions of value called comparative market analyses (CMAs). Note that a real estate licensee may not call their CMA an appraisal unless the licensee is also a licensed real estate appraiser.

Licensees must be familiar with the valuation of real property. While licensees do not prepare formal real estate appraisals, they will go through the appraisal process to some degree when listing properties. Licensees must have a good working knowledge of the market in which they operate to be able to use evaluation methods competently.

■ OPINION OF VALUE VERSUS CERTIFIED APPRAISAL

Real estate licensees may not refer to themselves as appraisers unless they are licensed appraisers. Licensees may be paid for providing opinions of value or competitive market analysis (CMA) services as long as they do not represent themselves or their reports as being certified appraisals. This unit focuses primarily on preparing opinions of value.

> **Remember, Rule E-42 states** *When a real estate licensee prepares a competitive market analysis (CMA) for any reason other than the anticipated sale or purchase of the property, the licensee must include a notice stating: "The preparer of this evaluation is not registered, licensed, or certified as a real estate appraiser in the state of Colorado."*

Basic Principles of Value

Many economic principles influence the value of real property. They are interrelated, and their relative importance varies, depending on local conditions. The following principles are important to licensees attempting to estimate market value:

- Substitution
- Highest and best use
- Law of supply and demand
- Conformity
- Contribution
- Law of increasing and diminishing returns
- Competition
- Change
- Anticipation

Substitution   Substitution is probably the most important factor in pricing residential property in a neighborhood with an active market. The value of a given parcel of real property is determined using the principle of substitution. The maximum worth of the real estate is influenced by the cost of acquiring a substitute or comparable property.

■ **EXAMPLE 3.1**   You have prepared a CMA for Savannah Cooley. Your opinion of value, based on sales of comparable homes, falls in a range between $192,000 and $203,000. Cooley needs $215,000 from the sale of her home to pay a number of obligations and requests that you list it at that price. Give four persuasive arguments for listing her property at market value.

Highest and best use   Of all the factors that influence market value, the primary consideration is the highest and best use of the real estate. A property's highest and best use is its most legally profitable and physically permitted use—that is, the use that provides the highest present value.

Law of supply and demand   As it does with any marketable commodity, the law of supply and demand affects real estate. Property values rise as demand increases or supply decreases. For example, when interest rates declined recently, demand for residential property increased significantly, resulting in dramatic increases in prices throughout most of Colorado.

Conformity   In neighborhoods of single-family houses, buildings normally should follow the principle of conformity; that is, they should be similar in design, construction, and age to other buildings in the neighborhood to realize their maximum value. An elaborate mansion on a large lot with a spacious lawn is worth more in a neighborhood of similar homes than it would be in a neighborhood of more modest homes on smaller lots. Subdivision restrictive covenants are designed to promote the principle of conformity to maintain and enhance values.

Contribution   Any improvement to a property, whether to vacant land or a building, is worth only what it adds to the property's market value. An improvement's contribution to the value of the entire property may be greater or smaller than its cost. A licensee's opinion should be governed by a feature's contribution to value, not its actual cost.

■   **EXAMPLE 3.2**   You have prepared a CMA for Phyllis, who lives in Scenic Heights, an area of $200,000 homes. Phyllis reviews the recent sales and sees that her house has a large deck and hot tub, a feature that is not present in the homes in the report. She produces the invoices for the cost of her deck and hot tub, which total $15,000, and suggests a $215,000 list price. You believe that decks and hot tubs in the neighborhood add about $5,000 to the properties' list prices.

Do a role-playing exercise, with another person taking Phyllis's part, and discuss the principles involved.

Law of increasing and diminishing returns   Improvements to land and structures reach a point at which they have no positive effect on property values. As long as money spent on such improvements produces a proportionate increase in income or value, the law of increasing returns is in effect. When additional improvements bring no corresponding increase in income or value, one can observe the law of diminishing returns.

Smaller homes in a neighborhood of larger homes may experience increasing returns by improvement. Homes that are the same size or larger than surrounding homes should not be improved significantly until the owners have considered the economics of their decisions.

■ **EXAMPLE 3.3** Sandy Brantly purchased a two-bedroom home in Betton Hills for $200,000. She builds an extra bedroom and bath and finds that the value has increased by much more than the cost of the improvements. She continues improving the property by adding two more bedrooms and a large family room with a fireplace. Sandy decides to sell, and she calls you to list the property. Your CMA shows that the value increase was much less than the construction cost. Sandy disagrees with your findings.

Do a role-playing exercise, with another person playing the part of Sandy, while you explain to her why the value may not have increased as much as the cost of the improvements.

Competition All residential properties are susceptible to competition, some more than others. The only house for sale in a nice, well-maintained neighborhood has a better chance of selling at or near market value than if several houses on the same street are for sale.

Change All property is influenced by the principle of change. No physical or economic condition remains constant. Licensees must be aware of market forces when preparing opinions of value.

Anticipation Most buyers purchase real estate with the expectation that its value will increase—and they have been rewarded when the anticipation proves correct. In inflationary times, the anticipation of higher prices creates a multitude of buyers, driving prices higher than can be supported for long periods. In Colorado, the prices for mountain properties have increased dramatically, especially if they are in or near a ski resort area.

But when the market begins to top out, the anticipation of a price recession can cause investors to dump property on the market, forcing prices lower. Anticipation also is important to prices of property in times of decreasing interest rates, when builders rush to fill the expected demand. Licensees must be aware of the importance of anticipation when valuing property for sale.

■ COMPARATIVE MARKET ANALYSIS

Most licensees use a **comparative market analysis (CMA)** to arrive at an opinion of value. A CMA is the process of gathering and analyzing the **property characteristics** of homes currently for sale, homes recently sold, and homes listed that did not sell. It may range in form from a simple list of recent sales with no adjustments to a detailed adjustment grid. Whether taking a simple or a complex approach, a licensee needs to ensure that all of the conditions for selecting comparables has been met.

Gathering CMA data

First, the broker associate must have knowledge of the **subject property.** If it is a standard floor plan subdivision home, it may be possible to complete a market analysis without a property inspection. However, if the seller has made many improvements or if the home has other amenities not typical of the market, it may be difficult to make adjustments during the CMA's presentation phase. The truly professional approach is to inspect the property before completing the CMA.

Once the property inspection has been completed, the licensee should select the best properties for comparison. Three categories of comparison help sellers and buyers better understand the market:

- Properties that have sold
- Properties that are now on the market
- Property listings that have expired

The CMA will be a good indication of value only when comparables exist in a reasonably active market and where sufficient, reliable market sales information is available.

A **comparable property** should meet four conditions before it is used in a CMA:

- It should be similar to the subject property.
- If this is a sale, it should have sold recently (within the past year).
- It should be located in the same market area as the subject property.
- It should have changed owners as a result of an arm's-length transaction.

Reviewing actual sales prices of comparable properties helps buyers and sellers see what buyers actually pay in the marketplace. Comparable sales data are important when new financing is necessary because an appraiser relies on these data to estimate market value. Many sales are contingent on financing the purchase price, so it is of no value to overprice a property only to lose the sale when the lender and buyer receive the appraisal report.

Reviewing the prices of comparable properties now on the market shows the seller what owners of properties with similar characteristics are asking. These are the properties that will compete with the seller's. The principle of substitution means that a buyer will select the property with the best price, all other things being equal. A seller who wishes to position the property in the most effective price window values it just above recent sales and just below competing properties. A properly priced listing should experience a reasonably quick sale at the optimum price.

The listing prices of properties that do not sell tell a great deal about the resistance level of buyers to overpriced listings. In almost every case, the expired listing has been priced too high for the amenities offered. The best sources for gathering CMA information include

- multiple listing service (MLS) records,
- company files,
- public records,
- other licensees, and
- data service companies.

MLS records are the most convenient and comprehensive method of getting listings and sales information. MLS computer records can be searched by address and subdivision for ease in finding comparable sales. The information can be retrieved for sold, current, or expired property listings.

Company files are limited in scope but may be more complete as to property descriptions and financing used in purchases.

Public records include information recorded in the clerk's office and information on file with the tax appraiser. Except for verification of sales data and identities of the parties, the information from the clerk's office is not as important as the information available at the tax appraiser's office. While the information from the property appraiser's records is sometimes outdated, the records are still a useful source of data. Because the "sold" section of the CMA should include for-sale-by-owner properties, the appraiser's office is often the best information source for such sales.

Licensees often know of properties that have just closed. The information given should be verified and added to the report to include current sales.

Data service companies compile property sales data and sell the information to interested parties. This information does not give complete property descriptions and is best used as a checklist to ensure that all sales have been considered.

Selecting Comparable Properties

A licensee preparing a CMA has two choices when selecting properties to compare. The first is to report every sale and every listing in the neighborhood, together with features and prices. The other is to analyze only the properties that are comparable.

Reporting all properties gives the seller an overview of the entire neighborhood market. Some sellers believe a list is incomplete if they know of a neighbor's home that sold recently that is not on the list; therefore, a complete list may make sellers more comfortable. However, problems sometimes arise with this all-inclusive list. Properties that are not comparable may mislead a seller concerning values. Properties that should not be used as comparables when making CMA adjustments include those that have significant differences in construction quality or size. Properties sold to relatives may be suspect as to fair value of the price and should be excluded from consideration.

Listing only three or four comparable properties makes a clearer presentation for a seller and reduces the chance for confusion about values. This is the approach appraisers use.

Perhaps the best approach for the licensee is to prepare a comprehensive list of all properties that have sold, are listed currently, or have expired and then select the most comparable properties from that list for analysis. This method satisfies the needs of completeness and clarity. The characteristics for comparison are described in the following.

Common Elements of Comparison

Clearly, the accuracy of the comparable sales approach relies on the elements of comparison selected for adjustment. The elements listed on the CMA chart in Figure 3.1 are some of the most common and significant factors that affect value in standard residential appraisals. In any given analysis, it may be necessary to include other adjustments. The easiest way to fill out the CMA is to list all of the details of the subject property, then evaluate each comparable with the data that have been gathered.

FIGURE 3.1

**Sample Property
Characteristics**

Location	Number of rooms
Size and shape of lot	Number of bedrooms
Landscaping	Number of bathrooms
Style	Kitchen characteristics
Construction quality	Condition of exterior
Design	Condition of interior
Age	Garage
Square feet of gross living area	Other improvements

*These are selected examples only; more or fewer characteristics may be applicable.

Location   What are the three most important determinants of property value? The old expression "location, location, location" is the best answer. Location is so important that only in very unusual circumstances would a licensee use a property outside the subject's neighborhood as a comparable sale. In such a case, the comparable should come from a similar neighborhood. Even within the same neighborhood, locations can result in significant variances. A property across the street from a park is more valuable than one across the street from a commercial area.

■ **EXAMPLE 3.4**   Sara Bilina wants a for-sale-by-owner to list with her, but the FSBO says that the commission added to his price would make the property overpriced. Sara really wants the listing, so she finds several homes the same size as the FSBO's property and prepares a CMA. However, the comparables she uses are located in another, more upscale neighborhood. The owner looks at the CMA and lists with Sara.

Has Sara prepared an acceptable CMA? Why or why not?

Has Sara violated any ethical or legal code? Why or why not?

Size and shape of lot   Irregularities can make portions of a site unusable for building, impair privacy, or restrict on-site parking, which could require major adjustments. Street frontage and total square footage are other important considerations.

Landscaping   Trees, plantings, and other types of landscaping should be evaluated as to maturity, quantity, and quality.

Construction quality   If construction quality of a comparable is not equivalent to that of the subject property, a major adjustment must be made. It is possible that the difference in quality might disqualify the property as a comparable.

Style   Generally, the style of a house follows the rule of conformity (a house should not be the only one of its type in the neighborhood). An important aspect of style is the number of floors of the residence. A one-story ranch house probably could be compared to a split-level, with some adjustment made. However, a three-story house is not comparable to a one-story ranch house. The best comparison is always a ranch to a ranch, two-story to two-story, and so on.

Design   Design must be viewed from both functional and aesthetic standpoints. Functional aspects include the existing traffic patterns in the house, placement of doors and windows, room-to-room relationships, and the usefulness of rooms. Aesthetic aspects focus on how pleasant and attractive an interior appears to an observer.

Age   Because most subdivisions are built within a relatively short period of time, there may not be significant age differences among comparables. A brand-new home is likely valued by the builder according to actual costs, overhead, and profit. While overall upkeep is important, the home's age may alert the licensee to outmoded design and fixtures or to needed repairs.

Square feet of gross living area   Square footage of the home is one of the most common areas for making adjustments because size differences among homes can be calculated easily. If licensees make adjustments for square footage, they also must be careful when adjusting for the number of rooms or bedrooms as this could lead to double counting. Adjustments for gross living area can be misleading if all properties are not comparable. For instance, a small house normally sells for more per square foot than a large house in the same area. A one-story house has a higher cost per square foot than a two-story house. Be sure that all properties used are comparable to the subject property. Appraisers normally do not count any floor area that is below grade as gross living area, so do not use such properties unless the subject also has below grade area.

■ **EXAMPLE 3.5**   Silas Dean is trying to set a price for a 1,500-square-foot home in Green Hills. He finds the following comparable sales:

Price	Square Feet	Price per Square Foot
$49,500	980	$50.51
51,000	1,025	49.76
50,000	1,000	50.00
61,500	1,500	41.00

The average price per square foot for these properties is $47.82. Sam Williamson, who owns the home, asks, "What is it worth?" Dean replies, "Houses sell for $47.82 per square foot in this neighborhood. Based on that, your property should sell for about $71,700." Williamson agrees and lists at $71,500.

Do you agree with Dean's analysis? If not, why not?

Measuring practice   Measurement of a house is extremely important. An error could cause problems in pricing the property if the home's square footage is given to buyers. Calculate the square footage of gross living area of the house shown in Figure 3.2.

■ **EXAMPLE 3.6**   You have done a market report for the Meadows at Woodrun subdivision. Your analysis of property value, based on several 1,200-square-foot homes, indicates that homes sell at prices averaging $50 per square foot. When talking by phone with a prospective seller, you quote that figure after setting the listing appointment. When you arrive at the property with your listing information in hand, the seller proudly shows you the 500-square-foot two-car garage that has been converted into a heated and cooled family room. He indicates that the price at which you should list the home is $85,000, based on 1,700 square feet times your $50-per-square-foot figure. Role-play this situation and explain why it may be difficult to market this home at $85,000. Also determine some methods of arriving at a more realistic price.

FIGURE 3.2

Living Area Outline

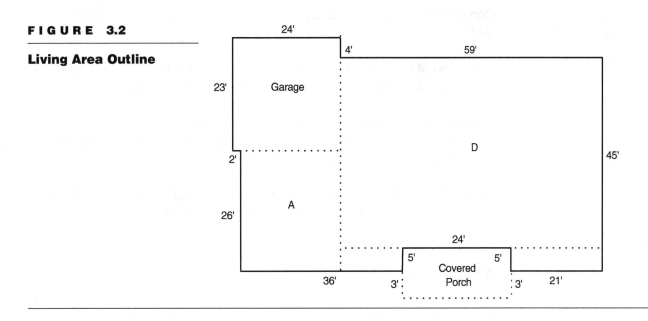

Number of rooms   The total number of rooms in a house does not include the foyer or bathrooms and generally does not include basement rooms. Don't double count when adjusting for square feet and number of bedrooms.

Number of bedrooms   A major adjustment is needed if the subject property has two bedrooms and the comparables have at least three, or vice versa. Don't double count when adjusting for square feet.

Number of baths   Full baths (lavatory, toilet, and tub, with or without shower), three-quarter baths (lavatory, toilet, and shower), and half baths (lavatory and toilet) comprise this category. Modern plumbing is assumed, so an adjustment must be made for out-of-date fixtures if different from the subject property.

Kitchen   Licensees should focus on the following key factors:

■ Location
■ Counter space and storage
■ Service triangle
■ Appliances

The location of the kitchen is an important factor, based on its convenience to dining areas and accessibility for unloading groceries. The market will not accept a kitchen with inadequate counter and storage space. The service triangle is calculated by drawing straight lines connecting refrigerator, range, and sink. Most consumer polls show that the total length of the three lines should be greater than 12 feet but should not exceed 22 feet. Appliances represent a sizable portion of the home's cost, and their age and condition are important.

Other space Unfinished attic, porch, utility room, enclosed sun porch, or any other room not part of the primary house area is included in this category. If it is not heated it is typically not included in the gross square footage.

Condition of exterior An adjustment should be made for any needed repair work.

Condition of interior An adjustment should be made for needed repairs. Luxurious finishing such as real wood paneling adds to a home's value.

Garage If the subject does not have one, any garage on a comparable property requires an adjustment. Garages on the subject and comparable properties must be compared for type of construction and size.

Other improvements An adjustment should be made for differences between the subject property and the comparable. Landscaping, driveways, trees, and views should be adjusted based on their contribution to value.

Adjusting for Differences

Ideally, the licensee wants to find comparable sales that are identical in characteristics to the subject property. In the real world, this doesn't always happen. While the CMA is not meant to be an appraisal, it is necessary to make **adjustments** for some of the differences discussed above. A major difference between the subject property and comparable property, such as a new kitchen, could make an opinion of value very misleading if no adjustment is made for the new kitchen. Many licensees recognize the difficulty in doing a CMA because when they look at a sold property, they see it as it is *today*, not how it looked when it went under contract. The important consideration in adjusting the comparable sale is how it looked at the time of sale.

■ **EXAMPLE 3.7** Whitney Cooley, a licensed broker associate, is preparing a CMA for Brian Edwards' three-bedroom, two-bath home in Eastgate. One of the comparable properties with the same floor plan sold recently for $73,000. The only difference between the properties is that the comparable property has an updated kitchen. Whitney has done CMAs in Eastgate before and estimates that an updated kitchen contributes about $4,000 to value. The subject property doesn't have an updated kitchen so Whitney makes a minus adjustment of $4,000 to the comparable's sales price. This indicates a value of $69,000 for the subject.

How did Whitney determine that an updated kitchen contributes $4,000 to value in that neighborhood? The matched pair technique helped her make the estimate. She examined two recent sales in which the only difference was the fact that one property had an updated kitchen. The property with the newer kitchen sold for $4,000 more than the home without the update. Because the kitchen was the only difference, the

$4,000 must be attributable to that amenity. It would be better to make the comparison with several matched pairs to support the conclusion, but the technique is valid. The cost to update the kitchen is not added, just the value buyers and sellers place on the newer kitchen.

Adjustments are always made to the comparable property, never to the subject. Adjustments are subtracted from the comparable property if the comparable is bigger or better. Adjustments are added if the comparable is smaller or less desirable. An easy way to remember is "CIA, CBS":

■ If the comparable is inferior, add.

■ If the comparable is better, subtract.

Adjustments should be made for sold properties, listed properties, and expired properties; then each category should be reconciled.

Reconciliation

Reconciliation is the resolution of several adjusted values on CMAs into a single estimate of value. While an appraiser is expected to report a single market value amount, a licensee making an opinion of value may prefer to report a range of values, from lowest to highest adjusted value of the comparables. Presenting a range rather than a single estimate of value allows a seller to price the property somewhat higher than the sold properties would indicate. The seller should understand that the home will likely sell at some price other than the list price and should consider all offers within the range of values.

Reconciliation enables the licensee to set the range differently. The first step is to estimate the value for each section of the report (sold properties, listed properties, and expired listings). Reconciliation is not simply the averaging of these values. The process requires the licensee to examine carefully the similarity of each comparable property to the subject property. If one comparable is nearly identical to the subject, including all relevant **transactional characteristics,** the sales price of that comparable might be the subject's estimated market value. When the comparables vary in their degree of similarity to the subject, the comparable property judged most similar is assigned the greatest weight in the reconciliation process.

The estimates for each section are rounded. The range is then calculated from the reconciled value of sold properties and the reconciled value of properties listed currently.

Another method for setting a range of values is to reconcile the sold properties to a value estimate, check to see what properties sell for as a percentage of list price, then divide the value estimate by that amount. The two values comprise the range high and low.

■ **EXAMPLE 3.8**   You have just completed a CMA for Tim Palmer's home at 1112 Bristol Court. The reconciled market value of his home is $127,500. MLS statistics indicate that homes sell at approximately 95 percent of list price.

What is the range of value you quote to Tim?

A Visual Aid to the CMA

"A picture is worth a thousand words" is a timeworn expression because it is true. Sellers who review CMAs with licensees often have difficulty visualizing the comparable properties. The licensee who provides visual data can make a clearer presentation, which may result in more realistic pricing. Owners who are motivated to sell do not set out to overprice their properties. Overpricing is usually the result of an inadequate understanding of the market, and that responsibility belongs to the listing broker associate.

Valuable visual aids include plat maps of the subdivision and pictures of the comparable properties. (See Figure 3.3.) The plat map should be color-coded to show which properties were sold, which properties are now for sale, and which listings have expired. Photos can be clipped from an MLS book, printed from the MLS computer system, or taken with a digital camera. The licensee who wants the listing should not fail to also include a photo of the seller's home. The seller will appreciate your personal touch and the extra photo for a scrapbook. Leaving a family home of some years can be a sentimental experience, and the seller will remember a licensee who is sensitive to those feelings.

CMAs Using Comparable Sales and Listings (No Adjustments)

Licensees commonly use this method to price property. It involves listing properties for sale now, properties sold in the previous year, and expired listings, without adjustments. Its simplicity is appealing to licensees and sellers alike because it provides an overview of the market. However, if properties on the chart are not comparable and the subject property is priced from an average of sales prices or square foot calculations, the pricing method can be misleading.

FIGURE 3.3

Plat Map of Neighborhood

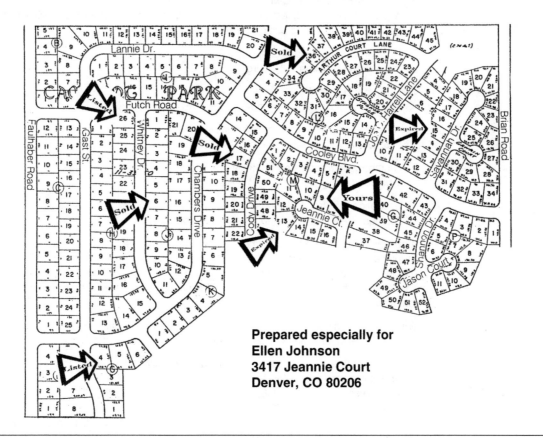

**Prepared especially for
Ellen Johnson
3417 Jeannie Court
Denver, CO 80206**

Getting Information from the Owner

You have just received a request from John Seburg to discuss listing his family's home. Mr. Seburg gives you the following basic information:

- The full name of all persons on the deed
  John Seburg and Susan C. Seburg

- The property address
  4316 Landtowne Drive, Lakewood

- The owner's home and office phone number
  720-555-3557; 720-555-3917

- The number of bedrooms and baths in the home
  Four bedrooms, two baths

- A description of extras in the home
  1,920 square feet of gross living area, two-car garage

- A convenient time for an appointment. This is the time to decide whether to do a prepresentation inspection of the property (two appointments required: one to inspect the property, one to present the CMA).
  You decide to have one appointment at 6:20 this evening and will inspect the property at that time.

Gathering Information from the Online Tax Rolls through the MLS System
The tax rolls for Jefferson County show the following information for the property

Legal description:	Lot 14, Block H, Landover Hills, Unit 2–Jefferson County
Property tax appraisal:	$149,300
Annual taxes:	$2,986.45
Year built:	1989
Base area:	1,920 square feet (later verified by physical measurement)
Total area:	2,420 square feet (includes two-car garage)
Last sale:	1996
Last sale price:	$128,000
Mortgage:	Sun Title Bank

A search of the tax records shows seven sales in the subdivision within the previous year, ranging from $168,000 to $174,800. Six of the seven sales were reported in the MLS. The sales are shown in the first section of the CMA in Figure 3.4.

There are four properties currently for sale in the MLS, shown in the second section of the CMA, and three listings have expired within the last 12 months, shown in the third section.

Analysis of Amounts Contributed by Amenities

Over a period of time, in reviewing data on sold properties, we can estimate what an updated kitchen, a garage, an extra bedroom, or a gas fireplace contributes to value. The matched pair technique would compare similar houses with and without a particular feature. The difference in price would tend to show what the feature contributes in value.

Comparative Market Analysis (continued)

For purposes of this CMA, we shall assume that sold properties in the neighborhood have shown the following value contributions over time:

■ The contribution of an updated kitchen is $4,000.

■ The contribution of a gas fireplace is $800.

■ The contribution of an extra garage stall (two cars, rather than one) is $2,800.

■ The contribution of extra square footage differences is $50/sq. ft.

■ The contribution of a large deck is $2,000.

The CMA has been filled in with the exception of the adjustments shown above. Please compare the subject property with the comparable properties and make adjustments to the comparable properties. Then complete the analysis and estimate the marketing range for the property. Presenting this CMA to the sellers will be discussed in Course 3, Unit 4.

■ **EXAMPLE 3.9** In this role-playing session, assume the CMA has been explained but the seller is attempting to set an unreasonably high listing price. Find as many persuasive points as possible to encourage the seller to price the property in the range suggested.

Computer-Generated CMAs

As computers have become more important in every phase of the real estate business, software programs have been written that make impressive presentations to buyers and sellers. Many of these programs are formatted to print out an entire listing presentation to the seller, tailored to a customer's specific needs. In many cases, the time required is less than that of handwriting the old CMA grids. Most of the programs are designed to interface directly with the MLS system program and download the necessary data. This saves the licensee time because information does not have to be typed in. Most programs provide raw sales data without adjustments, although the broker associate, by selecting only comparable properties, can come quite close to market value.

■ SUMMARY

Normally, when listing or selling property, licensees prepare a comparative market analysis and give their opinion of value. Many important principles of value exist, including highest and best use, substitution, supply and demand, contribution, and conformity.

The comparable sales approach to estimating value is the most appropriate method appraisers use to value homes and vacant sites. The comparative market analysis is the method most licensees use to prepare an opinion of value. The three sections of a CMA are properties that have sold recently, properties for sale now, and properties that did not sell during the listing periods (expired listings). Data for the CMA are gathered primarily from the MLS and county property appraiser's records. Only comparable properties should be used in the analysis. A range of values is provided to the seller because it is more meaningful than a single value.

FIGURE 3.4

Comparative Market Analysis

Comparative Market Analysis
Prepared by: _____
Date: _____

Prepared for: _____
Property Address: _____
Features: _____

Properties sold within the previous 12 months

Property Address	Sales Price	List Price	Days on Mkt	Living Area	Features	Estimated Adjustment	Adjusted Sales Price	Comments
1816 Hibiscus	172,800	180,000	120	1,820	Updated Kitchen, FP, Large Deck			
2412 Nasturtium	169,900	177,900	71	1,920	FP			
1763 Camellia	173,500	182,000	45	1,900	Updated Kitchen			
1421 Azalea	168,900	175,000	52	2,000	Large Deck			
1640 Clover	171,200	179,500	61	2,000	1 Car Garage			
2210 Hibiscus	168,000	175,900	32	1,900				
1240 Camellia	174,800	182,500	70	1,920	Large Deck, FP			
Percent sales price/list price	_____ %							

Properties currently on the market

Property Address	List Price	Days on Mkt	Living Area	Features	Estimated Adjustment	As Adjusted	Comments
1818 Azalea	191,000	75	2,100	Updated Kitchen			
1740 Hibiscus	178,800	120	1,900	FP			
2210 Clover	185,000	38	1,820	Large Deck, Updated Kitchen			
1604 Magnolia	177,000	45	1,920	Large Deck			

Properties that were listed but failed to sell during the previous 12 months

Property Address	List Price	Days on Mkt	Living Area	Features	Estimated Adjustment	As Adjusted	Comments
221 Camellia	192,800	180	1,900	Updated Kitchen, FP, Large Deck			
1812 Hibiscus	185,500	240	2,000	Large Deck			
2211 Azalea	186,600	140	1,800	FP			

Median $ _____

The suggested marketing range is
$ _____ to $ _____

This information is believed to be accurate, but is not warranted.
This is an opinion of value and should not be considered an appraisal.

■ KEY TERMS

adjustments
appraisal
comparable property

comparative market
  analysis (CMA)
opinion of value
property characteristic

reconciliation
subject property
transactional characteristic

Making the Listing Presentation

■ **LEARNING OBJECTIVES**   *Upon completion of this unit, you should be able to*

- ■ **list** at least four requirements for a proper listing presentation,
- ■ **list** the five major steps in a listing presentation,
- ■ **describe** the steps in explaining a CMA,
- ■ **list** two visual aids for a CMA presentation,
- ■ **list** the three major sections in a Seller's Net Proceeds Form,
- ■ **list** at least eight costs that a seller may be expected to pay at closing,
- ■ **explain** why insurance and escrow amounts usually are not included in the Seller's Net Proceeds Form,
- ■ **explain** the reasons for rounding all figures used in the Seller's Net Proceeds Form,
- ■ **prepare** a Seller's Net Proceeds Form, and
- ■ **describe** the problems a FSBO may face when selling a house.

■ OVERVIEW

When a licensee is able to deliver an effective listing presentation, the "close" rate for listing appointments will be much higher. Prospecting is a numbers game. It may take up to 50 calls to get one listing appointment. What a shame it would be to have all that effort rendered worthless by failing to prepare carefully before sitting down with the sellers.

REQUIREMENTS FOR THE PRESENTATION

The **listing presentation** is a "sit down at the dining room table" discussion at which all property owners and decision makers are present. It will be successful only if you

- know all the parties who need to sign your listing are available;
- are fully prepared to list the property, which means you must have all the forms ready for signature when the parties agree to list;
- know the presentation thoroughly;
- know about the house you are trying to list—use the information from the tax appraiser's office, the plat books, or from your own personal inspection;
- have prepared a comparative market analysis that will help you show the sellers a fair value for their house and to protect you from the "overpriced listing," which will cost you time, aggravation, and unhappy customers;
- have your information organized in a businesslike fashion and your mind organized as well;
- are properly dressed and professional in appearance and manner; and
- are on time for the appointment.

THE FIVE MAJOR SEGMENTS OF THE PRESENTATION

A listing presentation consists of the following five major segments:

- Building rapport with the sellers
- Explaining the pricing process (going over the CMA)
- Showing the sellers how much they might receive from the sale (the Seller's Net Proceeds Form)
- Discussing the importance of listing the property with you
- Asking for the listing

Building Rapport with the Sellers

1. Greet the sellers at the door with a smile and be yourself. Thank them for the opportunity to visit their home, and after some initial small talk, begin taking control of the interview.
2. If you haven't already made a preliminary visit to the property, ask the sellers to give you a tour. Have a notepad to record your observations for each room. Ask questions about the house while on the tour. If you see any features that indicate the sellers' hobbies, awards, or family photos, try to acknowledge them. Show the owners that you've done your homework by confirming some of the information you've gotten from the tax appraiser.
3. Inspect the property boundaries; make notes of exterior features, then ask the sellers to help you measure the exterior of the house. Confirm that total with the information you have from the tax appraiser.
4. After returning indoors, arrange to have all parties sit at a dining or kitchen table. Suggest that the TV be turned down (or off) so that you can hear them well.
5. Find out why they are selling. If they are moving to a new town, find out how they feel (not think) about the move. Is it scary? Has the seller met

the new boss? How do they feel about the new job? Let them know you care about them as individuals.

Explaining the Pricing Process

The presentation should provide the information the sellers need to fully understand the listing process. Agents who give a value without first going over the CMA may lose the opportunity for realistic pricing if the sellers are surprised and offended at the value. A proper presentation should proceed in the following sequence:

1. Help the sellers understand current market conditions. You can get this information from MLS statistics or from your broker. Give statistics for the overall market. The CMA will help show the neighborhood statistics. For example, tell the sellers the
   a. number of houses currently listed;
   b. number of homes sold last month; or
   c. month's supply of homes on the market (divide listed homes by sales).
2. Give the sellers your analysis of the market:
   a. Is it a buyers' or a sellers' market?
   b. Are prices rising or falling?
   c. What is likely to happen if interest rates rise (or fall)?
3. Explain the importance of pricing the property within the selling range.
4. Inform the sellers that the purpose of the CMA is to determine the best list price for the property.
5. Explain the report and how you researched the material in it. If your conclusions of market value are less than the sellers' desired price, you may have a problem. Do not state your conclusions at this time. Wait to see what the sellers conclude from the comparable sales. (Often sellers will quickly realize that their price is too high and, if motivated to sell, will agree to reduce the price.)
6. Explain how each section of the CMA is important in the decision-making process by giving the sellers an overview of the following:
   a. Sold listings prove what selling prices have been and what bank appraisals might show.
   b. Homes now for sale illustrate the importance of competitive pricing.
   c. Expired listings demonstrate the futility of pricing property at an unrealistically high price.
7. Review individual properties on the report while referring to visual aids such as a subdivision map and photos.
8. Ask the sellers for questions or comments.
9. Give the sellers time to arrive at a range of values independently.
10. If the sellers want to price the property too high, discuss the reasons why that approach is unproductive.
11. When a realistic listing price has been agreed upon, complete the Seller's Net Proceeds Form.

Assumptions

Use the CMA from Course 3, Unit 3.

You visited the house yesterday when Mrs. Seburg was home to measure it, evaluate its features, and take some digital photos for the presentation this evening. This allowed you to prepare a CMA with confidence that there would be no surprises.

Cast:

Sales Associate: Alice Newby

Sellers: John Seburg, Susan Seburg

Alice: Mr. and Mrs. Seburg, thanks for inviting me into your home. Helping you get the most dollars for your home in a reasonable time is one of my most important responsibilities in my real estate practice. One of the ways I can really be helpful is by carefully preparing a market report. It's called a comparative market analysis. Have you seen one of these before? [Hand them a copy of the CMA.]

John: No, we haven't. But this is our first home.

Alice: OK, it will take us a few minutes to go over it, but it's well worth the time. The decisions we make based on this analysis are going to be very important to you as we go forward.

You can see I've put your names and addresses here at the top.

You can see that the report is broken into three main sections [pointing]: Here are the sales in your neighborhood for the last 12 months. The sold properties section tells us which homes appraisers can use and gives us an idea of the value for a homebuyer's bank appraisal. The section on properties that are now listed shows your competitors. And here are the properties that failed to sell, usually because they were overpriced. All of these properties are going to help us decide at what price we should offer your home. Here's a map of the neighborhood so you can see where each of these homes is located. Do you have any questions so far?

Susan: Well, I don't see one of our neighbor's homes on your list, and I know he sold his house last May. The address is 4425 Landtowne Drive.

Alice: Right. Let me see [looks at another list of every sale in the area]. Yes, you're right. Here it is on this list [shows list]. As you can see, his house had only 1,500 square feet, while yours has more than 1,900. I didn't use it in our pricing guide because it's just not comparable, don't you agree?

Susan: Yes, I see.

Presentation of a CMA (continued)

Alice: On each of the homes included on our list, I've made some adjustments based on major differences from your house. For example, the house at 1640 Clover has only a one-car garage, and yours has a two-car garage. The price difference for that feature is about $2,800, so your house should sell for about $2,800 more.

John: OK, that makes sense.

Alice: You can see that in the first section, sold properties, the median sales price of properties—and what yours will probably appraise for—is about $167,500. In the second section, your competition has a median listed price of $177,500. Now our best chance at a sale within reasonable time frames is to price your home somewhere above the sold properties and below the competing properties. Does that make sense?

John: Sure does.

Alice: Here are the properties that were overpriced and stayed on the market a long time. They didn't sell. You can see they had a median price of $183,000. We want to avoid being in this group, don't you agree? Let me show you the Pricing Pyramid. [Shows them the pyramid (See Figure 4.1).] As you can see, if you price the home at the median of the sold homes in your area, you'll attract the most buyers. If you price at what the other homes are listed for, you'll get some activity, but not as much. And if you price it too high, you won't see many buyers at all. The more buyers we can get to look, the better the chance of a sale.

John: Yes, we'd like to get sold within the next few months.

Alice: Great. Based on what you've seen here, what price do you think would be the best price for us to put it on the market?

Susan: Well, I think we've got to be somewhere between the sold ones and the listed ones. Do you think we could list it at the higher end, like $177,500?

Alice: What do you think, John?

John: I'd like to get as much as possible, Susan, but two of the homes for sale now are at $175,000. I think maybe $174,500 might get it sold faster.

Susan: Yes, that's true. I'm comfortable with $174,500.

Alice: I wholeheartedly agree. Could we schedule your home for our office inspection on Monday or will the following week give you more time to get ready? (This is the first time you ask for the order.)

Susan: Well, we may not be quite ready to do anything yet. Can we think about it and let you know?

Alice: Absolutely. Perhaps I could review with you what you are likely to clear from the sale after paying off the mortgage and all your expenses. Would that be helpful?

John: Sure would.

FIGURE 4.1

The Pricing Pyramid

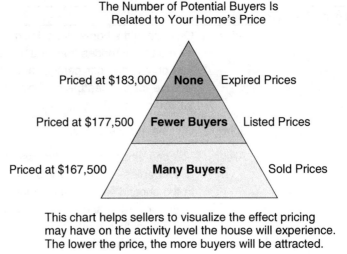

The Number of Potential Buyers Is
Related to Your Home's Price

Priced at $183,000 — **None** — Expired Prices

Priced at $177,500 — **Fewer Buyers** — Listed Prices

Priced at $167,500 — **Many Buyers** — Sold Prices

This chart helps sellers to visualize the effect pricing
may have on the activity level the house will experience.
The lower the price, the more buyers will be attracted.

■ **EXAMPLE 4.1**   Using the CMA report in Figure 3.4, role-play the complete presentation of a CMA without referring to the previous script. With another person, present the different sections of the material. Assign one person to represent a "reasonably motivated" seller who is kind to the agent.

Estimating the Seller's Proceeds

A seller generally is reluctant to enter into a listing agreement until understanding what expenses must be paid at closing. The **net proceeds** after paying off the mortgage and expenses of a sale are of primary interest to the seller and are often a factor in setting a list price. It is extremely important that a licensee use skill, care, and diligence in estimating the seller's proceeds from the sale. Following is a discussion of the **Seller's Net Proceeds Form** (see Figure 4.2).

On the Seller's Net Proceeds Form, a section for the seller's name and the property address should be completed. The left side of the form itemizes income and expenses related to the sale. Two columns are provided for calculations:

■ *When listing the property.* The licensee uses column 1 when calculating an estimate based on a recommended price; the licensee uses column 2 if the seller wants to know how much a different list price would net.

■ *When giving the seller a range of values.* The broker associate could provide for the seller a high-end list price and a low-end list price.

■ *At the time of listing.* Column 1 is used for showing the net proceeds if customary seller's expenses are to be paid; column 2 is used if the seller is asked to pay the buyer's loan closing costs. This is much like a best-case/worst-case scenario.

■ *For estimates given at the time of listing.* Column 1 is for listing proceeds; column 2 is used when an offer is submitted.

■ *At the time an offer is submitted.* Column 1 shows the seller's net if the offer is accepted; column 2 shows the seller's net if a counteroffer is accepted.

Seller's Net Proceeds Form

Seller's Name: _____		
Property Address: _____		
Selling Price	$	$
Less: 1st Mortgage 　　　2nd Mortgage 　　　Other		
Seller's Equity	$	$
Less: Expenses		
Title Insurance		
Homeowner's Warranty		
Buyer's Closing Costs Buyer's Origination Fee Buyer's Discount Points		
Repairs and Replacements		
Seller's Attorney Fee		
Brokerage Fee		
Other Miscellaneous Costs		
Other		
Total Expenses	$	$
Less: Prorations		
Property Taxes		
Interest		
Homeowner's Dues		
Rents and Deposits		
Total Prorations	$	$
Net Proceeds to Seller	$	$

These figures are estimates and intended only as a guide. They will vary at closing because of prorations, the mortgage balance, and unforeseen costs. An exact itemization will be provided to you at closing. Please read this and all other documents relating to this sale carefully. If you require further explanation, please consult an attorney.

Date: _____　　　Prepared by: _____

Seller: _____　　　Seller: _____

Seller's equity section   The seller's **equity** section consists of the sales price less mortgage balances and other encumbrances. Special assessment liens and construction liens are shown in the space provided for other encumbrances. All items should be rounded because this is an estimate. An exact mortgage balance is unnecessary because of the closing date's uncertainty. Uneven dollars and cents amounts should not be included. Exact amounts imply an accuracy that does not exist in the estimate.

Expenses section   Any expenses that the seller might be required to pay should be listed. It is better to overestimate than to underestimate the expenses. A seller will not be unhappy to receive more at the time of closing than expected, but likely will be upset if expenses have been underestimated. Even though the bottom of the form provides a disclaimer, the licensee must be careful to avoid errors. Some expenses that should be discussed include the following:

- When making the seller's statement, the licensee should include the typical charge a seller might be expected to pay for title insurance and related costs based on local practice.
- Homeowner's warranty costs are often associated with the seller's need to assure the buyer that the home is in good condition and will be warranted against many defects by an independent home warranty company. Depending on the company, these costs may range from $300 to $500. The benefit is that most warranty companies will cover the seller for any problems that might occur during the listing period if the seller agrees to pay for the buyer's policy.
- Buyer's closing costs, the origination fee, and discount points can be very substantial expenses to the seller if the seller agrees to pay them. When taking a listing, a broker associate should include these items if the custom in the market area dictates. When preparing this estimate at the time of contract, the broker associate should take extra care if the seller is paying the buyer's costs. The licensee should use the lender's good-faith estimate, with a maximum amount agreed to in the contract. Leaving this open-ended in a contract can be a problem if the discount points or other costs increase between the time of acceptance and the time of closing.
- Repairs and replacements are usually those that a lender might require. They also could be the result of inspection issues or nonfunctioning appliances. The licensee should use a cushion for such contingencies.
- The seller's attorney fee is an expense left to the seller to determine with an attorney.
- The brokerage fee is the commission the brokerage firm charges.
- Other miscellaneous costs include items such as express mail fees for mortgage payoffs and recording mortgage satisfactions. The licensee should include a cushion here to allow for contingencies. A seller on a tight budget cannot afford unpleasant surprises. This line also could be used to round uneven expense amounts to even amounts. For example, if the expenses were $8,945.60, the miscellaneous costs could be estimated at $54.40, resulting in total estimated expenses of $9,000.

Prorations section   This section, if not carefully estimated, could result in an unpleasant surprise for the seller, because most prorations are debits (charges) to the seller. Because the closing date is not certain, it is not necessary to do exact prorations; approximations are satisfactory if amounts are rounded higher. The statement offers no provision for insurance prorations or proceeds from a lender's escrow account. Insurance should not be prorated; the buyer should purchase a separate policy, and the seller should get a cancellation refund. Because the insurance refund and escrow refund from loans paid off are not received at closing, the net proceeds statement does not include these items. (If the mortgage is to be assumed, the prorations could be offset by the amounts held in escrow, as the buyer will be expected to reimburse the seller for those amounts.) The following are typical items that will be prorated between the seller and buyer at closing:

- Property taxes should be estimated for the year if tax information is not available. An assumed closing date is used to estimate prorations. If the closing were anticipated for June 28, for example, the licensee would show a charge to the seller for half the year's taxes.
- Interest prorations can be difficult to calculate. The amount depends on the time of month of the closing. Most interest is paid in arrears, but not all loans have that feature. The safest practice (if the loan is current) is to show a charge for a full month's interest.
- Homeowner's dues can be substantial in some areas, particularly with condominiums and other properties that have substantial common maintenance areas. The dues may be paid in advance, but often are paid in arrears. The homeowner should be questioned about the status of the dues.
- Rents and deposits can be major charges to the seller of an income property. If the seller has collected rent in advance, the buyer is entitled to the rent for the part of the month after the closing. The buyer also should be paid the security deposits.

Net proceeds to seller   The net proceeds equal the seller's equity less expenses and prorations. The amount of the seller's proceeds should be rounded to the next lowest $100.

■ **EXAMPLE 4.2**   Estimating Net Proceeds to Seller

Estimating the seller's net proceeds properly is extremely important. This exercise should be completed carefully using the Seller's Net Proceeds Form in Figure 4.2. Round up on expenses, prorations, and mortgages, and do not use cents. The final estimate should be rounded to the lowest hundred, using the following information:

Seller's name	Cindy Lewis
Property address	1947 Oldfield Circle
Prepared by	Janice Brown
Estimated closing date	August 26
Sales price	$93,800.00
Existing first mortgage (8.5%)	$47,425.67
Home equity loan (11%)	$14,659.42
Brokerage fee	7%
Buyer's title insurance	$650.00
Repairs and replacements	$450.00
Seller's attorney fee	$350.00
Homeowner's warranty	$375.00
Discount points	$2,100.00
Annual taxes	$1,325.00
Interest	?
Annual homeowner's dues	$150.00

■ **E X A M P L E   4 . 3**   Using the Seller's Net Proceeds Form prepared in the previous exercise, role-play the presentation of the form to the seller. With another person, present the different sections of the material. The seller should be reasonably motivated and kind to the agent. The licensee should ask a closing question when showing the net proceeds from the sale.

Ask for the Order

Show the sellers the net amount to be received and ask, "Can you live with this figure?" If the answer is "yes," follow up with, "Do you have any objections to my making the property available to all the REALTORS® in the city through the multiple listing service?" If the answer is "OK," ask for the current mortgage information and proceed to fill out the listing forms. You have obtained the listing!

If the answer is "We are not ready to list at this time," say "I understand," then go to the next step.

■ DISCUSS THE REASONS MOST FSBOs DON'T SELL

The Problem of Showing the Property

1. Explain that the sign in front of the home invites any passersby to come to the front door and ask to be let inside. Normally, a resident of a home would never allow the person access, but it's now more difficult to say "no." Talk for a moment about the family security and that you'll escort all buyers after they are qualified.
2. Remind the owners that a buyer cannot know everything about their property by simply looking at the front of the house. This is a very important point, especially if the home has only average curb appeal but the inside is far nicer than average. Without knowing about the good features, a buyer might drive right by. You should explain that when you show the home, you will escort the potential buyers inside, the only place they can truly evaluate the home.
3. Remind the sellers that if they are not home all day, in the evening, and on weekends to show the home, the buyer may not call back. Every time they go shopping or to work, their property is "off the market." Explain that when they list with you, the property will be on the market 24 hours a day, because buyers can reach a licensee who has the information the buyer wants.

The Problem of Financing

Because the buyers will likely need financing on the property, you could explain that they may want assistance in deciding where to go for a home mortgage and may not understand the process. For this reason, many buyers ask for the help of a real estate professional.

The Problem of Verbal Negotiations

Discuss with the sellers the disadvantage of direct negotiations with a buyer. Many buyers buy direct because their negotiation skills give them an advantage. Buyers will ask questions about the reason for selling and about how much lower the sellers might go. If the sellers remain firm, explain that the buyers may leave. But the sellers should also know that if they give a buyer a lower figure, that buyer may later try to negotiate even lower.

The sellers should be told that when a buyer wants to make an offer, the licensee will put it in writing and ask for a good-faith deposit so that if the price offered by the buyer is acceptable, all the sellers need to do is sign the contract.

The Problem of Writing a Purchase Contract

You can ask sellers whether they have a contract form and whether they feel comfortable filling it in for the buyers to sign. If the sellers have a contract form and think they can fill it in, let them know about the education process most licensees undergo so they can write one that will not end up in court.

If the sellers say they have an attorney to write the contract, suggest that it's important for the attorney to be qualified in real estate practice. You might also raise the question of how quickly a good, but busy, attorney could get a contract written when a buyer is ready to buy.

The Major Problem: Saving the Commission

In this last part of your discussion, you want to get the sellers' agreement that they are willing to try to overcome these obstacles in order to save the commission. When they agree, you must answer their objection to listing with you by letting them see that their efforts won't save a commission. Ask the sellers why they believe a buyer would be willing to take the time and make the effort to buy a house directly from a seller when the buyer could get much more help from a licensee. Then explain to them that the reason is that the buyer is also buying direct solely to save the commission and that it won't be possible for both parties to save the full commission. In the unlikely event that both seller and buyer complete the transaction without help from a licensee, why couldn't both parties save the full commission?

Ask for the Business

A closing question such as "Can you see why most people who try to sell their homes turn to a real estate professional?" might generate a positive answer. You can then ask if they'd like you to try to get the home into the MLS as soon as possible, or bring your office staff over on Monday morning to see it, or whether they would like you to hold an open house next Sunday. If their response is positive, you can begin filling out listing paperwork.

In many cases, the sellers won't be ready to list with your company. You should ask for the reason, and if they want to think about it, you should tell them why, when they decide to list the property, the listing person should be you.

Show the seller why the Realtor® should be you   Tell the sellers that your brokerage firm and you

- are in a high traffic location,
- have a training program that makes all your associates more professional and successful,
- sponsor listing caravans to generate more sales,
- will put the home into the MLS,
- will extensively advertise the home,
- will hold open houses,
- are members of an out-of-town referral agency,
- offer a warranty program; then describe how that will help to sell the property,
- will call them each week to tell them of your progress, and
- will give them your special "Seven-Step Service" program.

■ SEVEN-STEP SERVICE

A seller wants to know what the brokerage firm will do to earn the commission. A chart similar to the one shown in Figure 4.3 may be helpful to explain the brokerage firm's services. While the chart itself is rather sparse for easy understanding, the broker associate should explain each step to the seller in more detail. After you have finished your presentation, you should clearly and directly ask for the order: "Mr. and Mrs. Seburg, may I help you sell your property?"

FIGURE 4.3

Seven-Step Service

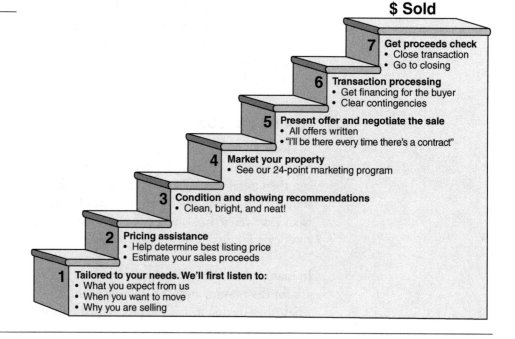

$ Sold

7 Get proceeds check
- Close transaction
- Go to closing

6 Transaction processing
- Get financing for the buyer
- Clear contingencies

5 Present offer and negotiate the sale
- All offers written
- "I'll be there every time there's a contract"

4 Market your property
- See our 24-point marketing program

3 Condition and showing recommendations
- Clean, bright, and neat!

2 Pricing assistance
- Help determine best listing price
- Estimate your sales proceeds

1 Tailored to your needs. We'll first listen to:
- What you expect from us
- When you want to move
- Why you are selling

If the answer is no, you should review every point of the presentation point-by-point, then ask for the order again. In many cases, the presentation will result in a listing. If for any reason you do not get a listing, arrange to visit again in three days. You may never get the listing, but it won't be because you gave up too soon.

■ SUMMARY

Making an effective listing presentation will result in a much higher close rate for listing appointments. Several conditions must be met in order to succeed:

- All parties on the deed must be present.
- All forms must be ready for the sellers' signature.
- The licensee must know each step of the presentation.
- The licensee must have complete information about the property to be listed.
- A comparative market analysis must be prepared.
- The licensee must be organized, have a professional appearance, and be on time.

The five major parts of a listing presentation are the following:

- Building rapport with the sellers
- Explaining the pricing process
- Explaining the Seller's Net Proceeds Form
- Discussing the importance of listing with your brokerage firm
- Asking for the listing

A seller usually is more interested in the net proceeds from the sale of the property than the home's actual sales price. The Seller's Net Proceeds Form—the financial disclosure to the seller—consists of three major sections. The seller's equity section provides the sales price less mortgage balances, with the difference being the seller's equity. The expenses section shows expenses the seller must pay at closing. The prorations section includes taxes, interest, rents, and homeowner's dues.

■ KEY TERMS

equity	net proceeds
listing presentation	Seller's Net Proceeds Form

UNIT 5

Brokerage Relationships and Listing Contracts in Colorado

■ **LEARNING OBJECTIVES**   *Upon completion of this unit, you should be able to*

- ■ **explain** to a seller or buyer how brokerage relationships work in Colorado,

- ■ **explain** the wording that could be used to protect both seller and broker from commission disputes caused by a buyer who improperly tries to leave the broker out of the transaction in an open listing,

- ■ **state** the legally required elements in a listing contract,

- ■ **explain** the distinguishing characteristics of each of the following types of listings: open, exclusive-brokerage, and exclusive-right-to-sell,

- ■ **explain** the steps required to complete a residential profile sheet,

- ■ **complete** the residential profile sheet,

- ■ **complete** a listing contract,

- ■ **explain** each paragraph of the listing agreement, and

- ■ **design** a listing servicing program for your personal listings.

■ OVERVIEW

Before a Colorado broker associate enters into a relationship with a member of the public the associate should have a full understanding of the duties and responsibilities they owe as an agent or transaction broker. Broker associates in Colorado are allowed to work with members of the public in different roles: both representative and nonrepresentative. The broker associate must be able to describe what each relationship means and help the member of the public decide how they wish to work with the licensee.

A listing contract is an agreement between a real estate broker and a property owner. The listing contract specifies the duties of both the broker and the owner in the sale of the owner's real property. Without listing contracts, there would be little or no inventory to sell, exchange, lease, rent, or auction. In Colorado, there are three approved listing contracts that can be used by broker associates when listing property for sale. Every written listing agreement must include a definite expiration date, a description of the property, the price and terms, the fee or commission, and the principal's signature. A legible, signed, true, and correct copy of the listing agreement must be given to the principal(s) once the listing agreement is signed. Also, a written listing contract may not contain a self-renewing or automatic renewal provision. It is important to understand that a listing agreement is a personal services (employment) contract that requires the brokerage firm to perform one or more professional services to fulfill the agreement. The listing broker associate may seek assistance from other licensees, but the primary responsibility remains with the listing broker associate and the brokerage firm that designated them to represent the seller. The listing contract is a broker's employment contract, and all listings should be in writing. If litigation should result from some misunderstanding, default, or breach, it is much easier to resolve by showing the terms of a written contract than by obtaining testimony to prove the terms or conditions of an oral listing.

■ BROKERAGE RELATIONSHIPS & CONFLICTS OF INTEREST

There are two levels of representation that a broker may offer a potential seller or buyer in Colorado: agency representation or transaction-brokerage representation. The broker is said to be either acting as an agent or as a transaction-broker. An agency relationship must be in writing (the exclusive-right-to-sell contract and the exclusive-right-to-buy contract both can be used to accomplish this agency relationship). If there is no written agreement and a broker is working with a potential buyer, Colorado law dictates that the broker is representing the buyer as a transaction-broker (the default relationship in Colorado in the absence of a written agreement). In both cases, the law prescribes certain dos and don'ts that the broker must observe with respect to the client (the seller or the buyer). An agent must adhere to a very strict list of duties and prohibitions. A transaction-broker must adhere to a more limited list of duties and prohibitions. In general, an agent can be thought of as an advocate and a consultant for the represented party, doing everything possible within the law to obtain the greatest advantage for the client. A transaction-broker, on the other hand, is more properly thought of as a facilitator or mediator, responsible for helping the seller or buyer complete the sale (or purchase) but stopping short of offering opinions and strategic advice.

Broker associates may also work with a member of the public in a nonrepresentation role in which they have no relationship or duty of representation and the member of the public will be an unrepresented customer. The broker associate owes the customer reasonable skill and care and accounting for any money received. Additionally, the licensee can help the customer write an offer to present to the seller. This type of relationship, however, must also be expressed in writing. The broker and member of the public who wish to work together without any level of representation must sign the required Brokerage Disclosure to Buyer or Brokerage Disclosure to Seller (FSBO) form. If there is no written agreement between a broker associate and the buyer she's working with, the broker associate is by default representing the buyer as a transaction-broker.

In certain situations, a broker associate or a brokerage firm may be in a position to represent both the buyer and the seller of a particular property. Often called "double-ending" the transaction, this situation presents a difficult legal issue regarding confidentiality and disclosure. The same broker associate representing both seller and buyer would be privy to confidential information about both parties, which could give rise to a conflict of interest. Typically, the seller's agent has a legal duty to tell the seller anything advantageous learned about a potential buyer and to keep certain information about the seller confidential, while the buyer's agent has the same duties with respect to the buyer. For example, the seller's agent (the listing broker) would know the absolute lowest price the seller is willing to sell the property for, even though the list price is higher. The law forbids the licensee from disclosing this information to a potential buyer (unless instructed to do so by the seller). On the other hand, the law requires the buyer's agent (the buyer's broker) to inform the buyer of material information learned, such as the fact that the seller would be willing to sell for a lower price than the list price. When the same broker represents both seller and buyer, how does the broker comply with these conflicting duties? Another situation that historically has given rise to a potential conflict of interest is one in which one broker associate in a firm lists a property for sale and another broker associate in the same firm finds a buyer for that listing. In some states, when one broker associate represents a buyer or seller, the entire brokerage firm is considered to be the seller's or buyer's agent. This gives rise to the same sort of potential conflict of interest described. Some states get around this issue by permitting dual agency. The broker double-ending the transaction or the firm with one broker representing the seller and another broker representing the buyer are deemed dual agents and the confidentiality and disclosure requirements are modified slightly to permit the agents to protect each client's interests without violating the law.

Colorado does not permit dual agency and has instead legislated a solution called designated brokerage. The brokerage firm is no longer seen as the agent or transaction-broker representing the seller or buyer. Instead, the firm simply owns the contract and designates one of their broker associates to represent the parties. Firms are required to have a written office policy that specifies which types of relationships their brokers can offer the public. Most firms allow their broker associates to negotiate the relationship with the party that is signing the agreement (seller or buyer) and offer agency or transaction-brokerage as they feel is appropriate to that transaction. This avoids a potential dual agency situation since only the individual designated broker associate is deemed to have the relationship with the party and they agree not to share confidential information about the party with any other brokers in the firm or outside of the firm. Should another broker in the same firm find a buyer for the property, this concept of designated brokerage would permit the second broker to represent the buyer with no conflict of interest.

In a situation in which the broker associate has the opportunity to double-end a deal, the broker must make a choice. Since Colorado designated brokerage law does not allow the broker to be agent to both parties, the broker can do one of two things: (1) move to the middle and act as a transaction-broker (facilitator) for both parties or (2) continue to be an agent for one party and treat the other party as an unrepresented customer. This situation most frequently arises when a broker lists a property for sale and establishes an agency relationship with the seller, then finds an interested buyer while marketing the property. The broker must have the seller's permission to change from agency representation to transaction-brokerage representation. This allows the broker associate to offer transaction-brokerage representation to the buyer as well, thereby representing both parties with no conflict of interest. This potential change of representation is one of the crucial concepts the listing broker associate must explain to the seller when they negotiate the listing agreement. The seller chooses the type of representation to hire the broker associate for (as an agent or as a transaction-broker). If the seller chooses an agency relationship, indication must be made in the listing agreement whether to permit the broker associate to change to a transaction-broker should that broker associate be the one to find a potential buyer. Some sellers may not wish their broker associate to offer any representation to potential buyers. More often, however, the broker associate will explain the options to the seller when completing the listing agreement and the seller will choose to allow the broker associate to switch to transaction-broker should the situation present itself.

The same issue must be discussed when a buyer wishes to hire a broker associate to help them find a home. The exclusive-right-to-buy contract requires the broker associate to explain the difference between agency representation and transaction brokerage. The buyer must indicate his choice in the appropriate section of the agreement. Again, some buyers will decide to allow the broker associate to change to a transaction-broker if that broker associate finds an unrepresented seller for a property the buyer wishes to purchase. Other buyers will require their broker associate to remain their agent and prohibit the broker associate from offering representation to any and all sellers they may find.

■ REPRESENTATION DUTIES

I. When a broker associate signs a listing agreement or buyer representation contract with a buyer or seller to act as an agent or transaction-broker, they are agreeing to perform a group of uniform duties.

   A. As stated in the Colorado Real Estate Manual, the uniform duties of an agent or transaction broker when representing the seller or buyer are:

   1. Broker shall exercise reasonable skill and care for seller or buyer, including, but not limited to

      a) performing the terms of any written or oral agreement with seller or buyer,

      b) presenting all offers to and from seller or buyer in a timely manner regardless of whether the property is subject to a contract for sale,

c)   disclosing to seller or buyer adverse material facts actually known by broker,

d)   advising seller or buyer regarding the transaction and to obtain expert advice as to material matters about which broker knows but the specifics of which are beyond the expertise of broker,

e)   accounting in a timely manner for all money and property received, and

f)   keeping seller or buyer fully informed regarding the transaction.

2.   Broker shall not disclose, the following information without the informed consent of seller or buyer

a)   that seller is willing to accept less or buyer is willing to pay more than the asking price for the property,

b)   what the motivating factors are for seller or buyer are to sell or buy the property,

c)   that seller or buyer will agree to financing terms other than those offered,

d)   any material information about seller or buyer unless disclosure is required by law or failure to disclose such information would constitute fraud or dishonest dealing, or

e)   any facts or suspicions regarding circumstances that could psychologically impact or stigmatize the property.

3.   Seller or buyer consents to broker's disclosure of seller's or buyer's confidential information to the supervising broker or designee for the purpose of proper supervision, provided such supervising broker or designee shall not further disclose such information without consent of seller, or use such information to the detriment of seller.

4.   Brokerage firm may have agreements with other sellers to market and sell their property or buyers to buy property. Broker may show alternative properties not owned by seller to other prospective buyers and list competing properties for sale. Broker may show properties in which the buyer is interested to other buyers without breaching their agreement.

5.   Broker shall not be obligated to seek additional offers or to find additional properties to purchase the property while the property is subject to a contract for sale.

6.   Broker has no duty to conduct an independent inspection of the property for the benefit of a buyer and has no duty to independently verify the accuracy or completeness of statements made by seller or independent inspectors. Broker has no duty to conduct an independent investigation of a buyer's financial condition or to verify the accuracy or completeness of any statement made by a buyer.

7.   Seller or buyer shall not be liable for the acts of broker unless such acts are approved, directed or ratified by seller.

■ ADDITIONAL DUTIES OF SELLER'S OR BUYER'S AGENT

If the Seller or Buyer Agency box at the top of page 1 of the representation contract is checked, the broker is a limited agent of seller (seller's agent) or buyer (buyer's agent) with the following additional duties:

■ Promoting the interests of seller or buyer with the utmost good faith, loyalty, and fidelity
■ Seeking a price and terms that are acceptable to seller or buyer
■ Counseling seller or buyer as to any material benefits or risks of a transaction that are actually known by broker

Disclosure of Brokerage Relationships

Rule E-35 requires a broker associate who is either an agent or a transaction-broker working with a seller to disclose that brokerage relationship to a potential buyer *in writing* before providing brokerage services to the buyer. The same is true if the broker associate is representing a buyer and approaches an unrepresented seller (FSBO). The broker associate is allowed to have rapport-building conversations and may have discussions of general terms and market conditions. It is imperative, however, that before eliciting or receiving any confidential information the broker associate discloses their brokerage relationship to the unrepresented member of the public.

The disclosure might start on the phone:

"Ms. Jones, I appreciate your calling on my listing. You seem to be very excited about the home and I would like to work with you. I need to tell you that at this time I represent the seller as an agent. This means that I would be required to take any confidential information that you give me to the seller. Colorado allows real estate brokers to work with buyers and sellers in a variety of ways. It is possible for me to work with both you and the seller and maintain your and the seller's confidential information. Could you meet me at my office to discuss how we can work together and then we can make arrangements for me to show you that home?"

Disclosure must be in writing at first physical contact. To continue from the previous example:

"Thank you for coming in, Ms. Jones. As we discussed on the phone, Colorado real estate brokers can work with buyers and sellers in a variety of ways. I would like to review the relationships we can offer using this form (Broker Disclosure to Buyer). When we've reviewed the form, we can discuss how we can work together and set a time to see the homes you are interested in."

The broker associate would then walk Ms. Jones through all the options that are available using the form to help Ms. Jones decide how she wanted to work with the broker associate. The broker associate should ask Ms. Jones to sign the disclosure form, give her a copy, and put the other copy in the file. If Ms. Jones will not sign the form the licensee should note that the disclosure was given, state the time and date and that signature was refused, and put the copy in the broker associate's file.

TYPES OF LISTING CONTRACTS

In this unit, three types of listing contracts are identified. We will briefly deal with open listings and exclusive-brokerage listings; however, the exclusive-right-to-sell contract is emphasized because of its predominance in residential property transactions.

Open Listing

An **open listing** is a contract in which an owner reserves the right to employ any number of brokers. Brokers may work simultaneously, but the first broker who produces a ready, willing, and able buyer at the terms accepted by the seller is the only one who earns a commission. If the owner sells the property without the aid of any of the brokers, the owner is not obligated to pay any commission; but if a broker can provide proof of being the procuring cause of the transaction, the broker may be entitled to a commission.

Exclusive-Brokerage Listing

While in law and practice this type of listing is called an exclusive-agency listing, in Colorado, because the listing does not represent the brokerage relationship but a type of brokerage service, it is called an exclusive brokerage. The seller and broker associate decide if the brokerage relationship is an agency or transaction-broker relationship by checking one of the boxes on page one of the listing.

The **exclusive-brokerage listing** is the preferred listing agreement of an owner who has selected one particular broker as an exclusive agent or transaction-broker, for a specified period of time, to sell real property according to the owner's stated terms. In an exclusive-brokerage listing, the owner appoints the broker but reserves the right to sell the property without paying a commission to the broker if the broker has not introduced or identified the buyer. If the broker performs by selling the property before the owner, the broker is entitled to a commission. Exclusive-brokerage residential listings are less common than exclusive-right-to-sell listings.

A common problem with exclusive-brokerage and open listings is the exposure to lawsuits for procuring cause between the broker and the seller.

■ **EXAMPLE 5.1** Arthur Cody lists Donald Wilson's home under an exclusive-brokerage listing agreement. Arthur shows the property to William Farkas. William notices that the seller has a sign on the property saying For Sale By Owner—555-1145. Arthur drops William off and writes a letter to Donald, registering William as a prospect. Immediately after Arthur drops him off, William calls Donald directly. Donald does not know that Arthur has shown the property and agrees to a reduced price since no commission is involved. Donald and William enter into a contract for sale. It is only after the contract is signed that Donald gets Arthur's prospect registration letter. When the sale closes, Arthur brings suit for commission as the procuring cause of the sale.

Role-play the court argument: Arthur, arguing for a commission on the sale, and Donald, explaining why no commission is due.

In Discussion Example 5.1, Donald, whom we assume to be an honest person, was sued because of the buyer's actions, not his own. How can a broker prevent this type of misunderstanding? Registration is not enough, because the notification may come after the parties have entered into a contract. A better method to help the seller receive fair disclosure is for the broker associate to recommend that the seller require the following words in all contracts the seller believes to be the procuring cause of the sale:

> *This property is listed with a broker under an agreement that the broker will be paid a commission for procuring a buyer for the property. Buyer warrants to seller that the buyer was not shown or made aware of this property by any real estate broker or broker associate. Buyer agrees that if a broker claiming a commission provides information to the contrary, buyer will reimburse seller for commissions due to said real estate broker as well as legal fees.*

A buyer who has seen the property with a broker will refuse to sign such a statement, putting the seller on notice that the buyer is trying to save the commission by excluding the broker.

Two other problems can arise from an exclusive-brokerage agreement. First, a broker is reluctant to show property to a buyer if the owner's phone number is displayed prominently on a sign in front of the property. The sign invites the buyer to exclude the broker to get a better price. If the broker takes the listing under an exclusive agency, the broker should get the owner's agreement to remove the sign.

Another problem the broker faces is the possibility of the owner's advertising a lower price (broker's price less commission). The broker likely will lose the buyer if the buyer sees the owner's ad. The broker and the owner should quote the same price.

Exclusive-Right-to-Sell Listing

The **exclusive-right-to-sell listing** is the most advantageous listing from the broker's viewpoint and the most common type of listing. The listing is given to a selected broker, who then becomes the exclusive broker for the sale of the property. The broker is due a commission regardless of who sells the property. That is, if the owner sells the property during the contract period, the broker still earns a commission. Also, if the owner sells the property within a designated time period after the listing contract has expired to a buyer originally introduced to the property by the broker, the owner usually is liable for a sales commission to the broker (the holdover or extension clause).

To be enforceable, this type of listing contract should be in writing and include valuable consideration. Only exclusive-right-to-sell and exclusive-brokerage listings may be entered into the MLS by the listing broker.

Warranties by the Owner

Both the broker and the seller have obligations under the listing agreement. The seller has legal obligations to the broker, including performance of all promises made in the contract, as well as the obligation to engage in honest, straightforward dealing. The actions and misrepresentations of a seller can become a liability to the agent. For example, if a seller tells a broker associate that the plumbing pipes are copper and the broker associate passes along that information to a buyer without qualification, both the seller and the brokerage firm may be liable for damages if the buyer later discovers the plumbing pipes are polybutylene. Litigation may result in damages assessed against both the seller and the broker.

The licensee is expected to be knowledgeable about and have a full understanding of all the contracts they use. A broker associate should be able to fully explain each section of the contract clearly and completely. Sellers lose confidence if the broker associate is unable to explain or doesn't understand a section. In the Contract and Regulations course we discuss what the each paragraph of the contract meant. In this section, we are going to discuss what is typically filled in the blanks and how to explain the document to the seller.

- Prior to filling out the listing agreement, the broker associate and the seller should have had a discussion in regard to what type of brokerage relationship the seller and broker associate are going to have. The Definitions of Working Relationships form is a helpful tool in this discussion. The broker associate can offer the seller any relationship that is allowed under their employing broker's office policy, usually either agency or transaction-broker. Then, through discussion between the seller and broker associate, the final decision on representation takes place.
- It is helpful to have the seller have available the documents that they received when buying the home. This will enable you to have the deed to verify the legal description, information on the lender, and so on.

Preparation of the Residential Profile Sheet

On December 13, John K. and Elizabeth J. Scott enter into a contractual agreement with you, a licensed real estate broker associate. You have a six-month exclusive-right-to-sell contract for their home. The house is a three-bedroom, two-bath, single-story structure, with an efficient traffic pattern. The master bath has an oversized, Roman-style bathtub. The house is brick with a Spanish tile roof and was built in 1938. Insulation used in the attic space has an R-36 rating. A new forced-air furnace with an air conditioner was installed in November.

The entire neighborhood is zoned R-1 and consists of quality homes on quiet, tree-lined streets, with city and county utilities and telephone and power lines underground. City bus service is two blocks away, and elementary, junior high, and high schools are all within six blocks of the property.

Use the following information to fill out a residential **profile sheet** and exclusive-right-to-sell contract available through the Colorado Division of Real Estate Web site: www.dora.state.co.us/real-estate (click **Real Estate Brokers** from the left column, and then click **Commission Approved Forms**).

The Scotts have decided that $271,500 is a fair selling price. The Scotts briefly considered an offer of a year's lease at $1,600 per month but decided to sell instead. The property, located at 1234 Sunny Circle, Sunshine City, is legally described as Lot 21, Block C, Mountain View Subdivision, Sunshine City, as recorded in Plat Book 39, Page 543, Lottery County, Colorado.

A utility room, foyer, pantry, hallway, two baths, and four large closets bring the total heated and air-conditioned living area to 1,776 square feet. An unusually large, 720-square-foot garage brings the total square footage under roof to 2,496.

The Scotts have paid the property taxes for the preceding year; the taxes for the current year will be prorated at closing. The property taxes for last year were $1,798.

The Scotts have just refinanced and now hold a 6 percent, 30-year, conventional mortgage in the amount of $155,000 with the Secured Profit Savings Association. Their monthly payment for principal and interest is $996.40. A comprehensive homeowner's hazard and liability policy with a face value of $356,500, purchased at a cost of $1,264 for one year is due to expire at midnight on October 18 of next year.

All floors except the kitchen and bathrooms have custom rugs and every window is equipped with custom-made draperies. The Scotts are willing to leave all rugs and draperies. The kitchen is all electric and the electric water heater is a 60-gallon, quick-recovery unit. The kitchen appliances include a large, beverage center–type refrigerator, a built-in food processor; a microwave oven; an electric oven over range; a disposal; a dishwasher; and a trash compactor. The Scotts have decided to leave all of the appliances except the refrigerator.

Preparation of the Residential Profile Sheet (continued)

The Scotts have stipulated that their home is to be shown by appointment only and have provided you with their telephone number (555-3210). They have indicated a willingness to take back a second mortgage, but they will not agree to any financing that results in a cost to them. Your employer, Super Real Estate, Inc. (555-6543), and the Scotts have agreed on a 6 percent sales commission on the gross sales price with the firm paying 2.8 percent to all cooperating brokers. The Scotts have agreed to give possession on day of closing. You agree to put the listing into the MLS and on all company Internet sites. If the Scotts decide to lease the property, your fee is 10 percent. The Scotts authorize you to put a **lockbox** on the home.

The Scotts agree to hire you as their agent, but will allow you to become a transaction-broker if you find a buyer. The earnest money is to be $2,000, payable to ABC Title, who will hold the funds for the seller.

In addition to the listing agreement and profile sheet, what other required disclosures will you need to complete the listing?

Preparation of an Exclusive-Right-to-Sell Contract

Once she has gathered and entered the property information on the profile sheet, the licensee should prepare the listing agreement. The broker associate should complete as much of the paperwork as possible before the listing appointment. Because the task can be done in a controlled environment without distractions, it is more likely to be correct. The advance preparation also results in a more efficient process once the broker associate is with the seller. However, it is not acceptable to fill in any items that are negotiable in the listing contract prior to discussing them with the seller. So the licensee can enter the legal names of the owners and the property's legal description but cannot enter the commission until it had been discussed and agreed to.

A listing contract is available through the Colorado Division of Real Estate Web site: www.dora.state.co.us/real-estate (click **Real Estate Brokers** from the left column, and then click **Commission Approved Forms**). Use it to complete the case study.

F I G U R E 5.1

Residential Profile Sheet

RES
PAGE 1   2 Sided Form

SUBMIT TO: **METROLIST, INC.** P.O. BOX 4875 ENGLEWOOD, CO 80155
Fax to: (303) 850-9637   Office: (303) 850-9613
"●" Items *MUST BE FILLED OUT or form will be returned.*

MLS P☐   #

●TAX COUNTY ●PIN

ADDRESS NUM   AD DIR ●STREET NAME *(Do Not Abbreviate)*

ST TYPE   ●CITY *(U.S. Postal - Do Not Abbreviate)*   ●ZIP CODE   UNINCORPORATED   ●ZONED *(Enter Code)*
Y ☐ Yes N ☐ No

● AREA   ●SUB AREA *(Do Not Abbreviate)*   ●PRICE *(No Commas, No Cents)* $

GRID INFORMATION
●NS DIR *(✔ One)*   ●NS#
N ☐ North
S ☐ South
O ☐ Out of Metro Area
●EW DIR *(✔ One)*   ●EW#
E ☐ East
W ☐ West
O ☐ Out of Metro Area

MAP#   SECTION
(See 2004 Mapsco Denver   *(Enter A-Z,*
Regional Street Atlas)   *excluding I and O)*

LOT SIZE *(Dimensions, Sq. Ft.)*

ACRES *(Approximate)*   FACES   *(Enter Direction Front Faces)*

TOTAL HOA FEES   ● FEE QUOTED *(✔ One)*
$ A ☐ Annual
                    M ☐ Monthly
MULTIPLE HOA'S   Q ☐ Quarterly
Y☐ Yes N☐ No   N ☐ None

FEE INCLUDES *(✔ Up to 10)*
CL ☐ Clubhouse   PL ☐ Comm Pool
CF ☐ Clubhouse w/Fitness SN ☐ Snow Rmvl
ER ☐ Ext Bldg&Roof Mnt   MO ☐ Mgt Only
EM ☐ Ext Bldg Mnt w/o Roof TN ☐ Tennis Courts
GM ☐ Grounds Mnt   TR ☐ Trash Removal
IN ☐ Insurance   WS ☐ Water/Sewer

HOA NAME

HOA PHONE #
(Area Code)

LOAN BALANCE *(Existing First Only) (No Commas, No Cents)*
$

● TAXES *(No Commas, No Cents)*
$

● TERMS *(✔ Up to 7)*
CV ☐ Conv   LP ☐ Lease Purchase
F ☐ FHA   TR ☐ Trade/Exchange
V ☐ VA   LO ☐ Lease Option
CA ☐ Cash   B ☐ Bond
O ☐ OWC   NQ ☐ Non Qual Asmpt
QA ☐ Qual Asmpt   DP ☐ Down Pmt Assistance

ADDITIONAL TERMS *(Special Financing, Not in Book)*

●TYPE *(✔ One) (Separate By Comma) (✔ One)*
DSF☐ Detached Single Fam HRS ☐ Horse Prop
ASF☐ Attached Single Fam AGR ☐ Agriculture
(Duplex, Triplex)   WTR ☐ Waterfront
CP ☐ Cluster/Patio   GLF ☐ Golf Course
                          PRK ☐ Park/Grnbelt

HORSES *(✔ Up to 4)*
Z ☐ Zoned For
C ☐ Covenants Allow For
W ☐ Well Allows For
S ☐ Water - Stream/Spring
N ☐ Water Not Provided

COOP COMPENSATION *(At least one $ or % must be offered)*
● BUYERS AGENCY
● TRANS BROKER

●BASEMENT *(✔ One)*   *(✔ One if applies)*
F ☐ Full   W ☐ Walk-Out
P ☐ Partial   G ☐ Garden Level
N ☐ None   C ☐ Cellar
SUBFLOOR *(✔ Up to 2)*
CR ☐ Crawl Space   SO☐ Structural Subfloor Other
SL ☐ Slab   ST☐ Structural Subfloor Wood
BSMT FINISHED *(✔ One)*   % BSMT FINISHED
F ☐ Fully Finished
P ☐ Partially Finished
O ☐ Open

FIREPLACE LOCation *(✔ Up to 2)*
L ☐ Living Room   D ☐ Dining Room
F ☐ Family Room   K ☐ Kitchen
B ☐ Bedroom   M ☐ Master Bedroom
OF FIREPLACES

●CAR STORAGE *(✔ Up To 5)*   SPACES
(Separate by Commas)   *(Enter # Of)*
G ☐ Garage   A ☐ Attached
C ☐ Carport   D ☐ Detached
F ☐ Off Street O ☐ Oversized
N ☐ None   T ☐ Tandem

●HEAT *(Primary Source)*
(✔ One) (Separate by Comma) (✔ One)
G ☐ Gas   FA ☐ Forced Air
P ☐ Propane   HW ☐ Hot Water
E ☐ Electric   BB ☐ Baseboard
S ☐ Solar   PE ☐ Pellet
W ☐ Wood   HP ☐ Heat Pump
C ☐ Coal   WH ☐ Wall Heater
O ☐ Oil   GR ☐ Gravity
               ST ☐ Stove
               SH ☐ Space Heater
AVG UTIL $ AC ☐ Active
(Excluding Water & Sewer) PS ☐ Passive
               SM ☐ Steam
               RA ☐ Radiant

SEWER *(✔ One)*   WATER *(✔ One)*
PUB ☐ Public   PUB ☐ Public
COM ☐ Community   COM ☐ Community
SEP ☐ Septic   WLD ☐ Well Domestic
                  WLH ☐ Well Household

LAUNDRY LOC   *(Enter U, M ,L or B)*

SCHOOL DISTRICT   *(School Codes*
●ELEMENTARY   *available on*
●JR HIGH/MIDDLE   *www.MYmls.com)*
●SR HIGH

DIMENSIONS *(Feet)*   LOCATION
(Enter Dimensions - 12x10) *(Enter U, M, L or B)*
MASTER BR   X
FAMILY ROOM   X
LIVING ROOM   X
DINING ROOM   X
KITCHEN   X
STUDY/DEN   X

●EXCLUSIVE AGCY *(✔ One)* ●VARIABLE COMM *(✔ One)*
EA ☐ Exclusive Agency   V ☐ Yes
ER ☐ Exclusive Right   N ☐ No

PROSPECT REServation   ●LIMITED SERVICE *(✔ One)*
(✔ One) P ☐ Yes   ☐ Yes ☐ No
          ☐ No   ●ENTRY ONLY *(✔ One)*
                         ☐ Yes ☐ No

BEDROOM   BATH *(F= Full, T= 3/4, H= 1/2, Q= 1/4, R=Rough)*
           (No #'s, No Commas, ex: 3 Full 2 Half=FFFHH)
U BR   U BA
M BR   M BA
L BR   L BA
B BR   B BA
● BEDROOMS TOTAL   ● BATHS TOTAL

APPROXIMATE SQUARE FEET   *U=Upper L=Lower M=Main B=Bsmt*
U SQ   *Ranch=M&B   Bi-Level=U&L*
M SQ   *2-Story=U&M&B Tri-Level=U&M&L*
L SQ   *4-Level=U&M&L&B*
●SQUARE FEET *(No comma)*   ● FINISH SQFT TOT
BSQ   ● TOTAL SQ FT
MEASUREMENT FROM *(✔ One)*
C ☐ County Records   B ☐ Builder
L ☐ Listor Measured   F ☐ Floor Plans
A ☐ Appraiser Measured
DATE MEASURED *(DD-MMM-YYYY e.g.: 01-JAN-2005)*

●CONSTRUCTION/Exterior Material
(✔ One) (Separate by Comma) (✔ One)
FR ☐ Frame   FK ☐ Frame/Rock
BR ☐ Brick   RK ☐ Rock
VY ☐ Vinyl Siding CO ☐ Concrete
FB ☐ Frame/Brick MO ☐ Modular
SU ☐ Stucco   MS ☐ Metal Siding
MR ☐ Moss Rock   CS ☐ Cedar Siding
BL ☐ Block   WS ☐ Wood Siding
AD ☐ Adobe   JM ☐ JM Asbestos
LG ☐ Log   MH ☐ Manufactured
SB ☐ Stucco/Brick OT ☐ Other

●STYLE *(✔ One)*   ARCHITECTURE *(✔ One)*
R ☐ Ranch/One-Story   A ☐ A-Frame
RR ☐ Raised Ranch   BU ☐ Bungalow
MH ☐ Mobile Home   CA ☐ Cabin
BI ☐ Bi-Level   CH ☐ Chalet
TR ☐ Tri-Level   CT ☐ Contemporary
FT ☐ Front/Back Tri-Lv DS ☐ Denver Square
4L ☐ Tri-Level w/Bsmt MC ☐ Mountain Contemp
F4 ☐ Front/Back 4L   RC ☐ Rustic Contemp
SH ☐ Story & 1/2   SP ☐ Spanish/SW
2S ☐ Two Story   TR ☐ Traditional
3S ☐ Three Story   TU ☐ Tudor
5L ☐ Four-Level w/Bsmt VC ☐ Victorian
                      OT ☐ Other

●YEAR
(Year Built, 2005 NOT 05: 4 Digits MUST Be Entered)

ROOFING MATERIAl *(✔ Up To 2)*
CO ☐ Composition Shingles *(Asphalt, Fiberglass, Organic)*
RR ☐ Rolled Roofing   BU ☐ Built-Up *(Tar & Gravel)*
WS ☐ Wood Shingles   SS ☐ Simulated Shake
CS ☐ Cement Shake   CT ☐ Concrete Tile
ME ☐ Metal   SL ☐ Slate
ST ☐ Spanish Tile   OT ☐ Other
DC ☐ Dimensional Comp UK ☐ Unknown

BUILDER

MODEL

●AGENT ID   ● LISTOR   ●PH L   *(Area Code)*
●OFFICE ID   ● OFFICE NAME
● PHONE#   *(Area Code)*   SHOWING PHONE#   *(Area Code)*   ●FAX#   *(Area Code)*
● CURR LIST DATE   ●EXP DATE   ● SIGNATURE
(DD-MMM-YYYY e.g.: 01-JAN-2005)   *(DD-MMM-YYYY e.g.: 01-JAN-2005)*

METROLIST inc   Res Form (Revised 11/05) Copyright 1999-2005   ● ENTERED WHERE *Enter BO for Broker Office*   ● ENTERED BY *Enter Initials of Entry Person*

F I G U R E   5.1

Residential Profile Sheet (continued)

RES
PAGE 2

REQUIRED ONLY IF FAXED OR MAILED TO METROLIST

Listing Address _____   Listor _____

Office _____   Office ID _____

Office Phone _____   Email _____

DESCRIPTION *(✔ Up to 34)*

AC ❑ Air Condition-Central	**CP** ❑ Covered Patio	**FX** ❑ Fix-Up	**LP** ❑ Landscaped Prof	**RM** ❑ Remodeled	**TO** ❑ Tenant Occupied
AG ❑ Age Restricted Cov	**CR** ❑ Corp Owned Relo	**5P** ❑ Five Piece Bath	**MB** ❑ Master Bathroom	**RV** ❑ RV Parking	**TP** ❑ Triple Pane Wndws
AF ❑ Attic Fan	**CT** ❑ Cook Top	**GA** ❑ Garden Area	**ML** ❑ Mother-In-Law Apt	**SA** ❑ Smoke Alarm	**TX** ❑ 1031 Exchange
AO ❑ Agent Owner	**CU** ❑ Cul-de-sac	**GC** ❑ Golf Community	**MO** ❑ Microwave Oven	**SC** ❑ Self-Cleaning Oven	**UD** ❑ Updated
AR ❑ Arena	**CV** ❑ Central Vacuum	**GD** ❑ Garage Door Opener	**MR** ❑ Media Room	**SD** ❑ Satellite Antenna	**UT** ❑ Utility Shed
AU ❑ Auction	**DB** ❑ Double Pane Windows	**GG** ❑ Gas Grill	**MS** ❑ Master Suite	**SE** ❑ Security Entrance	**VC** ❑ View City
BA ❑ Burglar Alarm	**DE** ❑ Deck	**GL** ❑ Gas Logs	**NC** ❑ Newer Carpet	**SF** ❑ Smoke Free	**VL** ❑ Vaulted Ceiling
BG ❑ Backs to Greenbelt	**DG** ❑ Dog Run	**GR** ❑ Great Room	**NH** ❑ New Home	**SH** ❑ Solar/Hot Wtr Heater	**VM** ❑ View Mountains
BL ❑ Balcony	**DO** ❑ Double Oven	**HC** ❑ Handicap Features	**NP** ❑ Newer Paint	**SK** ❑ Skylights	**WA** ❑ Washer
BO ❑ Backs to Open Space	**DR** ❑ Dryer	**HD** ❑ HUD Owned	**OG** ❑ On Golf Course	**SN** ❑ Sauna	**WB** ❑ Wet Bar
BR ❑ Barn	**DS** ❑ Disposal	**HS** ❑ High Speed Access	**PA** ❑ Parking Add'l Off St	**SO** ❑ Solar	**WC** ❑ Window Coverings
BW ❑ Buyer's Warranty	**DW** ❑ Dishwasher	**HT** ❑ Hot Tub	**PC** ❑ Pool Community	**SP** ❑ Sprinkler	**WD** ❑ Wood Floors
CA ❑ Cable Available	**EC** ❑ Evap Cooler(swamp)	**HU** ❑ Humidifier	**PF** ❑ Pet Free	**SS** ❑ Sun Room	**WI** ❑ Walk-in Closets
CF ❑ Ceiling Fan	**EF** ❑ Elec Air Filter	**IC** ❑ Intercom	**PL** ❑ Pool	**ST** ❑ Stove/Range/Oven	**WK** ❑ Work Shop
CH ❑ Carriage House	**ES** ❑ Eating Space/Kitchen	**JA** ❑ Jet Action Tub	**PR** ❑ Pet Restrictions	**SU** ❑ Sump Pump	**WP** ❑ Water Purifier
CI ❑ Cable Installed	**FD** ❑ Formal Dining	**JJ** ❑ Jack & Jill Bath	**PS** ❑ Pellet Stove	**SW** ❑ Storm Windows	**WR** ❑ Water Softener
CL ❑ Corner	**FE** ❑ Fence	**KI** ❑ Kitchen Island	**PT** ❑ Patio	**TC** ❑ Tennis Court	**WS** ❑ Wood Stove
CN ❑ No Covenants	**FI** ❑ Fireplace Insert	**LE** ❑ Lender Owned	**QP** ❑ Quick Possession	**TF** ❑ Tile Floor	**WT** ❑ Water Rights
CO ❑ Compactor	**FR** ❑ Freezer	**LO** ❑ Loft	**RF** ❑ Refrigerator	**TM** ❑ Two Master Bdrm	**WW** ❑ Wall to Wall Carpet

PUBLIC REMARKS
R1 _____
R2 _____
R3 _____
R4 _____
R5 _____
R6 _____

BROKER REMARKS *(PRIVATE)*
B1 _____
B2 _____

CONTRACT INFOrmation *(Online only-Data obtained through Print Everything or enter "Contract Info" in Custom Print)*

● LEGAL1 _____
LEGAL2 _____

● EXCLUSIONS1 _____
EXCLUSIONS2 _____

● EARNEST CK TO _____

MIN EARNEST *(No Commas, No Cents)*   POSSESSION
$ _____   _____

DIRECTIONS to property *(Online only-Data obtained through Print Everything or enter "Directions" in Custom Print)*

● D1 _____
D2 _____
D3 _____
D4 _____
D5 _____

● **PHOTOS** provided by *(✔ One)*   **PREVIOUS PHOTO** _____
B ❑ Broker Submitted Photo   **M** ❑ Metrolist Will Take Photo   Enter the old listing number of the desired photo

INTERNET ADS   **N** ❑ No

GHOST LISTING _____   *Enter Area(s) for Ghost Listing(s)*

All real estate advertised herein is subject to the Federal Fair Housing Act and the Colorado Fair Housing Act, which Acts make it illegal to make or publish any advertisement that indicates any preference, limitation, or discrimination based on race, color, religion, sex, handicap, familial status, or national origin. Metrolist, Inc. will not knowingly accept any advertising for real estate which is in violation of the law. All persons are hereby informed that all dwellings advertised are available on an equal opportunity basis.

Explaining the Agreement to the Seller

The presentation of the listing agreement to the seller needs to be thorough to ensure that the seller fully understands the agreement. Broker associates sometimes take a casual approach to explaining the listing agreement or offer no explanation at all to the seller. A broker associate may say, "Don't worry, it's the standard agreement. Sign here." Or the broker associate might try an explanation, even though the broker doesn't understand the agreement either. This misleads the seller and is not an acceptable practice. The licensee's job is to give the seller an understanding of the important provisions the agreement contains.

New broker associates should understand the agreement totally and explain each paragraph clearly. If a seller asks, "What happens during the listing period if I decide I want to lease the property to a tenant?" the broker associate should answer, "If you'll look at paragraph 18(d), you'll see that the property can be leased. You agree to pay my company a fee of _____ percent, but the fee does not include management."

The professional broker associate explains the listing agreement in language that the seller understands easily. Role-playing is an excellent method of learning this skill. When the role-playing results in wording that sounds appropriate the broker associate should write it down to be able to refer to the written explanation during the listing appointment.

The following scenario might result from a licensee's role-playing exercise:

"Mr. Jones, this is the standard agreement all Colorado brokers must use to list homes. Let's go over it together, paragraph by paragraph.

"This top section shows the standard headings. This is a binding contract and if you don't understand it or anything we discuss you should contact an attorney, tax professional, or other counsel before you sign. It also states that compensation to our firm is negotiable.

"As we discussed earlier, there are a number of relationships that are available with our firm. As you may recall, you and I decided that I would represent you as your agent, which is why I have checked that box.

"Section 1 says this is an exclusive and irrevocable contract for the time period we will agree on in a few minutes.

"Section 2 shows that I belong to a multiple-person firm and that I will be designated by my company to represent you in the sale of your property.

"Section 3 shows your name as the seller and ABC Realty as the brokerage firm and me as the broker. Do I have your names spelled correctly? Also, if you can give me a copy of your deed I will check to make sure that the legal description I copied from public records matches the deed."

The broker associate continues to explain sections 3 through 34 of the listing contract in a similar manner. She refers to the checklist in Figure 5.3 to be certain she has completed all the necessary documents and taken all the necessary actions in regard to the listing.

■ **EXAMPLE 5.2**   Using the listing agreement, paraphrase the legal words in everyday language that will help a seller understand the agreement better. In a group situation, each person should be assigned a paragraph. The person then explains the paragraph to the group in lay language and the group provides constructive criticism. Because each person would explain each paragraph differently, every broker associate should prepare his own written text for use in presentations.

Closing for the Listing

All necessary forms should be completed by this time. The best approach is to have the seller sign all forms at the same time rather than sign each as they are presented. A sample conversation is shown in Figure 5.2.

Marketing the Listing

The seller employs the listing broker to market the property. Many sellers believe that the licensee has not done the job unless the listing broker actually sells the listing. The licensee should discuss this misconception with the seller during the listing presentation. The seller should understand that if the licensee does the job properly, the house will sell through the licensee's marketing efforts—both to potential buyers and to other licensees, who will show the property to their buyers.

The broker has been hired to get the best price in the shortest time and with the least inconvenience to the seller. This requires the licensee to market

FIGURE 5.2

Getting Signatures on Listing Documents

Mr. and Mrs. Jackson, we agreed to market the property at $275,000. Based on that figure, we reviewed the statement showing your expenses of the sale and what you would receive as proceeds. Here's a copy for your records, and I need you to OK this form for our records. [After they sign the form, put it back in your stack.]

OK, you completed the disclosure statement that we'll give to buyers when they are interested in the home. This will protect you from later claims that you held back important information. I need your signatures here please. [After they sign the form, put it back in your stack.]

Great. We've gone over the agreement for us to market your home. I need your OK right here. [After they sign the form, put it back in your stack.]

I appreciate your confidence, and I'll start the marketing of your home right away. I'm going to try to get back to the office and prepare information to put the property into MLS. Before I leave, do you have any questions?

FIGURE 5.3

**Listing Procedure
Checklist**

Listing Procedure Checklist (Your company may have its own form)

Complete Brokerage Relationship Disclosures in accordance with Chapter 475, F.S.Rule E-35.

Do not need signed disclosures if you have a signed listing agreement.

This form should accompany all listings.

Property Address: _____

Listing Associate: _____

Listing Packet Contents (bold print indicates seller's signature is required):

❏ Comparative market analysis
❏ Brokerage relationship disclosures
❏ **EXCLUSIVE-RIGHT-TO-SELL CONTRACT**
❏ MLS profile sheet
❏ MORTGAGE STATUS REQUEST
❏ **SELLER'S PROPERTY DISCLOSURE**
❏ **HOME WARRANTY AGREEMENT if seller agrees to provide one**
❏ SELLER'S NET PROCEEDS FORM
❏ Survey, if available
❏ Copy of mortgage and note
❏ Copy of deed restrictions
❏ Title insurance policy
❏ Key to property
❏ Floor plan, if available
❏ Copy of seller or buyer referral sent out
❏ Three ads
❏ Sign installation form
❏ Lockbox installation form
❏ Client contact sheet
❏ Copy of MLS computer printout

Office Action:

❏ Get office manager's approval on listing forms.
❏ Enter listing data into computer.
❏ Put copy of printout into Floor Duty Book.
❏ Distribute copies of printout to all sales associates and broker associates.
❏ Turn in listing packet to secretary.

Follow-up Action:

❏ Return all original documents to seller.
❏ Send seller copy of the MLS listing book photo and information.
❏ Contact seller weekly.
❏ Send seller copy of mortgage status letter when received.
❏ Send copies of all ads to seller.
❏ Follow up on all showings.

the property in ways other than just showing it. Some of these activities include the following:

■ Disseminating the property information to all agents in the company
■ Putting the sign on the property

- Putting an MLS lockbox on the property (if approved by the seller)
- Arranging for all company broker associates to inspect the listing on caravan day
- Getting the information into the MLS service as soon as possible (It is unethical and self-serving to withhold the information from other brokers and broker associates while the agent attempts to sell the property)
- Announcing the listing at company sales meetings and at Board of REALTORS® marketing meetings
- Preparing a brochure to place in the home for prospective buyers and cooperating licensees
- Scheduling an open house if appropriate for the listing
- Writing at least three good ads to generate potential buyers
- Putting listing on Web sites (personal page, company page, and other advertisers' pages)
- Using e-mail auto responders to get immediate feedback for customers who ask for information from a Web site
- Preparing mail-outs to send to potential buyers
- Preparing a property brochure and a "Let's Make a Deal" package for potential buyers and other broker associates to be left on the property
- Telling 20 neighbors about the listing by mail
- Calling the neighbors to ask for help in finding buyers (search do-not-call list first)
- Holding a REALTORS® luncheon at the property to increase activity
- Reviewing sales and listing activity in the neighborhood and updating the CMA at least once a month

A detailed marketing program such as this could be the basis for a Satisfaction Guarantee or Steps to a Successful Sale listing presentation.

The purpose of the Let's Make a Deal package is to give the buyer's broker associate all the documents necessary to write an offer. Without these documents the offer would be contingent upon the buyer receiving and reviewing them to continue with the process. (See Figure 5.4.)

■ **EXAMPLE 5.3**   Prepare a 30-point marketing plan for a brochure you use in your listing presentation. Brainstorm to come up with different marketing ideas.

Servicing the Listing

Servicing the listing is often more important than acquiring it. "I never hear from my broker!" is probably the complaint sellers make most often about their broker associates. Sellers may perceive that listing broker associates are not completing their job if sellers do not hear from them.

Let's Make a Deal Package

Items to include:

A front page with:
- Property address including the zip code and the legal description
- The listing brokerage firm and broker associate's address and contact information
- The amount of earnest money and to whom the check is made payable to if other than the listing firm
- The possession date for the property
- A request to contact the listing broker before writing the offer

Copies with signatures of the following:
- Seller's property disclosure or source of water addendum
- Square footage
- Lead-based paint disclosure
- Closing instructions
- Earnest money receipt
- Any other items that might be needed such as surveys, easements, or any items that the buyer should have knowledge of prior to writing an offer

The purpose of the Let's Make a Deal package is to give the buyer's broker associate all the documents necessary to write an offer. Without these documents the offer would be contingent upon the buyer receiving and reviewing them to continue with the process.

■ **E X A M P L E   5 . 4**   You are a real estate broker associate who is quite busy and disorganized. You have had a listing for six months that is about to expire and you wish to renew it. Despite your best intentions, you have failed to contact your clients, Harold and Deidra, for more than two months. As time progressed, it became harder for you to make the call. You set an appointment to visit the home at 7:30 PM. Because you are caught in traffic, you are 20 minutes late when you walk up to the house. You are surprised to see that a competitor has listed the property next door. Even worse, it has a contract pending sign attached. Harold answers the door, nods his head seriously, and says, "Well, stranger. Long time no see!"

Role-play this situation. Try your best to re-establish the trust and rapport you had at the beginning of the listing period. It may be instructive enough that you will never allow this situation to happen in your career.

Professional licensees who are successful do not succeed on the strength of salesmanship alone. The licensees are successful because they provide service to their clients and customers. Often, a family's home is the largest asset it will ever have, so a broker associate must never take the marketing of the home lightly. Failure to maintain regular contact with a seller is a detriment to a broker associate's future success.

Several methods ensure that a broker associate will contact each seller at least once a week:

■ The broker associate selects one evening each week, such as Thursday night, to service listings.
■ The broker associate contacts every seller, in person, by phone or, if personal contact is not successful, by mail or e-mail. If the associate calls and the seller does not answer, the broker associate writes a card immediately to let them know the seller was called.

■ The broker associate clips every ad from every paper and homes magazine, then pastes it on a note card and mails it with a note that says, "Thought you'd like to see a recent ad on your home. Regards, Sally."

■ The broker associate calls the seller after every showing by a cooperating broker and gives feedback about the visit to the home. At a minimum, the broker associate should call once a week with feedback on all showings. If there have been no showings, this is another opportunity to discuss the market with the seller.

Often broker associates lose touch with sellers because they don't know what to talk about and feel that they sound like broken records because they say the same things over and over. But it's better to maintain consistent communication even if there is nothing new to report. Sellers have a lot at stake and feel better knowing their broker has not forgotten about them.

Each broker associate should prepare a Listing Servicing Schedule, which provides a basic format for the servicing of every listing. A sample form is shown in Figure 5.5.

FIGURE 5.5

Listing Servicing Schedule

Property Address: _____ H Phone: _____ W Phone: _____
Sellers' Names: _____ Children: _____

First Day:
❑ Verify tax information and legal description.
❑ Send out mortgage status request.
❑ Write three ads.
❑ Place listing on Web page.
❑ Send thank-you card to seller.
❑ Enter listing information in computer.
❑ Put copies of listing information in floor book.
❑ Distribute copies of listing information to all sales associates.
❑ Put sign and lockbox on property.

Second Day:
❑ Mail out notice of listing cards to at least 20 neighbors.
❑ Call or e-mail seller to tell of above steps.

End of First Week:
❑ Send letter to seller signed by employing broker.

Day after Caravan:
❑ Collect caravan comment sheets.
❑ Visit with seller to evaluate results of caravan and comments.

Second Week:
❑ Clip ads of property. Send to seller in postcard format.
❑ Check MLS information on computer, verify information, then e-mail to seller.
❑ Call seller to tell of progress. Ask seller to call when house is shown.

Listing Servicing Schedule (continued)

Third Week:
❏ Clip ads of property. Send to seller in postcard format.
❏ Run MLS computer check for new listings and listings under contract, then e-mail information to seller.
❏ Call or e-mail seller to find out who has seen home.
❏ Check with sales associates who have shown home; give feedback to seller.

Fourth Week:
❏ Clip ads of property. Send to seller in postcard format.
❏ Run MLS computer check for new listings and listings under contract, then e-mail information to seller.
❏ Call or e-mail seller to find out about who has seen home.
❏ Check with sales associates who have shown home; give feedback to seller.

Fifth Week:
❏ Clip ads of property. Send to seller in postcard format.
❏ Run MLS computer check for new listings and listings under contract, then e-mail information to seller.
❏ Visit seller in the home, and go over CMA. Get price reduction if appropriate.
❏ Walk through property again. Point out areas needing attention.

Sixth Week:
❏ Clip ads of property. Send to seller in postcard format.
❏ Run MLS computer check for new listings and listings under contract, then e-mail information to seller.
❏ Call or e-mail seller to find out who has seen home.
❏ Check with sales associates who have shown home; give feedback to seller.
❏ Schedule open house for the property, if appropriate.
❏ Send notice of open house to at least 20 neighbors.

Seventh Week:
❏ Run open house, and leave a note for seller on results. Call later.
❏ Clip ads of property. Send to seller in postcard format.
❏ Run MLS computer check for new listings and listings under contract, then e-mail information to seller.
❏ Call or e-mail seller to find out who has seen home.
❏ Check with sales associates who have shown home; give feedback to seller.
❏ Send out notice of listing to additional 20 homes in neighborhood.

Eighth Week:
❏ Clip ads of property. Send to seller in postcard format.
❏ Run MLS computer check for new listings and listings under contract, then e-mail information to seller.
❏ Call or e-mail seller to find out who has seen home.
❏ Check with sales associates who have shown home; give feedback to seller.

Ninth Week:
❏ Clip ads of property. Send to seller in postcard format.
❏ Run MLS computer check for new listings and listings under contract; then e-mail information to seller.
❏ Call or e-mail seller to find out who has seen home.
❏ Check with sales associates who have shown home; give feedback to seller.
❏ Do another CMA. Visit with seller, and get price reduction and extension.
❏ Schedule luncheon for sales agents.

Tenth Week:
❏ Clip ads of property. Send to seller in postcard format.
❏ Run MLS computer check for new listings and listings under contract, then e-mail information to seller.
❏ Call or e-mail seller to find out who has seen home.
❏ Check with sales associates who have shown home; give feedback to seller.

Continue this pattern until listing has been sold.

■ WHEN LISTINGS DON'T SELL

Occasionally, broker associates feel that they are wasting their time listing property. "I make more money working with buyers. I have ten listings and haven't earned a dime!"

Broker associates who feel that way may need to evaluate their listing inventory using the Listing Quality Report in Table 5.1. It is important to remember that one listing generates three sales: (1) the property itself, (2) the seller's new home, and (3) at least one buyer for another property that the listing broker meets while marketing the home. While buyers looking for a property often generate only the one sale, properly priced listings are the key to becoming a top-producing broker.

TABLE 5.1

Listing Quality Report

	123 Main St.		412 First St.		821 Jones St.	
	Yes	No	Yes	No	Yes	No
Listed at recommended CMA price?		✓	✓			✓
House in good condition?	✓		✓			✓
Seller motivated?	✓		✓			✓
Yard sign?	✓		✓		✓	
Easy showing access? (Lockbox, etc.)	✓		✓		✓	
Good curb appeal?		✓	✓			✓
Recommended price reduction	$10,000		$15,000		$17,500	

A. Address	B. Time Left	C. List Price	D. Chance of Sale During Term	E. Quality Volume [C × D]	F. Recommended Price Change
123 Main St.	3 months	$205,000	25%	$51,250	$10,000
412 Monroe St.	1 month	$178,200	10%	$17,820	$15,000
821 Jones St.	2 months	$312,500	40%	$125,000	$17,500
1250 Sipa Rd.	4 months	$285,000	60%	$171,000	$10,000
116 Third St.	5 months	$180,000	30%	$54,000	$10,000
TOTAL	**Avg 3 mo.**	**$1,160,700**	**1.65 listings**	**$419,070**	**$62,500**

Notice that the bottom part of the listing evaluation indicates that the broker associate who may have five listings has the equivalent of only 1.65 listings (adding the percentages of chance of sale). The associate may boast of a listing volume of $1,160,700 (average of $232,140) but really has the equivalent of only $419,070 (average of $83,814) when considering the chance of sale.

Overpriced listings result in frustration for the broker associate and resentment by the owner, who may become more demanding and tell friends of the lack of effort on the part of the broker associate. Sometimes, if the seller will not price the property appropriately, it may be best for the broker associate to give the listing back to the seller. An appropriate comment would be "We value our relationship with you and don't want you to feel we are not being productive. I feel you may be unhappy with us later on if we didn't give you the opportunity to talk with other agencies."

If the broker associate internalizes this evaluation and mentally reviews it when taking a listing, it is more likely that only salable listings would be taken thereafter.

■ SUMMARY

Three major types of listing agreements are open listings, exclusive-brokerage listings, and exclusive-right-to-sell listings. Licensees should carefully review and thoroughly understand the listing contracts they use. A licensee should be able to clearly explain to a seller the important provisions of a listing agreement.

A licensee must market property with skill, care, and diligence. A major part of the licensee's professional duties, in addition to listing and selling, is servicing listings and keeping in touch with sellers on a regular basis.

■ KEY TERMS

exclusive-brokerage listing	open listing	servicing the listing
exclusive-right-to-sell listing	profile sheet	
lockbox	Rule E-35	

■ APPLY WHAT YOU'VE LEARNED

The following actions reinforce the material in Course 3, Units 2 through 5:

■ Set up your power prospecting database. Start with your close friends and family, then list all the friends and past customers you can think of. After that, try to think of anyone even vaguely familiar that you have met and get the names down. You can get the addresses and contact information later.

■ If you own a home, estimate its current value, then prepare a CMA. If you do not own your home, do this exercise for a friend. Does the CMA support the value you guessed?

■ Based on the CMA you did on your or your friend's house; prepare a Seller's Net Proceeds Statement.

■ Complete a listing agreement for your home, along with other forms required by your broker. Ask your broker to review them.

■ Prepare an MLS computer input form describing the features of your house. Be certain it is complete.

■ Write three practice ads to market your home.

■ Pick a neighborhood in your city with homes priced from $200,000 to $250,000. Find as many sales as possible for the previous 12 months. Using the matched pair technique, identify the dollar contribution from
— a deck or mountain view,
— an extra bedroom,
— an enclosed garage, and
— a corner lot.

■ Using the same analysis, calculate the percentage difference between listing price and selling price.

■ Using MLS data, divide the number of houses on the market by the number of house sales last week to find how many weeks' supply of homes are on the market. Do this at least once a month. It's an excellent indicator of market activity.

■ Write a script for the explanation of a CMA to a prospective seller. Record your presentation on audiotape to hear how it sounds. Edit as necessary until it sounds just right.

■ Record your explanation of the approved exclusive-right-to-sell contract. Edit your remarks until you are satisfied.

6 UNIT

Working With Buyers

■ **explain** four different ways to enhance your product knowledge,

■ **list** at least five sources of buyers,

■ **give** at least three methods to show a buyer why an appointment with you will be beneficial,

■ **list** two important reasons for qualifying a buyer,

■ **explain** how prioritizing buyers benefits both the buyers and the broker associate,

■ **qualify** a buyer using the Fannie Mae/Freddie Mac housing expense ratio and the total obligations ratio,

■ **calculate** the total monthly payment (PITI) on a mortgage loan,

■ **qualify** a buyer using the do-it-yourself prequalification form,

■ **list** two benefits in having a buyer prequalify at a mortgage lender's office,

■ **list** the steps between setting up an initial appointment with a buyer and writing a contract for purchase, and

■ **explain** why you would show a limited number of homes to a potential buyer in one day.

■ OVERVIEW

Working with buyers is an important function of the professional real estate broker associate. Buyers are interested in working with knowledgeable, caring broker associates and generally are reluctant to make appointments without evaluating the broker associate's skills. A broker associate must be adept at handling telephone inquiries, know the inventory, and stay current with available financing plans. Above all, the broker associate must understand and observe the laws with respect to required disclosures and fair housing.

■ PRODUCT KNOWLEDGE

A buyer usually benefits from working with a licensee, regardless of the brokerage relationship, because of the licensee's product knowledge. It is hard work to acquire the extensive product knowledge that buyers expect. To become proficient, the broker associate should accomplish the following goals:

■ Spend a majority of the first few weeks in real estate looking at property
■ See at least 30 new properties each week
■ Keep a record of listings viewed by using one of the client follow-up programs and lead databases mentioned in Course 3, Unit 5 or even by using index cards grouped by price range and outstanding features. The broker associate may use the cards like flash cards to remember five good listings in each price range or five with pools or five fixer-uppers. With practice, the broker associate can remember more listings than five.
■ Constantly practice matching neighborhoods with price ranges or house sizes
■ Prepare a Five-Star Homes List showing the best-buys-on-the-market sheet for each price range (for instance, $175,000 to $200,000). A sample Five-Star Homes List is shown in Table 6.1.

If a buyer calls to ask for an address for one of the broker associate's listings, the broker associate should provide the information to the caller and, if needed, use "my five favorite homes on the market in your price range" to get an appointment with the buyer.

TABLE 6.1

Five-Star Homes List

★★★★★

FIVE-STAR HOMES
(BEST BUYS ON THE MARKET)
Price Range: $175,000–$200,000

Price	Address	MLS #	Comments
$176,900	116 Belmont Rd.	15432	Great deck, vaulted ceiling
$179,500	1272 Scenic Rd.	16523	Brick, large oak in front
$185,000	784 Wilson Ave.	16132	Wood frame colonial
$185,000	1216 Kara Dr.	15478	Huge back yard with hot tub
$188,500	8754 Skate Dr.	15843	Heavily wooded, secluded
$199,900	124 E. Call St.	16021	Downtown, arched doorways

■ **E X A M P L E   6 . 1**   If you actively sell residential properties, try to name from memory the location for at least three one-story, four-bedroom listings. Try to name the location for four listed homes with mountain or city views.

■ FINDING BUYERS

Some good sources of buyers include

- calls resulting from advertising,
- calls resulting from signs,
- past customers and clients,
- friends and family,
- open house visitors,
- canvassing prospects, and
- buyer seminar attendees.

■ **E X A M P L E   6 . 2**   Carol is on floor duty when she receives a call from a buyer who says, "I'm looking for a four-bedroom home with a deck, northeast, but it's got to have a large workshop. Do you have anything like that listed in the $150,000 range?"

"Yes, there are a number of properties in that area that may meet your needs," Carol responds. "How long have you been looking for a home?"

"Only a few weeks," the caller answers.

Carol then asks, "Would you be interested in learning about how I can make the buying process simple and save you a lot of time?"

Is Carol likely to get an appointment to meet with the buyer? Why or why not? Is there something she said that you would say differently?

Calls Resulting from Advertising

Advertisement calls are an extremely important source of buyers. A buyer calls for more information to determine whether a house is right. A buyer seldom calls to make an appointment with a broker associate, but the broker associate's objective is *always* to get the appointment with the buyer. The broker associate must remember two important points when answering buyer advertisement calls:

- It is difficult for the broker associate to talk intelligently about properties that she has not seen. For this reason, the broker associate should see every company listing before answering calls on ads or signs.
- The broker associate should review all company advertising in newspapers and homes magazines. The licensee should clip each ad and paste it on a separate piece of notebook paper or index card. A **fallback list,** sometimes called a *switch list* or *pivot list,* should be prepared for each ad. A fallback list comprises three to five properties that are similar to the property being advertised. The list can consist of the broker associate's personal listings, the brokerage firm's listings, or other brokers' listings. If a caller isn't satisfied after learning more about the property in question, the broker associate can

refer to the fallback list of other properties that might be suitable. The fallback list becomes invaluable in getting the appointment and helping the buyer find the right property. A sample fallback list is shown in Figure 6.2.

■ **EXAMPLE 6.3** Do a role-playing exercise with another person calling on an ad for 3415 Monitor Lane. Try to get an appointment using one of the methods discussed.

TABLE 6.2

Fallback List

Address	MLS #	Price	Comments
1546 Merrimac Dr.	16546	$89,500	Large workshop, lots of trees, 2 streets over
1247 Thresher Ln.	16478	$94,500	20' × 30' deck, spotless
1687 Woodgate Way	16521	$95,000	2 stories, 4 bedrooms, close to town
1856 Hoffman Dr.	16493	$85,000	Huge oak in front, lots of azaleas, big kitchen
1260 Dunston Ct.	16470	$92,500	Quiet street off Meridian, very clean, bright

Often, a caller wants a property's address but is unwilling to give a name or phone number. "I just want to ride by to see whether I like it," the caller says. The broker associate will not get the appointment unless the caller will benefit by meeting with the broker associate. The best-buys sheet and the fallback list may come in handy to get the appointment. Most buyers would then feel that the broker associate had market information that would make it worthwhile to make an appointment.

Another way to suggest to the caller that meeting with the broker associate would benefit the caller is to explain that many listings are not advertised. Many of the best properties are sold almost immediately by broker associates who watch carefully for new listings for their clients or customers. Many buyers want to know that someone constantly watches the market for the right properties for them. "Would you like to have first opportunity to see these prime properties?" is the question that can get the appointment.

When a caller is adamant about wanting an address but will not make an appointment, some broker associates do not give the address because they will lose the call. It is not worthwhile, however, to generate ill will with the consumer. Perhaps a better approach is to be helpful in every way. Ask how many property ads the caller has circled in the newspaper or homes magazine. Tell the caller you will provide an address and information on each listing advertisement, even though other real estate companies hold the listings. You should have a copy of the classified ad section and a homes magazine handy. Follow along with the caller, mark each ad, and set a time that you can get together. Prepare a list with addresses, prices, square footage, and other property features. The attraction to the buyer? One call gets it all because the consumer sees a benefit to meeting with the licensee. The attraction to the broker associate? The buyer places no calls to the competition and an appointment has been set.

Once an appointment is made, it is time to evaluate the buyer's needs and financial capabilities. This is called **qualifying** the buyer.

Often, the first visit with the buyer is simply a get-acquainted visit, meant for making required disclosures and for qualifying. After this is completed, a second appointment is set to show properties.

Calls Resulting from Signs

Another source of buyers is calls on property signs. Callers on real estate ads generally want the properties' addresses. Callers on signs generally want the prices because they already know the locations. A broker associate should handle a sign call like an ad call, with the exception of the information provided.

Past Customers and Clients

One of the best sources of buyers is past customers and clients because they already have enjoyed the benefits of the broker associate's services. Agency representation may be a problem, however. If the broker associate listed a client's property in a prior relationship, the person may feel that the same agency relationship exists in the purchase of a new home. The broker associate must give the buyer the appropriate brokerage relationship disclosures to recreate the relationship.

Friends and Family

Among the broker associate's first sources of buyers when starting out in real estate are friends and family. The agent should write to everyone he knows and stay in contact for news of potential customers. When working with a friend or family member, the broker associate must evaluate the loyalty issue to decide whether being a single agent for the buyer is more appropriate than being a transaction broker.

Open House Visitors

Holding open houses is a good way to find prospective buyers. The primary objective of an open house is not to make the seller happy (a sale makes the seller happy) but to get buyer prospects. If the buyer purchases the home on display, so much the better. The broker associate should prepare a brochure for the home with the broker associate's name and picture prominently placed.

Usually open house visitors are just looking. The broker associate should tell visitors that they are welcome to walk through the home but that there are few features that are not readily apparent. If this home is not right for the visitors, the licensee should have ready a list of the five best homes in the price range as well as a fallback list, then set an appointment to talk.

Canvassing Prospects

Canvassing is an excellent method of finding buyers and is discussed in detail in Course 3, Unit 2. The same canvassing call can be a source of either buyers or sellers. The broker associate might ask, "Do you know someone who may be getting ready to buy or sell real estate?" Often the answer is yes and the broker associate can set an appointment. Remember, you may not call anyone on the National Do Not Call Registry.

Buyer Seminar Attendees

Many broker associates and brokers consider buyer seminars to be outstanding prospecting tools and offer them to the public to attract large numbers of buyers at one time. Some real estate companies have impressive materials and workbooks for attendees of the classes, which run over two or three evenings. Often, attendees pay a nominal fee to cover the cost of books. Most seminars entitle an attendee to schedule a one-hour consultation with the seminar leader about a specific real estate problem or need. This can benefit both the consumer and the licensee if a business relationship results. Remember that the appropriate brokerage relationship disclosures must be made.

■ QUALIFYING THE BUYER

It is a waste of time to show properties the buyer does not like or cannot afford. So, before showing properties, the broker associate must get the answers to two important questions: (1) What are the buyers' housing objectives? (2) What can the buyer afford to pay?

What Are the Buyers' Housing Objectives?

Some of the information the broker associate should get from the buyers includes the following:

- What features do they want in the home?
- How quickly do they need to move?
- Must the buyers sell their current home?
- If they're leasing now, when does the lease expire?
- Have the buyers already spoken to a lender and been preapproved?
- Is there a specific area in which they want to live?

Desired features   The broker associate should ask the buyers what features the home *must have* and what features would be *nice to have.* The *must have* could be features such as a particular area of town, four bedrooms, or a two-car garage. The *nice to have* might be features such as high ceilings, updated kitchen, or a wood deck.

Urgency level   The broker associate also needs to know the buyer's urgency level. Each buyer should be classified based on urgency and motivation to purchase (see Table 6.3). A person needing to move within the next 30 days, for example, is a Priority 1 buyer, needing immediate attention. A person who doesn't have an immediate need, but who should not be ignored, is classified as Priority 2. A buyer who either will not or cannot purchase immediately is Priority 3 and should be contacted regularly for showings. If a buyer relocating to the city is in town just for the weekend to purchase a home, the broker associate knows this is a Priority 1 buyer. After financial qualifying shows the buyer to be capable of making a purchase, the broker associate might say, "It sounds like your situation needs my full attention. If you approve, I'll clear my calendar so we can find the right home for you." A buyer whose present lease expires in six months has less urgency to purchase now and is classified as Priority 3.

Current housing situation   If the buyers currently own a home that must be sold, one of the first actions should be to look at their home and make a listing presentation. After their home is listed, the best way to motivate the buyers-sellers to price their present home competitively is to show homes they might want to purchase during that listing period. When they see the right home, they will be prepared to sell their own quickly.

If the buyers are currently leasing, the licensee must determine when the lease expires. That will help in prioritizing the buyer.

Buyers' family helping in the decision   The broker associate must also find out whether someone other than the buyers will be involved in making the final purchasing decision. If the buyers' uncle will evaluate the final choice, the broker associate should try to get the uncle to see each property along with the buyers. Why? The uncle may have a better grasp of the market and of property values and may help the buyers reach a decision sooner.

T A B L E 6.3	**Buyer's Situation**	**Priority Level**
Prioritizing Your Buyers	Needs to move within 30 days or in town for the weekend to find a house	1
	Wants to buy a house within the next three to six months	2
	Can't buy right now but is just starting to look; perhaps on a lease expiring next year	3

Best times to see property   The licensee must find out what times are most convenient for the buyers to look at properties. Are they available during the day? Can they come immediately to see a property if the right one comes on the market? Or does their job situation require that they see property only in the evenings after work or on weekends?

Describing the Process to the Buyer

At the first meeting with the buyer, the broker associate should provide, in addition to the agency disclosure form, a clear picture of the entire process, from the time of this first meeting until the day the buyer moves into his new home. The buyer who understands the process is less likely to become uneasy or reluctant to purchase when finding the right property. The goal of this meeting is to have the buyer sign a buyer representation agreement. This lets the broker associate know the buyer is serious and makes sure the broker will get paid when the buyer buys. It is the first of many commitments the buyer will be asked to make in the process, and a very important one for the broker associate. The buyer should be given a copy of the purchase agreement and the broker associate should explain important provisions in the agreement. A buyer's cost disclosure should be prepared for the home the buyer desires. This also helps in the financial qualifying process.

Working with Buyers on a New Home Purchase

Nonstandard builder contracts   Builders or developers do not fall under the purview of the Colorado Real Estate Commission or Rule F and therefore rarely use the Commission-approved Contract to Buy and Sell. Typically, the attorney for the builder drafts a sale contract that is then used in the new home development. This contract usually favors the builders. Broker associates should be aware that the builder may or may not be willing to change any of this agreement, parts of which may not be in the buyer's best interest. Broker associates should counsel their buyer in regard to the different aspects of builder contracts before the buyer finds their dream property. The buyer should always be advised to seek legal or other counsel.

Earnest money not held in trust   Earnest money may be held by the brokerage firm or any other third party as long as the parties to the sales contract agree. Very often with new homes the builder will want to hold the earnest deposit. A discussion with the buyer prior to showing new home developments allows them the opportunity to determine if they are comfortable with the builder keeping the earnest money especially if the builder will be able to use the money for construction costs.

Warranties and completion dates   Typically, the builder will offer a warranty with the purchase of a new home. Broker associates should make sure the buyer clearly understands exactly what the warranty covers before entering into the contract. Additionally, it is important that the buyer understand what will happen if the builder does not meet the completion date. Discuss what the builder is willing to do for the buyer if the property is not completed on time. The broker associate should make sure that all of the agreements are in writing and signed by both parties.

Accompanying and Registering a Buyer

The majority of new home builders expect a licensee to be with a buyer at the first showing of the property. The broker associate should determine what is required to register the buyer with the builder. Registration allows the broker associate to be protected if the buyer returns without the broker to view the property. Many builders will not pay a broker associate who has not registered the buyer at the first showing. Buyers should be carefully counseled relating to this requirement when the buyer has signed an exclusive-right-to-buy contract with the broker associate. If the buyer buys any property without the broker's involvement, the buyer may still be obligated to pay the brokerage commission.

Soil report and required disclosure and warning Colorado Law states: (6-6.5-101 Disclosure to purchase—penalty)

■ At least 14 days prior to closing the sale of any new residence for human habitation, every developer or builder or their representatives shall provide the purchaser with a copy of a summary report of the analysis and the site recommendation. For sites in which significant potential for expansive soils is recognized, the builder or builder's representative shall supply each buyer with a copy of a publication detailing the problems associated with such soils, the building methods to address these problems during construction, and suggestions for care and maintenance to address such problems.

■ In addition to any other liability or penalty, any builder or developer failing to provide the report or publication required by subsection (1) of the section shall be subject to a civil penalty of five hundred dollars payable to the purchaser.

■ The requirements of this section shall not apply to any individual constructing a residential structure for his own residence.

Financial qualification Financial qualification is crucial to a successful sale. If the buyer contracts for a home and applies for a loan that is later denied, the seller, buyer, and broker associate have wasted time and effort. In addition, loan application fees ranging from $250 to $500, depending on the lender, could be lost. Licensees should explain both issues to their customers to help them understand the importance of financial qualifying.

Financial qualification is designed to determine how much money the buyer can borrow for the purchase of property. The broker associate has two ways to qualify a buyer financially:

■ Have a financial institution prequalify (or, better, preapprove) the buyer.
■ Use a do-it-yourself prequalification form.

Lender prequalifying versus preapproval Having a lender prequalify or pre-approve the buyer is the best approach and should be used whenever possible, but certainly before the buyer actually contracts for property. **Prequalification** is a lender's evaluation based on answers to questions given by the prospective buyer. Preapproval is given only after the buyer has been interviewed and the buyer's credit report has been reviewed and income verified.

A lender's preapproval letter makes the buyer's offer much stronger in the eyes of a seller and will result in more contracts.

Do-it-yourself prequalification form The prequalification form (See Figure 6.4) gives the licensee an opportunity to explain each entry on the form and thereby dispel some of the uneasiness that the potential borrower typically feels. This method should be used only when a buyer wants to see homes immediately after meeting with a broker associate and a lender's representative cannot be found for a prequalification interview.

Most lenders adhere to Fannie Mae/Freddie Mac standards in reviewing loan applicants. Those agencies recommend the maximum housing expense ratio (front) of

28 percent and the maximum total obligations ratio (back) of 36 percent for qualifying potential buyers for first mortgage (conforming) loans. The Federal Housing Administration's (FHA) maximum housing expense ratio is 29 percent and the maximum total obligations ratio is 41 percent. These figures are guidelines only. Many portfolio lenders will vary from these guidelines so that a prospective buyer who does not meet the guidelines may still be able to talk with a lender that will make the loan.

TABLE 6.4

Do-It-Yourself Prequalification Form (for Conventional Mortgage Loans)

Purchase price	$	115,000.00	(A)
Desired mortgage amount	$	92,000.00	(B)
Term of mortgage		30 years	
Mortgage rate		7.0%	
Loan-to-value ratio: (B) ÷ (A) =		80.0%	(C)
GROSS MONTHLY INCOME	$	3,000.00	(D)
Mortgage principal and interest payment: (Payment factor: 6.6530) × (B) ÷ 1,000 =	$	612.08	
Annual real estate taxes ÷ 12 =	+	110.21	
Homeowner's insurance premium ÷ 12 =	+	50.00	
MONTHLY HOUSING EXPENSES	$	772.29	(E)
Car payments	+	250.00	(D)
Alimony or child support payments	+	225.00	
Credit card or charge account payments	+	50.00	
Other loan payments	+		
FIXED MONTHLY OBLIGATIONS	$	1,297.29	(F)
HOUSING RATIO (E) ÷ (D) = 25.7%			
DEBT RATIO (F) ÷ (D) = 43.2%			

Source: Thomas C. Steinmetz, *The Mortgage Kit*, 4th ed. (New York: Kaplan Publishing, Inc., 1998), 33.

TABLE   6.4

Do-It-Yourself Prequalification Form (for Conventional Mortgage Loans) (continued)

Purchase price	(A)
Desired mortgage amount	(B)
Term of mortgage	
Mortgage rate	
Loan-to-value ratio: (B) ÷ (A) =	(C)
GROSS MONTHLY INCOME	(D)
Mortgage principal and interest payment: (Payment factor for a ___%, ___-year loan: ___) × (B) ÷ 1,000	
Annual real estate taxes ÷ 12 =	
Homeowner's insurance premium ÷ 12 =	
Mortgage insurance: (B) × 0.00025 (if (C) is more than 0.80)	(E)
MONTHLY HOUSING EXPENSES	(D)
Car payments	
Alimony or child support payments	
Credit card or charge account payments	
Other loan payments	(F)
FIXED MONTHLY OBLIGATIONS	
HOUSING RATIO (E) ÷ (D) = %	
DEBT RATIO (F) ÷ (D) = %	

Source: Thomas C. Steinmetz, *The Mortgage Kit*, 4th ed. (New York: Kaplan Publishing, 1998), 33.

The common reason buyers don't qualify under the Fannie Mae/Freddie Mac standards is usually the back ratio: total obligations. If that number is too high, perhaps a creative lender can still help by increasing the qualifying income or suggesting prepaying some installment debt to less than ten months so that it's no longer counted. A very high credit score could also help get the loan. Other compensating factors include the following:

- Having a good record of promotions and raises
- Having little or no installment debt if housing expense ratio is high
- Making a down payment greater than 20 percent
- Having saved money while making rent payments higher than the mortgage payments of the new mortgage
- Having a job with good benefits, such as a company car, free health plan, and high company contributions to a 401(k) plan

■ **EXAMPLE   6.4**   Sally and Will Cleare make $41,400 in gross annual income. They wish to purchase a $150,000 home, with $30,000 as a down payment. Fixed-rate, 30-year mortgages are at 7 percent. The monthly principal and interest payment is $798.36. Taxes for a home in this price range are approximately $1,440 per year. Insurance is approximately $540 per year. No private mortgage insurance is necessary because the loan-to-value ratio does not exceed 80 percent.

The Cleares have installment loan payments totaling $70 a month and a car payment of $320.

Using the Do-it-Yourself Prequalification Form, determine whether the Cleares qualify for this loan.

■ **EXAMPLE 6.5**   The following role-playing skit, designed to highlight mistakes some broker associates make in their first meetings with prospective buyers, allows both spectators and participants to learn from the process. Three actors are needed—a broker associate and two buyers. All persons in the skit should be as enthusiastic and realistic as possible. During the presentation, if the broker associate says something that may violate the law or ethics, group members should shout "Zap!" to signify their disapproval. At the end of the exercise, group members should be able to itemize the broker associate's errors and recommend responses to the buyers' questions.

Buyers' First Meeting with a Licensee

Buyers walk in, are greeted by broker associate.

Licensee:	Hello, may I help you?
Husband:	Yes, we are here to see Lee Wilson.
Licensee:	I'm Lee. You must be Mr. and Mrs. Camp?
Wife:	Yes, we are. Very nice to meet you.
Licensee:	Great. Please sit down. (*Pause while they sit.*)
Husband:	Our mutual friends, the Joneses, recommended we get in touch with you.
Licensee:	Yeah, the Joneses send me lots of people. By the way, if you send me anyone who buys a house, I'll give you $50.
Wife:	That's what they told us. I hope you can find us a good deal, too.
Licensee:	I love working with buyers, Mrs. Camp, and because I'm a transaction-broker, I can work harder on your behalf.
Wife:	Well, do you have any distress sales of houses in the $100,000 range that we could take advantage of?
Licensee:	As a matter of fact, my company just listed one. The listing broker associate suggested that I look at it. Confidentially, the owners' business is in trouble, and they need to sell quickly. I have heard they are desperate and probably would come off the price as much as $6,000, but we should start even lower to get the best counteroffer.
Husband:	Tell us about it.
Licensee:	Well, it's in Bent Tree Estates, close to Lake Jackson. It's got three bedrooms, two baths, a large lot, and a two-car garage. It's in absolutely perfect condition.
Wife:	The newspaper ran an article last week suggesting that buyers get a home inspection. Is that a good idea?

Licensee:	It is if you want to spend $300 for nothing. I've looked over the house, and it's just perfect. No problems whatsoever.
Husband:	I need to tell you that we may have a problem qualifying for a new loan. I had some credit problems last year, and we got turned down on another house we tried to buy. We really need to get an assumable loan with no qualifying.
Licensee:	Well, we're in luck again. If you like this house, you can buy it with less than $8,000 down. We'll have to structure a wraparound loan to beat the due-on-sale clause, but I do that all the time. Can you work with $8,000 down?
Husband:	I think we can come up with that much, if we can get the right price. Can we put some kind of contingency in the contract in case I can't get the money?
Licensee:	Hey! I can write up a contract with contingencies that will let you out at any time with no risk. Don't worry about that. But let's go see it.
Husband:	Should we have an attorney?
Licensee:	You know what's wrong with five attorneys up to their necks in sand?
Husband:	(*Smiles*) No, what?
Licensee:	Not enough sand. (*He laughs.*) Seriously, folks, you don't need an attorney. I can help you with anything an attorney can.
Wife:	Can we ask you some more questions first?
Licensee:	Sure. Go ahead.
Wife:	Is it a good neighborhood?
Licensee:	Oh, yeah, there are hardly any minorities living there!
Wife:	Well, I didn't mean that. I meant is it pleasant and well-maintained?
Licensee:	Oh, sorry. Yes, it's really nice.
Husband:	Do you need us to sign any disclosure forms now?
Licensee:	No, not really. Not until we write a contract for a house.
Husband:	Well, let's go looking. I hope it works out.
Licensee:	I'll do everything I can for you. (*The Camps leave; to an associate in the office*) Hey, Jim! I'll be back in a while. I've got some flakes with no money again, but I'm going to show a house!

Is it possible to learn from mistakes? The mistakes made in this skit may seem ridiculous, but these statements are actually made—although probably not all in a single transaction. Broker associates must be alert during their presentations and when answering questions to avoid these mistakes.

After qualifying the buyer, the broker associate has one more step to complete before showing properties.

■ PREPARING THE BUYER TO BUY

The successful broker associate will prepare the buyer for signing the contract long before the right property is found. After qualifying the buyer's needs, the broker associate should give the buyer a copy of the contract for purchase and sale and explain the more important paragraphs to the buyer. This serves two important functions:

- If the buyer receives important information from the broker associate at their first meeting, this works to cement the buyer's loyalty to the associate.
- Because the buyer is given a copy of the contract along with an explanation, the contract becomes the buyer's property. When the buyer becomes interested in a particular property, the buyer is not startled when the broker associate pulls out a contract form.

Many successful broker associates keep a contract on a clipboard along with the MLS information on the property. It's always in sight so the buyer can see it. If the buyer asks questions like, "Can the seller leave the draperies?" the broker associate would ask, "Shall I put that in the agreement?" while writing on the contract.

■ SHOWING THE PROPERTY

Once the buyer has been qualified and signed a buyer representation agreement, it is time to show properties that meet the buyer's needs. The broker associate should use the following sequence in the showing and contracting process:

1. Setting the appointment
2. Previewing the properties
3. Planning the route
4. Entering and showing the properties
5. Evaluating the buyer's level of interest
6. Estimating the buyer's costs and making required disclosures
7. Writing the contract

Steps 1 through 5 are discussed in the following sections. Step 7, writing the contract, is the subject of Course 3, Unit 7. Step 6, estimating the buyer's costs and making required disclosures, is covered in Course 3, Unit 8.

Setting the Appointment

This step is important not only for the obvious reason (nothing can happen until a meeting occurs) but also from a timing standpoint. Does the broker associate set the appointment before previewing prospective homes or after? Many times a broker associate will not set an appointment until previewing homes and is confident that good choices are available to show. The advantage of this method is that the broker associate can describe properties that meet the buyer's needs.

It is important to keep in contact with the buyer regularly, based on priority status. At least weekly, the broker associate should match the buyer's profile with new listings, then call the buyer for an appointment. If the broker associate wants a Saturday showing appointment, the appointment must be made far enough in advance that the buyer can make the necessary arrangements. Saturday morning is too late to make the call. Early in the week is the best time to call for weekend showing appointments.

The best way to match a buyer with property is to use one of the client follow-up programs or lead databases mentioned in Course 3, Unit 5. A separate card may be printed for each property. Match-ups between buyers and properties also are possible using some of the MLS system software. If the broker associate does not have access to a computer, it is simple to enter the buyer information onto prospect cards. Spread out the cards on a tabletop and group them by price range when reviewing new listings. Listings should be matched to the buyer, and the broker associate should call or e-mail the buyer regularly about properties that match the buyer's needs. The more frequently the broker associate makes the buyer aware that the broker associate is continually searching for the right property for the buyer, the more confident and comfortable the buyer will be with the broker associate and the buying process.

Previewing the Properties

The broker associate should **preview properties** before actually showing them to the buyers. The MLS system will often show a large number of properties that appear to meet the buyer's criteria. After previewing all the properties it often turns out that only three or four will really work for the buyer. Another advantage to previewing is that the licensee can walk very quickly through a property to determine if it will work. Either out of courtesy to the homeowner or out of general interest in viewing homes, buyers take more time to view even the properties they know immediately they don't like. Previewing saves time for the broker and the buyer. Additionally, it saves the broker associate the surprise and embarrassment of telling the buyers, "I think you'll like this next one!" only to find the property in terrible condition.

Each time the broker associate sees a new property, whether on a showing appointment, a preview day, or an office caravan of new listings, the broker associate should match that property with a buyer, taking careful notes before contacting the appropriate buyer.

Being Prepared to Show Properties

One of the most important factors in closing the sale is being prepared. That means having the objective firmly in mind that *today* you will write the contract. So, before showing property, you should have in your file folder:

- A copy of the lender's good-faith estimate for the top price the buyer can qualify for so you're ready to write the buyer's estimated cost disclosure
- All the necessary forms, including the cost disclosure estimate sheet and the contract for sale and purchase

Planning the Route

Normally, the broker associate should show no more than five properties in one tour. However, if a Priority 1 buyer is in town for the weekend for the purpose of buying a home, the broker associate must continue to show homes or risk losing the buyer.

When setting the appointment to show properties, the broker associate must consider in which order the homes will be shown. Buyers go through a continual evaluation process during the inspection tour, and the broker associate should help that process. Many broker associates like to schedule the home they consider just the right property as the last on the tour. While there are good arguments for this procedure, there are also disadvantages. The biggest problem is that if the houses get better between numbers one and five, and five is the best, the buyer wants to see house number six. Most brokers recommend showing the best house early in the tour. This sets a standard against which all other homes are measured. It usually makes the tour faster because the buyers can decide quickly that the home shown earlier was more to their liking.

Once the route has been decided, the broker associate should make appointments for the showings with the listing brokerage firm. The time scheduled for each showing should not be fixed but should fall in a range, because it is often difficult for the broker associate to judge how long the buyer will stay in each home on the tour. When calling the listing brokerage firm to set the showing, give them a time range of one to two hours. They will then set the showing and call all information back to the buyer's broker associate's office. The seller will be asked to vacate the property during the showing. This allows the buyer to relax and take "emotional possession" of the property during the showing. The broker associate should take careful notes about location of lockboxes and whether there are any pets. If the broker associate will be later than scheduled or must cancel, common courtesy as a professional dictates that the broker associate should call the listing company to explain the circumstances. Nothing is more disappointing to a seller than to needlessly prepare the home for a showing.

The route taken on the way to each property also is important. A trip past a beautiful park nearby makes the home site more interesting to the buyer, as does a trip past the shopping areas and schools closest to the home. While the initial route might avoid unsightly areas, they should be shown on the way out. Failure to show such surroundings is misrepresentation.

If the property has negative features, the licensee should discuss those features on the way to the property—for example, "When I previewed the home yesterday, the housekeeping was not up to its usual standard because the kids are out of school this week. I hope that's OK." This reduces the shock the buyer might feel when entering. Often, the buyer defends the property: "Considering everything, the house is surprisingly clean!"

The broker associate should avoid exaggerating a home's positive aspects to the buyer. This exaggeration may create an expectation that the house may not be able to meet. It is better that the buyer be pleasantly surprised when discovering the features.

Entering and Showing the Properties

This process depends on a property's general appearance. If the home's exterior is outstanding, the presentation should give the buyer time to appreciate this feature. Many broker associates park across the street so that a buyer's walk to a house is as pleasant as possible.

When highlighting a property's features, the broker associate must remember the most important words in any sales presentation:

- Fact
- Bridge
- Benefit
- Picture

The broker associate often points out facts that may be important to the buyer and expects the buyer to be able to translate each fact into a benefit. "This house is on a cul-de-sac" might be a typical comment when driving up to the property. The broker associate believes this is important information to the buyer. The buyer might be thinking, "Yes, that's quite obvious. So what?" The full presentation should include fact, bridge, benefit, and picture.

The *fact* is that the property is on the cul-de-sac. The *bridge* might be "What that means to you, Mr. and Mrs. Jones…" The *benefit* is the rest of the sentence: "is that because there is no through-traffic, automobiles travel very slowly, resulting in greater safety to your children." The *picture* is a word picture: "Imagine being out here on the street while your children roller skate safely."

■ **EXAMPLE 6.6**   Picture a house that you have been in recently. Try to think of as many features of the house as you can, then express those features to represent fact, bridge, benefit, and picture statements.

Or, with a group of people, set up a contest to see who can come up with the most fact-bridge-benefit-picture statements about a house that is familiar to all of you.

The broker associate should practice this technique whenever possible: when driving in the car alone, when previewing properties, or when on the office caravan of listings. Once it becomes a habit, buyers will find the broker associate's statements clearer and more interesting, and the broker associate will make more sales.

Many times, the listing office gives out the key to the back door or the back door key may be the only key provided in the lockbox, or **keysafe,** at the house. Although the broker associate must go in through the door for which the broker has a key, the buyer always should enter through the front door.

Finally, the broker associate should not overshow a property. The buyer should be allowed to discover some of the best features on his own. The classic example of overshowing is walking through a property making statements such as, "This is the dining room."

Making the Buyers' Decision Easier

Normally, a broker associate will only show five to seven homes during a showing appointment. This is usually recommended so that the buyer can have an opportunity to give feedback and not become confused by a large number of homes. In some cases, however, many homes are shown to a buyer during one appointment. This might happen if the buyer is making a trip from out of town and needs to find the right house during this trip.

If a buyer sees 20 to 30 homes in a tour, the buyer will certainly be confused about which home had what feature. To make it easier, an experienced associate will have the buyer make a decision after seeing each home. You would say, "Which home do you like best—this house or the house on Cherry Lane?" If the answer is "Cherry Lane," you would say, "OK, forget all the other homes." At the last home on the tour, it is then easy to close with the question, "Well, which home do you want to buy, this one or the one on Cherry Lane?"

If you show more homes the next day and the buyer liked Cherry Lane best, start the tour by taking the buyer back to Cherry Lane, with a comment such as, "OK, so this is the house we're ready to buy if we don't find one better today, right?"

Evaluating the Buyer's Level of Interest

A buyer usually knows when not interested shortly after entering the house. The broker associate should stop showing the property and proceed to the next. Because this is not the right house, it would be pointless to answer any of the buyer's objections. If the seller is at home, the broker associate should explain tactfully that the house does not satisfy the buyer's needs.

Handling Objections

Some important points to remember about objections include the following:

- An objection can be an opportunity to make the sale. Many objections can be turned into immediate selling points. "The house needs paint" could provoke an argument from an unprofessional broker associate. The empathetic broker associate simply asks, "Would you paint it yourself or would you hire someone to paint it for you?" With a positive response from the buyer, both parties are happy.
- Be certain you understand the objection; then restate it. For example, a buyer may say, "This house costs too much money!" You may follow with a question such as, "If I understand you, you feel that the house is overpriced?" The buyer may answer, "No, I'm just not certain I want to buy a house at this price level." By clarifying with a question, you avoid being argumentative.

Don't answer an objection until you have isolated it; if there are many more objections, this is not a suitable property. "If it were not for the problem about the house price, would you buy this house?" A yes answer tells you, "Satisfy me regarding this problem and I'll buy."

If you don't feel you can answer an objection to the buyer's satisfaction, especially if the objection is valid and you believe it is a deal-breaker, you shouldn't. You should agree with the buyer and go to the next property.

Make a list of as many objections as you can think of, then write out at least two plausible answers to the objection. Try them in your office sales meetings and practice them regularly.

Course 3, Unit 7 covers the legal document called a Contract for Sale and Purchase. It is important for licensees to understand the wording of the agreement they will ask buyers and sellers to sign. Course 3, Unit 8 discusses writing and presenting an offer.

■ SUMMARY

When working with a buyer, a broker associate must be certain to make required agency disclosures on a timely basis. A buyer benefits most when a licensee represents the buyer and no one else. Extensive product knowledge is necessary if a broker associate is to provide the best service to a consumer. The broker associate has many ways to acquire product knowledge, but all consist of looking at properties. Index cards or client contact software helps the licensee remember properties, and a best-buys-on-the-market list helps the broker associate better exhibit product knowledge.

Broker associates draw buyers from a number of sources: calls on ads or signs, past customers or clients, friends and family, open house visitors, canvassing, and buyer seminars. When handling an ad or a sign call, a licensee's primary objective is to get an appointment. Broker associates should prepare carefully for ad calls, know the properties advertised, and have fallback lists.

A broker associate should qualify a buyer's housing objectives and have the buyers preapproved for a loan, as well as prioritize buyers based on the immediacy of their needs. When showing properties, the broker associate should describe benefits and be careful not to overshow the properties. The broker associate can help reduce buyer confusion by helping the buyer decide which is the favored house after each house is shown.

■ KEY TERMS

buyer brokerage agreement	fallback list	previewing properties
canvassing	lockbox	qualifying
	prequalification	

UNIT 7

Sales and Option Contracts

- ■ **discuss** the unique features of a real estate contract,
- ■ **define** what is meant by a valid contract,
- ■ **distinguish** between an implied contract and an expressed contract,
- ■ **distinguish** between a voidable contract and a void contract,
- ■ **explain** the statute of frauds,
- ■ **name** and explain at least ten important sections or provisions in a real estate sales contract,
- ■ **complete** a sales contract, and
- ■ **list** the requirements for completing an option contract.

■ OVERVIEW

Contracts are part of our everyday lives. When a person orders telephone service, buys a refrigerator, or pays for an airline ticket, a contract has been formed.

Licensees regularly work with many different kinds of contracts. The broker's employment agreement, listing contracts, buyer brokerage agreements, leases, options, and sales contracts are just a few. Understanding the information in a contract and being able to correctly explain it to sellers and buyers is an important function of a sales associate. Licensees may legally prepare listing contracts, sales contracts, and option contracts.

ANALYSIS OF REAL ESTATE CONTRACTS

A **contract** is a promise or set of promises that must be performed. Once the promise is given, the law recognizes performance of that promise as a duty. If the promise is broken or breached, the law provides a legal remedy for the injured party. However, one promise, standing alone, does not constitute a contract. Some specific act by the party to whom the promise is made, or a mutual promise from that party, is required to conclude a contract. For example, if you promise to fix your neighbor's roof and the neighbor thanks you, no contract exists because you asked for nothing in return for your promise. If your neighbor promises to give you $1,000 to fix his roof and you promise to do it, mutual promises have been exchanged, and a contract has been made.

Types and Legal Standings of Contracts

A number of contract types and classifications exist, each having certain legal effects. Newly licensed sales associates will remember having been exposed to certain classifications of contracts and to the fact that a contract can change from one classification to another as **performance** progresses.

A **bilateral contract,** the most common type, is a mutual agreement by both sides to perform. A real estate sales contract is an example of a bilateral contract because the seller promises to sell a parcel of real property and to deliver title, and the buyer promises to pay a certain sum of money for the property. A **unilateral contract**, on the other hand, is a one-sided promise. One party makes an obligation to perform without receiving a promise to perform from the other party. In effect, it is an offer that can be accepted only by performance on the terms offered. An example of a unilateral contract is the ordinary option, in which the person granting the option (optionor) is obligated not to sell to anyone but the person asking for the option (optionee) during the life of the option. The optionee is not required to buy. Two additional examples of a unilateral contract are

- an open listing agreement, where the seller agrees to pay a commission if the broker performs, but the broker makes no promises to market the property, and
- a broker's promise to pay a $5,000 bonus to the broker associate who sells the most homes in a subdivision.

An **express contract** is a mutual agreement between parties stated in words, either oral or written. An **implied contract** is an unwritten agreement inferred from the actions or conduct of the parties that show intent to be bound by the agreement. For example, if a broker personally buys property on behalf of his principal, a promise is implied on the broker's part to deliver the property to the principal. A second example of an implied contract is a situation in which a broker tells a seller that there is a buyer willing and able to pay for the seller's property, and the seller accepts the buyer's offer. The law usually requires that the seller pay the broker a typical rate of commission because of the parties' acts.

An **executory contract** is an agreement in which some future act remains to be done by one or both parties. For example, a real estate sales contract, between signing and title closing, is an executory contract. An **executed contract,** on the other hand, is an agreement in which the parties have fulfilled their promises and thus performed the contract. For example, a sales contract becomes an executed agreement after title closing and after all parties have fully performed. (*Note:* Do not confuse the term *executed contract* with the use of the word *execute,* which refers to the signing of a legal document such as a contract.)

A **valid contract** is an agreement that contains all of the essential elements—contractual capacity, **offer** and acceptance, lawful purpose, **in** writing and signed, and consideration (COLIC)—and is binding and enforceable on both parties in a court of law.

A **voidable contract** is an agreement that appears to be valid and enforceable but may be rescinded by one of the parties. For example, an agreement entered into with a minor usually is voidable by the minor. The competent parties element of a valid contract is absent. For another example, a contract may contain a clause (provision) related to time of performance by both parties. If either party fails to perform on or before a specified date, the other party has the right to void or nullify the contract. Thus, a voidable contract may be seen as midway between a valid contract and a void contract: It remains valid until the party with the power to void the agreement chooses to do so. A **void contract** is an agreement that is unenforceable under the law. It has no legal force because it does not contain the essential elements of a contract. For example, a listing contract in which a broker agrees to illegal discrimination based on race, sex, color, religion, national origin, family status, or handicap probably voids the document.

■ **EXAMPLE 7.1**   You are a broker associate who has listed John Wilson's home in Foxcroft. Mr. Wilson would rather not repair several property defects (such as a cracked foundation). He suggests the use of an as is clause in the contract so that a buyer can do any inspection desired. "Based on this clause," Wilson tells you, "we have no need to disclose."

Does the use of an as is clause in a sales contract excuse a broker from disclosing material facts regarding a property? Explain.

Statute of Frauds

Before the enactment of the **statute of frauds,** it was not uncommon for a person to pay "witnesses" to falsify testimony to support a nonexistent oral contract for the sale of real property. The law commonly called the statute of frauds requires that certain types of contracts, in order to be enforceable, be in writing and be signed by the party against whom enforcement is sought. Contracts that must be in writing and signed are of two general types: those that will not be performed fully within a short period of time and those that deal with specific subjects.

In Colorado, an agreement to sell or the actual sale of any interest in real property is subject to the statute of frauds and must be in writing and signed by all parties bound by the contract to be enforceable. Witnesses are not required. The exception to the statute of frauds is a lease of less then 12 months.

■ SALES CONTRACTS

A **sales contract,** also called a **Contract to Buy and Sell** (CBS), is a written agreement setting forth the terms for the transfer of real property from seller to buyer, with both signing the document. The approved form was developed by the Colorado Real Estate Commission and is the required form for use by all broker associates in Colorado, which is available through the Colorado Division of Real Estate Web site: www.dora.state.co.us/real-estate (click **Real Estate Brokers** from the left column, and then click **Commission Approved Forms**). This section of the unit presents specific instructions for the correct preparation of that contract, providing licensees with hands-on practice in preparing contracts to increase their professional skills.

Completing the Contract to Buy and Sell

No two real estate transactions are exactly alike. Even two nearly identical houses located adjacent to one another may require different contractual handling. The earnest money deposits, mortgage sources, and prices, as well as many other items, must be considered. Even the tried-and-proven clauses in the approved form may need to be adapted to the requirements of a particular transaction. Therefore, licensees should use great care when completing all contracts.

Responsibility for Preparation

The sales contract is the most important instrument for closing a real estate transaction. Because it is the final agreement after all the offers and negotiations that have taken place, a licensee must be very careful when preparing it. Any time a licensee is not certain whether an attorney is required in preparing any special clause or type of contract, the best course of action is to advise the buyer and seller to consult an experienced real estate attorney.

The broker associate and the employing broker may be held financially responsible for any mistakes in the agreement. If any errors, omissions, or ambiguities exist regarding material terms, the courts will not go outside the contents of the contract to determine intent. The licensee who prepared the contract will not be allowed to explain later intent not indicated in the contract contents. If the contract is vague and unenforceable, the result could be no transaction at all, loss of commission, and a possible civil lawsuit against the licensee.

"Time Is of the Essence" Provision

A single sentence in Paragraph 21, "**Time is of the essence** for all provisions of this Contract," has important legal effects. If a party fails to perform the duties or promises made within the exact time limits in the contract, it causes an automatic default. This default then creates a right of cancellation on the part of the other party (voidable contract). Because of the importance of meeting requirements with dates and times, licensees should

- use realistic time periods,
- check that the time periods complement and are consistent with times in other blank spaces, and
- use the date and deadline chart in Section 2c to monitor performance by the parties to the sales contract once it has been signed.

Gathering Contract Data

Collecting the information required to complete all of the entry blanks in the CBS is a sizable task. Information may become available or should be obtained as the real estate licensee helps negotiate the contract. Once the licensee gathers all of the information, the licensee must verify it for accuracy and currency. Including obsolete information in a contract may be more harmful to a successful closing than having insufficient information to complete the contract. The licensee should pay particular attention to and be sure to verify the following two categories of data:

- *The owner/seller's name and address and the property's legal description.* MLS data, property appraiser information, and listing agreements have been in error on occasion. The listing broker should supply the legal description and they should place more reliance on an existing or a prior title insurance policy, a deed, or a survey for the information.
- *Financial information.* Financial data tend to change frequently and require last-minute updating. Check with the buyer's lender to make certain that times allowed for obtaining financial commitments are realistic and that the rates and terms contemplated actually are available.

The broker associate representing the buyer should have a conversation with the listing broker prior to writing the offer to make sure they have the most current disclosures and to determine certain dates and times. It doesn't make sense to have an offer countered over the closing or acceptance date if these could have been determined in an initial conversation.

■ OPTION CONTRACTS

An **option contract** is a contract between a property owner (optionor) and another (optionee) in which the optionee, for a consideration, has the right (not the obligation) to purchase or lease the property at a specified price during a designated period. To be enforceable, an option must contain all of the essential elements of a contract.

Strictly speaking, it is important to distinguish between an *option contract* and an *option* (in actual practice the terms are often used interchangeably). If you offer to sell your house to a friend for $100,000 and your friend wants to think about the offer for a day or so, your friend might have an option but does not have an option contract. Therefore, you could revoke your offer to sell and no breach of contract would occur because no contract exists when there is a lack of consideration (exchange of promises). Had your friend paid you $1,000 in option money in consideration of a 30-day or 60-day period to decide about your offer and you agreed to those terms, an option contract would have been concluded. The option money given legally may be applied as part of the purchase price in the event the option is **exercised**.

An option creates a contractual right; it does not create an estate in the optioned property. When first written and executed, an option contract is unilateral. The owner/optionor is obligated to sell if given proper notice by the buyer/optionee, but the buyer/optionee is not obligated to purchase and may allow the option to expire. Options frequently are used to give a developer or buyer time to resolve problems related to financing, zoning, title, or feasibility before committing to purchase or lease. Options also are useful instruments in the land assemblage process.

In addition to the required information in an option contract, other provisions should or may be included. For example, a statement of the method of notice required to exercise the option normally is provided. Also, some provision should be included concerning the option money (the consideration) if the option is not exercised. Unless expressly prohibited by the wording of the terms, an option normally is assignable.

Option contracts often are written with less care and attention than they deserve. Keep in mind that an option contract is converted into a sales contract when the option is exercised. However, if the option fails to include all the terms material to the transaction and leaves some terms or decisions for future agreement, the option contract normally is not enforceable. For example, if the option calls for a purchase-money mortgage as part of the method of payment and does not include the mortgage interest rate or the duration, courts normally would refuse to enforce the contract. Generally, it pays to have a competent real estate attorney construct an option agreement.

■ **EXAMPLE 7.2**   Oscar paid Silvio $2,000 for a 30-day option to buy Silvio's house for $160,000. Two weeks later, Silvio sold his house to Benny for $175,000.

Can Oscar enforce his option and require the property to be sold to him? Why or why not?

The optionee may wish to record the option. This establishes the optionee's rights back to the option date and gives priority over subsequent rights of third parties. Good title practice requires that a release of option be recorded later in the event a recorded option is not exercised. Otherwise, the expired option may create a cloud on the title. Many times, an option is constructed to include a defeasance clause stating that the recorded option will automatically cease to be a lien on the property upon expiration of the exercise date.

■ SUMMARY

A contract is a legally enforceable agreement that can be classified in a number of ways, such as bilateral, unilateral, express, implied, executory, executed, quasi, voidable, and void. Each classification has specific legal effects in a court of law. The licensee is permitted to prepare three types of real estate contracts: listing, sales, and option contracts. A sales contract is an agreement for the sale and purchase of real property. The various provisions and standards contained in a sales contract include information on the parties to the agreement, a legal description of the property, the purchase price and method of payment, deadline times and dates, information about financing, and riders to the contract.

■ KEY TERMS

abstract	express contract	time is of the essence
bilateral contract	implied contract	title insurance
Contract to Buy and Sell	negotiable	unilateral contract
contract	option contract	valid contract
executed contract	performance	voidable contract
executory contract	sales contract	void contract
exercised	statute of frauds	

UNIT 8

Writing and Presenting the Offer

■ **LEARNING OBJECTIVES** *Upon completion of this unit, you should be able to*

- ■ **prepare** and explain a buyer's cost disclosure,

- ■ **write** a contract for sale and purchase and be able to explain it in easy-to-understand language,

- ■ **list** the steps involved in presenting an offer,

- ■ **list** the three possible seller responses to an offer,

- ■ **prepare** a counteroffer using information given in the problem, and

- ■ **describe** the process involved when a seller makes a counteroffer.

■ OVERVIEW

Licensees hope that at the end of the showing process, the buyers will have found a house to buy. Sometimes the buyers will tell the licensee, "This is the house; we'd like to make an offer." More often a buyer will say "This is our favorite so far, but we'd like to think it over." The professional licensee can help the buyer make the decision by providing the buyer with information about financing, closing costs, and the process involved in making an offer. This unit will help broker associates become familiar with that process.

■ ESTIMATING THE BUYER'S COSTS AND MAKING REQUIRED DISCLOSURES

Most buyers are reluctant to make a buying decision until they see cash required to close and the monthly payment amount. To move the buyer closer to buying, the licensee should give the buyer a cost-disclosure statement. The licensee should get a good-faith estimate from the lender. Many broker associates go over this disclosure during the initial meeting so the buyers know what to expect. The following exercise shows how to prepare a buyers' cost disclosure.

■ **EXAMPLE 8.1** Using the blank form in Figure 8.1, estimate the buyer's closing costs and monthly payments based on the following information:

Purchaser	Kyle and Kari Buyers
Property address	1460 Lime Drive
	Denver, CO
Date of contract	March 20, 2007
Mortgage lender	Security First
Prepared by	(Your name)
Sales price	$200,000
First mortgage:	$160,000
Closing Costs:	
Mortgagee title insurance policy	$ 400
Origination fee	1%
Discount points	½
Documentary Fee (0.01 per $100)	$20
Recording fees	$60
Credit report	$50
Appraisal fee	$300
Survey	$180
Underwriting fee	$125
Express mail fee	$20
Attorney's fee	$300
Escrow/ Prepaid Items:	
Taxes—3 months	$600
Hazard insurance (1 year)	$900
Hazard insurance (2 months)	$150
Monthly mortgage insurance premium (2 months)	$44
Prepaid interest (1 month)	$935

Mr. and Mrs. Buyers will give a deposit of $4,000. The principal and interest on the 7 percent, 30-year, fixed-rate loan amount is $1,064.48.

F I G U R E   8.1

Buyer's Estimated Closing Costs

PURCHASER: _____ PROPERTY ADDRESS: _____

Date of Contract: _____   Sales Price $_____ $_____

Mortgage Lender: _____   1st Mortgage $_____   + _____ $_____

Prepared by: _____   2nd Mortgage $ _____   FHA MIP OR FUNDING   TOTAL LOAN AMOUNT

                                                                              $_____

                                    Estimated Down Payment   (1) $_____

Estimated closing costs:

1. Title Insurance: ❏ owner's ❏ mortgagee's
2. Title Insurance Endorsements
3. Origination Fee _____%
4. Discount Points Estimated _____%
5. Documentary Fees
6. Recording Fees
7. Credit Report
8. Appraisal Fee
9. Survey
10. Document Preparation Fee
11. Tax Certificate
12. Underwriting Fee
13. Express Mail Fee(s)
14. VA Funding Fee at _____%
15. Assumption Fee on Existing Mortgage
16. Purchase of Escrow Account
17. Home Inspection Fee
18. Homeowner's Warranty _____
19. Attorney's Fee (if any)
20. _____
21. _____

                    Total Estimated Closing Costs   (2) $_____

Estimated escrow/prepaid items:

1. Taxes _____ months   _____
2. Hazard Insurance, 1 year   _____
3. Hazard Insurance, 2 months   _____
4. First-Year Mortgage Insurance   _____
5. Mortgage Insurance, 2 months   _____
6. Flood Insurance, 14 months   _____
7. Prepaid Interest   _____
8. Homeowner's Assn. Dues   _____

                Total Estimated Escrow/Prepaid Items   (3) $_____

ESTIMATED MONTHLY PAYMENTS	
❏ Fixed ❏ ARM ____ % Interest Rate ____ Years	Total Lines 1, 2, and 3 $_____
Principal & Interest $_____	
Property Taxes _____	Less: Earnest Money Deposit $_____
Hazard Insurance _____	
Mortgage Insurance _____	
Other _____	Estimated Total Due at Closing $_____
TOTAL $_____	(Must be good funds)
Other Association fees may be due monthly	

■ WRITING THE REAL ESTATE CONTRACT

In the case study below, you will complete the cost disclosure forms and the contract. You are a broker associate for Sunny Hills Realty, Inc. In March of this year, a past customer referred Bob and Sandy Smith to you. At your request, they visited Security Atlantic Mortgage Company, which preapproved them for a mortgage loan of up to $200,000.

■ **EXAMPLE 8.2**   After the disclosure has been completed, role-play with two other people: two playing Mr. and Mrs. Smith and one playing the broker associate. The broker associate should present the completed form to the buyers, who should ask some simple questions in a positive way.

You learn that they want a three- or four-bedroom home with two baths and a two-car garage. They want a home in the northeast, less than five miles from the regional hospital where Bob is a pharmacist.

You describe the entire process of buying a home, from showing homes through moving into their new home. You tell them it is a sellers' market, and that listings sell almost as soon as they go on the market.

You explain the lender's good-faith estimate with them, and discuss the important clauses in the purchase agreement. You give them copies of the paperwork along with a transaction-broker notice. Because they have enough cash for a 20 percent down payment (80 percent loan), you can show homes in the $250,000 range ($200,000 ÷ 0.80).

Finding the Right Home

You set a showing appointment for Saturday and begin previewing homes that might satisfy their requirements. You find five houses that seem like real possibilities; one of them is just about perfect. It is located at 816 Harrison Court, a quiet street in a well-kept neighborhood, just two miles from the hospital. The owners have kept the home in wonderful condition. And it has great curb appeal. The home is listed by Blue Sky Realty, Inc., and is priced at $255,000. Perfect! You make appointments to show the homes.

On Saturday morning you show your favorite home first. They both love everything about it. You give them a copy of the seller's property disclosure statement, square footage disclosure, and lead-based paint disclosure that were available on the kitchen counter. The home has no apparent problems. After entering each house after that, it doesn't take long to walk through, because they love the first home. You suggest a return visit and clear it with the listing company who calls the sellers and then tells you the sellers are going out for several hours and the house will be available most of the day. After returning to the home, you stay unobtrusive and let the Smiths discover more features of the home. They want to think it over. You cover the market conditions with them again and explain that if they love it, it is likely that other buyers will, too.

Writing the Offer

You suggest that, even if they end up "sleeping" on the decision, it might be helpful if they had the contract filled out. Bob says to make the paperwork out as if they were paying $245,000. Bob wants to see the backyard again, so you suggest they look around some more while you complete the paperwork.

The sellers have requested an earnest money deposit of $5,000. Based on previous conversations, the Smiths will want to be in the home in 20 days. Because the sellers are in town, and because the market is so active, you will give them until 10 PM tonight to accept or reject the offer.

You call the listing broker to confirm that the time for acceptance and closing will work. The listing broker states that the time frame is fine if you get the offer by 1 PM today, but that seller will need 30 days to close. The two of you verify that all the other information you need is in the "Let's Make a Deal" package that you picked up on the property.

The package shows the following information:

Sellers' names: Larry and Wilma Palmer

Street address: 816 Harrison Court, Sunny Hills, CO

Legal description: Lot 18, Block C, Old Hills as recorded in book 126, page 368, Lake County

Title company: ABC Title Company, Inc.

Earnest money: $5,000 made payable to the title company

Personal property included: range, draperies, rods, and window treatments

Also in the package are the following forms:

- Seller's property disclosure form
- Lead-based paint disclosure form
- Square footage disclosure form

The buyers also want to include the refrigerator, washer and dryer, and the riding lawn mower. You explain that these items are not included in the sale, but they want to try for them anyway.

■ **EXAMPLE 8.3** **Preparing the Cost Disclosure Statement**

Using the Buyer's Estimated Closing Costs form on the following page, estimate the buyer's closing costs and monthly payments based on the following information given on a good-faith estimate given to the buyers by Security Atlantic Mortgage Co.

Closing Costs:

Mortgagee title insurance policy	$ 400
Origination fee	1%
Discount points	½
Documentary fee	$24.50
Recording fees	$60
Credit report	$50
Appraisal fee	$350
Survey	$250
Underwriting fee	$125
Express mail fee	$20
Attorney's fee	$300

Escrow/ Prepaid Items:

Taxes—3 months	$800
Hazard insurance (1 year)	$1,200
Hazard insurance (2 months)	$200
Monthly mortgage insurance premium (2 months)	$52
Prepaid interest (1 month)	?

The principal and interest on the 6 percent, 30-year, fixed-rate $200,000 loan amount is $1,199.10.

FIGURE 8.2

Buyer's Estimated Closing Costs

PURCHASER: _____   PROPERTY ADDRESS: _____

Date of Contract: _____   Sales Price $_____ $_____

Mortgage Lender: _____   1st Mortgage $_____   + _____ $_____

Prepared by: _____   2nd Mortgage $ _____   FHA MIP OR FUNDING   TOTAL LOAN AMOUNT

                                                                                                $_____

                                          Estimated Down Payment   (1) $_____

Estimated closing costs:

1. Title Insurance: ❏ owner's ❏ mortgagee's
2. Title Insurance Endorsements
3. Origination Fee _____%
4. Discount Points Estimated _____%
5. Documentary Fees
6. Recording Fees
7. Credit Report
8. Appraisal Fee
9. Survey
10. Document Preparation Fee
11. Tax Certificate
12. Underwriting Fee
13. Express Mail Fee(s)
14. VA Funding Fee at _____%
15. Assumption Fee on Existing Mortgage
16. Purchase of Escrow Account
17. Home Inspection Fee
18. Homeowner's Warranty _____
19. Attorney's Fee (if any)
20. _____
21. _____

                               Total Estimated Closing Costs   (2) $_____

Estimated escrow/prepaid items:

1. Taxes _____ months   _____
2. Hazard Insurance, 1 year   _____
3. Hazard Insurance, 2 months   _____
4. First-Year Mortgage Insurance   _____
5. Mortgage Insurance, 2 months   _____
6. Flood Insurance, 14 months   _____
7. Prepaid Interest   _____
8. Homeowner's Assn. Dues   _____

                           Total Estimated Escrow/Prepaid Items   (3) $_____

ESTIMATED MONTHLY PAYMENTS	
❏ Fixed ❏ ARM ____ % Interest Rate ____ Years	Total Lines 1, 2, and 3 $_____
Principal & Interest $_____	
Property Taxes _____	Less: Earnest Money Deposit $_____
Hazard Insurance _____	
Mortgage Insurance _____	
Other _____	Estimated Total Due at Closing $_____
TOTAL $_____	(Must be good funds)
Other Association fees may be due monthly	

■ **E X A M P L E 8 . 4** **Preparing the Contract to Buy and Sell (CBS)**

You will need to download and print out a copy of the current Contract to Buy & Sell for this exercise. Go to the Colorado Division of Real Estate at *www.dora.state.co.us/ real-estate*. Click **Real Estate Brokers** from the left column, and then click **Commission Approved Forms**.

Just as you are finishing the contract, Sandy and Bob return to the kitchen. You tell them it's a great home, and well priced at $255,000. You ask if there is anything they want to do to the home after they buy it and Bob says he wants to pour a concrete patio. At your request, they write a short note to the sellers about why they want to buy this house, then both sign it.

You go over the cost-disclosure statement and attach it to the lender's good-faith estimate. Then you go over the contract form carefully. Sandy says it all looks good. You say "You could go home and worry about this tonight or I could take this to the seller and you might have great news to celebrate tonight. Wouldn't it be better if we went ahead? " Wait for the answer, because in many cases, the buyer will agree.

If the Smiths agree, ask them to

1. approve the cost disclosure first;
2. sign lead paint disclosure, the sellers' property disclosure, and the square footage disclosure; and
3. approve the agreement with their signatures.

Ask for the earnest money deposit and clip all the paperwork together along with the lender letter stating that they can qualify for the home. To prepare them for a counteroffer, ask that they not be too disappointed if the seller does not accept the offer at $245,000. After dropping them off, you should immediately contact the listing agent, Hillary Jenkins, to let her know you have a signed offer.

Presenting the Offer

Hillary answers her mobile phone right away. After you tell her that you have the offer signed she asks if you'd like to fax it to her office. Because you want to present the offer with her, you arrange to meet at her office 45 minutes before the appointment. You ask if there are any other offers to be presented, and she says there are not. You request that you be called if that situation changes and she agrees. In some cases, especially if you are a buyers' agent, the listing broker associate will be reluctant to let you present your offer. Explain that you will not stay during the discussions, but that it may be helpful if you tell them about the buyer, present the offer, and see if they have any questions about the flexibility of the buyers, for example, on the closing date.

Hillary calls back and says she has an appointment with the Palmers at 7 PM, and will see you at her office at 6:15 PM.

Going to the Sellers' House

You make extra copies of the offer, gather all the documents, and arrive at the Blue Sky Realty office at 6:15 PM. You show Hillary the bank's preapproval letter and give her a copy of the offer. If she has no questions about the offer, you ask if she'd like you to present it to the sellers and she agrees. She also suggests that after presenting the contract, if the sellers have no questions, that you might excuse yourself so they have time to discuss the offer. This is very gracious on her part as she will not ask to you leave; it will be your idea.

You go in separate cars to the house. Hillary waits outside so you can go in together. You smile when you see her carrying a "sold" sign on top of her file folder.

At the door Hillary introduces you to the seller and takes charge, asking if we can all sit at the kitchen table. The sellers agree.

Hillary starts the presentation by complimenting you. You look at her with gratitude and admiration, beginning to understand why she is successful.

She continues: "I'm going to let _____ tell you a little about the prospective buyers and go over the offer with you, if that's OK." The sellers nod in agreement and look in your direction.

"Hi, Mr. and Mrs. Palmer," you say. "I'd like to say how pleased I am to be working with Hillary again. You made a great choice when you listed your home with her. Before I go over the offer, I'd like to tell you a little about the buyers. Their names are Robert and Sandy Smith. Robert is a pharmacist at Sunny Hills Regional Hospital. They have two children: Mary, who's 3, and Brett, who's 1.

"They have owned a condominium since they've been married, and this is their first single-family home. They have been approved for financing by the bank to buy your home. And they love it! They have written you a note about your house and why they want to buy it." Hand them the note. (See Figure 8.3.)

Mrs. Palmer says, "That is the sweetest thing! Larry, I hope this couple buys this house."

Mr. Palmer says, "Yes, they sound like pretty nice people. But let's see what they're willing to pay."

And you present the contract. Save the offered price until last. Ask if they will let you cover the highlights before starting a discussion on any one item, and that you'll give them copies of the agreement in a moment. Then cover the contingencies first before talking about price.

"The buyers can close in 20 days, but after talking with Hillary we decided to set closing for 30 days so you would have enough time to get into your new home. I've spoken with the lender who says they can close it on time and have included a letter showing they qualify for the loan.

"They're including your refrigerator, range, washer and dryer, riding mower, and the window treatments.

"They're getting new financing and have been preapproved for their loan."

Now tell them the offer is $245,000. Reassure the sellers that the buyers' offer is not meant to insult them, but they can qualify to buy a $250,000 home and are hoping to keep $5,000 to build a concrete patio. Give statistics about sales: price ratios in the MLS ("Listings sell at 96 percent of list price," etc.), so this offer is right on target.

FIGURE 8.3
 	
Handwritten Note
	Dear Mr. and Mrs. Palmer,
	
	We just want to tell you how much we love your home. We can tell that you love it too by the way you keep it so beautiful.
	   We can't think of a home that would be better to raise our two young children in. Their names are Mary and Brett.
	      We hope you will let us have it.
	      And we hope you'll be happy in your new home, too.
	
	Sandy Smith
	Bob Smith

Tell the sellers that if they have no questions for you about the buyers or the offer, you'd like to excuse yourself to give them an opportunity to discuss the offer with Hillary. You can tell them you have some calls to make anyway, and will do it from your car, so you'll be close by if any other questions arise.

Sellers' Responses to an Offer

Sellers who receive an offer on their home have several possible responses:

- Acceptance
- Rejection
- Counteroffer

Acceptance   Obviously, the buyer's broker associate hopes the response will be an acceptance. The offer is signed and becomes a contract between the buyer and the seller.

Rejection   If the price offered is very low and is obviously a "fishing expedition," the seller may be advised to reject the offer outright. A better approach might be to reject the offer with an invitation to come back with a more serious offer. In a strong sellers' market with many buyers bidding for the same properties, brokers report that sellers often reject offers unless they are very close to the asking price.

Counteroffer   If the offer is not acceptable but is close enough to be considered serious, a **counteroffer** should be used. A counteroffer keeps the parties "at the table," making continued negotiations easier.

The approved Colorado Counterproposal form must be used when countering an offer. The form is used only to note the changes to the original offer and must be attached to the offer to be valid. The earnest money is also still attached to these documents. Earnest money is not deposited until the offer is accepted.

Remember: The seller will just initial the box in the CBS marked Counter and will *not* sign the offer but will sign the Counterproposal.

In 15 minutes, Hillary comes to the door and motions you inside. Back at the table, Hillary says, "Mr. and Mrs. Palmer want the Smiths to have this home, but want to make several changes. First, they feel the house is worth the asking price of $255,000, but they will split the difference with the buyers at a price of $250,000. They will include the range and window treatments, but want to take the other items of personal property. I have a signed counterproposal for you to take to your buyers."

When you arrive at the Smiths' house, tell them you have great news. "The sellers came off the price by $5,000! Let's go over their counteroffer."

They agree to all terms of the counteroffer. You change the cost disclosure statement to reflect the new price. Call Hillary and tell her you are under contract and ask where she would like the contract to be delivered.

You have sold the house and made several people very happy.

Additional Points on Writing and Presenting Offers

- If the buyers' offer is much lower than the asking price, strongly recommend that the buyers not add many contingencies to the offer. Boil all the requirements into the offering price.
- If the market is very strong and there might be multiple offers for the property, don't add too many contingencies. Sometimes even if the offering price is good, a buyer may accept another offer that is simpler and more certain to close.
- If the market is very strong and you are aware that there will be competing offers for the property, recommend that the buyers not only remove most contingencies, but also consider making an offer that is higher than the asking price.
- Make the acceptance date fairly short so the seller makes a decision quickly, rather than waiting to "shop" the offer.
- Go with your contract. Present it with the listing agent. You may be busy, but you'll have many more accepted contracts if you help in the presentation. You are the only one who can answer questions about the buyers and give the buyers a "face" in the minds of the sellers. Sure, it takes more of your time. But this is top priority time, and your customer's lives and lots of your money is riding on your performance.
- If you are the listing associate and another associate has the offer, you want the cooperating associate to be with you when you present. You're a team. It also stops second-guessing about the quality of your presentation if the other associate's offer is not accepted. If the other associate is a buyers' agent, you should tell your sellers not to give any reaction during the presentation of the offer, as it may affect their negotiating position.
- If you are the listing broker associate, prepare your sellers for a low offer before the cooperating broker associate arrives to present the offer. If a seller

has raised expectations, a low offer may insult the sellers and make it very difficult to put a transaction together.

■ If the parties are far apart on the offered price, try to keep the buyers and sellers from taking it personally. It is your job to be sure personalities are not a factor in the negotiations.

■ Be courteous to the cooperating broker associate. Nothing can derail the presentation of an offer more than distrust and dissension between the licensees.

■ Don't give the offer out to all parties until you have summarized the important parts. It is hard to maintain control if the parties are all looking at different parts of the contract, interrupting by asking questions.

■ Make enough documents for everyone who will be at the presentation so they don't have to read over your shoulder.

■ Cover all points of the agreement, making price last. Have all the buyers' requirements depend on getting the price right.

■ Work the contract until it's either accepted or dead. Don't stop working it because it's nearly midnight. Sellers want to sell and buyers want to buy, and respect professionals who work hard. Working late brings an urgency that gets lots of offers accepted.

■ If you are the listing associate and the cooperating associate brings in a very low offer, have the cooperating associate present the offer to your sellers.

■ If the offer is low and the sellers are angry, let them vent their frustration before starting to work on a counteroffer.

■ If multiple offers are received the listing broker should present them all at the same time.

■ SUMMARY

Because buyers are reluctant to committing to buy without understanding the financial commitment they must make, a broker associate should understand how to prepare a cost disclosure statement. To reduce liability, the statement should be based on a lender's good-faith estimate of settlement costs.

A licensee should practice preparing offers on different types of properties with a variety of financing programs. Once the practice offer is written, you should role-play the explanation of the offer. Practice will give you the skills to help you get more transactions to the closing table.

■ KEY TERM

counteroffer

■ APPLY WHAT YOU'VE LEARNED

The following actions reinforce the material in Course 3, Units 6 through 8:

■ Preview at least five homes in your favorite price range. Try to see five each day for the next five days. Use a tape recorder to describe each home thoroughly and try to match it with a prospective buyer or type of buyer.

■ From your preview visits, list the best homes on the market. Pick your favorite home from that list.

■ Describe every characteristic of *your* favorite home from your preview trips as if you were writing a book on the house. Try to remember colors, room sizes and arrangements, and garage size. Describe each room in as much detail as possible. If you can't do it, go back to the house again and make careful notes. Try to increase your observation powers every time you preview homes.

■ When you visit a vacant home, thoroughly describe each room aloud as if your buyer were sight-impaired.

■ Keep a tape recorder near your phone. The next time you answer a call from a prospective buyer, turn on the recorder. (You must observe the law, however; record only *your* side of the conversation.) When you have completed the call, listen to the tape. Make written notes about what you would change about your side of the conversation.

■ Ride through a neighborhood you have not yet explored, describing into your tape recorder the details you see. Then do the same thing in the surrounding area to find shopping areas, libraries, car washes, schools, and houses of worship.

■ Write the features you think some close friends would like in a home. From memory, list the properties you would show them and give reasons for your decisions. Make a buyer's cost statement based on a 90 percent conventional loan.

■ Call your friends and tell them about the previous exercise. Ask whether they will let you show them the homes you chose for them. How well did you judge their tastes?

9
UNIT

Exploring Mortgage Alternatives

■ **LEARNING OBJECTIVES**   *Upon completion of this unit, you should be able to*

■ **describe** the components of the lender's required annual percentage rate (APR) disclosures,

■ **calculate** the effective interest rate on 30-year, fixed-rate loans and on loans for shorter periods,

■ **calculate** the PITI payment for a borrower,

■ **compare** the interest savings on a 15-year, fixed-rate mortgage versus a 30-year, fixed-rate mortgage,

■ **compare** the interest savings on a biweekly mortgage versus a 30-year, fixed-rate mortgage,

■ **discuss** the pros and cons of an adjustable-rate mortgage (ARM),

■ **explain** the five components of an ARM,

■ **explain** the advantages of FHA interest rate caps over conventional ARM caps, and

■ **calculate** interest rate adjustments.

■ **OVERVIEW**

The mortgage market has seen many significant changes in recent years. Twenty years ago, commercial banks and savings associations originated more than 80 percent of home mortgages. That share has dropped sharply and today mortgage companies are the dominant factor in the market, originating more than 50 percent of all home loans. Driven by market forces, lenders offer a wide variety of mortgage products tailored to the needs of consumers. Experts expect the changes to accelerate in the future.

A general knowledge of these changes can enhance the opportunities available to the real estate professional. Developing strong relationships with lenders who preapprove loans for prospective buyers saves licensees time and can significantly increase their income.

Steps before Loan Application

Before buyers begin calling or visiting lenders, they should have a good understanding of their own financial capabilities and housing objectives. Licensees should explain both issues to their customers to help them understand the importance of prequalifying. This is important because if a loan application is denied, the applicant may lose the opportunity to buy the desired home. In addition, some expense is involved in applying for a loan. Fees may range from $150 to $500, depending on the property and circumstances.

Mortgage Shopping

In shopping for a mortgage, licensees should advise buyers to look for competitive rates and a lender with a reputation for integrity and good service.

Surveys show that mortgage interest rates and closing costs vary in metropolitan markets for the same mortgage product. Comparing prices obviously is important, but it is not an easy task as lenders charge borrowers a variety of fees to submit a loan application. Discount points, usually one of the largest fees lenders charge, also vary from lender to lender in the same market area. The points change the effective interest rate, and just two points more on a loan can mean significant additional expense to the borrower.

Licensees must learn which lenders can be trusted to act with speed and service to borrowers. Licensees should use and recommend only those that provide good service.

Seller-Paid Closing Costs

A buyer must have the necessary income and debt ratios to afford a mortgage payment. Coming up with enough cash to close is another big hurdle. The closing costs and prepayments on a typical mortgage loan for $120,000 can reach $5,000 in addition to the down payment. Many qualified buyers are forced to rent in order to accumulate the savings necessary to close. Licensees who know lender standards on seller-paid closing costs are able to sell to these buyers much sooner. The seller can pay part of the closing costs for conventional, FHA, and VA mortgage loans. Table 9.1 shows the current allowed percentages.

A seller who could pay only 3 percent of the buyer's closing costs on a low down payment conventional loan for $120,000 would contribute $3,600. If a two-income family is saving $300 per month, the home purchase could be made 12 months sooner.

	Type of Loan	Percent
TABLE 9.1	Conventional	
	Less than 10% down payment	3
Maximum Seller-Paid Closing Costs That Can Be Applied to Buyer's Closing Costs, Prepaid Items, and Reserves, Expressed as a Percentage of the Purchase Price	19% or greater down payment	6
	FHA	6
	VA	6

■ **EXAMPLE 9.1**   Do you think most licensees guide potential borrowers to lenders with whom they have built relationships or to lenders who have the best mortgage rates on a given day?

Annual Percentage Rate (APR)

The Truth-in-Lending Act requires that mortgage lenders disclose their annual percentage rates to potential borrowers. The **annual percentage rate (APR)** is a standard expression of credit costs designed to give potential borrowers an easy method of comparing lenders' total finance charges. These financing costs include points and any other prepaid interest or fees charged to obtain the loan, in addition to the contract interest cost. By law, the APR must be the relationship of the total financing charge to the total amount financed and it must be computed to the nearest one-eighth of 1 percent. Perhaps the best and most accurate definition of the APR is that it is the effective interest rate for a mortgage loan repaid over its full term.

The law allows a lender three days after loan application to inform the applicant of the APR. When a lender gives the borrower a good-faith estimate of the annual percentage rate, the consumer should be aware that this is not a legally binding document; it is simply an estimate. Licensees should avoid lenders who frequently estimate a lower APR than the rate available at closing.

Another feature of this act is that it assumes that borrowers will keep their loans for the full number of years for which the loans are written. Records of mortgage lending, however, show that most borrowers either sell or refinance their homes in less than 12 years. The actual (effective) interest rate paid depends on the number of years a loan is kept.

■ **EXAMPLE 9.2**   If the borrower expects to keep the loan for longer than 12 years, divide the points by 8 and add the result to the note interest rate. For example, if a lender has offered a first mortgage for 30 years at 7.5 percent and 3 points, the effective interest rate would be 7.875 percent, computed as follows:

Note rate + (points ÷ 8) = Effective interest rate

7.5% + (0.03 ÷ 8) or 7.5% + 0.375% = 7.875%

When the lender gives a prospective borrower a rate quote, the borrower is often undecided about whether to pay discount points. Discount points can be considered prepaid interest that will reduce the interest rate on the note. In effect, a borrower has a "menu" of interest rates based on the amount paid as discount points. Figure 9.2 shows a sample market quote for a 30-year fixed-rate loan. Fluctuations in the market cause differences from day to day in the differential of discount points and yield.

From the example, it's obvious that a person who intends to occupy the property for three years should avoid paying points because it will take almost six years to break even. In some cases, a borrower should ask the lender to raise the interest rate not only to avoid discount points but also to avoid paying an origination fee.

TABLE 9.2

Comparison of Interest Rates and Discount Points (For a $100,000, 30-Year, Fixed-Rate Mortgage)

	A. Interest Rate	B. Discount Points	C. Principal and Interest Payment	D. Payment Difference from 7% Rate	E. Amount Paid in Discount Points	F. Months at Lower Rate for Points Payback (E ÷ D)
1.	7.000	0	$665.30	—	$0	0
2.	6.875	0.5	656.93	$8.37	500	59.7
3.	6.750	1.2	648.60	16.70	1,200	71.9
4.	6.625	1.7	640.31	24.99	1,700	68.0
5.	6.500	2.3	632.07	33.23	2,300	69.2

If a person expects to remain in the property for the full 30-year period and will not be refinancing or making an early loan payoff, the savings could be worth paying points. At line 5, for instance, the borrower breaks even at 69 months. The difference in payments of $33.23 for the remaining 291 months would total $9,670, well worth paying the points.

Of course, the better way to analyze points is by considering the time value of money. Using the 6.5 percent rate on line 5, the borrower pays $2,300 in *today's* dollars (that could be invested to return some interest) to get a savings sometime in the future. A financial calculator approach shows the payback period is longer (87 months versus 69.2 months).

Financial calculator keystrokes to find payback period for $2,300 in points with a 6.5 percent yield:

%I	PMT	PV	FV	Solve for N
0.54167	33.23	2,300	0	87 months

Where: % = monthly market interest rate: 6.5% ÷ 12 months = 0.54167
PMT = savings per monthly payment = –$33.23
PV = dollars paid in points = $2,300
FV = input zero for this problem = 0

Solve for: N = Number of months to pay back points

Solution is 87 months

■ **EXAMPLE 9.3** John has been transferred to Colorado Springs and expects to be in the location for about three years before being transferred again. He needs to borrow $200,000 for his new home. With no points he can get a 7.5 percent, fixed-rate mortgage with principal and interest payments of $1,398.43. The lender offers him a 7.125 percent mortgage (payments of $1,347.44) with two points.

Should John take the lower interest rate mortgage?

Using simple math, how many months will it take John to break even by paying the points if he takes the lower interest rate?

PITI Payment

Customers often ask licensees to calculate the monthly mortgage payment for a possible purchase or sale. Most lenders require an amount each month that includes principal and interest plus escrow items—property taxes, homeowner's insurance, and possibly mortgage insurance or homeowners'/condominium association dues. This entire package of payments commonly is referred to as the **PITI payment.**

Principal and interest payments on the mortgage are the largest part of the monthly PITI payment. Using the mortgage payment factor table shown in Table 9.1, multiply the loan amount by the appropriate factor to get the principal and interest portion of the payment.

For example, the payment factor for a 30-year mortgage at 8.5 percent is 0.0076891. To calculate the monthly principal and interest for a 30-year loan of $98,000 at 8.5 percent, use the following equation:

$$\$98{,}000 \times 0.0076891 = \$753.53$$

While the factor table has been included in this text to help calculate the monthly payment, most real estate licensees use a financial calculator to obtain a more accurate monthly mortgage payment of principal and interest.

In the previous example, the licensee with a financial calculator would solve the problem as shown:

N	%I	PV	FV	Solve for PMT
360	0.70833	98,000	0	$753.53

Where: N = number of monthly periods in loan term
%I = interest rate (8.5% ÷ 12 months = 0.70833)
PV = loan amount
FV = input zero when solving for present value

Solve for: **PMT = monthly mortgage payment**

Note: %I is calculated by dividing 8.5% by 12 months.

A PITI worksheet that licensees can use in helping their clients and customers calculate the PITI amount for a potential loan is shown in Figure 9.1.

■ FIXED-RATE MORTGAGES

Any mortgage written to preclude change in the interest rate throughout the duration of the loan is a **fixed-rate mortgage.** The term includes the traditional 30-year mortgage, the 15-year mortgage, and the biweekly mortgage. The use of a due-on-sale clause in a fixed-rate mortgage reserves the lender's right to make an interest rate change if a transfer of ownership takes place. Practically all conventional mortgages issued since the early 1980s contain such a clause.

Traditional 30-Year Mortgage

The fixed-rate, fully amortizing mortgage loan has been the standard of the real estate finance industry for the past 50 years. A 30-year term provides a reasonably low payment for the amount borrowed, while the interest rate, payment amount, and repayment schedule are set permanently at the beginning of the loan period. Fixed-rate loans often are sold in the secondary market because they appeal to pension funds and other investors searching for a relatively safe investment with a known interest rate and a long duration.

Advantages of a 30-year mortgage Monthly payments on the loan are spread over 30 years, offering the borrower protection against future increases in interest rates and inflation rates while providing for the orderly repayment of the amount borrowed. Household budgets are easier to manage when the borrower does not have to plan for changing payment amounts or interest rates.

TABLE 9.3

Mortgage Payment Factor Table

Interest Rate	Term of Loan				
	10 years	15 years	20 years	25 years	30 years
5.00%	0.0106066	0.0079079	0.0065996	0.0058459	0.0053682
5.25%	0.0107292	0.0080388	0.0067384	0.0059925	0.0055220
5.50%	0.0108526	0.0081708	0.0068789	0.0061409	0.0056779
5.75%	0.0109769	0.0083041	0.0070208	0.0062911	0.0058357
6.00%	0.0111021	0.0084386	0.0071643	0.0064430	0.0059955
6.25%	0.0112280	0.0085742	0.0073093	0.0065967	0.0061572
6.50%	0.0113548	0.0087111	0.0074557	0.0067521	0.0063207
6.75%	0.0114824	0.0088491	0.0076036	0.0069091	0.0064860
7.00%	0.0116108	0.0089883	0.0077530	0.0070678	0.0066530
7.25%	0.0117401	0.0091286	0.0079038	0.0072281	0.0068218
7.50%	0.0118702	0.0092701	0.0080559	0.0073899	0.0069921
7.75%	0.0120011	0.0094128	0.0082095	0.0075533	0.0071641
8.00%	0.0121328	0.0095565	0.0083644	0.0077182	0.0073376
8.25%	0.0122653	0.0097014	0.0085207	0.0078845	0.0075127
8.50%	0.0123986	0.0098474	0.0086782	0.0080523	0.0076891
8.75%	0.0125327	0.0099945	0.0088371	0.0082214	0.0078670
9.00%	0.0126676	0.0101427	0.0089973	0.0083920	0.0080462
9.25%	0.0128033	0.0102919	0.0091587	0.0085638	0.0082268
9.50%	0.0129398	0.0104422	0.0093213	0.0087370	0.0084085
9.75%	0.0130770	0.0105936	0.0094852	0.0089114	0.0085915
10.00%	0.0132151	0.0107461	0.0096502	0.0090870	0.0087757
10.25%	0.0133539	0.0108995	0.0098164	0.0092638	0.0089610
10.50%	0.0134935	0.0110540	0.0099838	0.0094418	0.0091474
10.75%	0.0136339	0.0112095	0.0101523	0.0096209	0.0093348
11.00%	0.0137750	0.0113660	0.0103219	0.0098011	0.0095232
11.25%	0.0139169	0.0115234	0.0104926	0.0099824	0.0097126
11.50%	0.0140595	0.0116819	0.0106643	0.0101647	0.0099029
11.75%	0.0142029	0.0118413	0.0108371	0.0103480	0.0100941

FIGURE 9.1

PITI Worksheet

Mortgage amount $_____

Interest rate   _____%

Term of loan   _____ years

Mortgage payment factor   _____

Principal and interest payment: $_____

($_____ _____)
     (mtg. amt.)   (factor)

Property taxes: $_____ ÷ 12   _____

Hazard insurance: $_____ ÷ 12   _____

Mortgage insurance: $_____

$ _____ × _____ ÷ 12
  (mtg. amt.)   (premium rate)

TOTAL MONTHLY MORTGAGE PAYMENT (PITI) $_____

Disadvantages of a 30-year mortgage   If overall interest rates drop, as they did in 2000–2001, the rate on a fixed-rate mortgage will not go down with them. To take advantage of lower interest rates, the original loan must be repaid with the proceeds of a new loan taken out at the lower rate. This procedure, called **refinancing**, usually requires that the borrower pay substantial closing costs on the new loan.

15-Year Mortgage

The 15-year, fixed-rate mortgage has become popular with both lenders and borrowers in recent years. It is just like a traditional 30-year loan, except that its monthly payment is higher, its interest rate typically is slightly lower, and it is paid off in 15 years. The 15-year mortgage saves the borrower thousands of dollars in interest payments.

The popular press sometimes compares the two mortgage plans, showing dramatic savings from the 15-year plan. The gross savings, however, usually are overstated. The higher payments on the 15-year plan have an opportunity cost. If the difference were invested, the return on the investment would reduce the net cost of the 30-year mortgage. The tax savings from mortgage interest deductions also would reduce the savings.

For many borrowers, the 15-year mortgage may be the best way to finance a home because, in addition to the overall savings in total cost, it forces a monthly saving in the form of extra equity and allows a person who needs it a sense of confidence that the home will be paid off in 15 years. This is true for those planning in advance for retirement. Also, many in the baby boomer generation are in their 40s, with a growing number eager to end their mortgage payments and own their homes free and clear.

Licensees should point out, however, that the 15-year mortgage robs the borrower of some flexibility. A 15-year mortgage cannot be extended to 30 years, but a 30-year mortgage can be paid off in 15 years if the borrower accelerates monthly payments to create a 15-year loan or remits a lump-sum payment on principal each year. The borrower retains the right to decide when, or if, to make extra payments. Borrowers must evaluate the benefits of the 15-year mortgage based on their personal situations.

Advantages of a 15-year mortgage   Because lenders get their money back sooner than they do with traditional 30-year mortgages, they charge slightly lower rates for 15-year loans. Also, the loans are paid off faster, less money is borrowed for less time, and less total interest is paid over the lives of the loans—more than 50 percent less. As with a 30-year, fixed-rate loan, the interest rate on a 15-year mortgage does not change, and the monthly principal and interest payment does not go up. Finally, the higher monthly payment results in forced savings in the form of faster equity buildup.

Disadvantages of a 15-year mortgage   The monthly payment on a 15-year loan is higher and the borrower forgoes investment opportunities voluntarily for the extra dollars paid on the loan each month. Some income-tax advantages related to home mortgages and investment opportunities are lost. Flexibility of mortgage payment is sacrificed and any future increase in income tax rates could increase the 15-year mortgage's net costs.

Biweekly Mortgage

The development of computer programs to service biweekly mortgages properly, the creation of a secondary market (Fannie Mae), increased familiarity with the product, and growing consumer demand all are combining to bring about a comeback for the biweekly mortgage. The **biweekly mortgage** alternative is a fixed-rate loan, amortized over a 30-year period, with payments made every two weeks instead of every month. Borrowers pay half the normal monthly payment every two weeks, which means a total of 26 payments each year, or the equivalent of 13 monthly payments. The extra month's payment each year reduces the principal faster and results in considerable savings in interest, as well as a reduction in the duration of the loan to between 19 and 21 years.

Normally, interest rates for biweekly mortgages are comparable to the rates charged for traditional 30-year mortgages. Most biweekly loans are scheduled to mature in 30 years even though the actual number of years to maturity depends on the interest rate. The higher the interest rate, the larger the monthly payment, and the more that is applied to reducing mortgage principal. A biweekly mortgage with a 7 percent interest rate, for example, would be paid off in approximately 23 years, 9 months.

Consumer Reports magazine analyzed several mortgage options and concluded that a $100,000 biweekly mortgage at 8 percent interest would save a borrower approximately $34,000 in interest, when compared with a traditional 30-year, fixed-rate mortgage at the same interest rate.

TABLE 9.4

Comparison of Interest Costs for Various Mortgage Plans (For a $100,000 Loan at 8 Percent Interest)

Payment Pattern	Regular Payment Amount	Total Paid Each Year	Time Until Paid Off	Total Interest Paid
30-Year Mortgage	$733.76	$8,805	30 years	$164,155
Added $25/Month	758.76	9,105	26 yrs. + 6 mos.	141,286
Added $100/Month	833.76	10,005	20 yrs. + 2 mos.	101,770
Biweekly Mortgage	366.88	9,539	22 yrs. + 10 mos.	117,804
15-Year Mortgage	955.65	11,468	15 yrs.	72,017

Table 9.4 compares the results of making scheduled payments on a traditional 30-year mortgage, of adding different amounts of additional principal payments each month, and of making scheduled payments on a biweekly mortgage amortized over 30 years.

Advantages of a biweekly mortgage A biweekly mortgage combines the benefits of a 30-year loan and 15-year loan without the increased payments of the 15-year loan. It offers borrowers the affordability of the 30-year loan because the two biweekly payments come within a few pennies of the one monthly payment on a 30-year loan.

Also, Fannie Mae requires that payments be deducted automatically from a borrower's checking or savings account every two weeks. Because more than half of the nation's workforce is paid on a biweekly basis, it is compatible with a large number of paychecks. Some lenders include a conversion clause that permits a borrower to change a biweekly mortgage to a traditional 30-year, fixed-rate, amortized mortgage at little or no cost with only 30 days' advance notice.

Disadvantages of a biweekly mortgage The biweekly mortgage has the same disadvantages as other fixed-rate mortgages. In addition, the biweekly loan threatens those borrowers who do not maintain stable checking or savings account balances. The biweekly mortgage also locks borrowers into payment plans that they could set up themselves, at their own discretion, with a traditional 30-year loan. Some lenders also charge a set-up fee.

■ **EXAMPLE 9.4** If a biweekly mortgage combines the good features of both the traditional 30-year, fixed-rate mortgage and a 15-year, fixed-rate mortgage, why is it so seldom used, comparatively speaking, to finance residential purchases?

■ ADJUSTABLE-RATE MORTGAGES

The **adjustable-rate mortgage (ARM)** has become a widely accepted alternative to the traditional 30-year, fixed-rate, level-payment mortgage. The popularity of ARMs noticeably increases when interest rates rise and they lose favor when interest rates fall. An adjustable-rate mortgage is, as the term implies, a financing instrument that allows the lender to increase or decrease the interest rate based on the rise or fall of a specified index.

Components of Adjustable-Rate Mortgages

The primary elements in determining the acceptability of an ARM from the borrower's viewpoint are the index, the lender's margin, the calculated interest rate, the initial interest rate, and the interest rate cap.

Lending institutions are legally permitted to link the interest rate of a conventional ARM to any recognized **index** (indicator of cost or value) that is not controlled by the lender and is verifiable by the borrower. The **margin,** also called the *spread,* is a percentage added to the index. The margin usually remains constant over the life of the loan, while the selected index may move up or down with fluctuations in the nation's economy. The calculated (or actual) interest rate is calculated by adding the selected index to the lender's margin (index plus margin equals calculated interest rate). This calculated interest rate may be discounted during the initial payment period, but it is the rate to which all future adjustments and caps apply.

To be competitive, lenders sometimes reduce the first year's earnings by discounting the calculated interest rate, thus creating a lower initial interest rate. This helps to qualify potential buyers at artificially low interest rates, which may or may not be a service to the borrowers, and establishes the amount of the monthly loan payment during the first time period of the loan. Be aware that many lenders now use the second year's interest rate rather than the discounted rate as the qualifier. Both Fannie Mae and Freddie Mac require borrowers with less than a 20 percent down payment on one-year, adjustable-rate loans to be qualified at the initial interest rate plus 2 percent.

The main appeal of ARM loans is the lower-than-market initial interest rates offered as inducements (teasers). But without some type of protection from unacceptable increases in interest rates, borrowers would be in danger of being unable to make future mortgage payments. To prevent this, most lenders and all federal housing agencies have established standards calling for ceilings on increases. Three types of **caps** (ceilings) limit increases in the calculated interest rates of ARM loans:

- ■ Amount of increase that can be applied at the time of the first adjustment (for example, a cap of 1 percent or 2 percent per adjustment period)
- ■ Amount of increase that can be applied during any one adjustment interval (for example, no more than 2 percent during any 1-year period)
- ■ Total amount the interest rate may be increased over the life of the loan (for example, no more than 6 percent)

Borrowers should be cautious when payments are capped and interest rates are not because of the probability that **negative amortization** will occur. Negative amortization occurs when the monthly payment is not enough to pay the interest on the loan. The shortfall is added to the mortgage balance.

Lenders must provide potential borrowers with a worst-case example at loan application. This disclosure must show the maximum possible payment increases if conditions should warrant maximum interest rate increases at the earliest opportunities.

TABLE 9.5

$100,000 Mortgage Loan, 30-Year Term, 8 Percent Fixed-Rate versus 5.5 Percent Adjustable-Rate Mortgage (Annual Cap 2 Percent, Lifetime Cap 6 Percent)

	Fixed Rate		Adjustable Rate		ARM Savings (Loss)	
Year	Payment	Rate	Payment	Rate	Monthly	Accumulated
1	$734	8%	$568	5.5%	$166	$1,992
2	734	8	699	7.5	35	2,412
3	734	8	841	9.5	(107)	1,128
4*	734	8	990	11.5	(256)	(1,944)

*ARM savings exhausted in fifth month of year 4.

Conventional ARM

Table 9.5 compares two approaches to a $100,000 conventional mortgage using a worst-case scenario for interest rate increases.

In this example, all monthly payment amounts are for principal and interest and the amounts are rounded to the nearest dollar. The upfront costs of points and fees will be discussed later.

ARM loans have lower initial rates than fixed-rate mortgages, primarily because lenders can avoid the risk of market interest changes for the full 30 years of the loan period. ARM loans reduce the risk, so lenders don't need as much cushion for contingencies. New ARM products are available that combine the ARM features of lower initial interest rate with a longer fixed-rate period between adjustments. For example, three-year, five-year, or ten-year ARMs are available at slightly higher initial rates than one-year ARMs, but at lower rates than 30-year fixed mortgages.

■ **EXAMPLE 9.5** In your opinion, do the lower initial rates offered on ARM loans cause borrowers to take on more mortgage debt than they can afford? Why or why not?

Interest rates and recognized indexes   The index to which a conventional ARM is tied can increase or decrease the volatility of interest rate changes. There are four principal indexes used for residential mortgages:

- The LIBOR (London Interbank Offered Rate) index is the base interest rate paid on deposits between banks in the Eurodollar market.
- MTA—Monthly Treasury Bill Average—This stable, slow-moving index is a 12-month moving average of the U.S. One-Year Treasury Bill.
- COFI—11th District Cost of Funds Index—Another stable, slow-moving index, consisting of the weighted average of deposits and borrowings between banks in the Federal Home Loan Bank District of San Francisco.
- PRIME rate is the rate charged to most favored customers by major banks. This rate is commonly used for adjustments to home equity or second mortgages and can be quite volatile.

Lenders must provide consumers with details on conventional ARMs to assist them in comparison shopping. Potential borrowers must be informed of the index used, how often the loan will be adjusted, and the maximum amount of loan payment increase allowed.

When helping prospective borrowers sort through the many factors to be considered in selecting a conventional adjustable-rate loan, licensees should make sure the borrowers know

- what rate will be used when interest rate caps are applied to an ARM loan;
- that the margin is one of the most important benchmarks in comparing lenders (most other ARM features are relatively similar, but the margins can vary considerably);
- to seek another lender if the one they are considering has policies that call for ARM increases exceeding the 2 percent annual cap or the 6 percent lifetime cap;
- not to consider loans that call for negative amortization;
- to compare upfront costs, such as underwriting fees, points, and origination fees, because some lenders offer lower interest rates but make up for it with inflated upfront costs; and
- not to stretch their borrowing to the limit, as they could with a fixed-rate loan, because the payments remain fixed and income should increase. Borrowing to the limit can become a disaster when an ARM is involved. Prospective borrowers should calculate their first-year payments at the initial interest rate plus 2 percent; otherwise, the first adjustment could hurt them financially.

Advantages of an ARM loan   The ARM's low initial interest rate and the borrower's ability to qualify for a larger mortgage top the list of advantages of adjustable-rate mortgages. ARMs appear to be most appropriate for those who plan to hold the mortgage loans for no more than four years. Also, anytime the interest rate gap between a fixed-rate loan and an adjustable-rate loan reaches 3 percent in favor of the ARM, an ARM loan with interest rate caps and a one-year Treasury bill constant maturity index should make sense to homebuyers. Many ARMs are now written with conversion privileges, allowing the mortgagors to convert to fixed-rate loans for a modest fee during a specified period. This enables borrowers to take advantage of falling interest rates if they desire to do so. One of the standard features of an ARM is that there is no prepayment penalty.

Longer adjustment periods are available   Many borrowers prefer an ARM loan that won't adjust for periods longer than a year. For example, the low initial rate may last for three, four, or seven, then adjust once each year. Such loans would be called 3/1, 5/1, or 7/1 ARMs. Other options would be for loans that had an initial rate that lasted five years, then went to a fixed-rate loan at the prevailing rates available for the fifth year. This would be called a 5/25. There are 3/27s, 5/25s, 7/23s, or 10/30 loans available. No one program suits everyone, so each borrower must evaluate the alternatives based on the personal situation.

■   **EXAMPLE 9.6**   Cindy has been transferred to Lakewood and is expecting to be in that location for about three years before being transferred again. She can get a 7.5 percent fixed-rate mortgage with no discount points or a 5 percent one-year adjustable-rate mortgage with no points. The ARM has a 2 percent annual cap and a 6 percent lifetime cap. She asks for your recommendation.

What should Cindy do based on her situation?

What calculations did you use to make your recommendation?

Disadvantages of the ARM loan   ARM borrowers bet against the lenders that interest rates will not rise to the extent that the maximum interest rate caps will be needed. The main disadvantages of the ARM loan are the uncertain amounts of future mortgage payments and the difficulty in calculating adjustments in interest rates as they occur. Lenders, of course, do the actual calculation of adjustments, but they have been known to make mistakes, and such mistakes can be expensive to the borrowers. Calculation details are spelled out in each loan document, but they are somewhat complicated and require the use of either a financial calculator or a handbook of ARM payment tables. For a borrower who wants to audit a lender's ARM adjustments without going to the trouble of research and math calculations, Loantech, Inc., a Gaithersburg, Maryland, mortgage consulting firm (800-888-6781), will do a complete individual ARM adjustment review for a fee, based on the terms of the loan document submitted.

FHA Adjustable-Rate Mortgage

Section 251 of the National Housing Act authorizes the Federal Housing Administration (FHA) to insure adjustable-rate mortgages on single-family properties. The interest rate is the sum of the index and the margin. The index changes but the margin will remain the same over the life of the loan. The initial interest rate may be a result of combining the current one-year Treasury bill index with the margin at the time the loan is closed. This combination of components produces what is often called the **calculated interest rate**. Each FHA-approved lender is allowed to discount the calculated interest rate to a lower figure if local competition requires it, or the calculated interest rate may become the initial interest rate. The initial interest rate cannot be a rate higher than the current index plus margin.

Once the initial interest rate is set, annual adjustments to FHA ARMs must be calculated. The first interest rate adjustment may not occur sooner than 12 months from the due date of the first monthly payment or later than 18 months from that first designated payment date. In other words, the first adjustment must be made during a six-month period or it is forfeited. This time frame permits lenders to complete the collection or pooling of many mortgages for sale to secondary market institutions. Whatever date is designated as the initial interest rate adjustment date, all subsequent rate adjustments must be made on the anniversary of that first adjustment date.

Unlike the conventional ARM choice of index, all FHA ARMs must use the published Constant Maturity of the One-Year Treasury Security index using the most recently available figure that applied exactly 30 calendar days before the designated change date. The new current index plus the constant margin rounded to the nearest one-eighth of 1 percent is the new calculated interest rate. It is then compared with the existing interest rate. If it is the same as the existing interest rate, no change is made to the existing rate. If it is up to 1 percent higher or lower than the existing interest rate, the new calculated interest rate becomes the new adjusted interest rate. If it is more than 1 percent higher or lower than the existing interest rate, the new adjusted interest rate is limited to a 1 percent increase or decrease of the existing interest rate.

The new adjusted interest rate becomes effective on the designated change date and is regarded as the existing interest rate until the next allowable change date. In no event may any future combination of interest rate adjustments exceed five percentage points higher or lower than the initial interest rate.

The FHA considers interest payable on the first day of the month following the month in which the interest accrued. Therefore, adjusted monthly mortgage payments resulting from the adjusted interest rate are not due until 30 days after the designated change date. No negative amortization is allowed with FHA ARMs. The FHA requires that payments be recalculated each year to provide for complete amortization of the outstanding principal balance over the remaining term of the loan at the new adjusted interest rate. Lenders must give borrowers at least 30 days' notice of any increase or decrease in the monthly mortgage payment amount. The adjustment notice must contain the date the adjustment notice is given, the ARM change date, the new existing interest rate, the amount of the new monthly mortgage payment, the current index used, the method of calculating the adjustment, and any other information that may be required to clarify the adjustment.

FHA required disclosure statement   All approved lenders making FHA adjustable-rate loans must provide each borrower with a mortgage loan information statement that includes a worst-case example form. The borrower must receive this statement and be given an opportunity to read the informative explanation before signing the borrower's certification on the loan application. Licensees are urged to obtain personal copies of the FHA adjustable-rate mortgage disclosure statement to use when counseling clients or advising customers.

Advantages of the FHA ARM   An FHA ARM has several advantages over a conventional ARM. Often, an FHA ARM bears a slightly lower interest rate because of the government insurance provided the lender. In addition, the FHA commonly uses more lenient qualification formulas. The down payment (required investment) also is lower in many cases, and the interest rate increase each year is limited to 1 percent, with an overall cap of 5 percent (conventional caps usually are 2 percent per year, with a 6 percent overall cap). FHA loans continue to be easier to assume than conventional loans, although the FHA has increased the requirements for assumption of FHA loans. The FHA now requires a review of the creditworthiness of each person seeking to assume an FHA-insured loan.

Disadvantages of an FHA ARM   The FHA imposes a maximum loan amount that differs from region to region, depending on the cost of living in each region. Also, the FHA requires an upfront mortgage insurance premium (UFMIP) of 1.5 percent, although this cost may be financed along with the mortgage. If FHA loans are repaid early, mortgagors may apply for partial refunds of the mortgage insurance premiums.

Bond Money for First-Time Homebuyers

States, counties, and cities can offer below-market mortgage financing by selling tax-free bonds. These loans are available to first-time homebuyers (who haven't owned a home for the previous three years). Sometimes divorced persons who want to buy their own home also qualify. These programs come and go so check with local lenders for availability.

■ MORTGAGE INSURANCE

Conventional lenders usually require that the borrower pay for private mortgage insurance (PMI). PMI protects the lender if the borrower defaults on the loan. The *Homeowners Protection Act of 1998*, which became effective in 1999, established rules for automatic termination and borrower cancellation of PMI on home mortgages. These protections apply to certain home mortgages signed on or after July 29, 1999. These protections do not apply to government-insured FHA or VA guaranteed loans or to loans with lender-paid PMI.

For conventional home mortgages signed on or after July 29, 1999, PMI must, with certain exceptions, be terminated automatically when the borrower has achieved 22 percent equity in the home based on the *purchase price*, if the mortgage payments are current. PMI also can be canceled when the borrower requests it—with certain exceptions—when the borrower achieves 20 percent equity in the home based on the original property value, if the mortgage payments are current.

There are three exceptions for which the PMI may continue:

- If the loan is high-risk
- If the borrower has not been current on the payments within the year prior to the time for termination or cancellation
- If the borrower has other liens on the property

The FHA Homebuyer Savings Plan has also reduced mortgage insurance premiums on loans originated after January 1, 2001, to 1.5 percent of the original loan amount from 2.25 percent. FHA has also eliminated the 0.5 percent premium for borrowers who have achieved 22 percent equity in their house, based on the lower of the purchase price or the appraisal.

■ RELATED WEB SITES

Fannie Mae: *www.fanniemae.com*
Freddie Mac: *www.freddiemac.com*
U.S. Department of Housing and Urban Development: FHA:
        www.hud.gov/fha/fhahome.html
Federal Reserve Board: *www.federalreserve.gov*
U.S. Department of Veterans Affairs: *www.va.gov*

■ SUMMARY

Real estate licensees should assist their clients and customers in the initial two steps of prequalifying and shopping for a mortgage loan. Too often, the process begins instead with the loan application. Various proven tools and techniques exist for doing both before applying to a lender for a loan.

Fixed-rate mortgages remain popular. While the 30-year, fixed-rate mortgage is the most common, 15-year and biweekly mortgages are gaining popularity. Adjustable-rate mortgages also are popular among lenders and borrowers. Conventional and FHA adjustable-rate mortgages are available. Each financing instrument has its own advantages and disadvantages, and licensees who understand the current and ever-changing mortgage market increase their chances for success in the business.

■ KEY TERMS

adjustable-rate mortgage (ARM)	calculated interest rate	margin
	cap	negative amortization
annual percentage rate (APR)	fixed-rate mortgage	PITI payment
	index	refinancing
biweekly mortgage		

UNIT
10

Acquiring Financing for the Property

■ **LEARNING OBJECTIVES** *Upon completion of this unit, you should be able to*

■ **list** three federal statutes that control the information a lender may obtain and consider when qualifying an applicant,

■ **list** the four basic loan processing procedures,

■ **list** two of the latest trends in mortgage lending due to computer technology,

■ **describe** the difference between qualifying the borrower and qualifying the property,

■ **describe** how lenders are using credit scoring to assist in the underwriting process,

■ **itemize** at least three sources of income that will be counted when qualifying a buyer,

■ **explain** what analyzing the title means and how it is accomplished,

■ **list** the components of a full title report,

■ **list** the two methods of obtaining assurance of good title, and

■ **describe** the difference between an owner's title insurance policy and a lender's title insurance policy.

■ OVERVIEW

The origination of a home mortgage is subject to a number of federal statutes, particularly the **Equal Credit Opportunity Act (ECOA),** the **Consumer Credit Protection Act** (Title I: Truth-in-Lending Act), and the **Real Estate Settlement Procedures Act (RESPA).** Together, these laws control the information a lender may obtain and consider in qualifying consumer mortgage loan applicants. They also dictate both the content and the form of information lenders must present to borrowers, the procedure for closing mortgage loan agreements, the documents to be used in closings, and the fees that may be charged.

In today's environment, lenders are required by the Civil Rights Acts, and the amendments to them, not to discriminate against consumer mortgage loan applicants on the basis of race, color, national origin, religion, sex, age, family status, or handicap. In addition, borrower rights have been better protected since passage of the Equal Credit Opportunity Act and the *Federal Reserve Board of Governor's Regulation B,* which implemented the act. The act requires fair consideration of consumer loan applications from women, minorities, part-time employees, and others who may have suffered prejudicial treatment in the past.

As a result of increasing concern about protection of consumer rights, most mortgage lenders have developed specific guidelines for loan underwriters to follow to ensure compliance with federal laws affecting consumer mortgage lending. Although the guidelines are protective of consumers' rights, they do not interfere with the analysis of an applicant's credit standing. The purpose of such guidelines is to prevent homebuyers from being victimized, not to guarantee that a loan will be approved. In the final analysis, good underwriting policies and practices by a lender combine compliance with the continual search for financial safety and streamlined processing. Licensees can serve themselves and their customers well by becoming knowledgeable about residential mortgage loan processing and closing.

To accomplish the above-stated goals of government agencies and originating lenders, four basic **loan processing procedures** have been developed:

1. Determining a borrower's ability to repay the loan
2. Estimating the value of the property being pledged as collateral to guarantee the repayment
3. Researching and analyzing the marketability of the collateral's title
4. Preparing the documents necessary to close the loan transaction

Most lenders follow loan processing procedures that reflect a combined concern for the borrower's credit ability and the collateral's value. Some loan transactions require an emphasis of one factor over another, but generally, both borrower credit and collateral value are essential determinants in the real estate finance loan processing equation.

Loan underwriting is the evaluation of the risks involved when issuing a new mortgage. This process involves qualifying the borrower and the property to determine whether they meet the minimum requirements established by the lender, investor, or secondary market in which the loan probably will be sold.

■ TRENDS IN THE MORTGAGE MARKET

The mortgage market is changing as rapidly as many other sectors of the real estate industry and technology is the engine of that change. The last two years have seen many lenders moving their loan programs to the Internet. Almost immediate loan approval is possible on the Web. Credit scoring, discussed later in this unit, is changing the way mortgage interest rates are quoted. Appraisers can make restricted drive-by appraisals when a loan application is strong.

Automated Underwriting

With **automated underwriting** a lender can enter loan application information into Fannie Mae's Desktop Underwriter software and receive a decision almost immediately. If the software determines that the buyer and the property are qualified, Fannie Mae is required to purchase the loan from the originator.

Because of the huge growth of people using the Internet, and the public's acceptance of the technology, lenders are moving toward so-called **paperless mortgages.** For example, a person who applies for a mortgage online can expect to take 15 minutes to complete the application, and the applicant will get an automated decision almost immediately. This bypasses the need for a lender to take the application. How does all this work? With **computer valuation** (automated valuation) and credit scoring.

Automated Valuation

Some years ago, a consortium of lending organizations including Fannie Mae, Freddie Mac, Citibank, Countrywide Funding, and others, formed an organization called the *National Property Data Service*. The purpose was to reduce time and costs for both consumers and lenders through **automated valuation**, which uses a computer-generated valuation program.

Each lender contributed all its residential appraisals to create a huge database of property descriptions and sale prices. A review of the database might show, for example, that 74 percent of all the homes in a given subdivision had been the subject of an appraisal over a ten-year period.

An appraiser employs matched pair analysis using two or three pairs of properties to estimate the value of a fourth bedroom, a swimming pool, or another feature. The Desktop Underwriter uses multiple linear regressions to do the same thing for that neighborhood. It uses precise dollar adjustments and, depending on the buyer's credit score, may allow an appraiser to do a streamlined property inspection (exterior only) to make an estimate of value. When Fannie Mae uses this method, it has judged the reasonableness of the sale price and has relied on the property value generated by the software.

■ QUALIFYING THE BORROWER

The framework for current real estate financing is the 30-year amortization schedule and regular monthly payments of principal and interest. In addition, mortgagees currently can lend up to 100 percent of a property's value. High loan-to-value ratios combined with long-term loan amortization payment schedules require that a lender look to the credit of the borrower as the primary protection.

Even though lenders using insured or guaranteed programs of real estate finance do not bear the risks of default directly, they still must follow the directions of their guaranteeing agencies and carefully screen loan applicants to derive some reasonable estimate of borrowers' ability to pay and their inclinations to meet their contractual obligations responsibly. Thus, a great effort is made to thoroughly check and evaluate a potential mortgagor's credit history and current financial status to predict her future economic stability. The mortgage loan process is shown in Figure 10.1.

FIGURE   10.1

Mortgage Loan Process

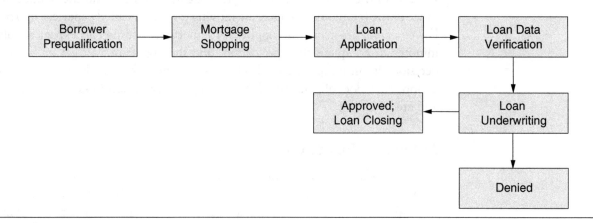

Loan Application

When a licensee works with a buyer, one of the services the licensee can offer is that of helping the buyer obtain financing. Before the buyer goes to the lender to make an application, the licensee should provide a list of items the buyer will need.

A Mortgage Loan Application Checklist is shown on the next page.

F I G U R E   10.2

Mortgage Loan Application Checklist

Place personal and company information/logo here	Mortgage Lender: _____ Address: _____ Loan Officer: _____ Phone: _____ Date of Application: _____ Time: _____

Thanks for using our real estate firm to find your home. To assist you in making your mortgage loan application, we have prepared the list of items that may be needed by the lender. Additional information may be requested

The Transaction:
- ❏ Copy of the signed purchase contract.
- ❏ If you have sold your present home, a copy of the HUD-1 closing statement. If the sale is not complete, a copy of the signed purchase contract.

Your Income:
- ❏ Original pay stubs for the latest 30-day period.
- ❏ Original W-2 forms for the previous two years.
- ❏ If you are self-employed or have commission income: a year-to-date profit and loss statement and balance sheet; copies of your last two years' personal and business signed federal tax returns.
- ❏ If you are using child support payments to qualify for mortgage: proof of receipt.

Your Assets:
- ❏ Original bank statements for all checking and savings accounts for the past three months. You should be able to explain all deposits not from payroll.
- ❏ Original statements from investment or brokerage firms for the last three months (if applicable).
- ❏ Original IRA or 401(k) statements (if applicable).
- ❏ List of real estate owned: address, market value, mortgage balance, name and address of mortgage company.
- ❏ List of life insurance policies with company name, face value, beneficiaries, and cash surrender value.
- ❏ List of automobiles, with make, model, value, amount owed, lender name, address and account number.
- ❏ Estimate of replacement value of household furniture and appliances.
- ❏ Value of other assets (collections, art, etc.).
- ❏ If you have sold a home in the past two years, a copy of the closing statement and a copy of the deed given.

Your Liabilities:
- ❏ Credit cards: name, address, account number, monthly payment, and present balance.
- ❏ Other liabilities: name, address, account number, monthly payment, and present balance.

Payments for Housing:
- ❏ List of addresses for previous two years, along with names, addresses, and phone numbers of landlords and/or mortgage companies where housing payments were made.
- ❏ Last 12 month's cancelled checks for housing payments (landlord or mortgage company).

If you are divorced:
- ❏ Copies of all divorce decrees, including any modifications or stipulations.
- ❏ Child support or alimony payments: amount, duration, and proof of payment for 12 months.

If you are applying for an FHA loan:
- ❏ Photocopy of driver's license or other acceptable photo ID.
- ❏ Photocopy of Social Security Card.

If you are applying for a VA loan:
- ❏ VA Certificate of Eligibility.
- ❏ Form DD-214.

For in-service veterans or those discharged within the past two years.
- ❏ Statement of Service.
- ❏ Most recent Leave and Earnings Statement.

Other items:
- ❏ If you have graduated from high school or college within the previous two years, a copy of your diploma or transcripts.
- ❏ If you have a gap in employment for 30 days or more, include a letter explaining the reason.
- ❏ If part of your down payment is a gift, the lender will give you a gift letter for signature when you apply.
- ❏ If you have filed bankruptcy in the last seven years, give a letter explaining the reasons, a copy of the Petition Decree, a Schedule of Creditors, and the Discharge document.
- ❏ If you have rental property, a copy of the current lease and two year's signed income tax returns.

Your Check:
- ❏ Your check for the appraisal and application fee.

Data Verification

The loan processor will verify the information included in the application by actually checking with the various references given, the banks where deposits are held, and the applicant's employer.

Deposits

The borrower must sign a separate deposit verification form for each bank account, authorizing the bank to reveal to the lender the current balance in the borrower's account. Under the *Federal Right to Privacy Act*, the bank cannot release such confidential information without a verification form. The knowledge that the loan processor can verify account amounts usually is enough incentive for the borrower to be truthful in reporting financial information. When the deposit balances are verified, the appropriate entries are made in the applicant's file.

Employment

The applicant also is required to sign an employment verification form authorizing the employer to reveal confidential information concerning the applicant's job status. Not only will the applicant's wages or salary and length of employment be verified but the employer also will be requested to offer an opinion of the applicant's job attitude and give a prognosis for continued employment and prospects for advancement. Employment may be checked again before closing.

Credit Report

Simultaneously with the gathering of financial and employment information, the loan processor sends a formal request for the borrower's credit report to a local company offering this service. The credit report is a central part of the loan approval process and the lender relies on it heavily. Of the two types of credit reports, consumer credit and mortgage credit, the discussion here centers on the latter.

A credit report is the result of the compilation of information accumulated from a thorough check of the creditors indicated on the loan application, as well as a check of public records to discover whether any lawsuits are pending against the applicant. When completed, the credit search company sends the loan processor a confidential report of its findings.

This report usually states the applicant's (and co-applicant's) age, address, status as a tenant or owner, and length of residency at his current address and includes a brief employment history and credit profile, both past and present. The credit profile itemizes the status of current and past accounts, usually identified by industry, such as banks, department and specialty stores, and finance companies. In addition, it indicates the quality and dates of the payments made, and their regularity; delinquency; any outstanding balances also are reported. This payment history is the most important part of the report because it indicates how well the applicant has managed debt over time. Underwriters view a person's past behavior as the best indicator of future attitude toward debt repayment. Research tends to reinforce these opinions, indicating that slow and erratic payers generally retain those attitudes when securing new loans and that prompt and steady payers also are consistent in meeting their future obligations. As a result, lenders pay careful attention to the last section of a credit report, which indicates an applicant's attitude toward debt and payment pattern.

When a credit report is returned revealing a series of erratic and delinquent payments, the loan is usually denied at this point and the file closed. If an applicant is denied a loan because of adverse information in a credit report, the applicant has the right to inspect a summary of that report, to challenge inaccuracies, and to require corrections to be made (see the most current RESPA-required brochure, *Settlement Costs: A HUD Guide*). If one or two unusual entries stand out in a group of otherwise satisfactory transactions, the applicant will be asked to explain these deviations.

As with many standardized procedures, credit reporting has become computerized, dramatically shortening the time needed for completing a check. In exchange for time efficiency, however, credit-reporting bureaus risk sacrificing the borrower's confidentiality. The fraudulent use of credit reports is increasing now that information is so easily accessible. Credit reports should be used only by the persons or institutions requesting the information and only for the purposes stated. As a result of increased seller financing, credit bureaus are receiving more requests from agents and sellers to check the credit of potential purchasers. To protect a buyer's confidentiality, most credit agencies insist on seeing the buyer's written permission before issuing any information.

After the deposit and employment verifications are returned with acceptable information, and a favorable credit report is obtained, the lending officer makes a thorough credit evaluation of the data collected before continuing with the loan process.

Evaluation of Credit Ability

Despite the standardization of the detailed guidelines used in the lending process, the one area allowing for the greatest amount of latitude in interpretation is the analysis and evaluation of a borrower's credit ability. A degree of subjective personal involvement may be introduced into an otherwise strongly objective and structured format by an evaluator's unintentional bias or by a loan company's changing policies.

In addition, credit standards are altered periodically to reflect a lender's changing monetary position. When money is scarce, standards are more stringent; when money is plentiful, standards are lowered. An applicant who qualifies for a loan at one time may not at another. Thus, although a credit analyst is governed by guidelines, rules, and regulations, the criteria fluctuate with the analyst's discretionary powers. In the long run, a lender's success is demonstrated by a low rate of default on approved loans and by the fact that no discrimination complaints have been filed.

Credit Scoring

One of the most significant changes in mortgage lending has been the use of credit scores to better evaluate a borrower's ability to repay. Many borrowers who would have been turned down for a loan five years ago can buy today, but at higher rates.

A major reason Fannie Mae and Freddie Mac lenders are willing to make immediate loan decisions is credit scoring. **Credit scoring** uses statistical samples to predict how likely it is that a borrower will pay back a loan. To develop a model, the lender selects a large random sample of its borrowers, analyzing characteristics that relate to creditworthiness. Each of the characteristics is assigned a weight based on how strong a predictor it is. Credit scores treat each person objectively because the same standards apply to everyone. Credit scores are blind to demographic or cultural differences among people.

The most commonly used credit score today is known as a **FICO score**, named after the company that developed it, Fair Isaac Corporation. FICO scores range from 300 to 850. The lower the score, the greater the risk of default. A recent study by the Federal Reserve Board found that borrowers with low credit scores accounted for 1.5 percent of new mortgages, but 17 percent of delinquencies.

Freddie Mac has found that borrowers with credit scores above 660 are likely to repay the mortgage, and underwriters can do a basic review of the file for completeness. For applicants with scores between 620 and 660, the underwriter is required to do a comprehensive review. A very cautious review would be made for persons with credit scores below 620.

Is Credit Scoring Valid?

With credit scoring, lenders can evaluate millions of applicants consistently and impartially on many different characteristics. To be statistically valid, the system must be based on a big enough sample. When properly designed, the system promotes fast, impartial decisions.

Fair Isaac has recently completed *NextGen®*, designed to more precisely define the risk of borrowers because it analyzes more criteria than the old model. Using the new model, lenders can evaluate credit profiles of high-risk borrowers in terms of degrees, rather than lumping them into the same category.

What Information Does Credit Scoring Use?

The scoring models use the following information when evaluating a score:

- Thirty-five percent of the score is determined by payment history, with higher weight for recent history. If late payments, collections, and/or bankruptcy appear in the credit report, they are subtracted from the score.
- Outstanding debt is very close in importance to payment history (30 percent of the total score). Many scoring models evaluate the amount of debt compared with the credit limits. If the amount owed is close to the credit limit, it affects the score negatively.

- Fifteen percent of the score is the result of credit history. A long history is better if payments are always on time.
- Ten percent of the score is very recent history and inquiries for new credit. If the applicant has applied for credit in many places recently, it will negatively affect the score. This problem occurs when a person goes car shopping. Broker associates at each car lot will ask for the consumer's Social Security number in order to pull a credit report ("no charge"). The shopper has no idea that as more reports are ordered, the shopper's credit rating declines.
- Ten percent of the score is based on the mix of credit, including car loans, credit cards, and mortgages. Too many credit cards will hurt a person's credit score. In some models, loans from finance companies or title loan companies will also hurt the score.

To improve the credit score, persons should pay bills on time, pay down outstanding balances, and not take on new debt. It may take a long time to improve the score significantly.

How Is Credit Scoring Being Used?

Residential lenders now use credit scoring the same way it is used in automobile financing and consumer loans. Interest rates on home mortgages are based on the credit score. In theory, a person with a very high score should expect to get the best rate, but typically the rate is the same for anyone with a FICO score higher than 620. Below the 620 line, several grades and interest rates have resulted.

For example, when an A+ borrower can obtain a 30-year fixed rate mortgage at 7 percent, an A− borrower pays 8.4 percent, a B borrower pays 8.7 percent, a C borrower pays 9.15 percent, and a D borrower pays 9.95 percent. Before credit scoring, however, these borrowers might not have been able to get a loan at all.

Many people who go to subprime lenders have only slight credit problems and end up paying 2 percent higher than they need to. Those borrowers may qualify for standard rates and should find out their credit scores before making a decision on a lender. If individuals cannot get their FICO score, E-Loan Corp. provides a credit score using basically the same techniques. Individuals can get one free credit score by logging into E-Loan and requesting the information.

■ RELATED WEB SITES

E-Loan (for prequalifying and credit scores): *www.eloan.com*
HSH Associates, Financial Publishers: *www.hsh.com*
Fair Isaac Corporation: *www.fairisaac.com*

The quantity and quality of an applicant's income are the two major considerations in determining ability to support a family and make the required monthly loan payments. Analysts consider the **quantity of income**—the total income—when they review a loan application. Not only is the regular salary of a family's primary supporter basic to the analysis but also a spouse's full income usually is accepted. Extra sources of income also may be included in the analysis if circumstances warrant it.

Any bonuses will be accepted as income only if they are received on a regular basis. If commissions are a large part of an applicant's income base, the history of past earnings will be scrutinized to estimate the stability of this income as a regular source for an extended time period. Overtime wages are not included in the analysis unless they have been—and will be—earned consistently. Pensions, interest, and dividends are treated as full income, although it is recognized that interest and dividends fluctuate over time and could stop if an investment were cashed out.

A second job is accepted as part of the regular monthly income if it can be established that the job has existed for approximately two years and there is good reason to believe it will continue. Child support also can be included in the determination of monthly income, but only if it is the result of a court order and has a proven track record. Government entitlement funds must also be considered.

In addition to its total quantity, a loan analyst pays careful attention to the **quality of income.** An applicant's employer will be asked for an opinion of job stability and possible advancement. Length of time on the job no longer carries the importance it once did. Applicants whose employment records show frequent shifts in job situations that result in upward mobility each time will be given full consideration. Lenders will, however, be wary of an applicant who drifts from one job classification to another and cannot seem to become established in any specific type of work.

When the accumulated data strongly support a positive or negative decision, the loan underwriter's decision is easy and minimal use of discretion is needed. However, numerous borderline cases make it difficult for a loan officer to form objective judgments. In such a case, the loan officer schedules an in-depth personal interview with the applicant during which questions regarding data appearing on the credit report are clarified or mistakes in bank balances can be explained. More often, however, the loan officer merely wishes to visit with the applicant to observe and probe his attitudes regarding the purchase of the property and the repayment of the prospective loan. Thus, although a person's credit character can be measured objectively, personal character is subject to interpretation.

After reviewing all of the information provided in the application as well as the other data collected, the loan officer decides either to approve or to disapprove the loan application. If the officer judges a loan application to be unacceptable, the officer states the reasons for the rejection, the parties to the loan are informed, and the file is closed.

■ QUALIFYING THE COLLATERAL

Despite the current trend toward emphasizing a borrower's financial ability as the loan-granting criterion, real estate lenders and guarantors are practical and fully understand that life is filled with events beyond one's control. Death is a possibility that can abruptly eliminate a family's wage earner. Economic conditions can exert devastating financial impact. Corporate downsizing and layoffs have resulted in hardship for many families. Honest mistakes in personal decisions can result in bankruptcies, often damaging or destroying credit.

■ **EXAMPLE 10.1** You are at an open house on Sunday afternoon. A young couple asks whether they could qualify to buy the house. Based on the home's price of $156,000, you estimate a 90 percent loan would be about $140,000. You tell them you can give them your best estimate, but that they will know for sure only after they see a lender to become preapproved. They give you the following monthly financial information:

Gross monthly income	$4,300
Mortgage principal and interest payment @ 6 percent for 30 years	$839
Real estate tax escrow	$150
Homeowner's insurance escrow	$50
Private mortgage insurance	$45
Car payment	$250
Credit card payments (average)	$50

The borrower's housing expense ratio is: _____

The borrower's total obligations ratio is: _____

What is your informal opinion on their chances to qualify? _____

To reduce the risk of loss, real estate lenders look to the value of the collateral (the real property) as the basic underlying assurance for recovery of their investment in a default situation.

Unique financing terms or an active local housing market in which the number of potential buyers briefly exceeds the number of available properties may cause prices to rise above actual market values. Therefore, each parcel of property pledged for collateral must be inspected and appraised carefully to estimate its current market value because this amount will be used as the basis for determining the mortgage loan amount. Depending on the type of loan to be issued and its loan-to-value ratio, either the amount determined through the formal or certified appraisal made as part of the loan process or the purchase price, whichever is less, determines the loan's amount.

Some financial institutions maintain appraisers on their staffs, but most lenders engage certified appraisers for estimates of value. All three approaches to estimating a property's value are addressed. When an appraisal is completed, it is delivered to the loan officer to aid in the final loan decision. As noted previously, a loan amount is based on the lesser of either this appraised value or the purchase price of the property.

■ **EXAMPLE 10.2** Which do you consider the more important factor in granting or denying a mortgage application: the borrower's ability to make the required payments or the value of the collateral? Why?

■ ANALYZING THE TITLE

The assurance of good title is as essential to a loan's completion as are the borrower's credit and the collateral's value. Once the property is under contract, the listing broker will order the title commitment. The buyer's broker (representing the buyer) should make sure that the buyer's lender is included in the commitment. The lender may also require a survey or improvement location certificate (ILC). The components of a full title report are a survey, a physical inspection of the collateral, and a search of the records to determine all the interests in a property. Normally, property interests are perfected through the appropriate filing and recording of standard notices. A recorded deed notifies the world that a grantee has the legal fee simple title to the property. A recorded construction lien, for example, is notice of another's interest in the property.

In Colorado, two methods can been used to obtain assurance of good title: (1) the abstract and opinion of title and (2) title insurance. In the majority of transactions title insurance is preferred. Whichever method is used, the title report should provide the loan officer and the lender's attorney with all available information relevant to the legal status of the subject property, as well as any interests revealed by constructive notice. This title search requirement represents another effort by the lender to protect the loan investment. Because title insurance is most lenders' and buyers' method of choice, it is discussed here.

Title Insurance

Title insurance companies combine the abstracting process with a program of insurance that guarantees the validity and accuracy of the title search. A purchaser of title insurance can rely on the insurance company's assets to back up its guarantee of a property's marketable title. This guarantee is evidenced by a policy of title insurance. Most financial institutions now require that a title policy be issued to them for the face amount of a loan. Insurance is defined simply as coverage against loss. Standard practice in Colorado is for the seller to pay for the owner or buyer policy at closing. The buyer then pays for the mortgagee's policy, which protects the lender; this policy will also be paid for at closing.

When a title insurance policy is issued to a lender, it is usually in the American Land Title Association (ALTA) form. While a standard title policy insures against losses overlooked in the search of the recorded chain of title, an ALTA policy expands this standard coverage to include many unusual risks, such as forgeries, incompetence of parties involved in issuing documents pertaining to the transfer of ownership, legal status of parties involved in the specific loan negotiations, surveying errors, and other possible off-record defects. Some additional risks can be and usually are covered by an extended coverage insurance policy. These include protection against any unrecorded easements or liens, rights of parties in possession of the subject property, and additional negotiated special items pertinent to the property involved. Participants in the secondary mortgage market (Fannie Mae, Freddie Mac, and Ginnie Mae) generally require the expanded ALTA policy for the added protection it provides. Many lenders use the phrase "an ALTA policy" when describing an extended-coverage policy.

Surveys or Improvement Location Certificates (ILC)

Whether the abstract and opinion of title method or the title insurance policy method is used, a property's title is searched by an experienced abstractor who prepares a report of those recorded documents that clearly affect the quality of ownership. In addition, lenders sometimes require a survey or ILC for the collateral property as a condition for a new loan. Although many properties are part of subdivisions that have been engineered and described by licensed and registered surveyors and engineers, some owners might have enlarged their homes or made additions to the improvements since the original survey. These might not meet the various setback restrictions set forth in local zoning laws. Some properties might have been resubdivided, while others might have encroachment issues. A survey will identify the property boundaries and all improvements, while an ILC will simply locate the improvements relative to the property line. Both will note any encroachments. Typically for urban property a survey or ILC is not required. The broker associate should check with the lender and title company to see if they are going to require a survey or ILC prior to ordering them, since this can save their buyer or seller anywhere from $150 to $2,000 at closing if one is not required.

Defects

If a defect, sometimes called a *cloud on the title*, is found, the loan process does not continue until the cloud is cleared to the buyer's and lender's satisfaction. Such a cloud could be an unsatisfied construction lien, an income tax lien, a property tax lien, an easement infraction, an encroachment, or a zoning violation. Sometimes a borrower's name is not correct on the deed, an error exists in the legal description, or the deed has a faulty acknowledgment or lacks the appropriate signature(s). Because of the many complexities in a real estate transaction, there are possibilities for defects to appear in a title search and property survey. It is the abstractor's responsibility to discover and report them.

In certain instances where clouds are difficult to remove by ordinary means, they must be cleared by filing suit to quiet title. After appropriate evidence is submitted, a judge removes or modifies an otherwise damaging defect in a title. The loan process can continue when a clear chain of title is shown on the public records.

■ SUMMARY

The process of obtaining a real estate loan includes four steps: qualifying a borrower, evaluating the collateral, analyzing the title, and closing the loan transaction.

Beginning with an application to obtain a loan, the borrower's credit, financial condition, and personal attitudes are analyzed to determine ability and willingness to honor debts and repay the loan as agreed. Current assets and employment are verified, a credit rating is obtained, and often a private interview is held between the borrower and loan officer to estimate certain credit characteristics. Other basic criteria used to determine the applicant's creditworthiness include gross monthly earnings of approximately four times the required monthly mortgage payment (sometimes higher for large loans), stability of earnings, and a good prognosis for continued employment and advancement.

Once the loan applicant's credit is accepted, either a staff appraiser or an independent fee appraiser analyzes the value of the real estate to be pledged as collateral. A certified appraisal report offering the appraiser's opinion of the subject property's value is submitted to the loan officer.

After the borrower's credit and the collateral's value are verified, the legal status of the property's title is examined and analyzed carefully, usually by a trained abstractor. The title commitment or title report is delivered to the lender's attorney for an opinion of accuracy and validity. Because of the growing activity of this nation's secondary mortgage market and its concurrent necessity for added protection, lenders generally require title insurance to guarantee the title search.

Finally, after approval of the borrower's credit, the collateral's value, and the title's marketability, the loan processor prepares the documents necessary for closing. With the delivery of the funds to the seller and the recording of the necessary papers transferring title, the loan transaction is completed.

■ KEY TERMS

automated underwriting

automated valuation

computer valuation

Consumer Credit Protection Act

credit scoring

Equal Credit Opportunity Act (ECOA)

FICO score

loan processing procedures

loan underwriting

paperless mortgage

quality of income

quantity of income

Real Estate Settlement Procedures Act (RESPA)

UNIT 11

Closing Real Estate Transactions

- **name** the steps that a broker associate must follow after writing a contract to ensure a timely closing,

- **list** the tasks that a broker associate should complete after a closing,

- **describe** the reasons why a licensee might not want to personally order repairs on a property and what steps can be taken to protect the broker associate from liability,

- **list** at least four objectives of a preclosing inspection,

- **describe** the reasons a real estate broker associate should provide closing documents to the buyer and seller at least one day in advance of a closing,

- **list** the proration items paid in advance and those paid in arrears,

- **prorate** rent, interest, and property taxes,

- **describe** the methods lenders use to set up an escrow account for prepaid taxes, hazard insurance, and private mortgage insurance,

- **calculate** prepaid interest for a new loan,

- **calculate** the expenses on the closing statement, and

- **prepare** and review a HUD-1 Settlement Statement.

■ OVERVIEW

Closing the transaction is the final and most important step in the transaction. The listing brokerage firm and designated listing broker are responsible for the overall closing. In addition, the designated buyer's broker will be responsible for the buyer's closing statements. Brokerage firms and employing brokers are responsible for training their broker associates on the closing process and must be available for new agents by either attending the closing or being available to answer questions. Upon completing this unit broker associates should be familiar with the closing process and closing documents and be ready for that special day when they have their first closing.

■ THE CLOSING PROCESS

Once the real estate contract has been signed, the licensee's work has just begun. The parties to a transaction expect their broker associate to personally monitor and coordinate all the details of their closing. While the licensee may believe he has "passed the torch" to the next group of professionals (lenders and closing agents), the buyer and seller continue to look to their broker associate to coordinate all the details of the transaction. A smooth transition from contract to closing enhances the reputations of the firm and the sales associate. This section is intended to help licensees better understand the process and to follow the "road to closing" successfully. (See Figure 11.1.)

FIGURE 11.1

The Road to Closing

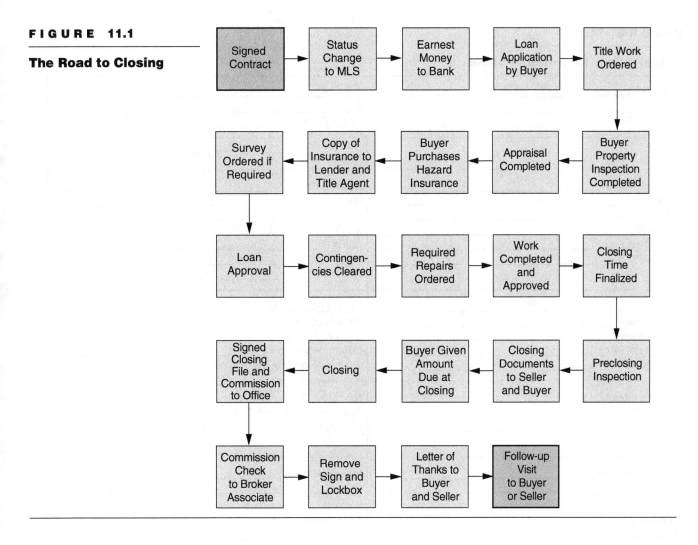

Some important steps a licensee may take to reduce problems with title closing include the following:

- Disclose everything to all parties that will affect their decisions before the buyer and seller sign the contract; surprises after a contract is signed almost certainly will result in one party wanting to get out of the contract
- Write the contract carefully and properly explain it to the parties
- Recommend that buyers and sellers select lenders and title closing agents who are organized professionals able to meet deadlines
- Tell the loan officer and closing agent what the licensee expects in the way of communication and performance
- Prepare a Property Sale Information Sheet from your company or use the one on the following page
- Give the closing agent a copy of the prior title insurance policy, if possible
- Provide a complete legal description of the property to the closing agent
- Ask a lender and title agent to communicate by e-mail, speeding the process while also giving written documentation of the transaction
- Use a checklist of duties, such as the Closing Progress Chart provided in Figure 11.3

FIGURE 11.2

Property Sale Information Sheet

Property Address:_____

Seller: _____   Buyer:_____

Contract Date: _____   Closing Date (Est.): _____

Seller	Buyer
Listing Broker:_____ Phone: _____ Fax: _____ Listing broker associate:_____ Home Ph.: _____ Office Ph.: _____ Mobile Ph.: _____	**Buyer's Broker:**_____ Phone: _____ Fax: _____ Buyer's broker associate:_____ Home Ph.: _____ Office Ph.: _____ Mobile Ph.: _____
Seller:_____ Old address: _____ New address:_____ City, State, Zip:_____ Current Home Ph.: _____ Ofc.: _____	**Buyer:**_____ Present address:_____ City, State, Zip:_____ Current Home Ph.: _____ Ofc.: _____ Will buyer occupy new home?_____
Existing mortgage for Payoff (P) Assumption (A) 1st Mortgage holder:_____ 2nd Mortgage holder:_____	New Mortgage Lender: _____ Type (Fixed; ARM: FHA, VA, Conv.):_____ LTV Ratio: ____ % Interest Rate: ___% Yrs: ___
Seller's Attorney:_____ Ph.:_____	Buyer's Attorney:_____ Ph.:_____
Lender:_____ **Title Company:**_____ **Appraiser:**_____ **Date Schedules to Close:**_____ **Service Providers:** Pest inspection: _____ Home inspection: _____ Roof inspection: _____ Contractor: _____ Surveyor: _____	**Loan Officer:**_____ **Closing Agent:**_____ Ph.: _____ Ph.: _____ Ph.: _____ Ph.: _____ Ph.: _____

Buyer's Insurance Company:

_____

Agent: _____   Phone:_____

Property status: ❑ Occupied by seller ❑ Occupied by tenant ❑ Vacant

Key to property for inspection: ❑ At listing office ❑ In lockbox at property ❑ Call seller for appointment

F I G U R E   11.3

Closing Progress Chart

Listing Broker Associate								
#	Sched Date	Actual Date	X	Closing Duties	Done	X	Sched Date	Actual Date
1				"Sale Pending" sign on listing				
2				Notice of under contract to MLS				
3				Binder deposited in bank $_____				
4				Additional binder received, if required $_____				
5				Loan application made by buyer				
6				Contingencies cleared in writing:				
7				Home inspection By: _____				
8				Soil test from: _____				
9				Roof inspection By: _____				
10				Other (describe): _____				
11				Appraisal By: _____				
12				Loan approval From: _____				
13				Title insurance ordered from: _____				
14				Report received and delivered to buyer				
15				Report received and delivered to lender				
16				Treatment ordered, if required				
17				Structure inspection ordered, if necessary				
18				Work completed and approved				
19				Required repairs ordered				
20				Required repairs completed				
21				Survey ordered (After loan approval)				
22				Survey completed. Results . . .				
23				Encroachments, survey problems cleared				
24				Buyer to get hazard insurance				
25				Insurance policy to title closing agent				
26				Buyer/seller contacted for closing appointment				
27				Pre-closing inspection				
28				Closing papers reviewed with buyer/seller 1 day prior				
29				Buyer given figure for certified check for closing				
30				Binder check prepared to take to closing				
31				Closing date				
32				Signed closing papers received by broker associate				
33				Post-closing duties:				
34				Commission check to broker				
35				Sign/lockbox picked up from property				
36				Buyer/seller letter of thanks				
37				Follow-up visit to buyer/seller				
38				Notice of closed sale to MLS				

A broker associate must be familiar with the documents that will be presented to the parties at the closing table. One of the most important documents, the HUD-1 Settlement Statement, relates to the financial side of the transaction. A closing statement is, in effect, the purchase and sales agreement reduced to numbers. The broker associate must understand each number in the statement and be able to explain it clearly to the buyer or seller.

The Sales Information Sheet

To organize the work program, the broker associate needs to complete the Property Sale Information Sheet. The brokerage firm or a contract computer software program may have this form. It provides necessary data about the sale, the cooperating agent, the lender, the title company, and more. This form should be clipped inside the closing file and referred to as necessary when servicing the sale.

Establishing a Plan of Action

One of the first steps after both buyer and seller sign the contract is to set up a plan for closing. This step is even more important if another broker associate is involved because miscommunication often delays closings and causes unnecessary problems. Organization and attention to detail are key to a successful closing.

The Closing Progress Chart

The closing progress chart will help the licensee organize the details of the closing. If there is a cooperating licensee, the chart should be a joint effort so that licensees agree about which licensee will handle certain duties and when the tasks should be completed. Once agreement has been reached, each broker associate should place a copy of the chart in the closing file. Additionally, each date scheduled should be transferred to the broker associate's appointment book. As each task is completed, the broker associate should place a check mark in the appropriate row. An "X" in the chart indicates that comments have been made on the back of the form. A discussion of each item follows.

Preclosing Duties

Sold or Sale Pending sign on listing   Placing a sold or sale pending sign on the listed property is a function of the listing sales associate. Some sellers prefer a sold sign so that prospective buyers are no longer escorted through the property, while others do not want to discourage activity until at least after the buyer's loan approval.

Notice of under contract to MLS   Most multiple listing services require that all offices be notified of a listed property's status change within one business after the change occurs. Failure to change the status to under contract or to taking backups can result in agents from other offices wasting time trying to set showings and is against MLS rules and regulations.

Earnest money deposited in bank   The listing broker associate should give the earnest money deposit to the employing broker as soon as the offer has become a contract. If the buyer's broker faxed a copy of the earnest money check when submitting the offer, the broker should be sure to get the earnest money check to the listing broker immediately upon acceptance. Colorado Real Estate Commission rules require that the buyer's earnest money deposit be placed in a bank no later than three business days after acceptance of the offer. If a title-closing agent will hold the deposit, the broker must deliver the deposit to the title-closing agent within the same time frame allowed by the Commission for depositing the funds in a brokerage account. The broker should get a closing instructions earnest money receipt form signed when delivering the funds to the title company.

Earnest money promissory note   If the buyer has given a promissory note, the listing broker is responsible for collecting the funds prior to closing and by the date listed in the promissory note. If the listing broker cannot collect the money from the buyer, notification must be sent to the seller.

Remember: The promissory note does not have any specific amount the buyer will be charged in interest should the seller be required to collect the promised deposit from a delinquent buyer. The buyer when making the note agrees to ALL reasonable fees with no set limit.

If the contract requires that the buyer put up additional earnest money as a good-faith deposit, it is the broker associate's responsibility to ensure that the funds are received and deposited on a timely basis. The buyer's failure to comply with contract requirements is a default. The seller must be notified and the seller's instructions followed.

Loan application made by buyer   The Contract to Buy and Sell requires that the buyer make application for the loan by a certain date. The buyer's failure to comply with contract terms is a default. The seller must be notified and the buyer may lose their earnest money.

Contingencies cleared in writing   The broker associate must ensure that contingencies are satisfied as soon as possible. Some normal contingencies include a home inspection, a soil test, a roof inspection, and financing. If a problem arises with one of the contingencies, the broker associate should do everything possible to correct the problem, and all parties should be made aware of the situation. If more time is needed, the brokers should extend the deadlines for the contingencies, with agreement of the seller and buyer, using the amend/extend contract form.

Appraisal   The appraisal normally is ordered and paid for at the time of loan application. The broker associate wants to be certain that the appraiser selected by the financial institution has complete cooperation, particularly with respect to access to the property. Failure to provide access wastes the appraiser's time and may delay the closing.

Loan approval   The Contract to Buy and Sell requires a loan commitment within a certain number of days from the contract's effective date. The licensee must monitor the lender's progress and provide to the lender without delay any information or documents requested. The lender's failure to provide the commitment within the required time may put the buyer's earnest money in jeopardy.

Title insurance ordered   Typically, the listing broker will order the title insurance after having discussed which company to use with their seller. Once the offer has been accepted, the buyer's broker should deliver the contract, earnest money, and financing information immediately to the listing broker if they have not already done so. The listing broker should ask for a title request and closing sheet from the title company and then use the form to give the title company and closing entity all the necessary information requested. Typically, the following items will be requested when a title insurance order is placed:

- A signed and dated sales contract with all attachments
- A previous title insurance policy on the property, if available
- Enough information about the sellers, buyers, property, and lender to process and close the transaction, including the following:
  — The sellers' and buyers' full names, contact information and addresses if not specified in the contract
  — A complete legal description, for example, lot, block, subdivision name, phase or unit, recording information, and county
  — Street address including ZIP code
  — Terms of any legal documents the title company must prepare
    Remember: The title company acts as a "scrivener" to fill out these documents. The listing broker hires the title company to complete these documents using the closing instructions and earnest money receipt form. This MUST be completed by the title deadline.
  — Closing date and information about whether all parties will attend
  — Information on commission to broker and commission splits between brokers

Inspection ordered   The inspection should be ordered as soon as possible after contract acceptance. The inspection must be completed on or before the inspection objection deadline. If the buyer has any requests for repairs or if they wish to terminate the contract, the buyer's broker associate must give a completed and signed Inspection Notice form with the buyer's request to the listing broker associate before the inspection objection deadline. If the buyer has requested repairs, the buyer and seller will then have until the inspection resolution deadline to negotiate what will done and how. For example; the seller may choose to offer monetary compensation at closing in lieu of doing the actual work. The buyer and seller are also agreeing on the date that the repairs will be completed by, typically, a few days or the week before closing. The parties must resolve what is to happen with all the inspection issues by the resolution deadline, but if the buyer and seller cannot come to an agreement, the contract will terminate 24 hours after the resolution deadline and the buyer's earnest money will be returned, unless the buyer removes their request for repairs.

Required repairs   Ordered once the inspection notice has been completed and any requested repairs agreed to, the listing broker should work with the seller to make sure the repairs are completed by the walk-through date listed. If the repairs are not complete, the brokers will need to extend the contract using the amend/extend contract form.

A note of caution to licensees   A licensee sometimes orders major repair items without the seller's authorization to do so. A failed closing can have adverse financial consequences for the broker associate aside from the loss of commission. While a broker associate might facilitate some of the legwork required in getting estimates, the broker should not order the work without written approval. The seller or buyer, as appropriate, should contract for the work. This also makes the contractor responsible to the appropriate party if any warranty work is necessary later.

A sample form, the authorization for broker associate to order work, is on the next page.

FIGURE 11.4

Authorization for Broker Associate to Order Work and Customer's Agreement to Pay

Re: Property Address: _____

Responsible Person: _____ as ❏ Owner ❏ Buyer

Address: _____

Phone Number: _____

I hereby authorize _____ of _____ to order on my behalf the item specified below and agree to pay for said item upon demand as required by supplier regardless of the outcome of this property transaction. I understand that these arrangements are being made by the broker associate as a courtesy to me. I shall look to the supplier only for performance and workmanship and absolve broker associate and the brokerage firm for the performance and workmanship of the supplier.

Item to be ordered by broker associate:

_____

_____

Supplier: _____ Price Quoted: _____

Signature: _____ Date: _____

Supplier Agreement to Provide Service And
To Look Only To Responsible Party For Payment

Re: Property Address: _____

City: _____

Supplier: _____

Phone Number: _____

I agree to provide the item/service specified below and agree to seek compensation from "responsible party" shown above. I understand that these arrangements are being made by the broker associate in this transaction as a courtesy to me. I agree to look to the "responsible party" only for compensation and absolve broker associate and brokerage firm for the cost of the item/service.

Item to be ordered by broker associate:

_____

_____

Supplier: _____ Price Quoted: _____

Signature: _____ Date: _____

Required repairs completed and approved   When the work has been completed, the appropriate party should inspect the work on the date listed in the agreement to be sure that it has been done properly. A licensee who takes on this responsibility may be held responsible if deficiencies are discovered later.

Survey ordered   Prior to writing the offer the broker should verify whether the title company or lender will require a survey or ILC. If neither the title company nor the lender require one and the buyer does not want one, this expense can be removed by not ordering these items. If the lender or the title company does request a survey, the survey should be conducted after the loan commitment deadline date.

A licensee who orders the survey without written approval may be liable for the fee if the sale does not close. In case of survey problems such as encroachments, the broker associate must act quickly to help clear up the problems.

Buyer purchases hazard insurance   The buyer should purchase hazard insurance policy as soon as possible in the transaction and certainly must know by the property insurance objection deadline whether they are going to be able to obtain coverage on the property. In years with wildfires in the mountain areas of Colorado, some buyers have found that they cannot get insurance at an affordable rate and have had to terminate the contract.

Preclosing inspection   The buyer should make a **preclosing walk-through inspection** on the date detailed in the contract. The inspection is to ensure that

- the property is ready for occupancy;
- personal property the seller is required to leave remains on the property;
- all required repairs and maintenance have been completed; and
- the property has been maintained in the condition as it existed at the time of contract, ordinary wear and tear excepted.

The broker associate should not conduct such an inspection because of the liability involved. When the inspection has been completed to the buyer's satisfaction, the broker associate should ask the buyer to sign a preclosing walk-through inspection results form.

A copy of the preclosing walk-through inspection results form is on the next page.

FIGURE 11.5

Preclosing Walk-Through Inspection Results

Property Address: _____ Date of Inspection: _____

Seller: _____ Buyer: _____

I have made a walk-through inspection of the property. I acknowledge that the broker associate has accompanied me to the property to make it available, and not to conduct the inspection. I take complete responsibility for the inspection and agree to hold harmless the broker associate and the brokerage firm from any liability in connection with the inspection.

My inspection shows that:

1. Personal property items required by the contract to be left are present in the property ❏ Yes ❏ No

2. Required repairs, if any, have been completed ❏ Yes ❏ No

3. The property has been maintained in the condition as it existed at the time ❏ Yes ❏ No
   of the contract, reasonable wear and tear excepted

Comments _____

_____

I accept the property as inspected and release the sellers, broker associates, and brokers in this transaction of any further responsibility for the property. I have been notified of the benefits of having the property covered by a homeowner's warranty. If the seller has not provided such a warranty, I ❏ accept ❏ decline to purchase coverage at a cost of $ _____.

Buyer: _____ Date: _____

Buyer: _____ Date: _____

Closing papers reviewed with the buyer and seller one day before closing A broker associate should attempt to work with lenders and title-closing agents who understand the broker associate's need to provide the highest level of service to the customers. Those lenders and title agents work diligently to provide all documents for the closing one day in advance. The broker associate must monitor all phases of the closing, including a careful review of the closing statements. Many buyers and sellers attend their closings—at which large sums of money are disbursed—without having seen any of the documents beforehand. They are expected to sign all documents after a cursory review at the closing table. This is not fair to the participants and can lead to embarrassment for their broker associates. Often a broker associate gets little more than the dollar amount that the buyer must bring in the form of a **certified** or cashier's **check**. This is simply not satisfactory to the broker associate who wishes to handle the closing professionally.

Upon receiving the documents, the broker associate should arrange an appointment to visit the buyer or seller and deliver copies of all documents that the person will sign. The broker associate should review the closing statement carefully to ensure that all items are correct and should explain each item to the buyer or seller at the appointment. The broker associate working with the buyer should compare the closing statement with the lender's good-faith estimate. The broker associate working with the seller should compare the figures to those given to the seller on the approximate seller's net proceeds form. The closing will go more quickly and pleasantly for the person who has reviewed all documents the evening before.

Closing statements are covered later in this unit.

Buyer given figure for certified check for closing   This figure should be provided to the buyer as soon as possible to allow for time to get a certified check for the proper amount from his bank. The check should be made payable to the buyer. At closing it will be signed over to the closing company, but making the check out to the buyer will make it easier for the buyer to keep his money if for some reason the transaction fails to close.

Earnest money check prepared to take to closing   If the listing brokerage firm has the earnest money in their trust account, at least one day before closing the listing broker associate should arrange to get a good funds earnest money check from their employing broker and clip it to the file folder that will be taken to the closing. Good funds are required at closing. Any bank certified check is considered good funds. Personal checks are not considered good funds. Also included in the folder will be the contract and other related materials for this closing. If the earnest money was given to the title company and not deposited in the brokerage firm's trust account, the listing broker will not need to bring the money to closing since the title company already has it.

■ THE CLOSING STATEMENT

Buyers and sellers expect their broker associates to coordinate and monitor every step of the closing process. The last step is the closing itself. A broker associate must be familiar with the documents that will be presented to the parties at the closing table. One of the most important documents, the HUD-1 Settlement Statement, relates to the financial side of the transaction.

A closing statement is, in effect, the purchase and sales agreement reduced to numbers. The broker associate must understand each number in the statement and be able to explain it clearly to the buyer or seller. Understanding the settlement statement will make the process easier.

■ PRORATIONS AND PREPAYMENTS

In every closing, property income and expenses should be prorated between the buyer and the seller. In Colorado, the 365-day method is used for prorations of annual expenses. The annual cost is divided by 365 days to get a daily rate. That rate is then multiplied by the number of days involved to get the amount due. When calculating prorations using the 30-day month method (as on the national portion of the Colorado real estate licensing exam), the annual cost is divided by 360 days; that rate is then multiplied by the number of days involved to get the amount due.

Proration calculations should be based on the last day of seller ownership. The day of closing is charged to the buyer in Colorado (and to the seller for the national portion of the exam).

The most common items prorated on a closing statement are rents, property taxes, and interest on assumed mortgages. While insurance can be prorated between the parties, it is not recommended and usually is not allowed by the insurer. The buyer should purchase a new policy and the seller should cancel the existing policy. The full amount of the security deposits, which belong to the tenant, will be transferred from the seller to the buyer at closing.

Prorating Rent

If the property is an income property, the seller should pay the buyer any rent that applies for the period after closing. The first step is to see the problem graphically by drawing a timeline. The rental period is shown, as is the day of closing. The following example illustrates the various aspects of prorations and prepayments. In the example, if the seller had collected the rent in advance, the seller would owe the buyer 16 days of the rent.

Closing date—April 15

Rent collected for April—$450

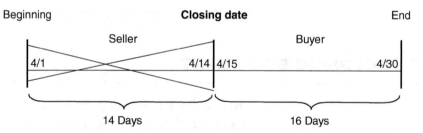

Since the rent was paid by the tenant for the month, the seller will owe the buyer for the 16 days the buyer is the new owner. Draw an X through the side that does not apply as a reminder of which side to work the proration.

Daily rate—$450 ÷ 30 days = $15

Proration—$15 × 16 days = $240

Debit the seller $240, credit the buyer $240.

■ **EXAMPLE 11.1** Calculate the following rent prorations:

Closing Date	Rent Received	Debit	Credit	Amount
July 12	$760			$
November 12	$900			$
January 6	$425			$

Prorating Property Taxes

In Colorado, property taxes are paid in arrears so they would be a debit to the seller and a credit to the buyer. If the seller has not paid the taxes for the previous year, the seller alone owes the entire amount due from the previous year (unpaid taxes from prior years are not prorated between buyer and seller—these are debts the seller owes and must pay). Typically, the tax amount from last year will be used to prorate the amount of this year's tax unless there has been a more recent mill levy and the Contract to Buy and Sell calls for the newer levy amount to be used.

Closing date—April 15

Property taxes—$2,275

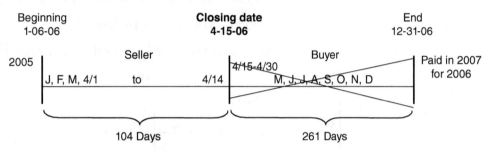

Since the taxes are paid in arrears and the seller owes the buyer, draw an X through the side that does not apply as a reminder of which side to work.

Number of days from January 1 through April 15:

January	31
February	28
March	31
April	14
Total	104

Daily rate—$2,275 ÷ 365 days = $6.23288 per day

Proration—$6.23288 × 104 days = $648.22

Debit the seller $648.22, credit the buyer $648.22.

■ **EXAMPLE 11.2** Calculate the following property tax prorations:

Closing Date	Taxes	Debit	Credit	Amount
September 12	$2,567.00			$
November 18	$4,260.00			$
April 24	$1,892.56			$

Prorating Interest

Interest is prorated between the parties when a loan is to be assumed. Interest is paid in arrears. For example, when the mortgage payment is made on May 1, it pays the principal due on May 1 and the interest for the month of April.

Closing date is April 15.

Mortgage balance on April 1 is $67,125.

The interest rate is 8 percent.

Interest for April is $447.50 ($67,125 × 0.08 ÷ 12 months).

Daily rate—$447.50 ÷ 30 days = $14.91667 per day.

Proration—$14.91667 × 14 days = $208.83.

Debit the seller $208.83, credit the buyer $208.83.

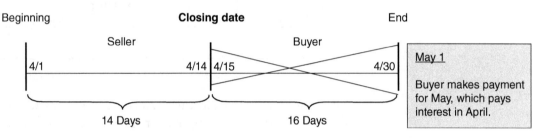

■ **EXAMPLE 11.3** Calculate the following interest prorations for these assumed mortgages:

Closing	Mortgage balance	Interest rate	Debit	Credit	Amount
October 12	$137,500.00	9.0%			$
November 18	$246,532.50	8.5%			$
April 24	$91,892.56	10.0%			$

■ RESPA SETTLEMENT STATEMENT (HUD-1)

The HUD-1 Settlement Statement provides an itemized listing of the funds payable at closing (see Figure 11.6). Closing agents must prepare the HUD-1 for the parties in a federally related mortgage loan. The HUD-1 is used in nearly all residential closings, whether or not the form is legally required. Each item in the statement is assigned a separate number within a standardized numbering system. The totals at the bottom of page 1 of the HUD-1 statement show the seller's net proceeds and the amount due from the buyer at closing.

The HUD-1 statement has two pages. Page 1 shows the parties, the property description, the lender, the settlement agent, and a summary of the borrower's and seller's transactions. Page 2 (Section L) itemizes the settlement charges for each party, such as the broker's commission, loan closing costs, prepaid items, escrow account setup, title charges, and recording charges. The totals for each party on page 2 are transferred to the summary on page 1. When explaining the statement to the buyer and seller, the closing agents start at page 2, then go to page 1. A discussion of the lines on the statement follows.

FIGURE 11.6

HUD-1 Settlement Statement

A. Settlement Statement

B. Type of Loan

U.S. Department of Housing
and Urban Development

OMB No. 2502-0265

1. ☐FHA	2. ☐FmHA	3. ☐Conv. Unins.	6. File Number	7. Loan Number	8. Mortgage Insurance Case Number
4. ☐VA	5. ☒Conv. Ins.		EDODONNELL8LBM	12345678	

C. Note: This form is furnished to give you a statement of actual settlement costs. Amounts paid to and by the settlement agent are shown. Items marked "(p.o.c.)" were paid outside the closing; they are shown here for information purposes and are not included in the totals. WARNING: It is a crime to knowingly make false statements to the United States on this or any other similar form. Penalties upon conviction can include a fine and imprisonment. For details see: Title 18 U. S. Code Section 1001 and Section 1010.

D. NAME OF BORROWER:	KYLE BYERS and KARI BYERS
ADDRESS:	1460 LIME DRIVE
E. NAME OF SELLER:	JOHN SELLARS and SUSAN SELLARS
ADDRESS:	
F. NAME OF LENDER:	FIRST SOUTH BANK, A FEDERAL SAVINGS BANK
ADDRESS:	3020 HARTLEY ROAD, SUITE 330
G. PROPERTY ADDRESS:	1460 LIME DRIVE,
	LOT 8, ORANGE PARK SUBDIVISION
H. SETTLEMENT AGENT:	ABC TITLE COMPANY
PLACE OF SETTLEMENT:	7889 Thomasville Rd
I. SETTLEMENT DATE:	05/15/05

J. SUMMARY OF BORROWER'S TRANSACTION:		K. SUMMARY OF SELLER'S TRANSACTION:	
100. GROSS AMOUNT DUE FROM BORROWER		**400. GROSS AMOUNT DUE TO SELLER:**	
101. Contract sales price	120,000.00	401. Contract sales price	120,000.00
102. Personal Property		402. Personal Property	
103. Settlement charges to borrower (line 1400)	7,039.76	403.	
104.		404.	
105.		405.	
Adjustments for items paid by seller in advance		*Adjustments for items paid by seller in advance*	
106. City/town taxes		406. City/town taxes	
107. County taxes 05/15/05 to 12/31/05	1,329.04	407. County taxes 05/15/05 to 12/31/05	1,329.04
108. Assessments		408. Assessments	
109.		409.	
110.		410.	
111.		411.	
112.		412.	
120. GROSS AMOUNT DUE FROM BORROWER	128,368.80	**420. GROSS AMOUNT DUE TO SELLER:**	121,329.04
200. AMOUNTS PAID BY OR ON BEHALF OF BORROWER		**500. REDUCTIONS IN AMOUNT DUE TO SELLER**	
201. Deposit or earnest money	4,000.00	501. Excess Deposit (see instructions)	
202. Principal Amount of new loans	108,000.00	502. Settlement charges to seller (line 1400)	9,515.50
203. Existing loan(s) taken subject to		503. Existing loan(s) taken subject to	
204.		504. Payoff of First Mortgage Loan	45,452.65
		BARNETT BANK	
205.		505. Payoff of Second Mortgage Loan	
206.		506.	
207.		507.	
208.		508.	
209.		509.	
Adjustments for items unpaid by seller		*Adjustments for items unpaid by seller*	
210. City/town taxes		510. City/town taxes	
211. County taxes		511. County taxes	
212. Assessments		512. Assessments	
213.		513.	
214.		514.	
215.		515.	
216.		516.	
217.		517.	
218.		518.	
219.		519.	
220. TOTAL PAID BY/FOR BORROWER	112,000.00	**520. TOTAL REDUCTION AMOUNT DUE SELLER**	54,768.15
300. CASH AT SETTLEMENT FROM OR TO BORROWER		**600. CASH AT SETTLEMENT TO OR FROM SELLER**	
301. Gross amount due from borrower (line 120)	128,368.80	601. Gross amount due to seller (line 420)	121,329.04
302. Less amounts paid by/for borrower (line 220)	112,000.00	602. Less reduction amount due seller (line 520)	54,768.15
303. **CASH FROM BORROWER**	16,368.80	603. **CASH TO SELLER**	66,560.89

F I G U R E 11.6

HUD-1 Settlement Statement (continued)

U.S. DEPARTMENT OF HOUSING AND URBAN DEVELOPMENT
SETTLEMENT STATEMENT

File Number: EDODONNELL8
PAGE 2

L. SETTLEMENT CHARGES				PAID FROM BORROWER'S FUNDS AT SETTLEMENT	PAID FROM SELLER'S FUNDS AT SETTLEMENT
700. TOTAL SALES/BROKER'S COMMISSION based on price $ 120,000.00 @ 7.000 = 8,400.00					
Division of commission (line 700) as follows:					
701. $ 8,400.00 to BIG BEND REALTY					
702. $ to					
703. Commission paid at Settlement					8,400.00
800. ITEMS PAYABLE IN CONNECTION WITH LOAN					
801. Loan Origination Fee 1.000 % FIRST SOUTH BANK				1,200.00	
802. Loan Discount 1.000 % FIRST SOUTH BANK				1,200.00	
803. Appraisal Fee to TALLAHASSEE APPRAISAL COMPANY (P.O.C.) 300.00 Buyer					
804. Credit Report to CREDCO				55.00	
805. Lender's Inspection Fee					
806. Mortgage Application Fee					
807. Assumption Fee					
808. AMORTIZATION SCHEDULE to FIRST SOUTH BANK				25.00	
809.					
810.					
811.					
900. ITEMS REQUIRED BY LENDER TO BE PAID IN ADVANCE					
901. Interest From 05/15/05 to 06/01/05 @$ 22.1917 /day 17 Days				377.26	
902. Mortgage Insurance Premium for to					
903. Hazard Insurance Premium for 12 to STATE FARM				840.00	
904.					
905.					
1000. RESERVES DEPOSITED WITH LENDER FOR					
1001. Hazard Insurance 2 mo. @ $ 70.00 /mo				140.00	
1002. Mortgage Insurance 2 mo. @ $ 45.00 /mo				90.00	
1003. City Property Taxes mo. @ $ /mo					
1004. County Property Taxes 8 mo. @ $ 175.00 /mo				1,400.00	
1005. Annual Assessments mo. @ $ /mo					
1009. Aggregate Analysis Adjustment					
1100. TITLE CHARGES					
1101. Settlement or closing fee to ABC TITLE COMPANY				100.00	
1102. Abstract or title search to ABC TITLE COMPANY				100.00	
1103. Title examination to ABC TITLE COMPANY				75.00	
1104. Title insurance binder					
1105. Document Preparation					
1106. Notary Fees					
1107. Attorney's fees					
(includes above items No:)					
1108. Title Insurance to SMITH, JONES AND ADAMS, P.A.				700.00	
(includes above items No:)					
1109. Lender's Coverage $ 108,000.00 - 25.00					
1110. Owner's Coverage $ 120,000.00 - 675.00					
1111.					
1112. ALTA 8.1 to SMITH, JONES AND ADAMS, P.A.				25.00	
1113. COURIER FEE to SMITH, JONES AND ADAMS, P.A.				20.00	20.00
1200. GOVERNMENT RECORDING AND TRANSFER CHARGES					
1201. Recording Fees Deed $ 10.50 ; Mortgage $ 42.00 ; Release $ 10.50				52.50	10.50
1202. City/County tax/stamps Deed $ 840.00 ; Mortgage $ 378.00				378.00	840.00
1203. State Tax/stamps Doc Fees Deed $ 12.00 ; Mortgage $				12.00	
1204.					
1205.					
1300. ADDITIONAL SETTLEMENT CHARGES					
1301. Survey to ALL CORNERS SURVEYOR				250.00	
1302. Pest Inspection to NO REQUIRED PER CONTRACT AND LENDER					
1303. MISC REPAIRS to FIX IT ALL, INC.					245.00
1304.					
1305.					
1306.					
1307.					
1308.					
1400. TOTAL SETTLEMENT CHARGES (enter on lines 103, Section J and 502, Section K)				7,039.76	9,515.50

Page 2

700. **Sales/broker's commission**

This section shows the total dollar amount of sales commission, usually paid by the seller. If more than one broker is involved, the split is shown on the next lines.

701–702. **Division of commission**

Cooperating brokers normally split commissions. The total charge is listed on line 703.

703. **Commission paid at settlement**

This is the total commission to be paid; it is charged to the buyer, the seller, or both.

800. **Items payable in connection with loan**

In this section, the fees the lender charges to process, approve, and make the mortgage loan are itemized.

801. **Loan origination**

The lender charges this fee for processing. It is often expressed as a percentage of the loan and varies among lenders and from locality to locality. Generally, the borrower pays the loan origination fee, but the contract will determine who has agreed to pay this fee.

802. **Loan discount**

The loan discount is a one-time charge used to adjust the yield on the loan to what market conditions demand. It usually is expressed as points. Each point equals 1 percent of the mortgage amount. For example, if a lender charges 2 points on a $100,000 loan, this amounts to a fee of $2,000. On a 30-year loan, this fee increases the lender's yield by approximately one-fourth of 1 percent.

803. **Appraisal fee**

This fee is paid to a state-certified appraiser who prepares an estimate of value of the property that will be mortgaged. The borrower usually pays the appraisal fee, but either party may pay it as agreed in the sales contract. May be shown as P.O.C. (paid outside of closing).

804. **Credit report fee**

This fee covers the cost of the credit report, which shows the lender the borrower's attitude and willingness to pay debt on time. Often P.O.C.

805. **Lender's inspection fee**

This charge covers inspections, often of newly constructed housing, made by personnel of the lending institution or an outside inspector.

806. **Mortgage insurance application fee**

This fee covers processing of the application for **private mortgage insurance**, which may be required on certain loans.

807. **Assumption fee**

The assumption fee is charged for processing when the buyer takes over the seller's mortgage obligations.

900.   **Items required by lender to be paid in advance**

This section lists prepaid items such as interest, mortgage insurance premium, and hazard insurance premium at the time of settlement.

901.   **Interest**

Lenders usually require that borrowers pay at settlement the interest on the mortgage from the date of closing to the beginning of the period covered by the first monthly payment. For example, if a closing takes place on August 12 and the first regular monthly payment is due October 1, the lender collects enough for interest from August 12 through August 31. September's interest is included in the October 1 payment.

902.   **Mortgage insurance premium (MIP)**

Mortgage insurance protects the lender from loss if the borrower defaults. The premium may cover a specific number of months, a year in advance, or the total amount. This type of insurance should not be confused with mortgage life, credit life, or disability insurance designed to pay off a mortgage in case of the borrower's disability or death.

903.   **Hazard insurance premium**

This prepayment is for insurance protection against loss due to fire, windstorm, or natural hazards. Lenders usually require payment of the first year's premium at closing.

904.   **Flood insurance premium**

If the property is located within a flood hazard area identified by Federal Emergency Management Agency (FEMA), the borrower may be required to carry flood insurance. The first year's premium must be paid in advance.

1000.   **Reserves deposited with lenders**

Lenders normally require *reserves* if the loan-to-value ratio is more than 80 percent. Reserves are escrow accounts the lender holds to ensure future payment for recurring costs such as real estate taxes, mortgage insurance, and hazard insurance. An initial amount for each of these items is collected to start the reserve account. Then part of each monthly payment is added to the reserve account.

1001.   **Hazard insurance**

The lender determines how much money must be placed in the reserve to pay the next insurance premium when due. Normally, two months' premiums are collected.

1002.   **Mortgage insurance**

The lender may require that part of the total annual premium be placed in the reserve account at settlement. Normally, two months' premiums are collected.

1003–1004.   **City/county property taxes**

The lender may require a regular monthly payment to the reserve account for property taxes. The lender pays the taxes either in two payments (February and June) or in full in April so a full year's taxes should be available by then. The lender collects an amount each month equal to one-twelfth of the estimated taxes.

1005. Annual assessments

This reserve item covers assessments that may be imposed by subdivisions or municipalities for special improvements (such as sidewalks, sewers, or paving) or fees (such as homeowners' association fees).

1009. Aggregate analysis adjustment

This adjustment ensures that the lender has set up enough, but not too much, in reserves.

1100. Title charges

Title charges may cover a variety of services the closing agent performs.

1101. Settlement or closing fee

Most often this fee is split equally between the buyer and seller at closing; however, it is negotiable and must be specified in the contract.

1102–1104. Abstract of title search, title examination, title insurance binder

These charges cover the costs of the search and examination of the public records to learn whether the seller can convey clear title to the property.

1105. Document preparation

This document fee covers preparation of final legal papers, such as a mortgage, deed of trust, note, deed, or bill of sale.

1106. Notary fee

If the notary charges for affixing a name and seal to various documents authenticating the parties' execution of these documents, the fee is shown here. Typically the person whose signature is being notarized will pay the notary fee for that document. Therefore, while the closing company will record the warranty deed for the buyer, it is the seller who will pay the notary fee as they are the only one required to sign the deed.

1107. Attorney's fees

The buyer and seller are advised to retain attorneys to check the various documents and to represent them at all stages of the transaction, including closing. If this service is not required and is paid for outside closing, the person conducting settlement is not obligated to record the fee on the settlement form.

1108. Title insurance

The total cost of the owner's and lender's title insurance is shown here. Usually in Colorado the seller will pay for the buyer's (new owner's) policy and the buyer will pay for the mortgagee's (lender's) policy.

1109. Lender's title insurance

A one-time premium may be charged at closing for a lender's title policy that protects the lender against loss due to problems or defects concerning the title. The insurance usually is written for the amount of the mortgage loan and covers losses due to defects or problems not identified by title search and examination. This is typically a debit to the buyer.

1110. Owner's title insurance

This charge protects the new owner (the buyer) against losses due to title defects and is usually a debit to the seller.

1113.   **Endorsements**

These are additional coverages added to the mortgagee's policy to protect the lender against issues such as encroachments or parties in possession that a title search alone would not reveal.

1200.   **Government recording and transfer charges**

The buyer will pay the documentary fee ($0.01 per $100 of sales price) and the recording fees for the new deed and deed of trust (line 1201–1203). Seller will pay for the reconveyance deed releasing their deed of trust.

1300.   **Additional settlement charges**

1301.   **Survey**

Usually, the borrower pays the surveyor's fee, but sometimes the seller pays it, if agreed to in the contract.

1302.   **Pest and other inspections**

Pest inspections are not typical in Colorado. The buyer usually pays for their own property inspection at the time it is conducted. The charge would be shown here if the buyer did not pay for the inspection at the time it was done or if the seller agreed to pay for it at closing.

1400.   **Total settlement charges**

All the fees in the borrower's column entitled Paid from Borrower's Funds at Settlement are totaled here and transferred to line 103 of Section J, settlement charges to borrower, in the summary of borrower's transaction on page 1 of the HUD-1 settlement statement. All the settlement fees the seller pays are transferred to line 502 of Section K, summary of seller's transaction, on page 1 of the HUD-1.

Page 1

Section J summarizes the borrower's transaction.

100.   **Gross amount due from borrower**

101.   **Contract sales price**

This ultimate closing cost is taken directly from the sales contract.

102.   **Personal property**

The total price of items of personal property being sold to the buyer is entered on this line.

103.   **Settlement charges to borrower**

This total closing cost is carried forward from page 2.

107.   **County taxes**

This line is used only if the seller paid the annual taxes before closing.

108.   **Assessments**

This line is used if a seller prepaid a county or homeowners' association assessment.

120.   **Gross amounts due from borrower**

This is a subtotal of the above items.

200.   **Amounts paid by or in behalf of borrower**

201.   **Deposit or earnest money**
The buyer gets a credit for the earnest money deposit given at the time the contract was signed.

202.   **Principal amount of new loan**
The buyer is credited with the loan amount, which the lender gives to the closing agent.

203.   **Existing loan(s) taken subject to**
If the buyer assumes or buys subject to a mortgage, the current principal balance is entered on this line.

211.   **County taxes**
The amount due from the borrower is reduced by the amount of the seller's share of annual ad valorem taxes.

212.   **Assessments**
This line is used for amounts due to the buyer for assessments the seller has not paid.

220.   **Total paid by/for borrower**
This is the subtotal of lines 200 through 218.

300.   **Cash at settlement to/from borrower**
This section summarizes the transaction.

301.   **Gross amount due from borrower (line 120)**

302.   **Less amounts paid by/for borrower (line 220)**

303.   **Cash ❑ from ❑ to borrower**
This is the grand total of the borrower's transaction.

Section K summarizes the seller's transaction. Lines 400 through 420 are the seller's credits, which increase the amount due to the seller; lines 500 through 520 reduce the amount due to the seller; and lines 600 through 602 show the check due to the seller at closing.

400.   **Gross amount due to seller**

401.   **Contract sales price**
The sum is taken directly from the sales contract.

402.   **Personal property**
The total price of items of personal property being sold to the buyer is entered on this line.

407.   **County taxes**
This line is used only in the case in which the seller has paid the annual taxes before closing.

408.   **Assessments**
This line is used if a seller has prepaid a county or homeowners' association assessment.

420.   **Gross amount due to seller**
This is a subtotal of the above items.

500.   **Reductions in amount due to seller**

501.   **Excess deposit**
If the buyer pays the earnest money deposit directly to the seller, not to the broker or title-closing agent, it is shown on this line.

502.   **Settlement charges to seller**
This is the seller's total closing costs carried forward from page 2.

503.   **Existing loan(s) taken subject to**
If the buyer assumes or buys subject to a mortgage, the current principal balance is entered on this line.

504–505.   **Payoff of mortgage loan**
This is the balance due on the seller's deed of trust that the closing agent must pay off.

511.   **County taxes**
The amount due from the borrower is reduced by the amount of the seller's share of annual ad valorem taxes.

512.   **Assessments**
This line is used for amounts due to the buyer for assessments the seller has not paid.

520.   **Total reductions in amount due seller**
This is the subtotal of lines 500 through 519.

600.   **Cash at settlement to/ from seller**
This section summarizes the transaction.

601.   **Gross amount due to seller (Line 420)**

602.   **Less reductions in amount due seller (Line 520)**

603.   **Cash ❑ to ❑ from seller**
This is the grand total of the seller's transaction.

■ AT THE CLOSING TABLE

The closing normally includes the buyers, the sellers, and their respective licensees, if any. Sometimes attorneys of the parties attend, and occasionally a lender's representative. The title company closer conducts the closing, starting with closing the real estate side where the deed is transferred. The closer typically goes over the seller's closing statement with them first. The closing statement and all the seller's documents are signed by the seller and, when required, by the listing broker. The closer will close the buyer's side next. This entails not only the real estate documents but often also the loan documents. The buyer and, when required, the buyer's broker will sign all the documents. Once the paperwork is completed the closer will then deliver or collect checks from the appropriate parties.

Closing Disputes

The title closer is not an advocate for any of the parties. It is the title closer's job to close the transaction based on the contract and the lender's closing instructions. The designated broker for each party should be at the closing and be prepared to solve any problems that might arise. Each broker is responsible for their party's closing statement being correct. If there is a problem between the buyer and the lender, the broker gets them together on the phone. If there is a dispute between the buyer and the seller, the brokers should work to help the parties settle the dispute.

The General Warranty Deed

The general warranty deed is the most common deed for residential property, with the seller guaranteeing to the buyer a good title, without material defects or encumbrances, and will stand by the guarantee forever. Special attention should be given to the names and legal description and to any items in the subject to section, such as restrictive covenants and unsatisfied mortgages.

Truth-in-Lending Disclosure

If there is an institutional loan, the first document to be reviewed must be the truth-in-lending (TIL) disclosure. If the buyers were informed by the lender or the licensee when they applied for the loan that the annual percentage rate (APR) shown on the TIL would be higher than the interest rate on their note, this will not be a problem.

If they were not informed, however, some buyers, upon seeing a 7.875 percent APR on the disclosure form, would say, "Wait a minute! I was supposed to be getting a 7.5 percent loan!" The closer must explain that origination fees and discount points are included to calculate the APR, but the loan rate remains the same.

Loan Application

Usually, the lender will want a typed loan application signed at closing, verifying the information given to the lender at the time of application.

Note

The closer presents the note for the buyer's signature. The note shows the principal balance, number of payments, and the dates and the amount of the payments. The amount will be for principal and interest only. The first payment date will normally be the first day of the second month after closing. The note is not witnessed or notarized. If a signature appears on the face of the note along with the borrower's signature, that person becomes a cosigner on the note.

Deed of Trust

The deed of trust is the security for the note. It is the document that may require that the borrower pay one-twelfth of the ad valorem taxes and the hazard insurance and mortgage insurance premiums, along with the principal and interest. It requires that payments be made on time, that taxes be paid, and that the property be covered by insurance and describes prepayment options. It also probably states that a sale or alienation of the property will make the loan due immediately.

Other Documents

Some of the other documents the buyer may sign include an anti-coercion statement that says the lender did not require that the buyer choose a certain insurance company. The lender and title insurance company will want a compliance agreement that the parties will do anything necessary to give the lender an acceptable loan package, such as signing new documents, if required. If the loan is above 80 percent of a home's value, the lender will want an affidavit that the buyer will occupy the property. The seller will be required to sign an affidavit that the seller (1) owns the property, (2) has the right to convey it, and (3) it is not encumbered by any lien or right to a lien, such as a construction lien. If there is a new loan the buyer may be asked to waive homestead rights so the deed of trust lien can be in first position.

Disbursements at Closing

Everyone expects to be paid at closing. This is not always possible and licensees should be prepared to explain the problem to the sellers. Perhaps an example using a broker's trust account is easier to understand. Many real estate brokers have hundreds of thousands of dollars in their escrow accounts. A broker, who disburses from the escrow account before making a deposit into the account, even if the future deposit would be in certified funds, is guilty of a serious violation, because the broker would be using funds that belong to others.

Title insurance companies are faced with a similar problem. Some title insurance companies agree to disburse the proceeds at closing if the certified checks will be deposited by the close of business that day. (A real estate broker may never do this.) Many title insurance companies will not disburse if the closing takes place too late to make a same-day deposit or if the lender is holding the loan proceeds check until the loan package is delivered.

Signed Closing Papers Received by Sales Associate

The broker associate should be careful that the office file is fully documented. This includes any walk-through clearance papers the buyer signs for the seller and the closing statements all parties must sign. If disbursement is made at closing, the commission check also is received at this time. Typically, the broker associate will have a closing control sheet given to them by their office. The broker associate should go through their file prior to the closing and note any documents they will need to obtain at closing on the control sheet. It is very difficult to get required signatures from the buyer and seller after closing so the licensee must be sure they have all their required documents properly signed before leaving the closing.

Post Closing Duties

Commission check to broker   Upon returning to the office, the broker associate should give the closing file and the commission check to the broker.

Sign and lockbox picked up from property   The listing broker associate should ensure that the sign and lockbox are removed from the property and returned to the office. Often the associate does this just before closing. Many broker associates remove the lockbox for security reasons immediately after the contract has been signed.

Letter of thanks to buyer or seller and their broker   The letter, which should include both the broker associate's and the employing broker's signatures, will be appreciated by the customer, will foster goodwill, and likely will result in future business. Many companies request that the buyer or seller complete a questionnaire about the level of service provided in the transaction. A thank-you note to the other broker will also foster good will and help establish future networking opportunities.

Follow-up visit to buyer or seller   The broker associate who calls on the customer after the closing demonstrates the careful attention needed to ensure that all details of the transaction have been completed satisfactorily.

Notice of closed sale to MLS   Most MLS systems require that listing status changes be submitted as soon as possible. This provides brokers and broker associates in the area with the most current information about listing availability and comparable sales information.

■ SUMMARY

The broker associate's job really is just beginning when the parties sign the contract. Much work must be completed to ensure a successful closing. One of the first steps is to plan for each required task and enter it on a time line. Each broker associate and broker involved should agree about who must do what, and when it must be done.

Licensees must complete tasks like attaching a contract pending sign, notifying the MLS, making the binder deposit, helping the buyer with the loan application, and taking care of inspections and repairs. A major part of the broker associate's duties is reviewing the closing documents with the buyer or seller before closing.

■ KEY TERMS

certified check
documentary fee
mortgage insurance
   premium (MIP)

preclosing walk-through
   inspection

private mortgage insurance

■ APPLY WHAT YOU'VE LEARNED

The following actions reinforce the material in Course 3, Units 9 though 11.

■ Select a three-bedroom home that is currently for sale that you would like to own. Calculate the PITI payment, assuming you pay the listed price and make a 10 percent down payment. Use current interest rates.

■ Based on the previous action, divide the PITI payment by the mortgage amount. This will give you the mortgage payment factor including taxes, insurance, and PMI. It will probably be just under 1 percent.

■ Using the factor calculated above, quickly figure the payment for a $165,000 mortgage (1% × $165,000 = $1,650, quote just under that and estimate $1,634). Now quickly estimate the PITI payments for the following mortgage amounts:

Loan Amount	Payment (PITI)
$189,000	$_____
$238,000	$_____
$298,500	$_____
$212,000	$_____

■ Ask a title-closing officer to show you the entire closing process (usually the end of the month is a bad time for this). Ask to watch a title search to see what the title company looks for. Examine the closing officer's checklist for closings. See what an instruction package from the lender looks like. Watch as the closing officer enters information into the computer for the HUD-1 settlement statement.

■ With your employing broker's approval, randomly select five file folders for closed transactions. Thoroughly review each file and list every document in the file. Do some files seem more complete to you? Are there any that you believe are *not* complete? Check these against the firms required list. Note what documents you want in all your closed files.

■ Start again at the first file folder. Inspect the contract, the good-faith buyer's estimate of settlement costs, payment amounts, and the HUD-1 form. Check to see whether the amount the sales associate estimated for the seller or buyer matched the actual amount on the HUD-1 form. Can you account for any material differences?

■ Next, check every entry on the HUD-1 form for accuracy.

■ If you have not yet had a closing, arrange with a broker associate to attend another closing. Remember, you should listen, not talk, at the closing.

UNIT 12

Practical Applications
Lecture Slides

Instructions:

■ Refer to the following lecture slides to follow along in class or with the online lecture.

Practical Applications

© 2013 Kaplan, Inc.

Tools to help you get a fast start in real estate

- Kaplan Professional Schools offers a Career Starter Pack—three useful books for $59 ($71 if purchased individually) *www.kpscolorado.com*
  - *Up and Running in 30 Days: A Proven Plan for Financial Success in Real Estate*
  - *21 Things I Wish My Broker Had Told Me*
  - *The Language of Real Estate*

© 2013 Kaplan, Inc.

Tools to help you get a fast start in real estate

- Kaplan Connection – *www.kaplanconnection.com*
  - Set up your profile preferences
  - Brokers looking to hire will contact you
  - It's free

© 2013 Kaplan, Inc.

KAPLAN REAL ESTATE EDUCATION

Course overview

- Competency
- Independent contractor versus employee
- Choosing a brokerage firm
- Getting started in your new career

© 2013 Kaplan, Inc.

KAPLAN REAL ESTATE EDUCATION

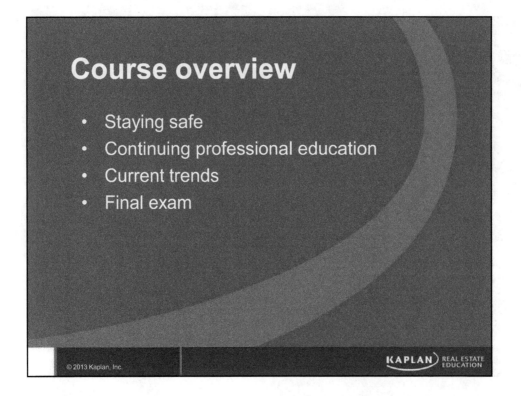

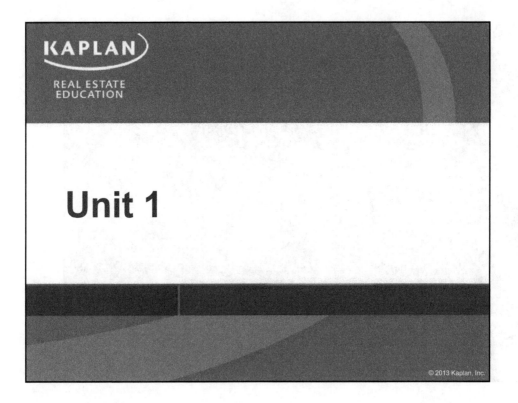

I. COMPETENCY

© 2013 Kaplan, Inc.

A. Competency levels

1. Are you experienced, trained, and qualified to do what you've been asked to do?

© 2013 Kaplan, Inc.

KAPLAN REAL ESTATE EDUCATION

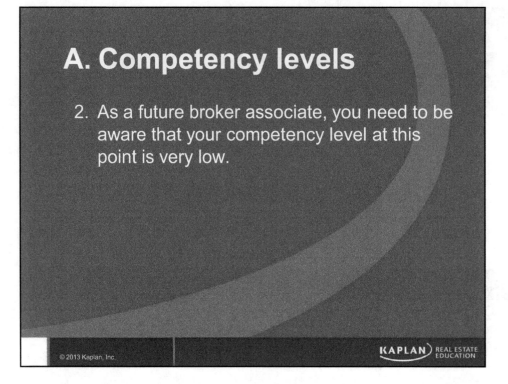

A. Competency levels

2. As a future broker associate, you need to be aware that your competency level at this point is very low.

© 2013 Kaplan, Inc.

KAPLAN REAL ESTATE EDUCATION

A. Competency levels

3. Specialties and competency requirements
   a) Commercial real estate is highly specialized and requires additional training.
   b) Property management can involve commercial and residential properties.

© 2013 Kaplan, Inc.

KAPLAN REAL ESTATE EDUCATION

A. Competency levels

c) Property management frequently requires an employing broker's license.

d) Farm and ranch can involve water rights and/or mineral rights.

© 2013 Kaplan, Inc.

KAPLAN REAL ESTATE EDUCATION

A. Competency levels

4. Because there are no standards for competency, it is the broker's responsibility to determine your areas of competence.

   a) Commission position 41 can be a guide.

© 2013 Kaplan, Inc.

KAPLAN REAL ESTATE EDUCATION

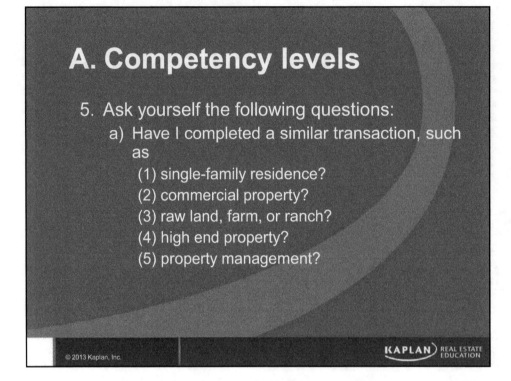

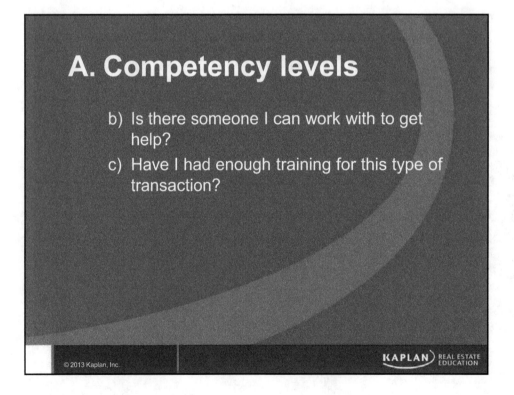

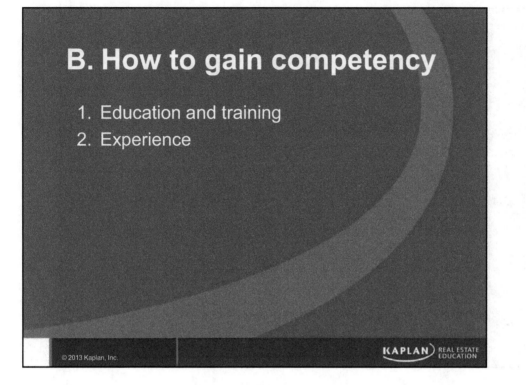

A. Types of property management
1. Residential property management
a) Single-family homes
b) Multifamily homes
c) Apartment complexes
© 2013 Kaplan, Inc.
KAPLAN REAL ESTATE EDUCATION

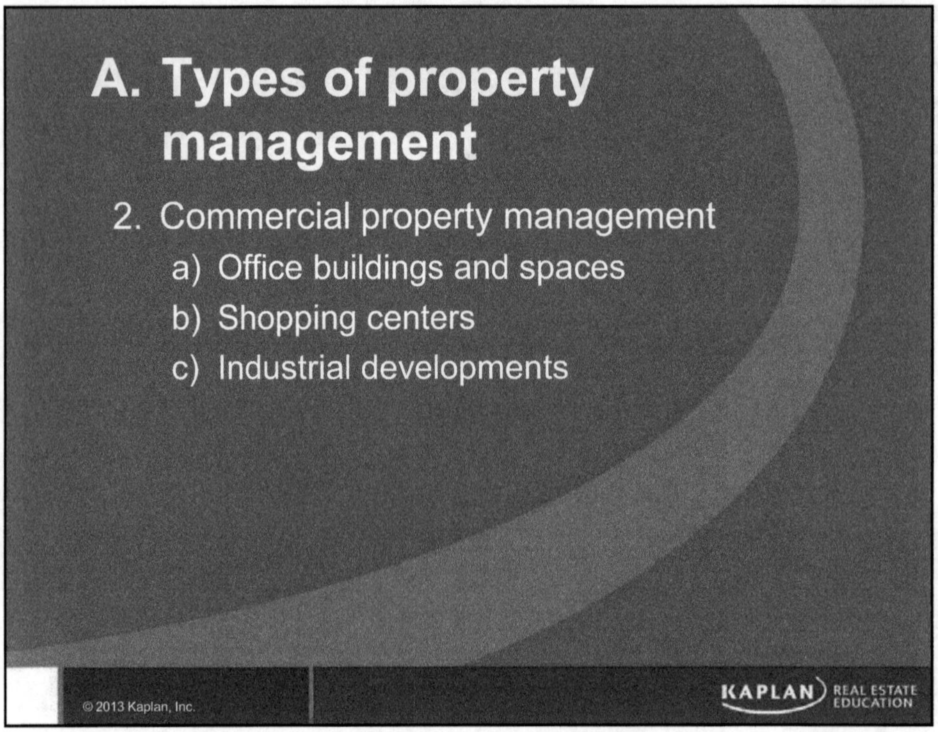
A. Types of property management
2. Commercial property management
a) Office buildings and spaces
b) Shopping centers
c) Industrial developments
© 2013 Kaplan, Inc.
KAPLAN REAL ESTATE EDUCATION

B. Leasing versus property management

1. First, it is necessary to determine the difference between leasing and property management.

© 2013 Kaplan, Inc.

KAPLAN REAL ESTATE EDUCATION

B. Leasing versus property management

2. Leasing is a one-time activity in which a licensee (broker associate) works with a seller/owner to find a tenant for the property.

   a) The licensee would check box 3.5.2 in the Exclusive Right-to-Sell Listing Contract or could use the Exclusive Right-to-Lease Listing Contract.

© 2013 Kaplan, Inc.

KAPLAN REAL ESTATE EDUCATION

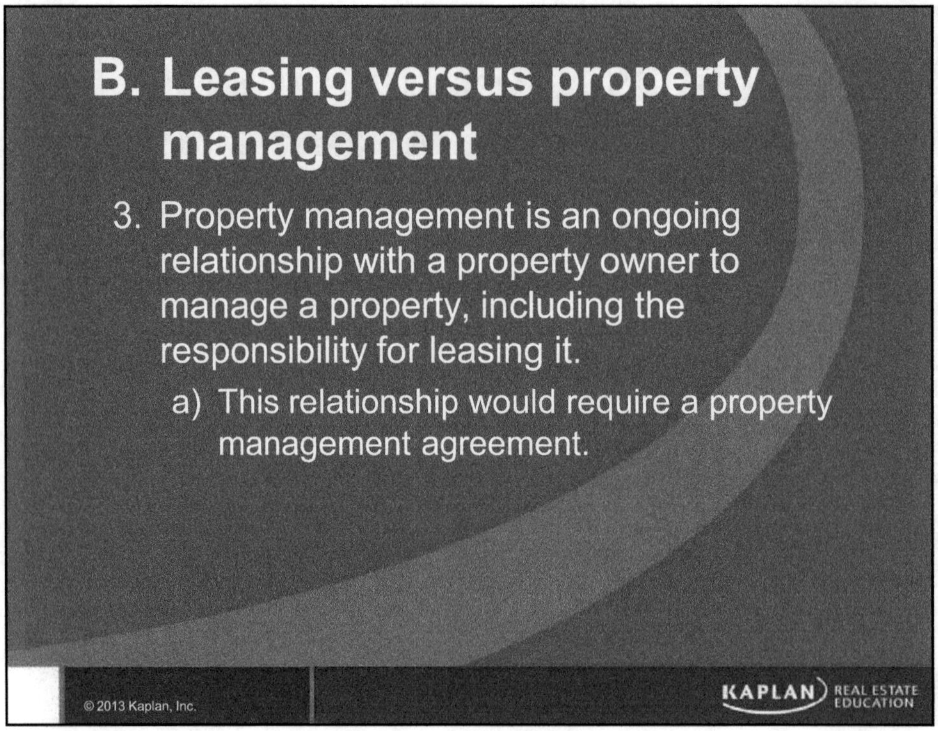

B. Leasing versus property management

3. Property management is an ongoing relationship with a property owner to manage a property, including the responsibility for leasing it.
   a) This relationship would require a property management agreement.

© 2013 Kaplan, Inc.

KAPLAN REAL ESTATE EDUCATION

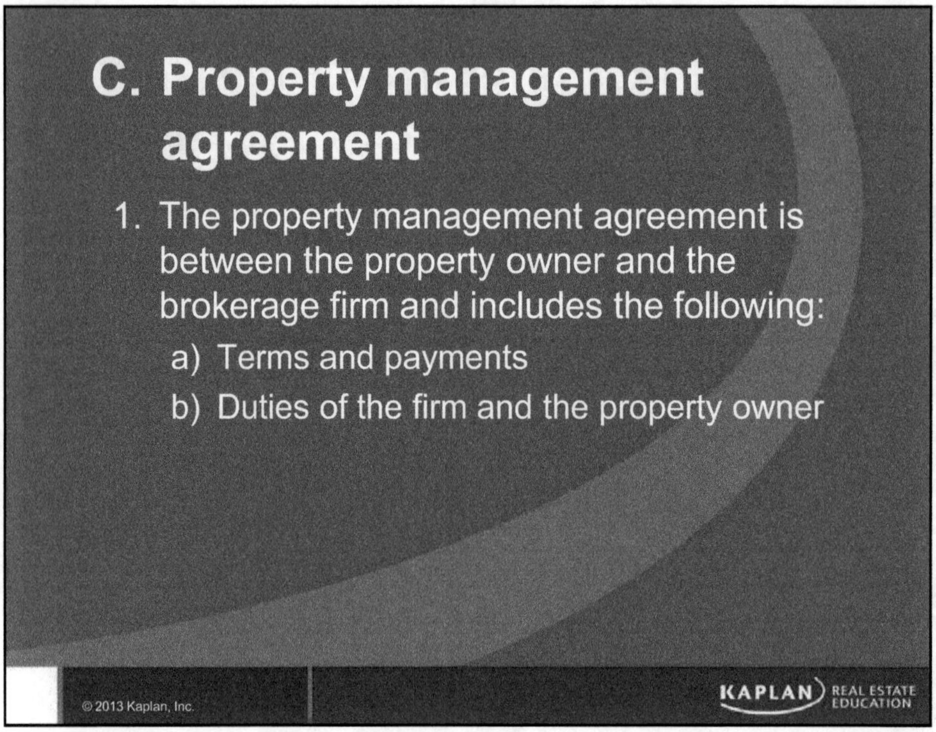

C. Property management agreement

1. The property management agreement is between the property owner and the brokerage firm and includes the following:
   a) Terms and payments
   b) Duties of the firm and the property owner

© 2013 Kaplan, Inc.

KAPLAN REAL ESTATE EDUCATION

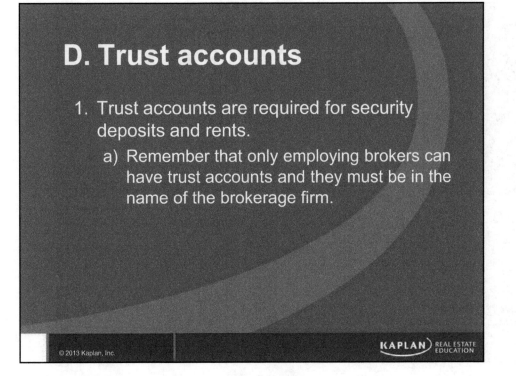

D. Trust accounts

1. Trust accounts are required for security deposits and rents.

   a) Remember that only employing brokers can have trust accounts and they must be in the name of the brokerage firm.

© 2013 Kaplan, Inc.

KAPLAN REAL ESTATE EDUCATION

E. Broker associates

1. According to the DORA 2012 Commission Update, "Broker associates may not manage any property without the knowledge, consent, and supervision of their employing broker."

© 2013 Kaplan, Inc.

KAPLAN REAL ESTATE EDUCATION

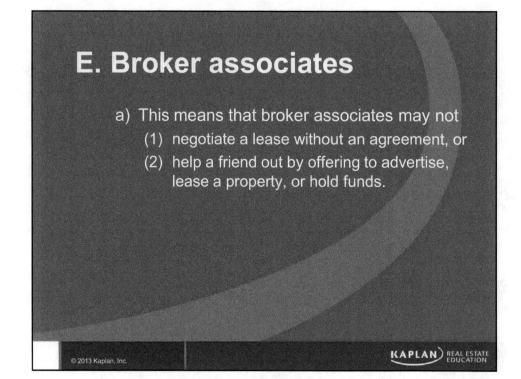

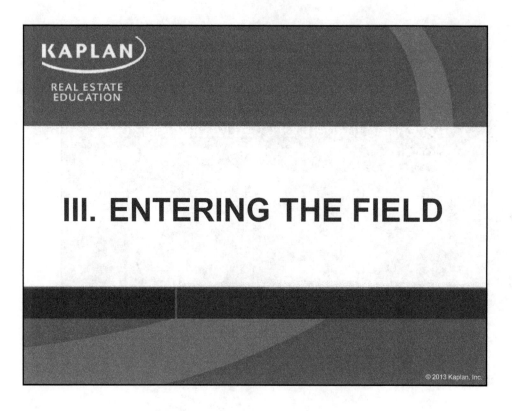

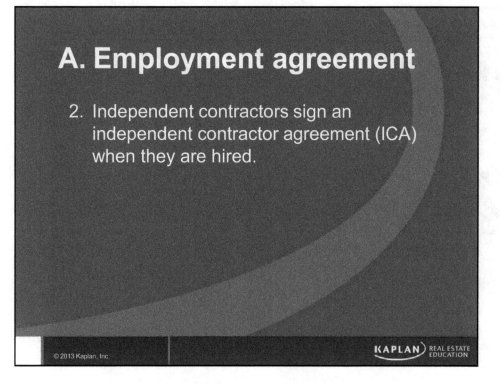

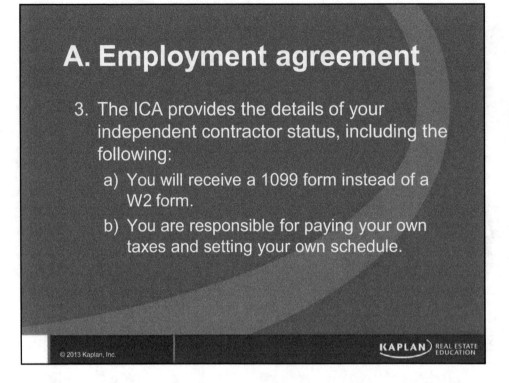

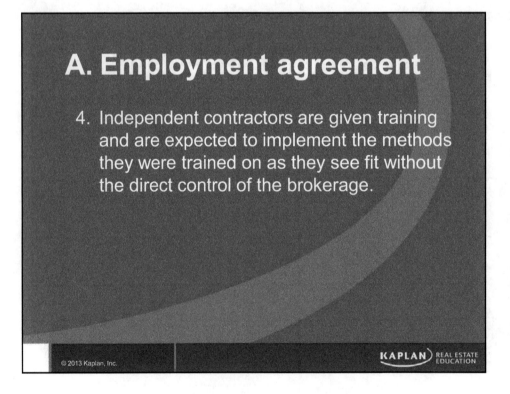

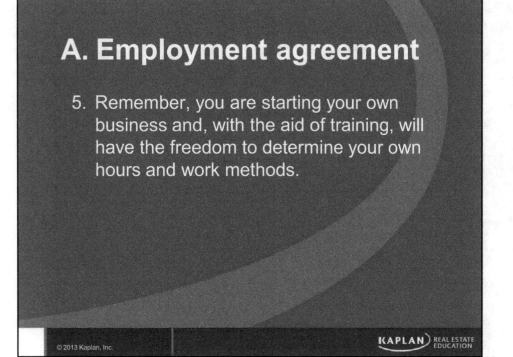

A. Employment agreement

5. Remember, you are starting your own business and, with the aid of training, will have the freedom to determine your own hours and work methods.

© 2013 Kaplan, Inc.

KAPLAN) REAL ESTATE EDUCATION

B. Choosing a brokerage

1. Top three issues when choosing a broker
   a) Training
   b) Relationship with the employing broker, manager, or mentor
   c) Convenient location

© 2013 Kaplan, Inc.

KAPLAN) REAL ESTATE EDUCATION

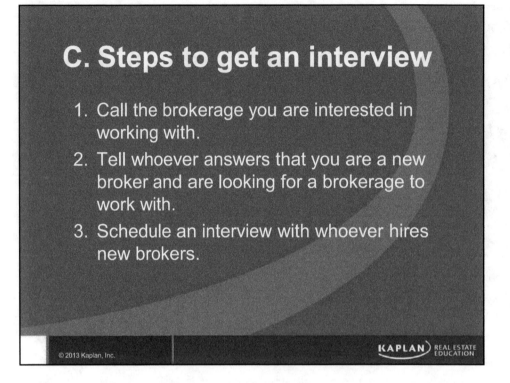

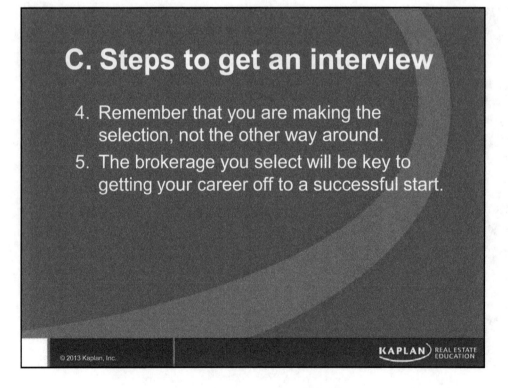

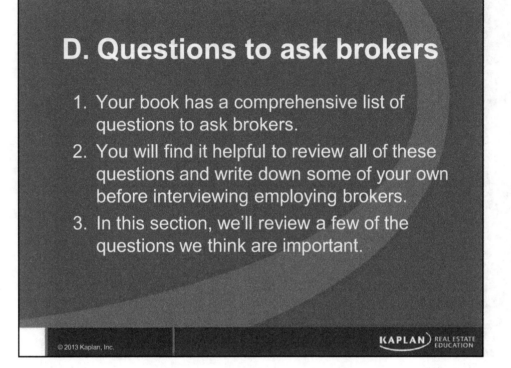

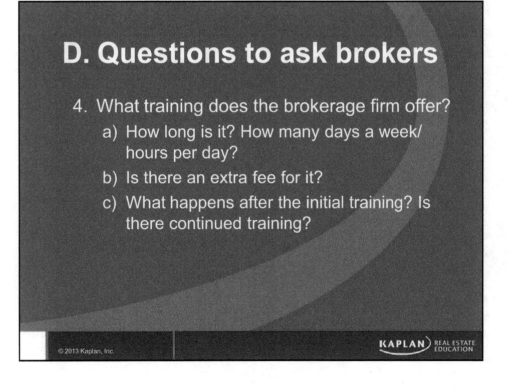

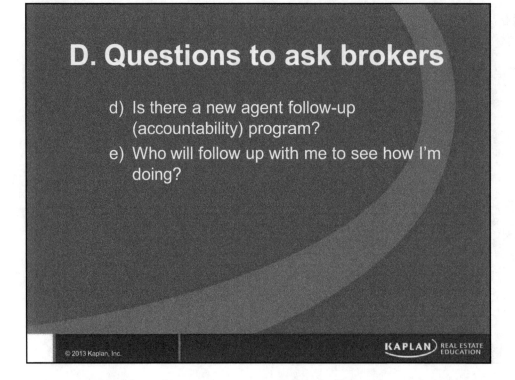

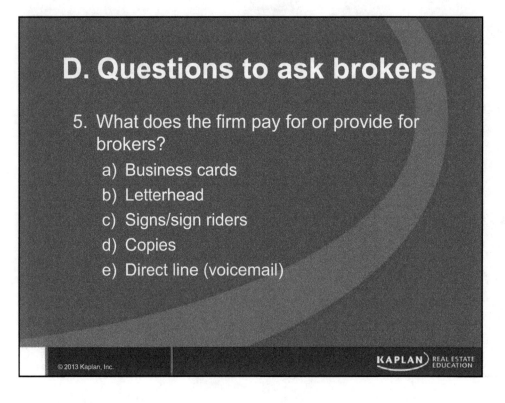

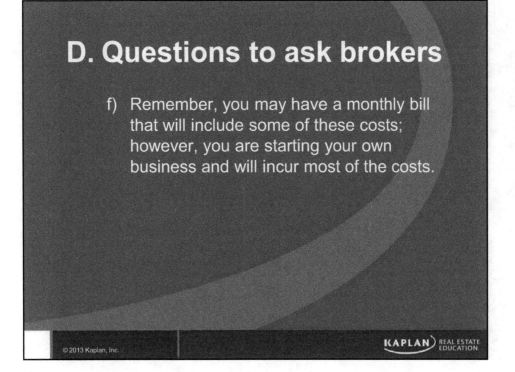

D. Questions to ask brokers

f) Remember, you may have a monthly bill that will include some of these costs; however, you are starting your own business and will incur most of the costs.

© 2013 Kaplan, Inc.

KAPLAN REAL ESTATE EDUCATION

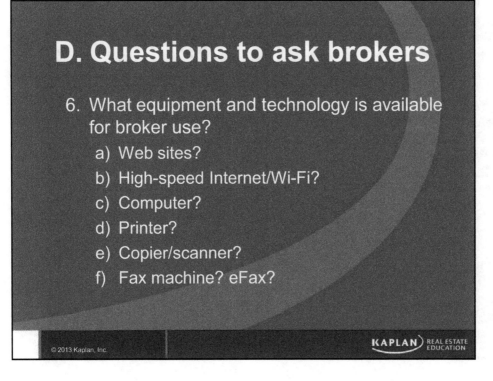

D. Questions to ask brokers

6. What equipment and technology is available for broker use?
   a) Web sites?
   b) High-speed Internet/Wi-Fi?
   c) Computer?
   d) Printer?
   e) Copier/scanner?
   f) Fax machine? eFax?

© 2013 Kaplan, Inc.

KAPLAN REAL ESTATE EDUCATION

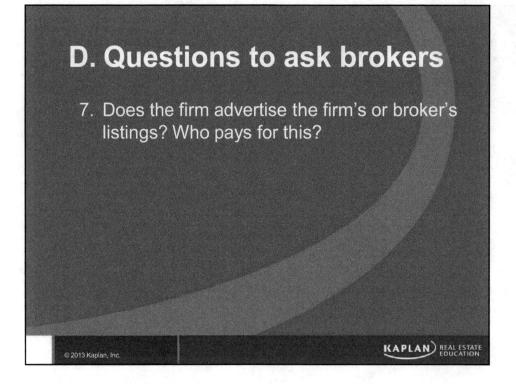

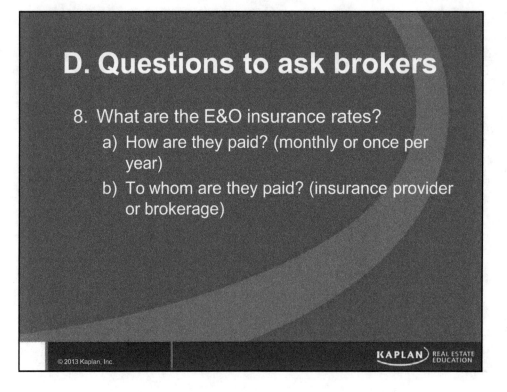

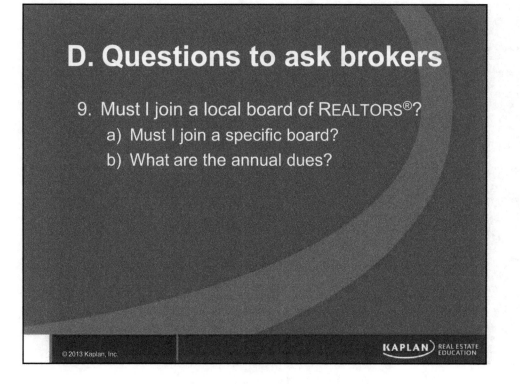

D. Questions to ask brokers

9. Must I join a local board of REALTORS®?
   a) Must I join a specific board?
   b) What are the annual dues?

© 2013 Kaplan, Inc.

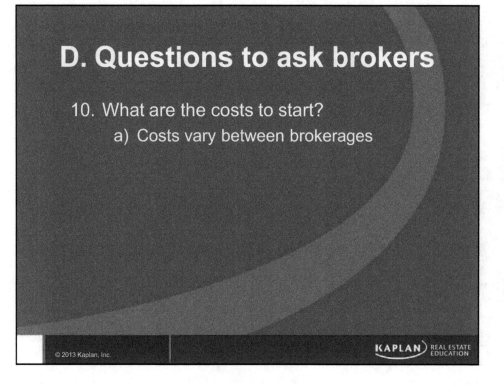

D. Questions to ask brokers

10. What are the costs to start?
    a) Costs vary between brokerages

© 2013 Kaplan, Inc.

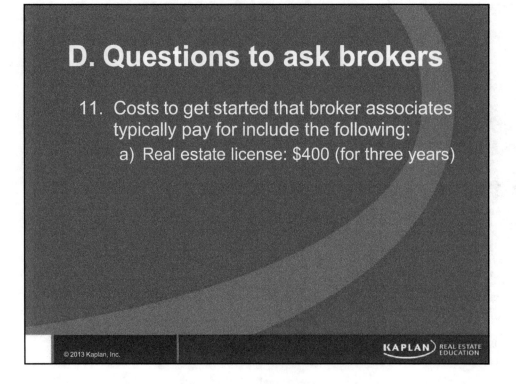

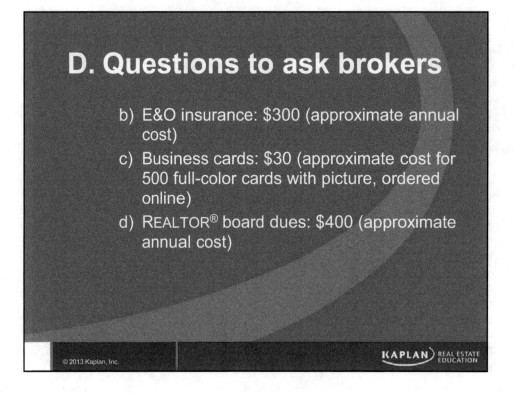

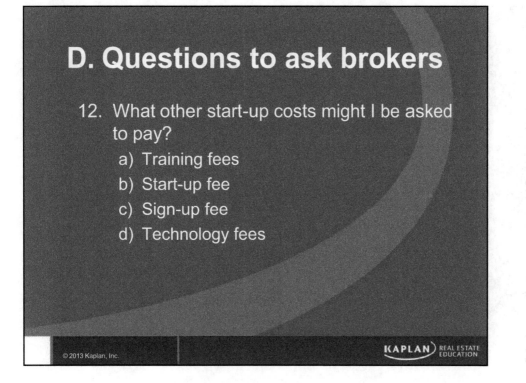

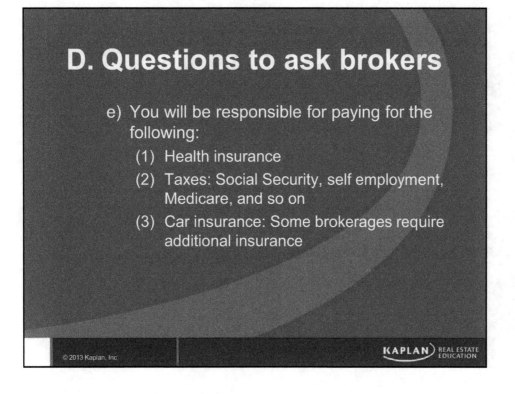

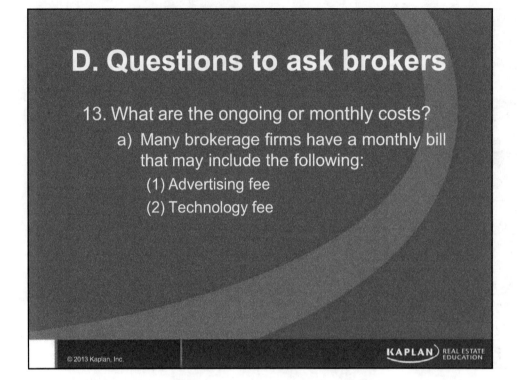

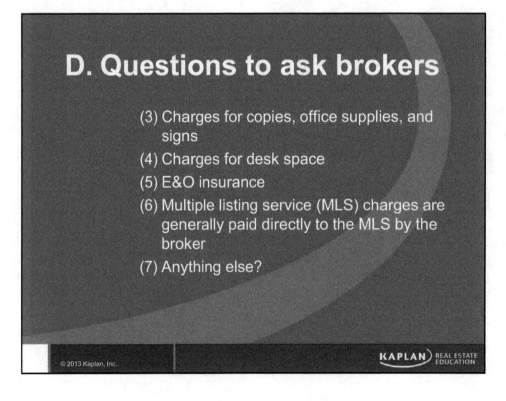

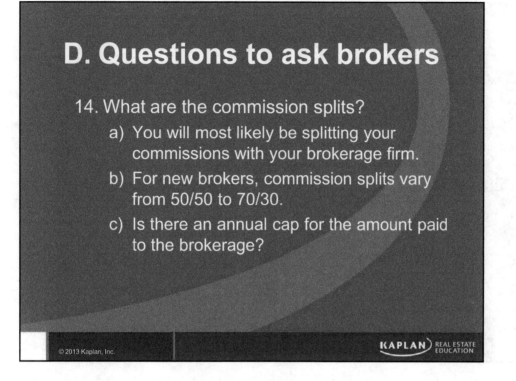

D. Questions to ask brokers

14. What are the commission splits?
   a) You will most likely be splitting your commissions with your brokerage firm.
   b) For new brokers, commission splits vary from 50/50 to 70/30.
   c) Is there an annual cap for the amount paid to the brokerage?

© 2013 Kaplan, Inc.
KAPLAN REAL ESTATE EDUCATION

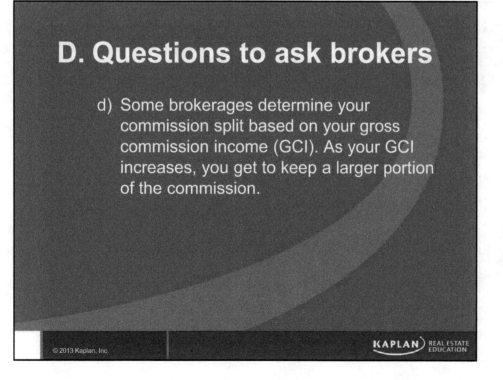

D. Questions to ask brokers

   d) Some brokerages determine your commission split based on your gross commission income (GCI). As your GCI increases, you get to keep a larger portion of the commission.

© 2013 Kaplan, Inc.
KAPLAN REAL ESTATE EDUCATION

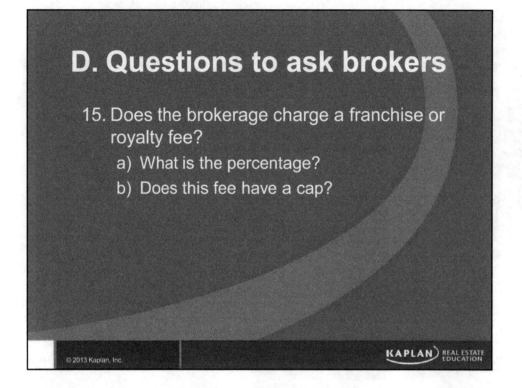

D. Questions to ask brokers

15. Does the brokerage charge a franchise or royalty fee?
    a) What is the percentage?
    b) Does this fee have a cap?

© 2013 Kaplan, Inc.   KAPLAN REAL ESTATE EDUCATION

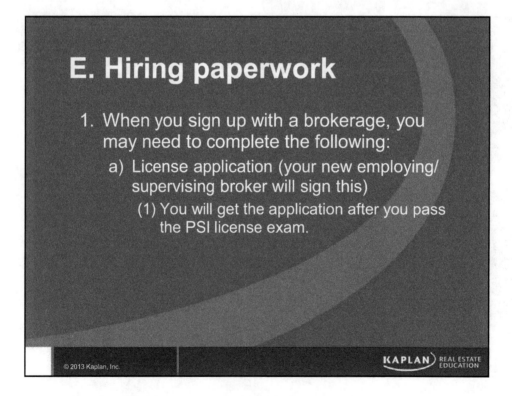

E. Hiring paperwork

1. When you sign up with a brokerage, you may need to complete the following:
    a) License application (your new employing/ supervising broker will sign this)
        (1) You will get the application after you pass the PSI license exam.

© 2013 Kaplan, Inc.   KAPLAN REAL ESTATE EDUCATION

E. Hiring paperwork

b) Application for E&O insurance (wait for your new broker to tell you how to do this, as it varies from brokerage to brokerage)

© 2013 Kaplan, Inc.

KAPLAN REAL ESTATE EDUCATION

E. Hiring paperwork

c) Independent contractor agreement

d) Commission agreement

e) Agreement to pay fees

f) Agreement to read the policies and procedures manual

© 2013 Kaplan, Inc.

KAPLAN REAL ESTATE EDUCATION

F. What is your job description?

1. Find buyers and sellers with whom to do business

   a) **Prospecting**: Going out and finding someone who wants to buy or sell now or in the near future

   b) **Marketing**: Attracting buyers and sellers to you

KAPLAN REAL ESTATE EDUCATION

F. What is your job description?

2. Know what to do when someone says yes

   a) Be prepared to give a credible presentation to buyers and sellers so they want to work with you

   b) Study scripts and dialogues so you know what to say

KAPLAN REAL ESTATE EDUCATION

F. What is your job description?

c) Know who to go to when you need help

d) Attend all the training offered so you're ready when the call comes

© 2013 Kaplan, Inc.

KAPLAN) REAL ESTATE EDUCATION

G. Treat your new career like a job

1. Create a business plan—hit or miss doesn't work
2. Think *systems*

© 2013 Kaplan, Inc.

KAPLAN) REAL ESTATE EDUCATION

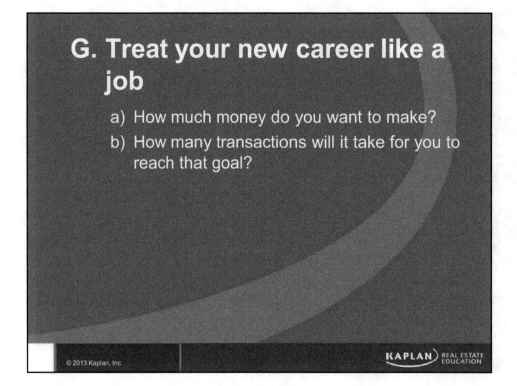

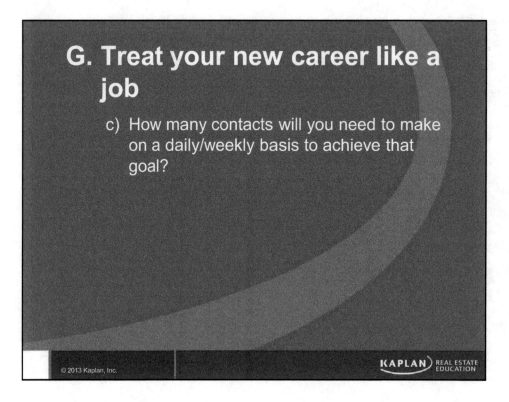

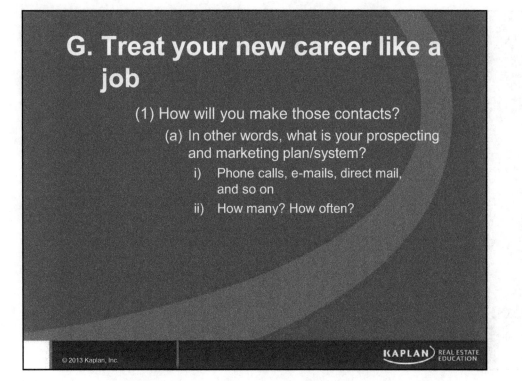

G. Treat your new career like a job

4. How will you track your leads?

    a) Follow-up is key.

    b) What lead tracking system should you use?

       (1) The tracking system you use does not matter unless you use it and follow up with leads daily.

© 2013 Kaplan, Inc.

KAPLAN) REAL ESTATE EDUCATION

G. Treat your new career like a job

5. Prioritize your activities so that the most important tasks get done every day.

© 2013 Kaplan, Inc.

KAPLAN) REAL ESTATE EDUCATION

H. Prospecting and marketing plan

1. Prospecting

   a) Knock on doors in a neighborhood

© 2013 Kaplan, Inc.

KAPLAN REAL ESTATE EDUCATION

H. Prospecting and marketing plan

   b) Call everyone you know (sphere of influence) to ask if they or someone they know wants to buy or sell

   c) Join a leads group

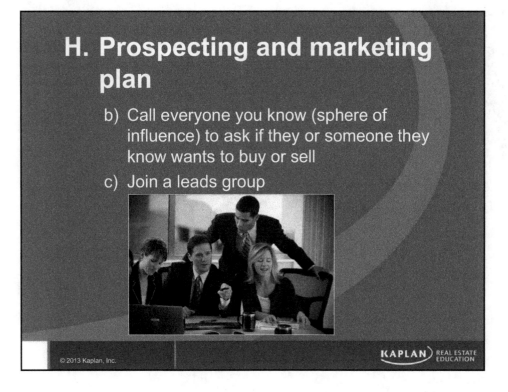

© 2013 Kaplan, Inc.

KAPLAN REAL ESTATE EDUCATION

H. Prospecting and marketing plan

d) Call for sale by owners (FSBOs)

© 2013 Kaplan, Inc.

KAPLAN REAL ESTATE EDUCATION

H. Prospecting and marketing plan

e) Contact expired listings
f) Hold open houses

© 2013 Kaplan, Inc.

KAPLAN REAL ESTATE EDUCATION

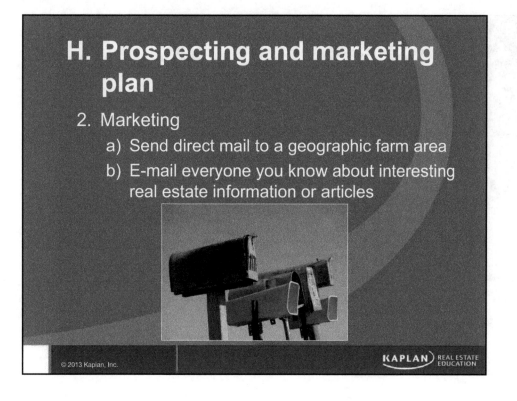

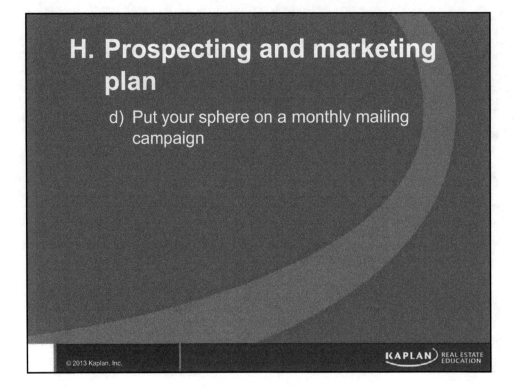

I. Prospecting and marketing ideas

1. Farming (geographic or people)
2. Internet (e-mail and social networks)
3. Sphere (referrals)
4. Buyer/investor seminars
5. Floor calls

© 2013 Kaplan, Inc.

KAPLAN REAL ESTATE EDUCATION

I. Prospecting and marketing ideas

6. Develop a niche market
   a) Seniors
   b) Downsizers
   c) Green buyers
   d) Builders
   e) Renters
   f) First-time homebuyers

© 2013 Kaplan, Inc.

KAPLAN REAL ESTATE EDUCATION

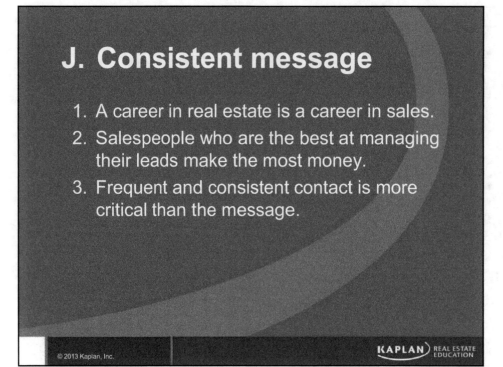

J. Consistent message

1. A career in real estate is a career in sales.
2. Salespeople who are the best at managing their leads make the most money.
3. Frequent and consistent contact is more critical than the message.

© 2013 Kaplan, Inc.

KAPLAN REAL ESTATE EDUCATION

K. Presenting your product— you!

1. Most brokerage firms have prepared presentations you can customize to tell buyers and sellers what you and your company can offer them.
2. Practice, practice, practice

© 2013 Kaplan, Inc.

KAPLAN REAL ESTATE EDUCATION

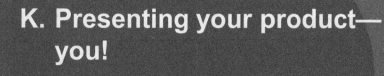

K. Presenting your product— you!

3. Handling objections: You will hear the same objections often, such as "we want to think about it."

   a) A skilled salesperson knows that "no" doesn't always mean "no" and has practiced an appropriate response to discover the real issue.

© 2013 Kaplan, Inc.

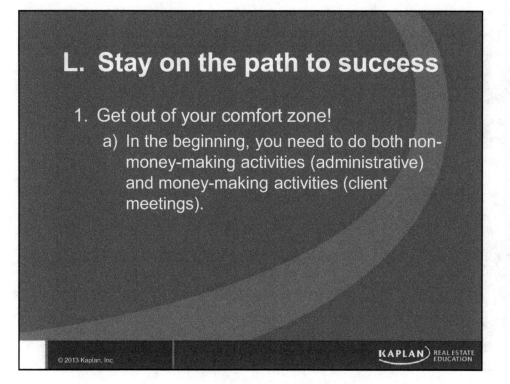

L. Stay on the path to success

1. Get out of your comfort zone!

   a) In the beginning, you need to do both non-money-making activities (administrative) and money-making activities (client meetings).

© 2013 Kaplan, Inc

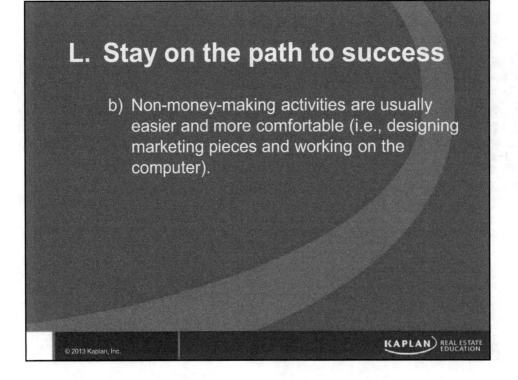

L. Stay on the path to success

b) Non-money-making activities are usually easier and more comfortable (i.e., designing marketing pieces and working on the computer).

© 2013 Kaplan, Inc.

KAPLAN REAL ESTATE EDUCATION

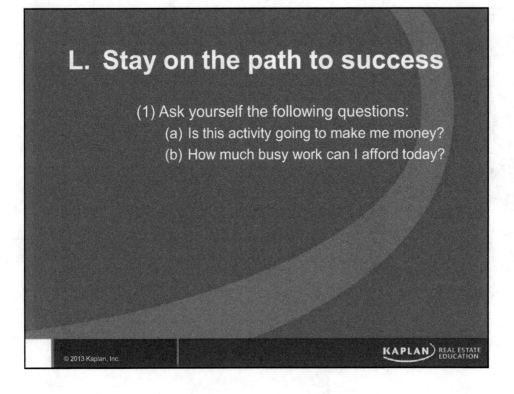

L. Stay on the path to success

(1) Ask yourself the following questions:
    (a) Is this activity going to make me money?
    (b) How much busy work can I afford today?

© 2013 Kaplan, Inc.

KAPLAN REAL ESTATE EDUCATION

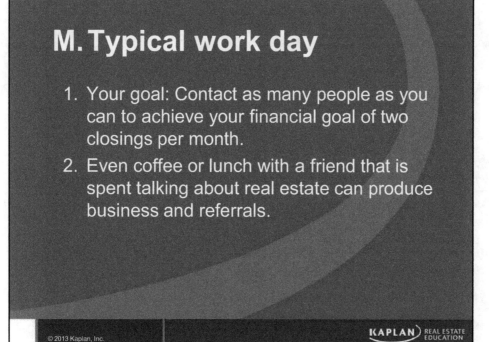

M. Typical work day

1. Your goal: Contact as many people as you can to achieve your financial goal of two closings per month.

2. Even coffee or lunch with a friend that is spent talking about real estate can produce business and referrals.

© 2013 Kaplan, Inc.

KAPLAN REAL ESTATE EDUCATION

M. Typical work day

3. Contacts turn into leads and leads turn into appointments.

4. Practicing your presentation pays off with higher conversion rates from appointments to listings and buyer agencies.

© 2013 Kaplan, Inc.

KAPLAN REAL ESTATE EDUCATION

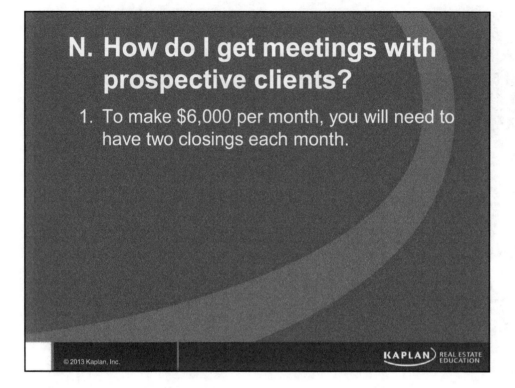

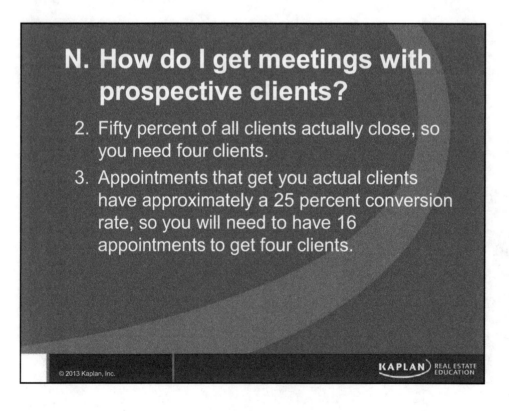

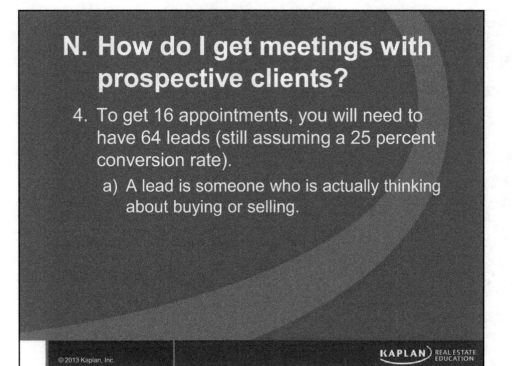

N. How do I get meetings with prospective clients?

4. To get 16 appointments, you will need to have 64 leads (still assuming a 25 percent conversion rate).

   a) A lead is someone who is actually thinking about buying or selling.

© 2013 Kaplan, Inc.

KAPLAN REAL ESTATE EDUCATION

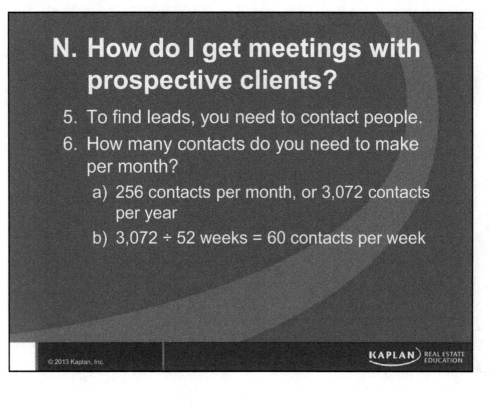

N. How do I get meetings with prospective clients?

5. To find leads, you need to contact people.

6. How many contacts do you need to make per month?

   a) 256 contacts per month, or 3,072 contacts per year

   b) 3,072 ÷ 52 weeks = 60 contacts per week

© 2013 Kaplan, Inc.

KAPLAN REAL ESTATE EDUCATION

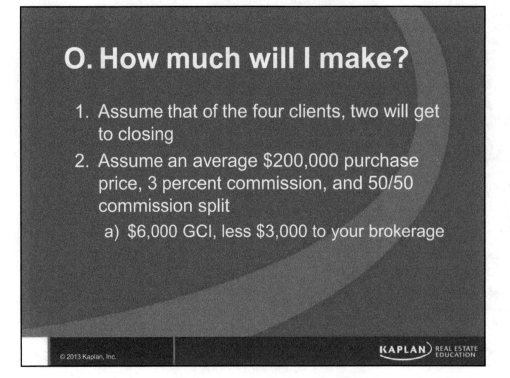

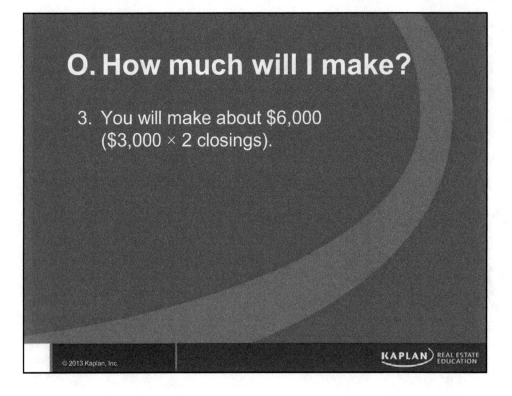

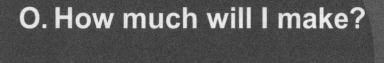

O. How much will I make?

4. Remember, as an independent contractor, you are responsible for paying your own taxes.

5. Be sure to contact your tax advisor in advance to find out how to best handle paying your taxes.

© 2013 Kaplan, Inc.

KAPLAN REAL ESTATE EDUCATION

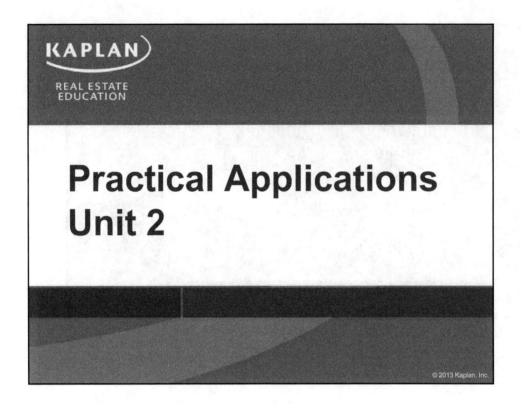

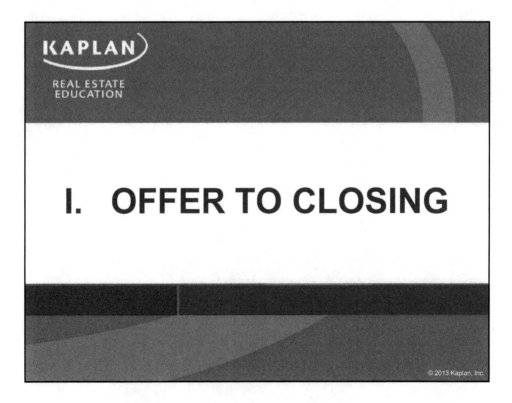

A. Working with buyers and sellers

1. The next section will give you a broad overview of the process of working with buyers and sellers.

    a) This is where your book will come in handy.

© 2013 Kaplan, Inc.

KAPLAN) REAL ESTATE EDUCATION

A. Working with buyers and sellers

2. This is where your company training will pay off (i.e., practicing presentation skills, completing a CMA, writing a contract, setting showings).

3. Be sure to get help from your mentor, coach, or managing broker.

© 2013 Kaplan, Inc.

KAPLAN) REAL ESTATE EDUCATION

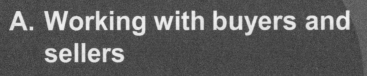

A. Working with buyers and sellers

4. Education: Use your buyer/listing presentation to educate buyers and sellers (and keep you on track).

© 2013 Kaplan, Inc.

KAPLAN REAL ESTATE EDUCATION

A. Working with buyers and sellers

5. Customer service: What will you do to provide top-quality service?

© 2013 Kaplan, Inc.

KAPLAN REAL ESTATE EDUCATION

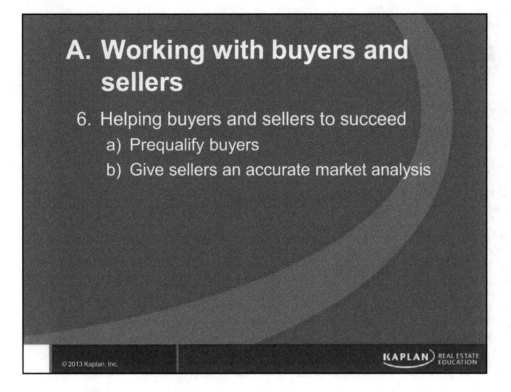

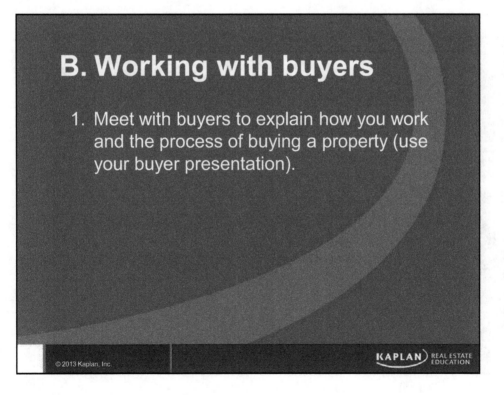

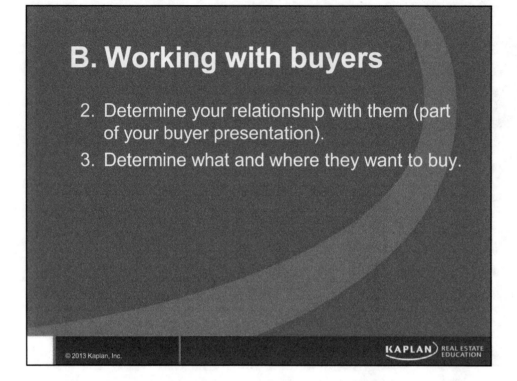

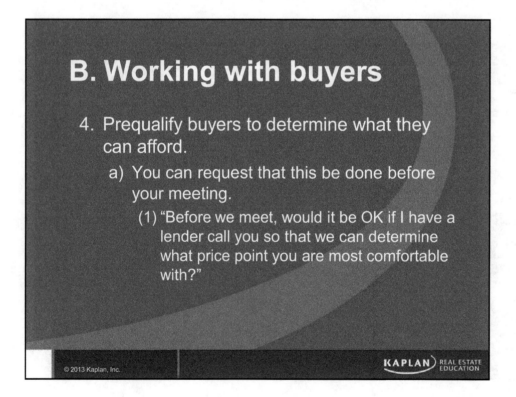

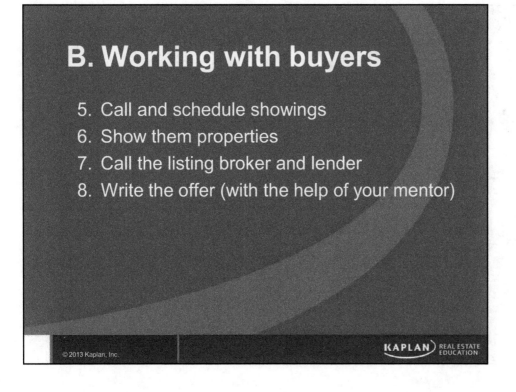

B. Working with buyers

5. Call and schedule showings
6. Show them properties
7. Call the listing broker and lender
8. Write the offer (with the help of your mentor)

© 2013 Kaplan, Inc. KAPLAN REAL ESTATE EDUCATION

C. Working with sellers

1. Do your homework (i.e., CMA, seller's net sheet) in advance so you are ready to make a great presentation and take the listing.

    a) You don't have to see the property to know the sales price range; most of the information you need is available on the MLS.

© 2013 Kaplan, Inc. KAPLAN REAL ESTATE EDUCATION

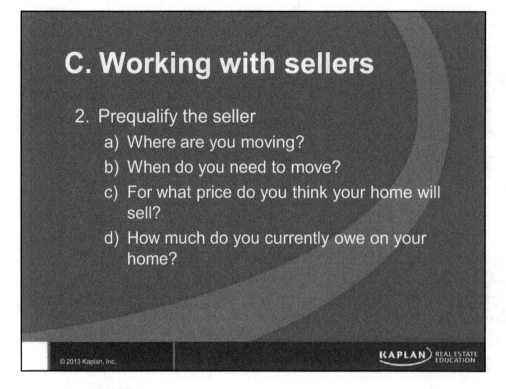

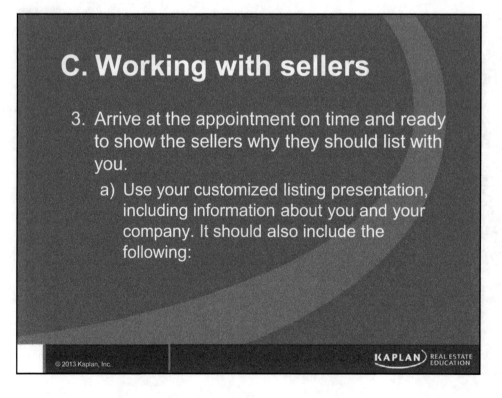

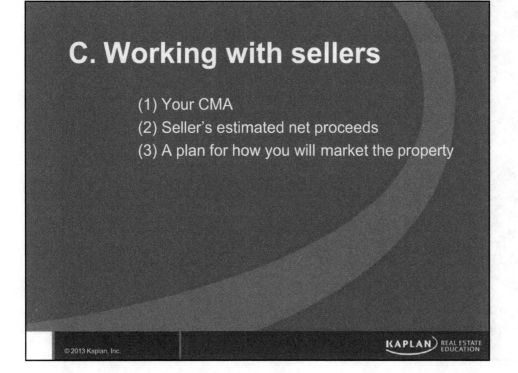

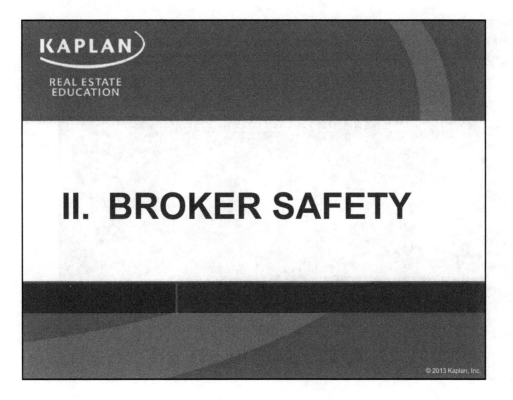

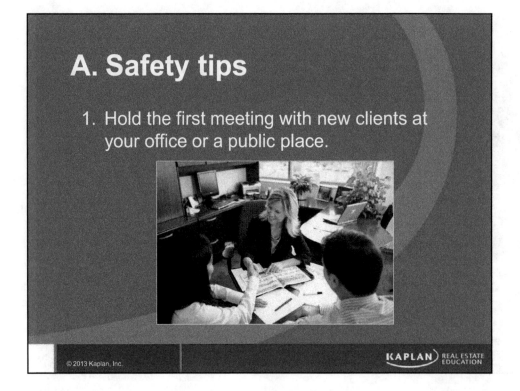

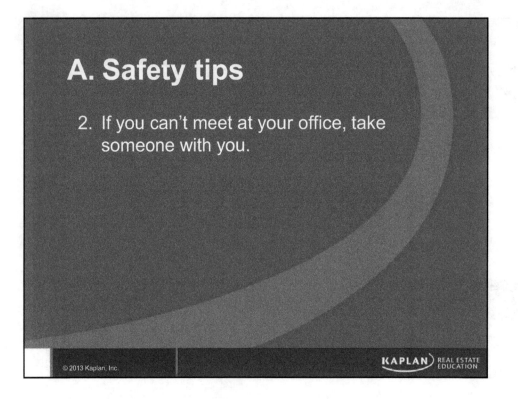

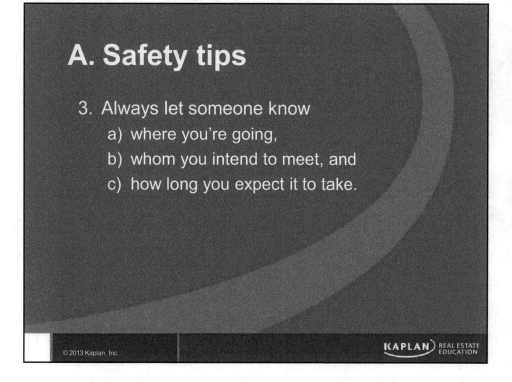

A. Safety tips

3. Always let someone know
   a) where you're going,
   b) whom you intend to meet, and
   c) how long you expect it to take.

© 2013 Kaplan, Inc.

KAPLAN REAL ESTATE EDUCATION

A. Safety tips

4. Arrange for a family member, friend, or colleague to check in with you by phone at a predetermined time, and use code words to convey your comfort level.

© 2013 Kaplan, Inc.

KAPLAN REAL ESTATE EDUCATION

A. Safety tips

5. When hosting an open house, invite someone along. Never do it alone.

6. Avoid going into closets, attics, and basements, and never allow a stranger to get between you and the door.

© 2013 Kaplan, Inc.

KAPLAN) REAL ESTATE EDUCATION

A. Safety tips

7. Be assertive and confident. When you feel uncomfortable or sense any threat, excuse yourself for a call or to retrieve something from your car.

© 2013 Kaplan, Inc.

KAPLAN) REAL ESTATE EDUCATION

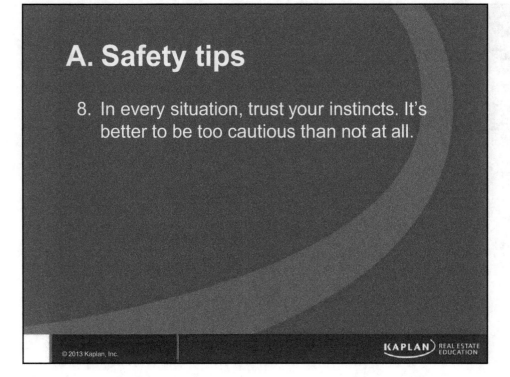

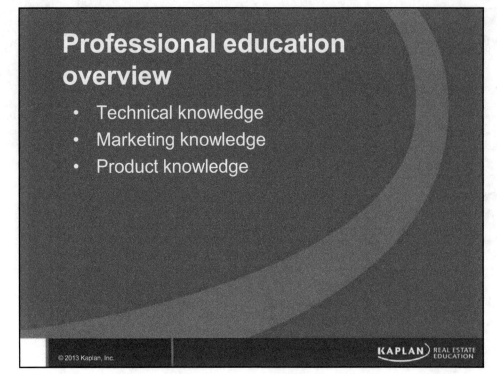

Professional education overview

- Technical knowledge
- Marketing knowledge
- Product knowledge

© 2013 Kaplan, Inc.

KAPLAN) REAL ESTATE EDUCATION

A. Technical knowledge

1. Using the MLS system
2. Preparing CMAs
3. Preparing listing/buyer contracts
4. Preparing required documents
5. Reviewing closing statements

© 2013 Kaplan, Inc.

KAPLAN) REAL ESTATE EDUCATION

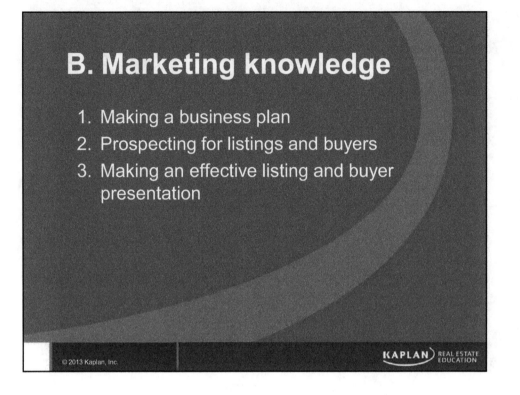

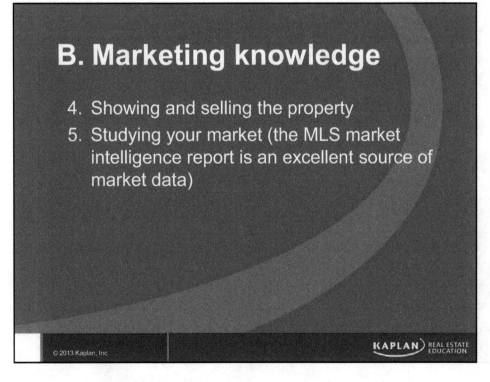

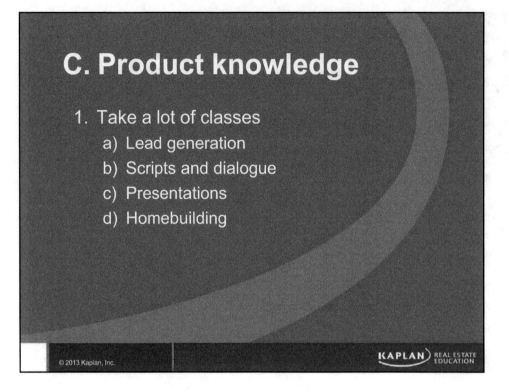

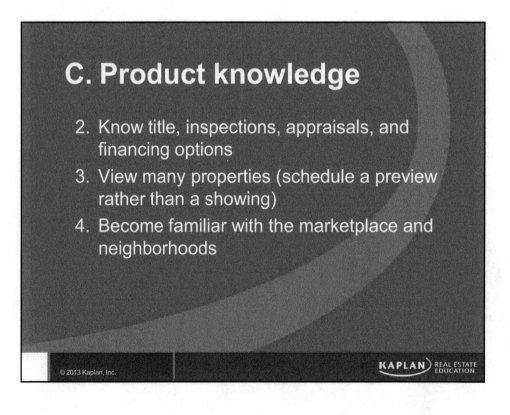

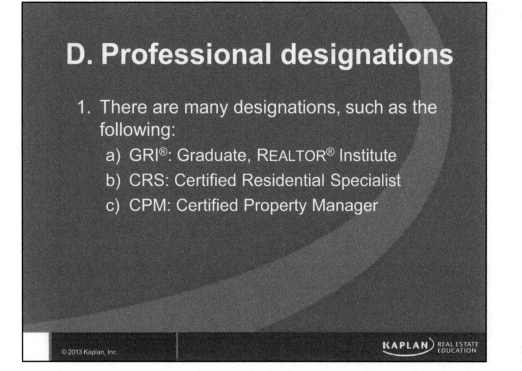

D. Professional designations

1. There are many designations, such as the following:
   a) GRI®: Graduate, REALTOR® Institute
   b) CRS: Certified Residential Specialist
   c) CPM: Certified Property Manager

© 2013 Kaplan, Inc.

KAPLAN) REAL ESTATE EDUCATION

D. Professional designations

   d) CCIM: Certified Commercial Investment Member
   e) SRES®: Seniors Real Estate Specialist
   f) NAR's GREEN designation or the EcoBroker designation: Green and sustainable issues
   g) SFR: Short Sales and Foreclosure Resource

© 2013 Kaplan, Inc.

KAPLAN) REAL ESTATE EDUCATION

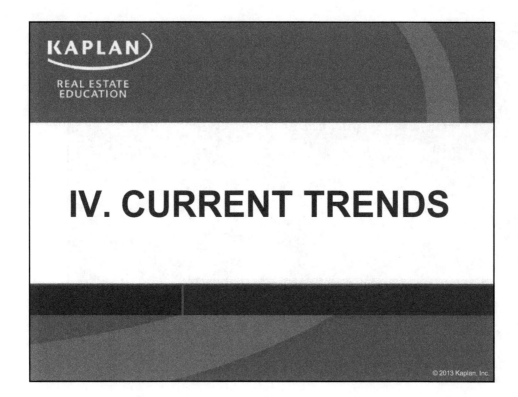

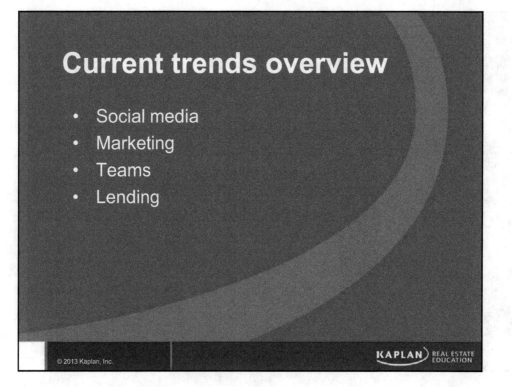

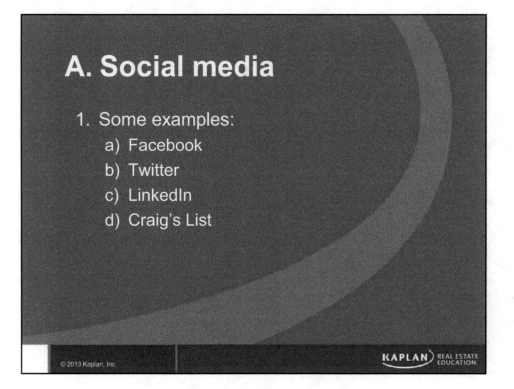

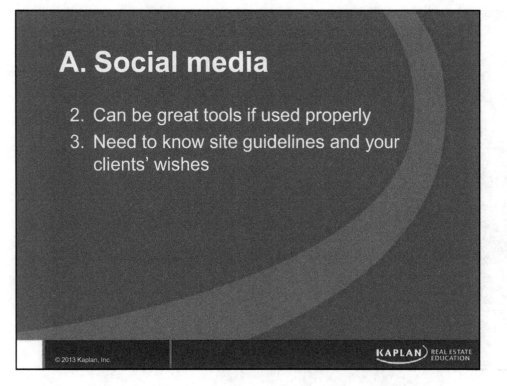

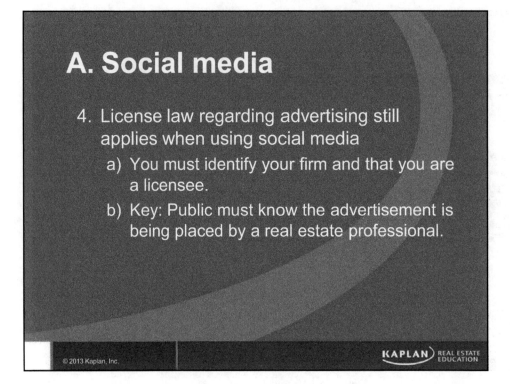

A. Social media

4. License law regarding advertising still applies when using social media
   a) You must identify your firm and that you are a licensee.
   b) Key: Public must know the advertisement is being placed by a real estate professional.

© 2013 Kaplan, Inc.

KAPLAN REAL ESTATE EDUCATION

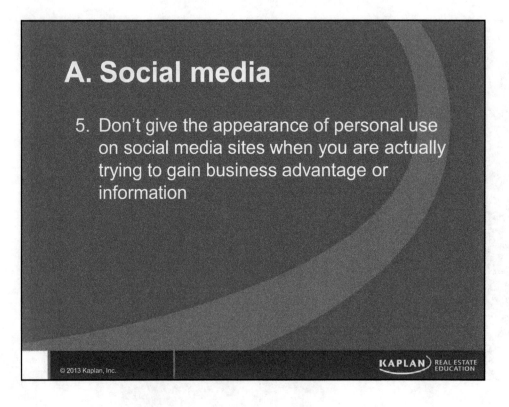

A. Social media

5. Don't give the appearance of personal use on social media sites when you are actually trying to gain business advantage or information

© 2013 Kaplan, Inc.

KAPLAN REAL ESTATE EDUCATION

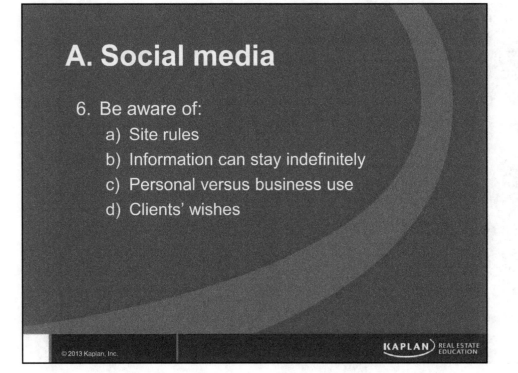

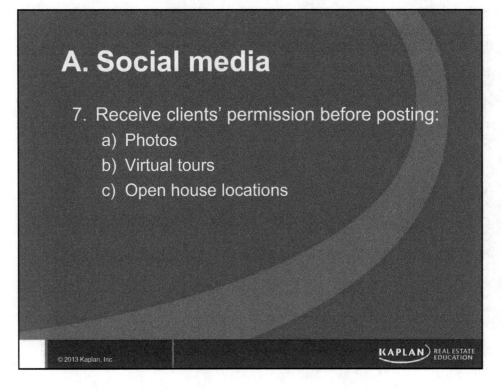

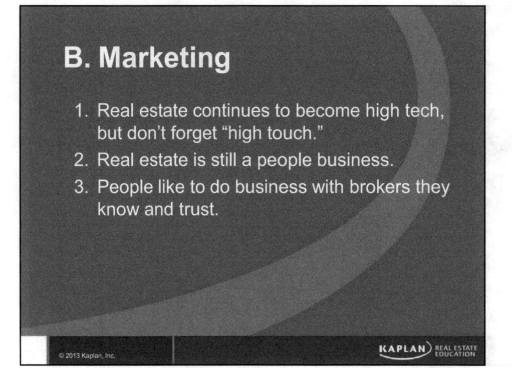

B. Marketing

1. Real estate continues to become high tech, but don't forget "high touch."
2. Real estate is still a people business.
3. People like to do business with brokers they know and trust.

© 2013 Kaplan, Inc.

KAPLAN REAL ESTATE EDUCATION

B. Marketing

4. Use technology with a personal touch.
5. Often a call can move a client forward.
6. Make sure you are easy to find in Internet searches.

© 2013 Kaplan, Inc.

KAPLAN REAL ESTATE EDUCATION

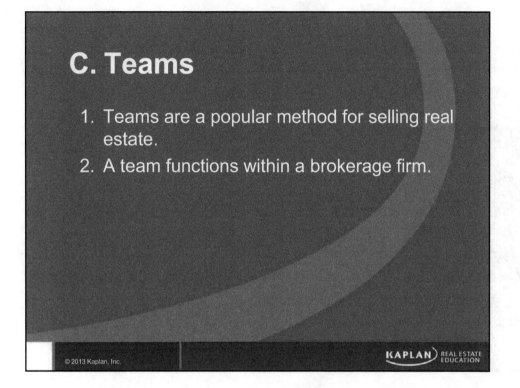

C. Teams

1. Teams are a popular method for selling real estate.
2. A team functions within a brokerage firm.

© 2013 Kaplan, Inc.   KAPLAN REAL ESTATE EDUCATION

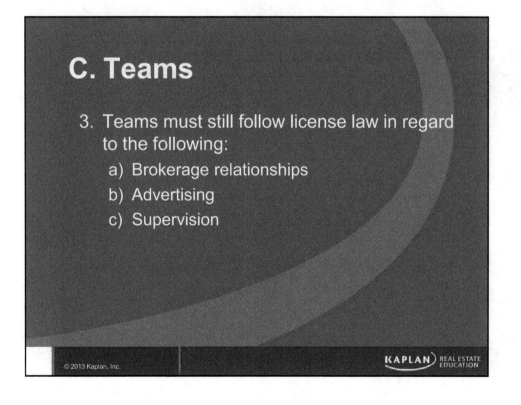

C. Teams

3. Teams must still follow license law in regard to the following:
   a) Brokerage relationships
   b) Advertising
   c) Supervision

© 2013 Kaplan, Inc.   KAPLAN REAL ESTATE EDUCATION

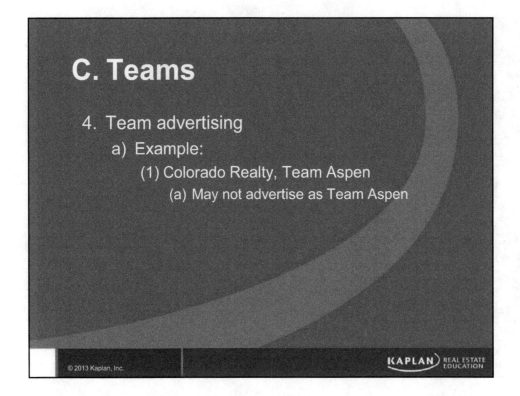

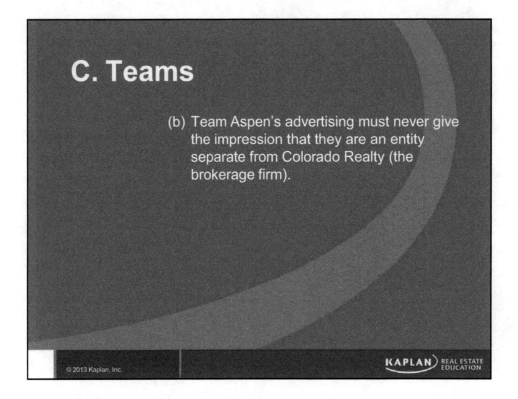

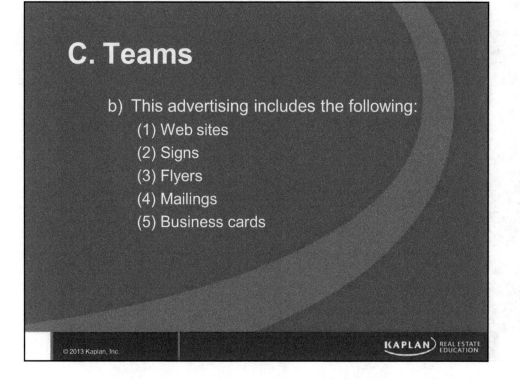

C. Teams

b) This advertising includes the following:
    (1) Web sites
    (2) Signs
    (3) Flyers
    (4) Mailings
    (5) Business cards

© 2013 Kaplan, Inc.

KAPLAN REAL ESTATE EDUCATION

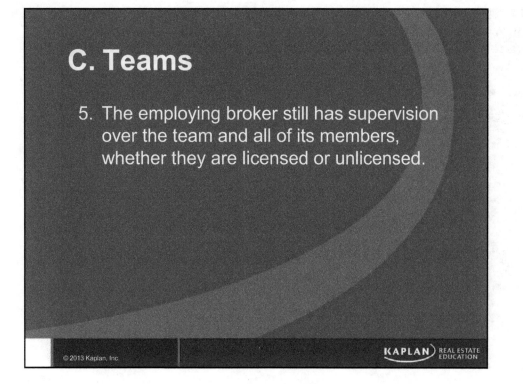

C. Teams

5. The employing broker still has supervision over the team and all of its members, whether they are licensed or unlicensed.

© 2013 Kaplan, Inc.

KAPLAN REAL ESTATE EDUCATION

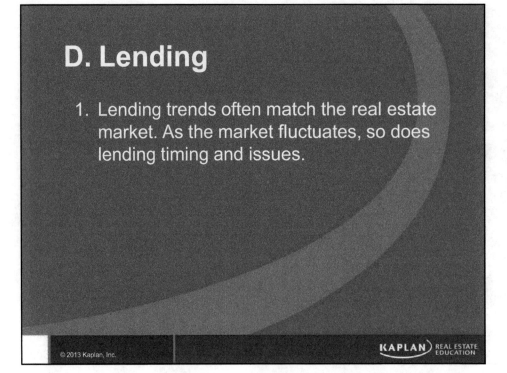

D. Lending

1. Lending trends often match the real estate market. As the market fluctuates, so does lending timing and issues.

© 2013 Kaplan, Inc.

KAPLAN REAL ESTATE EDUCATION

D. Lending

2. An improving market tends to increase volume and thus can increase the length of time to close.

3. It is important to check with a lender to properly advise buyers and sellers.

© 2013 Kaplan, Inc.

KAPLAN REAL ESTATE EDUCATION

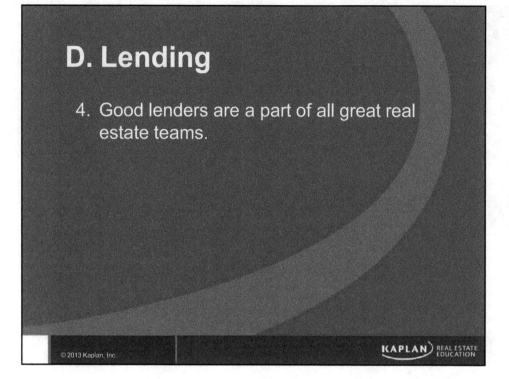

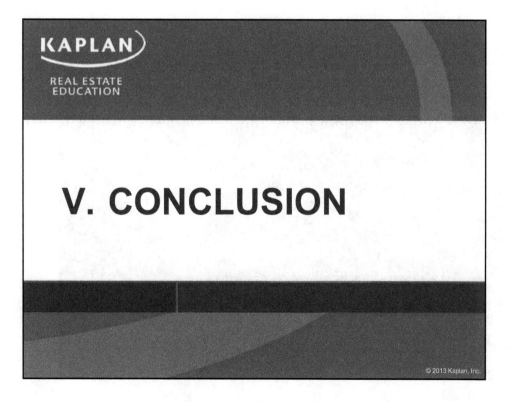

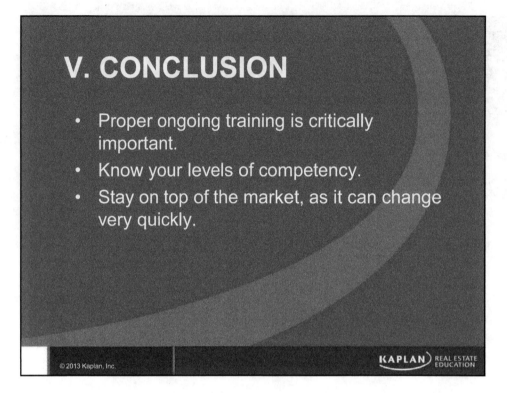

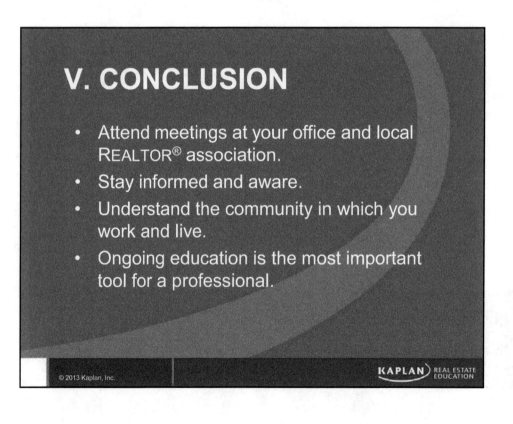

TRUST ACCOUNTS AND RECORD KEEPING

While a great deal of care has been taken to provide accurate and current information, the ideas, suggestions, general principles, and conclusions presented in this text are subject to local, state, and federal laws and regulations, court cases, and any revisions of same. The reader is thus urged to consult legal counsel regarding any points of law—this publication should not be used as a substitute for competent legal advice.

Trust Accounts and Record Keeping

■ FOCUS ON UNDERSTANDING

- ■ Definition of a trust account
- ■ Requirements for trust accounts
- ■ Types of trust accounts
- ■ Requirements for earnest money deposits and earnest money promissory notes
- ■ Record keeping rules and safeguards
- ■ Property management trust accounts

■ STUDY PLAN

Before Class:

- ■ Read the Trust Accounts & Record Keeping text.
- ■ Complete the Trust Accounts & Record Keeping Review Exam.
- ■ Complete the reading assignment in the Colorado Real Estate Manual (CREM) (included in *Colorado Real Estate Principles Volume 1*) that is listed in the Colorado Prelicense Reading Guide.

During Class:

- ■ Lecture Outline
- ■ Final Exam

After Class:

■ Prepare for Closings Class
— See Closings section for pre-class reading.

Key Terms

Account journal	Good funds	Transaction files
Audit	Operation account	Trust account
Beneficiary ledger card	Reconcile	

■ OVERVIEW OF TRUST ACCOUNTS

A trust account is a separate bank account established to hold money for the benefit of others. The money in the trust account belongs to other people—called beneficiaries—and it is only in the temporary custody of the trustee or fiduciary. Because the money belongs to others, it is subject to very specific controls and requires a high level of accuracy and care. Trust accounts have strict accounting requirements, in addition to the requirements on how the account can be established at a bank. Colorado real estate trust accounts must follow specific statutes and Commission rules.

Real estate brokerage firms frequently maintain one or more trust accounts to hold money they receive as part of real estate transactions or the *management* of properties. As part of protecting the public, the Colorado Real Estate Commission takes very seriously the accounting of monies collected by principal brokers, collected by broker associates, and held by brokerage firms or title companies as part of real estate transactions. In Colorado, only principal brokers who are either an employing or independent broker may have trust accounts. Broker associates, at any license level, are not allowed to keep trust accounts [Rule E-1(c)]. This means for new broker associates, there is no worrying about setting up trust accounts. However, all licensed brokers are responsible for collecting earnest money and other funds and seeing the funds are delivered or deposited correctly. Additionally, property managers are responsible for making sure all security deposits, rents, and funds used for property maintenance are properly accounted for in the brokerage firms property management trust account.

Typically, each brokerage firm will also have a company operating account, which is not a trust account. The funds in the operating account will be the property of the principal broker or brokerage firm and used for operating expenses. When the firm earns a commission and splits it with a broker associate, the employing broker deposits the commission check into the operating account and then writes an operating account check for the commission split to the broker associate. Brokerage firm operating expenses cannot be paid directly into or out of the trust account. These funds must be separate from the funds held in trust. Combining operating and trust funds is called *commingling* and is illegal.

After two years, a broker associate can choose to become an independent broker and at that time become responsible for maintaining proper trust accounts. In this course, we will discuss what trust accounts are, the rules that must be followed in maintaining a trust account, record keeping issues, and the handling of earnest money. Through out the course, when the term *principal broker* is used, it is referring to employing or independent brokers who are required to have trust accounts.

Establishing Trust Accounts

If the principal broker is going to hold trust funds in a brokerage firm account, the principal broker must establish a trust account at least by the time money belonging to others is first received. Good business practice would dictate that principal brokers establish trust accounts as part of first establishing their brokerage firm so such accounts will be already available when the need arises.

If a principal broker holds no money belonging to others, no separate trust account is required [Rule E-1(u)]. The brokerage firm and principal broker may choose to allow a title company to hold the trust funds; however, the brokerage firm and principal broker remain responsible for the funds and what happens to them. This means if the title company closes, loses the funds, or improperly handles the money, the principal broker is also considered a responsible party.

The principal broker has a great deal of personal responsibility for the trust accounts that bear the brokerage and principal broker's name. The principal broker is required to actively supervise the accounting procedures used to keep track of the accounts and to maintain adequate security over the money in the accounts. The principal broker is also charged with the supervision of all employed broker associates and making sure that they properly handle all money received [C.R.S. 12-61-103(8) and 12-61-113(1)(g)(n) and (o)]. The principal broker may delegate, in writing, the accounting for trust accounts to another responsible party in the company. The principal broker is of course still responsible and must maintain control over all the accounts and accounting.

An additional requirement is the principal broker must be able to withdraw funds from the trust account without a cosigner. The principal broker may authorize other signers on the account who may be licensed or unlicensed. An unlicensed assistant or office manager may sign checks if authorized by the principal broker.

The principal broker's (or firm's) funds must not be commingled with funds belonging to beneficiaries of the trust account. For example, the brokerage firm may not keep trust funds and operation funds in the same account. However, brokerage firm funds sufficient to open and operate the account may be kept in a trust account. While the amount of brokerage funds permitted in the trust account is not specified by the Commission, it should not be in excess of what might be considered a reasonable amount. A broker's or brokerage ledger card will keep track of how much of the brokerage funds are being used in the firm's trust accounts.

Types of Trust Accounts Used

Trust accounts contain earnest money, rents, and security deposits, among other funds. Depending upon the needs of the brokerage firm, the number and types of accounts needed will vary. A large company or one performing many types of real estate brokerage services may need a number of trust accounts to assure that funds for various purposes and beneficiaries are not improperly mixed. A small brokerage specializing in residential sales may require only one account or none at all. The number is determined by the requirement to assure the funds are properly accounted for, not by, the amount of money in the trust account.

The type of funds to be held are the deciding factor, and the number of accounts can range from none to unlimited. The most common trust accounts are the

- sales trust account—for money held in connection with sales transactions pending closing (earnest money);
- management trust account—for money held in connection with property management services (rents and other income belonging to the property owner);
- security deposit trust account—for refundable security deposits collected from tenants or short term occupants, for lease, and rental units under management by the principal broker (tenant's money, which is fully accountable to the tenant);
- advance rental—for rental money collected in advance, especially for short-term rentals as experienced in resort and vacation rentals (this is not security deposit money); and
- homeowners' association trust account—for funds held on behalf of condominium or planned community associations, use a separate account for each association and identify the account with the tax identification number of each association (this money belongs to the all owners as a group and is differentiated from an individual property owner).

Most sales firms will have a sales trust account for earnest money, or they will not have any trust accounts and simply use the title company to hold these funds. A property management company will typically have a management account and a security deposit account. If the company also does sales, the principal broker may decide to establish a sales trust account for earnest money.

Accounts and Systems Used to Account for Brokerage Firm Money

The operations account is used by the brokerage firm to take care of day-to-day expenses to run the office. Once a commission is earned, the funds are deposited into the firm's operation account, and a check to the broker associate is then written for the broker associate's share of the commission.

The funds going into a trust account come from a written document, and the accounting system used to maintain and reconcile the trust account must make note from what document or documents the funds came. This documentation is kept in a transaction file. For example, the Contract to Buy and Sell states the listing brokerage firm will hold the earnest money until termination, closing, or default. Additionally, the amount and form of the earnest money is also listed.

The Contact to Buy and Sell is kept in the transaction file, and the principal broker would create a new beneficiary ledger card that details where the funds are from, what document gave the brokerage permission to hold the earnest money, the property information, and so forth. All trust funds must be traceable back to the written agreement, bill, or invoice.

The beneficiary ledger is used to keep track of the money for a property. The amount and address are also entered into the account journal, which is used to keep track of all the funds within a trust account. A typical firm might be holding money from 20 or more different properties. The ledger card tells the principal broker the details of the property and funds, while the account journal keeps track of all the funds within the trust account.

The trust account should not be used to hold funds belonging to broker associates except as part of an executory sales contract to which the broker associate is a party. Employee benefit funds and tax withholding funds shall not be deposited in these types of trust accounts [Rule E-1(f)(2) and (3)].

If a principal broker advances funds for the benefit of a client, the funds may be placed in the trust account and identified as an advance. The funds may not be withdrawn except on behalf of the client. The funds may be repaid to the principal broker or withdrawn for the principal broker's use only with the consent of the client [Rule E-1(f)(4)].

FIGURE 1.1

Sales Trust Account

Sales Trust Account
Holds other people's money in trust

Broker Ledger $50.00

Account Journal

Brokers funds	$50.00
143 Ash	$1,000.00
621 Elm	$5,000.00
Balance in account	$6,050.00

Ledger Card 143 Ash Street
$1,000
Balance for property

Ledger Card 621 Elm Street
$5,000
Balance for property

Requirements of Trust Accounts

Trust accounts must be in a bank or recognized depository in Colorado that is insured by an agency of the U.S. government. The most likely agency is the Federal Deposit Insurance Corporation (FDIC), which insures deposits in both commercial banks and savings and loans. While credit unions do have insurance through the National Credit Union Association (NCUA), that insurance only protects members of the credit union. While the principal broker might be a member, typically the beneficiaries (seller, buyer, landlord, and tenant) of the trust account would not be members of that credit union. Therefore, the Colorado Real Estate Commission prohibits principal brokers from utilizing credit unions for their trust accounts, because all parties might not be insured against loss [Rule E-1(b)].

The Colorado Real Estate Commission requires separate trust accounts for each type of activity when a brokerage firm is holding money belonging to others. In addition, each account must have the type of account clearly labeled in the documents used to establish the account to reflect the fiduciary nature of the account (Rule E-1).

All trust accounts must be identified in the bank records and on bank statements with the following specific information:

1. The company name as registered with the Commission
2. The personal name and capacity of the principal broker responsible for the account
3. The type of trust account, such as sales or property management
4. The account records, checks, and deposit slips stating that it is a trust or trustee account

A company trust account might be identified as follows:

- For a sole proprietor brokerage (licensed under a trade name) sales trust account:
  — Integrity Realty Company
  Susan R. Smith, Broker,
  Sales Escrow Account
  1234 Main Street
  Hometown, Colorado 80999
- For a corporate property management firm's management and security deposit accounts:
  — Verygood Management, Inc.
  William A. Johnson, Broker
  Property Management Trust Account
  1 Priority Blvd., Ste 222
  Uptown, Colorado 81111
  — Verygood Management, Inc.
  William A. Johnson, Broker
  Security Deposits Trustee Account
  1 Priority Blvd., Ste 222
  Uptown, Colorado 80111

The principal broker setting up the trust account(s) must assure that the name of the account is specific enough that the bank recognizes it as a trust account. This type of account is protected from actions against the principal broker because the money belongs to beneficiaries, not the principal broker. A Notice of Escrow or Trust Account form is executed between the principal broker and the banking institution to document this protection. This notice can be created using the principal broker's letterhead and must be maintained in the principal broker's files. Additionally, funds must be available for immediate withdrawal without penalty from these accounts [Rule E-1(d)].

Any real estate firm may have other operating accounts in the name of the firm or the principal broker of record, but the Real Estate Commission is primarily concerned with the safety of money belonging to others. The Commission auditing staff will not ordinarily scrutinize operating accounts.

Other locations or branch offices of a brokerage firm may use the trust account(s) of the primary office. If a branch office maintains separate trust accounts, a separate record-keeping system must be maintained in each branch office [Rule E-1(s)].

Interest-Bearing Trust Accounts

A principal broker may not use trust account funds to earn undisclosed profits [C.R.S. 12-61-113(1)(q)]. The statute and the Commission rules permit the funds to be held in interest-bearing accounts under the following conditions:

■ If the principal broker or one party to the transaction is to benefit from the interest income, all parties with an interest in the funds must provide their informed consent. They must agree to any risks or penalties for early withdrawal. They must also agree to who the interest will go to in the event the transaction is either consummated or defeated.

If an *affordable housing program* benefiting Colorado residents will receive the interest, the principal broker must post a notice in the office indicating that the company participates in such a program. The most used program is operated through the Colorado Association of REALTORS® and is called Colorado Association of REALTORS® Housing Opportunity Fund (CARHOF). The seller and buyer give permission for the transfer in the Contract to Buy and Sell.

■ EARNEST MONEY

Earnest Money Deposits

Earnest money can be anything the seller will accept: cash, personal check, or property. The most typical is a personal check from the buyer to be held by the listing brokerage for the seller. Earnest money received must be deposited in the trust account not later than the **third business day following notice of acceptance** of the offer. The offer must clearly define who will hold the funds, the type of funds used, and where the funds are being held. If a check is to be withheld from deposit for any reason, the reason for holding the deposit must be disclosed in the contract, or the seller should provide written instructions to withhold deposit of the check [Rule E-1(m) and (n)].

If the offer was sent electronically and the buyer's broker is holding the earnest money instead of delivering it to the listing broker, the buyer's broker is obligated to deliver the money to the listing broker immediately upon acceptance of the offer. The buyer's broker should have sent a copy of the buyer's check or other verification that the buyer's broker has the funds, along with the offer. It is important the buyer's broker actually collect the funds per the terms of the contract before the offer is made; this allows the buyer's broker to easily deliver the funds upon acceptance. It would be inappropriate to collect the earnest money funds after the offer was accepted, unless it was clearly stated in the contract the earnest money was to be delivered by the buyer after acceptance.

If the purchase does not close and there is no dispute regarding the earnest money, it is to be returned to the appropriate party. The principal broker may **not** require the parties to sign a release in order to disburse the money if there is no dispute as to who is to receive the money. Of particular concern to the Commission is a broker requiring all parties to sign a release that holds the broker harmless and uses exculpatory provisions to limit the broker's liability (Commission Position CP-6). There is an approved Earnest Money Release form (EMR 83-5-04) that may be used to show all parties are in agreement with the return of earnest money. If an Earnest Money Release is used, the seller will have three days to sign and return the release to the brokerage firm or buyer. Per the Closing Instructions, the holder of the earnest money will then have five days to return the money to the buyer. The Commission is concerned that brokerage firms not unduly hold funds for more time than necessary to obtain release signatures.

If there is a dispute regarding the earnest money, the broker may hold the money in the trust account until the parties provide mutual written instructions. The broker may also choose to interplead the money (surrendering it to the court if a lawsuit is pending or has commenced). This action can result in the broker forfeiting any claim to the money and also being removed as a defendant in the litigation. In the case of this court action, the broker may recover associated court costs and attorney's fees.

In the event the parties do not reach an agreement and no lawsuit is initiated, the broker holding the earnest money could be required to hold the earnest money indefinitely. To address this potential problem, the real estate commission has inserted language in the Contract to Buy and Sell to assist the holder of the earnest money should this situation arise. This wording provides for the broker to notify the parties that, unless an agreement is reached or a lawsuit is initiated within 120 calendar days of the notice, the broker is authorized to disburse the earnest money to the buyer.

FIGURE 1.2

The Trail of Earnest Money to Commission Check

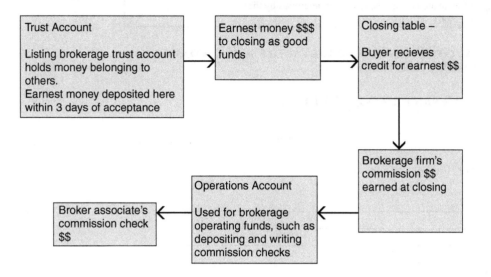

F I G U R E   1.3

Earnest Money Release

The printed portions of this form, except differentiated additions, have been approved by the Colorado Real Estate Commission (EMR 83-5-04)

THIS FORM HAS IMPORTANT LEGAL CONSEQUENCES AND THE PARTIES SHOULD CONSULT LEGAL AND TAX OR OTHER COUNSEL BEFORE SIGNING.

EARNEST MONEY RELEASE

Date:_____

1.   Parties, Property, Contract, Earnest Money Deposit:

        a.   Seller_____

        b.   Buyer_____

        c.   Property_____

        d.   Date of Contract_____

        e.   Earnest Money $_____

2.   Buyer and Seller agree that the Contract is terminated. Buyer and Seller agree that the Earnest Money shall be distributed as follows:

        a. $_____ payable to: _____

        b. $_____ payable to: _____

        c.   Other:

      If the Contract required the Earnest Money to be placed in an interest bearing account, the interest shall be disbursed as follows:

      This Earnest Money Release may affect legal rights or claims of the parties. Buyer and Seller are advised of their right to obtain legal counsel.

Date: _____   Date: _____

_____   _____
Buyer   Buyer

Date: _____   Date: _____

_____   _____
Seller   Seller

EMR 83-5-04 EARNEST MONEY RELEASE

Earnest Money Promissory Note

The earnest money promissory note is used when the prospective purchaser is not providing earnest money in cash, check, or property. There are many reasons the purchaser may not wish to or may not be able to provide liquid earnest money at the time the offer is made. For example, the purchaser may have funds tied up in a certificate of deposit with an early withdrawal penalty and does not wish to liquidate the funds until the offer is accepted. In discussion prior to the offer being made, the listing broker should help the seller evaluate the reasons and the amount of security provided by a note, and then the seller should decide whether the promissory note is acceptable. If the seller will accept the note, the listing broker will then inform the buyer's broker who will then write the offer and clearly identify that an earnest money promissory note is being used, as well as, including the due date and the signed note attached to the offer [Rule E-1(m)].

The listing broker is responsible to present the note for payment in a timely manner for redemption and inform the seller if it is not paid. Notes or checks for earnest money are to be made payable to the listing brokerage firm that is responsible for timely collection of the note [Rule E-1(m)]. Any costs associated with collecting the note are the responsibility of the buyer without limitation.

A signed promissory note **must be due prior to closing** so the funds will be available in the broker's trust account as *good funds* to be disbursed at closing. Once the note is paid, the money is then deposited into the broker's trust account or otherwise as agreed by the parties.

F I G U R E   1.4

Earnest Money Promissory Note – Sample Only

The printed portions of this form, except differentiated additions, have been approved by the Colorado Real Estate Commission (EMP 80-5-04)

EARNEST MONEY
Promissory Note

U.S. $ _____

_____, _____   Date:_____
City   State

FOR VALUE RECEIVED,

_____
Name(s) of Maker(s)

_____,
Address

jointly and severally, promise to pay to the order of

_____

the sum of

_____Dollars,

with interest at _____ per cent per annum from _____until paid.

Both principal and interest are payable in U.S. dollars on or before_____, payable at

or at such other address as note holder may designate. Presentment, notice of dishonor, and protest are hereby waived. If this note is not paid when due, I/we agree to pay all reasonable costs of collection, including attorney's fees.

_____
Maker's signature

_____
Maker's signature

This note is given as earnest money for the contract on the following property:

■ RECORD KEEPING

Trust Account Records and Record-Keeping Systems

Every real estate brokerage firm or independent broker is required to keep transaction files with copies of various documents and supporting information. Commission Rules E-4 and E-5 describe the contents of the required closing files, for listing/buyer's brokers whether acting as agent, transaction broker or when the seller or buyer is a customer. All files and records must be retained for **four years** by the brokerage firm.

Every brokerage firm who maintains a trust account must maintain a record keeping system for **each** trust account. The accounting system may be manual or computerized, but it must contain all of the following types of records and historical reports.

Account records   In addition to the bank account agreement and Notice of Maintaining a Trust Account form for each trust account, the broker must maintain the following records:

1. Account journal of all cash receipts/disbursements—a chronological record of all money going into and out of the account plus a running balance of the account at any one time. All entries come from matching ledger cards. The journal is used to account for all the ledger cards and the balance of all money in the trust account. It does **not** contain specific information, such as Social Security or tax identification numbers.
2. Beneficiary ledger card system—a series of individual records segregating receipts and disbursements as they affect individual beneficiaries or transactions. The ledger contains transaction specific information, such as Social Security and tax identification numbers.
3. Broker ledger card—a record of brokerage funds used to open and maintain the account and cover related service charges as they are incurred.
4. Bank reconciliation records—the trust account must be reconciled to the bank statement at least once a month in any month where there is account activity. The reconciliation records must be retained with the account records.

Transaction files   No funds may go into or out of a trust account without proper documentation. Individual transaction files are where the required documentation is kept and used to support the financial activity in the account including invoices or other documents to support disbursements. These would include the Contract to Buy and Sell, management agreements, bills, and so forth—any financial paperwork for the property. This file's monetary documentation should match what is noted on the beneficiary ledger card.

Samples of these records for a manual accounting system can be found in the Colorado Real Estate Manual. If a principal broker uses a computerized accounting system, the broker must assure that the various reports and other records required by the Commission can be generated by the system.

Account journal entries must sufficiently identify the funds and include the date, the name of the party giving the money, the name of the beneficiary (seller, tenant, owner, and so forth), property identification, document reference, and amount. Disbursements must also include the check number. The ledger entries also include the specific details for the property and the parties, such as Social Security number and contact information and so forth.

Transaction files should include bids, invoices, contracts, or other written documents that must support disbursement of funds from a trust account. Deposit slips should be accompanied with details about the type of funds tendered, such as earnest money, the name(s) of who tendered the funds, and for what transaction or property. Disbursements should be accompanied by receipts or invoices identifying the purpose of the payment, the property address, and the account or principal involved. All documents pertinent to the sale, management agreements, and so forth are to be maintained in the transaction file [Rule E-1(p)(6)].

The following page depicts an example of a principal broker of a small company who does property management and also lists real estate all within one trust account. A brokerage firm that manages less than seven (six or less) rental properties may manage the properties, hold the security deposits, and hold earnest money within one trust account [Rule E-1(I) less than seven rule]. More typical would be a brokerage firm having separate sales trust, management trust, and security deposit trust accounts. The flow of funds through the trust account is shown and how the various records are impacted by the process. Entries in the account journal are shown along with individual beneficiary ledger card entries for a listed property and managed property owners and the broker's ledger as well as the broker's operating account journal. Employed brokers' commissions are not to be paid from the trust account. The following diagram represents the flow of the money through the trust account and payment of the commissions to the firm.

FIGURE 1.5

Journal and Ledger Card Example

Journal–Chronological record of all ledgers within the account

Broker funds
Deposit to maintain account   50   50

Property	Action		Balance
Ash St	Sec. Deposit	$1,000	1,050
Ash St	Nov Rent	1,000	2,050
Ash St	ck to owner	(900)	1,150
Ash St	ck to ABC	(100)	1,050
Main St	Deposit	$1,500	2,550
Main St	ck to plumber	(200)	2,350
Main St	ck to owner	(1,150)	1,200
Main St	ck to ABC	(150)	1,050
Elm St	Earnest Money In	$5,000	6,050
Balance			6,050

Broker Ledger–ABC Brokerage

		Balance
Deposit, maintain property management account	$50	$50

Ledger–Property/Person Specific

143 Ash St
Jane Smith owner
112 Maple
Somewhere, CN
SSN# 233-00-0000

		Balance
Sec. Deposit Held	1,000	1,000
Rent 11-06	1,000	2,000
Ck to Smith	(900)	1,100
Ck to ABC	(100)	1,000
(management fee)		

Ledger–Property/Person Specific

643 Main St
Sherry Jones owner
112 Maple
Wowtown, CA
Tax Id 0010202
Seller holding Security Deposit of $1,500

		Balance
Rent 11-06	1,500	1,500
Ck to plumber	(200)	1,300
Ck to Jones	(1,150)	150
Ck to ABC	(150)	0
(management fee)		

ABC Operations Account

Commission from property
Management account 11-06

		Balance
Ash	$100	$100
Main	$150	$250
Check to Broker Associate		
50/50 split		$175
Balance		$175

Ledger–Property/Person Specific

621 Elm St
Colorado Town, CO
Robert & Mary Smith, Sellers
Fred & Martha Jones, Buyers

	Balance
Earnest Money Dep	5,000

Commissions earned by the firm and payable from funds in the trust account must be withdrawn from the trust account to avoid commingling of these funds. While the Commission does not state a period of time for this withdrawal to occur, it requires the funds to be withdrawn **promptly** and moved to the operating account once they are earned. Failure to do so is an improper commingling of funds [Rule E-1(f)(1)].

Safeguards

Even in a corporate brokerage firm, the principal broker has personal responsibility for the proper maintenance and security of the trust accounts. Several specific practices can help reduce the risk of loss through accidental clerical errors, improper practices, and employee dishonesty. Too often a principal broker with a trust account shortage did not know it was short and does not know where the money went. Often it stems from poor record keeping or improper accounting. Safeguards include the following:

1. **Frequent reconciliation** to the bank. Because the bank statement reflects the funds actually present in the account, frequent reconciliation will point out any inconsistencies soon after they happen. A proper reconciliation balances all of the ledger cards with the journal balance and with the actual cash balance in the bank. If the account does not balance, the principal broker must quickly determine what the issue is and rectify the problem.
2. **Separation of duties.** The person who is in charge of the everyday bookkeeping should not normally do the bank reconciliation. As an alternative, the bank reconciliation may be reviewed in detail by the principal broker. If the principal broker does all the bookkeeping, a review by an accountant could spot problems the broker does not notice.
3. **An outside audit.** A broker with a large or very active trust account may wish to have a company auditor or CPA review the account status on an annual basis to catch problems before they become serious. Homeowners' associations are required to have such an audit on their accounts.

Commingling/Conversion of Trust Funds

Commingling of funds is simply defined as the **improper mixing** of funds within an account. In a sales trust account, the most common type of commingling (mixing) of funds is between broker funds and trust funds. For example, once a commission or fee that is paid from trust account funds, it is earned and becomes the broker's money. It must then be withdrawn from the trust account **promptly** and transferred to the broker's operating account [Rule E-1(f)]. Failure to do so results in funds that now belong to the broker commingling with trust funds.

Conversion is defined as the **illegal** use of one party's funds to the benefit of another party. In property management accounts, conversion can occur in several ways. In an account where funds are held for several beneficiaries, using funds belonging to one beneficiary for the benefit of another is conversion.

■ **EXAMPLE 1.1**   If a broker managing two properties pays a bill for owner Ann at a time when there is sufficient money in the trust account to cover the check, but not enough on Ann's ledger card to pay the bill, this results in a negative balance in

Ann's ledger. The shortage must come from the other owners' funds. Now, the second owner's funds have been **converted** to benefit Ann. The broker should have requested Ann send money to cover the bill, so funds would not have been converted.

In order to avoid this kind of illegal act, each owner's ledger card must be reconciled before funds are disbursed either for the benefit of an owner or paid directly to an owner [Rule E-1(q)].

A single bank account may be used for a number of managed properties, but the ledger accounting must be accurate for each of the different properties and must avoid a negative balance for any property or owner as described above. Various arrangements could be used in the event an owner's obligation needs to be paid when insufficient funds are available. The bill could be sent to the owner for payment by the owner, the owner could be notified to remit additional funds into the trust in order for the broker to pay the bill, or the broker could advance funds by making a deposit into the trust the benefit of the property owner. Any of these procedures would avoid a negative balance in the owner's ledger, which would automatically result in the illegal conversion of funds. A ledger card may often have a zero balance but should never have a negative balance.

The principal broker must furnish accurate and timely accounting reports to the owner within 30 days after the end of the month in which funds were received or disbursed. The management agreement may provide for a specific accounting schedule, which may be more or less frequent than this [Rule E-1(p)(4)].

■ PROPERTY MANAGEMENT

Principal brokers engaged in property management have additional rules they must comply with because of the more complex financial arrangements common in property management agreements. The concerns of the Commission are the same: the protection of other people's money and the accurate accounting for funds held in trust. **Funds received in connection with property management activities must be deposited within five business days of receipt.**

Property Management Transaction Files

- Current/past management or short-term reservation agreements
- Current/past lease or rental occupancy agreement
- Lead-Based Paint Disclosure for residential property built before 1978
- Disclosure of brokerage relationships and/or listing contracts to lease
- Disclosure of compensation/service income from affiliated entities
- Accounting/tax reports/records required by Commission regulations or other laws
- Ongoing contracts, bids, invoices from vendors, service providers, travel agents, or marketing organizations
- Legal notices, actions, accounting reports affecting owner/occupant/tenant funds
- Documentation for commissions/fees earned versus taken/charged to others

■ Evidence of prompt assessment and timely (45–90 days) collection and resti-
tution of all money due to the broker's trust account from any source

■ Documentation verifying reported receipts, income, and all expenses paid for
another

Accounts

In addition to the sales trust account, a property management broker will usually require the management trust account and security deposits trust account,
described previously. In certain circumstances, an advance rental account or an
other association trust account may be required.

Less than seven rule   By Real Estate Commission policy, a broker may use
the sales trust account for those funds involving management of a small number
of single family properties. Rule E-1(I) refers to "less than seven (7) single family
residential units (6 or less) . . . ." In that instance, the rents and security deposits
may flow through the sales trust account with proper record keeping.

Security Deposits

Security deposits are one of the most common causes for complaints regarding
property management firms. These deposits may have been held over a long period
of time, through a change of management companies, and possibly even different
property owners. Colorado law and Commission rules and position statements
provide guidance for most circumstances.

1. A security deposit must be held in a separate trust account set aside for
   security deposits. They may not be kept in the same trust account with
   management funds unless the brokerage meets the less than seven exception
   mentioned previously.
2. The brokerage is responsible for the security deposit funds and is expected to
   keep them in a trust account under the principal broker's control. Security
   deposits may be turned over to the property owner only with tenant authorization in the lease or after written notice to the tenant by first class mail.
   This rule assures that the tenant knows how to seek return of the deposit if
   the lease is carried out faithfully (Rule E-16).
3. If security deposit funds are transferred to a new property manager, tenants
   must be notified in writing of the change along with instructions for contacting the new manager. The previous property manager must account fully for
   the funds to the owner and the new property management firm. Failure to
   provide notice of the transfer of the security deposits to the owner or to a
   new manager could result in the previous management firm being liable for
   return of the funds to the tenants.
4. If the property is sold, per the Contract to Buy and Sell, the seller is required
   to give the tenant notice of the new owner's name and address, so the tenant
   will know by whom and where their deposit is being held.

Colorado law is definite about the procedures for the return of security deposits.
A landlord or property manager, as agent for the landlord, must return the deposit
within one month after the termination of a lease or surrender and acceptance of
the premises. The lease may specify a longer period but not more than 60 days. If

there is reason to keep all or part of the deposit, the landlord must provide a statement listing the exact reasons for keeping any part of the deposit. Payment of the balance of the deposit must accompany the list.

If the landlord or property manager, as agent, does not provide the return of the deposit or the required statement of deductions, he may be liable for damages of triple (or treble) the amount wrongfully withheld. The law places the responsibility on the landlord to prove that the deposit was not wrongfully withheld.

The lease should clearly state that the security deposit is not an advance payment of rent. Some municipalities in Colorado require the payment of interest on advance rent payments. Accepting the deposit as the last month's rent could also create a liability to pay interest as it is advance rent.

Short-Term Occupancy Agreements

Brokers engaged in property management may collect deposits or advance rental payments for short-term occupancy agreements. These would be common in the management of resort condominiums and other resort properties. The Real Estate Commission has taken the position that these funds need to be held in appropriate trust accounts. Since the short-term agreements are usually more like hotel rentals than leases, a real estate license may not be required in order to receive the funds. Some resort management firms have elected to set up separate nonlicensed companies to handle this part of their business. However, if a licensed broker receives them, they must be in a trust account (CP-19, Commission Position on Short Term Occupancy Agreements).

Principal Broker-Owned Properties

Principal brokers may manage properties in which they have a part ownership interest, such as real estate partnerships, joint ventures, and syndications. They may also receive compensation for selling or leasing the property. Brokers who receive compensation for managing properties in which they have ownership interest must maintain a separate trust account for these properties to keep the broker's funds segregated from any other managed property [Rule E-1(f)(5)].

Homeowners' Association Management

The Real Estate Commission rules mandate the retention of required records for a period of four years. However, brokers managing common-interest community properties have different record retention requirements.

A principal broker managing a common interest (homeowners') association is generally the **temporary custodian** and trustee for the association records. Such records generally pertain to any budgeting, financial, or ongoing administration of the association business and related operating policies, conducted by the broker pursuant to the management agreement. These records belong to the association, not the broker. Rule E-3 requires that all such records be promptly returned to the association upon termination of the broker's employment. **A broker may retain file copies at the broker's own expense.**

It is recommended that the broker obtain an itemized receipt from any new manager or the association board, stating they have received all records and accounts that were previously in the broker's custody. This statement should acknowledge the statutory requirement applicable to the broker for retention of these records for four years and waive any claim against the broker for release of such records in the event of subsequent loss or destruction.

■ CLOSING

Transaction Records

Real Estate Commission Rules and good business practices determine what a principal broker should keep in transaction files. The following lists relate to sales transactions whether they are residential or commercial. Lease and rental transactions will have similar requirements to retain all of the relevant contracts, agreements, and supporting documents, such as inspection reports.

The following is a list for common records to be retained in both the listing and buyer's broker's transaction files. Documents, records, and agreements executed by the parties with the closing entity or lender that are not listed below need not be copied or retained in the listing and buyer's broker's file.

Sales Files

- Lead-Based Paint Disclosure for residential property built before 1978
- Exclusive Right-to-Buy Listing Contract (buyer's broker only)
- Exclusive Right-to-Sell Listing Contract (listing broker only)
- Brokerage Relationships Disclosure Form—Brokerage Disclosure to Buyer or to FSBO
- Disclosure of compensation for services and income from affiliated entities
- Square Footage Disclosure for residential property
- The correct Contract to Buy and Sell (e.g., residential, commercial, etc.)
- Current marketing/MLS information used in the transaction
- Inspection Notice
- Seller's Property Disclosure
- Approved Closing Instructions form—negotiated before the actual date of closing
- Copy of Power-of-Attorney (show recording data if closed in-house)
- Earnest Money Promissory Note (copy)
- Earnest Money Receipt held by third-party closing entity
- Buyer's financial information—owner-carry financing
- Rental/occupancy agreement before closing date
- Estimated closing costs/estimated monthly expenses
- Closing statement (for the party represented or assisted)
- Side agreement/amendment to revise a closing statement
- Closing entity commission check remittance less earnest money amount if applicable
- Escrow receipts or collection agreements—continuing after closing
- Accountings for use of advance retainer fees (Rule E-2)

The following are also required to be retained in the files if the broker personally prepares the document or conducts the closing (in-house without use of a title company) and/or is responsible for the recording of any documents:

- Six-column worksheet for settlement or equivalent form
- Deed (copy showing recording data if closed in-house)
- Deed of trust (copy showing recording data in-house)
- Promissory note (unsigned marked "COPY")
- Other legal documents prepared by the broker
- Transaction/tax reports required by government agencies

Broker associates attending a closing without their employing broker must deliver all closing and related documents to the employing broker **immediately** following the closing for proper filing. Commission required records and files must be maintained in good order by the principal brokerage firm for at least **four years**. Broker associates may maintain separate personal files and have no requirement on how long the files are to be held.

If the brokerage is a corporation, partnership, or limited liability company, this business entity is responsible for the records. If the entity dissolves, the final acting broker retains personal responsibility for records retention.

If an individual proprietorship dissolves, the records maintenance remains the responsibility of the individual proprietor broker and heirs.

■ CLOSING FUNDS

Good Funds

Rule E-36 requires that *good funds* be available before money is disbursed at a closing. This includes the earnest money held by the brokerage firm. *Good funds* generally means that a bank will immediately issue cash for whatever form the funds are in. This is obviously not true for a personal, business, or trust account check. Good funds will normally include wire transfers, telephone transfers between accounts in the same bank, cashier's checks, certified checks, teller's checks (from a savings and loan or credit union), and special agreements by which a bank agrees to accept and guarantee a particular check. Even cashier's checks are not foolproof because they could be from a nonexistent bank or otherwise fraudulently created. Many title companies will not take an out-of-town cashier's check without verification, which could include investigating the bank itself. It is the designated broker associate's responsibility to assure that the parties appear with the proper form of funds acceptable to the closing agent.

The earnest money, if being held by the brokerage firm, can be transferred to the title company early in order for the title company to have good funds. The broker associate can bring the earnest money to the closing as a cashier's or teller's check or applicable good funds. The earnest money is going to be credited to the buyer at closing because the buyer has met the requirements of the contract. If a transaction is to be closed by a title insurance company, attorney, or other closing agent, the broker may transfer funds to the closing agent from the broker's trust account with enough lead time for the check to clear and provide good funds.

■ CONFIDENTIAL INFORMATION

Real Estate Commission Position Statement CP-22 provides brokers and brokerage firms with guidance about maintaining confidentiality of various records and files. The advent of *designated brokerage* created the necessity to keep files confidential from others **within the brokerage firm** as well as anyone outside the firm.

Prior to designated brokerage, it was common practice to discuss clients' needs and motivations with others within the company typically in a company sales meeting. Because the company owned the contract and the relationship was with the brokerage firm, there was *imputed knowledge* among all brokers in the firm, and sharing this information was appropriate. Designated brokerage ended that by allowing designated brokers within the firm to each establish a relationship with their own clients. There is no longer imputed knowledge with others in the firm—including the employing broker. This permits all designated brokers within the firm to maintain an agency or transaction brokerage relationships with their respective clients without compromising their clients' interests. For example, one designated broker can be the listing broker with seller agency with the seller, and another designated broker can have buyer agency with the buyer in the same transaction because confidential information is no longer shared with others in the firm.

Brokerage firms must now take extra care with all common files of client records and **communications** to protect the confidentiality of the firm's clients. CP-22 addresses the Commission's concerns regarding the types of precautions brokerage firms are expected to take.

REVIEW EXAM FOR TRUST ACCOUNTS AND RECORD KEEPING

(Complete this review exam and check your answers using the answer key provided)

1. In a cooperative transaction in which one broker holds an exclusive-right-to-sell listing contract and another broker is the buyer's broker, the
   a. buyer's broker must place the earnest money in a trust account within one business day after acceptance of the offer.
   b. listing broker must place the earnest money in a trust account immediately upon receipt of the offer.
   c. any earnest money promissory note will be the responsibility of the buyer's broker to redeem.
   d. buyer's broker must deliver the earnest money deposit to the listing broker immediately upon acceptance.

2. In the event a dispute arises between a seller and a buyer regarding the earnest money, the principal broker
   a. must return the earnest money to the buyer immediately.
   b. should notify the Real Estate Commission.
   c. may interplead the earnest money into court.
   d. should disburse the earnest money to the seller.

3. In a real estate sale, if the broker places the earnest money deposit in an interest-bearing account, any accrued interest
   a. belongs to the listing broker.
   b. belongs to the seller.
   c. must be agreed to in writing by the principals.
   d. is shared by the listing and selling broker.

4. A chronological summary of the cash receipts and disbursements made by the broker, which affect the cash balance of the trust account, is the
   a. property file.
   b. account journal.
   c. management file.
   d. ledger.

5. Which of the following details receipts and disbursements as they affect a particular property?
   a. Property file
   b. Journal
   c. Management file
   d. Beneficiary ledger

6. The employing broker should pay the associate brokers' commissions from the
   a. business operating account.
   b. trust account.
   c. management account.
   d. sales trust account.

7. After the closing of a property transaction, the balance on the beneficiary ledger card
   a. should be zero.
   b. might be negative if bills were paid before closing.
   c. should be the same as the balance reflected on the broker's ledger card.
   d. should be equal to the check the buyer must bring to closing.

8. The broker must maintain a separate transaction file for each property under a lease, purchase, sale, or exchange of real property. This file must be kept for how many years?
   a. 5
   b. 4
   c. 7
   d. 12

9. Which of the following documents must the listing broker keep in the property file? A signed copy of the
   a. good faith estimate provided by the lender.
   b. promissory note if prepared by the broker.
   c. listing contract, sale contract, and closing statements.
   d. loan application and deed of trust.

10. A broker managing how many properties must maintain a property management trust account?
    - a. 2
    - b. 4
    - c. 6
    - d. 8

11. A broker must first open a trust account
    - a. prior to applying for a license.
    - b. before going to work for an employing broker.
    - c. before activating an inactive license.
    - d. when first receiving earnest money for deposit.

12. The document that reports all specific income and expenses associated with a particular owner's property is the
    - a. account journal.
    - b. beneficiary ledger card.
    - c. tenant record.
    - d. property management file.

13. Security deposits collected from tenants in connection with property management must be held in the
    - a. property management trust account.
    - b. security deposits trust account.
    - c. operating account until returned.
    - d. advance rental trust account.

14. In the case of an interest-bearing sales trust account, interest
    - a. earned belongs to the broker.
    - b. may be paid to a non-profit affordable housing fund.
    - c. earned must be paid to the seller.
    - d. may be applied to closing costs.

15. The Real Estate Commission has the authority to audit a broker's files
    - a. at any time.
    - b. only if written notification is received by the broker at least 24 hours in advance.
    - c. only if the broker has received verbal notification at least 24 hours in advance.
    - d. only after receipt of a verified written complaint.

16. Earnest money received by a listing broker must be
    - a. delivered to the buyer's broker.
    - b. deposited in the sales trust account no later than the third business day following notice of acceptance of the contract.
    - c. deposited in a trust account no later than the third business day following receipt.
    - d. held by the buyer's agent for the buyer.

REVIEW EXAM ANSWER KEY

#	Answer	Rationale
1.	D	In a cooperative transaction, the listing broker or title company will hold the earnest money. The buyer's broker must deliver the funds immediately after acceptance of the offer.
2.	C	The principal broker in an earnest money dispute may interplead the money to court if no resolution has been found during mediation.
3.	C	Earnest money in an interest-bearing account must be agreed to in writing by all parties. The interest may go to an affordable housing program with notice from the principal broker to the parties.
4.	B	Account journals are a chronological summary of all ledger records in the trust account.
5.	D	The beneficiary ledger accounts for all property details.
6.	A	Commissions to broker associates may only be paid from the principal broker's operating account.
7.	A	Upon closing, the property ledger card should have a zero balance. A negative balance reflects conversion of funds from one owner to another.
8.	B	The principal broker must retain all records for four years.
9.	C	A listing broker's file should have the listing contract, sales contract, and closing statements.
10.	D	A principal broker may manage six or less properties in one account. Managing seven or more will require a security deposit and a management account.
11.	D	Principal brokers must have a trust account prior to receiving trust funds.
12.	B	Beneficiary ledger cards record specific information for each property.
13.	B	Security deposits are held in the security deposit account.
14.	B	Interest maybe paid to affordable housing programs.
15.	A	The Commission may audit accounts at any time.
16.	B	Earnest money must be deposited in the listing brokerage or title company trust account three business days after acceptance of the offer.

■ LECTURE OUTLINE

I.   TRUST ACCOUNTS

A. Overview

1. Trust accounts are required any time a real estate brokerage firm is going to hold money that belongs to other people.

2. Trust accounts must follow specific rules established by statute and the Real Estate Commission and are subject to audit by the Real Estate Commission.

B. Establishing Brokerage Accounts

1. Brokerage firms typically have two types of accounts:

   a) ___*Operations*___ used for running the firm

   b) ___*Trust Accounts*___ used to hold money for the benefit of others

2. A principal broker, who is any employing or independent broker who holds money for others, is required to put these funds in a trust account.

3. The principal broker must establish an account prior to receiving money belonging to others.

4. Employed or broker associates are ___*not*___ permitted to have trust accounts.

5. If the principal broker is not holding money belonging to others, no trust accounts are required.

   a) If the principal broker chooses to have a title company hold the funds, the principal broker will still be responsible for making sure the funds are in safe and proper keeping.

6. Principal brokers who have trust accounts must follow specific rules. The principal broker

   a) must use a ___*High level*___ of accuracy and care;

   b) is personally responsible for the funds in the trust account;

   c) is subject to commission audit ___*at any time*___ ; and

   d) should establish the trust account ___*prior*___ to receiving money belonging to others.

C. Operating a Trust Account

1. Principal brokers are responsible for supervising their trust accounts.

2. Principal brokers must be able to withdraw funds without a cosigner.

3. The trust account ___*may not contain operating funds*___ funds or any funds belonging to employed broker associates.

a) Employed brokers' commissions are paid from the broker's _operations account_.

4. Care must be taken to not commingle the broker's funds with trust funds.

   a) The account may contain _sufficient funds_ to open and operate the account.

   b) Commissions or other funds _that have been earned_ and belong to the broker must be removed from trust account _promptly_.

D. How Many Trust Accounts Does a Broker Need?

1. A broker needs enough trust accounts to assure that funds will not be _commingled_.

2. The Commission requires the following types of separate accounts when the broker is holding funds for others:

   a) _Sales_ trust account—for money held in connection with sales transactions pending closing, which is also known as _earnest money_.

   b) _Management_ trust account—for money held in connection with property management services.

   c) _Security Deposit_ trust account—for refundable security deposits collected from tenants for lease and rental units under management by the broker.

   d) Advance rental—for rental money collected in advance, especially for short-term rentals as experienced in resort and vacation rentals.

   e) Owners' association trust account—for funds held on behalf of condominium or planned-community associations. Use a separate account for each association and identify the account with the tax identification number of each association.

E. Requirements for a Trust Account

1. Trust accounts must be in a bank or appropriate institution located in _Colorado_.

2. They must be insured by a government agency, such as the _FDIC_.

3. Trust accounts cannot be held in a _Credit Union_ because only members' funds are insured.

4. Trust accounts must follow specific requirements of the Commission.

   a) The brokerage firm name and _the principal Brokers'_ personal name must be on account records.

5. The bank must recognize that the account is a trust account.

   a) Checks and _deposits_ slips must indicate that it is a trust account.

   b) Branch offices do not need trust accounts separate from main office unless they maintain separate bookkeeping systems as well.

F. Interest-Bearing Trust Accounts

1. The parties must agree if the account is to be interest bearing.

   a) Details of interest, fees, penalties, and disposition of interest are negotiated and
      written into the contract.

   b) These funds are placed in a trust account _seperate_ from all other funds held
      by broker.

2. Exception

   a) The broker's sales trust account may be an interest-bearing account if the interest benefits an
      affordable housing program.

      (1) Colorado Association of REALTORS® Housing Opportunity Fund (CARHOF)

   b) The brokerage must have a sign in the office indicating participation in this program.

      (1) The seller and buyer will approve the transfer in the Contract to Buy and Sell.

II. EARNEST MONEY

A. Earnest Money Deposits

1. Earnest money deposits are typically payable to the _listing broker_
   _____ and presented with the contract offer.

2. The type of the _earnest money_ (such as check or promissory
   note) is identified in the Contract to Buy and Sell.

   a) Earnest money is anything the seller will _accept_.

3. Checks must be deposited not later than the _3rd business day_
   following notice of _acceptance_ of the offer.

4. Earnest money can be held in the trust account of a _third party_, such as a
   title company, with the permission of the parties.

5. The holder of the earnest money is identified in the contract and is often shown in the
   MLS. Listing brokers must advise buyer's brokers if the earnest money is to be held by a
   third party.

6. If a contract _terminates_ under a provision of the contract or ends due to an
   undisputed default of either party, the broker is required to disburse the funds to the proper party
   without delay.

7. If there is a dispute regarding disbursement of the earnest money, broker may

   a) hold the funds until it is resolved;

   b) interplead the funds to the court if the dispute is not resolved; and

c) deliver notice to the parties of the intent to disburse funds to buyer if no action is taken within 120 calendar days of notice.

B. Earnest Money Promissory Note

1. A note is a reasonable alternative when the _buyer_ has limited funds available when the offer is submitted.

2. Notes are made payable to the _listing brokerage_ and must be identified with the due date specified in the Contract to Buy and Sell.

3. The due date must be before closing in time for the funds to be _good funds_ at closing.

4. If the note cannot be collected when due, the _listing broker_ must inform the seller immediately and is responsible for the collection of the funds.

   a) The seller can choose to declare the contract in default or agree to _extend_ the contract.

   b) Costs of collecting the promissory note are the responsibility of the buyer.

III. RECORD KEEPING

A. Records and Record-Keeping Systems

1. Principal brokers must have trust account records that include the following:

   a) Account journal of all cash receipts/disbursements—a _chronological record_ of all activity in the account

   b) _Beneficiary ledger_ account system—records with specific details regarding the parties for each transaction

   c) Broker ledger card—for funds _belonging to the Brokerage funds_

   d) Bank reconciliation records

      (1) Trust accounts must be reconciled _every month_ that there is activity in the account.

      (2) All disbursements and receipts must be supported by appropriate documentation in the transaction file.

2. The transaction file will include all support documents for any funds held in the trust account. At minimum, these records include copies of the following documents:

   a) Contract, _earnest money check_, Seller's Property Disclosure, listing or buyer representation agreement

   b) Copies of the _closing statements_ and other closing documents signed at closing for the parties they represented

   c)   Copies of other documents or checks (at the principal broker's option)

3.   Employing brokers are responsible to make sure that they have a complete file of all required documents and agreements made during the transaction.

   a)   Employed brokers are required to return files to the employing broker for review and filing _____*immediately*_____ after the closing.

4.   Brokers must maintain required records for a minimum of ____*4*____ years.

5.   The __*listing broker*__, must have the exclusive-right-to-sell listing contract in its file and the __*buyers broker*__ agreement or brokerage disclosure must be in the selling brokerage firm's file.

   a)   Both brokers' files are to have copies of the rest of the required documents.

6.   Most employing brokers will not disburse commission checks until the file is complete.

7.   Sole proprietors are responsible to retain their records for four years even if they leave the business entirely or close their office to join another brokerage firm. (If deceased, the heirs are responsible for records retention.)

B. Safeguards

1.   __*Frequent reconciliation*__

2.   Separation of duties

3.   Outside audits

4.   Real estate commission assistance

C. Commingling/Conversion of Trust Account Funds

1.   __*Commingly*__ is the improper mixing of operating account funds with trust account funds.

   a)   Not removing earned commissions or fees from the trust account __*promptly*__ is an example of commingling.

2.   The illegal practice of __*Conversion*__ is the use of one party's funds for the benefit of another party.

   a)   Paying bills for a property owner whose __*ledger card*__ does not have sufficient funds, even though the check will clear the bank, is an example of this.

3.   An owner's ledger card can have __*a zero balance*__ at times—this is not commingling or conversion. However, a negative balance for an owner is most likely an example of conversion.

4.   Brokers are responsible for accurate accounting for all funds held in their trust accounts.

5.   Business funds including payroll taxes or other employee withholdings do not belong in the real estate trust accounts.

D. Property Management

1. Accounts

   a) The management account holds funds belonging to the _property owners_ _____ and it is used to manage the property.

      (1) Deposits including rents or other income and payments of bills, including the broker's fee, flow through this account.

   b) Security deposits must be held in an account separate from the owner's account because the funds belong to the _tenants_ (unless meeting the less than seven rule).

   c) Property management-related funds must be deposited into the appropriate trust account not later than _five business_ days following receipt of the money.

   d) Principal brokers who hold earnest money and manage properties must have the following:

      (1) A sales trust account to hold _earnest money_

      (2) At least one property management account for owners' funds

      (3) At least one _Security deposit_ trust account for tenants' funds

      (4) A broker can have an unlimited number of deposits for each type of funds in the above accounts—separate accounting using the _ledger card_ identifies the individual transactions and properties.

2. Security deposits

   a) The lease and management agreement specify who holds the deposit—owner or broker—as tenants must know who has their money.

   b) The broker can turn the deposit over to the owner

      (1) with written authorization of tenant;

      (2) if the _lease_ calls for it; or

      (3) after notifying the tenant in writing that the owner is holding the deposit.

   c) The broker is responsible for security deposits and _must notify tenants_ _____ if no longer managing the property and advise tenants how to contact the new manager.

   d) The security deposit must be returned in full or an accounting of the reason the deposit was kept must be sent to the tenant within one month or within _60_ if the lease calls for it.

3. Short-term occupancy funds and advance rental payments are not security deposits and are held in management trust accounts.

4. Brokers who receive compensation for managing a property in which they have an ownership interest are required to use a separate management account for those properties.

5. Homeowners' association records belong to the association not the brokerage firm. Rule E-3 requires that all such records be promptly returned to the association upon termination of the broker's employment. A broker may retain file copies at the _Brokers own_ _Expens_.

IV. CLOSING FUNDS

A. _Good Funds_ **must be available for closing.**

1. Good funds include

a) wire transfers;

b) cashier's checks; and

c) teller's checks (savings and loan or credit union).

2. Good funds are NOT personal checks or company checks.

B. Clients must bring their funds in good funds.

1. A check made payable _to the client_ is recommended.

C. The broker may deliver earnest money to closing entity prior to closing.

1. The broker gets a receipt for earnest money—closing instructions or Earnest Money Receipt form.

V. CONFIDENTIAL INFORMATION

A. Client's confidential information, such as _motivating_ **factors or the willingness to consider different price or terms, must be filed so as to protect the client's information.**

1. Confidential information must be protected from _other brokers_ within the firm.

2. _Designated brokerage_ eliminates imputed knowledge within the firm; other brokers are not presumed to have access to confidential information.

3. Commission Position Statement CP-22 discusses policies necessary to protect information within the firm.

CLOSINGS AND SETTLEMENT

■ CLOSINGS AND SETTLEMENT OVERVIEW

Objectives:

Colorado real estate brokers are obligated to provide the party they represent with a closing statement. This course is designed to give a new licensee competency in closing issues, including the following:

■ The basic skills required to properly close a real estate transaction
■ An understanding of the broker associates and employing broker's responsibilities, from the sales contract through and after the closing
■ The knowledge required to account for all funds received and disbursed
■ A comprehensive review of the legal documents the broker prepares

■ CLOSINGS AND SETTLEMENT DESCRIPTION

Closings and Settlement reviews the basic concepts needed to close a real estate transaction. Also known as *closing* or **settlement**, this process completes the financial transaction between a buyer and seller. It also ensures the necessary documents are prepared to carry out the transfer of ownership.

Important: By Colorado law, designated brokers are responsible for the closing statements for the party they represent.

Before class, or for Home Study Students:

1. Learn the Important Terms at the beginning of the unit.
2. Read the unit text (for example, before coming to the first classroom session, read Unit 1).
3. Complete the Glossary Review for the unit.

After class, or for Home Study Students:

Some units include **assignments that must be completed** as part of the course credit. Be sure to read and follow the instructions provided in each unit.

UNIT 1

Closings: The Big Picture

■ FOCUS ON UNDERSTANDING

- ■ The broker's role/responsibilities in a closing
- ■ Accounting for typical buyer, seller, and broker closing items
- ■ Prorating expenses between seller and buyer

■ ASSIGNMENTS AND STUDY PLAN

Before Unit 1:

1. Look up **Important Terms** (see next page) in the Glossary at the end of this workbook.
2. Read Unit 1 text.
3. Read section listed in the Colorado Prelicense Reading Guide.
4. Complete the Unit 1 Glossary Review.
5. Complete Exercise 1: Debit and Credits.

After Unit 1:

1. Complete Closing Exercise 1.
2. Read Unit 2 text (if you haven't already).

■ IMPORTANT TERMS

Buyer's broker	Deficit closing	Loan assumption
Broker's escrow account	Designated broker	Mortgage insurance
Certificate of taxes due	Documentary fee	Notary
Closing	Hazard insurance	Proration
Closing Statement	Homeowners' association	Recording
CREDIT	Lender reserve (impound)	Six-column closing
DEBIT	account	worksheet
Deed of trust (trust deed)	Listing broker	Trust account

■ CLOSING A REAL ESTATE TRANSACTION

The Big Picture

Closing day is an exciting day for all involved. The seller will convey title to the property and get a check for equity. The buyer is finally going to own the property and the brokers will get a paycheck. This course covers the financial piece of the real estate transaction: the final step the real estate broker is responsible for in order to collect the commission that is owed the brokerage.

The requirements of the closing are created in the Contract to Buy and Sell. The seller, in exchange for the money the buyer brings, will convey title by giving the buyer a deed. The closing would be very simple if there were no liens, taxes, or other charges. The buyer would just hand the seller a check for the sales price and the seller would give the buyer the deed to the property.

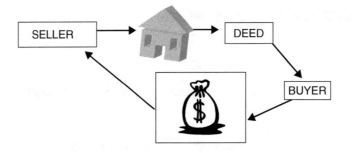

Even if the seller has no liens or debt against the property and the buyer is paying all cash, there will be a minimum number of charges, called *entries*, that have to be taken care of at closing. These entries are called DEBITS (money owed) and CREDITS (money received).

A simple cash closing One of the entries the seller will be asked to pay for is title insurance for the buyer. Remember: this is standard in the Contract to Buy and Sell. Additionally, the seller will need to pay a share of the tax bill for the current year and may owe some water or other fees. The seller also typically pays the broker's fee and the fee to notarize their signature on the warranty deed. All of these are amounts that are owed and will be DEBITS to the seller.

The seller's side of closing

Seller will receive the sales price	+ $CREDIT to seller
Seller will owe broker and notary fees, and a prorated share of water	– $DEBIT what seller owes +/– based on when the bill is owed advance or arrears
Taxes for the current year—**always paid in arrears so the seller will owe the buyer**	– $<u>DEBIT</u> the seller portion of the year
Remaining balance of money to seller.	**The check the seller takes with them—called "net proceeds"**

The buyer's side of closing

The buyer will pay money for recording the deed, tax certificate, and documentary fee, which will be a DEBIT to them and CREDIT to the broker. The Broker will write the checks to pay the bill for the buyer. The buyer may owe the seller for water (if the bill was paid in advance), but should receive from the seller the seller's portion of taxes for the current year. These prorations are shared between the buyer and seller depending upon when the bill is due. For example, taxes, which are paid in arrears in Colorado, will always be a DEBIT to the seller, who owes the bill, and a CREDIT to the buyer, who will pay the bill when it comes due next year.

The buyer will receive the deed in exchange for the money the buyer brings, in this case, cash.

Buyer will receive deed but must give cash	–$DEBIT sales price from buyer
Buyer will owe tax certificate, recording, and notary fee	–$DEBIT from buyer
Prorated share of water	<u>DEBIT or CREDIT based on if the bill is paid in advance or arrears</u>
Total is the balance of the cash the buyer will need to bring to closing	**Good funds check from buyer**

Closing is simply the seller paying the bills so the property can be conveyed according to the Contract to Buy and Sell. Additionally, the broker or title closer will need to determine the total amount the buyer will need to bring to closing, in order to meet the bills and pay the seller the agreed sales price.

■ UNDERSTANDING THE REAL ESTATE SETTLEMENT

The buyer and seller negotiate a purchase contract that includes various items to be charged at the closing table and identifies various responsibilities for each party before the sale of the property can be finalized. The transaction may involve a variety of parties and service providers including the following:

- Seller
- Buyer
- Designated listing broker (working with the seller)
- Designated buyer's broker (working with the buyer)
- Current and/or new lender
- Many service providers such as title insurance companies, attorneys, appraisers, surveyors, inspectors, etc.

The designated brokers working with the seller and buyer must ensure all parties meet their obligations and are compensated as specified in the contract.

To the average buyer and seller, the closing is a blizzard of paperwork they may or may not understand but must sign, an overwhelming amount of numbers, and a large check they either bring to, or take away from, closing. They rely on their real estate professional to guide and educate them through the contract and closing process. Even more importantly, they rely on their real estate broker to ensure the transaction is closed properly.

What Happens at Closing?

At a real estate closing, the brokers and the closing company have the duty to ensure title to the real estate is correctly passed from the seller to the buyer. The buyer and seller must meet their obligations set forth in the Contract to Buy and Sell. The seller may have to pay off prior obligations and liens. The buyer will probably get a new loan, or assume (take over) an existing loan now held by the seller. The brokers' and closing company's responsibilities include ensuring the correct paperwork is drafted then signed by the appropriate parties and often recorded with the County Clerk and Recorder. The brokers are responsible to check that each party has paid for any services they agreed to in the contract and the payment for the property is in place before the deed is delivered and accepted.

The majority of closings are handled by title insurance companies in Colorado, but the Colorado Real Estate Commission holds licensed brokers responsible to either perform the closing, or check it thoroughly prior to the actual transfer of title. Every closing is different, but they all involve a lot of very specific paperwork and financial accounting.

Listing Brokerage and Listing Broker

The listing brokerage firm and listing broker have an overall responsibility to ensure a proper closing happens. The designated buyer's broker should deliver earnest money to the listing broker either with the offer, or immediately upon acceptance of the offer, when it becomes an executory contract. The listing broker will have three days to deposit the earnest money into an escrow account, belonging to either the brokerage firm or the title company.

Designated Broker Responsibilities

The broker designated by an employing broker to assist or represent the seller or buyer is responsible for the "proper closing of the transaction" and shall "sign and be responsible for" a Closing Statement as it applies to the party with whom that broker has a *brokerage relationship*. This means that an associate broker who has been appointed by the employing broker in writing or by written company policy as the designated broker for the seller or buyer is personally responsible for the accuracy and completeness of the seller's or buyer's closing documents and finances. Thus, the designated listing broker is responsible for the overall closing and the seller's Closing Statement and the designated buyer's broker is responsible for the buyer's Closing Statement.

License law requires Closing Statements be delivered to the parties at the time of delivery and acceptance of the title at closing. The 2-column Closing Statement is designed to meet this requirement. Other forms prepared by a title company or other closing entity are acceptable, but must meet the minimum requirements of the Commission rules.

What if a broker can't make it to the closing?   Brokers for both parties are expected to attend closing. If they cannot attend, they may have their employing broker designate another broker to attend in their place. The employing broker, the original broker, and the newly appointed broker will all share the responsibility of the closing being accurate.

Title Company or Other Closing Entity

The parties to the contract may, and most often do, engage a company other than the listing brokerage to carry out the settlement services. The Real Estate Commission has approved a form to use in setting up this relationship. The *Closing Instructions* document reproduced on the next pages identifies and allocates the proper responsibilities. The document can be completed**, prior to, or with the delivery of, the earnest money.**

The closing company then becomes responsible to the parties for their work in preparing the paperwork. The Real Estate Commission rules **do not however, permit the brokers to escape responsibility.** The designated brokers are still responsible for checking the closing company's work, on behalf of the party they represent.

The last two sections of the *Closing Instructions* form are separate agreements between the closing company and the listing brokerage firm. The firm hires the closing company as *scrivener* to prepare the legal documents. The closing company is not authorized to perform this limited practice of law, so the closing company does it under the authority (and responsibility) of the listing broker. The listing broker is also obligated to pay for the legal documents the closing company prepares as scrivener, such as the deed, bill of sale or promissory note, and deed of trust.

F I G U R E   1.1

Closing Instructions

1 The printed portions of this form, except differentiated additions, have been approved by the Colorado Real Estate Commission.
2 (CL8-8-10) (Mandatory 1-11)

3

4 **THIS FORM HAS IMPORTANT LEGAL CONSEQUENCES AND THE PARTIES SHOULD CONSULT LEGAL AND TAX OR**
5 **OTHER COUNSEL BEFORE SIGNING.**

6

7   # CLOSING INSTRUCTIONS

8

9   Date: _____

10

11 **1.   PARTIES, PROPERTY.** _____, Seller, and
12 _____, Buyer,
13 engage _____, Closing Company, who agrees to provide
14 closing and settlement services in connection with the Closing of the transaction for the sale and purchase of the Property

15 known as No. _____,
16   Street Address   City   State   Zip

17 and more fully described in the Contract to Buy and Sell Real Estate, dated _____, including any
18 counterproposals and amendments (Contract).

19 **2.   INFORMATION, PREPARATION.** Closing Company is authorized to obtain any information necessary for the Closing.
20 Closing Company agrees to prepare, deliver and record those documents (excluding legal documents), and disburse all funds
21 pursuant to the Contract that are necessary to carry out the terms and conditions of the Contract.

22 **3.   CLOSING FEE.** Closing Company will receive a fee not to exceed $_____ for providing these closing and
23 settlement services.

24 **4.   RELEASE, DISBURSEMENT.** Closing Company is not authorized to release any signed documents or things of value
25 prior to receipt and disbursement of Good Funds, except as provided in §§ 8, 9 and 10.

26 **5.   DISBURSER.** Closing Company shall disburse all funds, including real estate commissions, except those funds as may be
27 separately disclosed in writing to Buyer and Seller by Closing Company or Buyer's lender on or before Closing. All parties agree
28 that no one other than the disburser can assure that payoff of loans and other disbursements will actually be made.

29 **6.   SELLER'S NET PROCEEDS.** Seller will receive the net proceeds of Closing as indicated: ☐ **Cashier's Check,** at
30 Seller's expense ☐ **Funds Electronically Transferred** (wire transfer) to an account specified by Seller, at Seller's expense ☐
31 **Closing Company's** trust account check.

32 **7.   CLOSING STATEMENT.** Closing Company will prepare and deliver an accurate, complete and detailed closing
33 statement to Buyer and Seller at time of Closing.

34 **8.   FAILURE OF CLOSING.** If Closing or disbursement does not occur on or before Closing Date set forth in the Contract,
35 Closing Company, except as provided herein, is authorized and agrees to return all documents, monies, and things of value to the
36 depositing party, upon which Closing Company will be relieved from any further duty, responsibility or liability in connection
37 with these Closing Instructions. In addition, any promissory note, deed of trust or other evidence of indebtedness signed by Buyer
38 shall be voided by Closing Company, with the originals returned to Buyer and a copy to Buyer's lender.

39 **9.   RETURN OF EARNEST MONEY.** Except as otherwise provided in § 10, Earnest Money Dispute, if the Earnest Money
40 has not already been returned following receipt of a Notice to Terminate or other written notice of termination, Earnest Money
41 Holder shall release the Earnest Money as directed by the written mutual instructions. Such release of Earnest Money shall be
42 made within five days of Earnest Money Holder's receipt of the written mutual instructions signed by both Buyer and Seller,
43 provided the Earnest Money check has cleared.

44 **10.   EARNEST MONEY DISPUTE.** In the event of any controversy regarding the Earnest Money (notwithstanding any
45 termination of the Contract), Earnest Money Holder shall not be required to take any action. Earnest Money Holder, at its option
46 and sole subjective discretion, may (1) await any proceeding, (2) interplead all parties and deposit Earnest Money into a court of
47 competent jurisdiction and shall recover court costs and reasonable attorney and legal fees, or (3) provide notice to Buyer and
48 Seller that unless Earnest Money Holder receives a copy of the Summons and Complaint or Claim (between Buyer and Seller)
49 containing the case number of the lawsuit (Lawsuit) within one hundred twenty days of Earnest Money Holder's notice to the
50 parties, Earnest Money Holder shall be authorized to return the Earnest Money to Buyer. In the event Earnest Money Holder does
51 receive a copy of the Lawsuit, and has not interpled the monies at the time of any Order, Earnest Money Holder shall disburse the
52 Earnest Money pursuant to the Order of the Court.

F I G U R E   1.1

Closing Instructions (continued)

53 **11.   SUBSEQUENT AMENDMENTS.** Any amendments to, or termination of, these Closing Instructions must be in writing
54 and signed by Buyer, Seller and Closing Company.

55 **12.   CHANGE IN OWNERSHIP OF WATER WELL.** Within sixty days after Closing, Closing Company shall submit any
56 required Change in Ownership form or registration of existing well form to the Division of Water Resources in the Department of
57 Natural Resources (Division), with as much information as is available, and the Division shall be responsible for obtaining the
58 necessary well registration information directly from Buyer. Closing Company shall not be liable for delaying Closing to ensure
59 Buyer completes any required form.

60 **13.   WITHHOLDING.** The Internal Revenue Service and the Colorado Department of Revenue may require Closing Company
61 to withhold a substantial portion of the proceeds of this sale when Seller either (a) is a foreign person or (b) will not be a Colorado
62 resident after Closing. Seller should inquire of Seller's tax advisor to determine if withholding applies or if an exemption exists.

63 **14.   ADDITIONAL PROVISIONS.** (The following additional provisions have not been approved by the Colorado Real Estate
64 Commission.)
65
66
67

68 **15.   COUNTERPARTS.** This document may be executed by each party, separately, and when each party has executed a copy,
69 such copies taken together shall be deemed to be a full and complete contract between the parties.

70 **16.   BROKER'S COPIES.** Closing Company shall provide, to each broker in this transaction, copies of all signed documents
71 that such brokers are required to maintain pursuant to the rules of the Colorado Real Estate Commission.

72 **17.   NOTICE, DELIVERY AND CHOICE OF LAW.**
73   **17.1.   Physical Delivery.** Except as provided in § 17.2, all notices must be in writing. Any notice or document to Buyer
74 shall be effective when physically received by Buyer, any individual buyer, any representative of Buyer, or Brokerage Firm of
75 Broker working with Buyer. Any notice or document to Seller shall be effective when physically received by Seller, any individual
76 seller, any representative of Seller, or Brokerage Firm of Broker working with Seller. Any notice or document to Closing
77 Company shall be effective when physically received by Closing Company, any individual of Closing Company, or any
78 representative of Closing Company.
79   **17.2.   Electronic Delivery.** As an alternative to physical delivery, any signed documents and written notice may be
80 delivered in electronic form by the following indicated methods only: ☐ **Facsimile** ☐ **Email** ☐ **Internet** ☐ **No Electronic**
81 **Delivery**. Documents with original signatures shall be provided upon request of any party.
82   **17.3.   Choice of Law.** This contract and all disputes arising hereunder shall be governed by and construed in accordance
83 with the laws of the State of Colorado that would be applicable to Colorado residents who sign a contract in this state for property
84 located in Colorado.

Buyer's Name: _____   Buyer's Name: _____

_____   _____   _____   _____
Buyer's Signature   Date   Buyer's Signature   Date

Address: _____   Address: _____

_____   _____

Phone No.: _____   Phone No.: _____
Fax No.: _____   Fax No.: _____
Electronic Address: _____   Electronic Address: _____

Seller's Name: _____   Seller's Name: _____

_____   _____   _____   _____
Seller's Signature   Date   Seller's Signature   Date

■ DEBITS AND CREDITS

The Settlement Closing worksheet and other closing documents use the terms *DEBIT* for items that are owed, and *CREDIT* for items or amounts received for the buyer and seller. They are given special meaning in real estate settlement that is not quite the same as in standard bookkeeping practice. Use the terms in this course as follows:

DEBIT: Items Owed

The word *DEBIT* means a bill **due from or charged** to either the buyer or seller on the day of closing.

■ A DEBIT for the seller reduces the amount of cash the seller takes away from closing.
■ A DEBIT for the buyer will increase the amount of cash the buyer will bring.

A DEBIT is **bad** (disadvantage) for that party's bottom line on closing day.

A **seller DEBIT** decreases the check the seller will receive at closing.

Typical seller DEBITS—bills—could include the following:

■ Owner's title insurance—paid for by the seller and given to the buyer
■ Unpaid property taxes for the preceding year
■ Prorated property taxes for the portion of the current year the seller owes
■ Notary fee for the warranty deed
■ Broker's commission—as agreed to in the listing agreement
■ Prorated water and homeowners' association (HOA) dues if paid in arrears
■ Loans of the seller are assumed by the buyer*
■ Seller's loans that have to be paid off*
■ New seller-carry loans (the amount of the loan the seller carries for the buyer at closing is money the seller will not receive at closing)*
■ Closing fees as determined by the Contract to Buy and Sell

*Note: If the seller is involved in the loan, it will be a seller DEBIT.

A **buyer DEBIT** increases the amount of **cash** the buyer must bring to closing.

Typical buyer DEBITS—items owed—could include the following:

■ Selling price of the property as determined by the contract
■ Loan closing costs as agreed to in the contract in conjunction with the lender
■ Premium for new hazard insurance
■ Recording fees for the warranty deed and deed of trust
■ Documentary fee based on the sales price
■ Notary fee for documents the buyer signs that require notarizing, such as the note and deed of trust
■ Closing fees
■ Tax certificate
■ Prorated water and HOA dues if paid in advance

CREDIT: Amounts Received

The word *CREDIT* means money **received** by either the buyer or seller on the day of closing

■ A CREDIT to the seller increases the amount the seller will receive
■ A CREDIT to the buyer reduces the amount the buyer must bring to closing

A CREDIT is **good** (advantage) for that party's bottom line on closing day.

A **seller CREDIT—amount received**—makes the seller's check on closing day larger.

Typical seller CREDITS include the following:

■ Selling price of the property as determined by the contract
■ Proration of bills paid in advance (already paid) by the seller such as homeowners' fees, water, etc.

A **buyer CREDIT** helps the buyer pay for property without bringing more **cash** to the closing.

Typical buyer CREDITS could include the following:

■ Earnest money already deposited by the buyer and held by the listing broker or closing company; the listing broker will be responsible for making sure this money is brought to closing if it is in the listing company escrow account
■ Security deposits transferred from a seller on an investment property
■ Current year's property taxes, (a prorated amount paid by the seller to the buyer, for the amount of time the seller lived in the property)
■ The amount of any loans assumed by the buyer or any new loans created as part of the purchase; **all** loans are a CREDIT to the buyer to pay off many of the bills at closing

Remember: DEBIT and CREDIT always relate to the seller's and buyer's cash position at closing.

■ A DEBIT—item owed—is a disadvantage (bad) for that party's cash at closing.
■ A CREDIT—amount received—is an advantage for that party's cash at closing.

The DEBIT and CREDIT columns for the broker refer to the broker's escrow account or ledger card for that particular transaction and have different meanings than they do for the buyer or seller.

A **broker DEBIT** is money to be **deposited** into the broker escrow account.

The two common broker **debits/deposits** are

■ buyer's earnest money, which will be credited to the buyer at closing; and
■ net loan proceeds, a deposit of funds from the lender when the buyer uses a new loan.

A **broker CREDIT** represents **money out of** the broker's escrow account to pay a bill. Think of it as a CHECK the broker will write to pay a bill for either the seller or the buyer. Remember, they charge the amount of the bill as a DEBIT to the responsible party.

Typical bills the broker will pay on behalf of the seller or buyer include

- title insurance;
- pay off to a lender; and
- recording, documentary, and notary fees.

Broker DEBIT = DEPOSIT/money in
Broker CREDIT = CHECK/money out

Closing forms

The buyer and seller will each receive a Closing Statement at the closing, which reflect their DEBITS and CREDITS only. The individual Closing Statements are created from the six-column closing worksheet we will be using throughout this course. The listing brokerage and the listing broker are responsible for the overall closing. The designated brokers are responsible for the Closing Statements for the party they represent. This means the listing broker will be responsible for the overall closing and the seller's Closing Statement but the designated buyer's broker will be responsible for making sure the figures on the buyer's Closing Statement are correct.

It is important to remember that all the forms, closing worksheet, and Closing Statements reflect only what happens at the closing table—the money in and out on that day. Items paid for before or after the closing will not be reflected in the cash the party brings or receives. For example: if the buyer assumes the seller's loan, the seller will be given a DEBIT for that amount since the seller will not be receiving those funds at the end of the closing, and the buyer will be given a CREDIT as the buyer will not have to bring money to cover the loan being assumed.

WORK SHEET FOR CLOSING STATEMENT

SELLER_____ BUYER_____
PROPERTY ADDRESS_____
SETTLEMENT DATE_____ DATE OF PROPATION _____
LEGAL DESCRIPTIONS:

	SELLER		BUYER		BROKER	
	Debit	Credit	Debit	Credit	Debit	Credit
1. Purchase Price						
2. Deposit (Earnest Money) Paid to						
3. Principal amount of new 1ˢᵗ loan payable to						
4. Principal amount of new 2ⁿᵈ loan payable to						
5. 1st loan Payoff to						
6. 2nd loan Payoff to						
7. Taxes for Preceding Year(s)						
8. Taxes for Current Year						
9. Presonal Property Tax						
10. Transaction Fee						
11. Loan Origination Fee						
12. Loan Discount Fee						
13. Appraisal Fee						

A broker preparing to close at the office would use the six-column worksheet to determine all the DEBITS and CREDITS for each of the three parties. The broker column is used to keep track of bills the broker needs to pay for the responsible party or to note the earnest money that will be a CREDIT to the buyer. Once the closing worksheet is complete, a separate Closing Statement is created for the buyer and the seller. At closing, only the individual Closing Statements will be reviewed and signed. More typically, the Closing Statements are created by the title company closer and reviewed prior to closing by each designated broker.

Closing Statement for seller or buyer

One statement is created for each party or side of the closing. No Closing Statement is created for the broker column, as these represent checks (CREDIT) the closer/broker will write to pay the bills for the responsible party or deposits (DEBIT) the broker receives, so no separate statement is needed.

The printed portions of this form, except differentiated additions, have been approved by the Colorado Real Estate Commission. (SS60-9-08)(Mandatory 1-09)

☐ESTIMATE	☐FINAL

CLOSING STATEMENT
☐SELLER'S   ☐BUYER'S

PROPERTY ADDRESS_____

SELLER_____   BUYER_____
SETTLEMENT DATE_____   DATE OF PROPATION _____
LEGAL DESCRIPTION:

	Debit	Credit
1. Purchase Price		
2. Deposit (Earnest Money) Paid to		
3. Principal amount of new 1st loan payable to		
4. Principal amount of new 2nd loan payable to		
5. 1st loan Payoff to		
6. 2nd loan Payoff to		

■ UNDERSTANDING THE REAL ESTATE SIX-COLUMN CLOSING WORKSHEET

The purpose of the closing is to finalize the sales contract as well as fulfill the broker's statutory obligation to furnish the buyer and the seller proper Closing Statements accounting for the transaction. Most of the major money amounts and their distribution are a direct result of what the buyer and seller have agreed to in the Contract to Buy and Sell Real Estate. Other items may depend upon state or federal law, tradition, requirements of a specific loan program, the lender, or who will benefit from the expense charged.

The **six-column closing worksheet** (shown on next page) is provided for the broker's convenience. Use of the form is **not mandatory**. It is used by the closer or broker to keep track of all the items that need to be debited and credited between the parties to create the closing documents. Once all the expenses are accounted for and the closing worksheet balances, then the broker will create the individual

Closing Statements for the buyer and seller. If the brokerage uses a title company all of these figures are in a computer program. There is no actual six-column closing worksheet produced, only the Closing Statements.

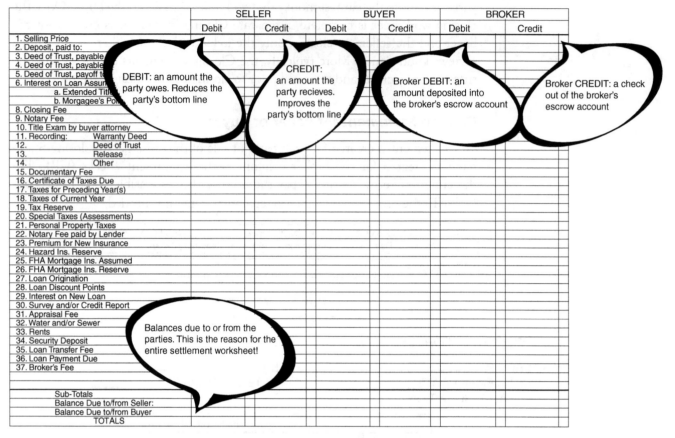

How to Use the Six-Column Closing Worksheet

We will discuss, later in this unit, how the broker DEBIT and CREDIT columns work. For now, we will focus on just the seller and buyer items.

Item	Seller		Buyer	
	Debit	Credit	Debit	Credit

Who has the debit? Who owes the money?

Note:

- The word *ALWAYS* is used for DEBITS and CREDITS when 99 percent of the time this is how the DEBIT or CREDIT is handled at closing.
- The word *TYPICALLY* is used when the majority of the time the party named pays for the item.
- The word *NEGOTIABLE* is used when the Contract to Buy and Sell has a check box that clearly makes the item negotiable.

These generalities, always, typically, and negotiable, are used to help in teaching the concepts. However, the terms of the Contract to Buy and Sell are the final determinant of who is obligated in any closing for a bill and should always be reviewed. **Remember: all items in the Contract to Buy and Sell can be negotiated.**

The six-column worksheet:

The numbers used below all correspond to the six-column worksheet used in the closing process. In the back of this workbook are worksheets you can remove in order to familiarize yourself with these various items.

Line 1. Selling Price: Paid by the buyer, in order to obtain the deed.

■ Always DEBIT the Buyer.

Line 5. Seller loans to be paid off (Deed of Trust, payoff to:)

■ Any current loans the seller has, that the buyer will not assume, will need to be paid off at closing.
■ Always DEBIT the seller.

		WHO PAYS?	Seller		Buyer	
			Debit	Credit	Debit	Credit
1.	Selling Price	**BUYER**			**XXX.XX**	
5.	Deed of Trust, payoff to:	**SELLER**	**XXX.XX**			

Line 7. Title Insurance: Owners Title Insurance Premium: The approved *Contract to Buy and Sell* specifies that the seller will pay for the owner's (buyer's) **standard** title insurance policy.

■ Always DEBIT the seller.

Line 7a. Extended Title Insurance Coverage: The approved *Contract to Buy and Sell* determines if the seller or buyer pays for the extended coverage.

■ Negotiable: DEBIT seller or buyer per the contract.

Line 7b. Mortgagee's Policy Premium: The mortgagee's title insurance policy (lender's policy) is part of the cost of borrowing and is paid by the borrower/buyer.

■ Always DEBIT the buyer.

Line 10. Title Examination by: Buyer's Attorney: The buyer's attorney would review the title insurance commitment for possible problems. If the buyer has an attorney, the buyer will pay this bill.

■ Always DEBIT the buyer.

		WHO PAYS?	Seller		Buyer	
			Debit	Credit	Debit	Credit
7.	Owner's Title Insurance Premium	**SELLER**	**XXX.XX**			
	a. Extended Title Coverage	**SELLER/ BUYER**	**XXX.XX**		**XXX.XX**	
	b. Mortgagee's Title Insurance	**BUYER**			**XXX.XX**	
10.	Title Exam by: Buyer's Attorney	**BUYER**			**XXX.XX**	

Recording Fees: In Colorado, a buyer normally pays recording charges, except for the recording of any release (payoff) of prior liens.

Line 11. Recording the Warranty Deed: This benefits the buyer by providing constructive notice of the buyer's interest and ownership of the property.

■ Always DEBIT the buyer.

Line 12. Recording the Deed of Trust: The buyer/borrower pays for this loan cost, the deed of trust is the document that protects the lender and creates the lien on the property.

■ Always DEBIT the buyer.

Line 13. Recording a Release of Deed of Trust: If a prior loan is being paid off as part of the closing, the seller has the obligation to convey the property cleared of this lien. The release must be recorded, so it is the seller's obligation. There will also be a corresponding DEBIT under loan payoff for the amount of any liens being paid off by the seller.

■ Always DEBIT the seller.

		WHO PAYS?	Seller		Buyer	
			Debit	Credit	Debit	Credit
11.	Recording: Warranty Deed	*BUYER*			*XXX.XX*	
12.	Recording: Trust Deed	*BUYER*			*XXX.XX*	
13.	Recording: Release	*SELLER*	*XXX.XX*			

Line 15. Documentary Fee: A fee required by state law and paid to the county with the recording of any conveyance deed (a deed conveying property from a grantor to a grantee).

■ The amount is $.01 per $100 of purchase price (a penny per one hundred).
  — Divide the Selling Price by $10,000.
    or
  — Move the decimal point in the selling price four places to the left.
  For example: $230,000.00 = $23.00
■ **Every closing** has a documentary fee because there will be a conveyance deed that needs to be recorded. State law requires the party that records a document of conveyance to pay the documentary fee.
  Always DEBIT the buyer (who benefits from recording the deed).

Line 16. Certificate of Taxes Due: This certificate from the County Treasurer **verifies the current status of taxes** due on the property and the amount of the previous year's taxes.

■ This benefits the buyer by assuring all unpaid taxes will be paid off at closing and there are no other taxes due at closing.
■ Always DEBIT the buyer.

Line 17. Unpaid Taxes for Preceding Year(s):

- Preceding year taxes (i.e., 2010)
  - Seller owes if unpaid
    - If any taxes for years preceding the year of closing are due, they are entirely the seller's responsibility as they have created a lien on the property that must be cleared.
  - 2010 taxes are due and payable on January 1, 2011.

- Current year taxes (i.e., 2011)
  - Prorated at Closing

- Always DEBIT the seller.
  - If taxes for preceding, or earlier, years have been paid, this line will be blank.

Tip: If the prior year's taxes have been paid, note the amount in the left margin. This amount will be used in calculating the tax proration for the year of closing. Remember: in real life closings, taxes could be prorated using the most current mill levy and assessment. How taxes are prorated is determined by the Contract to Buy and Sell.

		WHO PAYS?	Seller		Buyer	
			Debit	Credit	Debit	Credit
15.	Documentary Fee	*BUYER*			*XXX.XX*	
16.	Certificate of Taxes Due	*BUYER*			*XXX.XX*	
17.	Taxes for the Preceding Year(s)	*SELLER*	*XXX.XX*			

Line 20. Special Taxes/Assessments: These are amounts due on government special assessments or tax for local improvements. These assessments are one-time charges typically paid to the government over several years, in addition to the general property taxes.

- If a special tax/assessment is to be *paid off* at closing, it is the seller's responsibility to pay off the full amount that is owed.

Always DEBIT the seller for **the FULL** amount of the special assessment.

- If the special tax is assumed by the buyer (not paid off), it will not impact the cash at closing and will not appear on the settlement sheet. The buyer has agreed to take over the payments and therefore since nothing is being paid off, it will not show on the closing worksheet.

  Special rule: If seller pays, DEBIT seller. If buyer assumes it <u>does</u> <u>NOT</u> show at closing.

Line 37. Broker's fee: The broker's fee is a seller cost based on the listing contract.

- Always DEBIT the seller.

		WHO PAYS?	Seller		Buyer	
			Debit	Credit	Debit	Credit
20.	Special Taxes **(if paid off)**	*SELLER*	*XXX.XX*			
37.	Broker's fee	*SELLER*	*XXX.XX*			

Loan Costs

Line 27. Loan Origination Fee (or Loan Service Fee): This is a fee charged by the lender for services related to creating a new loan. Normally, it is a DEBIT to the buyer because it is a requirement of getting the loan. Think of it as the commission the lender is receiving for originating the loan.

■ Typically DEBIT the buyer.

Line 28. Loan Discount Points: The sales contract states the buyer will pay this cost; it is a DEBIT to the buyer because it is a requirement of getting the loan at a certain interest rate.

■ The Discount Points are a percentage of the loan amount, not the sales price.
■ 1 point = 1 percent of the loan amount.
■ DEBIT buyer unless the contract states differently.

Line 30. Survey: The sales contract states who will pay for the survey.

■ Negotiable: DEBIT seller or buyer per the contract.

Line 30. Credit report: If the seller or the lender wishes to determine the credit worthiness of the buyer, a credit report may be ordered. This is charged to the buyer as a cost of getting a loan.

■ Always DEBIT the buyer.

Line 31. Appraisal fee: The sales contract states who will pay for the appraisal, but normally it is a DEBIT to the buyer because it is a cost for getting a loan.

■ Negotiable: DEBIT seller or buyer per the contract.

Line 35. Loan transfer fee: In an assumption, the lending institution usually requires a fee for changing the loan records (i.e., transferring the loan from the seller's information to the buyer's).

■ Typically DEBIT the buyer.

Line 36. Loan payment due: All payments on the loan must be up to date before the loan can be assumed. The payment reduces the amount of principal owed by the seller on the loan. Since loan payments are made in arrears, the seller will owe the full amount of the payment due for the preceding month.

■ <u>Never prorate</u> the monthly payment that is past due.
■ Always DEBIT the seller.

Lines 19 & 24. Lender Reserve Impound Accounts: For most loans, the lender will require the buyer to give the lender funds to establish reserve accounts to pay the taxes and property insurance when the bills come due. Remember, property taxes have priority over all other liens if not paid. Property insurance would be used to pay off the debt if the property is damaged. The lender will require the buyer to collect for and pay these bills for most loans. The lender will always collect for the month of closing.

Buyer/borrower funds may be held for the following:
- Annual property taxes are typically paid on April 30.
- Annual hazard insurance premium is paid based on the policy date typically due one year from the closing date.
- Always DEBIT the buyer.

Line 23. Premium for new insurance: The buyer will provide insurance.

- Always DEBIT the buyer.

		WHO PAYS?	Seller		Buyer	
			Debit	Credit	Debit	Credit
19.	Tax Reserve	**BUYER**			**XXX.XX**	
23.	Premium for New Insurance	**BUYER**			**XXX.XX**	
24.	Hazard Insurance Reserve	**BUYER**			**XXX.XX**	

Line 8. Closing Fee: Typically, there will be a closing fee to be split between the buyer and the seller, but in some cases one party, either the buyer or seller, will pay the entire fee. In either case, the sales contract and the closing instructions will provide the needed information.

- Negotiable: DEBIT seller or buyer per contract.

Line 9. Notary Fees:

Special Rule: A notary fee is paid by the party who **signs** the document.

The party actually signing the document would owe the bill for the notary fee, which will then be a CREDIT to the broker who writes the CHECK and pays the bill for the responsible party.

- DEBIT party signing
- The seller/grantor signs warranty deed, thus they will ALWAYS be charged for a notary fee.
- The buyer/borrower signs the deed of trust and will ALWAYS be charged if there is a new loan.
- The broker will be credited the **combined amounts** to pay the bill.
  - Example: The notary fee is $1.00 per document and each party needs to have the signature notarized. The seller and buyer will each be debited $1.00 with the broker receiving a CREDIT of $2.00 to pay the notary bill in full.

		Seller		Buyer		Broker	
		Debit	Credit	Debit	Credit	Debit	Credit
8.	Closing Fee	*X*		*X*			*X X*
9.	Notary fee	*X*		*X*			*X X*

Summary of Debits: Who Pays Which Bills?

	Bill to be paid	WHO PAYS?	Seller		Buyer	
			Debit	Credit	Debit	Credit
1.	Selling Price	**BUYER**			XXX.XX	
7b.	Mortgagee's Title Insurance	**BUYER**			XXX.XX	
10.	Title Exam by: Buyer's Attorney	**BUYER**			XXX.XX	
11.	Recording: Warranty Deed	**BUYER**			XXX.XX	
12.	Recording: Trust Deed	**BUYER**			XXX.XX	
15.	Documentary Fee	**BUYER**			XXX.XX	
16.	Certificate of Taxes Due	**BUYER**			XXX.XX	
19.	Tax Reserve	**BUYER**			XXX.XX	
24.	Hazard Insurance Reserve	**BUYER**			XXX.XX	
25.	Loan Transfer Fee	**BUYER**			XXX.XX	
23.	Premium for New Insurance	**BUYER**			XXX.XX	
27.	Loan Origination Fee	**BUYER**			XXX.XX	
30.	Credit Report	**BUYER**			XXX.XX	
28.	Loan Discount Points	**BUYER**			XXX.XX	
8.	Closing Fee*	**BUYER/SELLER**	XXX.XX		XXX.XX	
9.	Notary fee	**BUYER/SELLER**	XXX.XX		XXX.XX	
30.	Survey*	**BUYER/SELLER**	XXX.XX		XXX.XX	
31.	Appraisal Fee*	**BUYER/SELLER**	XXX.XX		XXX.XX	
7a.	Extended Title Ins. Coverage*	**BUYER/SELLER**	XXX.XX		XXX.XX	
7.	Owner's Title Insurance Premium	**SELLER**	XXX.XX			
13.	Recording Release of Lien	**SELLER**	XXX.XX			
17.	Taxes for the Preceding Year(s)	**SELLER**	XXX.XX			
5.	Seller loan to be paid off	**SELLER**	XXX.XX			
20.	Special Taxes/Assessments	**SELLER**	XXX.XX			
36.	Loan Payment Due	**SELLER**	XXX.XX			
37.	Broker's Fee	**SELLER**	XXX.XX			
38.	Seller Attorney	**SELLER**	XXX.XX			

Reminder: *Payment for any Appraisal, Survey, and Closing service costs is negotiable in the contract so either party may have these items as a debit! (Remember: ASC what was negotiated.)

The majority of these items are DEBITS for bills to be paid. These items will become CREDITS to the broker who will write a check to pay the various bills owed by each party.

Who Receives What? Who gets the CREDIT—money received?

Selling Price: Paid to the seller by the buyer, therefore CREDIT the seller.

■ Always CREDIT the seller.

Earnest Money Deposit: Earnest money is provided by the buyer prior to closing and held in an escrow account. At closing, the buyer will receive a CREDIT (reducing the amount of cash they need to bring to closing).

■ Always CREDIT the buyer.

DEBIT versus CREDIT for the Cash Closing

Below is a closing worksheet based on a cash closing between a seller and buyer

(**Note:** Only the items that apply to the closing are in the following table.)

	SELLER		BUYER		BROKER	
	Debit	Credit	Debit	Credit	Debit	Credit
1. Selling Price		X	X			
2. Deposit, paid to				X	X	
7. Title Insurance Premium Owners	X					X
8. Closing Fee Split 50-50	X		X			XX
9. Notary	X		X			XX
10. Title Exam by: Buyer's Attorney			X			X
11. Recording: Warranty Deed			X			X
12. Recording: Trust Deed			X			X
13. Recording Release of Lien	X					X
15. Documentary Fee			X			X
16. Certificate of Taxes Due			X			X
18. Taxes for Current Year **Prorated** between the parties	X			X		
23. Premium for New Insurance			X			X
37. Broker's Fee	X					X

Negotiated in the contract

Notice how each DEBIT has a matching CREDIT in another column. These DEBITS and CREDITS are also always equal dollar amounts. For example: if the title insurance costs $1,000, there is a DEBIT to the seller, who owes the bill and a CREDIT of $1,000 to the broker who will write a check to pay the bill for the seller.

Steps for Balancing a Seller's Closing Statement

Subtotals:

1. Once all of the entries on the worksheet, both the seller columns are subtotaled.

Balance Due to/from Seller:

2. Once a subtotal of the seller's DEBIT and CREDIT columns is complete, the broker will analyze the situation. If the seller has more CREDITS than DEBITS (as in the example), the seller will receive some money at the closing.
3. Compute the difference between the CREDITS and DEBITS and enter the amount ($130,586.49) under the smaller of the two numbers on the "Balance due to the seller" line, thus forcing a balance for the seller's Total DEBITS and Total CREDITS.
    Since the broker will collect and disburse all money, a balance due to the seller means the broker who is closing the transaction must write a check to the seller for net proceeds, so this amount is also noted in the broker's CREDIT column.

4. If the seller has more DEBITS than CREDITS (which sometimes happens), this is known as a **deficit closing**. Again, compute the difference between the DEBITS and CREDITS and enter that amount on the smaller side, forcing a balance. This difference is the amount the seller will need to bring to closing in good funds which the broker will deposit into the escrow account to pay bills owed.

	SELLER		BUYER		BROKER	
	Debit	Credit	Debit	Credit	Debit	Credit
Subtotals	11,430.55	142,017.04				
Balance Due TO/from Seller	130,586.49					130,586.49
Balance Due to/FROM Buyer						
Totals	142,017.04	142,017.04				

Since the balance is due TO seller, the amount due goes to the left side to balance the two columns.

The same number is also put into the broker CREDIT column, as this is the check the broker will write to the seller at closing.

Totals:

Once the balance due to/from the seller is completed, add the subtotal figure to any balance due to/from figure in that column to obtain the totals, which must be the same or the seller side does not balance.

Important: The seller's totals of DEBITS and CREDITS must be the same. If not, the Closing Statement is incorrect and does not balance.

Steps for Balancing the Buyer's *Closing Statement*

Subtotals:

1. Once all the entries are made on the *Closing Statement*, subtotal both columns.

Balance Due to/from Buyer:

2. Once a subtotal of the buyer's DEBIT and CREDIT columns is complete, the broker must again analyze the situation.
3. If the buyer has more DEBITS than CREDITS (as in the example), the buyer will be bringing money to closing.
4. Compute the difference between the CREDITS and DEBITS and enter the amount ($140,596.69) under the smaller of the two numbers on the "Balance due from the buyer" line, thus forcing a balance for the buyer's Total DEBITS and Total CREDITS. These must balance or there is an error. Since the broker will collect and disburse all money, a "balance due *from* the buyer" means the broker must receive and DEPOSIT that amount in good funds from the buyer at closing. The amount the buyer must bring is also noted in the broker's DEBIT column.

	SELLER		BUYER		BROKER	
	Debit	Credit	Debit	Credit	Debit	Credit
Subtotals			142,767.24	2,170.55		
Balance Due TO/from Seller						
Balance Due to/FROM Buyer				140,596.69	140,596.69	
Totals			142,767.24	142,767.24		

Since the balance is due FROM the buyer the amount due goes on the right side to balance the two columns.

The same number is also put into the broker DEBIT column. This is the check the broker will deposit from the buyer to cover what is due to the seller.

Totals:

1. Once the balance due to/from the buyer is complete, add the subtotal figure to any balance due to/from figure in that column to obtain the totals.
Important: The buyer's totals of DEBITS and CREDITS must be the same. If not, the Closing Statement is incorrect and does not balance.

Remember:

A Closing Statement that balances is not necessarily correct!

If you leave out an entire item or reverse a DEBIT and CREDIT entry on a line, the sheet may balance but be inaccurate. Do every settlement closing worksheet as though your career as a real estate licensee depended on it, it may.

Closing Statements must be signed as provided in Rule E-5.

Broker Totals: How to find the Subtotal and Total for each column

	SELLER		BUYER		BROKER	
	Debit	Credit	Debit	Credit	Debit	Credit
Subtotals	11,430.55	142,017.04	142,767.24	2,170.55	1,800	11,810.20
Balance Due TO/from Seller	130,586.49					130,586.49
Balance Due to/FROM Buyer				140,596.69	140,596.69	
Totals	142,017.04	142,017.04	142,767.24	142,767.24	142,396.69	142,396.69

Balance Due TO seller: Subtract DEBIT from CREDIT subtotal. (Enter balance TO on the left.) Once determined, put in broker CREDIT column as this is the amount the broker will have to write as a check to the seller for their net proceeds.

Balance Due from Buyer: Subtract CREDIT from DEBIT subtotal. (Enter balance FROM on the right.) Once determined, put in broker DEBIT column as this is the amount the broker will have to collect (deposit) from the buyer.

If broker columns do not balance, check the Seller and Buyer columns.

Seller and Broker Totals

■ Once the seller's "Balance Due Total" amount is found (seller DEBIT), this amount is also moved under the broker's CREDIT subtotal. Remember: this is the check the broker will write to the seller for the net proceeds.

Buyer and Broker Totals

■ Once the buyer's "Balance Due From" amount is found, this amount is also moved under the broker's DEBIT subtotal. Remember: this is the check the buyer will bring and the broker will deposit to pay the bills and the seller net proceeds. Now the broker columns are totaled and balanced.

Review the six-column worksheet on the next page. Notice how the debits and credits are charged. Examine how the lines are then totaled and balanced.

	SELLER			BUYER			BROKER		
	Debit		Credit		Debit		Credit		Debit		Credit	
1. Selling Price			142,000	00	142,000	00						
2. Deposit, paid to:							1,800	00	1,800	00		
3. Deed of Trust, payable to:												
4. Deed of Trust, payable to:												
5. Deed of Trust, payoff to:												
6. Interest on Loan Assumed												
7. Owner Title Insurance Premium	764	00									764	00
a. Extended Title Insurance												
b. Mortgagee's Policy												
8. Closing Fee	75	00			75	00					150	00
9. Notary Fee	1	00									1	00
10. Title Exam by buyer attorney					160	00					160	00
11. Recording: Warranty Deed					6	00					6	00
12. Deed of Trust												
13. Release												
14. Other												
15. Documentary Fee					14	20					14	20
16. Certificate of Taxes Due					15	00					15	00
17. Taxes for Preceding Year(s)												
18. Taxes for Current Year	370	55					370	55				
19. Tax Reserve												
20. Special Taxes (Assessments)	1,700	00									1,700	00
21. Personal Property Taxes												
22. Notary Fee paid by Lender												
23. Premium for New Insurance					480	00					480	00
24. Hazard Ins. Reserve												
25. FHA Mortgage Ins. Assumed												
26. FHA Mortgage Ins. Reserve												
27. Loan Origination												
28. Loan Discount Points												
29. Interest on New Loan												
30. Survey												
Credit Report												
31. Appraisal Fee												
32. Water and/or Sewer			17	04	17	04						
33. Rents												
34. Security Deposits												
35. Loan Transfer Fee												
36. Loan Payment Due												
37. Broker's Fee	8,520	00									8,520	00
38. Seller's Attorney												
39. **Net loan proceeds**												
Subtotals	11,430	55	142,017	04	142,767	24	2,170	55	1,800	00	11,810	20
Balance Due to/~~from~~ Seller	130,586	49									130,586	49
Balance Due ~~to~~/from Buyer							140,596	69	140,596	69		
TOTALS	142,017	04	142,017	04	142,767	24	142,797	24	142,396	69	142,396	69

Creation of Closing Statements

When the six-column worksheet is complete and balanced, the results are used to create the individual Closing Statements for seller and buyer to sign at closing. Note: the broker does not have a Closing Statement.

Closing Statements for the previous worksheet are on the next two pages.

F I G U R E   1.2

Statement of Settlement

The printed portions of this form, except differentiated additions, have been approved by the Colorado Real Estate Commission. (SS60-9-08) (Mandatory 1-09)

☐ **ESTIMATE**	☐ **FINAL**

CLOSING STATEMENT
☒ SELLER'S   PURCHASER'S

PROPERTY ADDRESS: *124 Any Street, Your town, Colorado 80999*
SELLER: *Stanley Seller and Myrtle Q. Seller*   BUYER: *Stanley E Bedford and Catherine J. Bedford*

SETTLEMENT DATE: *August 22, 2xxx*   DATE OF PRORATION*: August 22, 20xx*

LEGAL DESCRIPTION: *Lot 2, Filing 6, Horse property Subdivision, Weld County, Colorado*

	Debit	**Credit**
1. Selling Price		142,00.00
2. Deposit paid to		
3. Trust Deed payable to		
4. Trust Deed payable to		
5. Trust Deed, payoff to *previous lender*		
6. Interest on Loan Assumed *new second*		
7. Title Insurance Premium	764.00	
8. Closing Fee	75.00	
9. Notary Fees	1.00	
10. Title Exam by		
11. Recording: Warranty Deed		
12. Trust Deed		
13. Release		
14. Other		
15. Documentary Fee		
16. Certificate of Taxes Due		
17. Taxes for Preceding Years(s)		
18. Taxes for Current Year	370.55	
19. Tax Reserve		
20. Special Taxes	1,700.00	
21. Personal Property Taxes		
22. Notary Fee paid by Lender		
23. Premium for New Insurance		
24. Hazard Ins. Reserve		
25. FHA Mortgage Insurance Assumed		
26. FHA Mortgage Ins Reserve		
27. Loan Service Fee (Buyer)		
28. Loan Discount Fee		
29. Interest on New Loan		
30. Survey and/or Credit Report		
31. Appraisal Fee		
32. Water and/or Sewer Report		17.04
33. Rents		
34. Security Deposits		
35. Loan Transfer Fee		
36. Loan Payment Due		
37. Broker's Fee	8520.00	
Seller's Attorney		
Net Proceeds from a new loan		
Sub-Totals	11,430.55	142,017.04
1Balance Due to/~~from~~ Seller	130,586.49	
Balance Due to/from Buyer		
TOTAL	142,017.04	142,017.04

APPROVED AND ACCEPTED

Buyer/Seller: _____   Buyer/Seller: _____

Brokerage Firm's Name: _____   Broker: _____

F I G U R E 1.2

Statement of Settlement (continued)

The printed portions of this form, except differentiated additions, have been approved by the Colorado Real Estate Commission. (SS60-9-08) (Mandatory 1-09)

☐ **ESTIMATE**	☐ **FINAL**

CLOSING STATEMENT
SELLER'S ☒ BUYER'S

PROPERTY ADDRESS: *124 Any Street, Your town, Colorado 80999*
SELLER: *Stanley Seller and Myrtle Q. Seller*   BUYER: *Stanley E Bedford and Catherine J. Bedford*

SETTLEMENT DATE: *August 22, 2xxx*   DATE OF PRORATION: *August 22, 2xxx*

LEGAL DESCRIPTION: *Lot 2, Filing 6, Horse property Subdivision, Weld County, Colorado*

	Debit	Credit
1. Selling Price	142,000.00	
2. Deposit paid to *listing broker*		1,800.00
3. Trust Deed payable to		
4. Trust Deed payable to		
5. Trust Deed, payoff to		
6. Interest on Loan Assumed		
7. Title Insurance Premium		
8. Closing Fee	75.00	
9. Notary Fees		
10. Title Exam by *James Snow*	160.00	
11. Recording: Warranty Deed	6.00	
12. Trust Deed		
13. Release		
14. Other		
15. Documentary Fee	14.20	
16. Certificate of Taxes Due	15.00	
17. Taxes for Preceding Years(s)		
18. Taxes for Current Year		370.55
19. Tax Reserve		
20. Special Taxes		
21. Personal Property Taxes		
22. Notary Fee paid by Lender		
23. Premium for New Insurance	480.00	
24. Hazard Ins. Reserve		
25. PMI		
26. Mortgage Ins Reserve		
27. Loan Origination Fee		
28. Loan Discount Points		
29. Interest on New Loan		
30. Survey and/or		
Credit Report		
31. Appraisal Fee		
32. Water and/or Sewer	17.04	
33. Rents		
34. Security Deposits		
35. Closing Service		
36. Loan Payment Due		
37. Broker's Fee		
Sellers Attorney		
Net proceeds new loan		
Sub-Totals	142,767.24	2,170.55
Balance to/from Seller		
Balance to/from Buyer		140,596.69
TOTAL	142,767.24	142,767.24

APPROVED AND ACCEPTED

Buyer/Seller: _____   Buyer/Seller: _____

Brokerage Firm's Name: _____   Broker: _____

Prorations: Dividing Expenses between Buyer and Seller

Most existing properties have various ongoing expenses that must be divided between the seller and the buyer. These could include interest on a loan the buyer is assuming, general property taxes, water and sewer bills, rents collected in advance on a leased property, and homeowner's association dues. We will investigate each of these items individually.

Prorations will not normally include utilities such as electricity, telephone, or cable TV service since these are billed to the individual and can be stopped as of the date of closing, and a new account opened for the buyer. These companies do not have the right by law to place liens on the property, if the bill is left unpaid, without going to court. Water, sewer, and property tax bills can (by law) become a lien against the property, so the broker must ensure these are taken care of at closing.

Closings Prorations Helper

Proration Rules and Method

1. Whether the seller or the buyer should be charged for the day of closing varies from state to state.

   ■ The Colorado *Contract to Buy and Sell Real Estate* specifies that proration items "shall be apportioned TO the day of closing" (not THROUGH).
   ■ Therefore, the **buyer** owns the property all day on the day of closing.

2. When prorating in Colorado, a year has 365 days.

   ■ A leap year with February having 29 days has 366 days.
   ■ Calendar year begins January 1 and goes through December 31.

3. Every month must be calculated according to the exact number of days in that particular month. Do you remember:

   ■ "30 days has September, April, June, and November; all the rest have 31, and February's great with 28; Leap Year's February's fine with 29."

4. **Remember: Never prorate** the following:

   ■ Tax **Reserve**
   ■ Hazard Insurance **Reserve**
   ■ **Loan payment due**
   ■ Security Deposits
   ■ Mortgage Payment due for the month prior to closing
   ■ Special Taxes (assessments):
       — Colorado Sales Contract says seller pays the special assessments: If the buyer and seller modify the contract and have the buyer assume the special assessment, then it will not be part of the closing figures.

How To Prorate

	National Test	**State Test**
Who owns the day of closing	SELLER	BUYER
Days in the month	30 in every month	ACTUAL
How many days in the year	360	365/366 (leap)

Step One:

Draw a horizontal line representing the entire "billing period" for the item being prorated. Add short vertical lines at each end to show the limits with the beginning date just inside the left-hand vertical line and the last date just inside the right-hand line.

Step Two:

Draw another vertical line near the closing date (use rough proportions). Presume a closing date of June 10.

Step Three:

Put the closing date on the right side of the vertical line (buyer's first day of ownership).

Step Four:

Put the day before closing on the left side of the vertical line (seller's last day of ownership).

Step Four:

Determine if the item to be prorated is paid in arrears. The buyer will receive a bill later for a charge that will include time the seller was in the property, property taxes are an example. An item may be paid in advance. The seller has already paid a bill and the buyer will take over the property during that period. Water is often paid in advance. In either case, one party will owe the other for the period in which they are in the property but have not paid.

SOB SIDE (<u>Seller Owes Buyer</u>): Solve the <u>Left side</u> of time line

- Paid in arrears: buyer will pay the bill in the future
- Includes items such as: real estate taxes and interest on most real estate loans

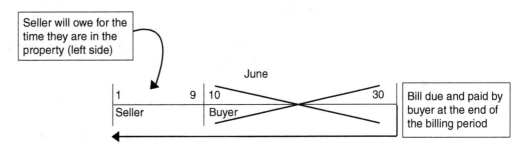

BOS SIDE (<u>Buyer Owes Seller</u>): Solve the <u>Right side</u> of time line

- Paid in advance (i.e. "prepaid," "paid," "was paid," "has already paid")
- Water and HOA fees are often paid in advance

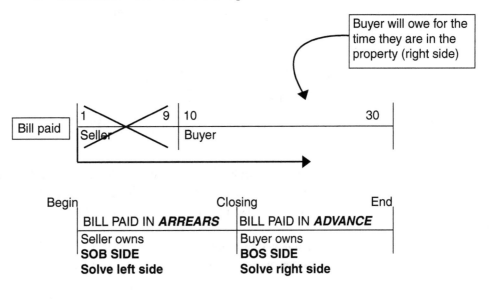

Begin		Closing		End
	BILL PAID IN *ARREARS*		BILL PAID IN *ADVANCE*	
	Seller owns **SOB SIDE** **Solve left side**		Buyer owns **BOS SIDE** **Solve right side**	

Step Five:

Cross off the side of the figure not being used. Now go to the appropriate side and count the days. Use actual number of days in each month.

June

1 ~~ARREARS~~ 9	10	ADVANCE	30
~~Seller owns~~ **~~SOB SIDE~~**		Buyer owns **BOS SIDE** Solve right side	

Determine the days that are owed for the side being worked. In this case, the buyer will be in the property 21 days

To find the buyer's ownership: 30 – 9 (seller's last day) = 21.

Do not do the common error of 30 – 10 (Buyer's first day) = 20.

For this item paid in advance, the buyer would owe the seller 21 days.

Step Six:

Calculate the share for the side owed. In this case, water is paid in advance so the buyer owes the seller for 21 days.

The formula we use to calculate is always the same:

RULE: Amount for billing period ($) divided by days in billing period multiplied by number of days the person owes.

$150.00 water bill paid in advance buyer owes seller how much?

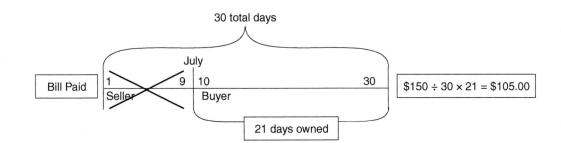

Tip 1: Start by dividing the bill's dollar amount for the total billing period by the **number** of days in the total billing period, and then multiply by the number of days the person owns. In our example above:

Total water amount was $150.00. Total billing period was 30 days and the buyer owns 21 days. $150.00 ÷ 30 × 21= $105.00

Tip 2: A proration is always an exchange between the buyer and the seller. **The DEBIT and CREDIT amounts will always be the same.** We would DEBIT the buyer, who owes the bill $105 and CREDIT the seller, who previously paid the bill, $105.

Tip 3: **The seller's last day will always be used to determine the number of days owed. For buyer's side, take total number of days minus the seller's last day to determine the number of days the buyer will own the property.**

Tip 4: Use your calculator for the math, rather than writing down the daily amount to enter on the calculator later. Most calculators easily retain the six decimal places needed to assure an accurate calculation.

TOTAL BILL ÷ TOTAL DAYS × DAYS OWNED = PRORATED $

Tip 5: On the top of the six-column worksheet, write the closing day and the number of days each party has. Remember, this will be different for each closing.

Example:

Real Estate Closing Worksheet: June 10, Seller = 9, Buyer = 21 days

▉ EXAMPLE 1.1:

The unmetered water and sewer bill from March 1 through May 31 has been paid in the amount of $23.00. (Paid in Advance BOS, right side of our drawing, buyer owes seller) Prorate for a closing on April 13.

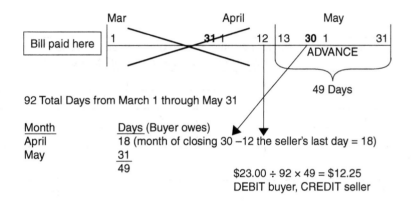

▉ EXAMPLE 1.2:

Homeowners' Association (HOA) fees for the month of April are $247 paid in arrears (SOB solve the left side). Prorate the HOA fees for a closing on April 13.

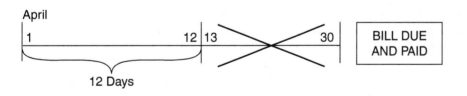

$247 ÷ 30 × 12 = $98.80, DEBIT seller who owes the bill for the time they owned the property, CREDIT buyer who will pay the bill when it becomes due.

DEBITS and CREDITS on a closing worksheet

Below is how the three prorations above would appear on a closing worksheet.

		WHO PAYS?	Seller		Buyer	
			Debit	Credit	Debit	Credit
Water paid in advance		*BOS*		$105.00	105.00	
Water/Sewer paid in advance		*BOS*		$12.25	$12.25	
HOA Dues in Arrears		*SOB*	$98.80			$98.80

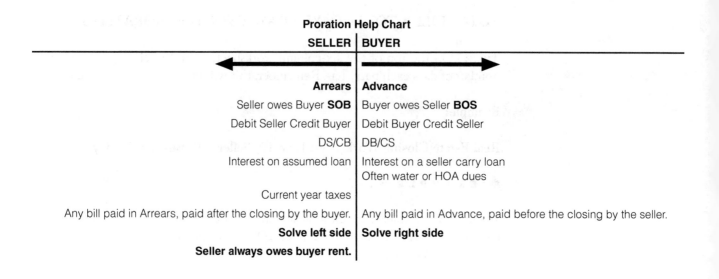

Proration Help Chart

SELLER	BUYER
Arrears	Advance
Seller owes Buyer **SOB**	Buyer owes Seller **BOS**
Debit Seller Credit Buyer	Debit Buyer Credit Seller
DS/CB	DB/CS
Interest on assumed loan	Interest on a seller carry loan
	Often water or HOA dues
Current year taxes	
Any bill paid in Arrears, paid after the closing by the buyer.	Any bill paid in Advance, paid before the closing by the seller.
Solve left side	**Solve right side**
Seller always owes buyer rent.	

		Seller		Buyer		Broker	
		Debit	Credit	Debit	Credit	DEBIT	Credit
1	Selling Price		**X**	**X**			
2	Deposit, paid to						
7	Title Insurance Premium Owners						
8	Closing Fee Split 50-50						
9	Notary						
10	Title Exam by: Buyer's Attorney						
11	Recording: Warranty Deed						
12	Recording: Trust Deed						
13	Recording Release of Lien						
15	Documentary Fee						
16	Certificate of Taxes Due						
18	Taxes for Current Year **Prorated** between the parties						
23	Premium for New Insurance						
37	Broker's Fee						

Exercise 1 Debits and Credits: Before Unit 1 class fill in the X's on this worksheet for the proper DEBIT and CREDIT for each party

Six-Column Worksheet Helper: on the next page, review how the various lines work on the six-column worksheet.

Real Estate Settlement Closing Worksheet - Helper

	All Closings — SELLER		Assumable — BUYER		New Loan — BROKER	
	Debit	Credit	Debit	Credit	Debit Deposit IN	Credit
Check Out						
1. Selling Price: Always use—what the closing is all about (Line 15)		XX	XX			
2. Deposit, paid to: Money the buyer gave the broker				XX	XX	
3. Deed of Trust, payable to: Lender in Assumable (Line 6)	XX			XX		
3. Deed of Trust, payable to: Gross loan amount—single entry				S		
4. Deed of Trust, payable to: Seller-carry loan	XX		XX			
5. Deed of Trust, payoff to: New loan single entry	S					
6. Interest on Loan Assumed: Seller will owe their portion of the month of closing	Prorate XX			Prorate XX		
7. Owner Title Insurance Premium: Seller agrees to pay per contract	XX					XX
a. Extended Title Insurance: Negotiable charge per the contract	????		????			
b. Mortgagee's Policy: Buyer cost in new loan single entry			S			
8. Closing Fee: Split between the parties—negotiable charge per contract	??		??			XX
9. Notary Fee: Charge person who signs the document	Warranty		Deed of Trust			XX
10. Title Exam by buyer attorney: Buyer owes Broker will pay the bill			XX			XX
11. Recording: Warranty Deed: Always Buyer's—New loan single entry			S OR XX			XX
12. Deed of Trust: Always a Buyer fee if one is used			S OR XX			XX
13. Release: Seller fee to clear title new loan single entry	S					XX
15. Documentary Fee: Move decimal four places to left in Sale's Price	XX					XX
16. Certificate of Taxes Due: Buyer debit—to find what seller might owe			XX			XX
17. Taxes for Preceding Year(s): Note if seller had paid and the amount	If owed					Only if not paid
18. Taxes for Current Year: Seller will owe buyer prorated share	Prorate XX			Prorate XX		
19. Tax Reserve: Lender impound buyer charge single entry			XX			
20. Special Taxes (Assessments): If seller agrees to pay, charge seller	XX					
21. Personal Property Taxes: Buyer fee if charged			XX			
22. Notary Fee paid by Lender: Buyer charge—new loan single entry			S			XX
23. Premium for New Insurance: Charge buyer for new policy			XX			XX
24. Hazard Ins. Reserve: Lender impound - buyer charge—new loan single entry			S			XX
27. Loan Origination: Charge to buyer—new loan single entry			S			
28. Loan Discount Points: Charge to buyer—new loan single entry			S			
29. Interest on New Loan: Buyer will owe prorated share month of closing			Prorate ?? / S			
31. Appraisal Fee: Charge buyer—new loan, single entry			S			
32. Water and/or Sewer: Prorate month of closing per bill	Prorate ??	Prorate ??	Prorate ??	Prorate ??		XX - if not paid
33. Rents: Prorate - Seller will always owe buyer for buyer's share	Prorate XX	Prorate ??	Prorate XX	Prorate XX		
34. Security Deposits: Transfer full amount from seller to buyer	XX			XX		
35. Loan Transfer Fee: Charge buyer fee to transfer in assumable loans			XX			XX
36. Loan Payment Due: Seller will owe, Credit Broker to pay	XX					XX
37. Broker's Fee: Seller will owe the brokerage	XX					XX
38. Seller's Attorney: Seller owes, Broker will pay the bill	XX					XX
39. Net loan proceeds: broker deposit, to pay the other new loan bills					S	

Notes

■ SUMMARY OF UNIT 1

1. Real estate brokers are responsible for making sure that the property is closed properly.

2. Closing includes preparing or reviewing all of the documents at a closing and checking the allocation of funds represented by the settlement worksheet.

3. The designated broker representing each party is responsible for accuracy of the figures on the client's Closing Statement.

4. Allocating expenses, fees, and other amounts is a complex process requiring skill and care in interpreting the contract as well as following law and local customs.

5. Prorating ongoing expenses between the seller and buyer is an essential skill in successfully completing a worksheet.

■ UNIT 1: GLOSSARY REVIEW

Match the terms with the definitions. Terms may be used more than once.

Certificate of Taxes Due   Equal
Closing   Lender Reserve Impound Account
Closing Statement   Pay a bill
Credit   Proration
Debit   Recording
Documentary Fee   Trust Account

1. An amount charged to a party to pay a bill is a __*debit*__.

2. The place where a broker holds money that belongs to other parties is a __*Trust Account*__.

3. An amount of $.01 per $100 charged when a deed is recorded is called the __*Documentary Fee*__.

4. The document from the county treasurer that summarizes the current status of taxes is the __*Certificate of Taxes Due (Tax Certificate)*__.

5. An amount received by a party to pay a bill is a __*Credit*__.

6. The final settlement created by the terms of the Contract to Buy and Sell is called __*Closing*__.

7. __*Recording*__ a document creates constructive notice of the contents of the document.

8. A CREDIT to the broker is used to __*Pay a Bill*__.

9. Dividing expenses between the buyer and seller based on ownership periods is called __*Proration*__.

10. A place where a lender holds borrower's funds to pay bills at a later time is a __*Lender Reserve Impound Account*__.

11. A summary of the financial part of a closing for one party to the transaction is a __*Closing Statement*__.

12. DEBITS and CREDITS are always in __*Equal*__ amounts.

UNIT 1: LECTURE OUTLINE

I.   HOW THE CLOSING IS CREATED:

A. The closing is created by the ___Contract to Buy and Sell___ along with other supporting documents, such as the closing instructions, tax certificates, and the title commitment.

B. There are ___four parties___ each with separate obligations that are involved in the closing process:

   1. ___The Seller___ who is obligated to ___clear all liens___ on the property that are not being assumed by the buyer.

   2. ___The Buyer___, who is obligated to meet all the requirements of the contract and ___bring good funds___ to closing.

   3. ___The Brokers___ who are obligated to verify the party they represent is meeting the obligations of the contract. The broker is also responsible for the ___closing Statement___ the party they have been ___designated to represent___.

   4. ___The closing entity___ hired by the buyer and seller in the ___closing instructions___ is obligated to complete the forms per these instructions.

C. The four most typical ways to close a real estate purchase are by using the following:

   1. ___Cash___, which is covered in this unit.

   2. ___Assumable loans___ in which the buyer takes over the seller's existing loan.

   3. ___Seller Carry loan___ often used with an assumable loan, which is covered in Unit 2.

   4. ___New Loans___, which are covered in Unit 3.

D. Creating the final figures for closing.

   1. A six-column worksheet is used to determine all the credits and debits for each of the three parties involved.

   2. From the worksheet, the broker/closer will create a separate Closing Statement for the seller and buyer.

E. Responsibility for the proper accounting at a closing:

   1. Overall responsibility belongs to the ___Listing Brokerage and Listing Broker___.

★ 2. Individual licensee responsibility: The ___*designated brokers*___ are responsible for the accuracy of the Closing Statement.

    a) The designated listing broker is responsible for the Closing Statement for the ___*seller*___.

    b) The designated buyer's broker is responsible for the Closing Statement for the _____.

★ 3. Brokers are expected to attend the closing. If a designated broker is unable to attend the ___*Employing broker may appoint*___ broker may appoint another broker to attend.

    a) In this instance, all three brokers, ___*Employ, original broke and appointed Broker*___, will be responsible for the accuracy of the Closing Statement for the party represented.

F. Closing Company or Other Closing Entity

1. A title insurance closing company, broker, or attorney may perform settlement services on behalf of the seller and buyer.

2. Such a closing entity (company) must be appointed by written closing instructions such as the approved *Closing Instructions* form.

    ★ a) 3-Party agreement: seller, buyer, and closing company

    b) Engages ___*the closing company*___ and outlines requirements for closing

    c) Lists responsibilities of closer, buyer, and seller

II. BUYER'S AND SELLER'S COLUMNS

A. DEBIT, item owed (disadvantage), means one of the following:

1. A ___*charge*___ to either the buyer or seller on the ___*day of closing*___. OR

2. If the DEBIT is to the seller, it reduces the amount of cash the ___*seller will take away from closing*___.

3. If the DEBIT is to the buyer, it increases the amount of cash the buyer must bring to closing.

B. Examples of seller DEBITS (items owed):
(Items that reduce the amount of cash the seller receives at closing)

1. Owner's title insurance policy

★ 2. Property taxes for the ___*preceding year*___; seller will owe the full amount

3. Current year's taxes: seller will owe buyer a prorated share (SOB) *seller owes buyer*

4. Broker's commission

5. Proration of rents collected for the month of closing, seller will ___*always owe the buyer a prorated share*___

    6. Security deposits are <u>transferred in full</u>

    7. Seller-carry loan

C. Examples of buyer DEBITS (items owed):
(Items that increase the amount of cash the buyer must bring to closing)

    1. <u>*Selling price*</u> of the property

    2. Loan closing costs

    3. Mortgagee's title policy

    4. Premium for new hazard insurance

D. Broker DEBIT: Deposit INTO the broker's column (escrow account)

    1. Earnest Money from the buyer

    2. <u>*Net loan Proceeds*</u> from the lender in a new loan

E. CREDIT: money received (advantage) means the following:

    1. A <u>*benefit*</u> to the buyer or seller (something they receive at closing)

    2. A reduction in the amount of cash the buyer must <u>*bring to closing*</u>

    3. An increase in the amount of cash the seller receives at closing

F. Examples of seller CREDITS:
(Items that increase the amount of cash the seller receives at closing)

    1. Selling price of the property

    2. Proration of bills paid in advance (<u>already paid</u>) by the seller (water and HOA dues)

G. Examples of buyer <u>CREDITS:</u>
(Items that reduce the amount of cash the buyer must bring to closing)

    1. <u>*Earnest*</u> money already deposited by the buyer and held by the broker or closing company

    2. Security deposits transferred from a seller on an investment property

    3. Proration of rent for the month of closing—from the seller

    4. Proration of property taxes for the current year to be paid in arrears (after the year for which they are collected)

    5. The amount of <u>any loans</u> assumed by the buyer or any new loans created as part of the purchase

H. Broker CREDITS: CHECKS out of the broker's column (escrow account)

    1. All the items the closer/broker pays at closing.

    2. Title insurance, recording and notary fees, documentary fee, etc.

III. OVERVIEW OF THE SIX-COLUMN WORKSHEET ENTRIES:

How DEBIT and CREDIT items are handled for closing. **Use the six-column helper worksheet from the back of your book.**

Line 1. Selling Price: Money the buyer owes the seller. **Used in all closings.**

Always _____ *used in all closing* _____
_____.

Line 2. Deposit paid to: (broker): The buyer's earnest money deposit which is owed to the buyer at closing.

Always _____ *Money the buyer gave the broker* _____
_____.

Line 3. Trust Deed, payable to: The name of the lender for the assumable loan or new loan is listed here. In an assumption, the buyer is assuming this obligation of the seller so this amount represents money the seller will not receive at the closing table. In a new loan, this amount is a single entry credit to the buyer.

Assumption: always _____
_____ the amount from the assumption statement.

New loan: single entry, CREDIT buyer.

Line 4. Trust Deed, payable to: Typically used for seller financing. This represents funds the seller will not receive at the closing table.

Always DEBIT seller, CREDIT buyer.

Line 5. Trust Deed, payoff to: This line is used when the seller is paying off the seller's current loan, when the buyer brings cash or a new loan.

Single entry DEBIT seller only.

Line 6. Interest on Loan Assumed: The seller will owe the buyer interest for the portion of the month the seller lives in the property.

Always _____
_____ the prorated share.

Line 7. Owner's Title Insurance Premium: The owner's title policy paid by the seller, per the terms of the Contract to Buy and Sell, and will only show on the seller's Closing Statement.

_____ who will pay the bill.

Line 7a. Extended Title Insurance: This additional coverage is negotiable per the terms of the contract. _____Negotiable charge per the contract_____
_____ and CREDIT broker who pays the bill. (check going out to
title company)

Line 7b. Mortgagee's Policy: The lender requires this policy as part of a new loan, it is a buyer obligation.

DEBIT buyer—Single entry

Line 8. Closing Fee: This is the fee charged by the title company to close the transaction and is negotiable per the contract, may be paid by the seller, buyer, or split between the parties.

DEBIT _____ per the terms of the contract. _Credit the_
_____broker_____ the full amount to pay the bill.

Line 9. Notary Fee: This fee is charged to the party that is signing the document.

DEBIT _____ and CREDIT broker.

DEBIT _____ and CREDIT broker.

Line 10. Title Exam by Buyer's Attorney: The fee for the buyer's attorney to review title.

DEBIT buyer, CREDIT broker.

✶ **Line 11. Recording: Warranty Deed:** Benefits the buyer by providing constructive notice of the buyer's new ownership of the property.

_____Debit Buyer , Credit Broker_____.

Line 12. Recording Deed of Trust: This is the buyer's obligation to pay. When used for a seller-carry loan, it is a double entry. When used in a new loan, it is a single entry.

Seller-carry loan: DEBIT buyer, CREDIT broker.

New loan: DEBIT buyer single entry.

Line 13. Release: The seller pays to record the release of deed of trust. Typically used in a new loan.

DEBIT seller (single entry).

Line 14. Other: Used for any other recording fees.

Line 15. Documentary Fee: A buyer's expense, paid at the time of recording the warranty deed. It is calculated by moving the decimal point four places to the left in the selling price. Remember: = $.01 per $100. (move it 4 spaces to the left of Sales price)
_____Credit Buyer ,_____.

Line 16. Certificate of Taxes Due: The certificate that is obtained from the county treasurer and confirms the current status of governmental taxes on the property.

_____ .

Line 17. Taxes for Preceding Year(s): If the taxes from the preceding year are unpaid, they are an obligation of the seller. ✗

Always _____ _Debit Seller_ , _Credit Broker_ _____

_____ to pay the bill to clear the lien.

Line 18. Taxes for Current Year: Will be a proration between the seller and the buyer. Since Colorado property taxes are paid in arrears, the seller will owe the buyer.

DEBIT seller, CREDIT _____ _buyer the prorated share_ (_SOB_) _____ .

Line 19. Tax Reserve: The lender will collect one month's taxes in each monthly installment. However, the lender will collect funds from the closing to prime the account (can collect an additional **three months** plus what is owed). This amount plus the monthly escrow installments will be sufficient to pay the taxes when they become due.

DEBIT buyer (single entry).

Line 20. Special Taxes/Assessments: This line refers to government special assessments. The rule: if listed in the contract, the seller will pay in full at closing. If the buyer is to assume the bill, there is NO deduction at closing.

_____ _Debit to Seller_ , _Credit to Broker_ (✗) _____ .

Line 21. Personal Property Taxes: Typically a buyer responsibility.

DEBIT buyer, CREDIT broker.

Line 22. Notary fee paid by Lender: In a new loan closing, the lender may collect and pay the notary from the buyer for the deed of trust.

DEBIT buyer (single entry).

Line 23. Premium for New Insurance: This is to cover the new hazard insurance policy. In a new loan, it would be a single entry DEBIT to the buyer.

Assumed loan DEBIT the buyer, CREDIT broker.

Line 24. Hazard Insurance Reserve: As with the tax reserve, the lender requires an amount up front to prime the escrow account.

DEBIT buyer (single entry).

Lines 25 and 26: Not used.

Line 27. Loan origination fee: This is the lender's fee for making the loan.

DEBIT buyer (single entry).

Line 28. Loan Discount Points: Charges by the lender to buy down the interest rate and increase the lender's yield. New loan single entry. *(could be concession by seller)*

DEBIT buyer.

Line 29. Interest on a new loan: At closing, the buyer must pay the interest adjustment for the month of closing, since the first payment will begin a month after closing. New loan requirement. *Calculation, not proration*

DEBIT buyer (single entry).

Line 30. Survey/Credit Report: If the lender requires any of these items, they would be a buyer obligation in a new loan or an assumption loan. *Survey is negotiable, but assumes buyer*

DEBIT buyer (single entry). *(credit report is a loan cost)*

DEBIT buyer, CREDIT broker (assumption).

Line 31. Appraisal fee: The cost of the appraisal is negotiable per the contract. Most often found in a new loan, this will be a single entry to the party that agreed to pay.

DEBIT seller or buyer (single entry).

DEBIT seller or buyer, CREDIT broker (assumption).

Line 32. Water and/or Sewer: The water/sewer bill can be paid in advance or arrears. It will be prorated between the seller and buyer. Determine how to prorate based upon the information given.

Prorated between the parties. If a bill is owed, ____*Credit Broker*____.

Line 33. Rents: The seller collects the rent from the tenant in advance for the month. The seller will always owe the buyer for the buyer's prorated share.

DEBIT _____.

Line 34. Security Deposits: The seller is holding the tenants security deposit and it must be transferred in full to the new buyer.

Always __*transfer full amount Debit Seller, Credit Buyer*__.

Line 35. Loan Transfer Fee: In an assumable loan, the lender may require the buyer pay a transfer fee.

DEBIT buyer, CREDIT broker.

Line 36. Loan Payment Due: If the seller on an assumable loan has a past due payment, the full amount is entered here. Remember, this pays for the previous month so the full amount is due.

DEBIT seller the full amount and CREDIT broker. (payment to lender)

Line 37. Broker's Fee: This fee is typically paid by the seller.

Debit Seller , Credit Broker

Line 38. Seller Attorney: If the seller has a bill from an attorney, DEBIT seller and CREDIT broker to pay the bill.

Line 39. Net Loan Proceeds: When a new loan is used, the broker will receive a DEBIT in this amount.

_____ (single entry).

IV. COMPLETING A SIX-COLUMN WORKSHEET:

	SELLER		BUYER		BROKER	
	Debit	Credit	Debit	Credit	Debit	Credit
1. Selling Price		100,000	100,000			
2. Deposit, paid to:				5,000	5,000	
7. Title Insurance Premium Owners	625					625
8. Closing Fee Split 50/50	75		75			150
9. Notary						
10. Title Exam by: Buyer's Attorney			200			200
11. Recording: Warranty Deed			12			12
12. Recording: Trust Deed			20			20
13. Recording: Release of Lien						
15. Documentary Fee			10			10
16. Cerificate of Taxes Due			15			15
Taxes for Current year **Prorated** 18. between parties	420			420		
20. Special Taxes	750					750
23. Premium for New Insurance			600			600
30. Credit Report			50			50
31. Appraisal Fee			350			350
37. Broker's Fee	6,000					6,000
Sub-Totals	7,871	100,000	101,332	5,420	5,000	8,784
Balance Due TO/from Seller	92,129					92,129
Balances Due to/FROM				95,912	95,912	
Totals	100,000	100,000	101,332	101,332	100,912	100,912

Negotiated in the contract

Balance Due TO seller: Subtract DEBIT from CREDIT subtotal. Once determined, put in broker CREDIT column as this is the amount the broker will have to write as a check to the seller.

Balance Due FROM buyer: Subtract CREDIT from DEBIT subtotal. Once determined, put in broker DEBIT column as this is the amount the broker will have to collect (deposit) from the buyer.

If Broker colums do not balance, check the seller and buyer columns.

V.   PRORATIONS

A. Colorado Rules and Methods

1. ___Buyer___ owns on day of closing.

2. Use ___365___ days in a year (366 for leap year). (360 in National)

★ a) Use calendar months—know how many days.

3. _Never Prorate_ the following:

a) Security deposits

b) ___Loan payment due_____,
since interest is paid in arrears a loan payment due pays the month before closing. The seller will owe the full amount.

c) Special taxes (special assessments)

★ (1) Contract says ___seller___ pays off special assessment.

(2) If both parties agree, could _be assumed by buyer_
and _will not show up_ on the Closing Statements.

2   (not entry)

B. How to Prorate

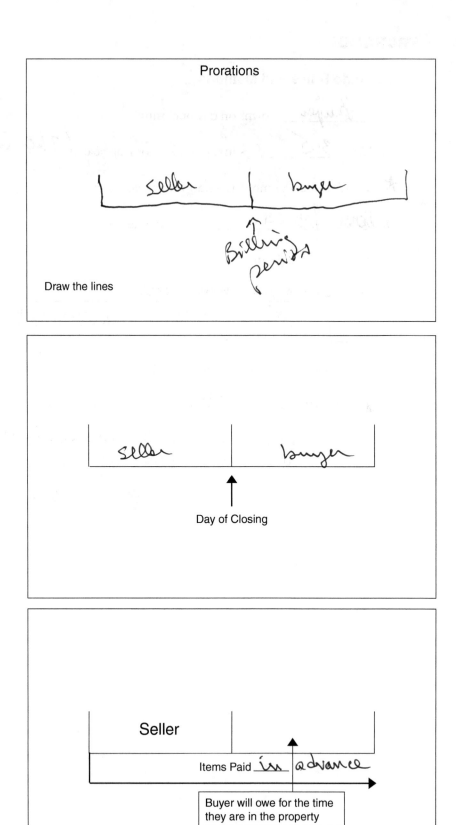

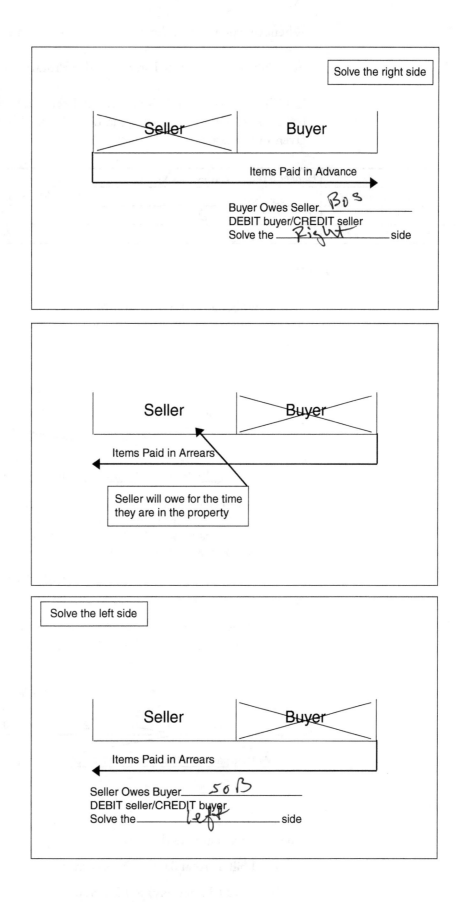

Whenever you prorate, the calculation is always the same:

Total bill ÷ Total days × Days owned = Prorated $

In Colorado, we use a 365-day year and the actual days in the month. February has 28 days, unless it is a leap year, not 30. **For either test, follow the directions given in the exam.**

	Banker's Year (*National*)	Actual Year
Who owns the day of closing?	*Seller*	*Buyer*
Days in the month	*30 in each*	*Actual*
How many days in the year?	*360*	*365*

C. Proration problem:

A property being sold has a water bill of $60.00 that has been paid in advance at the beginning of the month. What will be the DEBIT to the buyer at closing on June 21?

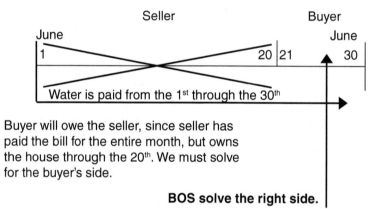

Buyer will owe the seller, since seller has paid the bill for the entire month, but owns the house through the 20th. We must solve for the buyer's side.

BOS solve the right side.

Buyer will owe the seller, since seller has paid the bill for the entire month and owns the house through the 20th. We must solve for the buyer's side.

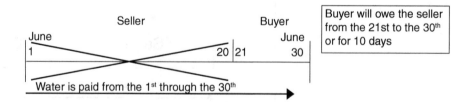

Buyer will owe the seller from the 21st to the 30th or for 10 days

The formula is always the same:

Total bill ÷ Total days × Days owned

$60 ÷ 30 ($2 per day) × 10 = $20

Buyer owes seller: DEBIT buyer and CREDIT seller

Big side versus little side

Some proration questions can be solved without having to do the math by simply looking for the big side versus little side.

In the problem we just did, the buyer owed the little side

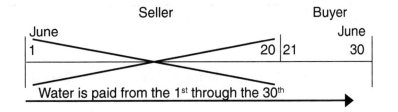

Let's see how this looks in a problem.

Big side versus little side

A property being sold has a water bill of $60 that has been paid in advance at the beginning of the month. What will be the DEBIT and CREDIT entries for a closing on June 21?

1. Debit buyer $40 credit seller $40
2. **Credit seller $20 debit buyer $20**
3. Debit seller $40 credit buyer $40
4. Credit buyer $20 debit seller $20

There is no need to do the math since you knew that the buyer owed (DEBIT the buyer) the seller (CREDIT the seller) the small side of the equations.

D. Proration example 1:

Prorate the Colorado general property taxes between buyer and seller if the tax amount for the preceding year was $1,366. The closing takes place on April 13. Which party is to be debited? Which will receive a CREDIT for the taxes?

Step 1:

Draw a horizontal line representing the entire billing period for the item you are prorating. Add short vertical lines at each end to show the limits with the beginning date just inside the left-hand vertical line and the last date just inside the right-hand line. Annual taxes billed on a calendar-year basis would look like this:

Step 2:

Draw another vertical line near the closing date (use rough proportions). Closing date is April 13.

Step 3:

1. Write the closing date on the right side of the vertical line (buyer's first day of ownership).

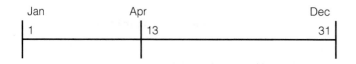

2. Write the day before closing on the left side of the vertical line (seller's last day of ownership).

Jan   Apr   Dec
1   12 | 13   31

Step 4:

Determine if the item to be prorated is paid in arrears (the buyer will receive a bill after closing that includes charges made during the seller's ownership period) or paid in advance (the seller has already paid a bill and the buyer owns the property during part of this period). In either case, one party will owe the other for a proportional share of time they owned the property.

SOB (Seller Owes Buyer) side: Left side of timeline

■ Paid in arrears (i.e., "unpaid," "not paid," or "owes")
■ Includes items such as: real estate taxes, personal property taxes, and interest on most real estate loans

BOS (Buyer Owes Seller) side: Right side of timeline

■ Paid in advance (i.e., "prepaid," "paid")
■ Most often water and home owner association bills

Begin		Closing		End
ARREARS		ADVANCE		
Seller owns		Buyer owns		
S.O.B side		**B.O.S side**		
DS CB		**DB CS**		

Step 5:

Go to the appropriate side (arrears or advance) and draw an X on the side that will **not** be worked—the side that does not owe the bill. Then count the days for the side that owes. Use actual number of days in each month.

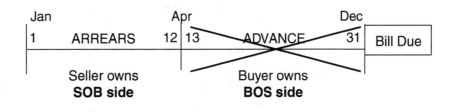

When calculating the days, use the figure on the left of the closing date line (usually) and not the actual date of closing.

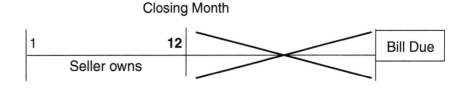

In our example, the number of days of seller's ownership in April is 12.

If we need to find the buyer's ownership something paid in advance: Take the number of days in April = 30 – 12 (seller's last day) = 18.

[**Not** the common error of 30 – 13 (buyer's first day) = 17.] Remember, always use the seller's last day.

For Colorado real estate taxes for the current year, always count the days on the SOB side:

Example:

January	31
February	28
March	31
April	12 (The buyer owns the property the day of closing.)
=	102

Note: Put the number for the month of closing first than other months, since the rest will all be full months.

Step 6:

Calculate one party's share. In this case, taxes are paid in arrears, so the seller owes the buyer for the seller's 102 days of ownership prior to the closing. **The formula is always the same:** _Total Bill ÷_

_____ .

Tip: Use your calculator for the calculation and don't write down the daily amount to re-enter later. Most calculators easily retain the six decimal places needed to ensure an accurate calculation.

$1,366 ÷ 365 × 102 days = _381.73_

DEBIT _Seller_ , CREDIT _Buyer_

Tips: remember the formula:

Total bill ÷ Total days × Days owned = Prorated $

Always use the seller's last day to determine the number of days owned. Cross off the person who pays the bill.

CLASSROOM EXERCISE: SETTLEMENT EXERCISE 1

Part A: Creating the closing worksheet for closing

1. Using the information on this page (from the sales contract and other sources), prepare a six-column worksheet for this closing.

   The closing will be April 13. The buyer is paying cash.

   Some items will be "prorated" between the parties. These are ongoing expenses of the property. Seller will be responsible for some of the money and buyer for the remainder.

   Sales Price (Line 1) $142,000

   Deposit paid to broker (Line 2).. 1,800

   Title Insurance Premium (Line 7)... 764 ·

   Closing fee split between the parties (Line 8) 150

   Notary charges per document signed (Line 9)... 1

   Title examination by buyer's attorney (Line 10)................................... 160

   Recording Warranty Deed (Line 11) 6

   Documentary fee (Line 15) .... ???? *14.20*

   Tax certificate (Line 16).. 15
   (shows the $1,326 taxes for last year were paid) (Line 17) ....Memo

   Don't forget the proration of taxes for the current year (Line 18)

   Special Assessment (that the seller has agreed to pay) (Line 20) 1,700

   New hazard insurance (Line 23) 480

   The unmetered water and sewer bill from March 1 through May 31
   has been paid in the amount of (Line 32)..$32

   Broker's fee: 6% (Line 37) 8,520

   Note: The brokerage fees are for illustration only and are not intended to imply standard fees. Actual brokerage fees are negotiated between brokers and the seller, buyers, landlords, or tenants who hire them.

	SELLER				BUYER				BROKER			
	Debit		Credit		Debit		Credit		Debit		Credit	
1. Selling Price			142,000	00	142,000	00						
2. Deposit, paid to:							1,800	00	1,800	00		
3. Deed of Trust, payable to:												
4. Deed of Trust, payable to:												
5. Deed of Trust, payoff to:												
6. Interest on Loan Assumed												
7. Owner Title Insurance Premium	764	00									764	00
a. Extended Title Insurance												
b. Mortgagee's Policy												
8. Closing Fee	75	00			75	00					150	00
9. Notary Fee	1	00									1	00
10. Title Exam by buyer attorney					160	00					160	00
11. Recording: Warranty Deed					6	00					6	00
12. Deed of Trust												
13. Release												
14. Other												
15. Documentary Fee					14	20					14	20
16. Certificate of Taxes Due					15	00					15	00
17. Taxes for Preceding Year(s)												
18. Taxes for Current Year	370	55					370	55				
19. Tax Reserve												
20. Special Taxes (Assessments)	1,700	00									1,700	00
21. Personal Property Taxes												
22. Notary Fee paid by Lender												
23. Premium for New Insurance					480	00					480	00
24. Hazard Ins. Reserve												
25. FHA Mortgage Ins. Assumed												
26. FHA Mortgage Ins. Reserve												
27. Loan Origination												
28. Loan Discount Points												
29. Interest on New Loan												
30. Survey												
Credit Report												
31. Appraisal Fee												
32. Water and/or Sewer			17	04	17	04						
33. Rents												
34. Security Deposits												
35. Loan Transfer Fee												
36. Loan Payment Due												
37. Broker's Fee	8,520	00									8,520	00
38. Seller's Attorney												
39. Net loan proceeds												
Subtotals	11,430	55	142,017	04	142,767	24	2,170	55	1,800	00	11,810	20
Balance Due to/~~from~~ Seller	130,586	49									130,586	49
Balance Due ~~to~~/from Buyer							140,596	69	140,596	69		
TOTALS	142,017	04			142,767	24	142,767	24				

■ DISCUSSION OF CLOSING WORKSHEET EXERCISE 1

The following discussion works through Exercise 1. The numbers refer to the lines on which you enter DEBITS and CREDITS on the worksheets.

1. Selling Price is $142,000. DEBIT the buyer and CREDIT the seller.

2. Deposit paid to: (broker) The buyer's earnest money deposit of $1,800, which is part payment of the purchase price and reduces the cash the buyer needs at closing. CREDIT the buyer and DEBIT the broker.

7. Title Insurance Premium refers to the owner's policy paid by the seller. DEBIT the seller and CREDIT the broker who will pay the bill.

8. Closing Fee this is the fee charged by the title company to close the transaction and is being split between the seller and buyer. DEBIT the buyer and seller each ½ of the fee ($75) and CREDIT the broker the full amount of $150.

9. Notary Fee this fee is charged to the party that is signing the document. In cash closing, the only document that it notarized is the warranty deed, signed by the seller. No fee will appear on the buyer's worksheet. DEBIT seller and CREDIT broker.

10. Title Exam by is the line for the fee for the buyer's attorney to review the title insurance commitment and advise the buyer on the merchantability of the title. The fee amount is $160. DEBIT the buyer and CREDIT broker.

11. Recording: Warranty Deed benefits the buyer by providing constructive notice of the buyer's new ownership of the property. DEBIT the buyer $6 and CREDIT the broker.

15. Documentary Fee A buyer's expense paid at the time of recording the warranty deed. It is calculated by moving the decimal point four places to the left in the selling price. $142,000 selling price yields $14.20 fee. DEBIT the buyer and CREDIT broker.

16. Certificate of Taxes Due refers to the certificate that is obtained from the county treasurer and confirms the current status of governmental taxes on the property. The buyer is assured that no other taxes are due. The $15 fee is a buyer DEBIT and CREDIT broker.

17. Taxes for Preceding Year(s) In this exercise, the tax certificate shows that last year's taxes are already paid in the amount of $1,326. It is customary to show a memo about this amount on line 17, but no DEBIT or CREDIT will show on either worksheet.

18. Taxes for Current Year are a proration between the seller and the buyer based on the $1,326 taxes of the preceding year. Prorate as illustrated in the Proration Helper and enter the seller's share of the taxes as a CREDIT to the buyer on line 18, with a corresponding DEBIT to the seller.

20. Special Taxes on Line 20 refers to government special assessments. The Contract to Buy and Sell provides that the seller will pay off these assessments unless the buyer agrees to assume the obligation. DEBIT seller and CREDIT broker.

23. Premium for New Insurance is for a new hazard insurance policy. The $480 premium is the buyer's expense. DEBIT the buyer and CREDIT broker.

32. Water and/or Sewer In this exercise, the unmetered water is already paid (in advance). Prorate the amount and charge (debit) the buyer for the buyer's ownership period. DEBIT buyer and CREDIT seller

37. Broker's Fee is typically paid by the seller, DEBIT seller and CREDIT broker.

Subtotals: Carefully add the DEBIT and CREDIT columns.

Which subtotal is larger? Normally the buyer has greater DEBITS than CREDITS which means the buyer will bring funds to closing. The opposite is true for the seller, who should have greater CREDITS than DEBITS.

The difference between the buyer's DEBITS and the buyer's CREDITS is the **Balance Due to/from Buyer**. Enter the amount on this line below the smaller of the two numbers (in this case, below the buyer's CREDITS).

1. Enter the difference between the **Subtotals** under the smaller (DEBIT) number and complete the **Total** line at the bottom of the sheet.
2. Complete the **Totals** by adding the Subtotal amounts to the Balance Due to/from Buyer and Balance Due to/from Seller. The result is equal Totals for the buyer's and seller's two columns at the very bottom which need to match. Now total the broker column. Note you will need to add the check from the seller total to the broker's CREDIT (check out) column to balance and the money brought by the buyer to the brokers DEBIT (deposit in) column to balance the broker side.

	Seller		Buyer		Broker	
	Debit	Credit	Debit	Credit	Debit	Credit
Subtotals	11,430.55	142,017.04	142,767.24	2,170.55	1,800.00	11,810.20
Balance Due **TO/from** Seller	130,586.49					130,586.49
Balance Due **to/FROM** Buyer				140,596.69	140,596.69	
Totals	142,017.04	142,017.04	142,767.24	142,767.24	142,396.69	142,396.69

Check the Buyer's Closing worksheet and the Prorations Solution to confirm your work on this part of the exercise.

■ SETTLEMENT EXERCISE 1—PRORATION SOLUTIONS

Line 18: Taxes for the preceding year were $1,326.

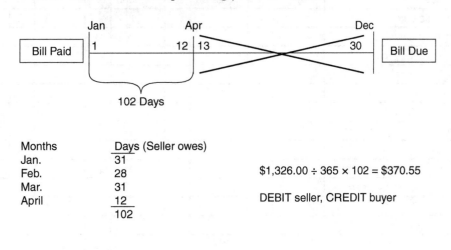

Months	Days (Seller owes)
Jan.	31
Feb.	28
Mar.	31
April	12
	102

$1,326.00 ÷ 365 × 102 = $370.55

DEBIT seller, CREDIT buyer

Line 32: Water and Sewer = $32

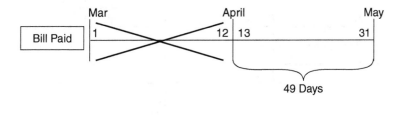

Months	Days (Buyer owes)
April	18
May	31
	49

$32.00 ÷ 92 × 49 = $17.04

DEBIT buyer, CREDIT seller

	SELLER				BUYER				BROKER			
	Debit		Credit		Debit		Credit		Debit		Credit	
1. Selling Price			142,000	00	142,000	00						
2. Deposit, paid to:							1,800	00	1,800	00		
3. Deed of Trust, payable to:												
4. Deed of Trust, payable to:												
5. Deed of Trust, payoff to:												
6. Interest on Loan Assumed												
7. Owner Title Insurance Premium	764	00									764	00
8. Closing Fee	75	00			75	00					150	00
9. Notary Fee	1	00									1	00
10. Title Exam by buyer attorney					160	00					160	00
11. Recording: Warranty Deed					6	00					6	00
12. Deed of Trust												
13. Release												
14. Other												
15. Documentary Fee					14	20					14	20
16. Certificate of Taxes Due					15	00					15	00
17. Taxes for Preceding Year(s)												
18. Taxes for Current Year	370	55					370	55				
19. Tax Reserve												
20. Special Taxes (Assessments)	1,700	00									1,700	00
21. Personal Property Taxes												
22. Notary Fee paid by Lender												
23. Premium for New Insurance					480	00					480	00
24. Hazard Ins. Reserve												
25. FHA Mortgage Ins. Assumed												
26. FHA Mortgage Ins. Reserve												
27. Loan Origination												
28. Loan Discount Points												
29. Interest on New Loan												
30. Survey												
Credit Report												
31. Appraisal Fee												
32. Water and/or Sewer			17	04	17	04						
33. Rents												
34. Security Deposits												
35. Loan Transfer Fee												
36. Loan Payment Due												
37. Broker's Fee	8,520	00									8,520	00
38. Seller's Attorney												
39. Net loan proceeds												
Subtotals	11,430	55	142,017	04	142,767	24	2,170	55	1,800	00	11,810	20
Balance Due to/~~from~~ Seller	130,586	49									130,586	49
Balance Due ~~to~~/from Buyer							140,596	69	140,596	69		
TOTALS	142,017	04	142,017	04	142,767	24	142,767	24	142,396	69	142,396	69

■ HOMEWORK BEFORE UNIT 2

Using Closing Exercise 1, see if you can do the closing worksheet and balance all six columns on your own. The understanding of these principles underlies what we will discuss in the rest of the course, so don't skip doing this work.

If you have Microsoft Excel, you can download an Excel version of the six-column worksheet at: *www.kpscolorado.com/homestudy*.

Read Unit 2 if you have not already done so and complete the glossary review.

UNIT 2

How Loans Affect the Buyer and Seller

■ FOCUS ON UNDERSTANDING

- ■ How loans affect a closing worksheet
- ■ Other prorations used in closings
- ■ The "Rules" for allocating expenses in a settlement

■ ASSIGNMENTS AND STUDY PLAN

Before Unit 2:

1. Complete Unit 1 homework
2. Look up **Important Terms** in Glossary
3. Read the Unit 2 text
4. Complete the Glossary Review for Unit 2

After Unit 2:

1. Prorations Practice 2
2. Contract to Buy and Sell Exercise
3. Settlement Exercise 3
4. Midterm Exam

■ IMPORTANT TERMS

Accrued interest	Hazard insurance	Tax certificate
Assumption balance	Notary fee	Title insurance premium
Colorado tax payment schedule	Seller-carry financing	VA loan
Documentary fee	Special taxes/ assessments	

Loans

Brokers should be familiar with the following two different types of loans:

■ New loans
■ Assumptions

A new loan begins on the day of closing. In an assumption, the buyer takes over (assumes) responsibility for the existing loan originated by the seller.

Most buyers finance their purchase with a **new loan**. For a new loan, the buyer will make a loan application and provide a credit report. The lender will normally require an appraisal, perhaps a survey, and most likely a mortgagee's (lender's) title insurance policy. The lender may charge a loan origination fee and/or charge discount points based on the loan amount. New loans may be conventional, VA guaranteed, FHA insured, or seller-carry loans. Each of these loan types may have specific fees or requirements unique to that loan program. Loan closing costs are normally the buyer's responsibility (buyer debits). (We will discuss new loans in Unit 3.)

An **assumed loan** (loan assumption) is an existing loan originally taken out when the seller purchased the home. If the lender agrees, or the terms of the original loan permit, the responsibility for the loan may be shifted to the buyer at closing. There may be a loan transfer fee, but there will not be a loan origination fee or discount points at the time the loan is assumed. Most lenders will not require an appraisal or a survey, and the lender's title insurance is already in place so there is no additional cost. In a rising interest rate market, an assumable loan that is a few years old may be an attractive marketing tool. By taking over the existing loan, the buyer uses the remaining balance at the time of closing as primary financing for the purchase.

If the seller's loan is several years old, the property may have appreciated and the loan balance reduced from the original loan amount. The buyer must come up with the difference between the assumed loan balance and the purchase price (the seller's equity). In that case, the seller may be willing to allow the buyer to pay for some of the seller's equity in the form of a **seller-carry second loan.** The seller agrees to accept the buyer's promissory note and record a deed of trust, which will be in second position behind the original deed of trust. The seller-carry loan helps the buyer with the down payment money but reduces the cash available to the seller at closing.

	Example:	Sales Price	$230,000
		Assumed Loan	175,000
		Seller's Equity	55,000
		Buyer Down Payment	25,000
		New Seller-Carry Loan	30,000

Loan Figures

For a closing, the lender's figures will be provided to the broker in a *New Loan Statement* (for new loans) or an *Assumption Statement* (for an assumption). Any figures presented in these statements **must be used exactly as provided** in the closing documents.

A broker who thinks the figures in a lender's *New Loan Statement* or *Assumption Statement* are incorrect, should do the following:

- Verify with the employing broker or closer that the figures are incorrect.
- Call the lender to get the figures checked (only the lender can change them).

Closing with an Assumed Loan

The Assumption Statement: The lender for the loan to be assumed supplies a statement of the current status of the loan. These figures must be used exactly as provided to calculate the closing adjustments (DEBITS and CREDITS).

Assumption Items

Loan Being Assumed (Line 3. Deed of Trust, payable to: Existing Lender):   This is the current principal balance of the first deed of trust or mortgage that is being assumed as of the month of closing. This loan is a debt the seller needs to clear and reduces the amount of cash they will take away from closing (DEBIT seller). The buyer's assumption of the loan results in a buyer CREDIT at closing (reducing the amount of cash the buyer needs to bring to closing). The buyer will take over payment of the loan after closing.

- Assumed Loan: DEBIT seller and CREDIT buyer

		Seller		Buyer	
		Debit	Credit	Debit	Credit
3	Deed of Trust, payable to: ABC Mortgage	**XXX.XX**			**XXX.XX**

Interest on loan assumed: Interest on loans is paid in arrears (i.e., the interest for a given month is due at the end of the month and the interest is included in the next month's payment). Since interest is collected in arrears, in an assumable loan the seller always owes the buyer their interest for the month of closing. (The exception being a closing on the first of the month when the seller would owe nothing provided that month's payment has been made.)

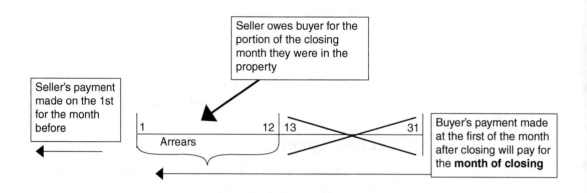

Seller <u>always</u> owes interest to the buyer for the month of closing if a loan is assumed.

1. Balance of Existing Loan × Interest Rate = One year's interest
2. One year's interest ÷ **12** = One month's interest
3. Prorate one month's interest amount by actual days within the month of closing.

Example: A buyer is assuming a loan balance of $36,143.24 on an 8 percent VA guaranteed loan. What is the settlement entry for interest at a closing on April 13?

Monthly interest is $36,143.24 × .08 ÷ 12 = $240.95 for April

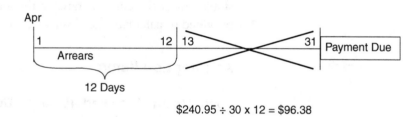

$240.95 ÷ 30 x 12 = $96.38

■ Always DEBIT the seller and CREDIT the buyer.

Special Rule: On assumed loans, interest is always divided by 12 months, since the loan payments have been amortized for the full loan. An assumed loan is the only time 12 months is used; in other interest proration calculations use 365 days. Formula: Loan amount × Interest rate ÷ 12 ÷ Days in month of closing × Days owed = Proration amount.

Line 9. Notary Fees: Notary fees are charged for having a witness (the notary) acknowledge the signing of a document. The party signing gives evidence of identity and the fact that they are signing willingly.

The party who signs the document pays for the notary fee.

■ **Notary Fee for a Warranty Deed is signed by the seller**
   — Always DEBIT the seller.
■ **Notary Fee for a Deed of Trust (Trust Deed) is signed by the buyer**
   — Always DEBIT the buyer.

Line 33. Water and/or Sewer: The proration of water and sewer charges must comply with the contract and the billing method. There are two common possibilities:

- Metered bill: The closer/broker will order the account to be switched to the buyer as of the date of closing. The seller will owe for the water used **to the** day of closing. Since that bill is not yet available, the broker withholds an adequate amount from the seller's proceeds to cover the bill. The amount withheld will show up on the seller's Closing Statement. The closer/broker will pay the bill when it arrives and return any excess to the seller.
- Unmetered bill: Paid as a flat rate either in advance or in arrears. Payment in advance is more common, but read the information provided by the utility, or in a test problem, carefully to determine whether it is paid in advance or in arrears.

Rental Properties

The sale of rental properties creates the need to account for items related to the tenants, primarily rents and security deposits.

Line 33. Rents: Rent is collected from a tenant on the first of the month in advance for that month. The buyer will want to be given a share of the rent. Remember: since the buyer will not have possession, they expect the rent that is owed them. Typically, this means the rent needs to be prorated. A tenant pays rent in advance and the seller will be required to CREDIT the buyer for the portion of the month the buyer owns the property. Rent is **always** a DEBIT to the seller and CREDIT to the buyer.

Closing Date: April 23rd

Monthly rent paid from April 1st to April 30th in the amount of $630.

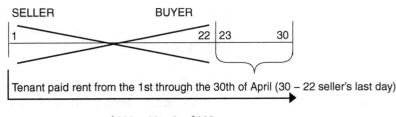

$630 ÷ 30 × 8 = $168

- Always DEBIT seller and CREDIT buyer the prorated share

Line 34. Security Deposits: The seller is holding all security deposits. This **tenant's money** is transferred in full to the new owner at the closing (DEBIT seller and CREDIT buyer the full amount). The Contract to Buy and Sell requires the seller notify the tenants as to who is holding the security deposit.

- Always DEBIT seller and CREDIT buyer **the full amount.**
- NEVER prorate security deposits.

Line 4. Deed of Trust, payable to: Seller-Second or Seller-Carry

- If a second Deed of Trust is to exist on the property after the closing, such as a seller-carry back, this needs to be included in the closing figures. The seller will receive this amount after closing from payments made by the buyer, but the **seller will not receive this as cash** at closing. Remember: the closing represents only funds brought to, or given out, on closing day.
- Always DEBIT seller and CREDIT buyer the full amount of the seller-carry loan.

Line 29. Interest on New Loan or Seller-Carry Second: In a new or seller-carry loan, because the ongoing monthly payments are amortized, the buyer will often owe the lender interest for the month of closing. In a seller-carry loan, the buyer will owe the seller (lender) this interest. The amount is for the days the buyer owns the property for the month of closing only. This is **not a proration** since it is money the buyer owes the lender and is not a bill being divided between the two parties. Interest is the buyer's responsibility because the loan starts as of the day of closing.

- Always DEBIT buyer (borrower) and CREDIT seller (lender) for the days owed for the month of closing.

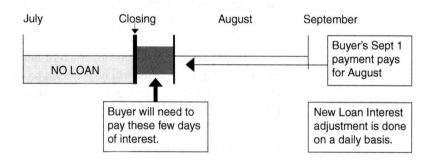

<u>Formula:</u> **Amount of New Loan × Interest Rate ÷ 365 × Days Owed**

Example: Seller-carry loan of $25,000 at 6 percent interest. Buyer owes five days for the month of closing. $25,000 × .06 ÷ 365 × 5 = $20.55. DEBIT buyer $20.55 and CREDIT seller $20.55.

Note: This method is not the same as the calculation of interest on the Loan Assumed in the closing! This is done using 365 days.

Buyer and Seller Transfers

As we have discussed before, many entries for a settlement involve just the buyer and seller. These are buyer and seller transfers of funds carried out on the six-column worksheet as part of the closing. Amounts are then summarized in the subtotals and totals at the bottom of the worksheet to determine the final funds needed for closing.

Review of Debits (items owed) and CREDITS (amounts received)

- **Sales price:**   CREDIT seller/DEBIT buyer
- **Loan assumption balance:**   DEBIT seller/CREDIT buyer

- **Seller-carry loan amount:**   DEBIT seller/CREDIT buyer
- **Security deposits:**   DEBIT seller/CREDIT buyer
- **Interest adjustment on
  a new or seller-carry loan:**   CREDIT seller/DEBIT buyer
- Prorations:
    - **Interest on a loan assumed: (SOB)** DEBIT seller/CREDIT buyer
    - **Taxes for the current year: (SOB)** DEBIT seller/CREDIT buyer
    - **Rents: (Seller always owes buyer)** DEBIT seller/CREDIT buyer
    - **HOA dues:** usually paid in advance so CREDIT seller/DEBIT buyer
    - **Flat rate water and/or sewer:** advance (BOS) or arrears (SOB)

Buyer Settlement Items

Many items are buyer-only items and do not affect the seller. These are mostly fees or obligations due to a person or company outside of the closing. As we saw in Unit 1, these are usually reflected in the broker's column as CREDITS to be paid. The broker or new lender will process payments to outside service providers.

Buyer settlement entries that affect only the buyer's Closing Statement include:

- **Earnest money deposits:**   Buyer CREDIT, because it will be deducted from the purchase price; DEBIT broker's escrow since this is where it was deposited and has been held.

- **Buyer's attorney:**   Buyer DEBIT to pay for this legal service; CREDIT broker to pay the bill.

- **Closing fee as negotiated in the contract:**   DEBIT buyer per terms; CREDIT broker.

- **Notary fee:**   DEBIT buyer for the Deed of Trust they sign; CREDIT broker.

- **Recording the warranty deed:**   DEBIT buyer since the buyer benefits from the constructive notice provided by recording; CREDIT broker to pay the bill.

- **Recording a new Deed of Trust:**   DEBIT buyer since the lender requires a Deed of Trust be signed at closing; CREDIT broker to pay the bill.

- **Documentary fee:**   DEBIT buyer by state law and because it will have to be paid at the time the warranty deed is recorded; CREDIT broker to pay the bill.

- **Tax certificate:**   DEBIT buyer as a benefit and future guarantee; CREDIT broker to pay the bill.

- Loan fees and costs—normally all buyer debits:
    - Mortgagee's title insurance
    - Loan origination fee
    - Loan discount points

— Loan transfer fee
— Appraisal—usually buyer, but negotiable in the contract
— Survey—negotiable in the contract
— Closing fee

Many of these DEBITS will be paid by the lender in a new loan, and reported to the broker/closer, which we will discuss later in the unit.

Seller Settlement Items

These items affect the seller's Closing Statement and not the buyer's. Again, the broker or new lender will make payments to outside service providers.

Seller settlement entries include:

■ **Deed of Trust Payoff:**	For a new loan closing, DEBIT seller to remove the lien.
■ **Owner's title insurance:**	DEBIT seller per terms of Contract to Buy and Sell Real Estate; CREDIT broker to pay the bill.
■ **Closing fee as negotiated in the contract:**	DEBIT seller per terms; CREDIT broker.
■ **Notary Fee:**	DEBIT seller for the Warranty Deed; CREDIT broker.
■ **Seller's attorney:**	DEBIT seller for this legal service; CREDIT broker to pay the bill.
■ **Recording Release of Deed of Trust:**	DEBIT seller to remove the lien; CREDIT broker to pay the bill.
■ **Taxes for the preceding year (if unpaid):**	DEBIT seller since they had possession of the year; CREDIT broker the full amount owed to pay the bill/lien.
■ **Loan payment due:**	DEBIT seller the full amount of loan payment due; CREDIT broker to pay the bill.
■ **Broker's Fee:**	DEBIT seller per terms of the listing contract. Listing Contract; CREDIT broker.
■ **Security Deposit:**	Since the security deposit belongs to the tenant, DEBIT seller the full amount and transfer to the buyer/new landlord (CREDIT buyer).

■ **Prorations:**
— Taxes for the current year: DEBIT seller; CREDIT buyer
— Flat rate water and/or sewer: advance (BOS) or arrears (SOB)
— Rents: DEBIT seller/CREDIT buyer
— HOA dues: usually in advance (BOS: buyer owes seller) so CREDIT seller/ DEBIT buyer

Broker items shown on the worksheet:

The last two columns of the six-column Settlement Closing worksheet represent the broker's escrow or trust account. The broker's two columns have the following meanings:

- ■ <u>DE</u>BIT (<u>D</u>eposit **into** the broker's escrow account)
- ■ <u>C</u>REDIT (<u>C</u>heck **out of** the broker's escrow account)

DEBIT (Deposit into the closer/broker's escrow account)   A DEBIT represents money deposited (or paid in) and held by the broker in the company's escrow account, or held by the closer in the title company escrow account until the day of closing. The money is held in trust for others and the broker owes it to someone; therefore it is a broker DEBIT. In the body of the settlement sheet, there are only two broker DEBITS we would expect to see in the main part of the worksheet above the Total lines:

- ■ **Line 2.** Deposit, paid to: Earnest money deposit (money provided by the buyer to the broker before closing)
- ■ **Line 39.** In a new loan **only**, Net Loan Proceeds: the net amount sent to closing by a new lender so the closer/broker can pay bills and write a check to the seller.

		BROKER	
		Debit	Credit
2	Earnest money deposit	XXX	
39	New Loan Net Loan Proceeds	XXX	

If the buyer (or seller in rare instances) will be bringing good funds to closing, this will show up as a broker debit/deposit on the Balance due to/from line (below the double line) for the respective party. It must be deposited **into** the trust account or the broker will not have sufficient money to complete the closing.

CREDIT (Check out of the closer/broker's escrow account)   A CREDIT represents a check written (an amount paid out) from the closer/broker's escrow account for that transaction. Writing a check to pay a bill on behalf of the buyer or seller reduces the money held for others, making the amount a broker CREDIT (think check out of the account).

When the closing worksheet is completed, the broker will have written checks in an amount equal to the money that was deposited in the escrow account, so the ledger for the transaction will have a **zero** balance.

Typical Broker CREDITS

DEBIT from Seller, Buyer, or Either			Debit		Credit	
Seller	Owner's Title Insurance Premium				XXX	XX
Either	Extended Title Insurance Premium				XXX	XX
Either	Title Exam by: (Attorney's Fees)				XXX	XX
Either	Closing Fees				XXX	XX
Both	Notary Fees				XXX	XX
Buyer	Recording: Warranty Deed				XXX	XX
Buyer	Recording: Trust Deed				XXX	XX
Buyer	Documentary Fee				XXX	XX
Buyer	Certificate of Taxes Due				XXX	XX
Seller	Taxes for the Preceding Year(s)				XXX	XX
Seller	Special Taxes				XXX	XX
Buyer	Premium for New Insurance				XXX	XX
Buyer	Loan Origination Fee				XXX	XX
Buyer	Loan Discount Points				XXX	XX
Either	Survey				XXX	XX
Buyer	Credit Report				XXX	XX
Either	Appraisal Fee				XXX	XX
Buyer	Loan Transfer Fee				XXX	XX
Seller	Loan Payment Due				XXX	XX
Seller	Broker's Fee				XXX	XX

Each of these CREDITS represents an amount the broker will pay out on behalf of one of the parties to the transaction.

Broker DEBIT = $ Deposit <u>into</u> trust account

Broker CREDIT = $ Check <u>out of</u> trust account

The broker's fee is a DEBIT seller and CREDIT broker. Remember: the broker has to write a check for the commission from the brokerage escrow account and deposit it into the brokerage operations account in order to write commission checks to a broker associate, and to avoid commingling of funds.

What is entered in the broker's columns?

Whenever there are funds deposited in the escrow account, there will be a broker DEBIT (deposit) noted. Whenever the closer/broker writes a check out of the escrow account, there will be a broker CREDIT.

All items in a closing will be handled by the closer/broker except any buyer/seller DEBITS or CREDITS **in the new loan statement,** which are handled by the lender.

Review of how to find the Subtotal and Total for each column

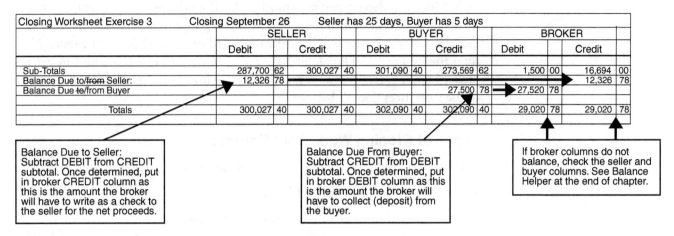

Seller's Subtotal and Total with the Broker's CREDIT Total

| | Seller | | | | Broker | |
	Debit	Credit			Debit	Credit
Subtotals	287,700 62	300,027 40				16,694 00
Balance Due TO/~~from~~ Seller	12,326 78	➡				12,326 78
Balance Due ~~to~~/FROM Buyer						
Totals	300,027 40	300,027 40				29,020 78

The seller's subtotals are all the DEBITS and CREDITS from the seller columns after everything has been entered. Typically the seller's CREDIT subtotal is larger than the DEBIT subtotal, meaning the seller will be receiving money at the closing table. Subtract the DEBIT from the CREDIT to determine how much is due the seller. Once complete, transfer the amount across to the broker CREDIT column as this represents the check the broker will have to write to the seller. Now total the broker CREDIT column add the seller's check amount to get the broker CREDIT total.

Buyer's Subtotal and Total with the Broker's DEBIT Total

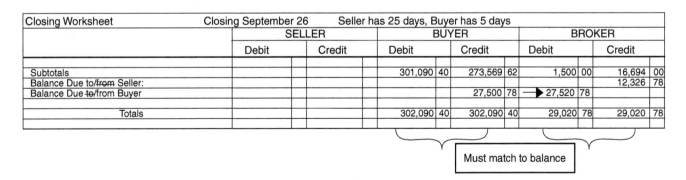

The buyer's subtotals are all the DEBITS and CREDITS from the buyer's columns after everything has been entered. Typically, the buyer's DEBIT subtotal is larger than the CREDIT subtotal, meaning the buyer will bring money to the closing table. Once it is determined how much is due from the buyer, transfer this amount across to the broker DEBIT column as this represents the deposit of funds into broker's account so they will have the money to write the check to the seller. Now, total the broker DEBIT column by adding the buyer's check amount to get the broker DEBIT total. This must match the total from the broker's CREDIT column or the worksheet doesn't balance.

Types of Closing Worksheet Entries:

All entries on the settlement closing worksheet fall into one of three categories:

1. Seller and Buyer Transfer of Funds

    - The selling price or prorations are examples.
    - For these entries, each line will have two off-setting entries. **Equal dollar value of DEBITS and CREDITS.** ($100 debit seller, $100 credit buyer; NOT $150 debit seller, $100 credit buyer.)

2. Funds Held By The Broker Until the Closing of a Transaction

    - Earnest money is the most common example.
    - It is a CREDIT to the buyer and a DEBIT to the broker (deposit **into** the escrow account) again, off-setting dollar value of DEBIT and CREDIT entries.

3. Bills Paid By the Broker, On Behalf of Seller or Buyer

    - A recording fee and attorney's fee are good examples.
    - These are a DEBIT to the party responsible for the item and a CREDIT to the broker (**out** of the escrow account) for writing the check. Equal off-setting dollar value entries again, except in new loans.

■ SETTLEMENT CLOSING WORKSHEET TIPS – ASSUMPTION LOANS

General Rule: ♦ *= proration items   Arrears = SOB-left side   Advance = BOS-right side*

Broker controls and pays. <u>DEBIT and CREDIT $$$ must be equal.</u>

	Debit / Credit	TIPS
1. Selling Price	Credit seller/Debit buyer	
2. Deposit, Paid to:	Credit buyer/Debit broker	
3. Deed of Trust, payable to:	Debit seller/Credit buyer	Seller's old loan being assumed
4. Deed of Trust, payable to **Seller**	Debit seller/Credit buyer	If seller is carrying a portion of selling price
5. Deed of Trust, payoff to:	N/A	
6. ♦ Interest on Loan Assumed	Debit seller/Credit buyer	SOB (solve left side)
7. Title Insurance Premium	Debit seller/Credit broker	
a. Extended Title Insurance		
b. Mortgagee's Policy		
8. Closing Fee	Debit seller and/or buyer/Credit broker	Verify how charged in the contract
9. Notary	Debit seller and buyer/Credit broker	Charge the person who signs the document
10. Title Exam by: Buyer Atty.	Debit buyer/Credit broker	
11. Recording: Warranty Deed	Debit buyer/Credit broker	
12. Deed of Trust New 2nd	Debit buyer/Credit broker	
13. Release	N/A	
14. Other	(depends on Contract)	Analyze carefully.
15. Documentary Fee	Debit buyer/Credit broker	Must have; .0001 × the sale price
16. Certificate of Taxes Due	Debit buyer/Credit broker	
17. Taxes for Preceding Year(s)	Debit seller/Credit broker	If unpaid
18. ♦ Taxes for Current Year	Debit seller/Credit buyer	SOB (solve left side)
19. Tax Reserve	Credit seller/Debit buyer	Assumption loan only // new loan D. Buyer
20. Special Taxes	Debit seller/Credit broker	If paid. If assumed, no entry.
21. Personal Property Taxes	N/A	
22. Hazard Ins. Prem.—Assumed	N/A	
23. Premium for New Hazard Insurance	Debit buyer/Credit broker	
24. Hazard Insurance Reserve	N/A	
25. FHA Mortgage Insurance—Assumed	N/A	
26. FHA Mortgage Insurance Reserve	N/A	
27. Loan Origination	N/A	New loans only
28. Loan Discount Points	N/A	New loans only
29. Interest on New Loan	Debit buyer/Credit seller	Seller-carry calculation
30. Survey	(depends on Contract)	Analyze carefully
Credit Report	Debit buyer/Credit broker	
31. Appraisal Fee	(depends on Contract)	Analyze carefully
32. ♦ Water and/or Sewer	(depends on how billed advance or arrears)	Analyze carefully
33. ♦ Rents	Debit seller/Credit buyer	Seller always owes buyer, solve right side
34. Security Deposits	Debit seller/Credit buyer	The full amount
35. Loan Transfer Fee	Debit buyer/Credit broker	
36. Loan Payment Due	Debit seller/Credit broker	Never prorate
37. Broker's Fee	Debit seller/Credit broker	From the listing contract
38. Seller Atty	Debit seller/Credit broker	
39. Net Loan Proceeds (from Lender)	N/A	New loans only; Debit broker
♦ Homeowner's Association Fees	(depends on how billed advance or arrears)	Analyze carefully
SUB-TOTALS		
Balance Due To / From Seller		
Balance Due To / From Buyer		
TOTALS		

	SELLER		BUYER		BROKER	
	Debit	Credit	Debit	Credit	Debit	Credit
1. Selling Price (**Linked to Line 15**)						
2. Deposit, paid to:						
3. Deed of Trust, payable to: (**Linked to Line 6**)						
4. Deed of Trust, payable to: (**Linked to Line 29**)						
5. Deed of Trust, payoff to:						
6. Interest on Loan Assumed	← Annual interest ÷ 12 then prorate					
7. Title Insurance Premium						
8. Closing Fee						
9. Notary Fee						
10. Title Exam by buyer attorney						
11. Recording: Warranty Deed						
12. Deed of Trust						
13. Release						
14. Other						
15. Documentary Fee	← Move decimal 4 to the left					
16. Certificate of Taxes Due						
17. Taxes for Preceding Yr (**Linked to Line 18**)						
18. Taxes of Current Year						
19. Tax Reserve						
20. Special Taxes						
21. Personal Property Taxes						
22. Hazard Ins. Premium Assumed						
23. Premium for New Insurance						
24. Hazard Ins. Reserve						
25. FHA Mortgage Ins. Assumed						
26. FHA Mortgage Ins. Reserve						
27. Loan Origination Fee (Buyer)						
28. Loan Discount Points (Buyer)						
29. Interest on New Loan	← Annual interest ÷ 365 then days owed					
30. Survey						
Credit Report						
31. Appraisal Fee						
32. Water and/or Sewer						
33. Rents	← Seller always owes buyer from closing to end of month					
34. Security Deposit						
35. Loan Transfer Fee						
36. Loan Payment Due						
37. Broker's Fee						
38. Seller's Attorney						

Sub-Totals	Place the balancing figures under the lower of the DEBIT & CREDIT subtotals (for both buyer and seller)
Balance Due to/from Seller:	Remember to match that entry with an opposing DEBIT or CREDIT in the broker columns
	Everything under the sub-total line is just a process for making the closing worksheet balance

■ SUMMARY OF UNIT 2

1. Information for a closing can come from many sources. A broker must be able to extract and coordinate information from lenders, the Contract to Buy and Sell, and directly from the parties.

2. Figures stated in any lender's statement (assumption or new loan) must be used exactly as provided.

3. There are two types of interest calculations (interest proration on a loan being assumed and interest adjustment on a seller-carry) it is important to be able to differentiate between the two calculations. Remember: assumed loans divide annual interest by 12 months; new loans divide annual interest by 365 days.

4. Many of the items listed on a *six-column worksheet* are buyer/seller exchanges (transfers of money between the buyer and seller). The rest are bills that have to be paid and will be a CREDIT to the broker who will pay them.

■ UNIT 2: GLOSSARY REVIEW

Match the terms with the definitions. Terms may be used more than once.

assumption balance	hazard insurance
Certificate of taxes due	lender reserve/impound account
CREDIT	loan assumption
DEBIT	notary fee
documentary fee	seller-carry financing
FHA loan *(insured)*	special taxes/assessments
FHA mortgage insurance	VA loan

1. The document from the county treasurer reporting the current status of taxes due on a property is the _____ *Certificate of taxes due* _____.

2. A loan from the seller to the buyer to help finance the sale is referred to as *Seller carry* _____ *financing* _____.

3. The fee paid to have the signature on a document witnessed and affirmed is the _____ *notary fee* _____.

4. A loan guaranteed by a government agency is a _____ *VA FHA loan* _____.

5. A lender may hold borrower's funds to pay future bills such as taxes and insurance in _____ *lender reserve/impound account* _____.

6. The exact amount of the _____ *loan assumption Assumption Balance* _____ reported by the existing lender is a CREDIT to the buyer at closing.

7. _____ *Hazard Insurance* _____ protects the owner from fire and other casualty losses.

8. _____ *Special taxes/assessments* _____ or localized improvements by the government will normally be paid off by the seller at closing.

9. A _____ *Credit* _____ in the broker's column typically represents a DEBIT from a buyer or seller.

10. When a buyer takes over responsibility for the seller's loan to help pay the purchase price of a property, this type of closing is called a _____ *loan assumption* _____ closing.

■ UNIT 2: LECTURE OUTLINE

I.   ASSUMPTION AND SELLER-CARRY LOANS

■ Mortgage interest is paid in ___*arrears*___ .

■ Payments are made on the ___1^st___ of the month (<u>unless otherwise stated</u>).

A. Assumption Statement

1. Includes all of the items related to the loan being assumed.

2. Use figures ___*exactly*___ as provided by the lender.

3. **Assumed Loans: (Line 3. Deed of Trust Payable to:)**

    The amount for the loan being assumed will always: *(loan is being transfered)*

    a) be a seller ___*Debit*___ because this is a loan that is owed and will not be part of the funds the seller will receive for the sale.

    b) be a buyer ___*Credit*___ because the buyer is taking over the loan and will not have to bring these funds to closing to pay for the property.

    c) appear on <u>both Closing Statements.</u>

4. When a loan is being assumed, expect to see a ___*Proration*___ of interest for the month of closing. Seller will owe buyer for the time the seller owns the property.

B. Prorating Interest on an Assumed Loan (Line 6. Interest on Loan Assumed)

1. A loan of $250,000 at 6 percent will be assumed by the buyer.

    $250,000 × .06 ÷ 12 = $1,250 per month

    Prorate the interest for a closing on June 6.

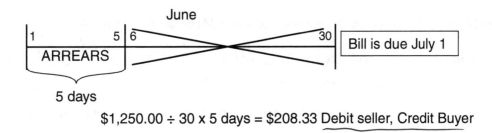

$1,250.00 ÷ 30 x 5 days = $208.33 <u>Debit seller, Credit Buyer</u>

Formula: loan amount × interest rate ÷ 12 ÷ days in month of closing × days owed = proration amount

2. For the proration of an assumed loan to be correct, it MUST be calculated using _____*Monthly interest*_____.

★ 3. **Special rule: Assumed interest is always annual interest divided by** _____*12*_____.

★ 4. Always DEBIT _____*Seller*_____ and CREDIT _____*Buyer*_____.

5. The amount for any loan payment due will always be:

 a) Seller _____*Debit*_____ = → *has not been made*

 b) Broker _____*Credit*_____ to pay the bill.

6. _____*Never prorate*_____ a loan payment that is due, as it pays for the month before closing and is the full obligation of the seller.

C. Lender Reserves: (Lines 19 Tax Reserve and 24 Hazard Insurance)

1. Lender reserves for taxes and insurance to set up new impound accounts are **always** a _____*Buyer*_____ DEBIT. ★

D. Notary Fees: (Line 9.)

★ 1. Notary fees are always paid by _____*the party that signs the document*_____.

 a) The warranty deed is signed by the _____*Seller*_____.

 b) The cost of any associated notary fee is a DEBIT to the _____*Seller*_____, CREDIT broker.

 ★ c) A deed of trust is signed by the _____*Buyer*_____.

 d) The cost of any associated notary fee is a DEBIT to the _____*Buyer*_____, CREDIT broker.

E. Insurance: (Line 23. Premium for New Insurance)

1. Hazard insurance is paid for a _____*policy year*_____ that starts the ~~month~~ *day* of closing.

2. **Always** DEBIT buyer, CREDIT broker, in an assumed loan.

F. Rental Properties (Line 33. Rents and Line 34. Security Deposits)

1. **Rent payments** are collected on the _____*first of the month in advance*_____ from the tenant.

2. The seller will **always** owe the buyer rent from closing to the end of the month.

 a) Rent is **always**:

★ Seller _____*Debit*_____ prorated share

 Buyer _____*Credit*_____ prorated share

3. A security deposit is the _____tenant's_____ money.

   a) It must be transferred __in full__ to the buyer/new owner.

★ b) Always DEBIT seller, CREDIT buyer the ___entire amount___.

G. Prorating Rent

1. Rent is income and not a bill, so it is handled differently than the proration rules about advance and arrears which apply only to transfers between the seller and buyer.

2. Rent is collected in advance by the seller from the tenant. This means the ___Seller___ will **always** owe the ___Buyer___ for the buyer's portion of the month.

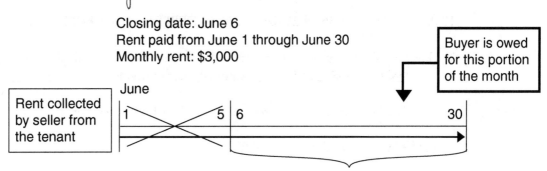

Closing date: June 6
Rent paid from June 1 through June 30
Monthly rent: $3,000

Buyer is owed for this portion of the month

Rent collected by seller from the tenant

June
1   5 6   30

June (30 – 5 seller's last day) = 25 days

$3,000 ÷ 30 x 25 days = $2,500. **Always** Debit seller, Credit Buyer

H. Seller-carry Loans; (Line 4. Deed of Trust, payable to: *Seller*)

1. When a seller agrees to lend the buyer part of the equity in the property, the closer/broker must handle the details of closing the seller-carry loan.

2. Amount of new seller-carry loan will always be a:

   a) ___Debit___ to seller because seller will not receive this amount in cash at closing. Instead, seller agrees to accept buyer's note and secure it with a Deed of Trust in this amount.

   b) ___Credit___ to buyer because the buyer does not bring this amount to closing in cash. Buyer signs the note and secures the debt with a Deed of Trust creating a lien on the property (usually in second position to an existing loan).

★ 3. Buyer will **always owe interest for the month of closing** on a seller-carry or new loan from the day of closing to the end of the month.

I. Calculating Interest Adjustment on a seller-carry loan or new loan: (Line 29. Interest on New Loan)

1. The seller has agreed to provide a second of $10,000 at 9 percent. Calculate the interest adjustment for a closing on June 6 where the first payment is due on August 1. Remember the first payment in August will pay for the month of July (mortgage interest in arrears). We must

collect interest for the portion of the closing month since it is not included in the amortization schedule.

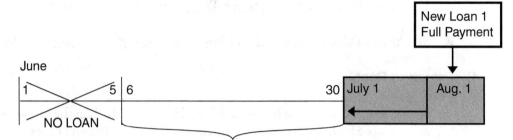

Buyer owes 25 days (30 - 5 seller's last day = 25)

10,000 × .09 (9%) ÷ 365 × 25 days = $61.64 DEBIT buyer, CREDIT seller

a) For the calculation of a seller-carry to be correct it **must** be calculated using _____daily interest_____ (annual interest divided by ___365___).

   (1) The buyer owes this interest to the lender who is the seller.

   (2) (Always) DEBIT the buyer. CREDIT the seller.

★ (3) **TIP: Only** Interest on **ASSUMED** loans is divided by 12.

★ b) Interest on **seller-carry or new loans** is divided by ___365___ .

II.   BUYER AND SELLER TRANSFERS

A. Buyer and seller transfers occur when money is transferred on paper at closing between the two parties to the transaction (the buyer and the seller). Common buyer and seller transfers include the following:

   1. Sales price: Always ____Credit____ seller, ____Debit____ buyer

   2. Loans in an assumption

      a) The loan being ___assumed___

      b) A ___Seller - carry___ second loan

      c) Always ___Debit___ seller, ___Credit___ buyer

   3. Prorations

      a) ___Interest___ on a loan assumed: SOB (solve left side and divide annual interest by 12).

★ b) ___Taxes___ for the current year: SOB (solve left side).

      c) Water and/or sewer ___flat rate___ bills—arrears or advance per the contract.

d) ___Interest___ on a new seller-carry loan: BOS (solve right side).

e) ___Rents___: Always seller owes buyer. (Remember: Security deposits are not prorated but will be transferred in full.)

f) HOA dues—arrears or advance per the contract.

4. Calculation of interest on new loans

a) ___Interest___ on a new seller-carry loan (divide annual interest by 365).

III. SELLER SETTLEMENT ITEMS

A. Seller Settlement items are CREDITS or DEBITS that will show on the ___Seller's___ Closing Statement and not on the ___Buyer's___ Closing Statement.

1. The majority of DEBITS have a corresponding CREDIT to the broker to pay the bill. Remember: all would show on the closing worksheet.

1.	Selling Price	Seller	(Both) Credit
5.	Deed of Trust Payoff	Seller	Debit
6.	Interest on Loan Assumed—Prorate what seller owes	Seller	(Both) Debit
7.	Owner's Title Insurance	Seller	Debit
8.	Closing Fee	Seller	Debit
9.	Notary Fee	Seller	Debit (warrantee Deed)
13.	Recording: Release	Seller	Debit
17	Unpaid Taxes for the Preceding Year	Seller	Debit
18.	Taxes for current year—Prorate what seller owes	Seller	Debit (Both)
34.	Security Deposit	Seller	Debit (Both)
36.	Loan Payment Due	Seller	Debit
37.	Broker's Fee	Seller	Debit
38.	Seller's Attorney	Seller	Debit

IV. BUYER SETTLEMENT ITEMS

A. Buyer settlement items are CREDITS or DEBITS that will show on the ___Buyer's___ Closing Statement and not on the ___Seller___ Closing Statement.

1. The majority of DEBITS have a corresponding CREDIT to the broker to pay the bill. Remember: all would show on the closing worksheet.

1.	Selling Price	Buyer	Debit (Both)
2.	Earnest Money Deposits:	Buyer	Credit ~~~~~~
8.	Closing Fee	Buyer	Debit
9.	Notary Fee	Buyer	Debit (Deed of Trust)
10.	Buyer's Attorney:	Buyer	Debit
11.	Recording: Warranty Deed:	Buyer	Debit
12.	Recording: Deed of Trust:	Buyer	Debit
15.	Documentary Fee:	Buyer	Debit
16.	Tax Certificate	Buyer	Debit
	Loan Costs:		
7b.	Mortgagee's Title Insurance	Buyer	
27.	Loan Origination Fee	Buyer	
28.	Loan Discount Points *Calculate*	Buyer	
29.	Interest on New Loan— ~~prorate~~ the amount owed for the month	Buyer	
35.	Loan Transfer Fee	Buyer	
30.	Survey	Buyer unless otherwise negotiated in the contract.	
31.	Appraisal	Buyer unless otherwise negotiated in the contract.	

negotiable
negotiable

2. Which buyer items are **negotiable** per the Contract to Buy and Sell?

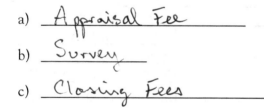

a) ___Appraisal Fee___

b) ___Survey___

c) ___Closing Fees___

★   Remember: ASC (ASK) what was negotiated.

V.   LOAN ASSUMPTION WORKSHEET

A. The lender provides a summary of the loan balance and other loan details to allow the broker to close the transaction.

1. Always close to the lender's **exact** figures

2. The assumption loan balance is a ___debit___ to the seller, and a ___Credit___ to the buyer.

B. The broker uses information from many sources, which may include the following:

1. The ___Contract to buy and Sell___

2. The loan assumption statement for the existing loan

3. The certificate of taxes due from the county

4. Bills and statements from service providers and utilities.

C. The six-column worksheet summarizes the financial transactions at the closing table and creates the information used to generate the _Closing Statements_ for the buyer and seller.

VI.   PRORATION PRACTICE:

Line 18. Current Year Taxes: Taxes for the preceding year were $2,970. For a June 6 closing, what will be the prorated share?

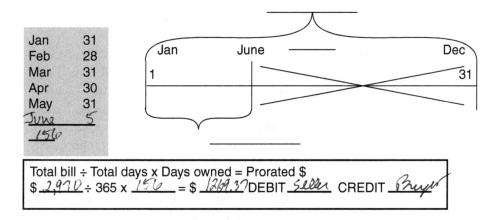

Jan	31
Feb	28
Mar	31
Apr	30
May	31
June	5
	156

Total bill ÷ Total days x Days owned = Prorated $
$ 2,970 ÷ 365 x 156 = $ 1269.37 DEBIT Seller CREDIT Buyer

Line 32. Water and/or Sewer: A water bill of $31.85 was paid in advance for the months of July through September. If the closing is September 20, what will the prorated entry be?

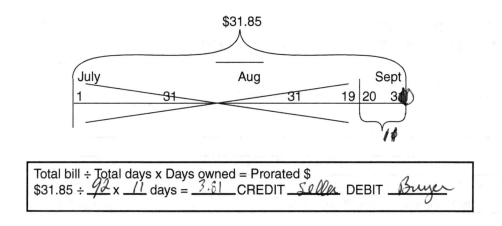

$31.85

July 1   31   Aug   31   19 20   Sept   30
11

Total bill ÷ Total days x Days owned = Prorated $
$31.85 ÷ 92 x 11 days = 3.81 CREDIT Seller DEBIT Buyer

■ SETTLEMENT EXERCISE 2: VA LOAN ASSUMPTION

To complete the six-column closing worksheet in this exercise, use the information below.

- The sellers have accepted an offer of $300,000 with closing on September 26.
- The buyers will provide $1,500 for earnest money.
- The buyers will assume the seller's loan in the amount of $250,000 (at 6 percent interest).
- The seller has agreed to provide a seller-carry of $20,000 at 10 percent with the first payment due on November 1.
- The cost of the new title insurance is $500.
- The buyer's attorney is charging $135.
- Recording fees: Warranty deed $6, New Deed of Trust (4 pages), $21.
- Notary fees: Warranty deed $1, Deed of Trust $1.
- Don't forget to collect documentary fee.
- The $15 tax certificate, verified there are no Special Taxes/Assessments on the property. and that last year's taxes are paid in full ($1,400).
- The lender required the buyer to supply a credit report, $65.
- The buyer's new homeowner insurance policy, starting the day of closing, is $600.
- The water and sewer charge is a flat rate for September 1 to October 1. The bill for $60 due in advance has **not** been paid.
- There is a loan transfer fee of $100.
- The sellers have agreed to pay a 5 percent commission.
- Closing fee $160 split between buyer and seller.

■ EMPIRE SAVINGS BANK STATEMENT FOR ASSUMPTION OF LOAN

Figures effective through September 30, 2xxx
The following must be paid before assumption can be completed:

September 1 payment has been received	$ 1,458.83
Loan Transfer Fee	$ 100.00
BALANCES:	
With October 1 payment the interest due in arrears will be	$ 1,250.00
Principal balance (after September 1 payment) at 6% interest	$250,000.00

	SELLER				BUYER				BROKER			
	Debit		Credit		Debit		Credit		Debit		Credit	
1. Selling Price			300,000	00	300,000	00						
2. Deposit, paid to: *Broker*							1,500	00	1,500	00		
3. Deed of Trust, payable to: *lender*	250k						250k					
4. Deed of Trust, payable to: *Seller*	20K						20K					
5. Deed of Trust, payoff to:												
6. Interest on Loan Assumed	1,041.67						1,041.67					
7. Owner Title Insurance Premium	500										500	
8. Closing Fee	80				80						160	
9. Notary Fee	1				1						2	
10. Title Exam by buyer attorney					135	00					135	00
11. Recording: Warranty Deed					6	00					6	00
12. Deed of Trust					21						21	
13. Release												
14. Other												
15. Documentary Fee					30						30	
16. Certificate of Taxes Due					15	00					15	00
17. Taxes for Preceding Year(s) *(1400 paid)*												
18. Taxes for Current Year	1627	95					1027	95				
19. Tax Reserve												
20. Special Taxes (Assessments)												
21. Personal Property Taxes												
22. Notary Fee paid by Lender												
23. Premium for New Insurance					600	00					600	00
24. Hazard Ins. Reserve												
25. FHA Mortgage Ins. Assumed												
26. FHA Mortgage Ins. Reserve												
27. Loan Origination												
28. Loan Discount Points												
29. Interest on New Loan			27	40	27.40							
30. Survey												
Credit Report					65	00					65	00
31. Appraisal Fee												
32. Water and/or Sewer	50.00				10	00					60	
33. Rents												
34. Security Deposits												
35. Loan Transfer Fee					100	00					100	00
36. Loan Payment Due												
37. Broker's Fee	15,000	00									15,000	00
38. Seller's Attorney												
Subtotals	287,700	62	300,027	40	301,090	40	273,569	62	1,500	00	16,694	00
Balance Due to/~~from~~ Seller	12,326										12,326	
Balance Due ~~to~~/from Buyer							27,520	78	27,520	78		
TOTALS												

Discussion of Settlement Exercise 2
Loan Assumption Closing

This settlement is for assumption of a VA loan.

Line 1. Selling Price and 2. Deposit, paid to:

Complete these as in previous exercises.

Line 3. Deed of Trust, payable to:

Use the balance reported by the lender.

Line 4. Deed of Trust, payable to:

Seller financing assists the buyer and reduces the cash the buyer brings to the closing table (DEBIT seller and CREDIT buyer). It also reduces the seller's cash proceeds at closing because the seller is allowing the buyer to borrow the seller's equity. They get a note for payment at a later time. Remember the settlement sheet is all about **cash at closing**. The buyer will owe interest on this loan.

Line 5. Deed of Trust, payoff to:

There is no existing loan being paid off.

Line 6. Interest on Loan Assumed:

The seller will owe the buyer interest for the portion of the month the seller lives in the property. Remember: since the payment is in arrears, seller will always owe the buyer this amount. In an assumption closing, an entry on line 6 is for this proration of the seller's interest owed to the day of closing. (DEBIT seller and CREDIT buyer.)

When lender provides only the loan balance and interest rate:

1. Calculate one month's interest as follows:

   Loan balance × Annual interest rate = Annual interest

   Annual interest ÷ 12 = One month's interest

■ **EXAMPLE** The loan is $250,000 at 6 percent interest and the closing is on September 26. The seller will owe 25 days.

One month's interest: $250,000 × .06 (6%) = $15,000 annual interest.

$15,000 ÷ 12 = $1,250. Closing months interest $1,250 ÷ 30 × 25 days the seller owes = $1,041.67

■ DEBIT the seller and CREDIT the buyer for this amount. (Remember: The buyer will make the payment at the beginning of the next month. Interest is always paid in arrears)

Line 7. Title Insurance Premium:

The title insurance premium is charged to the seller, based on the Contract to Buy and Sell.

Lines 8 through 14: are handled as was discussed in Unit 1.

Line 15. Documentary Fee:

A documentary fee is due whenever a warranty deed is recorded. Therefore, **every closing in this course and on the state exam will have a documentary fee.** This is the one entry that will always need to be made whether the fee is mentioned or not.

The documentary fee is one cent per hundred dollars of purchase price.

Calculate the documentary fee by moving the decimal **4 places** to the left in the purchase price:

$300,000.00 Selling Price = $30.00 Documentary Fee

Move decimal 4 places to the left.

Line 16. Certificate of Taxes Due:

The tax certificate is normally charged to the buyer.

Line 17. Taxes for Preceding Year:

This line determines the seller's responsibility for taxes for the year before the year of closing. These taxes are **always** entirely the seller's responsibility. The only question is whether they have been paid at the time of the closing.

If the taxes are truly delinquent, based on Colorado's payment schedule, the broker must arrange to collect the money from the seller and pay the taxes. This could happen with a free-and-clear property or a loan with no reserve accounts. The taxes represent a lien and must be cleared. DEBIT the **full** amount to the seller and CREDIT the broker the full amount, since the taxes are past due, so the broker can pay the bill to clear the tax lien.

Line 18. Taxes for the current year:

Do a normal proration of the general property taxes for the year of closing.

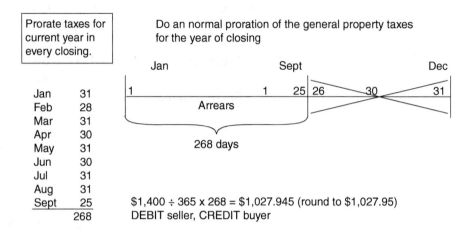

Prorate taxes for current year in every closing.		Do an normal proration of the general property taxes for the year of closing

Jan	31
Feb	28
Mar	31
Apr	30
May	31
Jun	30
Jul	31
Aug	31
Sept	25
	268

$1,400 ÷ 365 x 268 = $1,027.945 (round to $1,027.95)
DEBIT seller, CREDIT buyer

Line 23. Premium for New Insurance:

The buyer is responsible for paying for the new insurance policy. DEBIT buyer and CREDIT broker who will pay the bill.

Line 27. Loan Origination Fee and 28. Loan Discount Points: These lines are not used in an assumption closing.

Line 29. Interest on New Loan:

An assumption closing may include a new seller-carry loan originated to assist the buyer with the purchase. In that case, check for the possibility of an interest adjustment for a few days at the beginning of the loan term. The broker must calculate this adjustment since there is no institutional lender setting up the seller-carry loan.

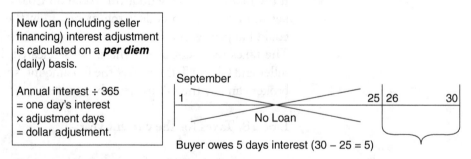

New loan (including seller financing) interest adjustment is calculated on a **per diem** (daily) basis.

Annual interest ÷ 365 = one day's interest × adjustment days = dollar adjustment.

Buyer owes 5 days interest (30 − 25 = 5)

Total loan $20,000 × .10 (10%) ÷ 365 × 5 = $27.40 DEBIT buyer CREDIT seller

If the first payment is more or less than one month after the closing date, an interest adjustment must be made. The first payment the buyer makes will be a full "regular" payment covering interest (in arrears) for a full month.

Line 30. Credit Report:

The credit report is always a buyer payment. DEBIT buyer, CREDIT broker

Line 32. Water/sewer:

Water can be paid in arrears or advance. In this case, it was due in advance for $60 however the seller has not paid the bill, which may become a lien. The seller will owe for a portion of the month that the seller owned the property, 25 days. The buyer will owe for the five days of ownership after closing. DEBIT seller and buyer, CREDIT the full amount to the broker to pay the bill.

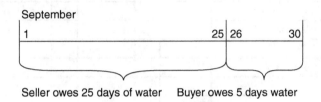

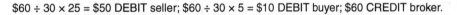

Seller owes 25 days of water   Buyer owes 5 days water

Seller days 1 – 25   Buyer 30 – 25 (seller's last day) = 5 days

$60 ÷ 30 × 25 = $50 DEBIT seller; $60 ÷ 30 × 5 = $10 DEBIT buyer; $60 CREDIT broker.

Line 36. Loan Payment Due:

In a loan assumption closing, the seller may not have made the payment due on the first day of the month of closing. This payment is entirely the seller's responsibility. It includes interest for the preceding month and a small payment to principal that is reflected in the assumption balance reported by the lender.

Collect any payment due. The amount is **never prorated** and must be collected to satisfy the lender. The broker will send a check to the lender. Check the loan assumption statement to determine if a payment is due. In this case it is not.

Never prorate a loan payment due. DEBIT the seller entire amount.

Below the Double Line:

Items below the double line on the closing worksheet are handled the same for all closings. Review the description in Unit 1 if you are unsure.

	SELLER				BUYER				BROKER			
	Debit		Credit		Debit		Credit		Debit		Credit	
1. Selling Price			300,000	00	300,000	00						
2. Deposit, paid to:							1,500	00	1,500	00		
3. Deed of Trust, payable to:	250,000	00					250,000	00				
4. Deed of Trust, payable to:	20,000	00					20,000	00				
5. Deed of Trust, payoff to:												
6. Interest on Loan Assumed	1,041	67					1,041	67				
7. Owner Title Insurance Premium	500	00									500	00
8. Closing Fee	80	00			80	00					160	00
9. Notary Fee	1	00			1	00					2	00
10. Title Exam by buyer attorney					135	00					135	00
11. Recording: Warranty Deed					6	00					6	00
12. Deed of Trust					21	00					21	00
13. Release												
14. Other												
15. Documentary Fee					30	00					30	00
16. Certificate of Taxes Due					15	00					15	00
17. Taxes for Preceding Year(s)												
18. Taxes for Current Year	1,027	95					1,027	95				
19. Tax Reserve												
20. Special Taxes (Assessments)												
21. Personal Property Taxes												
22. Notary Fee paid by Lender												
23. Premium for New Insurance					600	00					600	00
24. Hazard Ins. Reserve												
25. FHA Mortgage Ins. Assumed												
26. FHA Mortgage Ins. Reserve												
27. Loan Origination												
28. Loan Discount Points												
29. Interest on New Loan			27	40	27	40						
30. Survey												
Credit Report					65	00					65	00
31. Appraisal Fee												
32. Water and/or Sewer	50	00			10	00					60	00
33. Rents												
34. Security Deposits												
35. Loan Transfer Fee					100	00					100	00
36. Loan Payment Due												
37. Broker's Fee	15,000	00									15,000	00
38. Seller's Attorney												
Subtotals	287,700	62	300,027	40	301,090	40	273,569	62	1,500	00	16,694	00
Balance Due to/~~from~~ Seller	12,326	78									12,326	78
Balance Due ~~to~~/from Buyer							27,520	78	27,520	78		
TOTALS	300,027	40	300,027	40	301,090	40	301,090	40	29,020	78	29,020	78

After this Classroom Session and before Unit 3:

1. Prorations Practice 2
2. Contract to Buy and Sell Exercise
3. Settlement Exercise 3 using the Contract to Buy and Sell
4. Midterm Exam
5. Read Unit 3

Balance Helper

1. If you cannot balance the columns, the problem is usually on the broker side. Subtract the lower amount from the larger, then divide by two and look for that or a close number in the six-column worksheet in the seller or buyer columns.
2. If the column does not balance add from the bottom up to check figures before making changes.
3. It can also be something simple like inputting the figure(s) wrong in your calculator. Always double-check your calculations.

■ UNIT 2: PRORATIONS & CALCULATIONS PRACTICE

Practice these prorations before starting the midterm.

1041.67 Nov.

Line 6: Interest on Loan Assumed

33.60

Closing Date: October 25

$235.72
Oct

The FHA loan balance after the October payment is $125,000.

$1276.89

The interest rate is 10%.

DEBIT ____*840. Seller*____ CREDIT ____*Buyer*____

Closing Date: January 18

The VA loan balance after the January payment is $98,675.67.

The interest rate is 7.75%.

DEBIT _____ CREDIT _____

Line 18: Taxes for the Current Year

Closing Date: February 16

Last year's taxes: $1026.33

DEBIT ____*Seller*____ CREDIT ____*Buyer   132.10*____

Closing Date: August 13

Last year's taxes: $963.60

DEBIT _Seller_ CREDIT _Buyer_ 594

Line 29: Interest on New Loan

Closing Date: October 25

Seller is carrying a 2nd in the amount of $15,000.

The interest rate is 10%.

First payment is December 1.

DEBIT _____ CREDIT _____

Closing Date: January 18

Seller is carrying a 2nd in the amount of $12,000.

The interest rate is 9.75%.

First payment is March 1.

DEBIT _____ CREDIT _____

Line 32: Water and/or Sewer

Closing Date: June 20

The bill was due April 1 and is unpaid. (Broker to collect and pay the bill)

The water bill is for a 3-month period beginning April 1.

Flat rate: $95.55

DEBIT _____ CREDIT _____

Closing Date: October 13

Water/Sewer paid in two months in arrears on December 1

Flat rate: $58.50

DEBIT _____ CREDIT _____

Line 33. Rents

Closing Date: June 6th

Total rent collected on the first is $3,000.

DEBIT _____ CREDIT _____

HOA Fees

Closing Date: March 24

HOA fees paid from March 1 to April 1

Monthly HOA fees: $275

DEBIT _____ CREDIT _____

▪ PRORATIONS PRACTICE—SOLUTIONS

Line 6. Interest on Loan Assumed —SOB (solve left side)

Closing Date: October 25

The FHA loan balance after the October payment is $125,000

The interest rate is 10%

$125,00 × 10% ÷ 12 months ÷ 31 days × 24 days = $806.45
DEBIT the seller, CREDIT the buyer.

Closing Date: January 18
        The VA loan balance after the January payment is $98,675.67
        The interest rate is 7.75%

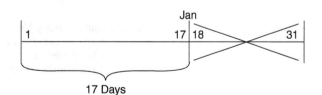

$98,675.67 × 7.75% ÷ 12 months ÷ 31 days × 17 days = $349.48
DEBIT the seller and CREDIT the buyer.

Line 17. Taxes—Paid in Arrears always SOB (solve left side)

Closing Date: February 16
Last year's taxes: $1026.33

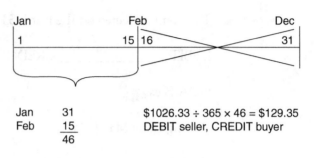

Jan		
31		$1026.33 \div 365 \times 46 = \$129.35$
Feb	15	DEBIT seller, CREDIT buyer
	46	

Closing Date: August 13
Last year's taxes: $963.60

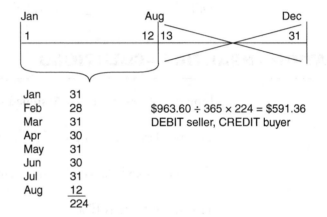

Jan	31	
Feb	28	$963.60 \div 365 \times 224 = \$591.36$
Mar	31	DEBIT seller, CREDIT buyer
Apr	30	
May	31	
Jun	30	
Jul	31	
Aug	12	
	224	

Line 29. Interest on New Loan—BOS (solve right side)

Closing Date: October 25
    Seller is carrying a 2nd in the amount of $15,000
    The interest rate is 0.10 (10%)
    1 payment is December 1

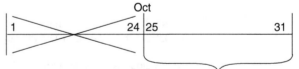

7 days

$\$15,000 \times 0.10 \ (10\%) \div 365 \times 7 = \$28.77$ DEBIT buyer, CREDIT seller

Closing Date: January 18
    Seller is carrying a 2nd in the amount of $12,000
    The interest rate is 0.975 (9.75%)
    1 payment is March 1

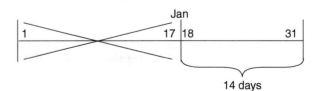

14 days

$\$12,000 \times 0.975 \ (9.75\%) \div 365 \times 14 = \$44.88$ DEBIT buyer, CREDIT seller

Line 32. WATER/SEWER - Read the question

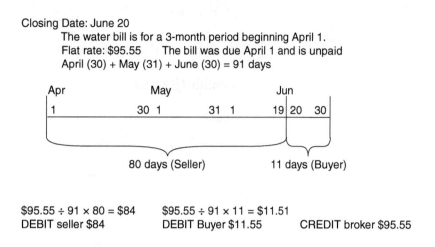

Closing Date: June 20
The water bill is for a 3-month period beginning April 1.
Flat rate: $95.55   The bill was due April 1 and is unpaid
April (30) + May (31) + June (30) = 91 days

Apr	May	Jun

80 days (Seller)   11 days (Buyer)

$95.55 ÷ 91 × 80 = $84 $95.55 ÷ 91 × 11 = $11.51
DEBIT seller $84   DEBIT Buyer $11.55   CREDIT broker $95.55

Because the bill is past due and unpaid, the broker must pay the bill.

Charge each party their share of the bill and pay the entire amount to the utility company.

This is not a proration. It is an allocation.

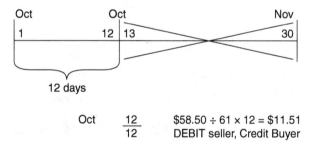

Closing Date: October 13
Water/Sewer paid two months in **arrears** on December 1
Flat rate: $58.50

Oct	Oct	Nov

12 days

Oct $\frac{12}{12}$ $58.50 ÷ 61 × 12 = $11.51
DEBIT seller, Credit Buyer

Line 33. Rents—Seller always owes buyer for month of closing

Closing date: June 6 seller will owe buyer the majority of the month.

$3,000 ÷ 30 × 25 = 2,500.00 DEBIT seller, CREDIT buyer

Jun

Collected in Advance 30 − 5 = 25 Days

HOA FEES—Read the question

Closing Date: March 24

HOA Fees paid from March 1 to April 1

Monthly HOA fees: $275

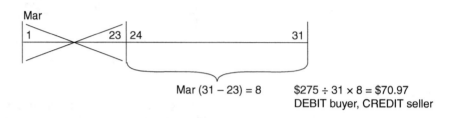

Mar (31 − 23) = 8 $275 ÷ 31 × 8 = $70.97
DEBIT buyer, CREDIT seller

■ CONTRACT TO BUY AND SELL EXERCISE

Use the *Contract to Buy and Sell Real Estate* from the next page to answer the following questions.

1. What date is closing?   6/6

2. What are the amounts for?

   a) Purchase price ___300,000___

   b) Earnest money ___6,000___

   c) Seller financing ___10,000___

3. Would it be correct to use the assumption balance figure in Section 4 if you were creating a settlement sheet?   yes   assumption

   Why or why not? ___there a balance 250 K___

4. What is the maximum amount the buyer has agreed to pay for the loan transfer fee?
   ___1,2000___

5. What is the interest rate on the seller-carry? ___9%___

6. If there is an appraisal, who has agreed to pay for it? ___Seller___

7. How will closing costs be paid?

   a) One-half by buyer and one-half by seller

   b) By the buyer

c) By the seller

This is agreed in Section ___15___

8. How will taxes be prorated? *midnight preceding closing*

This is agreed in Section ___16___

9. If the broker is to receive 5 percent, how much is the fee? ___15,000___

How will it appear on the closing worksheet? *C*

DEBIT ___Seller___   CREDIT ___Broker___

F I G U R E   2.1

Contract to Buy and Sell

1   The printed portions of this form, except differentiated additions, have been approved by the Colorado Real Estate Commission.
2   (CBS1-8-10) (Mandatory 1-11)

3
4   **THIS FORM HAS IMPORTANT LEGAL CONSEQUENCES AND THE PARTIES SHOULD CONSULT LEGAL AND TAX OR**
5   **OTHER COUNSEL BEFORE SIGNING.**

6
7   # CONTRACT TO BUY AND SELL REAL ESTATE
8   # (RESIDENTIAL)
9
10   Date: ___5/1/20--_____

11 | **AGREEMENT** |

12   **1.   AGREEMENT.** Buyer, identified in § 2.1, agrees to buy, and Seller, identified in § 2.3, agrees to sell, the Property
13   described below on the terms and conditions set forth in this contract (Contract).

14   **2.   PARTIES AND PROPERTY.**
15   **2.1.   Buyer.** Buyer, _____Dick M and Betty Jones_____, will take title to the Property
16   described below as ☒ **Joint Tenants** ☐ **Tenants In Common** ☐ **Other** _____.
17   **2.2.   Assignability and Inurement.** This Contract ☐ **Shall** ☒ **Shall Not** be assignable by Buyer without Seller's prior
18   written consent. Except as so restricted, this Contract shall inure to the benefit of and be binding upon the heirs, personal
19   representatives, successors and assigns of the parties.
20   **2.3.   Seller.** Seller, _____Mr. G and Mrs. S Winter_____, is the current owner of the
21   Property described below.
22   **2.4.   Property.** The Property is the following legally described real estate in the County of _____Baca_____, Colorado:
23
24   Lots 4 to 6 inclusive, Block 4, Sherry's Wild Acres.
25
26
27   known as No. ___321 Poco De Loco Lane_____   Wintertown   CO   80000___,
28   Street Address   City   State   Zip

29   together with the interests, easements, rights, benefits, improvements and attached fixtures appurtenant thereto, and all interest of
30   Seller in vacated streets and alleys adjacent thereto, except as herein excluded (Property).
31   **2.5.   Inclusions.** The Purchase Price includes the following items (Inclusions):
32   **2.5.1.   Fixtures.** If attached to the Property on the date of this Contract: lighting, heating, plumbing, ventilating
33   and air conditioning fixtures, TV antennas, inside telephone, network and coaxial (cable) wiring and connecting blocks/jacks,
34   plants, mirrors, floor coverings, intercom systems, built-in kitchen appliances, sprinkler systems and controls, built-in vacuum
35   systems (including accessories), garage door openers including ___2___ remote controls.
36   **Other Fixtures:**
37
38
39   If any fixtures are attached to the Property after the date of this Contract, such additional fixtures are also included in the Purchase
40   Price.
41   **2.5.2.   Personal Property.** If on the Property whether attached or not on the date of this Contract: storm windows,
42   storm doors, window and porch shades, awnings, blinds, screens, window coverings, curtain rods, drapery rods, fireplace inserts,
43   fireplace screens, fireplace grates, heating stoves, storage sheds, and all keys. If checked, the following are included: ☐ **Water**
44   **Softeners** ☒ **Smoke/Fire Detectors** ☒ **Security Systems** ☐ **Satellite Systems** (including satellite dishes).
45   **Other Personal Property:**
46
47   All personal property of seller, used to maintain the property, currently on the property.
48   The Personal Property to be conveyed at Closing shall be conveyed by Seller free and clear of all taxes (except
49   personal property taxes for the year of Closing), liens and encumbrances, except ___none_____.
50   Conveyance shall be by bill of sale or other applicable legal instrument.
51   **2.5.3.   Parking and Storage Facilities.** ☐ **Use Only** ☐ **Ownership** of the following parking facilities:
52   _____; and ☐ **Use Only** ☐ **Ownership** of the following storage facilities: _____.

F I G U R E   2.1

Contract to Buy and Sell (continued)

53   **2.5.4.   Water Rights, Water and Sewer Taps.** The following legally described water rights: n/a
54
55
56   Any water rights shall be conveyed by ☐ _____ **Deed** ☐ **Other** applicable legal instrument.
57   **2.5.4.1.** If any water well is to be transferred to Buyer, Seller agrees to supply required information about
58   such well to Buyer. Buyer understands that if the well to be transferred is a Small Capacity Well or a Domestic Exempt Water
59   Well used for ordinary household purposes, Buyer shall, prior to or at Closing, complete a Change in Ownership form for the well.
60   If an existing well has not been registered with the Colorado Division of Water Resources in the Department of Natural Resources
61   (Division), Buyer shall complete a registration of existing well form for the well and pay the cost of registration. If no person will
62   be providing a closing service in connection with the transaction, Buyer shall file the form with the Division within sixty days after
63   Closing. The Well Permit # is _____.
64   **2.5.4.2.** ☐ **Water Stock Certificates:**
65
66
67   **2.5.4.3.** ☐ **Water Tap**   ☐ **Sewer Tap**
68   **Note: Buyer is advised to obtain, from the provider, written confirmation of the amount remaining to be paid, if any, time**
69   **and other restrictions for transfer and use of the tap.**
70   **2.6.   Exclusions.** The following items are excluded (Exclusions):   Tenants personal property.
71
72

73   **3.   DATES AND DEADLINES.**

Item No.	Reference	Event	Date or Deadline
1	§ 4.2.1	Alternative Earnest Money Deadline	n/a
		Title and CIC	
2	§ 7.1	Title Deadline	5/8
3	§ 7.2	Exceptions Request Deadline	5/12
4	§ 8.1	Title Objection Deadline	5/15
5	§ 8.2	Off-Record Matters Deadline	5/8
6	§ 8.2	Off-Record Matters Objection Deadline	5/15
7	§ 7.4.4.1	CIC Documents Deadline	n/a
8	§ 7.4.5	CIC Documents Objection Deadline	n/a
9	§ 8.6	Right of First Refusal Deadline	n/a
		Seller's Property Disclosure	
10	§ 10.1	Seller's Property Disclosure Deadline	attached
		Loan and Credit	
11	§ 5.1	Loan Application Deadline	5/8
12	§ 5.2	Loan Conditions Deadline	n/a
13	§ 5.3	Buyer's Credit Information Deadline	5/8
14	§ 5.3	Disapproval of Buyer's Credit Information Deadline	5/12
15	§ 5.4	Existing Loan Documents Deadline	5/8
16	§ 5.4	Existing Loan Documents Objection Deadline	5/15
17	§ 5.4	Loan Transfer Approval Deadline	5/29
		Appraisal	
18	§ 6.2.2	Appraisal Deadline	5/15
19	§ 6.2.2	Appraisal Objection Deadline	5/19
		Survey	
20	§ 7.3	Survey Deadline	n/a
21	§ 8.3.2	Survey Objection Deadline	n/a
		Inspection and Due Diligence	
22	§ 10.2	Inspection Objection Deadline	5/8
23	§ 10.3	Inspection Resolution Deadline	5/12
24	§ 10.5	Property Insurance Objection Deadline	5/12
25	§ 10.7	Due Diligence Documents Delivery Deadline	5/8
26	§ 10.8.1	Due Diligence Documents Objection Deadline	5/15

F I G U R E   2.1

Contract to Buy and Sell (continued)

		Closing and Possession	
27	§ 12.3	**Closing Date**	6/6
28	§ 12.1	Closing Documents Delivery Deadline	6/5
29	§ 17	Possession Date	6/6
30	§ 17	Possession Time	following transfer of deed & funding
31	§ 28	**Acceptance Deadline Date**	5/2
32	§ 28	**Acceptance Deadline Time**	5:00 PM

74
75 **Note: Applicability of Terms.** A check or similar mark in a box means that such provision is applicable. The abbreviation "N/A"
76 or the word "Deleted" means not applicable and when inserted on any line in **Dates and Deadlines** (§ 3), means that the
77 corresponding provision of the Contract to which reference is made is deleted. The abbreviation "MEC" (mutual execution of this
78 Contract) means the date upon which both parties have signed this Contract.

79 **4.   PURCHASE PRICE AND TERMS.**
80   **4.1.   Price and Terms.** The Purchase Price set forth below shall be payable in U.S. Dollars by Buyer as follows:

Item No.	Reference	Item	Amount	Amount
1	§ 4.1	Purchase Price	$	300,000.00
2	§ 4.2	Earnest Money	6,000.00	$
3	§ 4.5	New Loan		
4	§ 4.6	Assumption Balance	250,000.00	
5	§ 4.7	Seller or Private Financing	10,000.00	
6				
7				
8	§ 4.3	Cash at Closing	34,000.00	
9		TOTAL	$ 300,000.00	$ 300,000.00

81
82   **4.2.   Earnest Money.** The Earnest Money set forth in this section, in the form of _____personal check_____,
83 shall be payable to and held by _____AV's Realty Company_____ (Earnest Money Holder), in its
84 trust account, on behalf of both Seller and Buyer. The Earnest Money deposit shall be tendered with this Contract unless the
85 parties mutually agree to an **Alternative Earnest Money Deadline** (§ 3) for its payment. If Earnest Money Holder is other than
86 the Brokerage Firm identified in § 32 or § 33, Closing Instructions signed by Buyer, Seller and Earnest Money Holder must be
87 obtained on or before delivery of Earnest Money to Earnest Money Holder. The parties authorize delivery of the Earnest Money
88 deposit to the company conducting the Closing (Closing Company), if any, at or before Closing. In the event Earnest Money
89 Holder has agreed to have interest on Earnest Money deposits transferred to a fund established for the purpose of providing
90 affordable housing to Colorado residents, Seller and Buyer acknowledge and agree that any interest accruing on the Earnest
91 Money deposited with the Earnest Money Holder in this transaction shall be transferred to such fund.
92   **4.2.1.   Alternative Earnest Money Deadline.** The deadline for delivering the Earnest Money, if other than at the
93 time of tender of the Contract is as set forth as the **Alternative Earnest Money Deadline** (§ 3).
94   **4.2.2.   Return of Earnest Money.** If Buyer has a right to terminate this Contract and timely terminates, Buyer
95 shall be entitled to the return of Earnest Money as provided in this Contract. If this Contract is terminated as set forth in § 25 and,
96 except as provided in § 24, if the Earnest Money has not already been returned following receipt of a Notice to Terminate or other
97 written notice of termination, Seller agrees to execute and return to Buyer or Broker working with Buyer, written mutual
98 instructions, i.e., Earnest Money Release form, within three days of Seller's receipt of such form.
99   **4.3.   Form of Funds; Time of Payment; Funds Available.**
100   **4.3.1.   Good Funds.** All amounts payable by the parties at Closing, including any loan proceeds, Cash at Closing
101 and closing costs, shall be in funds that comply with all applicable Colorado laws, including electronic transfer funds, certified
102 check, savings and loan teller's check and cashier's check (Good Funds).
103   **4.3.2.   Available Funds.** All funds required to be paid at Closing or as otherwise agreed in writing between the
104 parties shall be timely paid to allow disbursement by Closing Company at Closing or on such other date **OR SUCH PARTY**
105 **SHALL BE IN DEFAULT.** Buyer represents that Buyer, as of the date of this Contract, ☒ **Does** ☐ **Does Not** have funds that
106 are immediately verifiable and available in an amount not less than the amount stated as Cash at Closing in § 4.1.
107   **4.4.   Seller Concession.** Seller, at Closing, shall pay or credit, as directed by Buyer, an amount of $_____0_____ to
108 assist with Buyer's closing costs, loan discount points, loan origination fees, prepaid items (including any amounts that Seller
109 agrees to pay because Buyer is not allowed to pay due to FHA, CHFA, VA, etc.), and any other fee, cost, charge, expense or
110 expenditure related to Buyer's New Loan or other allowable Seller concession (collectively, Seller Concession). Seller Concession
111 is in addition to any sum Seller has agreed to pay or credit Buyer elsewhere in this Contract. Seller Concession shall be reduced to

FIGURE 2.1

Contract to Buy and Sell (continued)

112 the extent it exceeds the aggregate of what is allowed by Buyer's lender, but in no event shall Seller pay or credit an amount for
113 Seller Concession that exceeds the lesser of (1) the stated amount for Seller Concession or (2) Buyer's closing costs.
114   **4.5.**   **New Loan.**
115   **4.5.1.**   **Buyer to Pay Loan Costs.** Buyer, except as provided in § 4.4, if applicable, shall timely pay Buyer's loan
116 costs, loan discount points, prepaid items and loan origination fees, as required by lender.
117   **4.5.2.**   **Buyer May Select Financing.** Buyer may select financing appropriate and acceptable to Buyer, including a
118 different loan than initially sought, except as restricted in § 4.5.3 or § 29, Additional Provisions.
119   **4.5.3.**   **Loan Limitations.** Buyer may purchase the Property using any of the following types of loan:
120 ☐ **Conventional** ☐ **FHA** ☐ **VA** ☐ **Bond** ☐ **Other** _____.
121   **4.5.4.**   **Good Faith Estimate – Monthly Payment and Loan Costs.** Buyer is advised to review the terms,
122 conditions and costs of Buyer's New Loan carefully. If Buyer is applying for a residential loan, the lender generally must provide
123 Buyer with a good faith estimate of Buyer's closing costs within three days after Buyer completes a loan application. Buyer should
124 also obtain an estimate of the amount of Buyer's monthly mortgage payment. If the New Loan is unsatisfactory to Buyer, then
125 Buyer may terminate this Contract pursuant to § 5.2 no later than **Loan Conditions Deadline** (§ 3).
126   **4.6.**   **Assumption.** Buyer agrees to assume and pay an existing loan in the approximate amount of the Assumption
127 Balance set forth in § 4.1, presently payable at $___2,640.00___ per ___month___ including principal and interest
128 presently at the rate of ___6___ % per annum, and also including escrow for the following as indicated: ☒ **Real Estate Taxes**
129 ☒ **Property Insurance Premium** ☐ **Mortgage Insurance Premium** and ☐ ___N/A___.
130   Buyer agrees to pay a loan transfer fee not to exceed $___1,200.00___. At the time of assumption, the new interest rate shall
131 not exceed ___6___ % per annum and the new payment shall not exceed $___2,640.00___ per ___month___ principal and
132 interest, plus escrow, if any. If the actual principal balance of the existing loan at Closing is less than the Assumption Balance,
133 which causes the amount of cash required from Buyer at Closing to be increased by more than $___1,000.00___, then ☒ **Buyer**
134 **May Terminate** this Contract effective upon receipt by Seller of Buyer's written notice to terminate or ☐ _____.
135   Seller ☒ **Shall** ☐ **Shall Not** be released from liability on said loan. If applicable, compliance with the requirements for
136 release from liability shall be evidenced by delivery ☐ **on or before Loan Transfer Approval Deadline** ☒ **at Closing** of an
137 appropriate letter of commitment from lender. Any cost payable for release of liability shall be paid by _____seller_____
138 in an amount not to exceed $___1,000.00___.
139   **4.7.**   **Seller or Private Financing.** Buyer agrees to execute a promissory note payable to ___Mr. G and Mrs. S. Winter___,
140 as ☒ **Joint Tenants** ☐ **Tenants In Common** ☐ **Other** _____, on the note form as indicated:
141 ☒ **(Default Rate)** NTD81-10-06 ☐ **Other** _____ secured by a ___2nd___
142 (1st, 2nd, etc.) deed of trust encumbering the Property, using the form as indicated:
143 ☒ **Due on Transfer – Strict** (TD72-8-10) ☐ **Due on Transfer – Creditworthy** (TD73-8-10) ☐ **Assumable – Not Due on**
144 **Transfer** (TD74-8-10) ☐ **Other** _____.
145   The promissory note shall be amortized on the basis of ___5___ ☒ **Years** ☐ **Months**, payable at $___150.00___
146 per ___month___ including principal and interest at the rate of ___9___ % per annum. Payments shall commence
147 ___~~July~~ AUGUST___ and shall be due on the ___~~15th~~ 1ˢᵗ___ day of each succeeding ___month___. If not sooner
148 paid, the balance of principal and accrued interest shall be due and payable ___5 years___ after Closing.
149 Payments ☐ **Shall** ☒ **Shall Not** be increased by _____ of estimated annual real estate taxes, and ☐ **Shall** ☒ **Shall**
150 **Not** be increased by _____ of estimated annual property insurance premium. The loan shall also contain the following
151 terms: (1) if any payment is not received within ___5___ days after its due date, a late charge of ___5___ % of such payment
152 shall be due; (2) interest on lender disbursements under the deed of trust shall be ___10___ % per annum; (3) default interest rate
153 shall be ___15___ % per annum; (4) Buyer may prepay without a penalty except ___n/a___;
154 and (5) Buyer ☐ **Shall** ☐ **Shall Not** execute and deliver, at Closing, a Security Agreement and UCC-1 Financing Statement
155 granting the holder of the promissory note a _____ (1st, 2nd, etc.) lien on the personal property included in this sale.
156   Buyer ☐ **Shall** ☒ **Shall Not** provide a mortgagee's title insurance policy, at Buyer's expense.

157   **TRANSACTION PROVISIONS**

158 **5.**   **FINANCING CONDITIONS AND OBLIGATIONS.**
159   **5.1.**   **Loan Application.** If Buyer is to pay all or part of the Purchase Price by obtaining one or more new loans (New
160 Loan), or if an existing loan is not to be released at Closing, Buyer, if required by such lender, shall make an application verifiable
161 by such lender, on or before **Loan Application Deadline** (§ 3) and exercise reasonable efforts to obtain such loan or approval.
162   **5.2.**   **Loan Conditions.** If Buyer is to pay all or part of the Purchase Price with a New Loan, this Contract is conditional
163 upon Buyer determining, in Buyer's sole subjective discretion, whether the New Loan is satisfactory to Buyer, including its
164 availability, payments, interest rate, terms, conditions, and cost of such New Loan. This condition is for the benefit of Buyer. If
165 such New Loan is not satisfactory to Buyer, Seller must receive written notice to terminate from Buyer, no later than **Loan**
166 **Conditions Deadline** (§ 3), at which time this Contract shall terminate. **IF SELLER DOES NOT TIMELY RECEIVE**
167 **WRITTEN NOTICE TO TERMINATE, THIS CONDITION SHALL BE DEEMED WAIVED, AND BUYER'S**

Contract to Buy and Sell (continued)

168 **EARNEST MONEY SHALL BE NONREFUNDABLE, EXCEPT AS OTHERWISE PROVIDED IN THIS CONTRACT**
169 (e.g., Appraisal, Title, Survey).
170   **5.3.**   **Credit Information and Buyer's New Senior Loan.** If Buyer is to pay all or part of the Purchase Price by
171 executing a promissory note in favor of Seller, or if an existing loan is not to be released at Closing, this Contract is conditional
172 (for the benefit of Seller) upon Seller's approval of Buyer's financial ability and creditworthiness, which approval shall be at
173 Seller's sole subjective discretion. In such case: (1) Buyer shall supply to Seller by **Buyer's Credit Information Deadline** (§ 3),
174 at Buyer's expense, information and documents (including a current credit report) concerning Buyer's financial, employment and
175 credit condition and Buyer's New Senior Loan, defined below, if any; (2) Buyer consents that Seller may verify Buyer's financial
176 ability and creditworthiness; (3) any such information and documents received by Seller shall be held by Seller in confidence, and
177 not released to others except to protect Seller's interest in this transaction; and (4) in the event Buyer is to execute a promissory
178 note secured by a deed of trust in favor of Seller, this Contract is conditional (for the benefit of Seller) upon Seller's approval of
179 the terms and conditions of any New Loan to be obtained by Buyer if the deed of trust to Seller is to be subordinate to Buyer's
180 New Loan (Buyer's New Senior Loan). Additionally, Seller shall have the right to terminate, at or before Closing, if the Cash at
181 Closing is less than as set forth in § 4.1 of this Contract or Buyer's New Senior Loan changes from that approved by Seller. If
182 Seller does not deliver written notice to terminate to Buyer based on Seller's disapproval of Buyer's financial ability and
183 creditworthiness or of Buyer's New Senior Loan by **Disapproval of Buyer's Credit Information Deadline** (§ 3), then Seller
184 waives the conditions set forth in this section as to Buyer's New Senior Loan as supplied to Seller. If Seller delivers written notice
185 to terminate to Buyer on or before **Disapproval of Buyer's Credit Information Deadline** (§ 3), this Contract shall terminate.
186   **5.4.**   **Existing Loan Review.** If an existing loan is not to be released at Closing, Seller shall deliver copies of the loan
187 documents (including note, deed of trust, and any modifications) to Buyer by **Existing Loan Documents Deadline** (§ 3). For the
188 benefit of Buyer, this Contract is conditional upon Buyer's review and approval of the provisions of such loan documents, in
189 Buyer's sole subjective discretion. If written notice to terminate based on Buyer's objection to such loan documents is not received
190 by Seller by **Existing Loan Documents Objection Deadline** (§ 3), Buyer accepts the terms and conditions of the documents. If
191 the lender's approval of a transfer of the Property is required, this Contract is conditional upon Buyer's obtaining such approval
192 without change in the terms of such loan, except as set forth in § 4.6. If lender's approval is not obtained by **Loan Transfer**
193 **Approval Deadline** (§ 3), this Contract shall terminate on such deadline. If Seller is to be released from liability under such
194 existing loan and Buyer does not obtain such compliance as set forth in § 4.6, this Contract may be terminated at Seller's option.

195 **6.**   **APPRAISAL PROVISIONS.**
196   **6.1.**   **Property Approval.** If the lender imposes any requirements or repairs (Requirements) to be made to the Property
197 (e.g., roof repair, repainting), beyond those matters already agreed to by Seller in this Contract, Seller may terminate this Contract
198 (notwithstanding § 10 of this Contract) by delivering written notice to terminate to Buyer on or before three days following
199 Seller's receipt of the Requirements. Seller's right to terminate in this § 6.1 shall not apply if on or before any termination by
200 Seller pursuant to this § 6.1: (1) the parties enter into a written agreement regarding the Requirements; or (2) the Requirements are
201 completed by Seller; or (3) the satisfaction of the Requirements is waived in writing by Buyer.
202   **6.2.**   **Appraisal Condition.**
203   ☐   **6.2.1.**   **Not Applicable.** This § 6.2 shall not apply.
204   ☒   **6.2.2.**   **Conventional/Other.** Buyer shall have the sole option and election to terminate this Contract if the
205 Purchase Price exceeds the Property's valuation determined by an appraiser engaged by _____.
206 The appraisal shall be received by Buyer or Buyer's lender on or before **Appraisal Deadline** (§ 3). This Contract shall terminate
207 by Buyer delivering to Seller written notice to terminate and either a copy of such appraisal or written notice from lender that
208 confirms the Property's valuation is less than the Purchase Price, received by Seller on or before **Appraisal Objection Deadline**
209 (§ 3). If Seller does not receive Buyer's written notice to terminate on or before **Appraisal Objection Deadline** (§ 3), Buyer
210 waives any right to terminate under this section.
211   ☐   **6.2.3.**   **FHA.** It is expressly agreed that, notwithstanding any other provisions of this Contract, the Purchaser
212 (Buyer) shall not be obligated to complete the purchase of the Property described herein or to incur any penalty by forfeiture of
213 Earnest Money deposits or otherwise unless the Purchaser (Buyer) has been given in accordance with HUD/FHA or VA
214 requirements a written statement issued by the Federal Housing Commissioner, Department of Veterans Affairs, or a Direct
215 Endorsement lender, setting forth the appraised value of the Property of not less than $_____. The Purchaser (Buyer)
216 shall have the privilege and option of proceeding with the consummation of the Contract without regard to the amount of the
217 appraised valuation. The appraised valuation is arrived at to determine the maximum mortgage the Department of Housing and
218 Urban Development will insure. HUD does not warrant the value nor the condition of the Property. The Purchaser (Buyer) should
219 satisfy himself/herself that the price and condition of the Property are acceptable.
220   ☐   **6.2.4.**   **VA.** It is expressly agreed that, notwithstanding any other provisions of this Contract, the purchaser (Buyer)
221 shall not incur any penalty by forfeiture of Earnest Money or otherwise or be obligated to complete the purchase of the Property
222 described herein, if the Contract Purchase Price or cost exceeds the reasonable value of the Property established by the Department
223 of Veterans Affairs. The purchaser (Buyer) shall, however, have the privilege and option of proceeding with the consummation of
224 this Contract without regard to the amount of the reasonable value established by the Department of Veterans Affairs.

FIGURE   2.1

Contract to Buy and Sell (continued)

225   **6.3.   Cost of Appraisal.** Cost of any appraisal to be obtained after the date of this Contract shall be timely paid by
226   ☐ **Buyer** ☒ **Seller**.
227   **Note:** If **FHA** or **VA** Appraisal is checked, the **Appraisal Deadline** (§ 3) does **not** apply to **FHA** or **VA** guaranteed loans.

228   **7.   EVIDENCE OF TITLE, SURVEY AND CIC DOCUMENTS.**
229   **7.1.   Evidence of Title.** On or before **Title Deadline** (§ 3), Seller shall cause to be furnished to Buyer, at Seller's
230   expense, a current commitment for owner's title insurance policy (Title Commitment) in an amount equal to the Purchase Price, or
231   if this box is checked, ☐ **An Abstract** of title certified to a current date. If title insurance is furnished, Seller shall also deliver to
232   Buyer copies of any abstracts of title covering all or any portion of the Property (Abstract) in Seller's possession. At Seller's
233   expense, Seller shall cause the title insurance policy to be issued and delivered to Buyer as soon as practicable at or after Closing.
234   The title insurance commitment ☒ **Shall** ☐ **Shall Not** commit to delete or insure over the standard exceptions which relate to:
235   (1) parties in possession, (2) unrecorded easements, (3) survey matters, (4) any unrecorded mechanics' liens, (5) gap period
236   (effective date of commitment to date deed is recorded), and (6) unpaid taxes, assessments and unredeemed tax sales prior to the
237   year of Closing. Any additional premium expense to obtain this additional coverage shall be paid by ☐ **Buyer** ☒ **Seller**.
238   **Note:** The title insurance company may not agree to delete or insure over any or all of the standard exceptions. Buyer shall have
239   the right to review the Title Commitment, its provisions and Title Documents (defined in § 7.2), and if not satisfactory to Buyer,
240   Buyer may exercise Buyer's rights pursuant to § 8.1.
241   **7.2.   Copies of Exceptions.** On or before **Title Deadline** (§ 3), Seller, at Seller's expense, shall furnish to Buyer and
242   _____**Buyer's Broker**_____, (1) copies of any plats, declarations, covenants, conditions and restrictions
243   burdening the Property, and (2) if a Title Commitment is required to be furnished, and if this box is checked ☐ **Copies of any**
244   **Other Documents** (or, if illegible, summaries of such documents) listed in the schedule of exceptions (Exceptions). Even if the
245   box is not checked, Seller shall have the obligation to furnish these documents pursuant to this section if requested by Buyer any
246   time on or before **Exceptions Request Deadline** (§ 3). This requirement shall pertain only to documents as shown of record in the
247   office of the clerk and recorder in the county where the Property is located. The abstract or Title Commitment, together with any
248   copies or summaries of such documents furnished pursuant to this section, constitute the title documents (collectively, Title
249   Documents).
250   **7.3.   Survey.** On or before **Survey Deadline** (§ 3), ☐ **Seller** ☐ **Buyer** shall order or provide, and cause Buyer (and the
251   issuer of the Title Commitment or the provider of the opinion of title if an abstract) to receive, a current ☐ **Improvement Survey**
252   **Plat** ☐ **Improvement Location Certificate** ☐ ____**N/A**____ (the description checked is known
253   as Survey). An amount not to exceed $_____ for Survey shall be paid by ☐ **Buyer** ☐ **Seller**. If the cost exceeds this
254   amount, ☐ **Buyer** ☐ **Seller** shall pay the excess on or before Closing. Buyer shall not be obligated to pay the excess unless
255   Buyer is informed of the cost and delivers to Seller, before Survey is ordered, Buyer's written agreement to pay the required
256   amount to be paid by Buyer.
257   **7.4.   Common Interest Community Documents.** The term CIC Documents consists of all owners' associations
258   (Association) declarations, bylaws, operating agreements, rules and regulations, party wall agreements, minutes of most recent
259   annual owners' meeting and minutes of any directors' or managers' meetings during the six-month period immediately preceding
260   the date of this Contract, if any (Governing Documents), most recent financial documents consisting of (1) annual balance sheet,
261   (2) annual income and expenditures statement, and (3) annual budget (Financial Documents), if any (collectively, CIC
262   Documents).
263   ☒   **7.4.1.   Not Applicable.** This § 7.4 shall not apply.
264   **7.4.2.   Common Interest Community Disclosure. THE PROPERTY IS LOCATED WITHIN A COMMON**
265   **INTEREST COMMUNITY AND IS SUBJECT TO THE DECLARATION FOR SUCH COMMUNITY. THE OWNER**
266   **OF THE PROPERTY WILL BE REQUIRED TO BE A MEMBER OF THE OWNER'S ASSOCIATION FOR THE**
267   **COMMUNITY AND WILL BE SUBJECT TO THE BYLAWS AND RULES AND REGULATIONS OF THE**
268   **ASSOCIATION. THE DECLARATION, BYLAWS, AND RULES AND REGULATIONS WILL IMPOSE FINANCIAL**
269   **OBLIGATIONS UPON THE OWNER OF THE PROPERTY, INCLUDING AN OBLIGATION TO PAY**
270   **ASSESSMENTS OF THE ASSOCIATION. IF THE OWNER DOES NOT PAY THESE ASSESSMENTS, THE**
271   **ASSOCIATION COULD PLACE A LIEN ON THE PROPERTY AND POSSIBLY SELL IT TO PAY THE DEBT. THE**
272   **DECLARATION, BYLAWS, AND RULES AND REGULATIONS OF THE COMMUNITY MAY PROHIBIT THE**
273   **OWNER FROM MAKING CHANGES TO THE PROPERTY WITHOUT AN ARCHITECTURAL REVIEW BY THE**
274   **ASSOCIATION (OR A COMMITTEE OF THE ASSOCIATION) AND THE APPROVAL OF THE ASSOCIATION.**
275   **PURCHASERS OF PROPERTY WITHIN THE COMMON INTEREST COMMUNITY SHOULD INVESTIGATE THE**
276   **FINANCIAL OBLIGATIONS OF MEMBERS OF THE ASSOCIATION. PURCHASERS SHOULD CAREFULLY**
277   **READ THE DECLARATION FOR THE COMMUNITY AND THE BYLAWS AND RULES AND REGULATIONS OF**
278   **THE ASSOCIATION.**
279   ☐   **7.4.3.   Not Conditional on Review.** Buyer acknowledges that Buyer has received a copy of the CIC Documents.
280   Buyer has reviewed them, agrees to accept the benefits, obligations and restrictions that they impose upon the Property and its
281   owners and waives any right to terminate this Contract due to such documents, notwithstanding the provisions of § 8.5.

FIGURE 2.1

Contract to Buy and Sell (continued)

282   **7.4.4.**   **CIC Documents to Buyer.**

283   ☐   **7.4.4.1. Seller to Provide CIC Documents.** Seller shall cause the CIC Documents to be provided to
284 Buyer, at Seller's expense, on or before **CIC Documents Deadline** (§ 3).

285   ☐   **7.4.4.2. Seller Authorizes Association.** Seller authorizes the Association to provide the CIC Documents to
286 Buyer, at Seller's expense.

287   **7.4.4.3. Seller's Obligation.** Seller's obligation to provide the CIC Documents shall be fulfilled upon
288 Buyer's receipt of the CIC Documents, regardless of who provides such documents.

289   **7.4.5.**   **Conditional on Buyer's Review.** If the box in either § 7.4.4.1 or § 7.4.4.2 is checked, the provisions of this
290 § 7.4.5 shall apply. In the event of any unsatisfactory provision in any of the CIC Documents, in Buyer's sole subjective discretion,
291 and written notice to terminate by Buyer, or on behalf of Buyer, is delivered to Seller on or before **CIC Documents Objection**
292 **Deadline** (§ 3), this Contract shall terminate. If Seller does not receive Buyer's written notice to terminate on or before **CIC**
293 **Documents Objection Deadline** (§ 3), Buyer accepts the CIC Documents and waives the right to terminate for that reason.

294   Should Buyer receive the CIC Documents after **CIC Documents Deadline** (§ 3), Buyer shall have the right, at
295 Buyer's option, to terminate this Contract by written notice to terminate delivered to Seller on or before ten days after Buyer's
296 receipt of the CIC Documents. If Buyer does not receive the CIC Documents, or if such written notice to terminate would
297 otherwise be required to be delivered after **Closing Date** (§ 3), Buyer's written notice to terminate shall be received by Seller on or
298 before three days prior to **Closing Date** (§ 3). If Seller does not receive Buyer's written notice to terminate within such time,
299 Buyer accepts the provisions of the CIC Documents, and Buyer's right to terminate this Contract pursuant to this section is waived,
300 notwithstanding the provisions of § 8.5.

301 **Note:** If no box in this § 7.4 is checked, the provisions of § 7.4.4.1 shall apply.

302 **8.**   **TITLE AND SURVEY REVIEW.**

303   **8.1.**   **Title Review.** Buyer shall have the right to review the Title Documents. Buyer shall provide written notice to
304 terminate based on unmerchantability of title, unsatisfactory form or content of Title Commitment, or, notwithstanding § 13, of
305 any other unsatisfactory title condition, in Buyer's sole and subjective discretion, shown by the Title Documents (Notice of Title
306 Objection). Such Notice of Title Objection shall be delivered by or on behalf of Buyer and received by Seller on or before **Title**
307 **Objection Deadline** (§ 3), provided such Title Documents are received by Buyer in a timely manner. If there is an endorsement to
308 the Title Commitment that adds a new Exception to title, a copy of the new Exception to title and the modified Title Commitment
309 shall be delivered to Buyer. Provided however, Buyer shall have five days to deliver the Notice of Title Objection after receipt by
310 Buyer of the following documents: (1) any required Title Document not timely received by Buyer, (2) any change to the Title
311 Documents, or (3) endorsement to the Title Commitment. If Seller does not receive Buyer's Notice of Title Objection by the
312 applicable deadline specified above, Buyer accepts the condition of title as disclosed by the Title Documents as satisfactory.

313   **8.2.**   **Matters Not Shown by the Public Records.** Seller shall deliver to Buyer, on or before **Off-Record Matters**
314 **Deadline** (§ 3) true copies of all leases and surveys in Seller's possession pertaining to the Property and shall disclose to Buyer all
315 easements, liens (including, without limitation, governmental improvements approved, but not yet installed) or other title matters
316 (including, without limitation, rights of first refusal and options) not shown by the public records of which Seller has actual
317 knowledge. Buyer shall have the right to inspect the Property to investigate if any third party has any right in the Property not
318 shown by the public records (such as an unrecorded easement, unrecorded lease, boundary line discrepancy or water rights).
319 Written notice to terminate based on any unsatisfactory condition (whether disclosed by Seller or revealed by such inspection,
320 notwithstanding § 13), in Buyer's sole subjective discretion, by or on behalf of Buyer shall be delivered to Seller on or before **Off-**
321 **Record Matters Objection Deadline** (§ 3). If Seller does not receive Buyer's written notice to terminate on or before **Off-Record**
322 **Matters Objection Deadline** (§ 3), Buyer accepts title subject to such rights, if any, of third parties of which Buyer has actual
323 knowledge.

324   **8.3.**   **Survey Review.**

325   ☒   **8.3.1.**   **Not Applicable.** This § 8.3 shall not apply.

326   ☐   **8.3.2.**   **Conditional on Survey.** If the box in this § 8.3.2 is checked, Buyer shall have the right to review the
327 Survey. If written notice to terminate by or on behalf of Buyer based on any unsatisfactory condition, in Buyer's sole subjective
328 discretion, shown by the Survey, notwithstanding § 8.2 or § 13, is received by Seller on or before **Survey Objection Deadline**
329 (§ 3), this Contract shall terminate. If Seller does not receive Buyer's written notice to terminate by **Survey Objection Deadline**
330 (§ 3), Buyer accepts the Survey as satisfactory.

331   **8.4.**   **Special Taxing Districts.** **SPECIAL TAXING DISTRICTS MAY BE SUBJECT TO GENERAL OBLIGATION**
332 **INDEBTEDNESS THAT IS PAID BY REVENUES PRODUCED FROM ANNUAL TAX LEVIES ON THE TAXABLE**
333 **PROPERTY WITHIN SUCH DISTRICTS. PROPERTY OWNERS IN SUCH DISTRICTS MAY BE PLACED AT RISK**
334 **FOR INCREASED MILL LEVIES AND TAX TO SUPPORT THE SERVICING OF SUCH DEBT WHERE**
335 **CIRCUMSTANCES ARISE RESULTING IN THE INABILITY OF SUCH A DISTRICT TO DISCHARGE SUCH**
336 **INDEBTEDNESS WITHOUT SUCH AN INCREASE IN MILL LEVIES. BUYERS SHOULD INVESTIGATE THE**
337 **SPECIAL TAXING DISTRICTS IN WHICH THE PROPERTY IS LOCATED BY CONTACTING THE COUNTY**
338 **TREASURER, BY REVIEWING THE CERTIFICATE OF TAXES DUE FOR THE PROPERTY, AND BY OBTAINING**

FIGURE 2.1

Contract to Buy and Sell (continued)

339 **FURTHER INFORMATION FROM THE BOARD OF COUNTY COMMISSIONERS, THE COUNTY CLERK AND**
340 **RECORDER, OR THE COUNTY ASSESSOR.**
341   In the event the Property is located within a special taxing district and Buyer desires to terminate this Contract as the effect of
342 the special taxing district is unsatisfactory, in Buyer's sole subjective discretion, if written notice to terminate, by or on behalf of
343 Buyer, is received by Seller on or before **Off-Record Matters Objection Deadline** (§ 3), this Contract shall terminate. If Seller
344 does not receive Buyer's written notice to terminate on or before **Off-Record Matters Objection Deadline** (§ 3), Buyer accepts
345 the effect of the Property's inclusion in such special taxing district and waives the right to terminate for that reason.
346   **8.5.   Right to Object, Cure.** Buyer's right to object shall include, but not be limited to, those matters set forth in §§ 8 and
347 13. If Seller receives Buyer's written notice to terminate or notice of unmerchantability of title or any other unsatisfactory title
348 condition or commitment terms as provided in §§ 8.1, 8.2 and 8.3, Seller shall use reasonable efforts to correct said items and bear
349 any nominal expense to correct the same prior to Closing. If such unsatisfactory title condition is not corrected to Buyer's
350 satisfaction, in Buyer's sole subjective discretion, on or before Closing, this Contract shall terminate; provided, however, Buyer
351 may, by written notice received by Seller on or before Closing, waive objection to such items.
352   **8.6.   Right of First Refusal or Contract Approval.** If there is a right of first refusal on the Property, or a right to
353 approve this Contract, Seller shall promptly submit this Contract according to the terms and conditions of such right. If the holder
354 of the right of first refusal exercises such right or the holder of a right to approve disapproves this Contract, this Contract shall
355 terminate. If the right of first refusal is waived explicitly or expires, or the Contract is approved, this Contract shall remain in full
356 force and effect. Seller shall promptly notify Buyer in writing of the foregoing. If expiration or waiver of the right of first refusal
357 or Contract approval has not occurred on or before **Right of First Refusal Deadline** (§ 3), this Contract shall terminate.
358   **8.7.   Title Advisory.** The Title Documents affect the title, ownership and use of the Property and should be reviewed
359 carefully. Additionally, other matters not reflected in the Title Documents may affect the title, ownership and use of the Property,
360 including without limitation, boundary lines and encroachments, area, zoning, unrecorded easements and claims of easements,
361 leases and other unrecorded agreements, and various laws and governmental regulations concerning land use, development and
362 environmental matters. **The surface estate may be owned separately from the underlying mineral estate, and transfer of the**
363 **surface estate does not necessarily include transfer of the mineral rights or water rights. Third parties may hold interests in**
364 **oil, gas, other minerals, geothermal energy or water on or under the Property, which interests may give them rights to**
365 **enter and use the Property.** Such matters may be excluded from or not covered by the title insurance policy. Buyer is advised to
366 timely consult legal counsel with respect to all such matters as there are strict time limits provided in this Contract [e.g., **Title**
367 **Objection Deadline** (§ 3) and **Off-Record Matters Objection Deadline** (§ 3)].

368 **9.   GOOD FAITH.** Buyer and Seller acknowledge that each party has an obligation to act in good faith, including but not
369 limited to exercising the rights and obligations set forth in the provisions of **Financing Conditions and Obligations** (§ 5), **Title**
370 **and Survey Review** (§ 8) and **Property Disclosure, Inspection, Indemnity, Insurability, Due Diligence, Buyer Disclosure and**
371 **Source of Water** (§ 10).

372 **DISCLOSURE, INSPECTION AND DUE DILIGENCE**

373 **10.   PROPERTY DISCLOSURE, INSPECTION, INDEMNITY, INSURABILITY, DUE DILIGENCE, BUYER**
374 **DISCLOSURE AND SOURCE OF WATER.**
375   **10.1.   Seller's Property Disclosure Deadline.** On or before **Seller's Property Disclosure Deadline** (§ 3), Seller agrees to
376 deliver to Buyer the most current version of the applicable Colorado Real Estate Commission's Seller's Property Disclosure form
377 completed by Seller to Seller's actual knowledge, current as of the date of this Contract.
378   **10.2.   Inspection Objection Deadline.** Unless otherwise provided in this Contract, Buyer acknowledges that Seller is
379 conveying the Property to Buyer in an "as is" condition, "where is" and "with all faults". Seller shall disclose to Buyer, in writing,
380 any latent defects actually known by Seller. Buyer, acting in good faith, shall have the right to have inspections (by a third party,
381 personally or both) of the Property and Inclusions (Inspection), at Buyer's expense. If (1) the physical condition of the Property,
382 (2) the physical condition of the Inclusions, (3) service to the Property (including utilities and communication services), systems
383 and components of the Property, e.g. heating and plumbing, (4) any proposed or existing transportation project, road, street or
384 highway, or (5) any other activity, odor or noise (whether on or off the Property) and its effect or expected effect on the Property
385 or its occupants is unsatisfactory in Buyer's sole subjective discretion, Buyer shall, on or before **Inspection Objection Deadline**
386 (§ 3):
387   **10.2.1.   Notice to Terminate.** Notify Seller in writing that this Contract is terminated; or
388   **10.2.2.   Notice to Correct.** Deliver to Seller a written description of any unsatisfactory physical condition which
389 Buyer requires Seller to correct.
390   If written notice is not received by Seller on or before **Inspection Objection Deadline** (§ 3), the physical condition of the
391 Property and Inclusions shall be deemed to be satisfactory to Buyer.
392   **10.3.   Inspection Resolution Deadline.** If a Notice to Correct is received by Seller and if Buyer and Seller have not agreed
393 in writing to a settlement thereof on or before **Inspection Resolution Deadline** (§ 3), this Contract shall terminate on **Inspection**

FIGURE 2.1

Contract to Buy and Sell (continued)

394 **Resolution Deadline** (§ 3), unless Seller receives Buyer's written withdrawal of the Notice to Correct before such termination,
395 i.e., on or before expiration of **Inspection Resolution Deadline** (§ 3).
396   **10.4.** **Damage, Liens and Indemnity.** Buyer, except as otherwise provided in this Contract, is responsible for payment for
397 all inspections, tests, surveys, engineering reports, or any other work performed at Buyer's request (Work) and shall pay for any
398 damage that occurs to the Property and Inclusions as a result of such Work. Buyer shall not permit claims or liens of any kind
399 against the Property for Work performed on the Property at Buyer's request. Buyer agrees to indemnify, protect and hold Seller
400 harmless from and against any liability, damage, cost or expense incurred by Seller and caused by any such Work, claim, or lien.
401 This indemnity includes Seller's right to recover all costs and expenses incurred by Seller to defend against any such liability,
402 damage, cost or expense, or to enforce this section, including Seller's reasonable attorney fees, legal fees and expenses. The
403 provisions of this section shall survive the termination of this Contract.
404   **10.5.** **Insurability.** This Contract is conditional upon Buyer's satisfaction, in Buyer's sole subjective discretion, with the
405 availability, terms and conditions of and premium for property insurance. This Contract shall terminate upon Seller's receipt, on or
406 before **Property Insurance Objection Deadline** (§ 3), of Buyer's written notice to terminate based on such insurance being
407 unsatisfactory to Buyer. If Seller does not receive Buyer's written notice to terminate on or before **Property Insurance Objection
408 Deadline** (§ 3), Buyer shall have waived any right to terminate under this provision.
409   **10.6.** **Due Diligence–Physical Inspection.** Buyer's Inspection of the Property under § 10.2 shall also include, without
410 limitation, at Buyer's option, an inspection of the roof, walls, structural integrity of the Property and an inspection of the electrical,
411 plumbing, HVAC and other mechanical systems of the Property. If the condition of the Property or Inclusions are not satisfactory
412 to Buyer, in Buyer's sole subjective discretion, Buyer shall, on or before **Inspection Objection Deadline** (§ 3), provide the
413 applicable written notice pursuant to § 10.2.
414   **10.7.** **Due Diligence–Documents.** Seller agrees to deliver copies of the following documents and information (Due
415 Diligence Documents) to Buyer on or before **Due Diligence Documents Delivery Deadline** (§ 3) to the extent such Due Diligence
416 Documents exist and are in Seller's possession:
417
418
419
420   **10.8.** **Due Diligence Documents Conditions.** This Contract is subject to and expressly conditional upon Buyer, in Buyer's
421 sole subjective discretion, reviewing and approving the Due Diligence Documents, Survey and Leases. Buyer shall also have the
422 unilateral right to waive any condition herein.
423   **10.8.1.** **Due Diligence Documents.** If Buyer is not satisfied with the results of Buyer's review of the Due Diligence
424 Documents and written notice to terminate is received by Seller on or before **Due Diligence Documents Objection Deadline**
425 (§ 3), this Contract shall terminate.
426   **10.8.2.** **Survey.** If any unsatisfactory condition is shown by the Survey and written notice to terminate is received
427 by Seller on or before **Survey Objection Deadline** (§ 3), this Contract shall terminate.
428   **10.8.3.** **Leases.** If the Leases are not satisfactory to Buyer, Seller shall receive written notice to terminate on or
429 before **Off-Record Matters Objection Deadline** (§ 3), unless the Leases are not timely delivered under § 8.2, then Seller shall
430 receive written notice to terminate on or before **Due Diligence Documents Objection Deadline** (§ 3). If Seller timely receives
431 written notice to terminate, this Contract shall terminate.
432   If Buyer's written notice to terminate for any of the conditions set forth above is not timely received by Seller, then such
433 condition shall be deemed to be satisfactory to Buyer.
434   **10.9.** **Buyer Disclosure.** Buyer represents that Buyer ☐ **Does** ☒ **Does Not** need to sell and close a property to complete
435 this transaction.
436 **Note:** Any property sale contingency should appear in **Additional Provisions** (§ 29).
437   **10.10.** **Source of Potable Water (Residential Land and Residential Improvements Only).** Buyer ☒ **Does** ☐ **Does Not**
438 acknowledge receipt of a copy of Seller's Property Disclosure or Source of Water Addendum disclosing the source of potable water
439 for the Property. Buyer ☐ **Does** ☐ **Does Not** acknowledge receipt of a copy of the current well permit. ☒ There is **No Well**.
440 **Note to Buyer: SOME WATER PROVIDERS RELY, TO VARYING DEGREES, ON NONRENEWABLE GROUND
441 WATER. YOU MAY WISH TO CONTACT YOUR PROVIDER (OR INVESTIGATE THE DESCRIBED SOURCE) TO
442 DETERMINE THE LONG-TERM SUFFICIENCY OF THE PROVIDER'S WATER SUPPLIES.**
443   **10.11.** **Carbon Monoxide Alarms. Note:** If the improvements on the Property have a fuel-fired heater or appliance, a
444 fireplace, or an attached garage and include one or more rooms lawfully used for sleeping purposes (Bedroom), the parties
445 acknowledge that Colorado law requires that Seller assure the Property has an operational carbon monoxide alarm installed within
446 fifteen feet of the entrance to each Bedroom or in a location as required by the applicable building code.
447   **10.12.** **Lead-Based Paint.** Unless exempt, if the improvements on the Property include one or more residential dwellings
448 for which a building permit was issued prior to January 1, 1978, this Contract shall be void unless (1) a completed Lead-Based
449 Paint Disclosure (Sales) form is signed by Seller, the required real estate licensees and Buyer, and (2) Seller receives the
450 completed and fully executed form prior to the time when the Contract is signed by all parties. Buyer acknowledges timely receipt
451 of a completed Lead-Based Paint Disclosure (Sales) form signed by Seller and the real estate licensees.

FIGURE 2.1

Contract to Buy and Sell (continued)

452   **10.13. Methamphetamine Disclosure.** If Seller knows that methamphetamine was ever manufactured, processed, cooked,
453 disposed of, used or stored at the Property, Seller is required to disclose such fact. No disclosure is required if the Property was
454 remediated in accordance with state standards and other requirements are fulfilled pursuant to § 25-18.5-102, C.R.S. Buyer further
455 acknowledges that Buyer has the right to engage a certified hygienist or industrial hygienist to test whether the Property has ever
456 been used as a methamphetamine laboratory. If Buyer's test results indicate that the Property has been contaminated with
457 methamphetamine, but has not been remediated to meet the standards established by rules of the State Board of Health
458 promulgated pursuant to § 25-18.5-102, C.R.S., Buyer shall promptly give written notice to Seller of the results of the test, and
459 Buyer may terminate this Contract upon Seller's receipt of Buyer's written notice to terminate, notwithstanding any other
460 provision of this Contract.

461 **11. COLORADO FORECLOSURE PROTECTION ACT.** The Colorado Foreclosure Protection Act (Act) generally applies
462 if: (1) the Property is residential, (2) Seller resides in the Property as Seller's principal residence, (3) Buyer's purpose in purchase
463 of the Property is not to use the Property as Buyer's personal residence, and (4) the Property is in foreclosure or Buyer has notice
464 that any loan secured by the Property is at least thirty days delinquent or in default. If the transaction is a Short Sale transaction
465 and a Short Sale Addendum is part of this Contract, the Act does not apply. Each party is further advised to consult an attorney.

466   **CLOSING PROVISIONS**

467 **12. CLOSING DOCUMENTS, INSTRUCTIONS AND CLOSING.**
468   **12.1. Closing Documents and Closing Information.** Seller and Buyer shall cooperate with the Closing Company to
469 enable the Closing Company to deliver all documents required for Closing to Buyer and Seller and their designees by the **Closing**
470 **Documents Delivery Deadline** (§ 3). If Buyer is obtaining a new loan to purchase the Property, Buyer acknowledges Buyer's
471 lender shall be required to provide the Closing Company in a timely manner all required loan documents and financial information
472 concerning Buyer's new loan. Buyer and Seller will furnish any additional information and documents required by Closing
473 Company that will be necessary to complete this transaction. Buyer and Seller shall sign and complete all customary or reasonably
474 required documents at or before Closing.
475   **12.2. Closing Instructions.** Buyer and Seller agree to execute the Colorado Real Estate Commission's Closing Instructions.
476 Such Closing Instructions ☒ **Are** ☐ **Are Not** executed with this Contract. Upon mutual execution, ☐ **Seller** ☐ **Buyer** shall
477 deliver such Closing Instructions to the Closing Company.
478   **12.3. Closing.** Delivery of deed from Seller to Buyer shall be at closing (Closing). Closing shall be on the date specified
479 as the **Closing Date** (§ 3) or by mutual agreement at an earlier date. The hour and place of Closing shall be as designated by
480 ___mutual agreement_____.
481   **12.4. Disclosure of Settlement Costs.** Buyer and Seller acknowledge that costs, quality, and extent of service vary
482 between different settlement service providers (e.g., attorneys, lenders, inspectors and title companies).

483 **13. TRANSFER OF TITLE.** Subject to tender or payment at Closing as required herein and compliance by Buyer with the
484 other terms and provisions hereof, Seller shall execute and deliver a good and sufficient ___**general warranty**___ deed
485 to Buyer, at Closing, conveying the Property free and clear of all taxes except the general taxes for the year of Closing. Except as
486 provided herein, title shall be conveyed free and clear of all liens, including any governmental liens for special improvements
487 installed as of the date of Buyer's signature hereon, whether assessed or not. Title shall be conveyed subject to:
488   **13.1.** Those specific Exceptions described by reference to recorded documents as reflected in the Title Documents
489 accepted by Buyer in accordance with **Title Review** (§ 8.1),
490   **13.2.** Distribution utility easements (including cable TV),
491   **13.3.** Those specifically described rights of third parties not shown by the public records of which Buyer has actual
492 knowledge and which were accepted by Buyer in accordance with **Matters Not Shown by the Public Records** (§ 8.2) and **Survey**
493 **Review** (§ 8.3),
494   **13.4.** Inclusion of the Property within any special taxing district, and
495   **13.5.** Other _n/a_____.

496 **14. PAYMENT OF ENCUMBRANCES.** Any encumbrance required to be paid shall be paid at or before Closing from the
497 proceeds of this transaction or from any other source.

498 **15. CLOSING COSTS, CLOSING FEE, CIC FEES AND TAXES.**
499   **15.1. Closing Costs.** Buyer and Seller shall pay, in Good Funds, their respective closing costs and all other items required
500 to be paid at Closing, except as otherwise provided herein.
501   **15.2. Closing Services Fee.** The fee for real estate closing services shall be paid at Closing by ☐ **Buyer** ☐ **Seller**
502 ☒ **One-Half by Buyer and One-Half by Seller** ☐ **Other** _____.

CBS1-8-10. **CONTRACT TO BUY AND SELL REAL ESTATE (RESIDENTIAL)**   Page 10 of 15

FIGURE   2.1

Contract to Buy and Sell (continued)

503   **15.3.   Status Letter and Transfer Fees.** Any fees incident to the issuance of Association's statement of assessments
504   (Status Letter) shall be paid by ☐ **Buyer** ☐ **Seller** ☐ **One-Half by Buyer and One-Half by Seller**. Any transfer fees assessed
505   by the Association (Association's Transfer Fee) shall be paid by ☐ **Buyer** ☐ **Seller** ☐ **One-Half by Buyer and One-Half by**
506   **Seller**.
507   **15.4.   Local Transfer Tax.** ☐ **The Local Transfer Tax** of _____% of the Purchase Price shall be paid at Closing by
508   ☐ **Buyer** ☐ **Seller** ☐ **One-Half by Buyer and One-Half by Seller**.
509   **15.5.   Sales and Use Tax.** Any sales and use tax that may accrue because of this transaction shall be paid when due by
510   ☐ **Buyer** ☐ **Seller** ☐ **One-Half by Buyer and One-Half by Seller**.

511   **16.   PRORATIONS.** The following shall be prorated to **Closing Date** (§ 3), except as otherwise provided:
512   **16.1.   Taxes.** Personal property taxes, if any, and general real estate taxes for the year of Closing, based on ☒ **Taxes for**
513   **the Calendar Year Immediately Preceding Closing** ☒ ~~Most Recent Mill Levy and Most Recent Assessed Valuation~~, adjusted
514   by any applicable qualifying seniors property tax exemption, or ☐ **Other** _____.
515   **16.2.   Rents.** Rents based on ☒ **Rents Actually Received** ☐ **Accrued**. At Closing, Seller shall transfer or credit to
516   Buyer the security deposits for all leases assigned, or any remainder after lawful deductions, and notify all tenants in writing of
517   such transfer and of the transferee's name and address. Seller shall assign to Buyer all leases in effect at Closing and Buyer shall
518   assume such leases.
519   **16.3.   Association Assessments.** Current regular Association assessments and dues (Association Assessments) paid in
520   advance shall be credited to Seller at Closing. Cash reserves held out of the regular Association Assessments for deferred
521   maintenance by the Association shall not be credited to Seller except as may be otherwise provided by the Governing Documents.
522   Buyer acknowledges that Buyer may be obligated to pay the Association, at Closing, an amount for reserves or working capital.
523   Any special assessment by the Association for improvements that have been installed as of the date of Buyer's signature hereon
524   shall be the obligation of Seller. Any other special assessment assessed prior to **Closing Date** (§ 3) by the Association shall be the
525   obligation of ☐ **Buyer** ☐ **Seller**. Seller represents that the Association Assessments are currently payable at $_____
526   per _____ and that there are no unpaid regular or special assessments against the Property except the current regular
527   assessments and _____. Such assessments are subject to change as provided in the Governing
528   Documents. Seller agrees to promptly request the Association to deliver to Buyer before **Closing Date** (§ 3) a current Status Letter.
529   **16.4.   Other Prorations.** Water and sewer charges, interest on continuing loan, and _____ no others _____.
530   **16.5.   Final Settlement.** Unless otherwise agreed in writing, these prorations shall be final.

531   **17.   POSSESSION.** Possession of the Property shall be delivered to Buyer on **Possession Date** at **Possession Time** (§ 3),
532   subject to the following leases or tenancies: leases on both units.
533
534
535
536   If Seller, after Closing, fails to deliver possession as specified, Seller shall be subject to eviction and shall be additionally
537   liable to Buyer for payment of $ 500.00 per day (or any part of a day notwithstanding § 18.1) from **Possession Date** and
538   **Possession Time** (§ 3) until possession is delivered.
539   Buyer ☒ **Does** ☐ **Does Not** represent that Buyer will occupy the Property as Buyer's principal residence.

540   **GENERAL PROVISIONS**

541   **18.   DAY; COMPUTATION OF PERIOD OF DAYS, DEADLINE.**
542   **18.1.   Day.** As used in this Contract, the term "day" shall mean the entire day ending at 11:59 p.m., United States
543   Mountain Time (Standard or Daylight Savings as applicable).
544   **18.2.   Computation of Period of Days, Deadline.** In computing a period of days, when the ending date is not specified,
545   the first day is excluded and the last day is included, e.g., three days after MEC. If any deadline falls on a Saturday, Sunday or
546   federal or Colorado state holiday (Holiday), such deadline ☒ **Shall** ☐ **Shall Not** be extended to the next day that is not a
547   Saturday, Sunday or Holiday. Should neither box be checked, the deadline shall not be extended.

548   **19.   CAUSES OF LOSS, INSURANCE; CONDITION OF, DAMAGE TO PROPERTY AND INCLUSIONS AND**
549   **WALK-THROUGH.** Except as otherwise provided in this Contract, the Property, Inclusions or both shall be delivered in the
550   condition existing as of the date of this Contract, ordinary wear and tear excepted.
551   **19.1.   Causes of Loss, Insurance.** In the event the Property or Inclusions are damaged by fire, other perils or causes of
552   loss prior to Closing in an amount of not more than ten percent of the total Purchase Price, Seller shall be obligated to repair the
553   same before **Closing Date** (§ 3). In the event such damage is not repaired within said time or if the damage exceeds such sum, this
554   Contract may be terminated at the option of Buyer by delivering to Seller written notice to terminate on or before Closing. Should
555   Buyer elect to carry out this Contract despite such damage, Buyer shall be entitled to a credit at Closing for all insurance proceeds

FIGURE 2.1

Contract to Buy and Sell (continued)

556   that were received by Seller (but not the Association, if any) resulting from such damage to the Property and Inclusions, plus the
557   amount of any deductible provided for in such insurance policy. Such credit shall not exceed the Purchase Price. In the event Seller
558   has not received such insurance proceeds prior to Closing, then Seller shall assign such proceeds at Closing, plus credit Buyer the
559   amount of any deductible provided for in such insurance policy, but not to exceed the total Purchase Price.

560   **19.2.**   **Damage, Inclusions and Services.** Should any Inclusion or service (including utilities and communication
561   services), systems and components of the Property, e.g., heating or plumbing, fail or be damaged between the date of this Contract
562   and Closing or possession, whichever shall be earlier, then Seller shall be liable for the repair or replacement of such Inclusion ,
563   service, system, component or fixture of the Property with a unit of similar size, age and quality, or an equivalent credit, but only
564   to the extent that the maintenance or replacement of such Inclusion, service, system, component or fixture is not the responsibility
565   of the Association, if any, less any insurance proceeds received by Buyer covering such repair or replacement. Seller and Buyer
566   are aware of the existence of pre-owned home warranty programs that may be purchased and may cover the repair or replacement
567   of such Inclusions.

568   **19.3.**   **Condemnation.** In the event Seller receives actual notice prior to Closing that a pending condemnation action may
569   result in a taking of all or part of the Property or Inclusions, Seller shall promptly notify Buyer, in writing, of such condemnation
570   action. In such event, this Contract may be terminated at the option of Buyer, in Buyer's sole subjective discretion, by Buyer
571   delivering to Seller written notice to terminate on or before Closing. Should Buyer elect to consummate this Contract despite such
572   diminution of value to the Property and Inclusions, Buyer shall be entitled to a credit at Closing for all condemnation proceeds
573   awarded to Seller for the diminution in the value of the Property or Inclusions but such credit shall not include relocation benefits,
574   expenses or exceed the Purchase Price.

575   **19.4.**   **Walk-Through and Verification of Condition.** Buyer, upon reasonable notice, shall have the right to walk through
576   the Property prior to Closing to verify that the physical condition of the Property and Inclusions complies with this Contract.

577   **20.**   **RECOMMENDATION OF LEGAL AND TAX COUNSEL.** By signing this document, Buyer and Seller acknowledge
578   that the respective broker has advised that this document has important legal consequences and has recommended the examination
579   of title and consultation with legal and tax or other counsel before signing this Contract.

580   **21.**   **TIME OF ESSENCE, DEFAULT AND REMEDIES.** Time is of the essence hereof. If any note or check received as
581   Earnest Money hereunder or any other payment due hereunder is not paid, honored or tendered when due, or if any obligation
582   hereunder is not performed or waived as herein provided, there shall be the following remedies:

583   **21.1.**   **If Buyer is in Default:**

584   ☐   **21.1.1.**   **Specific Performance.** Seller may elect to treat this Contract as canceled, in which case all Earnest Money
585   (whether or not paid by Buyer) shall be paid to Seller and retained by Seller; and Seller may recover such damages as may be
586   proper; or Seller may elect to treat this Contract as being in full force and effect and Seller shall have the right to specific
587   performance or damages, or both.

588   **21.1.2.**   **Liquidated Damages, Applicable. This § 21.1.2 shall apply <u>unless the box in § 21.1.1. is checked</u>.** All
589   Earnest Money (whether or not paid by Buyer) shall be paid to Seller, and retained by Seller. Both parties shall thereafter be
590   released from all obligations hereunder. It is agreed that the Earnest Money specified in § 4.1 is LIQUIDATED DAMAGES, and
591   not a penalty, which amount the parties agree is fair and reasonable and (except as provided in §§ 10.4, 22, 23 and 24), said
592   payment of Earnest Money shall be SELLER'S SOLE AND ONLY REMEDY for Buyer's failure to perform the obligations of
593   this Contract. Seller expressly waives the remedies of specific performance and additional damages.

594   **21.2.**   **If Seller is in Default:** Buyer may elect to treat this Contract as canceled, in which case all Earnest Money received
595   hereunder shall be returned and Buyer may recover such damages as may be proper, or Buyer may elect to treat this Contract as
596   being in full force and effect and Buyer shall have the right to specific performance or damages, or both.

597   **22.**   **LEGAL FEES, COST AND EXPENSES.** Anything to the contrary herein notwithstanding, in the event of any arbitration
598   or litigation relating to this Contract, prior to or after **Closing Date** (§ 3), the arbitrator or court shall award to the prevailing party
599   all reasonable costs and expenses, including attorney fees, legal fees and expenses.

600   **23.**   **MEDIATION.** If a dispute arises relating to this Contract, prior to or after Closing, and is not resolved, the parties shall first
601   proceed in good faith to submit the matter to mediation. Mediation is a process in which the parties meet with an impartial person
602   who helps to resolve the dispute informally and confidentially. Mediators cannot impose binding decisions. The parties to the
603   dispute must agree, in writing, before any settlement is binding. The parties will jointly appoint an acceptable mediator and will
604   share equally in the cost of such mediation. The mediation, unless otherwise agreed, shall terminate in the event the entire dispute
605   is not resolved within thirty days of the date written notice requesting mediation is delivered by one party to the other at the party's
606   last known address. This section shall not alter any date in this Contract, unless otherwise agreed.

607   **24.**   **EARNEST MONEY DISPUTE.** Except as otherwise provided herein, Earnest Money Holder shall release the Earnest
608   Money as directed by written mutual instructions, signed by both Buyer and Seller. In the event of any controversy regarding the
609   Earnest Money (notwithstanding any termination of this Contract), Earnest Money Holder shall not be required to take any action.

FIGURE 2.1

Contract to Buy and Sell (continued)

610   Earnest Money Holder, at its option and sole subjective discretion, may (1) await any proceeding, (2) interplead all parties and
611   deposit Earnest Money into a court of competent jurisdiction and shall recover court costs and reasonable attorney and legal fees,
612   or (3) provide notice to Buyer and Seller that unless Earnest Money Holder receives a copy of the Summons and Complaint or
613   Claim (between Buyer and Seller) containing the case number of the lawsuit (Lawsuit) within one hundred twenty days of Earnest
614   Money Holder's notice to the parties, Earnest Money Holder shall be authorized to return the Earnest Money to Buyer. In the event
615   Earnest Money Holder does receive a copy of the Lawsuit, and has not interpled the monies at the time of any Order, Earnest
616   Money Holder shall disburse the Earnest Money pursuant to the Order of the Court. The parties reaffirm the obligation of
617   **Mediation** (§ 23). The provisions of this § 24 apply only if the Earnest Money Holder is one of the Brokerage Firms named in
618   § 32 or § 33.

619   **25.   TERMINATION.** In the event this Contract is terminated, all Earnest Money received hereunder shall be returned and the
620   parties shall be relieved of all obligations hereunder, subject to §§ 10.4, 22, 23 and 24.

621   **26.   ENTIRE AGREEMENT, MODIFICATION, SURVIVAL.** This Contract, its exhibits and specified addenda, constitute
622   the entire agreement between the parties relating to the subject hereof, and any prior agreements pertaining thereto, whether oral or
623   written, have been merged and integrated into this Contract. No subsequent modification of any of the terms of this Contract shall
624   be valid, binding upon the parties, or enforceable unless made in writing and signed by the parties. Any obligation in this Contract
625   that, by its terms, is intended to be performed after termination or Closing shall survive the same.

626   **27.   NOTICE, DELIVERY, AND CHOICE OF LAW.**
627   **27.1.   Physical Delivery.** All notices must be in writing, except as provided in § 27.2. Any document, including a signed
628   document or notice, delivered to Buyer shall be effective when physically received by Buyer, any signator on behalf of Buyer, any
629   named individual of Buyer, any representative of Buyer, or Brokerage Firm of Broker working with Buyer (except for delivery,
630   after Closing, of the notice requesting mediation described in § 23) and except as provided in § 27.2. Any document, including a
631   signed document or notice, delivered to Seller shall be effective when physically received by Seller, any signator on behalf of
632   Seller, any named individual of Seller, any representative of Seller, or Brokerage Firm of Broker working with Seller (except for
633   delivery, after Closing, of the notice requesting mediation described in § 23) and except as provided in § 27.2.
634   **27.2.   Electronic Delivery.** As an alternative to physical delivery, any document, including any signed document or
635   written notice may be delivered in electronic form only by the following indicated methods: ☒ **Facsimile** ☒ **Email**
636   ☒ **Internet** ☐ **No Electronic Delivery.** Documents with original signatures shall be provided upon request of any party.
637   **27.3.   Choice of Law.** This Contract and all disputes arising hereunder shall be governed by and construed in accordance
638   with the laws of the State of Colorado that would be applicable to Colorado residents who sign a contract in Colorado for property
639   located in Colorado.

640   **28.   NOTICE OF ACCEPTANCE, COUNTERPARTS.** This proposal shall expire unless accepted in writing, by Buyer and
641   Seller, as evidenced by their signatures below, and the offering party receives notice of such acceptance pursuant to § 27 on or
642   before **Acceptance Deadline Date** (§ 3) and **Acceptance Deadline Time** (§ 3). If accepted, this document shall become a contract
643   between Seller and Buyer. A copy of this document may be executed by each party, separately, and when each party has executed
644   a copy thereof, such copies taken together shall be deemed to be a full and complete contract between the parties.

645 | **ADDITIONAL PROVISIONS AND ATTACHMENTS** |

646   **29.   ADDITIONAL PROVISIONS.** (The following additional provisions have not been approved by the Colorado Real Estate
647   Commission.)
648
649   1. Seller to provide buyers' with current lease and operating expenses and any other
650   information on the current tenants, credit reports, applications, Lead Paint Disclosure
651   Rental signed by current tenants on or before Title Deadline.
652

653   **30.   ATTACHMENTS.** The following are a part of this Contract:
654
655   Lead Paint Disclosure-Sales
656
657   **Note:** The following disclosure forms **are attached** but are **not** a part of this Contract:
658
659   Seller Property Disclosure; Square Footage Disclosure; Closing Instructions
660

FIGURE **2.1**

Contract to Buy and Sell (continued)

661 | **SIGNATURES** |

662

Buyer's Name: Dick M. Jones   Buyer's Name: Betty Jones

Buyer's Signature   Date   Buyer's Signature   Date

Address: Address:

Phone No.:   Phone No.:
Fax No.:   Fax No.:
Electronic Address: Electronic Address:

663 **[NOTE: If this offer is being countered or rejected, do not sign this document. Refer to § 31]**

Seller's Name: Mr. G. Winter   Seller's Name: Mrs. S. Winter

Seller's Signature   Date   Seller's Signature   Date

Address: Address:

Phone No.:   Phone No.:
Fax No.:   Fax No.:
Electronic Address: Electronic Address:

664

665 **31.   COUNTER; REJECTION.** This offer is ☐ **Countered** ☐ **Rejected.**
666 **Initials only of party (Buyer or Seller) who countered or rejected offer** _____

667 | **END OF CONTRACT TO BUY AND SELL REAL ESTATE** |

32.   BROKER'S ACKNOWLEDGMENTS AND COMPENSATION DISCLOSURE.
(To be completed by Broker working with Buyer)

Broker ☒ **Does** ☐ **Does Not** acknowledge receipt of Earnest Money deposit specified in § 4.1 and, while not a party to the Contract, agrees to cooperate upon request with any mediation concluded under § 23. Broker agrees that if Brokerage Firm is the Earnest Money Holder and, except as provided in § 24, if the Earnest Money has not already been returned following receipt of a Notice to Terminate or other written notice of termination, Earnest Money Holder shall release the Earnest Money as directed by the written mutual instructions. Such release of Earnest Money shall be made within five days of Earnest Money Holder's receipt of the executed written mutual instructions, provided the Earnest Money check has cleared. Broker agrees that if Earnest Money Holder is other than the Brokerage Firm identified in § 32 or § 33, Closing Instructions signed by Buyer, Seller, and Earnest Money Holder must be obtained on or before delivery of Earnest Money to Earnest Money Holder.

Broker is working with Buyer as a ☒ **Buyer's Agent** ☐ **Seller's Agent** ☐ **Transaction-Broker** in this transaction.
☐ This is a **Change of Status**.

Brokerage Firm's compensation or commission is to be paid by ☒ **Listing Brokerage Firm** ☐ **Buyer** ☐ **Other** _____.

Brokerage Firm's Name: Your new home company
Broker's Name:

Broker's Signature   Date

■ CONTRACT TO BUY AND SELL EXERCISE—SOLUTIONS

1. What date is closing? <u>June 6</u>

2. What are the amounts for?

    a) Purchase price   <u>300,000 (Section 4)</u>

    b) Earnest money   <u>6,000 (Section 4)</u>

    c) Seller financing   <u>10,000 (Section 4)</u>

3. Would it be correct to use the assumption balance figure in Section 4 if you were creating a settlement sheet? <u>**NO**</u>

    Why or why not? <u>**The figure is just an estimate; the actual figure will be provided in the lender's assumption statement.**</u>

4. What is the maximum amount the buyer has agreed to pay for the loan transfer fee? <u>**$1,200**</u>

5. What is the interest rate on the seller-carry? <u>**9 percent**</u>

6. If there is an appraisal, who has agreed to pay for it? <u>**Seller**</u>

7. How will closing costs be paid?

    One-half by buyer and one-half by seller

    This is agreed in Section <u>**15**</u>

8. How will taxes be prorated?

    Based on the taxes for the calendar year immediately preceding closing

    This is agreed in Section <u>**16**</u>

9. If the broker is to receive 5 percent how much is the fee? <u>**$15,000**</u>

    How will it appear on the closing worksheet?

    DEBIT <u>seller</u> CREDIT broker

■ SETTLEMENT EXERCISE 3

Using the following information and the lender's Assumption Statement, complete this closing.

■ The seller has agreed to sell a duplex for $300,000. The closing date is June 6.

■ The earnest money deposit is $6,000.

■ The amount of the loan being assumed is listed in the assumption statement. The loan has an interest rate of 6 percent (don't forget to prorate interest if necessary).

■ The owner agrees to carry back a second of $10,000 at 9 percent with monthly payments to begin one month after closing (don't forget to calculate interest if necessary). *(June calculation)*

■ Title insurance full coverage will be $700 for standard and $90 for extended.

■ Closing fees are $150 and will be charged per the contract.

■ The fee for the seller's attorney is $200 and the buyer's is $175.

■ Recording costs are $20 for the warranty deed and $24 for the second deed of trust.

■ The tax certificate is $15.

■ Standard notary fees of $1 per ~~signature~~ *document* will apply.

■ Is there a documentary fee?

■ The Property Taxes of $2,970 for last year have not been paid.

■ Is there a tax proration? *yes*

■ The buyer is buying new hazard insurance for $500 per year.

■ The charge for the credit report is $35.

■ The buyer wants an appraisal and the cost is $350. Who per the contract is paying this fee?

■ Each half of the duplex is rented for $1,500 per month and has a $1,000 security deposit.

■ Make sure you check for any loan payments due or loan transfer fees.

■ The broker will receive a 5 percent commission.

■ ACME SAVINGS AND LOAN ASSOCIATION STATEMENT FOR ASSUMPTION OF LOAN

Figures effective through June 30, 2xxx

The following charges must be paid before the assumption can be completed:

June payment has not been received *interest* $2,640	$2,640.00	1,250
Loan transfer fee	$1,200.00	
Total amount needed to assume loan	$3,840.00	

Balances:

With July 1 payment the interest due in arrears will be	$2,640.00 *$1,250*
Principal balance (after June payment) at 6% interest	$250,000.00

To complete Exercise 3, use a worksheet from the back of the book or the downloadable Microsoft Excel worksheet from **www.kpscolorado.com/homestudy**. This exercise and the midterm also use the Contract to Buy and Sell. When finished, answer the questions on the midterm which is an **open book test**.

MIDTERM EXAM—OPEN BOOK

Classroom Students: Submit a bubble sheet for scoring with the following:

1. YOUR NAME, COURSE NAME (Closings); EXAM NAME (Midterm)
2. Write in and darken the ovals with your **Individual ID** (Your Student ID) (always start at the left-hand column of the box)
3. **Exam ID:** 10853 (always start at the left-hand column of the box)
4. **Today's Date**

Correspondence Students: Please take your exam online.

1. The buyer will assume a loan of $250,000 at 6 percent. For a closing on June 6th, what is the entry for Interest on Loan Assumed?
   a. $208.33 debit seller, credit broker
   b. $208.33 debit seller, credit buyer
   c. $1041.67 debit seller, credit buyer
   d. $1041.67 credit seller, debit buyer

2. When should a loan payment due be prorated?
   a. Never
   b. Only if requested by the buyer
   c. Only if requested by the seller
   d. This is the broker's decision

3. Who pays to record the deed of trust?
   a. Broker
   b. Seller
   c. Buyer
   d. Check section 4 of the contract

4. Taxes for the preceding year were $2,970. For a June 6th closing, how will taxes for the current year be entered?
   a. $1,700.63 credit seller, debit buyer
   b. $1,700.63 debit seller, credit buyer
   c. $1,269.37 credit seller, debit buyer
   d. $1,269.37 debit seller, credit buyer

5. How should you handle security deposits?
   a. Debit seller, credit buyer the full amount
   b. Debit seller, credit tenant
   c. Debit buyer, credit seller prorated amount
   d. Debit seller, credit broker

6. What is the charge for this appraisal?
   a. $350.00 debit seller, credit buyer
   b. $175.00 debit seller, credit broker
   c. $350.00 debit seller, credit broker
   d. $350.00 credit seller, debit buyer

7. Who will always be charged for unpaid taxes for the preceding year?
   a. Buyer
   b. Broker
   c. Seller
   d. There is no entry, this will be paid from the tax reserve

8. The entry for notary for the warranty deed is
   a. debit seller, credit buyer.
   b. credit seller, credit buyer, debit broker.
   c. credit seller, debit broker.
   d. debit seller, credit broker.

9. A duplex's rents are $1,500 per unit and have been paid. For a closing on June 6th, the pro-rated amount for both rents is
   a. $2,500 debit seller, credit buyer.
   b. $2,500 credit seller, debit buyer.
   c. $500 credit seller, debit buyer.
   d. $500 debit seller, credit buyer.

10. What is the entry for a loan being assumed?
    a. Credit seller, debit buyer
    b. Debit seller, debit buyer
    c. Debit seller, credit buyer
    d. Credit seller, credit buyer

11. If both the buyer and seller have subtotals with more debits than credits, what is the final result of the closing?

    a. The buyer will bring money to closing, the seller will take money away.
    b. The seller will bring money to closing, The buyer will take money away.
    c. The buyer and seller will take money away from closing.
    d. The buyer and seller will bring money to closing.

12. If the sales price is $300,000, then the documentary fee will be

    a. unnecessary.
    b. $300.
    c. $30.
    d. $3.

13. In a typical Contract to Buy and Sell, the person who pays for the appraisal is

    a. the buyer.
    b. negotiable.
    c. the seller.
    d. the lender.

14. The seller agreed to a seller-carry of $10,000 at 9 percent. For a closing June 6th, what is the entry for interest on the new loan if the first payment is due August 1?

    a. $61.64 debit buyer, credit seller
    b. $62.50 debit buyer, credit seller
    c. $12.33 debit seller, credit buyer
    d. $12.50 debit seller, credit buyer

15. Who always pays to start a lender reserve?

    a. The seller
    b. The lender
    c. The buyer
    d. Negotiable

16. A property has two special assessments. One for $263.00 that the seller has agreed to pay and another for $72.46 that buyer has agreed to assume. How should you handle the special assessments?

    a. $263.00 debit seller, credit broker
    b. $263.00 debit seller, $72.46 debit buyer
    c. $263.00 debit seller, credit buyer
    d. $72.46 debit buyer, credit broker

17. The broker credit total column is a combination of

    a. debits for bills paid and the amount of the check due the seller.
    b. credits for bills paid and the amount of the check due the seller.
    c. debits for bill due and the amount owed by the buyer.
    d. credits for bills paid and the amount of the check from the buyer.

18. A water bill of $31.85 was paid in advance for the months of July through September. What is the entry for the proration when closing is on September 20?

    a. $3.81 credit seller, debit buyer
    b. $3.81 debit seller, credit buyer
    c. $28.00 credit seller, debit buyer
    d. $28.00 debit seller, credit buyer

19. Which of the following is NOT part of every proration?

    a. Total amount for the billing period
    b. Total number of days in the billing period
    c. Annual interest
    d. Number of days owned by the person responsible

20. Who has overall responsibility for the proper accounting of a closing done in the listing broker's office?

    a. Buyer's broker
    b. Title company only
    c. Listing brokerage and listing broker
    d. Closer and buyer's broker

21. To verify that the DEBIT and CREDIT columns of each party balance, the "Totals" lines should

    a. be the same number.
    b. be the same as the broker's.
    c. depend on the amount of the earnest money deposit.
    d. have the same number in all six or the sheet does not balance.

22. The owner's title insurance premium will normally be entered on the six-column worksheet as a
    a. debit buyer, credit broker.
    b. debit seller, credit broker.
    c. debit seller, credit buyer.
    d. debit buyer, credit seller.

23. Which party normally pays for the recording of the warranty deed?
    a. Seller
    b. Listing broker
    c. Buyer
    d. Buyer's broker

24. If the buyer's subtotal of debits is $121,000 and subtotal of credits is $23,000, then
    a. the buyer is taking $98,000 away from closing.
    b. the buyer is bringing $98,000 to closing.
    c. the Closing Statement is wrong.
    d. the broker's commission will be $98,000.

25. How is the buyer's earnest money deposit treated at closing?
    a. The buyer gets credit for the deposit.
    b. The seller is debited the earnest money amount as already paid.
    c. The seller gets credited with the deposit that is brought to closing.
    d. The deposit has no effect on closing as it was already deposited.

3 UNIT

The New Loan Closing

■ FOCUS ON UNDERSTANDING

- The impact of a new loan on broker entries
- Use of lender's "Net Loan Proceeds" as a deposit to the escrow account to allow for the broker to pay any remaining bills and the final payout of amounts due to the seller

■ ASSIGNMENTS AND STUDY PLAN

Before Unit 3:

1. Complete Settlement Exercise 3 and the Midterm Exam
2. Look up **Important Terms**, found on the next page, in the Glossary
3. Read the Unit 3 text
4. Complete the Unit 3 Glossary Review

After Unit 3:

1. Settlement Exercise 4
2. Prepare for the final in Unit 4

■ IMPORTANT TERMS

Conventional loan	Loan origination fee	Realty tax service
First deed of trust	Loan underwriting fee	Release of deed of trust
Flood plain certification	Mortgagee title insurance policy	Second deed of trust
Loan discount points		Single entry

Summarizing the Transaction

In a **loan assumption** closing, the broker prepares the entire closing and the six-column summary, which shows all of the funds transferred, received and paid as part of the closing. Remember: this work is often done by another closing entity such as a title insurance company, but the broker remains responsible.

In a **new loan** closing, the lender will provide a statement of financial details and a list of bills the lender will pay from the gross loan proceeds. The broker will reconcile these lender adjustments and carry out the other contractual obligations as usual.

Review of the Important Factors for a Loan Assumption Worksheet

In a loan assumption, the buyer is taking over responsibility for the existing loan balance on the property. In most cases, the lender must review the buyer's qualifications and approve, or disapprove, the loan assumption. Upon approval, the lender will provide the broker with a detailed assumption statement to allow for the closing of the transaction, and the assumption of the loan. The broker works with the lender to assure the lender's requirements are met at closing.

Always close to the exact figures provided by the lender.

The balance of the loan being assumed is a DEBIT to the seller. This amount was not part of the seller's equity and the seller does not receive it at closing. The same loan balance is a CREDIT to the buyer because the buyer does not need to bring that amount to closing. They sign documents agreeing to take over payments on the loan balance.

- ■ The broker gets information from several sources:
  — The Contract to Buy and Sell Real Estate
  — A Loan Assumption Statement from the lender for the existing loan
  — Certificate of Taxes Due from the county government
  — Other service providers such as title insurance companies, attorneys, utility companies, etc.
- ■ The numbered lines of the closing worksheet are a checklist for most of the financial items from a closing. They summarize the DEBITS and CREDITS as described in Units 1 and 2.
- ■ Each line used on the six-column worksheet **for an assumption closing** will have an **equal dollar value** of DEBITS and CREDITS.
  — Transfers between the buyer and seller, such as the selling price, prorations, or reserve account balance transfers, will have the same dollar amount entered for each party.

— Bills for either party paid by the broker from the escrow account will be a DEBIT to the party who owes the bill and a CREDIT to the broker for the check written OUT of the escrow account.
■ Work in an orderly fashion from top to bottom on the worksheet.
  — Completing one line at a time helps keep track of where you are and helps prevent skipping important information.
  — When you reach the subtotal line on the closing worksheet, it will appear the broker does not have sufficient money to pay the checks that you have listed. That is true. When the summary is complete and the funds are shown coming from the buyer at the end, the broker will have enough money to disburse all of these amounts.
■ The completed closing worksheet shows a snapshot of all the financial matters that happen **at the closing table.** It represents the situation at the moment of closing after the buyer brings a check and the seller receives a check (in a normal closing).

Important Factors for a New Loan Worksheet

When the buyer is obtaining a new loan from a lending institution, the new loan amount and related loan costs become part of the closing. The broker must work with the new lender to ensure that all of the lender's requirements are met before closing the transaction. **Always close to the lender's exact figures.**

In a new loan closing the lender will pay, from the gross loan amount, some bills unique to the new loan closing; such as loan origination fees and loan discount points. In addition, the new lender may require the closing company to directly pay items that must be settled to ensure the lender's lien priority: paying off the seller's current loan, recording a lien release for the seller's loan, and recording a deed of trust for the new loan would be examples of these items. All of these things are paid from the gross loan amount before the lender provides the remaining money to the broker to complete the closing. This money will be a DEBIT to the broker column and is called Net Loan Proceeds.

The lender's New Loan Statement will show the gross loan amount approved for the buyer and list the various amounts paid by the lender from the loan. The buyer receives a CREDIT for the full amount of the new loan. The closing worksheet and Closing Statement show a single entry for this CREDIT.

When the new lender pays one of these bills of the seller or buyer, the broker does not need to write a check from the escrow account. Bills the lender paid must appear on the six-column closing worksheet as a DEBIT to either the seller or the buyer. The lender doesn't necessarily know which items the parties agreed to pay, thus the lender just lists them and the broker must allocate them to the appropriate party.

The lender's New Loan Statement is a bit like two invisible columns for the new lender. If we were to use an imaginary eight-column worksheet, the DEBIT and CREDIT columns for the lender would have a similar meaning as the DEBIT and CREDIT columns for the broker. When the lender pays something, there is a lender entry (in the invisible columns), and a DEBIT to the seller or the buyer, but

no broker entry. The six-column closing worksheet shows only the single entry charging the expense to the seller or buyer but no charges to the lender.

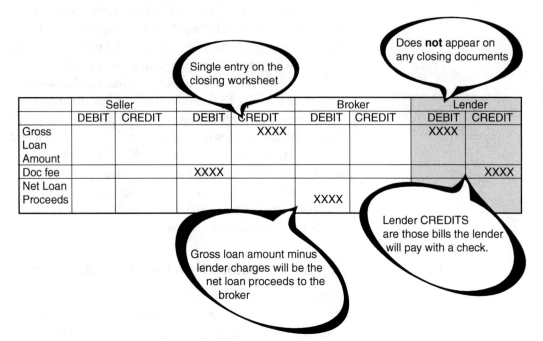

Items unique to a new loan closing:

■ Dollar amounts imported from the Lender's New Loan Statement will be **single entries** on the six-column worksheet.

■ **Line 3. "Deed of Trust Payable to:"** shows the gross amount of the **new loan**. This is the amount the buyer is borrowing to contribute to the purchase. The amount is a CREDIT to the buyer. This dollar amount does not impact either the seller or the broker—it is the first of the single entry items. Typically, this is the only entry from the new lender that will be a CREDIT.

■ **Line 5. "Deed of Trust Payoff to:"** shows loan payoff amounts owed by the seller. In the new loan closing, the amount to pay off this seller lien is included in the lender payout and is a single entry DEBIT to the seller.

■ Various expenses such as title insurance premiums, loan origination fees and recording fees are listed on the lender's New Loan Statement and also become single entries allocated to the appropriate party for each expense based on the Contract to Buy and Sell.

— An owner's title insurance policy is also a seller expense (by contract) and a seller DEBIT.

— Closing fees, the cost of the appraisal or a survey, can be negotiated. The broker will DEBIT these costs to party charged per the contract.

■ As a general rule, costs directly associated with borrowing money will be charged to the buyer unless the contract specifically indicates the seller has agreed to pay some or all of these costs.

Title Insurance Premiums:

Line 7. Owner's Title Insurance: The seller has agreed by contract to give evidence of merchantable title. This amount is a DEBIT to the seller [as noted in Unit 1].

The owner's title insurance is a policy that will protect the new buyer from defects in title to real estate. It, in effect, protects a policyholder, the new buyer/owner, against loss from an occurrence that has already happened, such as a forged deed, somewhere in the chain of title. In addition, the title company also agrees to defend the policyholder's title in court against any lawsuits that may arise from defects found after the policy is issued.

■ Always DEBIT seller.

Line 7a. Extended Title Insurance: Extended coverage eliminates or insures over the standard exceptions of parties in possession, unrecorded easements, survey matters, unrecorded mechanic's liens, the gap period (from the effective date of the commitment to the date the deed is recorded) unpaid taxes, and assessments. The fee for this coverage is small, usually $75 to $100 and payment is negotiated in the contract.

■ DEBIT buyer or seller as negotiated.

Line 7b. Mortgagee's (Lender's) Title Insurance: The new lender normally requires mortgagee's title insurance; therefore, it is the responsibility of the borrower to pay the premium.

The mortgagee's policy protects the lender against the same defects as an owner under an owner's policy but the insurer's liability is limited to the mortgage balance as of the date of the claim. Because of the reduced liability, and if the policy is ordered from the same company as the owner's policy, it usually costs less than the owner's policy.

Almost all major lenders now require, in addition to the mortgagee's policy, extra protection called a *Form 100 endorsement*. This form protects the lender against loss incurred due to any errors in the covenants, conditions, or restrictions, as well as loss due to any encroachments. In addition to the Form 100 endorsement, the lender may require other endorsements to cover other title concerns.

■ Always DEBIT the buyer.

Line 13. Release of Deed of Trust: The seller pays to record the release of the previous deed of trust. Recording the release clears the lien from the property as the seller promised, and will allow the new lenders loan to be in first position.

■ Always DEBIT the seller.

Line 27. Loan Origination Fee: This is the lender's fee for making the loan. Think of it as the lender's commission. It is typically expressed as a percentage of the loan amount (e.g., 1 percent origination fee).

■ DEBIT the buyer.

Line 28. Discount Points/Loan Discount Fee: The sales contract states the buyer will pay this fee, so it is a DEBIT to the buyer. The buyer can request the seller pay this fee in the Additional Provisions section of the Contract to Buy and Sell. The broker should always review the contract to determine who will be responsible for this charge. Discount points are expressed as a **percentage of the**

loan amount (3 points = 3% of the loan amount). In some instances, the seller in the sales contract may agree to pay for some or all of the discount points. The closer/broker must read the contract to determine who to charge.

■ DEBIT the buyer, unless otherwise stated in the contract.

Line 31. Appraisal Fee: When an appraisal fee is involved in closing a transaction, it is usually charged to the buyer since it is a requirement of obtaining the loan. In some instances, the seller in the sales contract may agree to pay for the appraisal. The closer/broker must review the contract to determine who to charge.

■ DEBIT the buyer or seller as negotiated.

Lines 19 & 24. Lender Reserves (in a new loan): For a new loan, the lender will collect funds from the closing to open the account with a starting balance. This amount plus the monthly installments (part of PITI) will be sufficient to pay the taxes when they become due.

■ Always DEBIT the buyer.

Line 29. Interest on New or a Seller-Carry Loan: Lenders insist every payment on a fully amortized loan must be the same amount. Lenders do not permit the first payment to be changed for part of a month.

■ **EXAMPLE 3.1**   If there is a closing on July 21 and the buyer's first payment will not be due until September 1, the lender requires that the interest be paid at closing from the day of closing to August 1. This is because the interest is payable in **arrears**. When the buyer makes the September payment, it will include the payment of interest for the entire month of August. This is also true on seller-carry loans.

■ Always DEBIT the buyer (for the gap between closing and the end of the month).

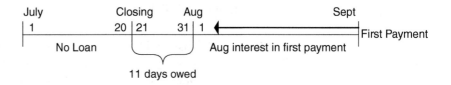

In a new institutional loan situation, the lender will calculate this adjustment for you. In most cases, it will result in a DEBIT to the buyer.

Net Loan Proceeds from a New Loan

After the lender has paid or withheld the items listed on the New Loan Statement, they prepare a check to the closing company (broker) for the *Net Loan Proceeds*. The lender must also provide *good funds*, often by wire transfer. This is simply the gross loan amount minus all of the items the lender deducts. The check for the Net Loan Proceeds is delivered to the broker and deposited **into** the broker column (single entry broker DEBIT). This amount, along with cash brought by the buyer, allows the broker to write the remainder of the checks to close the transaction. Traditionally, the Net Loan Proceeds figure is entered on the last line above the subtotals.

For a new loan closing, start the six-column closing worksheet with the New Loan Statement amounts. Remember: all items related to the new loan are single entries.

- On Line 3, enter the gross amount of the new loan—a buyer CREDIT.
- Continue with the various lender fees and disbursements—a number of single entry DEBITS allocated to the seller or buyer depending on who owns the bill.
- The final new loan entry, on Line 39, is the Net Loan Proceeds—a DEBIT to the broker for deposit into the escrow account.
- Taken together, these entries will result in a balanced closing worksheet with the total CREDIT equaling the combined DEBITS. The dollar values are balanced down the column, but not balanced on each line (across the sheet) as you saw in the loan assumption.

■ **EXAMPLE 3.2**

Line 3. Gross loan amount	$86,800.00
Minus Total lender payouts	($30,616.14)
Line 39. Net Loan Proceeds to broker	$56,186.86

The broker is still responsible to account for all of the remaining closing items, just as in the loan assumption closing. From the selling price on down, the broker must take care of the DEBITS and CREDITS for the closing. These remaining entries (non-new loan items) will all be balanced lines with equal dollar value of DEBITS and CREDITS.

New Loan Items Handled By the Lender and Not By the Broker

- Gross amount of the new loan is a CREDIT to the buyer (single entry).
- Lender payouts: recording the new deed of trust or payment of loan origination fees are good examples.
- There is no broker entry for these items and no offsetting CREDIT, just the DEBIT to the responsible party.
- The new lender actually pays these items and provides a detailed list to the broker or closing company. As usual, close to the lender's exact figures.

Classroom Exercise 4 will show a typical new loan closing in detail.

New Loans and Net Proceeds

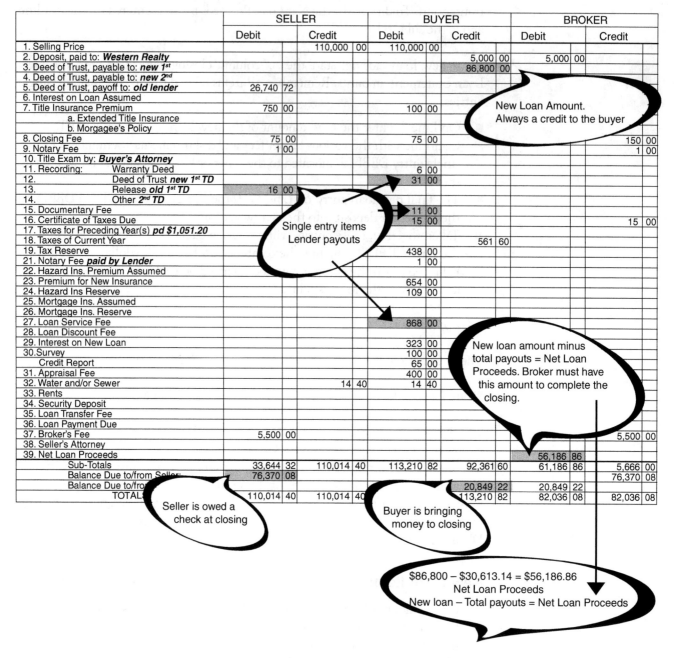

	SELLER		BUYER		BROKER	
	Debit	Credit	Debit	Credit	Debit	Credit
1. Selling Price		110,000 00	110,000 00			
2. Deposit, paid to: **Western Realty**				5,000 00	5,000 00	
3. Deed of Trust, payable to: **new 1ˢᵗ**				86,800 00		
4. Deed of Trust, payable to: **new 2ⁿᵈ**						
5. Deed of Trust, payoff to: **old lender**	26,740 72					
6. Interest on Loan Assumed						
7. Title Insurance Premium	750 00		100 00			
a. Extended Title Insurance						
b. Morgagee's Policy						
8. Closing Fee	75 00		75 00			150 00
9. Notary Fee	1 00					1 00
10. Title Exam by: **Buyer's Attorney**						
11. Recording: Warranty Deed			6 00			
12. Deed of Trust **new 1ˢᵗ TD**			31 00			
13. Release **old 1ˢᵗ TD**	16 00					
14. Other **2ⁿᵈ TD**						
15. Documentary Fee			11 00			
16. Certificate of Taxes Due			15 00			15 00
17. Taxes for Preceding Year(s) pd **$1,051.20**						
18. Taxes of Current Year				561 60		
19. Tax Reserve			438 00			
20. Notary Fee **paid by Lender**			1 00			
21. Hazard Ins. Premium Assumed						
23. Premium for New Insurance			654 00			
24. Hazard Ins Reserve			109 00			
25. Mortgage Ins. Assumed						
26. Mortgage Ins. Reserve						
27. Loan Service Fee			868 00			
28. Loan Discount Fee						
29. Interest on New Loan			323 00			
30. Survey			100 00			
Credit Report			65 00			
31. Appraisal Fee			400 00			
32. Water and/or Sewer		14 40	14 40			
33. Rents						
34. Security Deposit						
35. Loan Transfer Fee						
36. Loan Payment Due						
37. Broker's Fee	5,500 00					5,500 00
38. Seller's Attorney						
39. Net Loan Proceeds					56,186 86	
Sub-Totals	33,644 32	110,014 40	113,210 82	92,361 60	61,186 86	5,666 00
Balance Due to/from Seller:	76,370 08					76,370 08
Balance Due to/from				20,849 22	20,849 22	
TOTALS	110,014 40	110,014 40	113,210 82	113,210 82	82,036 08	82,036 08

Callouts in figure:
- New Loan Amount. Always a credit to the buyer
- Single entry items Lender payouts
- New loan amount minus total payouts = Net Loan Proceeds. Broker must have this amount to complete the closing.
- Seller is owed a check at closing
- Buyer is bringing money to closing
- $86,800 − $30,613.14 = $56,186.86 Net Loan Proceeds New loan − Total payouts = Net Loan Proceeds

Other Forms Used at Closing

Closing Statement is the two-column summary sheet. If the broker prepares the closing, this form or an equivalent is **mandatory**. One Closing Statement is prepared for the seller, and one for the buyer. These forms are checked and signed by the designated broker working with each party.

Closing worksheet for Real Estate Settlement is provided by the Real Estate Commission as a convenience to brokers. This is the six-column closing worksheet you used in Exercises 1 through 4. This sheet summarizes the DEBITS and CREDITS for both the seller and buyer and is the only sheet that **includes the broker escrow account DEBITS and CREDITS**. This summary may be completed with a computerized spreadsheet if desired. A balanced closing worksheet is the best way to ensure complete and accurate Statements of Settlement for the parties.

Real Property Transfer Declaration (TD-1000): This form is another responsibility of the Closing Company. It is a report to the County Assessor describing a transaction.

Purpose of the TD-1000: To "provide essential information to the county assessor **to help ensure fair and uniform assessments for all property for property tax purposes."**

Recordkeeping

Employing brokers and independent brokers must keep transaction records including the closing documentation for **four years**, to comply with Real Estate Commission rules.

Good Funds at Closing

Remember: all money brought to closing by any party must comply with the banking rules that define *good funds* as follows:

- Cashier's check from a recognized commercial bank
- Teller's check from a thrift institution such as a Savings and Loan or Credit Union
- Wire transfer via the Federal Reserve system

The seller **may** specify in the Closing Instructions want of good funds at closing as well. Normally, money coming **out** of the closing will be in the form of a wire transfer or a business check from the broker or closing company.

Note: The Contract to Buy and Sell does not recognize cash as good funds and most closing companies will not accept cash at the closing table. Buyers and sellers are expected to bring good funds as described above to closing.

Error at Closing

A broker that discovers any error before closing should have the error corrected. A relatively minor error discovered at closing can be adjusted between the parties, if they agree, using a check or cash to settle. A memorandum of this adjustment signed by both parties should be made and copies given to all parties. A major error is best handled by having the error corrected. The closing can be delayed, with agreement of all parties, until the figures can be corrected.

Additional Reporting Requirements: Non-resident Seller Withholding

State Law   When a seller is not a resident of Colorado, state law requires the *closing entity* to withhold potential **income tax** for sales in excess of $100,000. The withholding is 2 percent of the sales price or the entire *net proceeds* (balance due to seller) of the sale, **whichever is less.**

Exceptions There are a number of exceptions when the withholding law **does not apply** most notably if the property was the seller's principal residence.

■ **EXAMPLE 3.3** Assume the Nonresident Seller Withholding does apply. The seller will receive $123,000 at closing (without the withholding) and the selling price is $435,000. The closing entity must withhold 2 percent of the selling price or $8,700 from the seller's proceeds of sale.

The closing company will complete a report for the Colorado Department of Revenue and immediately forward the report and the money to the Department of Revenue. If the seller believes a refund is due, the seller files a state income tax return and requests a refund.

■ **EXAMPLE 3.4** Presume the same scenario as above and the withholding law still applies. This time, the seller is due to receive $7,000 net proceeds at closing, but the seller owes $8,700. The closing entity will withhold only $7,000. The seller is never required to bring additional money to closing to make up the full 2 percent withholding.

■ SUMMARY OF UNIT 3:

1. The six-column settlement closing worksheet summarizes the financial aspects of a closing for the seller, the buyer, and the broker.
2. In a loan assumption closing, DEBITS and CREDITS will be equal on each line of the six-column settlement worksheet.
3. Close assumptions to the exact lender figures. **Always** using double entry.
4. Lenders for new loan closings often pay some charges to protect their own interests.
5. On the settlement worksheet, the buyer receives a single entry CREDIT for the gross new loan amount. Items paid by the lender are a single DEBIT charge to one of the parties on the six-column worksheet. All items related to the new loan are single entry. Close new loans to the exact lender figures.

■ UNIT 3: GLOSSARY REVIEW

Match the terms with the definitions.

conventional loan	mortgagee's title insurance policy
designated broker	private mortgage insurance (PMI)
first deed of trust	release of deed of trust
loan discount points	second deed of trust
loan origination fee	single entry

1. The document recorded to indicate that a lien has been paid off is a _release of deed of trust_.

2. A document that creates a lien and has the highest priority is a _first deed of trust_.

3. The administrative fee charged by a lender to set up a loan is the _loan origination fee_.

4. To protect against defects in title, a lender will usually require the buyer to purchase a _mortgagee's title insurance policy_.

5. Fees usually quoted as a percentage of the loan amount and used to increase the lender's yield and/or acquire a lower interest rate for the buyer, is known as _loan discount points_.

6. A loan that is neither guaranteed nor insured by a government agency is called a _conventional loan_.

7. A loan created with a lower lien priority, such as a seller-carry loan, is often a _second deed of trust_.

8. A conventional loan with a loan-to-value ratio greater than 80 percent will typically require _PMI_.

9. An assumption close uses double entries, while a new loan close is mostly _single entry_.

10. The _designated broker_ is responsible for the Closing Statement for the party represented.

■ UNIT 3: LECTURE OUTLINE

I. REVIEW OF THE SIX-COLUMN REAL ESTATE SETTLEMENT WORKSHEET

A. Types of closing entries

There are four main types of entries on the settlement worksheet:

1. Seller and buyer exchanges of funds

   a) Examples are prorations and the _Selling price_.

   b) Each line has equal dollar values of DEBITS and CREDITS.

2. Funds held by the broker until the closing

   a) The most common example is _earnest money_

   b) This is a CREDIT to the buyer and _debit_ to the broker (deposit into escrow account) offsetting DEBIT and CREDITS.

3. Bills paid by the broker on behalf of seller or buyer

   a) Examples: attorney's fee or _recording_ fees.

   b) DEBIT to the responsible party for the item, and _Credit_ to the broker (out of the escrow account) for writing the check.

4. New loan items handled by the lender, not by the broker

   a) New loan gross amount

   b) Lender payouts of many fees including loan origination fees or recording the new deed of trust

   c) No broker entry for these items and no offsetting CREDIT. Only the DEBIT to the responsible party

   d) **Broker's Net Loan Proceeds, DEBIT into the broker's column.**

   e) The new lender has the closing company pay these items and provides a detailed list to the broker. Close using the lender's exact figures.

II. THE SIX-COLUMN CLOSING WORKSHEET—SUMMARIZING THE TRANSACTION

A. The six-column closing worksheet summarizes the transaction with DEBIT and CREDIT columns for the following parties:

1. _Buyer_

2. _Seller_

3. _Broker_

B. Items unique to the six-column worksheet

1. An optional form that may be done on a computer spreadsheet or other methods if desired.

2. Only the closing worksheet shows items going in and out of _Broker closing account_.

3. A properly balanced settlement closing worksheet provides the information for the Closing Statement for the buyer and seller.

C. _Loan Assumption_

1. Buyer assumes and agrees to pay the remaining balance on a seller's existing loan. Uses double entries.

D. _New loan_

1. When the buyer gets a new loan, _the new lender will withhold funds_ from the gross loan amount to pay some of the expenses of closing. Uses mostly single entries.

III. OTHER FORMS USED AT CLOSING

A. Seller or buyer Closing Statement

1. This form was reviewed in Units 1 and 2.

2. This form or a suitable substitute is _mandatory_ when the broker conducts the closing.

3. Shows all of the DEBITS and CREDITS for the _buyer_ or _seller_.

4. Must be maintained in employing broker's files for _4 years_.

5. _Listing Broker_ broker checks figures for the seller.

6. _Buyer's Broker_ broker checks figures for the buyer.

B. Real Property Transfer Declaration (TD-1000)

1. Helps ensure fair and uniform _assessment_ of property taxes.

2. Should be completed at closing

IV. GOOD FUNDS AT CLOSING

A. Good funds are:

1. _Cashiers Check_

2. _Teller's Check_ ~~Wire Transfer~~ from a savings and loan or credit union

3. _Wire Transfer_

B. A personal check or company business check is not classified as good funds.

C. Promissory note for earnest money

1. Must be honored in time to clear and be _good funds_ by closing.

V. ERRORS AT CLOSING

A. Found before closing

1. Have the _closing company_ correct the error.

B. Minor error found at closing

1. Parties may agree to _adjust the error or delay the_ closing (typically with a small check or cash).

C. Lender's figures (new or existing loan)

1. Close to lender's exact figures

2. Lender will adjust with appropriate party after closing.

VI. NON-RESIDENT SELLER WITHHOLDING

A. Colorado law calls for a possible withholding of potential income tax from the gain in the sale of a property sold by a non-Colorado resident.

B. The seller is subject to withholding tax if:

1. the seller lives outside of _Colorado_ ; and

2. the sales price is **greater than** _100,000_ .

C. There are several exemptions from this requirement including:

1. sale of a principal residence.

D. The amount of tax withheld will be the lower of:

1. _2 %_ of the sales price; or

2. the seller's entire net proceeds (balance due to the seller).

E. It is the responsibility of the _closing company_ to collect the withholding tax.

1. _Closing entity_ can be an attorney, a broker, or the closing/title company.

2. The closing entity is responsible for immediately forwarding the funds to the Colorado _Department of Revenue_.

VII. NEW LOAN CLOSINGS AND THE NEW LOAN STATEMENT

A. A new loan statement provides the broker the following information:

1. The amount of the loan

2. Specific bills the lender will withhold from the loan

3. Net amount of the check the lender will provide to fund the rest of the closing

B. Use lender figures _exactly_ as provided.

C. In a new loan, the lender brings the majority of the money for the buyer.

1. The new loan statement will show three sets of numbers the closer/broker needs.

   a) Gross or total new loan amount (Line 3)

   b) _lender payouts_

   c) _Net loan proceeds_ (Line 39)

2. Buyer will always have a large _Credit_ called the _gross loan amount_

3. From this amount, the lender will pay the majority of the bills, which are then totaled in _lender payouts_.

4. The difference between the gross loan amount and the lender payouts is the _net loan proceeds_, which will be a _Debit_ (deposit) into the closer/broker column so the final checks can be written.

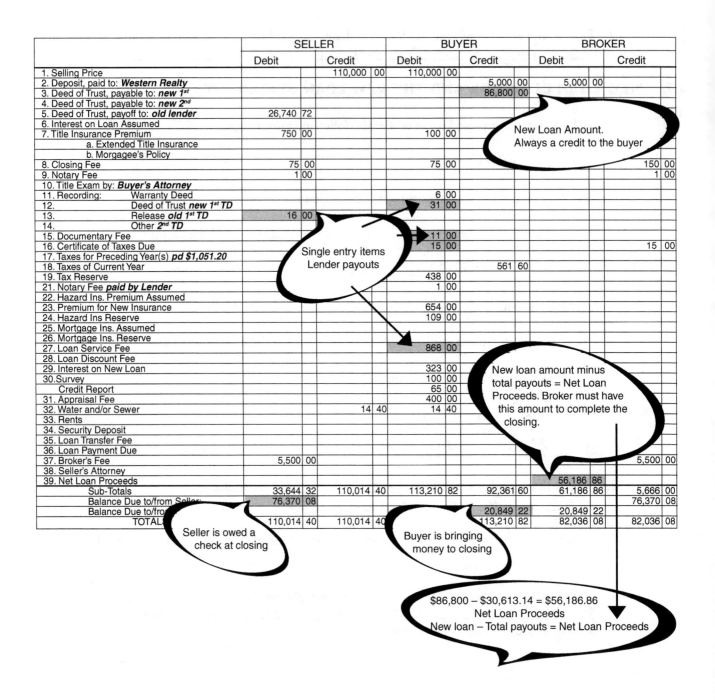

	SELLER				BUYER				BROKER			
	Debit		Credit		Debit		Credit		Debit		Credit	
1. Selling Price			110,000	00	110,000	00						
2. Deposit, paid to: **Western Realty**							5,000	00	5,000	00		
3. Deed of Trust, payable to: **new 1st**							86,800	00				
4. Deed of Trust, payable to: **new 2nd**												
5. Deed of Trust, payoff to: **old lender**	26,740	72										
6. Interest on Loan Assumed												
7. Title Insurance Premium	750	00			100	00						
a. Extended Title Insurance												
b. Morgagee's Policy												
8. Closing Fee	75	00			75	00					150	00
9. Notary Fee	1	00									1	00
10. Title Exam by: **Buyer's Attorney**												
11. Recording: Warranty Deed					6	00						
12. Deed of Trust **new 1st TD**					31	00						
13. Release **old 1st TD**	16	00										
14. Other **2nd TD**												
15. Documentary Fee					11	00						
16. Certificate of Taxes Due					15	00					15	00
17. Taxes for Preceding Year(s) **pd $1,051.20**												
18. Taxes of Current Year							561	60				
19. Tax Reserve					438	00						
21. Notary Fee **paid by Lender**					1	00						
22. Hazard Ins. Premium Assumed												
23. Premium for New Insurance					654	00						
24. Hazard Ins Reserve					109	00						
25. Mortgage Ins. Assumed												
26. Mortgage Ins. Reserve												
27. Loan Service Fee					868	00						
28. Loan Discount Fee												
29. Interest on New Loan					323	00						
30. Survey					100	00						
Credit Report					65	00						
31. Appraisal Fee					400	00						
32. Water and/or Sewer	14	40			14	40						
33. Rents												
34. Security Deposit												
35. Loan Transfer Fee												
36. Loan Payment Due												
37. Broker's Fee	5,500	00									5,500	00
38. Seller's Attorney												
39. Net Loan Proceeds									56,186	86		
Sub-Totals	33,644	32	110,014	40	113,210	82	92,361	60	61,186	86	5,666	00
Balance Due to/from Seller:	76,370	08									76,370	08
Balance Due to/from							20,849	22	20,849	22		
TOTAL	110,014	40	110,014	40	113,210	82			82,036	08	82,036	08

New Loan Amount. Always a credit to the buyer

Single entry items Lender payouts

New loan amount minus total payouts = Net Loan Proceeds. Broker must have this amount to complete the closing.

Seller is owed a check at closing

Buyer is bringing money to closing

*$86,800 − $30,613.14 = $56,186.86
Net Loan Proceeds
New loan − Total payouts = Net Loan Proceeds*

5. The new lender provides a New Loan Statement with information about financing and **items the lender is paying** from the gross loan amount.

6. The lender also provides a ___*net loan proceeds*___ number that represents what remains of the gross loan amount after the lender pays the bills listed in the New Loan Statement.

7. All of these numbers from the New Loan Statement are ___*single entry*___ on the six-column settlement worksheet.

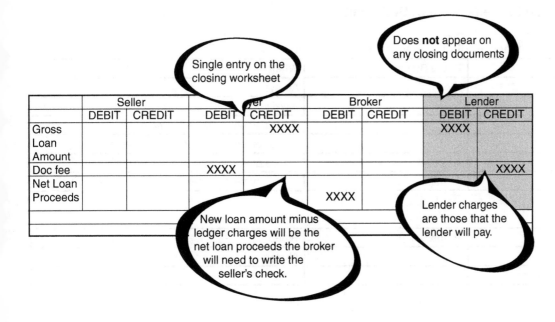

	Seller		Buyer		Broker		Lender	
	DEBIT	CREDIT	DEBIT	CREDIT	DEBIT	CREDIT	DEBIT	CREDIT
Gross Loan Amount				XXXX			XXXX	
Doc fee			XXXX					XXXX
Net Loan Proceeds					XXXX			

Speech bubbles:
- Single entry on the closing worksheet
- Does **not** appear on any closing documents
- New loan amount minus ledger charges will be the net loan proceeds the broker will need to write the seller's check.
- Lender charges are those that the lender will pay.

■ **EXAMPLE**

Line 3. Gross loan amount	$86,800.00
Minus total lender payouts	(30,613.14)
Line 39. Net Loan Proceeds to broker	$56,186.86

8. The broker records the lender single entry numbers on the closing worksheet _first_.

9. The closing entries not related to the new loan are all double entries and result in ___balanced lines___ with equal dollar values of DEBITS and CREDITS.

D. Items unique to a new loan closing

1. The gross amount of the **new loan** on Line 3 is a buyer ___Credit___ single entry.

2. A loan payoff on Line 5 to clear the seller's previous loan is a ___Seller___ DEBIT single entry.

3. Various expenses paid by the lender on behalf of both the seller and the buyer are single entry ___Debits___ to the party responsible for that obligation.

4. The Net Loan Proceeds from the lender's New Loan Statement is a single entry DEBIT to the ___broker___. It is a deposited into the escrow account and used to fund the closing.

E. Items Unique to the New Loan Statement

Items will be assigned as follows on a new loan statement:

Line	Item	To the Buyer	When
3	New loan amount		Always
7a.	Mortgagee policy		Always
31	Appraisal		Unless otherwise stated in the contract
27	Loan Origination Fee		Unless otherwise stated in the contract
28	Discount points		Unless otherwise stated in the contract
29	Interest on New Loan		If first payment more than one month after closing

	Item	To the Seller	When
5	Prior loan payoff		Always
13	Release of Deed of Trust		Always

■ CLASSROOM EXERCISE
SETTLEMENT EXERCISE 4: NEW CONVENTIONAL LOAN

Broker Details—Double Entries

Closing Date: July 15th

Sale price $110,000
Deposit 5,000
Tax certificate ordered and paid for by broker is $15.
Shows taxes for previous year are $1,051.20 and are paid.
Notary fee for the warranty deed is $1.
Water and sewer, paid quarterly in advance from June 1 through August 31, is $27.60..
Closing Fees of $150 split 50-50
Commission is 5 percent

NEW LOAN STATEMENT- Single Entries	
New loan at 8% interest..	$86,800.00
Payoff of present loan $26,625.52 including interest on present loan:	
10 days at $11.52 per day. Includes delivery time	26,740.72
Title policy (owners)	750.00
Mortgagee policy	100.00
Recording Warranty Deed...	6.00
Recording Deed of Trust	31.00
Release of Deed of Trust	16.00
Documentary fee...	??.00
New reserve for taxes (5 months: April through August)	438.00
Insurance premium	654.00
New insurance reserve (2 months)	109.00
Loan fee 1%	868.00
Interest to August 1st (First payment due: 9/1, interest in arrears)	323.42
Survey..	100.00
Credit report	65.00
Lender notary fee	1.00
Appraisal fee	400.00
Total amount of lender payouts	$30,613.14
NET LOAN PROCEEDS..	$56,186.86

Enter all of the new lender details as single entries before you enter the broker details.

Settlement Exercise 4

Exercise #4: New Loan (Net Proceeds)	SELLER DEBIT		SELLER CREDIT		BUYER DEBIT		BUYER CREDIT		BROKER DEBIT		BROKER CREDIT	
1. Selling Price			110,000	00	110,000	00						
2. Deposit, paid to: *Western Realty*							5,000	00	5,000	00		
3. Trust Deed, payable to: *new 1st*												
4. Trust Deed, payable to:												
5. Trust Deed, payoff to: *old lender*												
6. Interest on Loan Assumed												
7. Title Insurance Premium												
a. Extended Title Insurance												
b. Mortgagee's Policy												
8. Closing Fee	75	00									150	00
9. Notary	1	00									1	00
10. Title Exam by: *Buyer's Attorney*												
11. Recording: Warranty Deed												
12. Trust Deed *new 1st TD*												
13. Release *old 1st TD*	16	00										
14. Other *2nd TD*												
15. Documentary Fee												
16. Certificate of Taxes Due											15	00
17. Taxes – Preceding Year(s) *pd* $1,051.20												
18. Taxes for Current Year												
19. Tax Reserve												
20. Special Taxes												
21. Personal Property Taxes												
22. Notary Fees paid by lender												
23. Premium for New Insurance												
24. Hazard Ins. Reserve												
25. Mortgage Ins. Assumed												
26. Mortgage Ins. Reserve												
27. Loan Service Fee (Buyer)												
28. Loan Discount Fee												
29. Interest on New Loan												
30. Survey												
CREDIT Report												
31. Appraisal Fee												
32. Water and/or Sewer			14	40								
33. Rents												
34. Security Deposits												
35. Loan Transfer Fee												
36. Loan Payment Due												
37. Broker's Fee	5,500	00									5,500	00
38. Sellers attorney												
39. Net Loan Proceeds												
Subtotals	33,644	32	110,014	40	113,210	82	92,361	60	61,186	86	5,666	00
Balance Due to/~~from~~ Seller												
Balance Due ~~to~~/from Buyer												
TOTALS												

NEW LOAN DETAILS—All are single entries (broker entries covered after this section)

3. Trust Deed payable to: new lender. The new loan amount is a CREDIT to the buyer since it will be applied to the purchase price of the property. This item is a single entry since it appears on the lender's new loan statement and reduces the check the buyer must bring to close. It has no effect on either the seller or the broker. It may help to think the single entries are being accounted for on the lender's credit column, which can't be seen. These columns hold the offsetting entries for every item, which will be a single entry on our new loan closing.

New loan at 8% interest..$86,800.00

CREDIT buyer (single entry)

5. Trust Deed payoff. The payoff on the existing loan is a DEBIT to the seller because it is the seller's obligation to clear the existing lien from the property. To determine the amount of the payoff, the broker must request a payoff statement from the seller's loan company. This statement shows the balance after adjustments for interest, penalties and any CREDITS the seller may have in the way of tax or insurance reserves.

Note: The broker must always close to the figures provided by the new lender. If the broker disagrees with the lender's figures, the dispute must be settled with the lender ahead of time, or the disputed numbers are used to close and adjustment is sought after closing.

Payoff of present loan $26,625.52 including interest on present loan:

10 days at $11.52 per day. Includes delivery time............$26,740.72

DEBIT seller (single entry)

7. Title insurance premiums. The seller has agreed by contract to give evidence of merchantable title.

Title policy (owners) $750.00

DEBIT seller (single entry)

The new lender normally requires mortgagee's title insurance. It is the responsibility of the borrower to pay the premium.

7a. Mortgagee policy $100.00

DEBIT buyer (single entry)

11. and 12. Recording Warranty Deed and Trust Deed. It is the obligation of the buyer to pay for recording the new warranty deed and trust deed. These items are usually single entries since the new lender will pay them.

Recording Warranty Deed...$6.00

Recording Deed of Trust...$31.00

13. Release. The seller pays to record the release of deed of trust. Recording the release clears the lien from the property. DEBIT seller (single entry)

Release of Deed of Trust..$16.00

Line 15: Documentary Fee. DEBIT buyer (single entry).

Documentary fee..$11.00

17. Taxes for Preceding Year(s). If the tax certificate shows the taxes for the preceding year have been paid, no entry is required. If taxes are owed, the lender will pay them. DEBIT seller (single entry).

19. Tax reserve. After the closing, the lender will collect one month's taxes in each monthly installment. However, the lender will collect funds from the closing to prime the account. This amount plus the monthly escrow installments will be sufficient to pay the taxes when they become due. In this example, the lender is requesting five month's reserve (April through August) since the buyer will not make the first monthly payment until September 1. Most lenders escrow from April to April since they must pay the property taxes by April 30 each year.

New reserve for taxes (five months—April to August)........$438.00

21. Lender Notary. This is the notary charge witnessing the buyer signing the deed of trust.

23. Premium for new insurance. The lender requires a one-year hazard insurance policy be purchased, effective the day of closing. Since the policy is for the benefit of the buyer, the cost is a DEBIT to the buyer (single entry).

Insurance premium...$654.00

24. Hazard Insurance Reserve. As with the tax reserve, the lender requires an amount up front to prime the escrow account, usually a minimum of two months; DEBIT buyer.

New insurance reserve (two months) $109.00

27. Loan origination fee. This is the lender's fee for making the loan. DEBIT buyer (single entry).

Loan fee 1%...$868.00

29. Interest on a new loan. Since the buyer's first payment will not be due until September 1, the lender requires the interest be paid from the day of closing to August 1. Interest is payable in arrears. When the buyer makes the September payment, it includes the payment of interest for the entire month of August. At closing, the buyer must pay the interest adjustment beginning July 15 and ending July 31. DEBIT the buyer (single entry).

Interest to August $323.42

(First payment due on September 1. Interest in arrears.)

30. Survey/Credit Report. If the lender requires any of these items, they would be a DEBIT to the buyer (single entry).

Survey $100.00

Credit report $65.00

Enter the total of these items ($165.00) on Line 30

31. Appraisal fee. When an appraisal fee is involved in closing a transaction, it is usually charged to the buyer since it is a requirement of obtaining the loan. However, in some instances, the seller in the sales contract may agree to pay for the appraisal at closing. The broker must check the Contract to Buy and Sell in each situation.

Appraisal fee $400.00

Total amount of lender payouts. The total of payouts provided by the lender on the New Loan Statement does not go on the settlement sheet. It is merely the total of all of the DEBITS listed by the lender. The gross loan amount minus the total of charges is equal to the Net Proceeds.

Total payouts $30,613.14

Last line above Double Line. Traditionally, this Net Loan Proceeds figure is entered on the last line above the subtotals. It represents money the lender will actually provide to the closing. If the broker is closing the transaction, the lender will provide good funds (often by wire transfer).

The entry is a single entry **DEBIT** to the broker. It is actually deposited into the escrow account, allowing the broker to write the other checks (amount due to the seller, commission, etc.).

Net Loan Proceeds $56,186.86

At this point, much of the settlement sheet is filled in with single entries. The single entry DEBITS for seller, buyer, and broker must equal the gross loan amount on Line 3.

BROKER DETAILS—Double Entry

Now it is time to finish the closing worksheet by entering the rest of the financial details from the contract and other sources. These are things with which the lender is **not** involved. If there should be a duplicate entry mentioned, the lender is paying it, so do not duplicate the charges.

Working from Line 1 down to ensure that all lines have been considered:

1. Purchase price $110,000   CREDIT seller, DEBIT buyer.

2. Deposit $5,000   CREDIT buyer, DEBIT broker.

8. Closing Fee $150 split DEBIT seller and buyer each $75 CREDIT broker $150

9. Notary   Witness seller signing deed; DEBIT seller $1, CREDIT broker

16. Certificate of Taxes Due.   The tax certificate is normally charged to the buyer since it is for the benefit of the buyer. $15 DEBIT buyer, CREDIT broker

18. Taxes for Current Year.   DEBIT seller and CREDIT buyer the prorated amount as explained in Unit 1.

Taxes for current year = $1,051.20

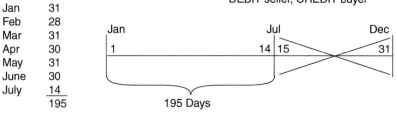

$$\$1,051.20 \div 365 \times 195 = \$561.60$$
DEBIT seller, CREDIT buyer

Jan	31
Feb	28
Mar	31
Apr	30
May	31
June	30
July	14
	195

195 Days

32. Water and/or sewer. Review Unit 1, Discussion for Settlement Exercise 1, Line 32. This item is not normally on the lender's statement so it would be a double entry.

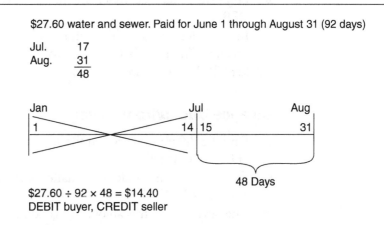

$27.60 water and sewer. Paid for June 1 through August 31 (92 days)

Jul.   17
Aug.   31
        ——
        48

Jan   Jul   Aug
1   14│15   31

                                      48 Days

$27.60 ÷ 92 × 48 = $14.40
DEBIT buyer, CREDIT seller

$27.60 water and sewer. Paid for June 1 through August 31 (92 days).

37. Broker's fee. DEBIT seller, CREDIT broker (the employing broker is writing a check from the escrow account to the brokerage operating account to disburse commissions).

$5,500 DEBIT seller, CREDIT broker

Other items not printed on the closing worksheet that may be found on a new loan closing:

- Realty Tax Service Fee (a service that provides property tax information to the lender on their reserve accounts)
- Underwriting Fee (a fee paid to the underwriter to analyze the loan documents)
- Loan Document Preparation Fee (a fee paid to the loan processor to prepare the loan documents for review)
- MIP (Mortgage Insurance for FHA loans), PMI (Private Mortgage Insurance for conventional loans)
- VA Funding Fee
- Flood Plain Certification (a fee to provide the lender with a certificate that the subject property is not in a flood plain). If the property were found to be in a flood plain, the buyer would be required to purchase flood insurance in addition to hazard insurance.

Below the Double Line

- The procedure for a new loan is the same as for an assumption closing.

Subtotals

- The subtotals are the sums of all the amounts in each column.

Balance Due to/from Seller

- Balance equals: subtotal of seller's CREDITS minus subtotal of seller's DEBITS
- Enter the difference under the smaller of the two numbers (usually seller's DEBIT).
- In most closings, the seller will receive a check from the broker's escrow account. Enter the Balance Due to/from Seller on the same line in the broker CREDIT column.

Balance Due to/from Buyer

- Find the difference between the subtotal of buyer's DEBITS and the subtotal of buyer's CREDITS.
- Enter the amount under the smaller of the two numbers (usually under buyer's CREDITS).
- The buyer brings this amount in good funds, usually in the form of a cashier's check.
- The check is deposited **into** the broker's escrow account. DEBIT the broker the amount of the check on the Balance Due to/from Buyer line.

Totals

- Total each line from subtotals down.
- Totals for each set of columns (seller, buyer, and broker) must be equal.
- The totals were forced to be equal for seller and buyer.
- When broker's totals are equal, the broker has accounted for all of the funds deposited into and withdrawn out of the escrow account.

■ SETTLEMENT EXERCISE 4
SETTLEMENT CLOSING WORKSHEET TIPS—NEW LOANS

1. Everything paid by the lender will be a single entry.

2. Total all single entry buyer and seller DEBITS, and balance with lender's dollar amounts paid out.

3. Study all facts carefully. Be alert to anything the broker handles.

4. Reconciliation will be the same as in an assumption.

5. Double entry indicates that entries are the same for assumptions and new loans.

	DEBIT / CREDIT	TIPS
1. Selling Price	CREDIT seller, DEBIT buyer	Double Entry
2. Deposit, Paid to:	CREDIT buyer, DEBIT broker	Double Entry
3. Trust Deed, payable to: *New Loan*	CREDIT buyer	**Single Entry** (lender will provide this amount)
4. Trust Deed, payable to: *Seller's second*	DEBIT seller, CREDIT buyer	Double Entry

5. Trust Deed, payoff to: *Old loan*	DEBIT seller	**Single Entry** (lender will pay)
6. • Interest on Loan Assumed	N/A	
7. Title Insurance Premium Mortgagee's Policy	DEBIT seller (Owner's Policy) DEBIT buyer (Mortgagee Policy)	Single Entry (lender will pay)
8. Closing Fee	DEBIT seller/buyer per contract CREDIT broker	Double Entry
9. Notary	DEBIT seller/buyer per document CREDIT broker	Double Entry
10. Title Exam by: Buyer's Attorney	DEBIT buyer, CREDIT broker	Double Entry
11. Recording: Warranty Deed	DEBIT buyer	**Single Entry** (lender will pay)
12. Trust Deed	DEBIT buyer	**Single Entry** (lender will pay)
13. Release	DEBIT seller	**Single Entry** (lender will pay)
14. Other		
15. Documentary Fee	DEBIT buyer	**Single Entry** (lender will pay); must have
16. Certificate of Taxes Due	DEBIT buyer	**Single Entry** (lender will pay)
17. Taxes for Preceding Year(s)	DEBIT seller	**Single Entry** (lender will pay)
18. • Taxes for Current Year	DEBIT seller, CREDIT buyer	Double Entry SOB
19. Tax Reserve *Prime Charge*	DEBIT buyer	Single Entry (lender will pay)
20. Special Taxes	(DEPENDS ON CONTRACT)	Analyze carefully (could be single or double entry)
21. Personal Property Taxes	N/A	
22. Hazard Insurance Premium Assumed	N/A	
23. Premium for New Hazard Insurance	DEBIT buyer	**Single Entry** (lender will pay)
24. Hazard Insurance Reserve	DEBIT buyer	**Single Entry** (lender will pay)
25. FHA Mortgage Insurance Assumed	N/A	
26. FHA Mortgage Insurance Reserve	N/A	
27. Loan Discount Points	(DEPENDS ON CONTRACT)	**Single Entry**—Analyze carefully
28. Loan Origination Fee	DEBIT buyer	**Single Entry** (lender will pay)
29. Interest on New Loan	DEBIT BUYER	**Single Entry** (lender will pay)
30. Survey	(depends on Contract)	**Single Entry** (lender will pay CREDIT report)
Credit Report	DEBIT buyer	**Single Entry** (lender will pay)
31. Appraisal Fee	(depends on Contract)	**Single Entry** (lender will pay)
32. •Water and/or Sewer	Analyze carefully	Double Entry
33. •Rent	DEBIT seller, CREDIT buyer	Assuming rent is prepaid. SOB
34. Security Deposits	DEBIT seller, CREDIT buyer	
35. Loan Transfer Fee	N/A	
36. Loan Payment Due	N/A	
37. Broker's Fee	DEBIT seller, CREDIT broker	Double Entry

38. **Seller's Attorney**	DEBIT seller, CREDIT broker	Double Entry
39. Net Loan Proceeds (from Lender)	DEBIT broker	**Single Entry** on broker DEBIT column
SUBTOTALS		Double Entry
Balance Due To / From Seller		Double Entry
Balance Due To / From Buyer		Double Entry
TOTALS		Double Entry

• = proration items   Arrears = SOB-solve left side   Advance = BOS- solve right side

■ DEBIT AND CREDIT CHART FOR CLOSINGS

Selected Items	*Details to Remember*	*Settlement Worksheet*	*Statement of Settlement*
Sales Price		**DEBIT buyer, CREDIT seller**	**Appears on both buyer's and seller's**
Earnest money		CREDIT buyer, DEBIT broker	Appears only on buyer's
Assumed loan amount	**Principal remaining on loan assumed by buyer**	**DEBIT seller, CREDIT buyer**	**Appears on both buyer's and seller's**
Seller-carry loan amount	Reduces seller's cash at closing	CREDIT buyer, DEBIT seller	Appears on both
Broker's commission	Negotiable Usually seller pays	DEBIT seller, CREDIT broker	Appears only on seller's
Owner's (buyer's) title insurance	**Seller's pays owner's policy**	**DEBIT seller, CREDIT broker**	**Appears on seller's**
Mortgagee's (lender's) title insurance	Buyer pays lender's policy	DEBIT buyer, CREDIT broker	Appears only on buyer's
Notary fee for warranty deed	**Who signs document pays notary; seller signs deed**	**DEBIT seller, CREDIT broker**	**Appears only on seller's**
Recording of warranty deed	**Recording deed benefits buyer/grantee**	**DEBIT buyer, CREDIT broker**	**Appears only on buyer's**
Notary fee for deed of trust	Buyer signs promissory note and deed of trust at closing	DEBIT buyer, CREDIT broker	Appears only on buyer's
Tenant security deposits	Not prorated; belong to tenants	DEBIT seller, CREDIT buyer	Appears on both buyer's and seller's
Rents	Prorated; collected in advance; Seller always owes buyer	DEBIT seller, CREDIT buyer	Appears on both buyer's and seller's
New loan amount	Figures from the new lender	CREDIT buyer, single entry	Appears only on buyer's
Net loan proceeds	**New loan closing**	**DEBIT broker only**	**Does not appear on either**
Taxes for the preceding year if unpaid	CREDIT broker to pay the lien in assumption; in New Loan—single entry	DEBIT seller, CREDIT broker in assumption	Appears only on seller's
Special taxes (special assessments)	May be paid off or assumed	If assumed, no entry.If paid, DEBIT seller	Appears only on seller's

■ SETTLEMENT EXERCISE 4—SOLUTION

Exercise #4: New Loan (Net Proceeds)	SELLER				BUYER				BROKER			
	DEBIT		CREDIT		DEBIT		CREDIT		DEBIT		CREDIT	
1. Selling Price			110,000	00	110,000	00						
2. Deposit, paid to: *Western Realty*							5,000	00	5,000	00		
3. Trust Deed, payable to: *new 1st*							86,800	00				
4. Trust Deed, payable to:												
5. Trust Deed, payoff to: *old lender*	26,740	72										
6. Interest on Loan Assumed												
7. Title Insurance Premium	750	00										
a. Extended Title Insurance												
b. Mortgagee's Policy					100	00						
8. Closing Fee	75	00			75	00					150	00
9. Notary	1	00									1	00
10. Title Exam by: *Buyer's Attorney*												
11. Recording: Warranty Deed					6	00						
12. Trust Deed *new 1st TD*					31	00						
13. Release *old 1st TD*	16	00										
14. Other *2nd TD*												
15. Documentary Fee					11	00						
16. Certificate of Taxes Due					15	00					15	00
17. Taxes – Preceding Year(s) *pd* $1,051.20												
18. Taxes for Current Year	561	60					561	60				
19. Tax Reserve					438	00						
20. Special Taxes												
21. Personal Property Taxes												
22. Notary Fees paid by lender					1	00						
23. Premium for New Insurance					654	00						
24. Hazard Ins. Reserve					109	00						
25. Mortgage Ins. Assumed												
26. Mortgage Ins. Reserve												
27. Loan Service Fee (Buyer)					868	00						
28. Loan Discount Fee												
29. Interest on New Loan					323	42						
30. Survey					100	00						
CREDIT Report					65	00						
31. Appraisal Fee					400	00						
32. Water and/or Sewer			14	40	14	40						
33. Rents												
34. Security Deposits												
35. Loan Transfer Fee												
36. Loan Payment Due												
37. Broker's Fee	5,500	00									5,500	00
38. Sellers attorney												
39. Net Loan Proceeds									56,186	86		
Subtotals	33,644	32	110,014	40	113,210	82	92,361	60	61,186	86	5,666	00
Balance Due to/~~from~~ Seller	76,370	08									76,370	08
Balance Due ~~to~~/from Buyer							20,849	22	20,848	22		
TOTALS	110,014	40	110,014	40	113,210	82	113,210	82	82,036	08	82,036	08

■ AFTER THIS CLASSROOM SESSION AND BEFORE UNIT 4:

1. Review **Settlement Closing Worksheet Tips—New Loans and Debit and Credit Chart for Closings** on pages 410–412.

2. Redo Exercise 4 on your own, as similar items will appear on the final.

3. Use the study guide in Unit 4 to prepare for the final exam.

UNIT 4

Final Exam Study Guide

■ ASSIGNMENTS AND STUDY PLAN

Before Unit 4:

1. Use the study guide on the next page to prepare for the Closings final exam.

■ CLOSINGS FINAL EXAM STUDY GUIDE

1. DEBIT and CREDIT chart in Unit 3
2. Proration of the following:
    a. Interest, taxes, rent, and water
    b. The different processes used to prorate in State and National questions
3. Special assessment taxes
4. The difference between the 6-column closing worksheet and closing statements
5. New loan entries
6. How points and loan origination fees are charged
7. Responsibility and obligations of brokers for the closing
8. How errors in lender figures or other items are handled at closing
9. How the Contract to Buy and Sell impacts the closing
10. Closing entity and non-resident withholding tax

Analyzing Real Estate Investments

■ **LEARNING OBJECTIVES**   *Upon completion of this unit, you should be able to*

- ■ **list** the three basic categories of changes and trends in the economy,
- ■ **itemize** the four phases of an economic cycle,
- ■ **name** four advantages of investing in real estate,
- ■ **list** at least four disadvantages of investing in real estate,
- ■ **itemize** five types of investment properties,
- ■ **enter** the major headings of an income property financial statement,
- ■ **list** and calculate four important income property ratios, and
- ■ **itemize** the three basic types of income tax deductions for investment property.

■ OVERVIEW

Investment in real estate has produced a substantial portion of the wealth of our country and its citizens. Real estate licensees should be prepared to assist buyers and sellers of investment real estate. Consumers expect their broker associates to have a basic understanding of the fundamentals of investment. An investment study includes analysis of the national and local economies, specifically as they relate to real estate.

Investing in real estate has advantages and disadvantages, and each investor must determine if an investment is suitable. This unit focuses primarily on investment opportunities in smaller income properties such as raw land and residential, office, and commercial properties.

Basic investment ratios help buyers analyze properties to help reduce risk. Several methods presented may help an investor use these ratios to determine the appropriate amount to offer for a property.

While federal income taxes are an important consideration when weighing an investment in real estate, the property's operating economics are more important.

■ THE GENERAL BUSINESS ECONOMY

Timing is important in real estate investment. A good property purchased at the wrong time may result in substantial losses to the investor. Many investors also understand that a rapidly appreciating real estate market can make even marginal properties show acceptable returns. Before deciding which type of real estate is right, the investor must try to understand the current economic trends.

Trends in the business economy may either originate from or result in changes in the real estate market. The condition of one directly affects the condition of the other. Changes and trends in the general economy fall into four basic categories: seasonal variations, **cyclic fluctuations**, specific cycles, and random changes.

Seasonal Variations

Changes that recur at regular intervals at least once a year are called **seasonal variations**. Such changes arise from both nature and custom. In the northern United States, for example, construction stops during the winter months; this seasonal change affects both the general economy and the real estate economy. Customs such as the nine-month school year have a seasonal effect on residential sales. Each year, the population of the mountain resorts increases during the ski season.

Cyclic Fluctuations

Business cycles usually are defined as wavelike movements of increasing and decreasing economic prosperity. A **cycle** consists of four phases: expansion, recession, contraction, and recovery.

Production increases during **expansion** periods. High employment levels, wages, and consumer purchasing power increase demand for goods and services. Prices rise because of greater demand and credit is easy, making more money available for purchasing.

Recession is defined as two successive quarterly declines in the **gross domestic product (GDP).** The GDP is the sum total of goods and services produced by the United States. The four major components of the GDP are consumption, investment, government purchases, and net exports.

Contraction begins immediately after recession. Confidence in the economy is shaken and consumers reduce spending in anticipation of lower earnings.

Slower sales cause reduced production, worker layoffs, and unemployment. Prices are reduced to clear out inventories of unsold goods.

Recovery, defined as two successive quarterly increases in the GDP, begins when consumers, lured by lower prices, venture back into the market. As business activity increases, confidence begins to return. Slowly, production facilities gear up to meet the new consumer demand, capital begins to flow back into business enterprises, and additional employees are hired. Finally, as the gradual rise in employment generates more spendable income and an increasing demand for more goods, the business cycle again enters the expansion phase.

Although business cycles technically consist of the four phases defined above, most discussions deal simply with expansion and contraction, measuring expansion from trough to peak and contraction from peak to trough. Business cycles are recurrent, but not periodic; that is, they vary in duration and timing. Economists have observed that a complete cycle in the general economy may vary from 1 to 12 years in length.

Specific Cycles

Specific cycles are wavelike movements similar to business cycles. They occur in specific sectors of the general economy, such as the real estate economy, and in individual sectors of the real estate economy, such as housing starts and real estate sales. Specific cycles do not always coincide with cycles of the general business economy, as the business cycle actually is a weighted average of all specific cycles.

Regardless of the state of the national economy, certain areas boom in recessions and stagnate in prosperous times because local demand runs counter to current broad economic trends. Colorado has long been affected by the cost of oil and gas, which has often created a boom and bust cycle.

■ **EXAMPLE A.1**   Review the following selected headlines from a major business newspaper. Then, with a group of others, discuss what the likely effects will be on real estate investment properties, real estate brokerage firms, and other investment possibilities. Discuss which businesses will suffer in the near term and which will prosper.

Selected headlines in an inflationary economy include the following:

"Strong business expansion under way, may lead to inflationary pressures on the economy"

"General Motors reports quarterly sales increase of 22%. Stock price surges!"

"Current rate of inflation is _____ %, expected to be at 9% within six months"

"Retail sales increase dramatically, paced by JC Penney, Wal-Mart, and The Limited"

"Federal Reserve Board raises discount rate ½%"

"Economists foresee higher interest rates soon"

"Travel industry sees bumpy road ahead if oil prices increase substantially"

"'Mortgage interest rates anticipated to rise to 12–14% in six months,' warns Citibank economist"

"Inflation will continue for at least two years, according to Congressional Budget Office"

"Oil prices in the $85 price range within two months, say industry sources"

Random Changes

Random changes are irregular fluctuations of the economy that may be caused by legislative and judicial decisions or by strikes, revolutions, wars, fires, storms, floods, or other catastrophes. These changes, impossible to predict or analyze, may affect one or more sectors of the aggregate economy. They may influence all industries in an area or one industry nationwide. Real estate activity, especially construction, is very vulnerable to labor strikes, political changes, and natural disasters. One example of a random change in regard to real estate is a zoning ordinance change allowing undeveloped land to be used for industrial purposes that would stimulate construction activity locally. Government policy changes and changes in tax laws also can cause random changes in real estate activity on a nationwide scale. Investors must be aware of what is happening on both the national and local levels and have contingency plans to cope with events as they occur.

■ THE REAL ESTATE ECONOMY

The real estate economy is an important component of the general business economy, subject to the same four types of fluctuations. Specific cycles are the most pronounced and important trends that appear in the real estate sector. They can be observed in all phases of real estate: land development, building, sales, finance, investment, rental, and redevelopment.

Most sectors of the real estate economy are subject to both long and short cycles. Long-term cycles last from 15 to 22 years and short-term cycles about 3 years.

A controlling factor in the building cycle is the availability of money and credit in the mortgage and construction markets. In general, when the economy is strong and prices are rising, the Federal Reserve tightens the money supply to control inflation. The resulting higher interest rates make real estate investment less attractive because builders must either pass the higher costs on to consumers or accept lower profits. Either situation slows the rate of construction. Conversely, interest rates decline during a recession, making construction of new projects more feasible.

An extremely important indicator for forecasting the economy is the monthly report of housing starts, published by the Census Bureau between the 16th and the 20th of each month. Housing starts, along with auto sales, are the first to rise in an economic recovery and the first to drop in a recession. Not only does new housing have a direct effect on the market but housing-related purchases such as furniture and appliances also fuel a rebounding economy.

Building permit data are released with the housing starts report. Because permits are secured about a month ahead of construction starts, reviewing the increase or decrease in building permits gives a pretty good idea of what housing starts will do in the next month.

Once investors have satisfied themselves that the general economic situation is sound, it may be time to review the advantages and disadvantages of investment in real estate.

■ REAL ESTATE INVESTMENT ANALYSIS

Most of the wealthy people in this country amassed their great fortunes from real estate investments. The most significant asset of most families is the equity in their homes. Real estate may not be the right investment for everyone, however. Advantages and disadvantages exist, and should be evaluated by each individual.

Advantages of Investing in Real Estate

The advantages of investing in real estate include leverage, good return, shelter from federal income taxes, and personal control of the asset.

Leverage   Leverage is the use of other people's money to increase the investor's return. Few other investments offer the high leverage real estate does. Stocks and bonds typically require at least a 50 percent down payment; mutual funds want 100 percent invested. Yet, real estate investments can be made with a 25 percent down payment and, in many cases, less. The following example shows the benefits of leverage.

■ **EXAMPLE A.2**   Jack Gormley is considering the purchase of a duplex in an attractive neighborhood. He has reviewed the rental records for the previous four years that the property manager provided. The property's net income has increased about 4 percent annually. Property values have increased at about the same rate. The property value is $100,000, with a $20,000 down payment. Based on the new financing, Jack anticipates before-tax cash flows of about $1,500 per year. He wants to compare this investment with a mutual fund that has averaged a 10 percent return over the previous five years. Assuming a holding period of five years and an annual property appreciation of 4 percent, how does the simple arithmetic look?

Property value at a 4 percent annual compound rate	$121,665
Less mortgage balance at year five	$73,800
Equals increase in equity	$47,865
Plus $1,500 per year for five years	$7,500
Equals total cash from investment	$55,365

The final figure averages $11,073 for each year. Divided by the original investment of $20,000, the average annual return is about 55 percent. The return from annual cash flows was only 7.5 percent ($1,500/$20,000); the balance came from the increase in equity.

This type of analysis would be more accurate using the discounted cash flow approach, but the mutual fund returns would come in about the same pattern, making the comparison valid. Because of leverage, Jack's clear choice is the real estate.

Good returns   Many careful and astute investors achieve excellent returns, often exceeding 20 percent.

Income tax shelter   Most investment opportunities such as savings accounts, bonds, stocks, and mutual funds require that the investor pay taxes on all current income (dividends). Real estate investments often provide tax-deferred cash flows, primarily because of cost recovery deductions (depreciation). This allows the investor to avoid paying taxes on the cash flows until the property is sold.

Exchanging and installment basis reporting are other ways to defer paying taxes. They will be discussed later in this section.

More personal control   Many investors are uncomfortable with the notion of entrusting their assets to other persons or companies with little or no control over the use of those assets. The purchase of real estate gives an investor much more control over the investment's operation and management. This is true even if the investor employs a property manager, as the manager is under the investor's control.

Disadvantages of Investing in Real Estate

Disadvantages of investing in real estate include management time, high capital requirements, poor liquidity, personal stress, and high risk.

Management time   Along with the advantage of personal control comes the disadvantage of the amount of time required to manage the property. Continuing review and management of an income property's operations is absolutely essential. A prudent investor takes an active role in overseeing management. The investor must seek a higher return on the investment to compensate for the time requirements.

High capital requirements   Real estate requires a substantial capital investment. The investor needs funds to acquire the property and must have reserve funds available to make major renovations when required or to cover unexpected events. If vacancy rates are high, the investor will find it difficult to sell the property and may need to inject more money into the real estate to pay its operating costs and debt service to carry through the hard times.

Poor liquidity   Investment real estate is a complicated purchase, even in the best markets. Land-use requirements, environmental audits, maintenance inspections, lease reviews, and new financing all take a substantial amount of time. A seller must understand that it could be a year or more after putting the property on the market before a sale is closed. In bad markets, however, it can be close to impossible to sell property at a fair price because so many other properties are available. This is a significant disadvantage of investment real estate.

Personal stress   Many first-time real estate investors suffer rude awakenings when they discover that property management isn't just about cash flow projections and planning, but also about personal interaction with tenants. Because an owner's first few properties usually are not large or profitable enough to justify hiring a manager, an owner is left with the task. When the mortgage payment is due, slow-paying tenants can become an irritation. Tenant complaints take time and interpersonal skills to resolve. Tenants sometimes leave a property in poor condition when they move, requiring a large contribution of time and money to restore the premises for the next tenant. Eviction is sometimes necessary and is usually distressing to both landlord and tenant.

High risk   It is said that the longer an asset is held, the greater the chance of catastrophe. Many examples exist of seemingly good real estate investments gone bad. It could result from overbuilding in the market causing high competition and lower rents. Environmental laws also may require expensive retrofitting. Or a major employer may relocate to another area, causing widespread unemployment. Insurance does not cover this dynamic risk. To overcome dynamic risk, the investor must analyze a property carefully before purchasing, then manage it effectively.

Static risk is risk that can be insured. Examples include fire, windstorm, accident liability, floods, appliance contracts, and workers' compensation.

TYPES OF INVESTMENT PROPERTY

A wide range of property is available for investment, and the type of property suitable for an investor often depends on the investor's age, assets, and risk profile. Young investors usually are willing to take greater risks. This may be due partly to optimism that has not been dimmed by hard knocks and partly to higher energy levels. Older investors want to keep what they have because they don't have a lot of time to get it back if it is lost. They avoid high risk and are more likely to look for attractive current cash flows as opposed to speculative appreciation.

Persons with very few assets have little to lose and are often risk-takers in their efforts to strike it rich. Persons who are financially comfortable usually are more conservative in their investment decisions.

Risk-averse investors ordinarily are not comfortable with industrial property, speculative land, or new construction of income property. They are more likely to want established income property with a proven record of income.

Types of investment property are raw land, residential income properties, office buildings, commercial properties, and industrial properties.

Raw Land

Investment in raw land can be extremely profitable if good research skills, good instincts, and good luck come together in one transaction. This type of property investment also can be extremely risky for the novice investor. Cities and counties in Colorado, when trying to get a handle on growth guidelines, often change land uses in an area, which may have either wonderful or disastrous consequences for the investor. Income tax laws can change the feasibility of many projects. Raw land usually does not offer a cash flow to the investor and requires continuing infusions of funds to pay property taxes and interest on mortgages. Timing is important because the longer the property is held, the lower the rate of return tends to be.

The most important determinant of value for a vacant site is location. If land is planned for commercial use, it must have access and visibility from a major arterial road. Shopping centers should have easy access to expressways. Topography is important because it can affect building costs to correct for heavily sloping land.

Residential Income Properties

A single-family home usually is the investor's initial purchase. A single-family rental home provides the investor with a breakeven cash flow or a little income if the investor combines good management with good luck. It also has some limited tax advantages from depreciation. Because the margins are so slim, however, a vacancy for even a month can wipe out all the profit for the year.

As the investor's assets and borrowing power grow, the next investment may be a multifamily property. Larger properties benefit from the efficiencies of land use and management. Where single-family homes usually are breakeven propositions for the investor, larger properties can bring substantially higher yields. Because of the much larger investment required, a buyer should make a complete and detailed investment analysis.

Office Buildings

In the 1980s, office building construction was spurred on by the tax code and by infusion of capital into the market through limited partnerships. As a result, the office market became overbuilt in almost every major city and vacancy rates of 25 percent were common. Many of the buildings were economically unsound and there were many foreclosure sales. The market finally began to recover in the late 1990s and developers are building again. Lenders, however, still are cautious and demand strong financial statements and tenant commitment to ensure reasonable occupancy rates when the buildings are complete.

Small investors must analyze the office building market carefully before committing their funds. What is the competition? How many new buildings are permitted? What's happening in the area economy? It is not enough to look at the overall occupancy rate. An investor should segment the market by age, location, and amenities. It is possible that vacancies are high in the older downtown buildings, while newer suburban office parks are nearly full. Prestige office buildings can be unprofitable for the investor. They're really pretty, but often have low yields.

When analyzing the rent rates for competitive properties, the investor should pay careful attention to the services and tenant improvements included. Many buildings pay for utilities and janitorial service and give each tenant an initial allowance for partitioning.

Many investors prefer office buildings to residential apartments because tenants tend to occupy the properties longer, tenant complaints usually are made during business hours, and fewer collection problems occur. Smaller office buildings tend to have somewhat higher tenant turnover than buildings rented by national tenants.

Commercial Properties

Many opportunities exist for small investors as well as shopping center developers to invest in commercial properties. Small strip shopping centers, because of their rectangular shape, lend themselves well to a variety of uses. They can be converted from storefronts to offices to restaurants with relatively little expense. A typical strip center consists of a 100 foot by 60 foot building with four 25 foot or five 20 foot wide bays. The market in many areas became very soft during the last economic downturn, making new construction loans difficult to obtain for some years. The market has improved in recent years, becoming attractive again to small investors.

Larger neighborhood shopping centers usually include a grocery store or a drugstore as the anchor, along with some personal service stores such as dry cleaners, laundromats, or restaurants.

Community shopping centers may include a Home Depot, Kmart, or Stein Mart as the anchor, along with a supermarket and other retailers, restaurants, and service companies. Management should try to arrange the mix of tenants so that each complements the others in the center; the overall effect is to generate additional traffic. Lease terms in these centers run longer than in strip centers. Professional property managers usually manage centers of this kind.

Regional shopping centers usually have three or more major department stores as anchors. They generally are located near expressways to draw more distant shoppers to the sites. The centers often have large numbers of general merchandise retailers. A professional manager is essential to enhance the value of this very large investment.

Industrial Properties

Industrial properties usually are located near expressways, airports, seaports, or railroad lines. Investment in industrial property requires substantial research and carries significant risk. Most small investors should be wary about investment in this market. Many industrial properties serve special purposes and are subject to long periods of vacancy in market downturns. However, with a successful company as a tenant, an industrial property can achieve reasonable returns.

▉ MARKET ANALYSIS

Once the investor is satisfied that the economy is sound and begins to target the type of property for investment, a market study is the next necessary step. A regional market analysis should include demographic and economic information such as population statistics and trends, a list of major employers in the area, and income and employment data. It should explore the economic base of the city and prospects for the future in that locale. A neighborhood market analysis should assess five major factors:

1. *Boundaries and land usage.* Rivers, lakes, railroad tracks, parks, or major highways may help define the neighborhood's boundaries.
2. *Transportation and utilities.* Transportation and utilities are crucial to the success of income property. The investor should analyze the effect of major traffic artery changes, as well as proposed or scheduled widening of streets, opening or closing of bridges, or new highway construction, all of which may enhance or hurt a location.

3. *Local economy.* The investor also should review the neighborhood's economic health. Rental rates in the neighborhood are a sound indicator of the real estate market's economic strength. The investor can obtain the most reliable current rental rate information by shopping the competition.
4. *Supply and demand.* A high occupancy rate indicates a shortage of space and the possibility of rental increases. A low rate, as evidenced by many for rent signs posted in the area, results in tenant demands for lower rents and other owner concessions.
5. *Neighborhood amenities and facilities.* The neighborhood's social, recreational, and cultural amenities can be important. Parks, theaters, restaurants, schools, and shopping centers attract potential tenants.

■ FINANCIAL ANALYSIS

After analyzing the market, the investor must examine the property's financial performance. This provides the basis for estimating the property's value, based on return criteria the investor establishes. Assembling the data is the most time-consuming part of the analysis process. The investor must review the property's financial history, as well as rent data, financial results, and amenities for competing properties. The first step after assembling the data is to prepare a one-year financial statement for the property.

Estimate Potential Gross Income

By multiplying the amount of space in the building by the base rental rate for that type of space, the investor can estimate rental income for each type of space found in the building. For example, the residential investor multiplies the number of studio, one-bedroom, and two-bedroom apartments by the rent for each type. The total of the estimated rent amounts from each type of space is the **potential gross income (PGI)** for the entire property.

Estimate Effective Gross Income

Effective gross income (EGI) is potential gross income minus vacancy and collection losses plus other income. Vacancy and collection losses are forecast from the experience of the subject property and of competing properties in the market, assuming typical, competent management. A good balance of supply and demand is a 95 percent occupancy rate. Occupancy rates change based on changing economic conditions, such as rising unemployment rates or overbuilding. Other income from sources such as vending machines and laundry areas is added to potential gross income *after* subtracting vacancy and collection losses.

Estimate Operating Expenses

The next step is to calculate the property's **operating expenses (OE)**. Operating expenses are divided into three categories: fixed expenses, variable expenses, and reserves for replacement (see the next paragraph). Ad valorem taxes and property insurance are examples of fixed operating expenses. Their amounts normally do not vary with the level of the property's operation. Variable expenses include items such as utilities, maintenance, trash removal, supplies, janitorial services, and management. These expenses are determined in direct relationship with the level of occupancy. Regional norms for these expenses are available through trade journals and professional property management associations.

Establish Necessary Reserves for Replacement

If the level of expenses fluctuates widely from year to year, based on major maintenance and replacements of property components, it is difficult for the analyst to get a clear picture of typical expenses. To be meaningful, the expense figure must be stabilized. This is accomplished by establishing a **reserves for replacement** category of expenses. It is not a current cash outlay but an annual charge that should account for future expenses. The most accurate way to establish reserves is to divide the cost of each item and piece of equipment by its expected useful life in years.

Estimate Net Operating Income

The **net operating income (NOI)** is obtained by deducting operating expenses (fixed, variable, and reserves) from effective gross income.

Determine Before-Tax Cash Flow

Income properties normally are purchased with mortgage financing, so owners must make mortgage payments from the NOI. When an annual mortgage payment is subtracted from NOI, the remaining amount is called **before-tax cash flow (BTCF),** sometimes called *cash throwoff.*

Constructing a Financial Statement for a Residential Investment

The following example describes the process of analyzing a residential investment. Sigrid Fleming is considering an investment in an apartment property. The property, which is about seven years old and well-maintained, is located near some office buildings and shopping. Many of the tenants are employed in clerical and secretarial positions. The rental rates are very competitive in the area. Sigrid's broker has given her the bookkeeper's statements for the previous two years. Based on those statements and information from competing properties, she has constructed an operating statement.

Ratio analysis   Sigrid's next step is to prepare a ratio analysis that helps her evaluate different investment opportunities. Some of the important ratios include capitalization rate, equity dividend rate, cash breakeven ratio, and debt coverage ratio.

The capitalization rate   Capitalizing net operating income is a basic approach to estimating value. While an appraiser uses a rate determined by verified sales in the marketplace, an investor sets the rate that provides an acceptable return using subjective criteria the investor establishes. The capitalization rate is the one-year before-tax operating return on a real property investment without considering debt service on the property. If an investor pays all cash for a $300,000 investment and the net operating income is $30,000, the rate of return is 10 percent.

This is calculated by dividing the net operating income by the value ($30,000 ÷ $300,000).

■ **EXAMPLE A.3**   What is the capitalization rate for the Villas Apartments?

If Sigrid desires a return of 14 percent, what will she pay for the property?

Assume, however, that the investor would not purchase the property unless it yielded 12 percent. By dividing the net operating income by the rate desired ($30,000 ÷ 0.12), the investor would agree to pay only $250,000.

Equity dividend rate   The equity dividend rate differs from the capitalization rate when a mortgage is considered in the analysis. If no mortgage exists, the capitalization rate is the same as the equity dividend rate. To calculate the equity dividend rate, divide the before-tax cash flow by the equity (value minus the mortgage).

Therefore, a property returning $14,000 after the owner makes the mortgage payment and having equity of $102,000 returns 13.7 percent on the equity ($14,000 ÷ $102,000). This percentage sometimes is called the *cash-on-cash return*.

Many investors believe that the equity should return 50 percent more than current mortgage rates. If mortgages are currently 8 percent, for example, the investor should look for at least a 12 percent return.

Assume that the above investor will purchase only if the property returns 16 percent on the equity. In that case, the investor would want to reduce the down payment from $102,000 to $87,500, determined by dividing the cash flow by the desired return ($14,000 ÷ 0.16). The price is determined by adding the down payment to the mortgage calculated originally.

■ **EXAMPLE A.4**   What is the equity dividend rate for the Villas Apartments?

If Sigrid desires a return of 16 percent, what down payment would she be willing to pay?

What price would she pay (add the down payment to the mortgage)?

Differences between the capitalization rate and the equity dividend rate   If the equity dividend rate is higher than the capitalization rate, the investor has achieved positive leverage. If the equity dividend rate is lower than the capitalization rate, negative leverage exists. Investors want positive leverage.

In the Villas Apartments, positive leverage exists. The capitalization rate is 11.67 percent, and the equity dividend rate is 14.75 percent. The investor increased the return by borrowing money with a favorable repayment rate. The repayment rate is called the **annual mortgage constant,** with a symbol of **k.** The annual constant is calculated by dividing the annual debt service by the original mortgage balance. In the Villas, the annual debt service is $87,235, and the mortgage is $800,000; *k* is

10.9 percent (the interest rate is 10 percent, and principal amortization accounts for the balance.) The rule then becomes simple: *To achieve positive leverage, k must be lower than the capitalization rate.*

Cash breakeven ratio   This ratio is extremely important to the investor because it shows the level of occupancy required to generate enough revenue to make the required payments for expenses and debt service. It is calculated by dividing the cash outflows (expenses and debt service) by the potential gross income. The operating expenses should show only those expenses required to be paid in cash. Reserves for replacements usually are not a cash expense.

Assume that a small retail strip center has potential gross income of $100,000, annual expenses of $40,000, including $4,000 in reserves for replacements, and annual debt service of $47,000. What is the breakeven ratio? Divide the total cash expenses ($40,000 – $4,000 = $36,000) plus the debt service by the potential gross income: $36,000 + $47,000 ÷ $100,000 = 0.83, or 83%.

If all bays in the center rent for the same amount, the developer knows that the occupancy rate must be greater than 83 percent or the developer will have to use his own funds to make up the shortfall.

■ **EXAMPLE A.5**   What is the cash breakeven ratio for the Villas Apartments? What will be the impact on the owner if the vacancy rate is 20 percent?

Debt service coverage ratio   A lender is concerned if a property has net operating income that is too low to allow the owner to make mortgage payments easily. The lender wants a cushion so that even if vacancies or expenses increase, enough income will remain to make the mortgage payment. The debt coverage ratio demonstrates the amount of cushion. It is calculated by dividing the net operating income by the annual debt service.

Assume the strip center discussed above has a 5 percent vacancy rate, the net operating income is $55,000, and the annual debt service is $47,000. The debt service coverage ratio is 1.17. That means the net operating income is 117 percent of the amount needed to cover the mortgage payment (a 17 percent cushion). A lender feels more comfortable with a coverage ratio of at least 1.3.

■ **EXAMPLE A.6**   What is the debt service coverage ratio for the Villas Apartments? Does it appear to be adequate?

The ratios discussed above should not be used solely to report on a property's status. Astute investors use the ratios to help them determine the prices they would be willing to pay based on income and cash flows. For instance, assume the seller's broker provided the statement on the Villas Apartments. After Sigrid Fleming verifies the statement for accuracy and prepares the ratio analysis as described above, she may be prepared to make an offer on the property. The following format uses two calculations to assist in that process. The first calculation estimates the amount of mortgage loan that would be available; the second determines how much down payment the investor is willing to make. When the two figures are added, the result is the purchase price.

Estimating the Amount of Available Financing Based on Lender Standards

To determine the financing, the investor needs to know the lender's requirements for the debt service coverage ratio and also needs to calculate the mortgage **loan constant** (k) based on current lending rates. Dividing the NOI by the required debt coverage ratio generates the allowable annual debt service. Dividing that figure by the loan constant results in the available loan amount.

Assume that the mortgage market will allow a commercial building a 25-year loan at a rate of 8 percent. The monthly payment factor is 0.00772 and the annual factor is 0.09261. The second factor is k. With a net operating income of $55,000, a required debt coverage ratio of 1.3, and an annual loan constant of 0.09261, the annual debt service can be $42,308, as shown below:

1. Net operating income ÷ Debt coverage ratio = Annual debt service

$$\$55,000 \div 1.3 = \$42,308$$

2. Annual debt service ÷ Mortgage loan constant = Mortgage loan amount

$$\$42,308 \div 0.09261 = \$456,840$$

Calculating the down payment based on investor return standards   The next step is to calculate the maximum down payment. Once the mortgage amount is determined, the investor subtracts the annual debt service from the net operating income to get before-tax cash flow. If the investor divides that figure by the required equity dividend rate, the result is the down payment the investor is willing to make.

In the example above, we estimated that the debt service allowed by the lender is $42,308. The net operating income is $55,000. Deducting the debt service of $42,308 results in a $12,692 cash flow. If the investor's required return is 15 percent, the down payment would be $84,613, as shown below:

1. Net operating income – Debt service = Before-tax cash flow

$$\$55,000 - \$42,308 = \$12,692$$

2. Before-tax cash flow ÷ Required rate of return = Down payment

$$\$12,692 \div 0.15 = \$84,613$$

Calculating the purchase price   Once the above two steps are complete, the purchase price is simply the addition of each figure. Continuing the above example, the calculation is as follows:

Mortgage amount available from lender	$456,840
Plus down payment from buyer	84,613
Equals purchase price offered	$541,453

This technique for valuing income property is superior to simply capitalizing net income.

Other Financial Analysis Techniques

More sophisticated discounted cash flow techniques require the use of financial tables or a financial calculator and include the *net present value*, the *internal rate of return*, and the *financial management rate of return*. In general, after-tax cash flows for future periods, including sales proceeds, are discounted back to the present value so that the pattern of receipts does not distort the analysis. While these techniques are important tools, they are beyond the scope of this text. The material is covered more fully in broker's courses and in commercial and investment real estate classes.

■ FEDERAL INCOME TAXES AND REAL ESTATE INVESTING

Real estate investors should not purchase property solely because of tax considerations. Many remember the large losses suffered by those who did so and were ruined financially by the 1986 Tax Reform Act. However, careful tax planning may help to maximize an investor's return on certain investments and should be considered when weighing alternative investments.

Income property owners enjoy certain tax advantages other investors do not. An owner is allowed three types of deductions from gross income when calculating taxable income from investment property: operating expenses, financing expenses, and depreciation.

Operating expenses include those cash outlays necessary for operating and maintaining the property. Financing expenses include interest on indebtedness and amortization of the costs of borrowing money, such as discount points.

Depreciation deduction is not related to the depreciation used in appraising, which is based on realistic improvement lives. This is an arbitrary method of allowing the investor to recover the cost of improvements over a specified period. Costs of residential income property may be recovered over a life of 27.5 years, and non-residential income property may be written off over 39 years. For example, if a person bought a duplex three years ago for $125,000, paid closing costs of $5,000, and obtained an appraisal showing that the building was worth 80 percent of the total, what is the depreciation deduction?

To determine the deduction, first allocate the acquisition costs to the building and the land, then divide the building's acquisition costs by the applicable depreciable life. The $125,000 purchase price plus the $5,000 in closing costs equals the acquisition cost of $130,000. Because the building is worth 80 percent of value, the building's depreciable basis is $104,000. Residential property is depreciated over 27.5 years, so $104,000 divided by 27.5 years equals a deduction for this year of $3,781.81.

■ **EXAMPLE A.7**   If closing costs on the Villas Apartments are $12,000 and the improvements are estimated to represent 75 percent of the total value, what is the depreciation deduction?

Tax-Deferred Exchange

While the new capital gains rates are attractive, most investors attempt to defer (not eliminate) paying any taxes by exchanging the property for *like* investment property. Like investment property includes real estate such as vacant land, residential income property, commercial income property, or industrial income property.

The rules do not require a barter of property. A person may sell investment property, escrow the proceeds out of his personal control, then identify another property to buy within 45 days, closing within 180 days.

Installment Basis Reporting

Taxes on the gain from the sale of a property need not be paid at once if the seller does not receive the proceeds in the year of sale. The law allows the taxpayer to pay taxes on the gain as the seller receives the proceeds. No minimum or maximum down payment is required. A loss on sale may not be reported using installment basis reporting.

■ SUMMARY

Real estate licensees are quite active in marketing investment properties. Most small investors concentrate initially on small residential properties but later may investigate the opportunities in the office and commercial markets.

An understanding of the general business economy is helpful in timing investment decisions. If the market is at the top of the cycle, buyers should be wary, but sellers might wish to market their properties aggressively. Specific cycles are the most important cycles that affect the real estate market. Low interest rates are a critical component to a strong real estate market.

Real estate investing offers many advantages, such as leverage, good returns, tax shelters, and personal control. However, those advantages are tempered by problems with stress, management time, risk, and poor liquidity.

After analyzing the market, an investor must prepare a careful financial statement, together with meaningful ratios. The investor can use the ratios to help determine what price to offer for the property.

Licensees have an opportunity to help their customers take one of the most important steps of their lives—beginning a program of real estate investment.

■ KEY TERMS

annual mortgage constant

before-tax cash flow
    (BTCF)

contraction

cycle

cyclic fluctuation

dynamic risk

effective gross income
    (EGI)

expansion

gross domestic product
    (GDP)

k

leverage

loan constant

net operating income (NOI)

operating expenses (OE)

potential gross income
    (PGI)

random changes

recession

recovery

reserves for replacements

seasonal variation

specific cycles

static risk

B
Professional Property Management

■ **LEARNING OBJECTIVES** *Upon completion of this unit, you should be able to*

- ■ **describe** the general duties of professional property managers;
- ■ **list** the four major classifications of rental properties;
- ■ **list** at least six important elements of a management contract;
- ■ **list** the four major property maintenance categories;
- ■ **describe** the requirements that determine the need for an on-site maintenance staff, contract services, or a resident manager;
- ■ **describe** the differences between a property manager and a resident manager;
- ■ **list** at least three different advertising media that help to market rental property;
- ■ **describe** the uses and benefits of a show list;
- ■ **identify** at least five of the essential elements of a valid lease; and
- ■ **identify** and explain the purpose of three of the financial reports an apartment building owner needs.

■ OVERVIEW

Investors generally agree that professional property management is the key to maximizing their returns. The professional property manager must have a comprehensive understanding of the economic forces at work in the real estate market and must be able to evaluate the property in terms of operating income, forecast its potential for the future, and construct a management plan that reflects the owner's objectives. The property manager must become a specialist skilled in space marketing, tenant psychology, the legal aspects of the landlord-tenant relationship, maintenance procedures, and accounting. This unit examines these topics.

■ INTRODUCTION TO PROPERTY MANAGEMENT

A professional property manager may be an individual licensee, a member of a real estate firm specializing in property management, or a member of the property management department of a large full-service real estate company. The professional property manager also may work within the trust department of a financial institution or within the real estate department of a large corporation or public institution. Regardless of their employment status, property managers pursue similar objectives and handle a wide variety of duties, including planning, merchandising, maintenance, and accounting. Although management duties vary according to the specific situation and particular property, a successful manager is competent in all of these areas.

Remember: A broker associate must have the permission of their employing broker to manage property. The employing broker will set up the trust accounts and will sign the management agreement.

The **Institute of Real Estate Management (IREM)** was created in 1933 by a group of property management firms as a subsidiary group of the National Association of REALTORS®. Currently, an individual wishing to join the institute must satisfy education and experience requirements, pass examinations given or approved by the institute, and adhere to a specific code of ethics. The individual is then awarded the prestigious designation **Certified Property Manager (CPM)** in recognition of reaching professional status as a property manager.

■ CLASSIFICATION OF REAL PROPERTY

Real estate property managers manage four major classifications of real property: residential, commercial, industrial, and special-purpose. Each classification can be further subdivided and requires a different combination of property management knowledge and skills. This unit introduces the field; it is not intended to be a complete discussion of property management. Residential property is emphasized in this introduction.

■ **EXAMPLE B.1** Relate a personal experience in renting or leasing residential property as a landlord or tenant.

Residential Property

Residential real estate is the largest source of demand for the services of professional property managers. Two principal categories of residential real estate exist: single-family homes and multifamily residences.

Single-family homes Freestanding, single-family homes are the most popular form of housing in the United States. According to the Census Bureau, more than 60 percent of housing in this country is owner-occupied and does not require professional management. Although homes that are rented to other parties often are managed directly by the owners, there is a growing trend toward professional management of such properties, particularly condominiums and vacation homes. Many large corporations and their relocation companies hire property managers for homes vacated by employees who have been transferred.

Rising construction costs and a decrease in the availability of usable land have resulted in the growing popularity of town houses, condominiums, and cooperatives. Although each unit is a single-family residence, the individual owners of the units share certain responsibilities, such as maintenance of the roof, common walls, grounds, and common facilities, for the development as a whole. They usually employ professional managers to handle these jobs and maintain accounting records.

Multifamily residences   The economy of design and land usage inherent in multifamily housing allows for a lower per-family cost of construction. Thus, multifamily residences are a rapidly growing segment of the national residential real estate market.

Multifamily residences can be held under various forms of ownership. Small properties of two to six units often are owner-occupied and owner-managed, whereas most large high-rise apartment communities are professionally managed for their owners. Cooperative and condominium apartments usually are owner-occupied buildings governed by boards of directors the owners elect. These boards generally hire professional managers for their properties.

Multifamily residences can be classified as garden apartments, walkup buildings, or high-rise apartments. Each type is unique in its location, design, construction, services, and amenities.

Owner-Broker Relationship

Three basic relationships can exist between the individual or corporate owner of a building and the property manager: owner-broker, employer-employee, and trustor-trustee. Property managers in all categories are considered professionals and their responsibilities are very similar. Because this section focuses on residential property management, only the principal-agent relationship is covered here.

Usually, when an owner engages a broker to be the property manager the broker acts as a single agent for the owner. The principal-agent relationship is created by a written contract signed by both parties that empowers the property manager, as agent, to act on behalf of the owner, or principal, in certain situations. Specifically, the agent acts for the principal to bring the principal into legal relations with third parties. Implicit in this fiduciary relationship are the legal and ethical considerations that any agent must accord to the principal. The property manager has the duties of skill, care, diligence, obedience, loyalty, accounting, disclosure, and confidentiality. Typically the property manager is considered to be a general agent for the principal.

■ THE MANAGEMENT CONTRACT

Once the property manager and the owner have agreed on principles, objectives, and a viable management plan, it is in both parties' best interests to formalize their accord. The manager and the owner must work out the structure of their relationship, their specific responsibilities and liabilities, the scope of the manager's authority, management fees, and the duration of the management agreement. In addition, the owner must turn over management records and other information to the manager to facilitate the property's operation.

Whether the property involved is a duplex or a high-rise complex, the responsibilities the manager assumes are of enough importance to warrant a written statement of intent. An agreement signed by both the manager and the owner defines the relationship between the parties, serves as a guide for the property's operation, and helps prevent misunderstandings. The terms of a management contract vary, but most share the following essential elements:

- Identification of the parties and the property
- The term of the contract
- Responsibilities of the manager
- Responsibilities of the owner
- Fees and leasing/sales commissions
- Signatures of the parties

■ PROPERTY MAINTENANCE

Maintenance is a continual process of balancing services and costs in an attempt to please the tenants, preserve the physical condition of the property, and improve the owner's long-term margin of profit. Efficient property maintenance demands careful assessment of the status of the building's condition. Staffing and scheduling requirements vary with the type, size, and regional location of the property, so owner and manager usually agree in advance on maintenance objectives for the property. In some cases, the owner instructs the manager to reduce rental rates and expenditures for services and maintenance. Under this shortsighted policy, the manager may encounter management problems and the manager's reputation may be affected adversely. Properties can command premium rental rates if they are kept in top condition and operated with all possible tenant services.

Types of Maintenance

The successful property manager must be able to function effectively at four different levels of maintenance operation:

- Preventive maintenance
- Corrective maintenance
- Routine maintenance
- New construction maintenance

Preventive maintenance is aimed at preserving the physical integrity of the premises and eliminating corrective maintenance costs. Regular maintenance activities and routine inspections of the building and its equipment disclose structural and mechanical problems before major repairs become necessary.

Corrective maintenance involves the actual repairs that keep the building's equipment, utilities, and amenities functioning as contracted for by the tenants. Fixing a leaky faucet and replacing a broken air-conditioning unit are corrective maintenance activities.

Routine maintenance is the most frequently recurring type of maintenance activity. Common areas and grounds must be cleaned and patrolled daily. Also, cleaning and housekeeping chores should be scheduled and controlled carefully because such costs easily can become excessive.

New construction maintenance, linked closely with leasing and tenant relations, is designed to increase the property's marketability. This may be as elementary as new wallpaper, light fixtures, and carpeting. If the new construction is extensive, it might include new entryways, the addition of a swimming pool, conversion of space to a meeting room, or renovation of a previously occupied space. New construction often is performed at a tenant's request and expense. Sometimes a landlord redecorates or rehabilitates a space for a tenant as a condition of lease renewal.

Deferred maintenance is necessary maintenance that cannot or will not be performed. Deferred maintenance results in physical deterioration, unhappy tenants, and reduced rent collections.

On-Site Maintenance Staff

The manager's hiring policy for on-site maintenance personnel usually is based on the cost differential between maintaining a permanent building staff and contracting for the needed services. For example, the amount of construction activity stemming from alterations tenants require determines the hiring policy. It makes sense to hire outside contractors for major construction jobs or for small buildings that cannot support permanent staffs.

The Building Owners and Managers Institute (BOMI) sponsors instruction that leads to professional designations for maintenance personnel and supervisors. These courses are particularly instructive for on-site maintenance personnel. Property managers who wish to learn more about the technical and mechanical aspects of their properties will find these courses a good source of information.

Contract Services

Services performed by outside persons on a regular basis for specified fees are known as **contract services.** For the protection of both the manager and the owner, a service contract always should be in writing and contain a termination provision. The latter stipulation becomes important if service is not satisfactory or if the property is sold.

Before entering into any service contract, the manager should solicit competitive bids on the job from several local contractors. The manager can then compare the cost of contracting with the expense of using on-site personnel. The management agreement terms often set a ceiling on the service contracts the manager can execute without owner approval. Window cleaning, refuse removal, pest control, and security are services that usually can be performed more efficiently and inexpensively by outside contractors. The manager should check a contracting firm's references and work history before employing them. The manager should determine whether the firm's employees are bonded and whether it has the necessary licenses or permits.

■ RESIDENT MANAGER—PROPERTY MANAGER RELATIONSHIP

Most properties of 20 units or more have a manager on the premises at all times. This **resident manager** is a salaried employee who usually coordinates rent collection, tenant relations, and maintenance work on the property. Obviously, these responsibilities increase with the building's size. The resident manager reports to the property manager. With this system, a single property manager can stay current with the operations of several large apartment properties without becoming consumed by the details. In addition to reviewing the reports submitted by resident managers, the property manager should visit each building regularly to gather information on necessary maintenance and repairs. Periodic inspections show the property manager how occupancy rates may be increased, indicate where operating costs can be cut, help improve tenant relations, and provide training and feedback reviews to the on-site manager.

In the past, building superintendents not only collected rents but also served as the maintenance staff. As the property management field grows more sophisticated and building equipment becomes more complicated, managers who perform all four maintenance functions have become the exception rather than the rule. Property managers are expected to recognize when maintenance is necessary and know where to turn for help with specific maintenance problems. While property managers need not be a jack-of-all-trades, they should understand the basic operation of mechanical and electrical systems well enough to make intelligent decisions about their care and operation. The managers also must understand the economics, staffing, and scheduling involved in the smooth performance of maintenance tasks.

The hiring and firing of employees should be under the control of the property manager, not the resident manager. When screening a potential employee or making a decision to terminate an employee, the property manager should ask for the resident manager's opinion of the person's integrity, industry, and skills.

■ MARKETING THE SPACE

Two basic principles of marketing are "Know your product" and "Your best source of new business is your present customer base." Thorough preparation is required to give a suitable presentation of the premises as well as to determine such items as rental rates and advertising methods necessary to attract tenants. Maximum use of referrals from satisfied tenants is the best and least expensive method of renting property and is essential to any marketing effort.

It is the property manager's responsibility to generate the maximum beautification and functional utility per dollar spent. Items such as an attractive lobby, well-landscaped grounds, and the use of pleasant colors inside and outside the building may not create greater functional utility, but they may increase marketability and profitability.

Rental space is a consumer good that can be marketed with promotional techniques like those used to sell cars or homes. Because most apartment renter prospects come to the property as a result of a neighborhood search, attractive signage and strong curb appeal is essential. Each residential property should display a tasteful sign on the premises identifying the community, the management firm, the type of apartment, the person to call for further information, and a telephone number. However, walk-ins alone will not supply all the prospects needed. Other types of advertising also are necessary to attract qualified tenants.

Advertising and Display

Even if the property is priced at the appropriate market level, the premises are clean and attractive, and the property has a good location, the building still may experience an unacceptable vacancy rate if prospective tenants are not attracted to inspect the premises. The most common advertising is newspaper classified and display ads and apartment guides. The broker should be careful to observe fair housing laws and restrictions when advertising; and be careful to discuss the house and not who should live there. Colorado license law requires that the brokerage name appear in all advertising.

Classified ads   Newspaper classified advertising is the most important advertising medium for renting apartments. The property manager must keep the prospective tenant's needs in mind when composing the ad. For example, in a neighborhood where three-bedroom apartments are difficult to rent, an ad may appeal to a broader segment of the market if it offers a two-bedroom apartment with den. The classified advertisement should include the amount of rent, apartment size, property address, and manager's phone number. A brief summary of the property's major amenities also is very effective.

Display ads   More prestigious residential projects, especially when newly built, find it advantageous to use display advertisements. These larger ads attract immediate attention, appeal to potential tenants' desire for attractive living space, and demonstrate the many amenities a building offers. The specific rental rates often are omitted, with reference to a general range.

■ **EXAMPLE B.2**   Find a copy of the entire classified ad section of your local newspaper. Examine the sections dealing with display ads for large residential properties and compare various ads' effectiveness. Also, examine the help wanted sections for property and resident managers.

Apartment Guides

Just as homes magazines are one of the most effective ways to market residential homes for sale, apartment guides appeal to potential tenants. Color photos make the property's presentation attractive and interesting. Many management firms report that the excellent response to ads in the guides is beginning to rival the effectiveness of newspaper classified advertising.

Broker Cooperation

While the ultimate objective of all selling activities is closing the sale or lease with the ultimate user, the property manager will want to take advantage of all opportunities for reaching customers. This means that sales efforts should be directed not only toward prospective buyers and tenants but also toward brokers and agents who can reach rental prospects.

Broker cooperation can be especially helpful when renting or leasing a new or very large development. Managers secure that cooperation by sending to key brokers brochures or newsletters describing available properties. Compensation usually is a split commission or referral fee. A manager also can make brokers aware of a property by making a personal presentation or by sponsoring an open house.

Rental Rate Strategy

Even when the space itself is clean, attractively decorated, and in good condition, market conditions may be such that some units cannot be leased. An alert manager quickly realizes which units are renting rapidly and which are not moving fast enough and either adjusts the price or changes the method of advertising and display.

The goal in establishing a rental fee schedule is to realize the maximum market price for each unit. If each apartment type is priced correctly, all types will have the same rate of demand; that is, demand for studio, one-bedroom, and two-bedroom units will be equal, and the manager will be able to achieve a balanced occupancy rate for all three types. However, this level of demand is the exception in the real market. More often than not, the manager will have to raise the base rent on the unit types that are fully occupied and decrease the rate for those units less in demand. An optimal price structure ensures a 95 percent occupancy level for all units. For this strategy to be economically sound, the revenue from the new 95 percent schedule must exceed the income that was collected when some types of units were fully occupied and others had tenant levels less than 95 percent. The optimum rental rates in a local market are best determined by market analysis.

Show List

To establish a reasonable rental price schedule like the one outlined above, the manager must follow certain organizational procedures, such as compiling a **show list.** This show list should designate a few specific apartments in the building that are currently available for inspection by prospects. No more than three apartments of each type and size should be on the list at any one time; when a unit is rented, it should be replaced by another vacated apartment that is ready for rental.

The manager should use the show list both as a control guide for the marketing program and as a source of feedback on its success or failure. The features of particular units are itemized on the list so that the manager can do a better and more informed selling job. The maintenance staff will have no problem keeping a small number of vacant units on the list in top-notch condition. The limited number of show units also suggests that space is at a premium and that the prospective tenant must make a decision quickly.

The show list and traffic count should be reviewed weekly to determine which units are not moving. Particular units may not rent even after several showings to prospects. The manager then should inspect these units personally to find out why they are hard to rent. All curable flaws (for example, worn carpeting or obsolete fixtures) should be corrected. If poor curb appeal is the problem, painting or cleaning up entranceways, planting new landscaping, cutting grass, and trimming shrubs often works wonders.

It is important that fair housing laws be observed carefully. The limited show list must never be used as a method of illegal steering within the property.

Selling the Customer

The best advertising programs, landscaping, decorating, and maintenance may be wasted if the rental agent is unresponsive or unprofessional or does not properly show the property. One of the most important ingredients in achieving occupancy targets is a well-trained rental staff who are personable, enthusiastic, and professional. Many large management organizations spend substantial time and money to ensure that rental agents have the technical knowledge and sales skills to best represent the property owner. The property manager should maintain records carefully, including guest books to record visitors' names. The rental agent should describe the result of each visit and record subsequent follow-up calls.

■ LEASES AND TENANT RELATIONS

Potential conflicts between property managers and tenants usually can be avoided when sound property management practices are employed. Sound management begins with negotiation between the property manager and the prospective tenant, the results of which should be in written form (the lease).

Essentials of a Valid Lease

The general requirements for a valid lease are similar to those for any legally enforceable contract:

- Complete and legal names of both parties (lessor and lessee)
- Legal description of the property
- Contractual capacity of the parties and legal purpose of the agreement
- Consideration or amount of rent
- Term of occupancy
- Use of the premises
- Rights and obligations of the lessor and lessee
- In writing and signed (if for more than one year)

Colorado does not have an approved lease form so licensees should use standard leases or one drafted by the owner, the owner's attorney, or the brokerage firm's attorney. The manager should explain the key points in the lease agreement. Rent collection policies should be covered. Tenants will usually pay rent promptly if the collection policy is efficient, effective, and reasonable. The manager should itemize other regulations that control the property and discuss the methods of enforcing them. The manager must be certain that the tenant understands maintenance policies and how responsibilities are divided between landlord and tenant. These policies and procedures are often outlined in a tenant brochure.

Most tenant-management problems center on maintenance service requests. When such a request is made, the tenant should be told immediately whether it will be granted. The tenant is the customer, not an adversary, and the staff should be reminded of that fact continually. Happy tenants remain in residence, eliminate expensive turnover, protect the owner's property (which lowers maintenance costs), and promote the property's reputation (which reduces vacancy losses and promotional expenses).

A tenant request for service should be entered on a standardized request form. The top copy and a copy to be left in the unit on completion of the work are assigned to the maintenance person answering the request. The manager keeps the third copy until the job is completed. An estimated completion date should be entered on the manager's copy for follow-up. The resident manager should contact the tenant to ensure that the work was completed properly.

OPERATING REPORTS

Owners of residential rental apartments need current operating reports to measure the profitability of their investments. The annual operating budget, cash flow statement, and profit and loss statement give an owner the data necessary to evaluate the property and its management.

Operating Budget

The property manager must prepare a meaningful annual operating budget that includes all anticipated income and expense items for the property. The starting point for this year's budget most often is based on the actual data from the previous year. The annual budget is helpful as a guide for overall profitability. It must, however, be broken down into monthly budgets if it is to be useful for controlling operations. There, the manager should produce monthly statements that compare actual and budgeted amounts and should be able to explain any significant variations.

Cash Flow Statement

Probably the most important operating record is the manager's monthly **cash flow report** on receipts and disbursements. This report includes all operating income, such as the income from parking, washing machines, dryers, and vending machines, and all operating expenses and debt service. The reports show the owner how the property is doing on a cash basis. The report also can include the annual budget as well as the previous year's results, providing a budgetary control and a cash control.

Profit and Loss Statement

A **profit and loss statement** is a financial report of a property's actual net profit, which may differ from the cash flow. The full mortgage payment is not shown; only the interest payment is an expense. The manager usually prepares a profit and loss statement quarterly, semiannually, and yearly. Monthly income and expense reports provide the raw data for these statements. The more detail provided in the report, the better the opportunity for meaningful analysis.

Additional Reports

Managers must be completely familiar with all phases of a property's operation. Other reports, such as vacancy ratios, bad-debt ratios, showings-to-rent ratios, and changes in tenant profiles, illustrate important trends that may require corrective action. Scrutiny of the budgets and actual expenditures per account from month to month and year to year can indicate the relative performance of management personnel.

LICENSING REQUIREMENTS IN COLORADO

Property managers, in general, must be licensed in Colorado. However, a regularly salaried on-site manager who reports to the owner or broker who manages the property need not be licensed. An unlicensed on-site manager may not negotiate the lease or other terms with tenants.

SUMMARY

When an owner hires a manager, the parties enter into one of three relationships: principal-agent, employer-employee, or trustor-trustee. Most management contracts share six basic characteristics and specify the duties and details of management operations that must be decided before responsibility for the property is transferred to the manager.

To handle the property's maintenance demands, the manager must know the building's needs and the number and type of personnel required to perform the maintenance functions. Staff and scheduling requirements vary with a property's type, size, and regional location.

Four types of maintenance operations exist: preventive maintenance, corrective maintenance, routine housekeeping, and new construction. Deferred maintenance is the term applied to accumulated postponed maintenance.

The hiring policy for on-site maintenance staff depends on the cost differential between maintaining a permanent building staff and contracting for needed services. A particular property's circumstances dictate which alternative is more efficient and economical.

Multifamily dwellings differ from one another in size, structure, location, and number of amenities provided. These differences exert a direct influence on the advertising techniques used to market each type of space. A show list of units available for inspection also is important to a property manager's marketing program, as is newspaper advertising, the most widely used medium for renting space because it reaches a large audience.

In addition to leasing, supervising the resident manager, and inspecting the maintenance of the premises, the property manager must provide the owner with regular financial reports. Various financial statements provide the owner with the data necessary to evaluate the performance of the manager and the property itself.

■ KEY TERMS

cash flow report
Certified Property Manager (CPM)
contract service
corrective maintenance
deferred maintenance

Institute of Real Estate Management (IREM)
new construction maintenance
preventive maintenance
profit and loss statement

resident manager
routine maintenance
show list

APPENDIX C

Answers to Lecture Outline Fill-Ins and Glossary Review

■ TRUST ACCOUNTS, UNIT 1: LECTURE OUTLINE

I.   TRUST ACCOUNTS

B. Establishing Brokerage Accounts

1. Brokerage firms typically have two types of accounts:

   a) <u>Operations</u> used for running the firm

   b) <u>Trust accounts</u> used to hold money for the benefit of others

4. Employed or broker associates are <u>not</u> permitted to have trust accounts.

6. Principal brokers who have trust accounts must follow specific rules. The principal broker

   a) must use a <u>high level</u> of accuracy and care;

   b) is personally responsible for the funds in the trust account;

   c) is subject to commission audit <u>at any time</u>; and

   d) should establish the trust account <u>prior</u> to receiving money belonging to others.

C. Operating a Trust Account

3. The trust account <u>may not contain operating</u> funds or any funds belonging to employed broker associates.

   a) Employed brokers' commissions are paid from the broker's <u>operations account</u>.

4. Care must be taken to not commingle the broker's funds with trust funds.

   a) The account may contain <u>sufficient brokerage funds</u> to open and operate the account.

   b) Commissions or other funds <u>that have been earned</u> and belong to the broker must be removed from trust account <u>promptly</u>.

D. How Many Trust Accounts Does a Broker Need?

1. A broker needs enough trust accounts to assure that funds will not be <u>commingled</u>.

2. The Commission requires the following types of separate accounts when the broker is holding funds for others:

   a) <u>Sales</u> trust account—for money held in connection with sales transactions pending closing, which is also known as <u>earnest money</u>.

   b) <u>Management</u> trust account—for money held in connection with property management services.

   c) <u>Security deposit</u> trust account—for refundable security deposits collected from tenants for lease and rental units under management by the broker.

E. Requirements for a Trust Account

1. Trust accounts must be in a bank or appropriate institution located in <u>Colorado</u>.

2. They must be insured by a government agency, such as the <u>FDIC</u>.

3. Trust accounts cannot be held in a <u>credit union</u> because only members' funds are insured.

4. Trust accounts must follow specific requirements of the Commission.

   a) The brokerage firm name and <u>principal broker's</u> personal name must be on account records.

5. The bank must recognize that the account is a trust account.

   a) Checks and <u>deposit</u> slips must indicate that it is a trust account.

F. Interest-Bearing Trust Accounts

1. The parties must agree if the account is to be interest bearing.

   a) Details of interest, fees, penalties, and disposition of interest are negotiated and <u>written into the contract</u>.

   b) These funds are placed in a trust account <u>separate</u> from all other funds held by broker.

2. Exception

   a) The broker's sales trust account may be an interest-bearing account if the interest benefits an <u>affordable housing program</u>.

II.   EARNEST MONEY

A. Earnest Money Deposits

1. Earnest money deposits are typically payable to the <u>listing brokerage firm</u> and presented with the contract offer.

2. The type of the <u>earnest money</u> (such as check or promissory note) is identified in the Contract to Buy and Sell.

   a) Earnest money is anything the seller will <u>accept</u>.

3. Checks must be deposited not later than the <u>third business day</u> following notice of <u>acceptance</u> of the offer.

4. Earnest money can be held in the trust account of a <u>third party</u>, such as a title company, with the permission of the parties.

5. The holder of the earnest money is identified in the contract and is often shown in the MLS. Listing brokers must advise buyer's brokers if the earnest money is to be held by a <u>third party</u>.

6. If a contract <u>terminates</u> under a provision of the contract or ends due to an undisputed default of either party, the broker is required to disburse the funds to the proper party without delay.

B. Earnest Money Promissory Note

1. A note is a reasonable alternative when the <u>buyer</u> has limited funds available when the offer is submitted.

2. Notes are made payable to the <u>listing brokerage</u> and must be identified with the due date specified in the Contract to Buy and Sell.

3. The due date must be before closing in time for the funds to be <u>good funds</u> at closing.

4. If the note cannot be collected when due, the <u>listing broker</u> must inform the seller immediately and is responsible for the collection of the funds.

   a) The seller can choose to declare the contract in default or agree to <u>extend</u> the contract.

   b) Costs of collecting the promissory note are the responsibility of the buyer.

III.   RECORD KEEPING

A. Records and Record-Keeping Systems

1. Principal brokers must have trust account records that include the following:

   a) Account journal of all cash receipts/disbursements—a <u>chronological record</u> of all activity in the account

b) <u>Beneficiary ledger</u> account system—records with specific details regarding the parties for each transaction

c) Broker ledger card—for funds <u>belonging to the brokerage firm</u>

d) Bank reconciliation records

(1) Trust accounts must be reconciled <u>every month</u> that there is activity in the account.

2. The transaction file will include all support documents for any funds held in the trust account. At minimum, these records include copies of the following documents:

a) Contract, <u>earnest money check</u>, Seller's Property Disclosure, listing or buyer representation agreement

b) Copies of the <u>closing statements</u> and other closing documents signed at closing for the parties they represented

3. Employing brokers are responsible to make sure that they have a complete file of all required documents and agreements made during the transaction.

a) Employed brokers are required to return files to the employing broker for review and filing <u>immediately</u> after the closing.

4. Brokers must maintain required records for a minimum of <u>four</u> years.

5. The <u>listing broker</u> must have the exclusive-right-to-sell listing contract in its file and the <u>buyer's broker</u> agreement or brokerage disclosure must be in the selling brokerage firm's file.

B. Safeguards

1. <u>Frequent reconciliation</u>

C. Commingling/Conversion of Trust Account Funds

1. <u>Commingling</u> is the improper mixing of operating account funds with trust account funds.

a) Not removing earned commissions or fees from the trust account <u>promptly</u> is an example of commingling.

2. The illegal practice of <u>conversion</u> is the use of one party's funds for the benefit of another party.

a) Paying bills for a property owner whose <u>ledger card</u> does not have sufficient funds, even though the check will clear the bank, is an example of this.

3. An owner's ledger card can have <u>a zero balance</u> at times—this is not commingling or conversion. However, a negative balance for an owner is most likely an example of conversion.

D. Property Management

1. Accounts

    a)   The management account holds funds belonging to the <u>property owners</u> and it is used to manage the property.

    b)   Security deposits must be held in an account separate from the owner's account because the funds belong to the <u>tenants</u> (unless meeting the less than seven rule).

    c)   Property management-related funds must be deposited into the appropriate trust account not later than <u>five business</u> days following receipt of the money.

    d)   Principal brokers who hold earnest money and manage properties must have the following:

        (1) A sales trust account to hold <u>earnest money</u>

        (2) At least one property management account for owners' funds

        (3) At least one <u>security deposit</u> trust account for tenants' funds

        (4) A broker can have an unlimited number of deposits for each type of funds in the above accounts—separate accounting using the <u>ledger card</u> identifies the individual transactions and properties.

2. Security deposits

    b)   The broker can turn the deposit over to the owner

        (1) with written authorization of tenant;

        (2) if the <u>lease</u> calls for it; or

        (3) after notifying the tenant in writing that the owner is holding the deposit.

    c)   The broker is responsible for security deposits and <u>must notify tenants</u> if no longer managing the property and advise tenants how to contact the new manager.

    d)   The security deposit must be returned in full or an accounting of the reason the deposit was kept must be sent to the tenant within one month or within <u>60 days</u> if the lease calls for it.

5. Homeowners' association records belong to the association not the brokerage firm. Rule E-3 requires that all such records be promptly returned to the association upon termination of the broker's employment. A broker may retain file copies at the <u>broker's own expense</u>.

IV. CLOSING FUNDS

A. <u>Good funds</u> must be available for closing.

B. Clients must bring their funds in good funds.

    1. A check made payable <u>to the client</u> is recommended.

V. CONFIDENTIAL INFORMATION

A. Client's confidential information, such as <u>motivating</u> factors or the willingness to consider different price or terms, must be filed so as to protect the client's information.

    1. Confidential information must be protected from <u>other brokers</u> within the firm.

    2. <u>Designated brokerage</u> eliminates imputed knowledge within the firm; other brokers are not presumed to have access to confidential information.

◼ CLOSINGS, UNIT 1: GLOSSARY REVIEW

1. An amount charged to a party to pay a bill is a <u>debit</u>.

2. The place where a broker holds money that belongs to other parties is a <u>trust account</u>.

3. An amount of $.01 per $100 charged when a deed is recorded is called the <u>documentary fee</u>.

4. The document from the county treasurer that summarizes the current status of taxes is the <u>certificate of taxes due</u>.

5. An amount received by a party to pay a bill is a <u>credit</u>.

6. The final settlement created by the terms of the Contract to Buy and Sell is called <u>closing</u>.

7. <u>Recording</u> a document creates constructive notice of the contents of the document.

8. A CREDIT to the broker is used to <u>pay a bill</u>.

9. Dividing expenses between the buyer and seller based on ownership periods is called <u>proration</u>.

10. A place where a lender holds borrower's funds to pay bills at a later time is a <u>lender reserve impound account</u>.

11. A summary of the financial part of a closing for one party to the transaction is a <u>closing statement</u>.

12. DEBITS and CREDITS are always in <u>equal</u> amounts.

■ CLOSINGS, UNIT 1: LECTURE OUTLINE

I.   **HOW THE CLOSING IS CREATED:**

A. The closing is created by the <u>Contract to Buy and Sell</u> along with other supporting documents, such as the closing instructions, tax certificates, and the title commitment.

B. There are <u>four parties</u> each with separate obligations that are involved in the closing process:

   1. <u>The seller</u> who is obligated to <u>clear all liens</u> on the property that are not being assumed by the buyer.

   2. <u>The buyer</u> who is obligated to meet all the requirements of the contract and <u>bring good funds</u> to closing.

   3. <u>The brokers</u> who are obligated to verify the party they represent is meeting the obligations of the contract. The broker is also responsible for the <u>closing statement</u> the party they have been <u>designated to represent</u>.

   4. <u>The closing company</u> hired by the buyer and seller in the <u>closing instructions</u> is obligated to complete the forms per these instructions.

C. The four most typical ways to close a real estate purchase are by using the following:

   1. <u>Cash</u>, which is covered in this unit.

   2. <u>Assumable loans</u> in which the buyer takes over the seller's existing loan.

   3. <u>Seller carry loans</u> often used with an assumable loan, which is covered in Unit 2.

   4. <u>New loans</u>, which are covered in Unit 3.

E. Responsibility for the proper accounting at a closing:

   1. Overall responsibility belongs to the <u>listing brokerage and listing broker</u>.

   2. Individual licensee responsibility: The <u>designated brokers</u> are responsible for the accuracy of the closing statement.

      a) The designated listing broker is responsible for the closing statement for the <u>seller</u>.

      b) The designated buyer's broker is responsible for the closing statement for the <u>seller</u>.

   3. Brokers are expected to attend the closing. If a designated broker is unable to attend, the <u>employing broker may appoint</u> broker may appoint another broker to attend.

      a) In this instance, all three brokers, <u>employing, original broker, and appointed broker</u>, will be responsible for the accuracy of the closing statement for the party represented.

F. Closing Company or Other Closing Entity

      b) Engages <u>the closing company</u> and outlines requirements for closing

II. BUYER'S AND SELLER'S COLUMNS

A. DEBIT, item owed (disadvantage), means one of the following:

    1. A <u>charge</u> to either the buyer or seller on the <u>day of closing</u>. OR

    2. If the DEBIT is to the seller, it reduces the amount of cash the <u>seller will take away from closing</u>.

B. Examples of seller DEBITS (items owed):
(Items that reduce the amount of cash the seller receives at closing)

    2. Property taxes for the <u>preceding year</u>; seller will owe the full amount

    5. Proration of rents collected for the month of closing, seller will <u>always owe the buyer a prorated share</u>

C. Examples of buyer DEBITS (items owed):
(Items that increase the amount of cash the buyer must bring to closing)

    1. <u>Selling price</u> of the property

D. Broker DEBIT: Deposit INTO the broker's column (escrow account)

    2. <u>Net Loan Proceeds</u> from the lender in a new loan

E. CREDIT: money received (advantage) means the following:

    1. A <u>benefit</u> to the buyer or seller (something they receive at closing)

    2. A reduction in the amount of cash the buyer must <u>bring to closing</u>

G. Examples of buyer CREDITS:
(Items that reduce the amount of cash the buyer must bring to closing)

    1. <u>Earnest</u> money already deposited by the buyer and held by the broker or closing company

III. OVERVIEW OF THE SIX-COLUMN WORKSHEET ENTRIES:

Line 1. Selling Price: Money the buyer owes the seller. **Used in all closings.**

Always <u>DEBIT buyer, CREDIT seller (DB CS)</u>.

Line 2. Deposit paid to: (broker): The buyer's earnest money deposit which is owed to the buyer at closing.

Always <u>CREDIT buyer, DEBIT broker (CB DBk)</u>.

Line 3. Trust Deed, payable to: The name of the lender for the assumable loan or new loan is listed here. In an assumption, the buyer is assuming this obligation of the seller so this amount represents money the seller will not receive at the closing table. In a new loan, this amount is a single entry credit to the buyer.

Assumption: always <u>DEBIT seller, CREDIT buyer (DS CB)</u> the amount from the assumption statement.

Line 6. Interest on Loan Assumed: The seller will owe the buyer interest for the portion of the month the seller lives in the property.

Always <u>DEBIT seller, credit buyer (DS CB)</u> the prorated share.

Line 7. Owner's Title Insurance Premium: The owner's title policy paid by the seller, per the terms of the Contract to Buy and Sell, and will only show on the seller's closing statement.

<u>DEBIT seller, CREDIT broker (DS CBk)</u> who will pay the bill.

> **Line 7a. Extended Title Insurance:** This additional coverage is negotiable per the terms of the contract. <u>DEBIT seller or buyer per the contract</u> and CREDIT broker who pays the bill.

Line 8. Closing Fee: This is the fee charged by the title company to close the transaction and is negotiable per the contract, may be paid by the seller, buyer, or split between the parties.

DEBIT <u>seller and/or buyer</u> per the terms of the contract. <u>CREDIT the broker</u> the full amount to pay the bill.

Line 9. Notary Fee: This fee is charged to the party that is signing the document.

DEBIT <u>seller for the warranty deed</u> and CREDIT broker.

DEBIT <u>buyer for the deed of trust</u> and CREDIT broker.

Line 11. Recording: Warranty Deed: Benefits the buyer by providing constructive notice of the buyer's new ownership of the property.

<u>DEBIT buyer, CREDIT broker (DB CBk)</u>.

Line 15. Documentary Fee: A buyer's expense, paid at the time of recording the warranty deed. It is calculated by moving the decimal point four places to the left in the selling price. Remember: = $.01 per $100.

<u>DEBIT buyer, CREDIT broker (DB CBk)</u>.

Line 16. Certificate of Taxes Due: The certificate that is obtained from the county treasurer and confirms the current status of governmental taxes on the property.

<u>DEBIT buyer, CREDIT broker (DB CBk)</u>.

Line 17. Taxes for Preceding Year(s): If the taxes from the preceding year are unpaid, they are an obligation of the seller.

Always <u>DEBIT seller, CREDIT broker (DB CBk)</u> to pay the bill to clear the lien.

Line 18. Taxes for Current Year: Will be a proration between the seller and the buyer. Since Colorado property taxes are paid in arrears, the seller will owe the buyer.

DEBIT seller, CREDIT <u>buyer the prorated share.</u>

Line 20. Special Taxes/Assessments: This line refers to government special assessments. The rule: if listed in the contract, the seller will pay in full at closing. If the buyer is to assume the bill, there is NO deduction at closing.

<u>DEBIT seller, CREDIT broker (DB CBk).</u>

Line 21. Personal Property Taxes: Typically a buyer responsibility.

DEBIT buyer, CREDIT broker.

Line 32. Water and/or Sewer: The water/sewer bill can be paid in advance or arrears. It will be prorated between the seller and buyer. Determine how to prorate based upon the information given.

Prorated between the parties. If a bill is owed, <u>CREDIT broker</u>.

Line 33. Rents: The seller collects the rent from the tenant in advance for the month. The seller will always owe the buyer for the buyer's prorated share.

DEBIT <u>seller, CREDIT buyer the prorated share.</u>

Line 34. Security Deposits: The seller is holding the tenants security deposit and it must be transferred in full to the new buyer.

Always <u>DEBIT seller, CREDIT buyer full amount.</u>

Line 37. Broker's Fee: This fee is typically paid by the seller.

<u>DEBIT seller, CREDIT broker (DS CBk).</u>

Line 39. Net Loan Proceeds: When a new loan is used, the broker will receive a DEBIT in this amount.

<u>DEBIT broker</u> (single entry).

V. PRORATIONS

1. <u>Buyer</u> owns on day of closing.

2. Use <u>365</u> days in a year (366 for leap year).

   a) Use calendar months—know how many days.

3. <u>Never prorate</u> the following:

    a) Security deposits

    b) <u>Loan payment due for month of closing,</u> since interest is paid in arrears a loan payment due pays the month before closing. The seller will owe the full amount.

    c) Special taxes (special assessments)

        (1) Contract says <u>seller</u> pays off special assessment.

        (2) If both parties agree, could <u>be assumed by the buyer</u> and <u>will not show up</u> on the Closing Statements.

B. How to Prorate

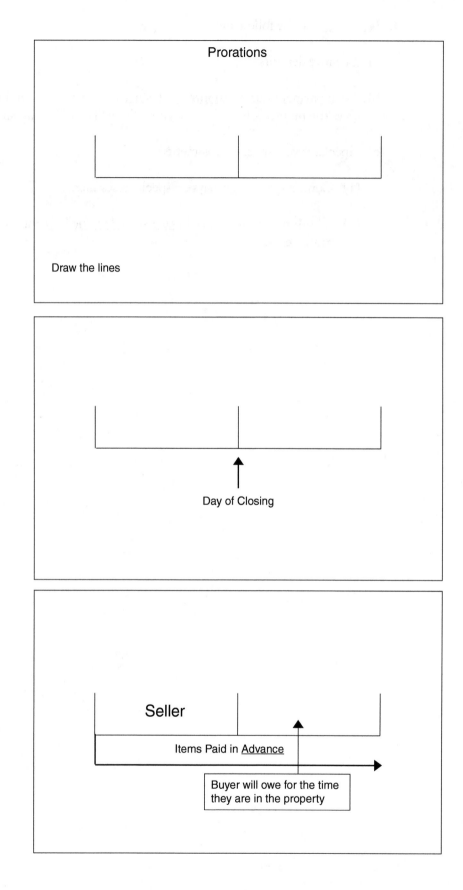

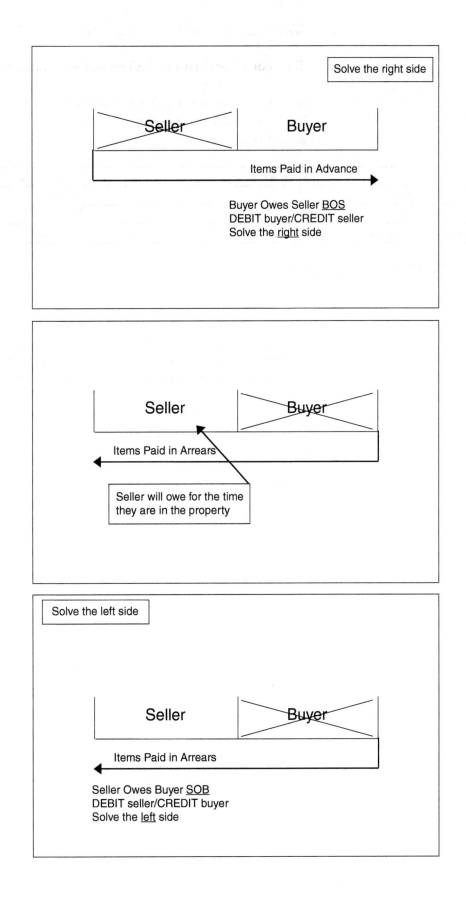

Whenever you prorate, the calculation is always the same:

Total bill ÷ Total days × Days owned = Prorated $

In Colorado, we use a 365-day year and the actual days in the month. February has 28 days, unless it is a leap year, not 30. For either test, follow the directions given in the exam.

	Banker's Year	Actual Year
Who owns the day of closing?	Seller	Buyer
Days in the month	30 in every month	Actual
How many days in the year?	360	365/366—leap

D. Proration example 1:

Step 6:

Calculate one party's share. In this case, taxes are paid in arrears, so the seller owes the buyer for the seller's 102 days of ownership prior to the closing. **The formula is always the same: Total bill ÷ Total days × Days owned.**

Tip: Use your calculator for the calculation and don't write down the daily amount to re-enter later. Most calculators easily retain the six decimal places needed to ensure an accurate calculation.

$1,366 ÷ 365 × 102 days = $381.73

DEBIT seller, CREDIT buyer

■ CLOSINGS, UNIT 2: GLOSSARY REVIEW

1. The document from the county treasurer reporting the current status of taxes due on a property is the <u>certificate of taxes due</u>.

2. A loan from the seller to the buyer to help finance the sale is referred to as <u>seller-carry financing</u>.

3. The fee paid to have the signature on a document witnessed and affirmed is the <u>notary fee</u>.

4. A loan guaranteed by a government agency is a <u>VA loan</u>.

5. A lender may hold borrower's funds to pay future bills such as taxes and insurance in <u>lender reserve / impound accounts</u>.

6. The exact amount of the <u>assumption balance</u> reported by the existing lender is a CREDIT to the buyer at closing.

7. <u>Hazard insurance</u> protects the owner from fire and other casualty losses.

8. <u>Special taxes/assessments</u> or localized improvements by the government will normally be paid off by the seller at closing.

9. A <u>CREDIT</u> in the broker's column typically represents a DEBIT from a buyer or seller.

10. When a buyer takes over responsibility for the seller's loan to help pay the purchase price of a property, this type of closing is called a <u>loan assumption</u> closing.

■ CLOSINGS, UNIT 2: LECTURE OUTLINE

I.   ASSUMPTION AND SELLER-CARRY LOANS

■ Mortgage interest is paid in <u>arrears</u>.

■ Payments are made on the <u>first</u> of the month (unless otherwise stated).

A. Assumption Statement

2. Use figures <u>exactly</u> as provided by the lender.

3. **Assumed Loans: (Line 3. Deed of Trust Payable to:)**

The amount for the loan being assumed will always:

a) be a seller <u>DEBIT</u> because this is a loan that is owed and will not be part of the funds the seller will receive for the sale.

b) be a buyer <u>CREDIT</u> because the buyer is taking over the loan and will not have to bring these funds to closing to pay for the property.

c) appear on both closing statements.

4. When a loan is being assumed, expect to see a <u>proration</u> of interest for the month of closing. Seller will owe buyer for the time the seller owns the property.

B. Prorating Interest on an Assumed Loan (Line 6. Interest on Loan Assumed)

2. For the proration of an assumed loan to be correct, it MUST be calculated using <u>monthly interest</u>.

3. **Special rule: Assumed interest is always annual interest divided by <u>12</u>.**

4. Always DEBIT <u>seller</u> and CREDIT <u>buyer</u>.

5. The amount for any loan payment due will always be:

a) Seller <u>DEBIT</u>

b) Broker <u>CREDIT</u> to pay the bill.

6. <u>Never prorate</u> a loan payment that is due, as it pays for the month before closing and is the full obligation of the seller.

C. Lender Reserves: (Lines 19 Tax Reserve and 24 Hazard Insurance)

1. Lender reserves for taxes and insurance to set up new impound accounts are **always** a <u>buyer</u> DEBIT.

D. Notary Fees: (Line 9.)

1. Notary fees are always paid by <u>the party that signs the document</u>.

   a) The warranty deed is signed by the <u>seller</u>.

   b) The cost of any associated notary fee is a DEBIT to the <u>seller</u>, CREDIT broker.

   c) A deed of trust is signed by the <u>buyer</u>.

   d) The cost of any associated notary fee is a DEBIT to the <u>buyer</u>, CREDIT broker.

E. Insurance: (Line 23. Premium for New Insurance)

1. Hazard insurance is paid for a <u>policy year</u> that starts the month of closing.

F. Rental Properties (Line 33. Rents and Line 34. Security Deposits)

1. **Rent payments** are collected on the <u>first of the month in advance</u> from the tenant.

2. The seller will **always** owe the buyer rent from closing to the end of the month.

   a) Rent is **always**:

   Seller <u>DEBIT</u> prorated share

   Buyer <u>CREDIT</u> prorated share

3. A security deposit is the <u>tenant's</u> money.

   a) It must be transferred <u>in full</u> to the buyer/new owner.

   b) Always DEBIT seller, CREDIT buyer the <u>entire amount</u>.

G. Prorating Rent

1. Rent is income and not a bill, so it is handled differently than the proration rules about advance and arrears which apply only to transfers between the seller and buyer.

2. Rent is collected in advance by the seller from the tenant. This means the <u>seller</u> will **always** owe the <u>buyer</u> for the buyer's portion of the month.

H. Seller-carry Loans; (Line 4. Deed of Trust, payable to: *Seller*)

2. Amount of new seller-carry loan will always be a:

   a) <u>DEBIT</u> to seller because seller will not receive this amount in cash at closing. Instead, seller agrees to accept buyer's note and secure it with a Deed of Trust in this amount.

b) <u>CREDIT</u> to buyer because the buyer does not bring this amount to closing in cash. Buyer signs the note and secures the debt with a Deed of Trust creating a lien on the property (usually in second position to an existing loan).

I.   Calculating Interest Adjustment on a seller-carry loan or new loan: (Line 29. Interest on New Loan)

a) For the calculation of a seller-carry to be correct it **must** be calculated using <u>daily interest</u> (annual interest divided by <u>365</u>).

b) Interest on **seller-carry or new loans** is divided by <u>365</u>.

II.   BUYER AND SELLER TRANSFERS

A. Buyer and seller transfers occur when money is transferred on paper at closing between the two parties to the transaction (the buyer and the seller). Common buyer and seller transfers include the following:

1. Sales price: Always <u>CREDIT</u> seller, <u>DEBIT</u> buyer

2. Loans in an assumption

   a) The loan being <u>assumed</u>

   b) A <u>seller-carry</u> second loan

   c) Always <u>DEBIT</u> seller, <u>CREDIT</u> buyer

3. Prorations

   a) <u>Interest</u> on a loan assumed: SOB (solve left side and divide annual interest by 12).

   b) <u>Taxes</u> for the current year: SOB (solve left side).

   c) Water and/or sewer <u>flat rate</u> bills—arrears or advance per the contract.

   d) <u>Interest</u> on a new seller-carry loan: BOS (solve right side).

   e) <u>Rents</u>: Always seller owes buyer. (Remember: Security deposits are not prorated but will be transferred in full.)

4. Calculation of interest on new loans

   a) <u>Interest</u> on a new seller-carry loan (divide annual interest by 365).

III.   SELLER SETTLEMENT ITEMS

A. Seller Settlement items are CREDITS or DEBITS that will show on the <u>seller's</u> closing statement and not on the <u>buyer's</u> closing statement.

1.	Selling Price	Seller CREDIT
5.	Deed of Trust Payoff	Seller DEBIT
6.	Interest on Loan Assumed—Prorate what seller owes	Seller DEBIT
7.	Owner's Title Insurance	Seller DEBIT
8.	Closing Fee	Seller DEBIT
9.	Notary Fee	Seller DEBIT
13.	Recording: Release	Seller DEBIT
17.	Unpaid Taxes for the Preceding Year	Seller DEBIT
18.	Taxes for current year—Prorate what seller owes	Seller DEBIT
34.	Security Deposit	Seller DEBIT
36.	Loan Payment Due	Seller DEBIT
37.	Broker's Fee	Seller DEBIT
38.	Seller's Attorney	Seller DEBIT

IV.   BUYER SETTLEMENT ITEMS

A. Buyer settlement items are CREDITS or DEBITS that will show on the buyer's closing statement and not on the seller's closing statement.

1.	Selling Price	Buyer DEBIT
2.	Earnest Money Deposits:	Buyer CREDIT
8.	Closing Fee	Buyer DEBIT
9.	Notary Fee	Buyer DEBIT
10.	Buyer's Attorney:	Buyer DEBIT
11.	Recording: Warranty Deed:	Buyer DEBIT
12.	Recording: Deed of Trust:	Buyer DEBIT
15.	Documentary Fee:	Buyer DEBIT
16.	Tax Certificate	Buyer DEBIT
	Loan Costs:	
7b.	Mortgagee's Title Insurance	Buyer DEBIT
27.	Loan Origination Fee	Buyer DEBIT
28.	Loan Discount Points	Buyer DEBIT
29.	Interest on New Loan—prorate the amount owed for the month	Buyer DEBIT
35.	Loan Transfer Fee	Buyer DEBIT
30.	Survey	Buyer DEBIT unless otherwise negotiated in the contract.
31.	Appraisal	Buyer DEBIT unless otherwise negotiated in the contract.

2. Which buyer items are **negotiable** per the Contract to Buy and Sell?

a) Appraisal fee

b) Survey

c) Closing fees

Remember: ASC (ASK) what was negotiated.

V.   LOAN ASSUMPTION WORKSHEET

A. The lender provides a summary of the loan balance and other loan details to allow the broker to close the transaction.

   2. The assumption loan balance is a <u>DEBIT</u> to the seller, and a <u>CREDIT</u> to the buyer.

B. The broker uses information from many sources, which may include the following:

   1. The <u>Contract to Buy and Sell</u>

C. The six-column worksheet summarizes the financial transactions at the closing table and creates the information used to generate the <u>closing statement</u> for the buyer and seller.

VI.   PRORATION PRACTICE:

Line 18. Current Year Taxes: Taxes for the preceding year were $2,970. For a June 6 closing, what will be the prorated share?

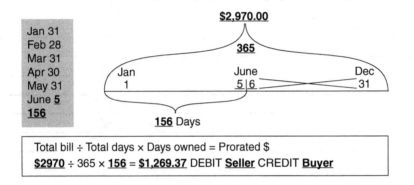

Total bill ÷ Total days × Days owned = Prorated $
$2970 ÷ 365 × **156** = **$1,269.37** DEBIT **Seller** CREDIT **Buyer**

Line 32. Water and/or Sewer: A water bill of $31.85 was paid in advance for the months of July through September. If the closing is September 20, what will the prorated entry be?

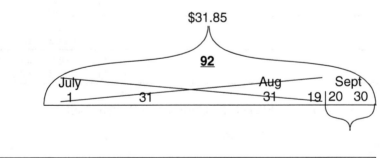

Total bill ÷ Total days × Days owned = Prorated $
$31.85 ÷ <u>92</u> × <u>11</u> days = <u>$3.81</u> CREDIT <u>seller</u> DEBIT <u>buyer</u>

■ CLOSINGS, UNIT 3: GLOSSARY REVIEW

1. The document recorded to indicate that a lien has been paid off is a <u>release of the deed of trust</u>.

2. A document that creates a lien and has the highest priority is a <u>first deed of trust</u>.

3. The administrative fee charged by a lender to set up a loan is the <u>loan origination fee</u>.

4. To protect against defects in title, a lender will usually require the buyer to purchase a <u>mortgagee's title insurance policy</u>.

5. Fees usually quoted as a percentage of the loan amount and used to increase the lender's yield and/or acquire a lower interest rate for the buyer, is known as <u>loan discount points</u>.

6. A loan that is neither guaranteed nor insured by a government agency is called a <u>conventional loan</u>.

7. A loan created with a lower lien priority, such as a seller-carry loan, is often a <u>second deed of trust</u>.

8. A conventional loan with a loan-to-value ratio greater than 80 percent will typically require <u>private mortgage insurance (PMI)</u>.

9. An assumption close uses double entries, while a new loan close is mostly <u>single entry</u>.

10. The <u>designated broker</u> is responsible for the closing statement for the party represented.

■ CLOSINGS, UNIT 3: LECTURE OUTLINE

I. REVIEW OF THE SIX-COLUMN REAL ESTATE SETTLEMENT WORKSHEET

A. Types of closing entries

There are four main types of entries on the settlement worksheet:

1. Seller and buyer exchanges of funds

   a) Examples are prorations and the <u>selling price</u>.

2. Funds held by the broker until the closing

   a) The most common example is <u>earnest money</u>.

   b) This is a CREDIT to the buyer and <u>DEBIT</u> to the broker (deposit into escrow account) off-setting DEBIT and CREDITS.

3. Bills paid by the broker on behalf of seller or buyer

   a) Examples: attorney's fee or <u>recording</u> fees.

   b) DEBIT to the responsible party for the item, and <u>CREDIT</u> to the broker (out of the escrow account) for writing the check.

II. THE SIX-COLUMN CLOSING WORKSHEET—SUMMARIZING THE TRANSACTION

A. The six-column closing worksheet summarizes the transaction with DEBIT and CREDIT columns for the following parties:

1. <u>Seller</u>

2. <u>Buyer</u>

3. <u>Broker</u>

B. Items unique to the six-column worksheet

2. Only the closing worksheet shows items going in and out of **the broker/closer escrow account**.

C. <u>Loan assumption</u>

1. Buyer assumes and agrees to pay the remaining balance on a seller's existing loan. Uses double entries.

D. **New loan**

    1. When the buyer gets a new loan, <u>the new lender will withhold funds</u> from the gross loan amount to pay some of the expenses of closing. Uses mostly single entries.

III. OTHER FORMS USED AT CLOSING

A. Seller or buyer closing statement

    2. This form or a suitable substitute is <u>mandatory</u> when the broker conducts the closing.

    3. Shows all of the DEBITS and CREDITS for the <u>seller</u> or <u>buyer</u>.

    4. Must be maintained in employing broker's files for <u>four years</u>.

    5. <u>Designated listing</u> broker checks figures for the seller.

    6. <u>Designated buyer's</u> broker checks figures for the buyer.

B. Real Property Transfer Declaration (TD-1000)

    1. Helps ensure fair and uniform <u>assessments</u> of property taxes.

IV. GOOD FUNDS AT CLOSING

A. Good funds are:

    1. <u>Cashier's check</u>

    2. <u>Teller's check</u> from a savings and loan or credit union

    3. <u>Wire transfer</u>

C. Promissory note for earnest money

    1. Must be honored in time to clear and be <u>good funds</u> by closing.

V. ERRORS AT CLOSING

A. Found before closing

    1. Have the <u>closing company</u> correct the error.

B. Minor error found at closing

    1. Parties may agree to <u>adjust the error or delay</u> closing (typically with a small check or cash).

VI. NON-RESIDENT SELLER WITHHOLDING

B. The seller is subject to withholding tax if:

1. the seller lives outside of <u>Colorado</u>; and

2. the sales price is **greater than** <u>$100,000.</u>

D. The amount of tax withheld will be the lower of:

1. <u>Two percent</u> of the sales price; or

2. the seller's entire net proceeds (balance due to the seller).

E. It is the responsibility of the <u>closing entity</u> to collect the withholding tax.

1. <u>The closing entity</u> can be an attorney, a broker, or the closing/title company.

2. The closing entity is responsible for immediately forwarding the funds to the Colorado <u>Department of Revenue.</u>

VII. NEW LOAN CLOSINGS AND THE NEW LOAN STATEMENT

A. A new loan statement provides the broker the following information:

1. The amount of the loan

2. Specific bills the lender will withhold from the loan

3. Net amount of the check the lender will provide to fund the rest of the closing

B. Use lender figures <u>exactly</u> as provided.

C. In a new loan, the lender brings the majority of the money for the buyer.

1. The new loan statement will show three sets of numbers the closer/broker needs.

   a) Gross or total new loan amount (Line 3)

   b) <u>Lender payouts</u>

   c) <u>Net loan proceeds</u> (Line 39)

2. Buyer will always have a large <u>CREDIT</u> called the <u>gross loan amount.</u>

3. From this amount, the lender will pay the majority of the bills, which are then totaled in <u>the lender payouts.</u>

4. The difference between the gross loan amount and the lender payouts is the <u>net loan proceeds</u>, which will be a <u>DEBIT</u> (deposit) into the closer/broker column so the final checks can be written.

5. The new lender provides a New Loan Statement with information about financing and **items the lender is paying** from the gross loan amount.

6. The lender also provides a <u>net loan proceeds</u> number that represents what remains of the gross loan amount after the lender pays the bills listed in the New Loan Statement.

7. All of these numbers from the New Loan Statement are <u>single entries</u> on the six-column settlement worksheet.

8. The broker records the lender single entry numbers on the closing worksheet <u>first</u>.

9. The closing entries not related to the new loan are all double entries and result in <u>balanced lines</u> with equal dollar values of DEBITS and CREDITS.

D. Items unique to a new loan closing

1. The gross amount of the **new loan** on Line 3 is a buyer <u>CREDIT</u> single entry.

2. A loan payoff on Line 5 to clear the seller's previous loan is a <u>seller</u> DEBIT single entry.

3. Various expenses paid by the lender on behalf of both the seller and the buyer are single entry <u>DEBITS</u> to the party responsible for that obligation.

4. The Net Loan Proceeds from the lender's New Loan Statement is a single entry DEBIT to the <u>broker</u>. It is a deposited into the escrow account and used to fund the closing.

E. Items Unique to the New Loan Statement

Items will be assigned as follows on a new loan statement:

Line	Item	To the Buyer	When
3	New loan amount	<u>Credit</u>	Always
7a.	Mortgagee policy	<u>Debit</u>	Always
31	Appraisal	<u>Debit</u>	Unless otherwise stated in the contract
27	Loan Origination Fee	<u>Debit</u>	Unless otherwise stated in the contract
28	Discount points	<u>Debit</u>	Unless otherwise stated in the contract
29	Interest on New Loan	<u>Debit</u>	If first payment more than one month after closing

	Item	To the Seller	When
5	Prior loan payoff	<u>Debit</u>	Always
13	Release of Deed of Trust	<u>Debit</u>	Always

Glossary

abstract A summary of all documents affecting title to a property shown by the public records used to give an opinion of title. Less frequently used today than title insurance.

accrued interest The amount of interest that has accumulated since the last payment was made. For a Colorado closing on the twentieth of the month, the seller would have accrued interest due for the first 19 days of the month. It is earned by the lender (accrued) but not payable until the next loan payment.

adjustable-rate mortgage (ARM) A loan that allows the borrower's interest rate to fluctuate based on some external index beyond the control of the lender.

adjustments The method used by brokers and appraisers to account for differences in comparable properties. If a subject property is superior, the appraiser makes a dollar adjustment increasing the sale price of the comparable. If the subject property is inferior to the comparable property, a negative adjustment is made.

advance See paid in advance

after-tax cash flow The amount remaining to an owner of income property after all expenses, debt service, and income taxes have been paid.

agency The relationship of agents and their principals.

agent A person who represents another person in a fiduciary relationship.

ambiguity A statement that is unclear or may have several meanings.

annual mortgage constant The factor that, if multiplied by the original loan balance, results in the annual mortgage payment; the mortgage payment's percentage of the original loan.

annual percentage rate (APR) An expression of credit costs over the life of a loan, taking into account the note interest rate plus lender fees for originating, processing, and closing a mortgage loan. The APR should be higher than the note rate.

antitrust Federal law that prohibits monopolistic practices such as price fixing.

appraisal An unbiased estimate of a property's market value.

appraising The process of estimating the market value of property.

arm's-length transaction A business transaction in which the parties are dealing in their own self-interest, not being under the control of the other party. One of the requirements before a comparable sale should be used in an appraisal.

assets Things of value owned by a person or organization.

assume a loan See loan assumption

assumption balance The remaining balance on a loan at the time of closing if the loan is being assumed by the buyer. The current lender provides this figure.

automated underwriting The evaluation of a mortgage loan application using predetermined formulas and credit scores. Fannie Mae's Desktop Underwriter performs automated underwriting.

automated valuation The use of computers and linear regression formulas to calculate the market value of property based on large numbers of comparable sales.

before-tax cash flow (BTCF) The amount of spendable income from an income property after paying operating expenses and debt service, but before the effect of income taxes.

bilateral contract A contract that requires both parties to perform, such as a sales contract.

biweekly mortgage A mortgage that requires that the borrower make payments every two weeks (26 payments per year). The payment is calculated by dividing the monthly mortgage payment by two. The effective result is that the borrower makes 13 monthly payments per year.

blockbusting The illegal act of a licensee who frightens homeowners into selling by raising fears that minority homeowners are moving into a neighborhood.

body language Nonverbal communication expressed by the position of the body, hands, arms, legs, or facial expressions.

Broker Disclosure to Buyer The disclosure form that is required when a licensee meets a potential buyer but has an agency or transaction-broker relationship with a seller.

Broker Disclosure to Seller (FSBO) The disclosure form that is required when a licensee meets an unrepresented seller of a property the licensee's buyer wishes to purchase. Since the licensee has an agency or transaction-broker relationship with the buyer, this form is used to disclose that relationship to the seller and could be used to make the seller a customer.

browser A software program that makes access to Web sites possible. Netscape and Internet Explorer are examples.

buyer agency The fiduciary relationship between a buyer and the buyer's single-agent broker.

buyer brokerage agreement An agreement between a buyer and a broker for the broker to provide services to a buyer for compensation. The broker may be acting as a single agent or a transaction-broker.

buyer's broker The broker representing the buyer. The buyer's broker is often appointed through an exclusive-right-to-buy contract. This broker will be responsible for the buyer's Statement of Settlement at closing.

calculated interest rate The interest rate in an adjustable-rate mortgage that is calculated by adding the margin to the index.

canvassing Prospecting for buyers or sellers by telephoning or walking door-to-door.

cap The maximum amount that an interest rate can increase per year or during the life of a loan.

capitalization rate The net operating income divided by the property value. A percentage representing the return on the investment, assuming the property was purchased for cash.

cash flow report A property manager's monthly report to the owner, showing cash receipts and cash disbursements of an income property.

Certificate of Taxes Due A certificate or report prepared by a county treasurer confirming the current status of general property taxes and governmental special assessments for a particular property.

certified check A check issued by a bank guaranteeing payment. The buyer is usually required to bring a certified check to closing by most title closing agents to speed disbursement at closing.

Certified Property Manager (CPM) A professional designation awarded by the Institute of Real Estate Management (IREM) to a property manager who has successfully completed required education and experience.

Change of Status Form This form is used to change from a single agent relationship to a transaction-broker when the licensee has an opportunity to represent both buyer and seller in the same transaction (double ending the deal).

closing statement Colorado Real Estate Commission approved form SS60. The form provides a two-column summary of the financial aspects of the closing for either a buyer or a seller. The form is marked at the top to indicate the party to whom it applies. The form is mandatory if a broker performs the closing through the brokerage office.

closing The consummation of the real estate transaction in which the seller delivers legal title to the buyer in exchange for the agreed payment or other consideration. Closing involves both the financial and the legal aspects of carrying out the agreement, created by the Contract to Buy and Sell, between the buyer and seller.

collateral Something of value given as security for a debt. In real estate, the mortgage or deed of trust pledges the property as collateral for the repayment of the loan.

Colorado Tax Payment Schedule In Colorado, general property taxes become a lien on the property on January 1 in arrears. They may be paid without penalty either the entire amount no later than April 30 or two equal payments with the first on or before the last day in February and the balance not later than June 15.

commission Compensation for professional services that is usually calculated as a percentage of the property's sales price.

compact disc (CD) drive A part of the computer that allows the user to access information or programs on a compact disc.

comparable property A similar property in the same market area that may be used to help estimate the value of the property being appraised.

comparative market analysis (CMA) Similar to the comparable sales approach used by appraisers, but usually less detailed. Used by broker associates to estimate the most likely selling price of properties they are listing or selling.

computer valuation The use of computers and linear regression formulas to estimate the market value of property based on large numbers of comparable sales.

computer-assisted design (CAD) A software program that assists the user in making technical drawings.

Consumer Credit Protection Act A federal statute that controls the information a lender may obtain and consider in qualifying consumer mortgage loan applicants.

contingency A condition in a contract that, unless satisfied, may make the contract voidable by one of the parties.

contract service A property maintenance service performed by an individual or company not in the employ of the property manager.

Contract to Buy and Sell See sales contract.

contract An agreement between two or more parties to do or not do a specific act.

contraction The phase of a business cycle that begins after a recession when economic conditions worsen.

conventional loan   a loan with no government guarantee or mortgage insurance.

cooperating broker   A broker working with a buyer (or tenant). The cooperating broker often receives compensation through an agreed division of the listing broker's transaction commission.

cooperative sale   Sale of a property by a broker who is not the listing broker. Normally, commissions are split between the two brokerage firms.

corrective maintenance   The repairs to a building's structure and equipment following breakdown.

counteroffer   A substitution for the original offer made by the offeree who changes the price or terms offered, sending it back to the offeror. The original offer is terminated. The original offeree becomes the offeror.

crash   The termination of a software program on a computer so that all unsaved data in random access memory is lost. Usually, the computer must be restarted.

credit (seller or buyer)   In closings, a credit is an amount received by a party or an amount such as a loan that the buyer does not bring to the closing in cash. A credit is "good" for the cash position of the party at closing.

credit scoring   A method of credit reporting using a numeric score. A higher score reflects a better credit history.

cross-defaulting clause   A mortgage clause that results in a default of a junior mortgage in case a senior mortgage becomes delinquent.

curb appeal   The impression, good or bad, that is made when a person first looks at a house from the street.

customer   A person who works with a broker associate and is not represented in the transaction. The person must sign a disclosure stating they agree to the relationship.

cycle   Periodic fluctuations of the overall economy, or any part of the economy, between good times and bad. The four parts of a general cycle are expansion, recession, contraction, and recovery.

cyclic fluctuation   Part of an economic cycle.

database   A listing of information in a form that allows easy manipulation and reporting. It is also the name for a software program that makes the organization of information easier.

debit (seller or buyer)   In closings, a debit is an amount charged to a specific party or a sum they will not receive in cash at closing. A debit is "bad" for the cash position of the party at the time of closing.

deed of trust   A deed of trust creates a lien on property to secure a note. In Colorado, the deed of trust is administered by a Public Trustee. The deed of trust will be accompanied by a promissory note both are signed by the buyer.

deferred maintenance   Maintenance that needs to be done, but has not been done for some reason, usually economic.

deficit closing   A closing in which the seller receives insufficient money to pay all of the obligations. The seller would be required to bring money to the closing in order to deliver title to the property.

designated broker   A broker associate who is appointed by their employing broker to be a single agent or transaction-broker for a buyer or seller. The designated broker will be the only representative that is considered to have imputed knowledge (confidential information given them by the buyer or seller) in the firm. Under Colorado law, no one else in the firm including the employing broker has any imputed knowledge.

designated broker   Under Colorado's designated brokerage law, the individual licensee (or team of licensed individuals) appointed by an employing broker to hold the brokerage relationship with a seller, landlord, buyer, or tenant.

digital camera   A camera that does not use conventional film, but instead stores images in a memory chip in the camera, ready to be loaded into a computer for display or printing.

disclosure   The revelation of information important to a transaction.

documentary fee   A fee charged when a warranty deed is recorded. In Colorado this fee is $0.01 per $100 of the sales price.

Documentary Fee   In Colorado, this fee in paid upon recording any deed conveying title from a grantor to a grantee. The fee is one cent per 100 dollars of consideration paid for the property. Determine the fee by moving the decimal point four places to the left in the selling price.

dual agent   An illegal arrangement whereby the broker tries to represent both the buyer and the seller in the same transaction.

dynamic risk   Uninsurable risk, such as that of an economic downturn.

Earnest Money Promissory Note   A personal note presented by a buyer as a form of earnest money. If acceptable to the seller, the note is made out to the listing broker and presented for payment when due.

earnest money   A deposit accompanying an offer to purchase that becomes earnest money (sometimes called good faith money). The earnest money may be identified in a contract as liquidated damages that would be forfeited if the buyer breaches the contract.

effective gross income (EGI)   The amount of rent and other income actually collected by the owner. When preparing an income statement, vacancy and collection losses are deducted from potential gross income as factors. The balance after this subtraction is effective gross income.

e-mail   Electronic mail that is sent over the Internet.

Equal Credit Opportunity Act   A federal statute that controls the information a lender may obtain and consider in qualifying consumer mortgage loan applications.

equity   The amount of the owner's portion of the property value after deducting mortgages and other liens.

escrow account   An account maintained by a broker to hold and account for money belonging to others. The account must meet strict requirements of real estate commission rules.

ethical   The right thing to do. Usually a higher standard than legality.

exclusive-brokerage (exclusive-agency) listing   A listing that requires that the owner pay the listing broker if the property is sold by any broker, but allows the owner to personally sell the property without being liable for a commission. Exclusive brokerage is used in Colorado while exclusive agency is used in other states and may be seen on the national portion of the Colorado real estate licensing exam.

exclusive-right-to-sell listing   A listing that requires that the owner pay the listing broker no matter who sells the property. The broker is automatically the procuring cause of the sale.

executed contract   A contract in which nothing else remains to be done. All requirements have been performed by the parties.

executory contract   A contract in which part of the agreement remains to be done. It has not yet closed.

exercised   Used in connection with an option contract. An option contract is a unilateral contract until the optionee agrees to purchase and is then said to have exercised the option; the contract is now considered to be bilateral.

expansion   The phase of a business cycle that begins after a recovery when economic conditions improve.

express contract   An oral or written agreement where the words specifically describe the intent of the parties.

Fair Housing Act   Federal law that prohibits discrimination in housing based on race, color, religion, sex, national origin, familial status, or handicap.

fallback list   A list of properties similar to the property being advertised that can be used by the licensee if the advertised property does not appeal to the person responding to the ad.

false or misleading statement   In real estate, a statement made by a licensee or party in a real estate transaction that is not factual.

farm   A geographic area selected for special prospecting attention by a real estate licensee.

federally related transaction   A real estate transaction financed by a lender insured by the federal government or a loan insured or guaranteed by the federal government that requires the services of an appraiser.

fee   Compensation, either as a fixed dollar amount or a percentage of the sale price.

FHA Loan   A loan that includes FHA Mortgage Insurance. The lending program is regulated by the Federal Housing Administration (FHA) and the borrower pays a mortgage insurance premium (MIP).

FHA Mortgage Insurance   An insurance program sponsored by the government and administered by HUD that insures lenders against default by a borrower. The mortgage insurance premium is paid by the borrower.

FICO score   A proprietary numeric credit score used to evaluate a prospective borrower, developed by Fair Isaac Corporation.

fiduciary relationship   A relationship of trust and confidence between an agent and principal.

First Deed of Trust   A deed of trust creating a lien to secure a real estate loan. A first deed of trust has priority over other private liens based on its date and time of recording.

fixed-rate mortgage   A loan secured by real estate that has the same rate of interest for the life of the loan.

Flood Plain Certification   Flood damage is excluded from normal homeowner hazard insurance. Lenders may require additional flood insurance if a property is located in a recognized flood plain. The certification service confirms whether the property is located in a flood plain. The cost of the service is normally a buyer's closing cost.

Foreign Investment in Real Property Tax Act (FIRPTA)   A federal law for aliens and alien corporations for U.S. income tax requiring that the buyer withhold a percentage of the sale price as taxes on the gain from the sale of a real property interest located in the United States.

for-rent-by-owner   An owner who attempts to rent his or her own property without using a broker.

for-sale-by-owner   An owner who attempts to sell his or her own property without using a broker.

funding fee   A charge levied by the Department of Veteran's Affairs to veterans who use VA loans.

good funds   Banking rules define certain types of funds as redeemable for cash immediately at any bank. Colorado law requires that a closing may only be done when all funds at closing are good funds. Cashier's checks, teller's checks, and federal funds wire transfers are the most common forms used for real estate closings.

gross domestic product (GDP) The sum total of goods and services produced by the United States. The four major components of GDP are consumption, investment, government purchases, and net exports.

hardware Tangible computer equipment that runs programs, called software.

hazard insurance The homeowner's insurance policy that protects against losses from fire and other hazards.

Homeowners Association (HOA) The association established by the declaration documents of a common-interest community. The association has the authority to levy mandatory assessments for maintenance of common elements in the community and to enforce unpaid levies with a lien on the property.

http A prefix for Web site addresses, meaning hypertext transport protocol.

hyperlink A link on a Web site that, when clicked, transports the user to another Web site.

hypertext The text, usually colored blue and underlined, on a Web site that is the hyperlink to another Web site.

implied contract An agreement not spelled out in words, where the agreement of the parties is demonstrated by their acts and conduct.

index An indicator beyond the control of a lender to which the interest rate on an adjustable-rate mortgage is tied.

infrastructure The system of public works for a country, state, or region, such as roads, schools, sewers, water treatment facilities, etc.

inkjet printer A printer that uses an ink spray for black and color printing.

innocent purchaser status An amendment to the Comprehensive Environmental Response, Compensation, and Liability Act (CERCLA) that exempts from liability landowners who made reasonable inquiries about hazardous substances before purchasing the property.

Institute of Real Estate Management (IREM) A national organization of property managers affiliated with the National Association of REALTORS®.

Internet service provider A company or organization that acts as the portal for a user to gain access to the Internet.

Internet The global network of computers connected by cable and phone lines.

jargon A word or expression related to a specific vocation that a layperson may not understand.

k The symbol for the annual mortgage constant, calculated by dividing the annual payment of principal and interest by the original amount of the loan.

keysafe Also called a lockbox, holds the key to the home, usually attached to a door handle allowing licensees who are members of the MLS easy access to the property.

laptop A small computer designed for travel that can run on battery power.

laser printer A printer using a toner bonded to the paper by laser and heat.

lender reserve (impound) account An account established by a lender to hold money collected in advance with monthly loan payments to pay later bills for property taxes and insurance. The funds belong to the borrower until the obligation is paid by the lender on behalf of the borrower.

leverage The use of borrowed money with the intent to increase the investor's return on the cash invested. If the return on the investment is greater than the interest rate paid by the borrower, the owner has positive leverage.

liabilities Amounts owed by a person.

listing agreement An agreement between a seller and a broker whereby the seller agrees to pay the broker a commission if the broker is successful in selling the property.

listing broker The broker hired by the seller to market a property. The listing broker is normally appointed through an exclusive-right-to-sell contract. This broker will be responsible for the seller's Statement of Settlement at closing.

listing presentation A "sit down at the dining room table" discussion at which the licensee builds rapport with a seller, explains the pricing process, and asks for the listing.

loan assumption With a lender's approval a buyer may be allowed to "assume and agree to pay" the seller's existing loan. The buyer then becomes responsible for the terms of the original agreement and the seller is relieved of liability.

loan constant Calculated by dividing the annual payment of principal and interest by the original amount of the loan.

loan discount fee This fee is also called points or discount points. It is a percentage of the loan amount collected as advance payment of interest. A buyer may use points to get a lower interest rate on the loan. A lender views a discount fee as a way to increase the income or yield on the loan. The amount of the fee will depend on the availability of mortgage money in the marketplace.

loan origination fee The administrative fee charged by a lender for the processing of a loan application. Also called a loan origination fee, it is usually quoted as a percentage of the loan amount. This fee is like the lender's commission.

loan processing procedures Steps taken by a lender to ensure that underwriting and documentation of a mortgage loan are done in a manner that reduces the lender's exposure to loss.

loan underwriting fee One of a number of specific fees charged by some lenders to offset specific expenses and increase their income or yield on a loan. Some of these fees are referred to as junk fees.

loan underwriting The evaluation of risk when a lender makes a mortgage loan to reduce the lender's exposure to loss.

lockbox A secure box holding the key to the home, usually attached to a door handle allowing licensees who are members of the MLS easy access to the property by using a special access key to the box.

margin The additional percentage added to the index on an adjustable-rate mortgage, resulting in the calculated interest rate.

marketing knowledge A licensee's knowledge of the sales process, including the psychology of selling, advertising, personal marketing, and prospecting.

material fact An important fact that may affect a buyer's decision to buy or a seller's decision to sell. Licensees must disclose facts that materially affect the value of residential property.

MIP or mortgage insurance premium The cost of mortgage insurance to protect the lender from borrower default. MIP is most commonly used when referring to FHA mortgage insurance.

misrepresentation A false or misleading statement made intentionally or unintentionally or the failure to disclose a material fact.

modem A device allowing a computer to communicate with other computers by phone lines or cable.

mortgage insurance premium (MIP) The amount paid by a borrower for insurance that protects the lender against loss in case of the borrower's default. FHA mortgage insurance is called MIP.

mortgage insurance An insurance policy that protects a lender against default by the borrower. The premium is normally paid by the borrower.

Mortgagee Title Insurance Policy A policy of title insurance to benefit a lender (mortgagee). The policy covers only the remaining balance on a loan and ceases when the loan is paid off. The premium is normally paid by the borrower.

mutual recognition An agreement between states to recognize a licensee's education obtained in another state.

negative amortization A situation occurring, usually under a graduated payment mortgage, where the payment on the loan is less than the amount required to pay the accrued interest. The unpaid interest is added to the principal balance of the loan and the loan balance gradually increases.

negotiable Open to discussion; the status of any item with a check box on the Contract to Buy and Sell.

net operating income (NOI) The income from an investment property remaining after operating expenses have been paid from the effective gross income.

net proceeds The amount remaining to the seller after paying off the mortgage and expenses of a sale.

net worth The amount remaining when liabilities are subtracted from assets.

new construction maintenance Work done on an income property designed to enhance the property's appeal to tenants. Includes adding new wallpaper, carpeting, and light fixtures.

nonverbal communication Unspoken communication expressed by the position of the body, hands, arms, legs, or facial expressions, commonly called body language.

notary fee The fee for notary service. This fee is paid by the party whose signature is acknowledged before the notary.

notary A notary public is an official authorized to receive acknowledgement of a signature and attest that it was given willingly by the party identified in the document.

Office of Foreign Assets Control (OFAC) "Specially Designated and Blocked Persons List" A list of persons suspected of aiding or committing terrorism against the Untied States. Brokers, buyers, and sellers agree in various approved Colorado contracts that they are not working with or aiding anyone on the list in the sale of real estate.

open listing A nonexclusive agreement in which a seller agrees to pay a broker if the broker sells the property. The broker is not paid if the seller or another broker sells the property.

operating expenses (OE) Costs of operating an income property. Includes property taxes, maintenance, insurance, payrolls, and reserves for replacements.

opinion of value A broker's price opinion, usually based on a comparative market analysis.

option contract An agreement that allows one party to buy, sell, or lease real property for specified terms within a specified time limit.

paid in advance Prepaid. A bill or obligation paid ahead of the time the service or product is delivered.

paid in arrears   A bill or obligation paid after the service or product is delivered.

paperless mortgage   A mortgage that is signed electronically, using digital signatures.

passive prospecting   A method of prospecting that does not include direct face-to-face or telephone conversations. Advertising and direct mail are examples of passive prospecting.

performance   The completion of a contract's requirements.

PITI payment   The payment required of a borrower that includes principal, interest, taxes, and insurance.

planned unit development (PUD)   A residential development designed to have mixed land uses and a high residential density.

point   A lender's charge to the borrower that increases the lender's yield. One point is equal to 1 percent of the loan amount.

potential gross income (PGI)   The total annual income a property would produce if it were 100 percent occupied, with no vacancy or collection loss.

power prospecting   A type of prospecting that seeks to make contact with many more buyers and sellers and that results in much higher income levels.

preclosing walk-through inspection   An inspection of the house by the buyer, done sometime before the sale closes, to determine that the property is in the same condition as it was when the contract was signed and to ensure that all required repairs have been completed.

prequalification   The preliminary process during which a prospective lender evaluates the buyer's ability to obtain a mortgage loan. Most licensees want a buyer to be prequalified or preapproved before showing properties.

preventive maintenance   A work program designed to preserve the physical integrity of the premises and eliminate the more costly corrective maintenance.

previewing properties   The activity a licensee uses to stay abreast of the market and to find specific properties to show to a prospective buyer.

principal   (1) The person who enters into a fiduciary relationship with a single-agent licensee. (2) The amount of money remaining due on a mortgage loan.

prioritize   To set up a list of activities in an order based on their importance.

private mortgage insurance (PMI)   The amount paid by a borrower for insurance that protects the lender against loss in case of the borrower's default. Conventional lenders use the term private mortgage insurance; FHA mortgage insurance is called MIP.

product knowledge   A licensee's familiarity with the real estate market and specific properties available for sale.

professional ethics   A body of accepted codes of behavior for a specific industry.

profile sheet   A form designed to organize the gathering and input of property listing information into the multiple listing service.

profit and loss statement   A detailed report of the income and expenses of an investment property over a stated period of time.

property characteristics   The features of a property that are used as a basis of comparison in an appraisal or comparative market analysis.

proration   In a closing, ongoing expenses of the property such as property taxes are divided between the parties in proportion to the period of ownership of the parties. Proration is the calculation of the appropriate amount and accounting for it in the closing documents.

qualifying   The process used by a licensee to determine whether to spend time working with a buyer or seller. For example, a buyer would first be qualified financially, then based on motivation to buy.

quality of income   A lender's analysis of factors that reveal the likelihood of the borrower's income continuing over a long period of time.

quantity of income   The total amount of a borrower's income from all sources.

radon gas   A colorless, odorless gas occurring from the natural breakdown of uranium in the soil. Many experts believe radon gas to be the second leading cause of lung cancer.

random access memory (RAM)   Dynamic memory in a computer that disappears when the computer is turned off. Information in the RAM would be lost if it were not saved on the hard drive.

random changes   Irregular fluctuations of the economy that may be caused by legislative and judicial decisions, wars, weather, etc.

Real Estate Settlement Procedures Act (RESPA)   A federal law requiring disclosure of loan closing costs in certain real estate financial transactions.

Real Property Transfer Declaration (TD-1000)   A form required by law to be submitted with the recording of a transfer deed and signed by the grantor or the grantee. Closing companies prepare the form for signature at the closing. The form provides information to the county assessor for use in ensuring fair and uniform assessments for real property taxation.

Realty Tax Service   A computerized service that keeps track of the general property tax obligations for a lender who collects tax and insurance monthly into reserve accounts. For a one-time fee paid at closing, the service ensures that taxes are paid to the right county on the correct schedule.

recession Two successive quarterly declines in the gross domestic product (GDP). This is the point at which economic activity has peaked and will be followed by a contraction.

reconciliation The final step in the appraisal process before the report is prepared. The correlation of property values derived from each of the three appraisal approaches into a single estimate of value.

recording A copy of a document is placed in the public record by the county clerk and recorder. Recording creates legal notice (constructive notice) of the contents of the document such as a deed conveying title or a lien encumbering the property.

recovery Two successive quarterly increases in the gross domestic product (GDP). This is the point at which economic activity has bottomed and will be followed by expansion.

redlining A lender's refusal to loan money in an area based on illegal discrimination.

refinancing Placing a new mortgage on a property to replace another mortgage.

Regulation Z The part of the Truth-in-Lending Act that requires that lenders calculate and disclose the effective annual percentage rate to the consumer.

Release of Deed of Trust When a real estate loan secured by a deed of trust is fully paid, the deed of trust continues to appear in the public record. Recording a Release of Deed of Trust shows that the lien has been released.

reserves for replacements A portion of an investment property's income that is set aside to pay the cost of replacing major building components when necessary.

resident manager A salaried individual employed for specific management functions for a single investment property.

rewritable CD drive (CD-RW) A computer device that writes information, graphics, or music onto a compact disc.

rider An attachment to a contract.

routine maintenance The most common maintenance performed on an investment property, such as grounds care and housekeeping.

Rule E-35 A rule that requires a broker associate who is either an agent or a transaction-broker working with a seller to disclose that brokerage relationship to a potential buyer in writing before providing brokerage services to the buyer.

sales contract (Contract to Buy and Sell) A bilateral agreement in which a buyer agrees to purchase a seller's property at a specified price and terms.

scanner A computer device that allows the user to copy a document or picture and for use in a computer.

scrivener A term from English common law referring to a person hired to complete forms exactly as directed. The scrivener is not responsible for the form; the party hiring the scrivener retains full responsibility.

search engine A Web site that has indexed millions of other Web sites, allowing users to locate information by entering key words.

seasonal variation Changes in the economy (for example, winter tourism in Colorado) that recur at regular intervals at least once a year.

Second Deed of Trust A deed of trust recorded later than the first deed of trust.

seller agency The relationship of a single agent and his principal, the seller.

Seller's Net Proceeds Form A form used to show the seller's equity, expenses, and prorations, as well as the net amount the seller is estimated to receive as proceeds from the sale of the property.

Seller's Property Disclosure Form A form designed for disclosure to a buyer of any property defects. The form is normally signed by the seller, and the buyer signs a receipt that the buyer has received the disclosure.

seller-carry financing A loan from the seller to the buyer to finance part of the purchase price of a property. The seller generally lends part of the equity they would normally have received in cash at closing.

selling broker More typically called the buyer's broker. The broker working with a buyer.

servicing the listing The actions of a licensee who stays in touch with a seller regularly, getting feedback from licensees who have shown the property, sending the seller copies of advertisements, and generally keeping the seller informed of the marketing efforts.

Settlement Services The collection of services provided by a broker or closing company to complete a Contract to Buy and Sell; pay bills related to the closing; prepare, record, and deliver documents required by the transaction; and ensure an orderly transfer of marketable title.

show list A selected inventory of apartments that are available for inspection by prospective tenants.

single agent A broker who represents either the seller or the buyer in a real estate transaction, but not both.

single entry (on a settlement worksheet) An entry on a settlement closing worksheet that has no offsetting entry. Most single entries are debits for an expense charged to one party of the transaction and paid on behalf of that party by the lender on a new loan.

Six-Column Settlement Closing Worksheet (also Closing worksheet for Real Estate Settlement) The six-column closing worksheet is provided by the Colorado Real Estate Commission. It is not mandatory but is available for a broker's convenience in calculating the financial aspects of a closing.

software Computer programs designed specifically to perform specialized functions.

special assessment A special improvement cost levied by a government entity for improvements benefiting a limited area. The properties that benefit pay a proportionate share, often based on street frontage. Typical improvements could be street lighting or new curb and gutter.

specific cycles Wavelike movements similar to business cycles that occur in specific sectors of the general economy, such as the real estate market.

spreadsheet A software program using columns and rows that allows the user to create formulas that act on the numbers stored in the spreadsheet. A change in one amount will change other numbers or totals in the spreadsheet, making what-if scenarios simple.

Square Footage Disclosure A required disclosure for all residential property in Colorado if the square footage of the property is listed in any sales information. Listing broker must specify how they measured the property or, if they used another source, that source must be identified.

static risk Risk that is quantifiable and insurable. For example, the risk of fire is a static risk. Fire insurance will transfer the risk from the owner to the insurance company.

statute of frauds A body of law that requires certain contracts, such as those for the sale of real property, to be written.

steering The illegal, discriminatory act of a sales associate who brings buyers into an area based on the racial or ethnic makeup of the neighborhood.

subject property The property being appraised.

surfing The actions of a person using the Internet who visits many Web sites.

targeted strangers Persons not known to a licensee who are qualified as prospects by income, occupation, or residence address.

Tax Certificate See Certificate of Taxes Due

TD-1000 Form See Real Property Transfer Declaration

technical knowledge The knowledge needed by licensees to properly conduct their business that relates to filling out contracts, preparing seller's proceeds estimates, doing comparative market analyses, etc.

thumbnail A picture reduced in size to save loading time that, when clicked on in a Web site, is converted to full size.

time is of the essence A contract clause that requires strict compliance with all dates and times specified in the contract. If a party fails to perform some act by the time specified, the person may be in default.

time management The organization of a person's day to maximize efficiency. It includes planning, scheduling, and prioritizing.

title insurance premium The cost of the title insurance policy. This amount is paid at closing and is a one-time charge.

title insurance A guarantee to reimburse a loss arising from defects in title or liens against real property.

to-do list A daily list, usually designed in priority order, of tasks to be completed that day.

transactional characteristics The factors related to a real estate transaction itself, such as time of sale, and financing terms.

transaction-broker A licensee who has limited representation to the buyer and/or the seller in a transaction. Instead of being an advocate for the buyer or the seller, the licensee is working for the contract. If the licensee is representing both sides in a single transaction they must be a transaction-broker in Colorado.

trust account See escrow account

Truth-in-Lending Act A federal law that requires that lenders inform consumers of exact credit costs before they make their purchases.

unconscionable contract An agreement that a court may declare unenforceable because it would be grossly unfair to one party if enforced.

Uniform Resource Locator (URL) A specific Web site address, such as *www.dearborn.com*.

Uniform Standards of Professional Appraisal Practice (USPAP) Strict requirements for appraisers interpreted and amended by the Appraisal Standards Board.

unilateral contract A contract in which only one of the parties is required to perform, such as an option contract. The optionor must sell if the optionee exercises the option, but the optionee is not required to buy.

VA Loan A loan guaranteed by the Department of Veterans Affairs. If a borrower defaults on the loan, the VA guarantees that the lender will not lose money in a foreclosure sale. The loan is available as a veteran's benefit to eligible veterans of military service.

valid contract An agreement that complies with all the essentials of a contract and is binding on all parties.

verbal communications skills The ability to speak effectively one-on-one or in a group presentation.

void contract An agreement that is not binding on either party.

voidable contract An agreement that may be canceled by the party who would be damaged if the contract were enforced. Minors, fraud, duress and misrepresentation make contracts voidable.

warranty of owner A hold harmless clause in a listing agreement whereby the seller warrants that all information given to the broker is correct.

World Wide Web A collection of millions of documents on the Internet.

written communication skills The ability to communicate effectively in letters, e-mails, and other documents.

Index

Real Estate Settlement Closing Worksheet

	SELLER		BUYER		BROKER	
	Debit	Credit	Debit	Credit	Debit	Credit
1. Selling Price						
2. Deposit, paid to:						
3. Deed of Trust, payable to:						
4. Deed of Trust, payable to:						
5. Deed of Trust, payoff to:						
6. Interest on Loan Assumed						
7. Owner Title Insurance Premium						
a. Extended Title Insurance						
b. Mortgagee's Policy						
8. Closing Fee						
9. Notary Fee						
10. Title Exam by buyer attorney						
11. Recording: Warranty Deed						
12. Deed of Trust						
13. Release						
14. Other						
15. Documentary Fee						
16. Certificate of Taxes Due						
17. Taxes for Preceding Year(s)						
18. Taxes for Current Year						
19. Tax Reserve						
20. Special Taxes (Assessments)						
21. Personal Property Taxes						
22. Notary Fee paid by Lender						
23. Premium for New Insurance						
24. Hazard Ins. Reserve						
25. FHA Mortgage Ins. Assumed						
26. FHA Mortgage Ins. Reserve						
27. Loan Origination						
28. Loan Discount Points						
29. Interest on New Loan						
30. Survey						
Credit Report						
31. Appraisal Fee						
32. Water and/or Sewer						
33. Rents						
34. Security Deposits						
35. Loan Transfer Fee						
36. Loan Payment Due						
37. Broker's Fee						
38. Seller's Attorney						
39. Net loan proceeds						
Subtotals						
Balance Due to/from Seller						
Balance Due to/from Buyer						
TOTALS						

Real Estate Settlement Closing Worksheet

	SELLER		BUYER		BROKER	
	Debit	Credit	Debit	Credit	Debit	Credit
1. Selling Price						
2. Deposit, paid to:						
3. Deed of Trust, payable to:						
4. Deed of Trust, payable to:						
5. Deed of Trust, payoff to:						
6. Interest on Loan Assumed						
7. Owner Title Insurance Premium						
a. Extended Title Insurance						
b. Mortgagee's Policy						
8. Closing Fee						
9. Notary Fee						
10. Title Exam by buyer attorney						
11. Recording: Warranty Deed						
12. Deed of Trust						
13. Release						
14. Other						
15. Documentary Fee						
16. Certificate of Taxes Due						
17. Taxes for Preceding Year(s)						
18. Taxes for Current Year						
19. Tax Reserve						
20. Special Taxes (Assessments)						
21. Personal Property Taxes						
22. Notary Fee paid by Lender						
23. Premium for New Insurance						
24. Hazard Ins. Reserve						
25. FHA Mortgage Ins. Assumed						
26. FHA Mortgage Ins. Reserve						
27. Loan Origination						
28. Loan Discount Points						
29. Interest on New Loan						
30. Survey						
Credit Report						
31. Appraisal Fee						
32. Water and/or Sewer						
33. Rents						
34. Security Deposits						
35. Loan Transfer Fee						
36. Loan Payment Due						
37. Broker's Fee						
38. Seller's Attorney						
39. Net loan proceeds						
Subtotals						
Balance Due to/from Seller						
Balance Due to/from Buyer						
TOTALS						

Real Estate Settlement Closing Worksheet

	SELLER		BUYER		BROKER	
	Debit	Credit	Debit	Credit	Debit	Credit
1. Selling Price						
2. Deposit, paid to:						
3. Deed of Trust, payable to:						
4. Deed of Trust, payable to:						
5. Deed of Trust, payoff to:						
6. Interest on Loan Assumed						
7. Owner Title Insurance Premium						
a. Extended Title Insurance						
b. Mortgagee's Policy						
8. Closing Fee						
9. Notary Fee						
10. Title Exam by buyer attorney						
11. Recording: Warranty Deed						
12. Deed of Trust						
13. Release						
14. Other						
15. Documentary Fee						
16. Certificate of Taxes Due						
17. Taxes for Preceding Year(s)						
18. Taxes for Current Year						
19. Tax Reserve						
20. Special Taxes (Assessments)						
21. Personal Property Taxes						
22. Notary Fee paid by Lender						
23. Premium for New Insurance						
24. Hazard Ins. Reserve						
25. FHA Mortgage Ins. Assumed						
26. FHA Mortgage Ins. Reserve						
27. Loan Origination						
28. Loan Discount Points						
29. Interest on New Loan						
30. Survey						
Credit Report						
31. Appraisal Fee						
32. Water and/or Sewer						
33. Rents						
34. Security Deposits						
35. Loan Transfer Fee						
36. Loan Payment Due						
37. Broker's Fee						
38. Seller's Attorney						
39. Net loan proceeds						
Subtotals						
Balance Due to/from Seller						
Balance Due to/from Buyer						
TOTALS						

Real Estate Settlement Closing Worksheet

	SELLER Debit	SELLER Credit	BUYER Debit	BUYER Credit	BROKER Debit	BROKER Credit
1. Selling Price						
2. Deposit, paid to:						
3. Deed of Trust, payable to:						
4. Deed of Trust, payable to:						
5. Deed of Trust, payoff to:						
6. Interest on Loan Assumed						
7. Owner Title Insurance Premium						
a. Extended Title Insurance						
b. Mortgagee's Policy						
8. Closing Fee						
9. Notary Fee						
10. Title Exam by buyer attorney						
11. Recording: Warranty Deed						
12. Deed of Trust						
13. Release						
14. Other						
15. Documentary Fee						
16. Certificate of Taxes Due						
17. Taxes for Preceding Year(s)						
18. Taxes for Current Year						
19. Tax Reserve						
20. Special Taxes (Assessments)						
21. Personal Property Taxes						
22. Notary Fee paid by Lender						
23. Premium for New Insurance						
24. Hazard Ins. Reserve						
25. FHA Mortgage Ins. Assumed						
26. FHA Mortgage Ins. Reserve						
27. Loan Origination						
28. Loan Discount Points						
29. Interest on New Loan						
30. Survey						
Credit Report						
31. Appraisal Fee						
32. Water and/or Sewer						
33. Rents						
34. Security Deposits						
35. Loan Transfer Fee						
36. Loan Payment Due						
37. Broker's Fee						
38. Seller's Attorney						
39. Net loan proceeds						
Subtotals						
Balance Due to/from Seller						
Balance Due to/from Buyer						
TOTALS						